# HANDBOOK OF DIGITAL ENTREPRENEURSHIP

T0317650

# Handbook of Digital Entrepreneurship

*Edited by*

## Mohammad Keyhani

*Associate Professor of Entrepreneurship and Innovation, Haskayne School of Business, University of Calgary, Canada*

## Tobias Kollmann

*Professor of Digital Business and Digital Entrepreneurship, University of Duisburg-Essen, Germany*

## Andishe Ashjari

*Doctoral Candidate in Entrepreneurship and Innovation, Haskayne School of Business, University of Calgary, Canada*

## Alina Sorgner

*Assistant Professor of Applied Data Analytics, John Cabot University, Rome, Italy, Research Affiliate, Institute of Labor Economics (IZA) and Research Fellow, Kiel Institute for the World Economy (IfW Kiel)*

## Clyde Eiríkur Hull

*Professor, Department of Management, Saunders College of Business, Rochester Institute of Technology, USA*

Edward Elgar
PUBLISHING

Cheltenham, UK • Northampton, MA, USA

Published by
Edward Elgar Publishing Limited
The Lypiatts
15 Lansdown Road
Cheltenham
Glos GL50 2JA
UK

Edward Elgar Publishing, Inc.
William Pratt House
9 Dewey Court
Northampton
Massachusetts 01060
USA

Paperback edition 2024

A catalogue record for this book
is available from the British Library

Library of Congress Control Number: 2022944500

This book is available electronically in the **Elgar**online
Business subject collection
http://dx.doi.org/10.4337/9781800373631

ISBN 978 1 80037 362 4 (Hardback)
ISBN 978 1 0353 3425 4 (Paperback)
ISBN 978 1 80037 363 1 (eBook)

Printed and bound by CPI Group (UK) Ltd, Croydon, CR0 4YY

# Contents

*v*

# Contributors

**Zoltan J. Acs**, George Mason University, USA

**Andishe Ashjari**, University of Calgary, Canada

**Giacomo Ciambotti**, Università Cattolica del Sacro Cuore, Italy

**Katharina de Cruppe**, University of Duisburg-Essen, Germany

**Angela Martinez Dy**, Loughborough University, UK

**Frank M. Fossen**, University of Nevada, Reno, USA

**Paolo Gerli**, Edinburgh Napier University, UK

**Vincent Göttel**, Heinrich Heine University Düsseldorf, Germany

**Alexander B. Hamrick**, Auburn University, USA

**Clyde Eiríkur Hull**, Rochester Institute of Technology, USA

**Zahra Jamshidi**, University of Calgary, Canada

**Philipp Benedikt Jung**, University of Duisburg-Essen, Germany

**Mohammad Keyhani**, University of Calgary, Canada

**Lucas Kleine-Stegemann**, University of Duisburg-Essen, Germany

**Lisa Klever**, Twitter Inc.

**Wolfgang Koehler**, University of Potsdam, Germany

**Tobias Kollmann**, University of Duisburg-Essen, Germany

**Éva Komlósi**, University of Pécs, Hungary

**Esteban Lafuente**, UPC Barcelona Tech, Spain

**Franz T. Lohrke**, Auburn University, USA

**Trevor McLemore**, University of Nevada, Reno, USA

**Anton Miglo**, University of Glasgow, UK

**Ben Mkalama**, University of Nairobi, Kenya

**Varun Nagaraj**, SPJIMR, India

**Bitange Ndemo**, University of Nairobi, Kenya

**Christoph Rasche**, University of Potsdam, Germany

**Bennet Schierstedt**, Heinrich Heine University Düsseldorf, Germany

**Christian Schultz**, Victoria International University of the Applied Sciences, Germany

**Eusebio Scornavacca**, Arizona State University, USA

**Abraham K. Song**, Pepperdine University, USA

**Alina Sorgner**, John Cabot University, Italy

**Christina Strauss (née Then-Bergh)**, University of Duisburg-Essen, Germany

**László Szerb**, University of Pécs, Hungary

**Jason Whalley**, Northumbria University, UK

**Qiongrui (Missy) Yao**, York College of Pennsylvania, USA

**Stefano Za**, Università Cattolica del Sacro Cuore, Italy

# PART I

# INTRODUCTION

# 1. An introduction to digital entrepreneurship: concepts and themes

*Mohammad Keyhani, Andishe Ashjari, Alina Sorgner, Tobias Kollmann, Clyde Eirikur Hull and Zahra Jamshidi*

## INTRODUCTION

Today, it is almost impossible to find an aspect of our lives that has not been touched by digitalization. Regardless of time and location, only having access to a *computer* (i.e., an electronic device capable of storing and processing data) and the Internet are enough for us to work, pay bills, rent or buy almost any goods or services, communicate, learn and even build a business from scratch. According to the International Communication Union (ITU), in the past decade, the number of individuals using the Internet has increased drastically from 2 billion in 2010 (29 percent of the world population) to 4.6 billion (59 percent of the population) in 2020[1] (Figure 1.1). Furthermore, the share of households with at least one personal computer at home increased from about 35 percent in 2009 to 47 percent in 2019[2] (Figure 1.2).

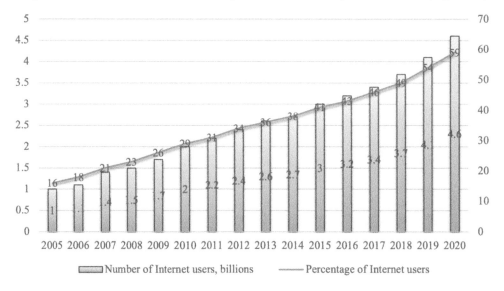

*Figure 1.1    Individuals using the Internet*

In the wake of this digital revolution, organizations are being transformed fundamentally across various industries, from manufacturing and retailing to health care and education. The current pandemic has further accelerated digital transformation to accommodate changes in people's behaviour. According to ITU, "in 2020, the first year of the pandemic, the number of

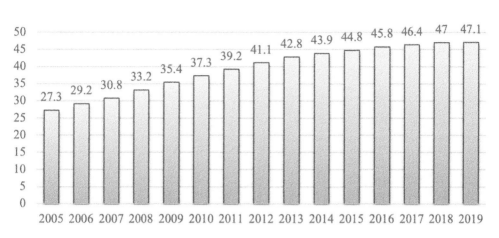

*Figure 1.2      Share of households with a computer at home*

[Internet] users grew by 10.2 percent, the largest increase in a decade."[3] As a consequence of this behavioral change, consumers become accustomed to *online everything*, from shopping and banking to education and dating.

Sparked by the COVID-19 pandemic, the digitalization of entrepreneurship has accelerated along with the digitalization of everything else. A survey by McKinsey found that as a result of the pandemic, companies have sped up the digitalization of their supply side and demand side interactions by three to four years and have fast-tracked the share of digital products in their portfolios by seven years (LaBerge, O'Toole, Schneider, & Smaje, 2020). The idea that COVID-19 has pushed the world beyond a tipping point is perhaps best seen in the rapid global transition to remote work. The number of job postings on the popular software industry website Hacker News that mention the word "remote" has skyrocketed from less than 30 percent before the pandemic to about 70 percent going into 2022[4] (Figure 1.3). In the startup world, many digital-focused business models proved to be essential in leading this transformation including startups providing solutions for remote work and video communication, ecommerce, online grocery shopping, online gaming, EdTech, FinTech, and other Software as a Service (SaaS) solutions.

If there was any doubt before the pandemic, it is now crystal clear that digital technology has brought major change to business and entrepreneurship. But academic research on digital entrepreneurship has lagged behind this change for several reasons. First, the allure of prestigious "grand theory" that is elegantly generalizable across contexts has prevented many researchers from focusing their research on issues specific to the "digital" context. This is despite calls from prominent scholars to contextualize entrepreneurship research (Baker & Welter, 2020; Zahra, 2007; Zahra, Wright, & Abdelgawad, 2014). Often, specific contexts introduce nuances and complexities that require more context-specific theory building. For example, the information technology industry has long realized that strategic issues such as switching costs, lock-in, zero marginal costs, network effects, two-sided markets, versioning, and standards wars are highly relevant to information goods and digital products (Shapiro & Varian, 1999; Varian, 2001) but not covered by generic generalizable theories that are not

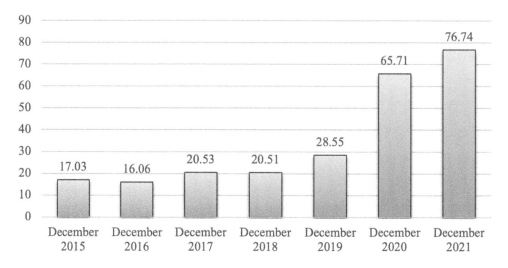

*Figure 1.3      Proportion of job postings on Hacker News that mention the word "remote"*

attuned to the specific characteristics of the digital context. In either case, given the rate at which digital is taking over the world (i.e., the rate of digital convergence), it is more and more difficult to describe digital entrepreneurship as being about a specific "context." Increasingly, almost all entrepreneurship is digital in some form or other (Hull, Hung, Hair, Perotti, & DeMartino, 2007).

Second, the rate at which digital technology is transforming entrepreneurship is so fast that it is often difficult for researchers to keep up. The lengthy publication process of peer-reviewed academic journals has barely changed and has perhaps become even lengthier and more difficult in recent years. It also takes time for substantial data to become available on emergent phenomena, and for armchair-inclined academics not entrenched in the world of practice to notice such phenomena and recognize their value as subjects of study. For example, the first exploratory study of crowdfunding published in a major entrepreneurship journal came out in 2014 (Mollick, 2014), a full five years after the launch of the Kickstarter platform. In such situations however, insights on these emergent phenomena can often be found published much earlier in lower-ranked academic journals, practitioner outlets, blogs and social media, which are unfortunately often discounted or unnoticed by much of academia. In many cases these early publications may even use different terminology to describe the phenomena compared to the terminology that eventually becomes dominant (Kollmann, Kleine-Stegemann, de Cruppe, & Then-Bergh, 2021).

This handbook is an effort to compile a diverse set of scholarly contributions to the literature on digital entrepreneurship in a way that provides an informative look into how digital entrepreneurship research has evolved over the years, and where it stands today. The aim is to provide a snapshot of many of the major themes in digital entrepreneurship research, highlight the diversity of topics and contributors to this line of work, and emphasize practice-engaged and practice-relevant works of academic scholarship on the topic. Furthermore, this handbook aims to help digital entrepreneurs and would-be digital entrepreneurs understand the history and theory of digital entrepreneurship while also sparking ideas for future research in digital entrepreneurship by highlighting emergent phenomena, and new ways to approach research in this broad area of study.

This introductory chapter aims to contextualize the remaining chapters by setting the stage in terms of key phenomena and key theoretical developments in digital entrepreneurship research. We highlight six themes in digital entrepreneurship research that serve as the organizing framework for the chapters in this handbook. Within the discussion of these themes, we provide brief summaries of each chapter and highlight the significance of their contributions. We end this introductory chapter with a summary of the editorial process.

## WHAT IS DIGITAL ENTREPRENEURSHIP?

There are many varieties of terms and definitions around the concept of digital entrepreneurship that are prevalent in the literature, and there is some value in this variety. That is why throughout this handbook we have followed a pluralist approach and have not attempted to consolidate definitions or advocate for the superiority of any one definition over others. However, here in this introduction to the handbook, it may be helpful to discuss the meaning of digital entrepreneurship and some of the issues that have arisen in the literature around attempts to define this concept.

First, the term "digital" itself typically refers broadly to the set of all technologies emanating from the invention of computers and their ability to process data and information as electronic signals. When analog signals are turned into digital ones, they are essentially decoupled from their physical storage medium and can be replicated, transmitted, and processed with much more flexibility, speed, and scale, and with much less boundaries from physical constraints and geographic distance. Naturally, given that the communication of information is at the heart of almost all processes of management, organization, and trade, it is no surprise that digitalization would deeply impact everything about business and entrepreneurship.

In practice, "digital" mainly refers to software and Internet technologies and is largely synonymous with the notion of Information Technology (IT). The reasons for why a term like "digital" starts to become the prevalent parlance when other terms already exist (e.g., "electronic" or "online") to describe the concept largely have little to do with research and scholarship and are mostly a function of the natural ways in which language evolves in society. For example, in the article "Eras of Digital Entrepreneurship – Connecting the Past, Present, and Future" by Kollmann, Kleine-Stegemann, de Cruppe, and Then-Bergh (2021) on the history of digital entrepreneurship (Chapter 3 in this handbook), the authors point out that up until 2015 the terms "Internet entrepreneur, "e-entrepreneur" or "net entrepreneur" were more popular labels for the concept that is now mostly called "digital entrepreneur." The authors provide some speculation about the reasons for this shift in terminology.

There are many narrow ways to define digital entrepreneurship, and often when the term is used in a particular context, one of these narrower definitions is implied. For example, simply creating digital products is a commonplace understanding of digital entrepreneurship in many contexts. However, scholars have noted that many different aspects of entrepreneurship are impacted by digital entrepreneurship to varying degrees in various contexts, and for this reason broader definitions are preferred. For example, von Briel et al. (2021, p. 287) provide one such broad definition as "creating new economic activities embodied in or enabled by digital technologies." Tackling definitional issues has been a major research theme in the digital entrepreneurship literature, as we discuss later in this chapter. In the article "What is Digital Entrepreneurship?" (Chapter 2 in this handbook), Kollmann and Jung (2022, p. 39) suggest that digital entrepreneurship "refers to establishing a new company with an innovative business idea within the Digital Economy, which, using a digital platform (also referred to as electronic platform) in data networks, offers its products and/or services based upon a purely digital creation of value."

## KEY CONCEPTS AND DEVELOPMENTS IN DIGITAL ENTREPRENEURSHIP RESEARCH

Entrepreneurship research has been an interdisciplinary field of study that has borrowed heavily from more mature disciplines to build its toolkit of theories of concepts. Most prominently, the fields of psychology, sociology, and economics are considered to be the main sources of theoretical insight in entrepreneurship research (Davidsson, 2016; Landström, 2005). Within the management and organization disciplines, the field of strategic management has been the one most in conversation with entrepreneurship (Hitt, Ireland, Sirmon, & Trahms, 2011; Keyhani, 2022; Meyer, 2009). Accordingly, many entrepreneurship scholars have a background as trained sociologists, economists, or researchers of psychology or strategic management.

However, with the exception of some concepts from economics, most of these "source disciplines" have had little to contribute to digital entrepreneurship research. That is why many entrepreneurship scholars unfamiliar with the information systems literature may feel that the conceptual toolkit of contemporary digital entrepreneurship research feels somewhat foreign to them. Nambisan (2017) has taken an important step to rectify this situation by introducing entrepreneurship researchers to a number of widely used theories and concepts in the information systems literature that are relevant to digital entrepreneurship. Toward a similar aim, in this section we briefly review an inevitably non-comprehensive and far-from-exhaustive but hopefully useful set of key concepts and theoretical developments that have shaped the study of digital entrepreneurship. Key concepts are emphasized in italic font.

### Information Goods, the Nature of Data, and Artificial Intelligence

One of the earliest and most impactful lines of work relevant to digital entrepreneurship is the literature on the economics of *information goods* (Shapiro & Varian, 1999; Varian, 2001). Along with the widespread adoption of personal computers, some economists started to notice certain peculiarities about the nature of software and digital products that completely upended the traditional economic calculations relevant to the production and manufacturing of physical goods. For example, the normal cost structure of information goods involves a constant fixed cost and virtually *zero marginal costs of production*. This leads to enormous *supply-side economies of scale*, which in turn gives rise of monopolies and intense competition to become the monopolist. On the other hand, *demand-side economies of scale* also known as *network effects* give rise to the *critical mass* phenomenon, and the importance of being the *first to scale* in a new market (Arthur, 1988; Hoffman & Yeh, 2018). The importance of scaling leads to the phenomenon of *penetration pricing*, which means *subsidizing* the demand side in order to increase adoption (Katz & Shapiro, 1994).

A good review of this literature is provided in Varian (2001). Shapiro and Varian (1999) popularized these ideas in their book *Information Rules* which had a noticeable impact on the evolution of Silicon Valley, such that practices recommended by this literature including price differentiation strategies, penetration pricing, bundling, increasing switching costs and creating lock-in were widespread in the industry by the 2000s. Hal Varian was hired as Chief Economist at Google in 2002.

In more recent years, the economists who studied information goods have turned their attention to the economics of artificial intelligence and machine learning (AI/ML) as these technologies gain center stage in the competition among the digital behemoths, for example Google (Alphabet), Facebook (Meta), Apple, Microsoft, and Amazon sometimes referred to as the "Frightful Five" (Manjoo, 2017) as well as geopolitical rivalry (especially among the US and China). It is becoming increasingly clear that in competition over AI, data becomes "the new oil" (Hirsch, 2014). However, data being a digital resource, is different from physical resources such as oil in that it is what economists call a *nonrival good* (Romer, 1990). Using it at any one time for any one application does not exclude it from any other use. However, where the scarcity comes into play is in *access* to the data, *excludability* (Benkler, 2000), the capabilities to model and process it, and to connect it to other data fruitfully. The cost structure of these activities and data access will be key determinants of the extent to which entrepreneurs and startups can engage with AI technology (Varian, 2019).

In general, it is interesting to ask if the nature of the digital technologies involved makes them the realm of competition between big players or if small entrepreneurial ventures will be able to compete. As a rule of thumb, in applications where the fixed costs are high or the data is difficult to access, the big players who already have access to the data and have the financial capabilities will have the upper hand and entrepreneurs will find it hard to enter. Examples include autonomous vehicles, virtual reality, Internet of things, and targeted advertising. This is why some observers have noted that the pendulum of digital technology today favors the big firms: "today's new technologies are complicated, expensive, and favor organizations that have huge amounts of scale and capital already" writes Jon Evans (2017) in *Techcrunch*. But in applications where the fixed costs are low and data is readily accessible, more startups are likely to arise. Examples include content generation and data analytics. The more that parts of the value chain can be outsourced or accessed as a service, the more entrepreneurial firms can enter and compete.

Current trends indicate an unprecedented ability to complete various tasks in digital value chains with less effort, time and money, and outsource other aspects of digital value chains by linking different software services together through API integrations. Developments along this trend include the availability of no-code software development platforms like Bubble. io, easy-to-use and easy-to-integrate database platforms like AirTable.com and Xano.com, API integration platforms like Zapier.com and Integromat.com, sheet-to-app solutions like GlideApps.com and Softr.io, and many other tools such as the ones discussed in the chapter on Startup Stacks by Keyhani (Chapter 7 in this handbook). Recently, complex AI models like GPT-3 by OpenAI.com have become available as a service, giving rise to a host of startups competing to find the best applications for language models in SaaS products. Examples include Copysmith.ai, HuggingFace.co, Latitude.io, OthersideAI.com, Deepset.ai, and Blogely.com. These trends point to an increasingly modular architecture of digital products, which is a topic we turn to in the next section.

**Decoupling and Modularity**

That fact that digitalization essentially decouples information from its physical medium acts as a first principle from which many implications relevant to digital entrepreneurship are derived. First, the *digital object* or *digital artifact* that exists solely as "bits" becomes an important unit of analysis (Kallinikos, Aaltonen, & Marton, 2013). It may be produced, copied, packaged, communicated, and consumed. It may be combined with or embedded in other digital artifacts or physical devices. And in all of these things it is unbounded by the traditional constraints of the physical world such as material scarcity and geographical distance. Varian (2010, p. 1) reflects on how these properties of digital artifacts led to an unprecedented scale and speed of *combinatorial innovation* with the rise of the Internet:

> Why was innovation so rapid on the Internet? The reason is that the component parts were all bits. They were programming languages, protocols, standards, software libraries, productivity tools and the like. There was no time to manufacture, no inventory management, and no shipping delay. You never run out of HTML, just like you never run out of e-mail. New tools could be sent around the world in seconds, and innovators could combine and recombine these bits to create new Web applications.

Because of theses properties, digital technologies bring an unprecedented level of scalability to entrepreneurial opportunities, and allow digital businesses to leverage extremely *fungible, scale-free capabilities* (Levinthal & Wu, 2010). However, while these capability and resource bundles may be extremely fungible across scale, they are often focused on narrow scopes or verticals. Giustiziero, Kretschmer, Somaya, and Wu (2021) refer to this phenomenon as *hyper-specialization* and *hyperscaling*. They argue that it is driven by incentives and opportunities to outsource complementary activities.

Baskerville, Myers, and Yoo (2020) point out that digital objects have two key properties with profound implications: First, they are *nonmaterial* and exist only in the form of bits. This means that humans can interact with them only through some sort of physical or device *interface*, but they can be processed or interact with each other without such an interface. Second, they are *computed*, meaning that they require the execution of algorithms to come into being. This computed nature gives rise to the *reprogrammable* nature of digital objects, as well as their indistinguishability from *digital actions*.

The relationship between digital objects and physical ones is interesting. The traditional way to think about digital objects is that they are representations of some physical reality. But in fact, digital technology often leads to an *ontological reversal* such that digital reality is decoupled from or takes precedence over the physical reality (Baskerville et al., 2020). While a regular vehicle in the physical world may be represented as a "blue dot" in navigation software, an autonomous vehicle in the physical world is itself controlled by the digital artifact in its navigation software. In other cases, the digital artifact may exist wholly independent of any physical reality and yet may be just as meaningful and impactful on our lives as anything in physical reality. Increasingly, more and more of the important and meaningful artifacts in our lives are digital, and less and less are physical, giving rise to a *"digital first"* world and creating opportunities for entrepreneurship in the *metaverse* (Park & Kim, 2022).

The flexible nature of digital artifacts allows for flexible levels of *modularity*, referring to the extent to which digital functionality is packaged in smaller modules (Yoo, Henfridsson, & Lyytinen, 2010). In modular architectures, smaller modules are decoupled from each other but can interact with other modules through standardized *interfaces*, thereby allowing innovators to experiment with different combinations of modules. On the other hand, integrated architectures group a large system of functions into a closed package that optimizes the connection among the modules for a specific combination but precludes alternative combinations of its component functions. The trade-offs between the benefits and costs of modular vs. integrated architectures is a prime example of the general *trade-off between openness and control* that is a recurring theme in the study of technology (Broekhuizen et al., 2021; Ethiraj & Levinthal, 2004; Fu, Sun, & Gao, 2022).

Almost all Software as a Service (SaaS) tools today provide standardized interfaces through documented *Application Programming Interfaces* (APIs) which allows them to be combined with other software. The emergence of API connector hub tools such as Zapier.com and Integromat.com in recent years has drastically increased the rate of combinatorial innovation made possible by combining functionality from different software components on the web. A host of new entrepreneurial opportunities have been created involving the patching together of various SaaS functionalities in novel combinations. At the same time, when a number of applications start to build on modular patchwork solutions, it often indicates an opportunity for other entrepreneurs to build integrated solution alternatives. Examples of integrated solutions that attempt to compete with modular ones include Kajabi.com in the online course management category and Outseta.com in the membership management category of SaaS products. However, even these integrated solutions are able to interact with other software through APIs.

## Digital Business Models and Platforms

The concept of *business models* has undoubtedly been one of the key contributions of entrepreneurship practice and scholarship to the management discipline. Widespread adoption of frameworks such as the business model canvas (Osterwalder & Pigneur, 2010) have expanded the meaning of business models to include a variety of elements such as value proposition, market segment, supply channels and others. This has resulted in business models sometimes being understood as more like a list of elements, whereas the main idea behind the concept is for it to describe a mechanism, sometimes referred to as the revenue generation mechanism (Chesbrough & Rosenbloom, 2002) or the profit formula (Johnson & Lafley, 2010). To describe these mechanisms, it is common in the business model literature to provide taxonomies of various business model archetypes or analogies that help us better understand the "formula." Examples of these analogies include the razor & blade model, brokerage, advertising, freemium, pay-as-you-go, commission, referral, and subscription (Afuah & Tucci, 2003; Gassmann, Frankenberger, & Csik, 2014; Johnson & Lafley, 2010).

Perhaps the most important aspect of digital entrepreneurship is how information processing gains center stage in the value chain and business model (Kollmann, 1998). Digital technology allows entrepreneurs and companies to implement new kinds of business models, have greater flexibility in changing and innovating with their business models, and leverage business models that take advantage of the particular properties of digital technology. As stated by Afuah and Tucci (2003, p. 7):

> An Internet business model … is the method by which a firm plans to make money long term using the Internet. The Internet business model is the system—components, linkages, and associated dynamics—that takes advantage of the properties of the Internet to make money. It takes advantage of the properties of the Internet in the way it builds each of the components—choice of profit site,

value, scope, revenue sources, pricing, connected activities, implementation capabilities, sustainability, and cost structure—and crafts the linkages among these components. For example, the Internet's universality and time-moderation properties allow employees of a firm located in different parts of the world to collaborate on product development, thus decreasing the time needed to bring a product to market. They also allow retailers to stay open 24 hours a day to shoppers, in the privacy of their homes, from different parts of the world.

Early in the life of the Internet, many had emphasized the opportunities for all kinds of disintermediation, envisioning that users would be able to use the Internet to interact directly and cut off many of the middlemen of the pre-Internet era. While this has occurred to some extent in some industries, to a large extent we have learned that various kinds of *intermediary* platforms are still needed, and in fact while they may not look like the traditional intermediaries, the Internet provides many lucrative opportunities for these kinds of digital business models referred to as "platforms" to arise and profit on a massive scale. There are multiple reasons for this, as for example outlined by Brousseau and Penard (2007, p. 82):

> These new business models contradict the prediction of a massive disintermediation caused by the strong development of digital technologies and of the Internet. Even if the Internet can reduce coordination costs, intermediaries are still needed. First, matching demand and supply plans, then performing transactions remains costly. Second, combining several digital goods to benefit from their interoperation – as is the case when a content is processed by a software run on a technical interface – is certainly much easier than it was in the past, thanks to standardized interfaces. However, it remains resource and time consuming to guarantee effective interoperability between digital goods to benefit from a value-added service. Third, while a profusion of information goods is available both on and off-line, it remains challenging to guarantee a user access to the information or piece of knowledge they need. Those who can provide knowledge should receive appropriate incentives. Potential users should be guaranteed access. These together led platforms to emerge to facilitate coordination in the production and marketing of information goods. Many of the Internet success stories – E-Bay, Amazon, Google, Yahoo, Autobytel – have developed business models based on the concept of platforms assembling components, then bundling them into packages that correspond to consumers' complex and specific needs.

A burgeoning literature in economics has developed around analyzing the properties of platform business models often under the label of two-sided markets or multi-sided markets (Eisenmann, Parker, & Alstyne, 2006; Rochet & Tirole, 2006; Roth & Sotomayor, 1990; Rysman, 2009) also referred to as "matching markets" (Abdulkadiroglu & Sönmez, 2013; Demange & Gale, 1985). An interesting phenomenon studied in this literature is *multi-sided network effects* where more than one of the sides being matched together through the platform exhibits network effects, and there are not only same-side network effects but also cross-side network effects at play. Careful analysis of the particular networks that operate in any given platform can lead to insights on which side of the market could or should be subsidized by the firm to optimize growth.

One of the most important issues in digital platform entrepreneurship is that in the presence of same-side and cross-side network effects, there is a *chicken-or-egg problem* when trying to attract users (Parker, Van Alstyne, & Choudary, 2016). Users on one side have little incentive to join unless there are enough users on the other side, but the other side users also have the same reservation. For example, not that many people would want to use Uber for rides if there were not enough Uber drivers, but not that many people would want to become Uber drivers if there were not enough demand. This chicken-or-egg problem is sometimes referred to as the *cold start problem* (Chen, 2021) and finding ways to address it is one of the most important challenges in digital platform entrepreneurship. Tiwana (2013) notes that most successful multi-sided platforms start out as a supplier on one side of the market, and then evolve into platforms only after a *critical mass* of adopters is reached.

Recently, industry observers have noted that traditional two-sided markets tend to rely on commodified products and services and short-term transactions. A new breed of digital business models referred to as *"market networks"* are attempting to innovate in this space by focusing on n-sided markets that combine elements of marketplaces and social networks, giving center stage to non-commoditized and more high-touch services, more professional profiles and salient identities for users, and longer-term relationships between parties (Currier, 2015). Examples of market network businesses include AngelList, HoneyBook.com and Houzz.com. Many recent startups such as OnDeck (BeOnDeck.com) have been inspired by the idea of market network business models (Yu, 2021).

The trade-off between openness and control surfaces in the study of platforms as well, for example in the question of whether a platform should be compatible with competing platforms (Rysman, 2009). In the case of smartphones, Android apps are not compatible with iOS and vice versa, resulting in some lock-in effects that benefit Google and Apple. If they were compatible however, there would be other benefits and other costs at play and therefore the optimal choice of the level of openness is not a trivial one.

**Unboundedness, Experimentation, and Generativity**

Nambisan (2017) characterizes the key impacts of digital technology on entrepreneurship in terms of *less bounded* entrepreneurial initiatives (in terms of outcomes and processes) and less bounded or less predefined entrepreneurial *agency*. One example of how digital technology *removes boundaries* is the way in which it allows *experimentation* at much higher scales and speeds through *automation*. While the entrepreneurship literature has long recognized the importance of experimentation, the popularity of the *lean startup* method has really emphasized the idea of rapid experimentation and *feedback* elicitation (Blank, 2013; Blank & Dorf, 2020; Ries, 2011). Digital technology makes such lean startup techniques much easier in many respects. In fact, it can be argued that in digital entrepreneurship, experimenting with ideas takes precedence over starting and incorporating a business as a legal entity at the center of entrepreneurship, with the key performance metric being the ability to *discover and validate customers*. In effect, the lean startup methodology envisions startups as a *search mechanism* for viable business models rather than full fledged organizations.

There are now a host of software tools available for various aspects of experimenting with ideas in the digital context. For example, a number of tools specialize in automated *A/B testing* of websites and digital products. A/B testing is a method of rapid experimentation with variations of product features on small sub-population samples to identify the optimal feature set for the broader population or for various segments. The technique gained popular attention after reports that Barack Obama's 2008 presidential campaign had successfully used the technique in their campaign emails and advertisements (Siroker & Koomen, 2013). Today, many digital businesses use automated or semi-automated A/B testing and it has been shown to have positive effects on performance (Koning, Hasan, Fuqua, & Chatterji, 2021). Interestingly, Koning et al. (2021) found that adoption of A/B testing is also associated with failing faster, thereby reducing the costs of failure.

Another prime example of how digital technology allows for the trespassing of traditional boundaries is the leveraging of crowds in the form of *crowdsourcing* or *crowdfunding*. Other than the obvious scale benefits, Tajedin, Madhok, and Keyhani (2019) delineate the important knowledge benefits of leveraging crowds. In other words, crowd-based business models and organizational techniques allow the firm to unchain and unburden itself from its own internal knowledge constraints, by tapping into the knowledge distributed in the broader population. Thinking in terms of problems and solutions, crowds are ideal for when the firm knows and can articulate the problem well, but wants to reduce the boundaries of its search parameters in the solution space. Most importantly, crowds allow firms to overcome *"unknown unknown"* problems by allowing others external to the organization to drive the search for the solutions, each using their own localized knowledge, and unchained from the knowledge boundaries of the crowdsourcing firm.

In fact, Tajedin et al. (2019) point out that marketplaces are in many ways taking this same phenomenon of unburdening the platform firm from the knowledge constraints of any one individual or organization. Viewed in this light, two-sided markets can be seen as mechanisms where both the search for problems and the search for solutions is delegated to crowds (one on each side of the market), and "unknown unknown" problems are avoided on both sides. For example, on smartphone app stores, the platform owner (e.g., Google or Apple) does not need to know or try to find out all the problems people have that could be solved with apps, and also does not need to know or try to find out what apps can solve those problems, let alone try to build them. Both the problem side and the solution side are delegated to the market.

The observation that marketplaces like the app store can endogenously produce innovations without direction from the platform leads Keyhani (2021) to refer to them as *"generative marketplaces."* The idea that dynamic market economies can act as *endogenous innovation machines* has been explored by economists in the past (Baumol, 2002; Phelps, 2013, 2017; Romer, 1990), but has rarely been viewed from the lens of *generativity* theory. The concept of generativity as mainly developed by law scholar Jonathan Zittrain is a key notion in modern information systems literature and the theories of digital technology. Generativity refers to "a system's capacity to produce unanticipated change through unfiltered contributions from broad and varied audiences" (Zittrain, 2008, p. 70). Importantly, generativity is conceptualized as a property of technology, not as an organizational method. Therefore, while the concepts of *"open innovation"* (Chesbrough, 2003) and *"user innovation"* (Thomke & von Hippel, 2002; von Hippel, 1986) are about leveraging external knowledge and innovations from broad and varied audiences (i.e., "crowds"), generativity is about automating these open innovation processes by taking advantage of the features of the technology (Keyhani, 2022; Keyhani & Hastings, 2021). Generativity can be embedded in a particular product (such as Microsoft Excel) which allows its users to innovate with it on a massive scale, or it can be leveraged through a marketplace mechanism like the app store. Importantly, the idea that a marketplace can be designed for generativity encourages us to avoid viewing platforms and two-sided markets as merely "matching" mechanisms. Matching is only one of their functions, and in fact may not even be the most important function if the generation of innovations is the main design objective of the platform. This is a key consideration for platform entrepreneurs.

# KEY THEMES IN DIGITAL ENTREPRENEURSHIP RESEARCH

## The Structure of this Handbook

In this handbook we have collected a range of research contributions covering many of the major prevalent themes in digital entrepreneurship research. In this section we provide a brief introduction to each theme, along with summaries of the handbooks in this chapter that contribute to that theme. It should be noted that the diversity of research in digital entrepreneurship is such that no brief introduction can do justice to the range of topics that have been covered, and that no short list of themes such as this one can be truly comprehensive. The themes or subheadings listed in this section mainly serve as the organizing structure of this handbook. Inevitably, many chapters are relevant to multiple themes but for organizational purposes had to be categorized under only one.

## Digital Entrepreneurship Overview and Definitions

One of the key themes in digital entrepreneurship research has been to tackle definitional issues, to clarify the meaning, and to delineate the boundaries of the concept relative to similar notions and adjacent concepts. These efforts have had varying degrees of success. Von Briel et al. (2021) outline some distinctions between the general notion of entrepreneurship, digital innovation, and digital entrepreneurship, although the distinctions are not always convincing. For example, they use the phrase "new economic activities" when describing entrepreneurship and "new and improved products, processes, or services" when describing innovation, which is arguably similar. Giones and Brem (2017) compare the notion of digital entrepreneurship with that of technology entrepreneurship, and define the intersecting construct of "digital technology entrepreneurship" which is a kind of entrepreneurship that builds on technological knowledge as input and produces *digital artefacts* as output.

The extent to which the digital component influences a particular entrepreneurial initiative may involve grey areas in terms of whether or not it surpasses a threshold that would allow it to be labelled as "digital entrepreneurship." Hull et al. (2007) take a deeper look at six different aspects of a business that may involve varying degrees of digitalization: (1) digital marketing, (2) digital selling, (3) digital offerings, (4) digital distribution, (5) digital interactions, and (6) digital operations. Importantly, any business or entrepreneurial initiative may involve varying degrees of digitalization in one or more of these aspects. Similarly, Steininger (2019) suggests that digital technology can be either a facilitator of venture operations, a mediator of venture communications, or an outcome of the venture such as digital products.

Three chapters in this handbook contribute to this theme. Chapter 2 titled "What is Digital Entrepreneurship? Fundamentals of Company Founding in the Digital Economy" by Kollmann and Jung challenges the idea that digital entrepreneurship is a new field, arguing that prior work explains the digital entrepreneurship phenomenon. They present the emergence and development of the digital economy based on information/communication technologies and define distinctive characteristics of companies established in this context. According to this chapter, the foundation of a new venture in the digital economy would rely on the managing of the information, the digital value chain, and the value-oriented processing of the information.

In Chapter 3 titled "Eras of Digital Entrepreneurship: Connecting the Past, Present, and Future" Kollmann, Kleine-Stegemann, de Cruppe and Strauss conduct a systematic literature review to analyze the roots and historical development of the term "digital entrepreneurship." The chapter identifies three eras in the terminological development of digital entrepreneurship: Seed-Era, Startup-Era, and Expansion-Era, and investigates the evolution and connection between nine different terms used for digital entrepreneurship through these eras. Understanding how these terms have been used in the digital entrepreneurship literature should help anyone interested in learning from its history. Note that this chapter is a reprint of Kollmann et al. (2021).

In Chapter 4, "Exploring the Field of Digital Entrepreneurship: A Bibliometric Analysis" Scornavacca, Kollmann, Za, Kleine-Stegemann, and Strauss analyze the literature on digital entrepreneurship with a bibliometric approach. The authors find nine relevant terms for digital entrepreneurship in the literature, noting that some keywords, such as "technopreneurship" and "e-entrepreneurship" were mostly used before the rise of the term "digital entrepreneurship." They analyze the shape of the digital entrepreneurship literature over time, tracing the 21 keywords most often used on this topic to show the connections among studies over time. This helps us gain a better understanding of the underpinnings of the current state of the digital entrepreneurship field.

## Digital Entrepreneurship Ecosystems

An *ecosystem* can be defined as "a purposeful collaborating network of dynamic interacting systems that have an ever-changing set of dependencies within a given context" (Sussan & Acs, 2017, p. 57). Given the desire of many policy makers, institutional and community leaders around the world to turn their own institutions, cities, regions and countries into thriving hotbeds for entrepreneurship akin to "the next Silicon Valley" (Victor & Greg, 2012) the idea of *entrepreneurial ecosystems* has become a subject of intense study. There have been multiple lines of research on the macro-level factors and institutions that shape an entrepreneurial ecosystem (Acs, Autio, & Szerb, 2014; Nelson, 1993; Porter, 1990), but the label of "ecosystem" borrowed from biology has gained increasing favor in recent years. The term implies a metaphor of life; the idea that if the system is designed properly and all the right components are in place, life will be born, the stale and inactive will turn into the dynamic and generative, and the system will to a large extent work autonomously as if it has "a life of its own" thereafter. Terms such as "*self-organizing*" or "*self-sustaining*" are often used to describe this property (Nicotra, Romano, Del Giudice, & Schillaci, 2018; Sussan & Acs, 2017).

Extending the concept of ecosystems to the digital realm, a line of work in the literature has started to discuss the notion of *digital ecosystems* comprised of both technological components often termed *digital infrastructure*, and social components such as *users*. Combining the notions of entrepreneurial ecosystems and digital ecosystems, Sussan and Acs (2017, p. 63) define *digital entrepreneurial ecosystems* as "the matching of digital customers (users and agents) on platforms in digital space through the creative use of digital ecosystem governance and business ecosystem management to create matchmaker value and social utility by reducing transactions cost." They suggest a framework for understanding digital entrepreneurship ecosystems consisting of four elements: (1) digital infrastructure governance, (2) digital user citizenship, (3) digital entrepreneurship, and (4) digital marketplace.

A commonly employed theoretical framework in digital entrepreneurship research is that of the theory of affordances and constraints (Chemero, 2003; Ingold, 2018; Majchrzak & Markus, 2013). Employing the language of affordances, Autio, Nambisan, Thomas, and

Wright (2018) argue that entrepreneurial ecosystems are unique from the notion of clusters in the way they take advantage of digital affordances "by their emphasis on the exploitation of digital affordances; by their organization around entrepreneurial opportunity discovery and pursuit; by their emphasis on business model innovation; by voluntary horizontal knowledge spillovers; and by cluster-external locus of entrepreneurial opportunities" (p. 72). Importantly, while previous literature on cluster and agglomeration emphasizes the importance of space and physical proximity, digital technology reduces this dependence on geographic distance and alters the role of location in entrepreneurial ecosystems. In this sense the Silicon Valley metaphor, given its reference to a specific location, may be a misleading one in thinking about digital entrepreneurial ecosystems. In this vein, Elia, Margherita, and Passiante (2020) view digital entrepreneurial ecosystems as virtually global and context-independent. On the other hand, many other researchers continue to emphasize the role of cities and locations in the development of digital entrepreneurial ecosystems (Du, Pan, Zhou, & Ouyang, 2018; Geissinger, Laurell, Sandström, Eriksson, & Nykvist, 2019).

Within the ecosystem theme, Chapter 5 "Measuring the Digital Platform Economy" by Acs, Szerb, Song, Lafuente, and Komlósi is an important and significant contribution to digital entrepreneurship research. A key reason for this importance being that the chapter develops an index that can be used in future empirical studies. The authors develop an integrated Digital Platform Economy (DPE) index based on the intersection of Digital Ecosystem (DE) and Entrepreneurial Ecosystem (EE), measuring this index for 116 countries. The DPE index includes 61 indicators, 24 variables, 12 pillars, 4 sub-indices, and 1 super index. They then make policy recommendations based on the country's development (i.e., GDP), DPE Index, and the balance between DE and EE scores. They find that in most countries the Digital Entrepreneurial Ecosystem (DEE) score reflects the development of the country.

In Chapter 6, "The Regional Impacts of Digitalization of Work on Entrepreneurship in the United States," Fossen, McLemore, and Sorgner look at the effects of digitalization on labor markets and entrepreneurship, with a specific focus on how different types of digital technologies, like Artificial Intelligence, shape the job market and entrepreneurial activities. They find that, at least in the US, regional digital entrepreneurial ecosystems are strongly related to the digitalization impact on the regional occupational structure. They also provide heat maps and state rankings, which may be of use to digital entrepreneurs, policy makers aiming to develop digital entrepreneurial ecosystems, as well as digital entrepreneurship scholars.

**Digital Entrepreneurship Technology**

Some of the major themes in digital entrepreneurship research have involved the underlying technologies themselves. We can identify at least one macro-level sub-theme and two micro-level sub-themes within this broader theme. First, at the macro level, a topic of interest has been the dynamics of technologies over time. Building on previous theories of technological change (Abernathy & Utterback, 1978), the lifecycle of technologies (Levitt, 1965), and disruptive innovation (Christensen, 1997), observers have begun to theorize how digital technology changes these dynamics. For example, Downes and Nunes (2014) argue that while traditional disruptive technologies started out as a cheap and simple alternative to incumbents and gradually encroaching upon the value provided to the incumbent's customers, new digital platforms are able to launch with greater value and lower prices from the very beginning, leading to a much faster pace of disruption.

At the micro-level, one line of research focuses on how new technologies give rise to change in industry dynamics and engender new opportunities. These studies typically focus on new burgeoning industries and specific technologies. For example Laplume, Petersen, and Pearce (2016) analyze the changes in global value chains sparked by the growth of 3D printing, and Chalmers, Matthews, and Hyslop (2021) study how the rise of blockchain technology enables new opportunities for music entrepreneurs.

Often specific technologies will be used to create services for all startups, thereby allowing "technology entrepreneurs" to develop "entrepreneurship technology." This is sometimes referred to as the "Startups for startups" phenomenon as noted by Paul Graham in a YCombinator memo (Keyhani, Chapter 7 in this handbook). Hence it becomes important to ask how the nature of all entrepreneurship is becoming increasingly digital and how digital technologies are changing and supporting the entrepreneurial process for all entrepreneurs. This is the main sub-theme focused on by the two contributions in this part of the handbook.

Chapter 7 in this handbook by Keyhani titled "Startup Stacks: Understanding the New Landscape of Digital Entrepreneurship Technology" is an early exploratory study of entrepreneurship technology. The author is the first to define the term "entrepreneurship technology" as the set of technological tools which support, improve and transform the entrepreneurship process. The chapter lists, and classifies directories of software tools for startups, pointing out the cost, time, and human resource savings that they enable. The author points out that given this landscape of technologies, any entrepreneur attempting to launch a business without taking advantage of these tools will be at a severe disadvantage.

In Chapter 8 "Digital Product-Assisted Learning: Transforming Entrepreneurial Learning with Product Usage Analytics," Nagaraj makes an important contribution to the lean startup literature by asking "what if the product itself were designed to help in the feedback and learning process?" The author discusses the impacts of digitization on the scale, speed, and scope of entrepreneurial learning. Drawing on the entrepreneurial learning and lean startup methodology literature, the chapter conceptualizes a framework for digital product-assisted learning. Based on two fast-growing lean startup case studies involving the agile development process, the paper proposes an enhanced Build–Measure–Learn process that facilitates digital product-assisted learning. This process provides useful data and information to the entrepreneurial venture, leading to rapid and continuous learning and product innovation.

**Digital Entrepreneurship Adoption and Outcomes**

Given the role of digital technologies in supporting and enabling entrepreneurs and startups, it becomes important to study how entrepreneurs make the decision to use or adopt certain technologies and what are the outcomes of such decisions. For app entrepreneurs or startups that develop apps within the platforms of other companies, a key adoption question is which platform to choose in the first place. For example, if we want to develop a mobile game, we have to choose whether we want to develop it for Android, iOS, other less popular platforms, or multiple platforms. Intuitively, it would make sense that linking to more dominant platforms increases the chances of success (Srinivasan & Venkatraman, 2018), but the costs and benefits of developing exclusively for one platform rather than for multiple platforms are less straightforward.

The impact of adopting specific tools or specific categories of tools is also an interesting topic of study. The availability of data sources like BuiltWith.com allows researchers to identify whether or not a particular website or SaaS startup uses a particular tool. Koning et al. (2021) take advantage of this rich data source to study the impact of adopting A/B testing technology. They find that relatively few firms have adopted this technology, but those that did have enjoyed performance benefits on multiple metrics such as page views and new product features.

Adoption of digital technologies also has broader societal level impacts that have been of interest to researchers. Galindo-Martín, Castaño-Martínez, and Méndez-Picazo (2019) argue that digital transformation returns digital dividends, referring to the broader development benefits from using new technologies. In their study of 29 European countries, they find that digital transformation stimulates and facilitates entrepreneurship, and entrepreneurship in turn produces innovations that further digital transformation.

Two chapters in this handbook can be categorized within this theme. Chapter 9 by Lohrke, Hamrick, and Yao titled "Punching Above Their Weight Class: Assessing How Digital Technologies Enhance New and Small Firm Survival and Competitiveness" investigates the effects of digital technologies on the challenges of newness and smallness faced by New Ventures (NVs) and Small and Medium-sized Enterprises (SMEs), suggesting that the emergence of digital artifacts, platforms, and infrastructures can enhance the position of NVs and SMEs. The authors point out ways in which digital technologies can help entrepreneurs with entrepreneurship, engineering, and administrative issues that historically have represented critical challenges to these firms' survival and growth.

In Chapter 10 by Mkalama, Ciambotti, and Ndemo titled "Digital Adoption in Micro and Small Enterprise Clusters: A Dependency Theory Study in Kenya," the authors investigate the outcomes of digital technology adoption within micro and small enterprises in Kenya through qualitative research and a multiple-case design approach. Analyzing the presence of psycho-social, socio-economic, and technological capability factors, they found that adopting digital technologies helped business owners grow their sales. Entrepreneurs use these technologies for advertising, opportunity identification, and data generation as well as accounting, tracking, and communication. The chapter also finds that a lack of technical training and education in information technology skills limits entrepreneurs' adoption of digital technologies.

## Digital Entrepreneurship and Financing

Although digital technology has given rise to new possibilities in the world of startup financing, digital entrepreneurs still make extensive use of traditional financing methods as well. The commonplace process perhaps still reflects the mainstream financial life of a digital startup: starting with funding from founders, friends and family, moving on to bank loans and credit in conjunction with seed investment from business angels and other seed funds, followed by further investment rounds from venture capitalists, and finally moving to an Initial Public Offering (IPO) or acquisition.

Some of the ways in which the digital age has given rise to novel forms of financing are reviewed in Klein, Neitzert, Hartmann-Wendels, and Kraus (2019). These include:

- Accelerators and incubators, many of which have now become important seed and pre-seed investors. The Silicon Valley based Y Combinator founded by Paul Graham is often considered a model in this space. The training and networking benefits provided by these organizations often exposes founders to leading edge best practices in digital entrepreneurship beyond what is taught at most educational institutions.

- Crowdfunding, which is dominated by reward-based platforms such as Kickstarter but is increasingly open to equity-based investment. A novel form of crowdfunding is based on blockchain-based cryptocurrencies and Initial Coin Offerings (Adhami, Giudici, & Martinazzi, 2018; Fisch, 2019). Peer-to-peer lending is also sometimes referred to as lending-based crowdfunding, and is made increasingly easy and widespread with digital platforms (Bachmann et al., 2011).
- Business angel groups and networks, enabled by digital platforms such as AngelList are now able to operate in coordination whereas previously angel investors mostly operated as individuals.
- Patent-based investment funds are a relatively novel form of financing where they invest in startups that hold valuable patents or patentable inventions, or provide credit financing based on such patents. These funds sometimes also provide expertise in commercializing early-stage technology.

Some additional new forms of financing such as indie or bootstrap financing, private equity platforms, and recurring revenue financing have been pointed out by Keyhani, Robinson, Lehar, and Ashjari (2022). From the above, three contributions in this handbook focus on crowdfunding and ICOs. Chapter 11 by Ashjari (2022) titled "Crowdfunding: A Competency Framework for Creators" proposes a competency-based framework to define crowdfunding, through its similarities with entrepreneurial activities, as a value creation process. These competencies consist of opportunity, strategic, organizing, relational, conceptual, ethical, digital, and narrative, categorized in pre-campaign, in-campaign, and post-campaign phases. The digital and narrative competencies are new in this context. The overall framework helps answer questions such as "who could be a capable crowdfunder?" or, for the practicing digital entrepreneur, "what do I need to be able to do in order to be a capable crowdfunder?"

Chapter 12 titled "Backers: Consumers or Investors? Crowdfunding vs. Traditional Financing as an Optimal Security Design Problem" by Miglo (2022) tackles the choice between digital financing (e.g., crowdfunding) and traditional financing through a mathematical model. The model incorporates aspects of the decision such as the presence of moral hazard problems regarding the choice of production scale, asymmetric information about firm quality, and market demand uncertainty. According to the model, a two-stage financing process involving reward-based crowdfunding followed by loan financing is optimal for entrepreneurs. This is particularly the case for digital entrepreneurs developing innovative or high-risk products.

Chapter 13 by Schierstedt, Göttel, and Klever (2022) titled "Blockchain Economy: The Challenges and Opportunities of Initial Coin Offerings" provides a great introduction to ICOs, which is the emerging phenomenon whereby startups are beginning to sell security in the form of currency or utility tokens to a crowd of investors. The ICO form of financing and its challenges and opportunities for digital entrepreneurs are analyzed to provide a better understanding of blockchain-based business models for digital entrepreneurs. Legal and regulatory issues are the main challenges of raising funding through ICOs, and the main benefits include access to financing in very early stages, low cost of raising capital, and high-speed transactions.

## Digital Entrepreneurship and Social Issues

There are a multitude of issues relating to ethics, social justice, and environmental sustainability that are relevant to digital entrepreneurship. Practitioners in the world of digital technology as well as entrepreneurs often have an optimistic bend (Dunne, Clark, Berns, & McDowell, 2019; Dushnitsky, 2010; Hmieleski & Baron, 2009). This results in a sometimes-blind faith and idealism that shapes their perspective about social issues. For example, the ideas that digital technology can significantly reduce costs, remove physical barriers, and reward competence may overshadow the fact that these benefits still accrue differentially to advantaged vs. disadvantaged segments of society. As pointed out by Dy, Marlow, and Martin (2017, p. 286): "it is purported that the emerging field of digital entrepreneurship may act as a 'great leveller' owing to perceived lower barriers to entry, disembodiment of the entrepreneurial actor and the absence of visible markers of disadvantage online" but that deeper analysis "reveals how the privileges and disadvantages arising from intersecting social positions of gender, race and class status are experienced" such that "offline inequality, in the form of marked bodies, social positionality and associated resource constraints, is produced and reproduced in the online environment."

In a similar vein Fossen and Sorgner (2021) find that while digitalization is significantly associated with entrepreneurial entry, this effect is mostly the result of high-skilled individuals and employees in ICT occupations becoming entrepreneurs as opposed to low-skilled individuals. Internationally, an increasingly large "digital divide" is being created between the richer and poorer countries (Arendt, 2008; Murthy, Kalsie, & Shankar, 2021). Digital entrepreneurship may also be a way to help sustainable entrepreneurship advance more quickly, but again, the sustainable entrepreneurs may well be high-skilled, wealthy individuals from more developed nations (Heinze, 2020; Pilgeram, 2011).

Both the theory of socio-materiality and the theory of affordances and constraints are useful perspectives to apply in the study of social issues in digital entrepreneurship. Socio-materiality emphasizes the idea that the social context of a technology is a key determinant of the entrepreneurial possibilities that may arise from the technology (Davidson & Vaast, 2010; Orlikowski, 2010). The theory of affordances and constraints reminds us that any technology that may be enabling in some ways also comes with boundaries and constraints (Chemero, 2003; Ingold, 2018; Majchrzak & Markus, 2013) as most of the digital entrepreneurship literature has an obvious bend toward affordances and opportunities, tending to neglect the dark side of digital entrepreneurship (Berger, von Briel, Davidsson, & Kuckertz, 2021). This is not to say that the study of social issues in digital entrepreneurship necessarily must always uncover a dark side. For example, McAdam, Crowley, and Harrison (2020) find that for women in Saudi Arabia, digital entrepreneurship is empowering, provides them with financial independence, social status, an online "safe space," and access to opportunities.

Three chapters in this handbook roughly fall into this theme of research. Chapter 14 by Martinez Dy titled "Agentifying the Body Algorithmic: Digital Entrepreneurial Agency and Accountability Gaps" provides a ground-breaking theoretical investigation of ethical issues arising from human reliance on non-human agents in the context of digital entrepreneurship. It examines the current status of rights and obligations for algorithmic agents as they manifest in several roles, such as Oracle, Trader, Manager, and Enforcer, and explores means by which to increase the possibility of algorithmic accountability and reduce their potential harm. Her arguments encourage us to embrace the idea that digital technology expands the very nature of entrepreneurial agency, and opens our minds to the potential consequences of such an expansion.

In Chapter 15, Gerli and Whalley (2022) study "Digital Entrepreneurship in a Rural Context: The Implications of the Rural–Urban Digital Divide." This chapter examines digital entrepreneurship in rural areas and the digital divide in Italy and the UK. Access to superfast broadband and the quality of Internet connection is critical for rural entrepreneurs. They argue that training to increase the digital skills of entrepreneurs in rural areas can support rural digital entrepreneurship and reduce the digital divide. The chapter also builds on the dynamic interplay between access divide, skill divide, and digital entrepreneurship to provide ideas for policymaking in support of digital entrepreneurship for rural areas.

Finally, Chapter 16 by Koehler, Schultz, and Rasche (2022) titled "Data are the Fuel for Digital Entrepreneurship – But what about data privacy?" takes a deeper look at the significance of data, data privacy, and privacy laws in today's economy. Large digital platforms with access to privileged data face increasingly serious questions of legitimacy from the public and from governments. On the other hand, data privacy legislation creates business opportunities for digital entrepreneurs in terms of providing solutions for enterprises facing this issue.

## CONCLUDING REMARKS

This chapter has aimed to provide a brief introduction to the field of digital entrepreneurship research and to position the remaining chapters of this handbook within some of the main research themes in this literature. We have been fortunate to receive high quality contributions from an eclectic and global group of scholars. Due to space limitations, the editorial team had to be selective and after a detailed review process ultimately chose 15 chapters to include in this volume. The included chapters are authored by scholars from institutions in 11 different countries and three different continents. Together, they highlight and discuss a diverse set of questions, contexts, theories, methods, and phenomena that is reflective of the diversity in the broader digital entrepreneurship literature.

Scholars who engage in research in the field of digital entrepreneurship often sacrifice some generality in exchange for context-richness and relevance to practical matters. This means that unfortunately much of the material in this type of research may go obsolete faster than other areas that are less embedded in such a rapidly changing context. On the other hand, this dynamism is inherent in the context of rapidly advancing digital technologies and the major impact they have on the work and life of everyone in the world. This sense of dynamism and advancement imbued in the subject matter being studied, infuses digital entrepreneurship research with a sense of forward-looking optimism, hope, and wonder about the possibilities that the future will bring. We hope that most readers of this handbook will share with us this general sense of positivity, even if it is qualified by a healthy dose of critical skepticism, as it well should be.

## NOTES

1.    Data source: https://www.itu.int/en/ITU-D/Statistics/Pages/stat/default.aspx.
2.    Data source: https://www.statista.com/statistics/748551/worldwide-households-with-computer/.
3.    See https://www.itu.int/itu-d/reports/statistics/2021/11/15/internet-use/.
4.    Data source: https://www.hntrends.com/2021/dec-remote-work-trend-still-climbing.html.

# REFERENCES

Abdulkadiroglu, A., & Sönmez, T. (2013). Matching markets: Theory and practice. *Advances in Economics and Econometrics, 1*, 3–47.

Abernathy, W. J., & Utterback, J. M. (1978). Patterns of industrial innovation. *Technology Review, 80*(7), 40–47.

Acs, Z. J., Autio, E., & Szerb, L. (2014). National systems of entrepreneurship: Measurement issues and policy implications. *Research Policy, 43*(3), 476–494.

Adhami, S., Giudici, G., & Martinazzi, S. (2018). Why do businesses go crypto? An empirical analysis of initial coin offerings. *Journal of Economics and Business, 100*, 64–75.

Afuah, A., & Tucci, C. L. (2003). *Internet Business Models and Strategies: Text and Cases* (2nd ed.). Boston: McGraw-Hill.

Arendt, L. (2008). Barriers to ICT adoption in SMEs: How to bridge the digital divide? *Journal of Systems and Information Technology, 10*(2), 93.

Arthur, W. B. (1988). Competing technologies: An overview. In G. Dosi, C. Freeman, R. Nelson, G. Silverberg, & L. Soete (Eds.), *Technical Change and Economic Theory* (pp. 590–607). London: Pinter Publishers.

Autio, E., Nambisan, S., Thomas, L. D., & Wright, M. (2018). Digital affordances, spatial affordances, and the genesis of entrepreneurial ecosystems. *Strategic Entrepreneurship Journal, 12*(1), 72–95.

Bachmann, A., Becker, A., Buerckner, D., Hilker, M., Kock, F., Lehmann, M., ... Funk, B. (2011). Online peer-to-peer lending: A literature review. *Journal of Internet Banking and Commerce, 16*(2), 1.

Baker, T., & Welter, F. (2020). *Contextualizing Entrepreneurship Theory*. New York: Routledge.

Baskerville, R. L., Myers, M. D., & Yoo, Y. (2020). Digital first: The ontological reversal and new challenges for information systems research. *Management Information Systems Quarterly, 44*(2), 509–523.

Baumol, W. J. (2002). *The Free-Market Innovation Machine: Analyzing the Growth Miracle of Capitalism*, Princeton, NJ: Princeton University Press.

Benkler, Y. (2000). Unhurried view of private ordering in information transactions. *Vanderbilt Law Review, 53*(6), art. 32.

Berger, E. S., von Briel, F., Davidsson, P., & Kuckertz, A. (2021). Digital or not: The future of entrepreneurship and innovation: Introduction to the special issue. *Journal of Business Research, 125*, 436–442.

Blank, S. (2013). Why the lean start-up changes everything. *Harvard Business Review, 91*(5), 65–72.

Blank, S., & Dorf, B. (2020). *The Startup Owner's Manual: The Step-By-Step Guide for Building a Great Company*, New York: John Wiley & Sons.

Broekhuizen, T. L., Emrich, O., Gijsenberg, M. J., Broekhuis, M., Donkers, B., & Sloot, L. M. (2021). Digital platform openness: Drivers, dimensions and outcomes. *Journal of Business Research, 122*, 902–914.

Brousseau, E., & Penard, T. (2007). The economics of digital business models: A framework for analyzing the economics of platforms. *Review of Network Economics, 6*(2), 81–114.

Chalmers, D., Matthews, R., & Hyslop, A. (2021). Blockchain as an external enabler of new venture ideas: Digital entrepreneurs and the disintermediation of the global music industry. *Journal of Business Research, 125*, 577–591.

Chemero, A. (2003). An outline of a theory of affordances. *Ecological Psychology, 15*(2), 181–195

Chen, A. (2021). *The Cold Start Problem: How to Start and Scale Network Effects*. New York: Harper Business.

Chesbrough, H. (2003). *Open innovation: The New Imperative for Creating and Profiting From Technology*. Boston, MA: Harvard Business School Press.

Chesbrough, H., & Rosenbloom, R. S. (2002). The role of the business model in capturing value from innovation: Evidence from Xerox Corporation's technology spin-off companies. *Industrial and Corporate Change, 11*(3), 529–555.

Christensen, C. M. (1997). *The Innovator's Dilemma: When New Technologies Cause Great Firms to Fail*. Boston, MA: Harvard Business School Press.

Currier, J. (2015). The Next 10 Years Will Be About "Market Networks." *NFX.com Blog Posts*. https://www.nfx.com/post/10-years-about-market-networks/.

Davidson, E., & Vaast, E. (2010). *Digital entrepreneurship and its sociomaterial enactment.* Paper presented at the 2010 43rd Hawaii International Conference on System Sciences.

Davidsson, P. (2016). *Researching Entrepreneurship.* New York: Springer Science.

Demange, G., & Gale, D. (1985). The strategy structure of two-sided matching markets. *Econometrica: Journal of the Econometric Society, 873–888.*

Downes, L., & Nunes, P. (2014). *Big Bang Disruption: Strategy in the Age of Devastating Innovation.* London: Penguin.

Du, W., Pan, S. L., Zhou, N., & Ouyang, T. (2018). From a marketplace of electronics to a digital entrepreneurial ecosystem (DEE): The emergence of a meta-organization in Zhongguancun, China. *Information Systems Journal, 28*(6), 1158–1175.

Dunne, T. C., Clark, B. B., Berns, J. P., & McDowell, W. C. (2019). The technology bias in entrepreneur–investor negotiations. *Journal of Business Research, 105,* 258–269.

Dushnitsky, G. (2010). Entrepreneurial optimism in the market for technological inventions. *Organization Science, 21*(1), 150–167.

Dy, A. M., Marlow, S., & Martin, L. (2017). A Web of opportunity or the same old story? Women digital entrepreneurs and intersectionality theory. *Human Relations, 70*(3), 286–311.

Eisenmann, T., Parker, G., & Alstyne, M. W. V. (2006). Strategies for two-sided markets. *Harvard Business Review, 84*(10), 92–101.

Elia, G., Margherita, A., & Passiante, G. (2020). Digital entrepreneurship ecosystem: How digital technologies and collective intelligence are reshaping the entrepreneurial process. *Technological Forecasting and Social Change, 150,* 119791.

Ethiraj, S. K., & Levinthal, D. (2004). Modularity and innovation in complex systems. *Management Science, 50*(2), 159–173.

Evans, J. (2017). After the end of the startup era. *Techcrunch.* https://techcrunch.com/2017/10/22/ask-not-for-whom-the-deadpool-tolls/.

Fisch, C. (2019). Initial coin offerings (ICOs) to finance new ventures. *Journal of Business Venturing, 34*(1), 1–22.

Fossen, F. M., & Sorgner, A. (2021). Digitalization of work and entry into entrepreneurship. *Journal of Business Research, 125,* 548–563.

Fu, S., Sun, Y., & Gao, X. (2022). Balancing openness and control to improve the performance of crowd-sourcing contests for product innovation: A configurational perspective. *Technological Forecasting and Social Change, 174,* 121194.

Galindo-Martín, M.-Á., Castaño-Martínez, M.-S., & Méndez-Picazo, M.-T. (2019). Digital transformation, digital dividends and entrepreneurship: A quantitative analysis. *Journal of Business Research, 101,* 522–527.

Gassmann, O., Frankenberger, K., & Csik, M. (2014). *The Business Model Navigator: 55 Models That Will Revolutionise Your Business.* London: Pearson.

Geissinger, A., Laurell, C., Sandström, C., Eriksson, K., & Nykvist, R. (2019). Digital entrepreneurship and field conditions for institutional change: Investigating the enabling role of cities. *Technological Forecasting and Social Change, 146,* 877–886.

Giones, F., & Brem, A. (2017). Digital technology entrepreneurship: A definition and research agenda. *Technology Innovation Management Review, 7*(5), 44–51.

Giustiziero, G., Kretschmer, T., Somaya, D., & Wu, B. (2021). Hyperspecialization and hyperscaling: A resource-based theory of the digital firm. *Strategic Management Journal.* Early view. https://onlinelibrary.wiley.com/doi/full/10.1002/smj.3365.

Heinze, L. (2020). Fashion with heart: Sustainable fashion entrepreneurs, emotional labour and implications for a sustainable fashion system. *Sustainable Development, 28*(6), 1554–1563.

Hirsch, D. D. (2014). The glass house effect: Big data, the new oil, and the power of analogy. *Maine Law Review, 66*(2), 373–395.

Hitt, M. A., Ireland, R. D., Sirmon, D. G., & Trahms, C. A. (2011). Strategic entrepreneurship: Creating value for individuals, organizations, and society. *Academy of Management Perspectives, 25*(2), 57–75.

Hmieleski, K. M., & Baron, R. A. (2009). Entrepreneurs' optimism and new venture performance: A social cognitive perspective. *Academy of Management Journal, 52*(3), 473–488.

Hoffman, R., & Yeh, C. (2018). *Blitzscaling: The Lightning-fast Path to Building Massively Valuable Businesses.* London: Broadway Business.

Hull, C. E., Hung, Y.-T. C., Hair, N., Perotti, V., & DeMartino, R. (2007). Taking advantage of digital opportunities: A typology of digital entrepreneurship. *International Journal of Networking and Virtual Organisations, 4*(3), 290–303.

Ingold, T. (2018). Back to the future with the theory of affordances. *HAU: Journal of Ethnographic Theory, 8*(1–2), 39–44.

Johnson, M. W., & Lafley, A. G. (2010). *Seizing the White Space: Business Model Innovation for Growth and Renewal.* Boston, MA: Harvard Business Press.

Kallinikos, J., Aaltonen, A., & Marton, A. (2013). The ambivalent ontology of digital artifacts. *Mis Quarterly*, 357–370.

Katz, M. L., & Shapiro, C. (1994). Systems competition and network effects. *Journal of Economic Perspectives, 8*(2), 93–115.

Keyhani, M. (2021). *The Architecture of Generative Marketplaces: Two-Sided Markets as Distributed Innovation Machines.* Paper presented at the Annual conference of the Administrative Sciences Association of Canada (ASAC), June 12–15, Virtual.

Keyhani, M. (2022). The logic of strategic entrepreneurship. *Strategic Organization.* doi:10.1177 %2F14761270211057571.

Keyhani, M., & Hastings, H. (2021). Implications of generativity for entrepreneurship and strategy. *ERENET Profile, 16*(1), 3–12.

Keyhani, M., Robinson, M. J., Lehar, A., & Ashjari, A. (2022). Digital Entrepreneurship and capital acquisition in the global economy. In M. Munoz (Ed.), *Digital Entrepreneurship and the Global Economy* (Chapter 8). London: Taylor & Francis.

Klein, M., Neitzert, F., Hartmann-Wendels, T., & Kraus, S. (2019). Start-up financing in the digital age: A systematic review and comparison of new forms of financing. *The Journal of Entrepreneurial Finance, 21*(2), 45–98.

Kollmann, T. (1998). The information triple jump as the measure of success in electronic commerce. *Electronic Markets, 8*(4), 44–49.

Kollmann, T., Kleine-Stegemann, L., de Cruppe, K., & Then-Bergh, C. (2021). Eras of digital entrepreneurship – connecting the past, present, and future. *Business & Information Systems Engineering*, 1–17.

Koning, R., Hasan, S., Fuqua, D., & Chatterji, A. (2021). Digital experimentation and startup performance: Evidence from A/B testing. Harvard Business School Working Paper 20-018. https://www.hbs .edu/ris/Publication%20Files/20-018_0e319556-b28a-4528-bfa1-51db6d5831b8.pdf.

LaBerge, L., O'Toole, C., Schneider, J., & Smaje, K. (2020). *How COVID-19 has pushed companies over the technology tipping point—and transformed business forever.* https://www.mckinsey.com/ business-functions/strategy-and-corporate-finance/our-insights/how-covid-19-has-pushed-companies -over-the-technology-tipping-point-and-transformed-business-forever.

Landström, H. (2005). *Pioneers in Entrepreneurship and Small Business Research.* New York: Springer Science.

Laplume, A. O., Petersen, B., & Pearce, J. M. (2016). Global value chains from a 3D printing perspective. *Journal of International Business Studies, 47*(5), 595–609.

Levinthal, D. A., & Wu, B. (2010). Opportunity costs and non-scale free capabilities: Profit maximization, corporate scope, and profit margins. *Strategic Management Journal, 31*(7), 780–801. doi:10 .1002/Smj.845.

Levitt, T. (1965). Exploit the product life cycle. *Harvard Business Review, 43*, 81–94.

Majchrzak, A., & Markus, M. L. (2013). Technology affordances and constraints theory (of MIS). In E. H. Kessler (Ed.), *Encyclopedia of Management Theory* (Vol. 1, pp. 832–836). Thousand Oaks, CA: Sage.

Manjoo, F. (2017). How the frightful five put start-ups in a lose-lose situation. *New York Times.* https:// www.nytimes.com/2017/10/18/technology/frightful-five-startups.html.

McAdam, M., Crowley, C., & Harrison, R. T. (2020). Digital girl: Cyberfeminism and the emancipatory potential of digital entrepreneurship in emerging economies. *Small Business Economics, 55*(2), 349–362.

Meyer, G. D. (2009). Commentary: On the integration of strategic management and entrepreneurship: Views of a contrarian. *Entrepreneurship Theory and Practice, 33*(1), 341–351. doi:10.1111/j.1540 -6520.2008.00292.x.

Mollick, E. (2014). The dynamics of crowdfunding: An exploratory study. *Journal of Business Venturing, 29*(1), 1–16.

Murthy, K. B., Kalsie, A., & Shankar, R. (2021). Digital economy in a global perspective: Is there a digital divide? *Transnational Corporations Review, 13*(1), 1–15.

Nambisan, S. (2017). Digital entrepreneurship: Toward a digital technology perspective of entrepreneurship. *Entrepreneurship Theory and Practice, 41*(6).

Nelson, R. R. (1993). *National Innovation Systems: A Comparative Analysis*. Oxford University Press on Demand.

Nicotra, M., Romano, M., Del Giudice, M., & Schillaci, C. E. (2018). The causal relation between entrepreneurial ecosystem and productive entrepreneurship: A measurement framework. *The Journal of Technology Transfer, 43*(3), 640–673.

Orlikowski, W. J. (2010). The sociomateriality of organisational life: Considering technology in management research. *Cambridge Journal of Economics, 34*(1), 125–141.

Osterwalder, A., & Pigneur, Y. (2010). *Business Model Generation: A Handbook for Visionaries, Game Changers, and Challengers*, New York: Wiley.

Park, S.-M., & Kim, Y.-G. (2022). A metaverse: Taxonomy, components, applications, and open challenges. *IEEE Access*.

Parker, G. G., Van Alstyne, M. W., & Choudary, S. P. (2016). *Platform Revolution: How Networked Markets Are Transforming the Economy and How to Make Them Work for You*. New York: WW Norton & Company.

Phelps, E. S. (2013). *Mass Flourishing: How Grassroots Innovation Created Jobs, Challenge, and Change*. Princeton, NJ: Princeton University Press.

Phelps, E. S. (2017). The dynamism of nations: Toward a theory of indigenous innovation. *Capitalism and Society, 12*(1), art. 3.

Pilgeram, R. (2011). "The only thing that isn't sustainable … is the farmer": Social sustainability and the politics of class among Pacific Northwest farmers engaged in sustainable farming. *Rural Sociology, 76*(3), 375–393.

Porter, M. (1990). *The Competitive Advantage of Nations*. New York: Free Press.

Ries, E. (2011). *The Lean Startup: How Today's Entrepreneurs Use Continuous Innovation to Create Radically Successful Businesses* (1st ed.). New York: Crown Business.

Rochet, J. C., & Tirole, J. (2006). Two-sided markets: a progress report. *The Rand Journal of Economics, 37*(3), 645–667.

Romer, P. M. (1990). Endogenous technological change. *Journal of Political Economy, 98*(5, Part 2), S71–S102.

Roth, A. E., & Sotomayor, M. A. O. (1990). *Two-Sided Matching: A Study in Game-Theoretic Modeling and Analysis*. Cambridge, UK and New York: Cambridge University Press.

Rysman, M. (2009). The economics of two-sided markets. *Journal of Economic Perspectives, 23*(3), 125–143.

Shapiro, C., & Varian, H. R. (1999). *Information Rules: A Strategic Guide to the Network Economy*. Boston, MA: Harvard Business School Press.

Siroker, D., & Koomen, P. (2013). *A/B testing: The Most Powerful Way to Turn Clicks into Customers*. New York: John Wiley & Sons.

Srinivasan, A., & Venkatraman, N. (2018). Entrepreneurship in digital platforms: A network-centric view. *Strategic Entrepreneurship Journal, 12*(1), 54–71.

Steininger, D. M. (2019). Linking information systems and entrepreneurship: A review and agenda for IT-associated and digital entrepreneurship research. *Information Systems Journal, 29*(2), 363–407.

Sussan, F., & Acs, Z. J. (2017). The digital entrepreneurial ecosystem. *Small Business Economics, 49*(1), 55–73.

Tajedin, H., Madhok, A., & Keyhani, M. (2019). A theory of digital firm-designed markets: Defying knowledge constraints with crowds and marketplaces. *Strategy Science, 4*(4), 323–342.

Thomke, S., & von Hippel, E. (2002). Customers as innovators: A new way to create value. *Harvard Business Review, 80*(4), 74–81.

Tiwana, A. (2013). *Platform Ecosystems: Aligning Architecture, Governance, and Strategy*: Oxford: Newnes.

Varian, H. R. (2001). High-technology industries and market structure. http://people.ischool.berkeley.edu/~hal/Papers/structure.pdf.

Varian, H. R. (2010). Computer mediated transactions. *The American Economic Review, 100*(2), 1–10.

Varian, H. R. (2019). Artificial intelligence, economics, and industrial organization. In A. Agrawal, J. Gans, & A. Goldfarb (Eds.), *The Economics of Artificial Intelligence: An Agenda* (pp. 399–419). Chicago: University of Chicago Press.

Victor, W., & Greg, H. (2012). *The Rainforest: The Secret to Building the Next Silicon Valley.* Regenwald.

von Briel, F., Recker, J., Selander, L., Jarvenpaa, S. L., Hukal, P., Yoo, Y., ... Alpar, P. (2021). Researching digital entrepreneurship: Current issues and suggestions for future directions. *Communications of the Association for Information Systems, 48*(33), 284–304.

von Hippel, E. (1986). Lead users: A source of novel product concepts. *Management Science, 32*(7), 791–805.

Yoo, Y., Henfridsson, O., & Lyytinen, K. (2010). The new organizing logic of digital innovation: An agenda for information systems research. *Information Systems Research, 21*(4), 724–735.

Yu, A. (2021). The power of market networks. https://www.linkedin.com/pulse/power-market-networks-andrew-yu/.

Zahra, S. A. (2007). Contextualizing theory building in entrepreneurship research. *Journal of Business Venturing, 22*(3), 443–452.

Zahra, S. A., Wright, M., & Abdelgawad, S. G. (2014). Contextualization and the advancement of entrepreneurship research. *International Small Business Journal, 32*(5), 479–500.

Zittrain, J. (2008). *The Future of the Internet—And How to Stop It.* New Haven, CT: Yale University Press.

# PART II

# DIGITAL ENTREPRENEURSHIP AND DEFINITIONS

# 2. What is digital entrepreneurship? Fundamentals of company founding in the digital economy

*Tobias Kollmann and Philipp Benedikt Jung*

## INTRODUCTION

New Ventures play a key role in the social and economic development of a country and are often based on technological innovations. The underlying idea is that each new start-up represents a new market player that has a stimulating effect on competition and thus drives economic momentum forward. At the same time, internal and external information and communication processes at enterprises across almost every industry sector have been increasingly supported by digital information technologies. These technologies (e.g. internet, interactive television and mobile communications) have triggered the founding of numerous start-ups in the Digital Economy. In this context, primarily young and innovative enterprises in the sector of information and communication technologies have the economic function to identify and realize innovation potentials and to transform them into competitive business models. Against this background, the term "Digital Entrepreneurship" respectively describes the act of establishing new companies specifically in the Digital Economy (Kollmann, 2006, 2020; Matlay, 2004).

It is a positive development that the topic of Digital Entrepreneurship receives increased attention (e.g. Ghezzi & Cavallo, 2020; Nambisan, 2017) as research in this important field enhances knowledge. At this point, however, it must be noted that several recent studies mistakenly regard Digital Entrepreneurship as a newly emerging field (e.g. Beliaeva et al., 2019; Kraus, Palmer et al., 2019; Kraus, Roig-Tierno et al., 2019). In so doing, these contributions neglect previous research contributions on this topic, which clearly laid the foundation for all subsequent considerations and discussions (Jones et al., 2021). Thus, the assumption that the research field of Digital Entrepreneurship is a new phenomenon must be disagreed with. It can rather be understood as a new common ground that merges the wording in this field, which has previously generated fragmented designations. Before relabeling the research topic into "Digital Entrepreneurship," the substantive foundation was already covered using preceding terms such as "Virtual-," "Cyber-," "IT-," "Techno-," "Online-," "E-Commerce-," "Internet-" or, particularly often, "E-Entrepreneurship." Hence, the roots of this field go back much further. The chapter "Eras of Digital Entrepreneurship" in this handbook precisely outlines the antecedents of the term Digital Entrepreneurship along with its historical development phases.

In the present work, we exemplify the true roots of Digital Entrepreneurship by presenting the core of one of the major foundational articles in this field (see "Eras of Digital Entrepreneurship" and "Exploring the Field of Digital Entrepreneurship" in this handbook).

The original article from Kollmann with the title "What is e-entrepreneurship? – Fundamentals of company founding in the net economy" was published in 2006 in the *International Journal of Technology Management* and explains the different facets of the phenomenon, which literature nowadays refers to as "Digital Entrepreneurship." In the presented version of the article, the term "Electronic" (in short "E-") and the word "Net" is replaced by the now more commonly used term "Digital." Additionally, only outdated contextual descriptions about the Digital Economy as well as references were updated. As these changes do not alter the content of the article, but only its wording, we exemplify that true roots of Digital Entrepreneurship lie further in the past than partially claimed.

It is therefore precisely the research-didactic and the research-historical goal that the following update of the 2006 contribution (with a first revision in 2009 in the *Handbook of Research on Techno-Entrepreneurship*; 2nd edition 2014) deliberately overlaps in content, except for the wording. This is intended to show that the content considerations from the past also retain their validity under the new terminology of a "digital entrepreneurship" and must therefore not be disregarded under the new terminology. Thus, we are pleased to enrich the subject area of Digital Entrepreneurship by shedding light on its relevant historical basis with updated sources and examples.

The original article "What is e-entrepreneurship? – Fundamentals of company founding in the net economy" (Kollmann, 2006) answers several questions, that were raised by the expansion of the classical use of the term "entrepreneurship":

- Which environment and which possibilities does the Digital Economy offer for new and innovative entrepreneurial activities?
- What is different or what unusual features can be found in establishing companies in the Digital Economy?
- What are the building blocks and phases of development involved in setting up a company in the Digital Economy?

## THE DIGITAL ECONOMY

The basis of the Digital Economy is formed by four technological innovations: telecommunication, information technology, media technology and entertainment (the so-called TIME markets). These innovations had, and continue to, significantly impact the possible ways in which information, communication and transactions are managed (Kollmann, 2001). According to BITKOM (2020), the associated German ICT sector in 2019 generated sales of 169.1 billion euros, demonstrating the importance of this field. Against this backdrop, business start-ups are often based on technological innovations and play an outstanding role in the social and economic development of a country. Information technologies in particular, have enabled numerous business start-ups within the Digital Economy. With every new foundation, a new market participant is born, which stimulates competition and thereby further advances economic dynamics. The ICT sector heavily relies on small and medium-sized enterprises, as specifically young and newly founded companies (start-ups in the young Digital Economy) play a key role as innovation drivers (Kollmann, Jung et al., 2020). Empirical evidence indicates that large, established companies in the ICT sector, oftentimes neglect a number of innovation potentials (Kollmann et al., 2021). Young and newly founded companies have the economic function of realizing such innovation potentials and converting them into marketable business models. Against this backdrop, the German Federal Ministry of Economics and Energy (Bundesministerium für Wirtschaft und Energie, 2018) investigated this field in its Digital Economic Monitoring Report and identified that nearly 6,000 ICT ventures are founded (Digital Entrepreneurship) only in Germany every year. Not only in Germany, but also in Europe and throughout the world, the dynamic environments of ICT ventures take a critical role in in the economic function by realizing innovation potentials (Keil et al., 2008; Kollmann et al., 2016). These findings further underline that we are talking about a critical field encompassing one of the most important technologies of the present and future (Kollmann, 2020).

Therefore, the increased support of business processes using digital systems takes center stage in this chapter. There are a number of terms for this that can be identified (e.g. digital business, digital commerce, information economics, network economics), which can, to some degree, be used synonymously (Jelassi & Enders, 2005). It is easiest to structure and clarify the terms, define their boundaries and field of application by using the shell model of the Digital Economy, which will subsequently be described in more detail (see Figure 2.1).

The initial assumption in the shell model is the general development towards an information society (see Figure 2.1). Since the beginning in the 1990s, innovative information technology induced a structural change in both social and economic spheres especially through the digitalization of information and the networking of computers (Hagel & Singer, 1997; Tapscott, 1996). Whereas just a few years ago, computers and networks were reserved for only a few specialists, today they are already an integral part of daily life: digital technologies and their influence on the transfer of information are ubiquitous. The results of this development are clear – innovative information technologies such as the internet/WWW, mobile telecommunications and interactive television (ITV). These technologies are changing the world as radically as the steam engine, loom, railways and tractor once did (Pruden, 1978). The digitalization and spread of information via digital data pathways or networks serve as a pacemaker for future economic growth that is comparable with the significance of the printing press in the 15th century or motorization in the 20th century. The information society is respectively characterized by the intensive use of information technologies and the resulting change from an industrial to a knowledge society (Evans & Wurster, 1997). Analogously, from a global economic point of view, there is an obvious shifting from the traditional economic sectors of agriculture, production and (non-virtual or rendered) services towards the information industry sector.

Against this background, one of the central characteristics of the post-industrial computer society is the systematic use of information technology (IT) as well as the acquisition and application of information that complements work-life and capital as an exclusive source of value, production and profit. Information becomes an independent factor of production (Porter & Millar, 1985; Weiber & Kollmann, 1998) and thus establishes the information economy (see Figure 2.1). From a historical perspective, initially, only the product characteristics (quality) and corresponding product conditions (e.g. price, discount) determined if a product was successful (Kirzner, 1973; Porter, 1985). At that point, it was important to either offer products or services to the customer that were either cheaper than (cost leadership) or qualitatively superior (quality leadership) to the competitor's product. Thereafter, the first major successes, two additional factors joined the scene–time (speed) and flexibility (Meyer, 2001; Stalk, 1988). At this point, it was important to offer products/services at a certain point in time at a certain place (availability leadership). Additionally, it became crucial to allow for customer-oriented product differentiation of important product characteristics (demand leadership). Information

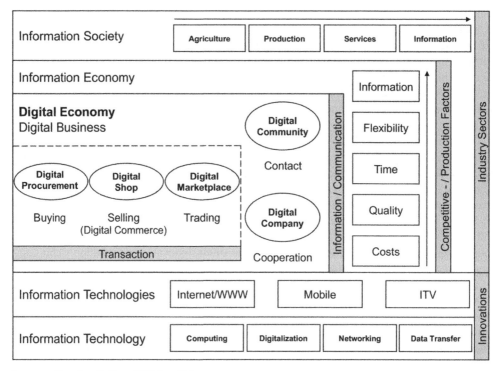

*Source:*    Based on Kollman (2006), p. 324.

*Figure 2.1    The shell model of the Digital Economy*

technologies have now created an environment in which information is more easily accessible and can be increasingly used for commercial purposes. The source of a competitive advantage will be determined in the future, as a result of the technological development presented here, by achieving knowledge and information superiority over the competition (information leadership). Those who possess better information about the market and their customers (potential customers) will be more successful than the competition. Whereas information previously held merely a supporting function for physical production processes, in the future it will become an independent factor for production and competitiveness (Weiber & Kollmann, 1998).

The growing relevance of IT and the expansion of digital data networks have created a new commercial/business dimension that can be called the Digital Economy (see Figure 2.1). It is especially influenced by the area of digital business processes that are concluded over digital data pathways (Kollmann, 2001; Taylor & Murphy, 2004; Zwass, 2003). Due to the importance of information as a supporting and independent competitive factor, as well as the increase in digital data networks, it must be assumed that there will be a division of the relevant trade levels on which the world does business in the future (Weiber & Kollmann, 1998): in addition to the real level of physical products and/or services (Real Economy), a digital level for digital data and communication networks (Digital Economy) will evolve. The commercial possibilities resulting from this development can be called, in this context, digital business (see Figure 2.1), which means the use of digital information technologies for supporting business processes in the preparation, negotiation and conclusion phases (Kollmann, 2001). The necessary building blocks, including information, communication and transaction are in this case transferred and respectively concluded between the participating trade partners over digital networks (Kollmann, 2019c).

Three central platforms have been formed which serve as a basis for these digital business processes in digital business (see Figure 2.1) that include the exchange of all three building blocks (information, communication and transaction).

- A Digital Procurement (also referred to as E-Procurement) enables the digital purchasing of products and services from a company via digital networks. This uses the integration of innovative information and communication technologies to support and respectively conclude both operative and strategic tasks in the area of procurement. An example for a Digital Procurement platform is SAP Ariba. It offers a complete solution for the digital transformation of the procurement process of companies (Kollmann, 2019b).
- A Digital Shop (also referred to as E-Shop) allows the digital sales of products and services by a company using digital networks. This allows innovative information and communication technologies to be used in supporting and concluding the operative and strategic tasks for the area of sales. An example for a Digital Shop platform is Zalando, which is an online fashion shop. Zalando developed its own shop system under the name "Zalando E-Commerce Operation System" (abbreviated to ZEOS) store system. According to the company, "Zalando Technology" is the basis for all internal processes and forms the core for all products and services (Kollmann, 2019b).
- A Digital Marketplace (also referred to as E-Marketplace) allows digital trade with products and/or services via digital networks. This represents the integration of innovative information and communication technologies to support and conclude respectively the matching process of the supply and demand sides. An example for a Digital Marketplace platform is Opodo. The company provides a wide range of travel services on the internet. Opodo's goal is to offer a wide selection of flights, hotels and vacation packages at particularly attractive and competitive prices by combining offers from different airlines, hotels, and other participants at their Digital Marketplace (Kollmann, 2019b).

Certainly, it must be understood that these terms are subject to overlapping. As a result of this, Digital Procurement can most certainly be offered as a marketplace solution. In addition to this, two further platforms exist that are also attributed to the Digital Economy, which, however, do not emphasize all three building blocks equally – but concentrate rather more heavily on information and communication.

- A Digital Community (also referred to as E-Community) enables digital contact between persons and/or institutions using digital networks. What occurs here is an integration of innovative information and communication technologies to support the exchange of data and knowledge. An example for a Digital Community platform is Instagram. This social network with a focus on video and photo sharing offers an associated communication exchange between community members.
- A Digital Company (also referred to as E-Company) enables digital cooperation between companies using digital networks. This involves an integration of innovative information and communication technologies to link together individual business activities to form a virtual company that presents a bundled offer. An example for a Digital Company

platform is Star Alliance, an aviation alliance of 26 airlines. One of the main goals of this alliance is digital efficiency gains, for example, via coordinated scheduled flights with the establishment of a global network.

In view of the topic area of establishing a company, it appears suitable to hereafter view the entire field of the Digital Economy and, thus, all platforms, as a basis for new business ideas. This builds upon the fact that website operators in the internet can generate income with all platforms and, in doing this, establish new companies. Against this background, the following definition can be determined (based on Kollmann 2006, p. 326):

> The 'Digital Economy' refers to the commercial use of digital data networks, that is to say, a digital network economy, which, via various digital platforms (also referred to as electronic platform), allows the conclusion of information, communication and transaction processes.

## THE DIGITAL VALUE CHAIN

With the establishment of the Digital Economy and the heightened importance of the factor, "information," new possibilities emerged with respect to how enterprises create value (for further details see Amit & Zott, 2001; Lumpkin & Dess, 2004). An enterprise can create customer value not only through physical activities on the real level, but also through the creation of value on the digital level. The value chain of the Real Economy, represented by the first case, is based upon the approach used by Porter (1985): the value chain divides a company into strategically relevant activities and identifies physically and technologically differentiable value activities (see Figure 2.2), for which the customer is prepared to pay. Value activities are, according to this, those basic building blocks from which the company produces a "valuable product" in the eyes of the customer. This product can then form the basis for establishing an enterprise in the Real Economy (see Figure 2.2). In this model – a sequence of value generating or value increasing activities – the individual steps are analyzed in order to efficiently and effectively structure and develop primary and supporting processes. Even here, information is extremely important when striving to be more successful than the competition. Information can be used to better analyze and monitor existing processes. The crucial point here is that information has previously been regarded only as a supporting element, not however as an independent "source of customer and/or corporate value."

The value chain of the Digital Economy presented in the second example is based on the approach proposed by Weiber and Kollmann (1998): through the newly created dimension of information as an independent source of competitive advantage, value can be created through digital business activities in digital data networks independent from a physical value chain. These digital value added activities are, however, not comparable with the physical value creation activities presented by Porter (1985), rather they are characterized by the way in which information is used. Such value activities might include, for example, the collection, systemization, selection, composing and distribution of information (see Figure 2.2). A "digital value chain" manifests itself through these specific activities of creating value within digital data networks that originates in and impacts only the Digital Economy. The result: based on this new value creation level, innovative business ideas evolve through the use of the various platforms and new "digital products" are created. Customers are willing to pay for the value created by this product and the product can form the basis for establishing a company in the Digital Economy (see Figure 2.2).

**Value Chain of the Real Economy**

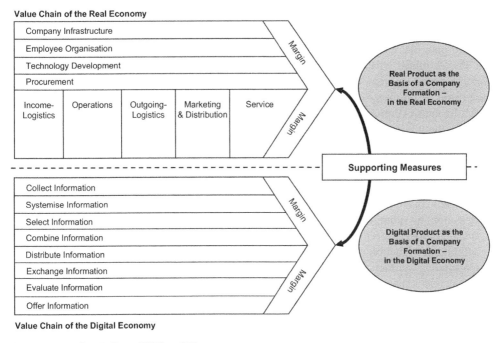

*Source:*    Based on Kollman (2006), p. 327.

*Figure 2.2     The concept of the digital value chain in the Real versus Digital Economy*

An example of the digital value chain can be seen in Autoscout24.de. In this Digital Marketplace, car sellers and buyers deal in used cars offered over the internet. User value is not necessarily just the used car. Value also rests in the provided overview, selection and mediation functions of the information related to the car and its availability, regardless of temporal and spatial restrictions. This "digital product" is made possible only through the use of information technologies. The website autoscout24.de is therefore a company of the Digital Economy as the creation of customer value only occurs at the digital level. This is similar to the example of Amazon.com, in which for instance the object "book" does not create added value, but by their processes enabling digital selection and ordering in a distinct and value adding way. However, this is an information product (overview, mediation, transaction) and thus amazon.com is a Digital Economy company with its Digital Shop. This does not mean that companies such as Autoscout24.de and Amazon.com do not require real resources (personnel, logistics, etc.). They also possess a real value chain, but it has a supporting role (see Figure 2.2) in order to successfully offer the digital creation of value. These correlations do not apply to an offer such as the one at Seat.com. In this case, value is created for the customer through the real product "car" and the shop in the internet is "merely" an additional distribution channel. This simplifies the ordering process, yet there is no independent value created for which the customer would be willing to pay extra. The car is not purchased due to the company's website.

Its internet presentation plays a supporting role for sales as a part of the real value chain (see Figure 2.2). Thus, Seat.com is not a company of the Digital Economy.

**The Digital Creation of Value**

Building upon the underlying value chain in the Digital Economy (see Figure 2.2), it must also be determined what form of digital value is "created" in the eyes of the customer for which he would be prepared to pay, that is, what makes an online offer attractive in the first place (from the customer's point of view). The most pertinent question for the company in the Digital Economy (digital ventures) is the question (see Figure 2.3): what value is created for the customer within the Digital Economy? In the example of the digital creation of value, this might include the following aspects.

- Overview: the aspect that an online offer provides an overview of a large amount of information that would otherwise involve the arduous gathering of information. By offering an overview, the digital venture creates value through structuring.
- Selection: by submitting database queries, consumers can locate exactly the desired information/products/services more quickly with an online offer and, thus, more efficiently. By offering this function, the digital venture creates selection value.
- Concluding transactions: this aspect refers to the possibility created by an online offer to design and structure business activities more efficiently and effectively (e.g. from the cost aspect or payment possibilities). The digital venture creates, in this way, transaction value.
- Cooperation: this aspect deals with the ability, using an online offer, for various vendors or companies to more efficiently and effectively interlink their service or product offers with each other. By doing this, the digital venture creates matching value.
- Exchange: in this case, an online offer allows different consumers to communicate more efficiently and effectively with each other. Through this, the digital venture creates communication value.

Considering these aspects, it is certainly possible that a digital venture creates several different types of value and that both structuring value as well as selection and mediation value are created. After the identification of the creation of value, the perspective changes to the entrepreneur's point of view. The question then remains (see Figure 2.3): how is this value created? For the purpose of answering this question, the previously presented digital value chain can once again be applied (see Figure 2.2). The digital value chain separates a digital venture into strategically relevant activities in order to better understand cost behavior and recognize present and potential sources of differentiation. Thus, the digital value chain represents respectively those value activities, which, for example, involve collecting, systemizing and distributing information (see Figure 2.2). Through specific value activities such as these within digital data networks, a "digital information product" is created that presents value for which the customer is hopefully willing to pay. The digital value chain embodies therefore the total value that is generated by the individual digital value activities plus the profit margin. Now, those value activities within the value chain will be identified that are especially relevant for the creation of value. These value activities, once identified, form, in turn, the basis of a digital value creation process within a company (see Figure 2.3). Thereafter, real work processes must be conceptualized to realize the digital process of value creation.

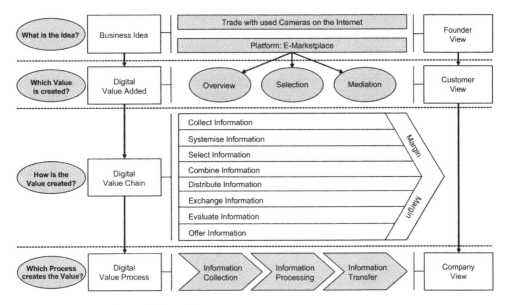

*Source:* Based on Kollman (2006), p. 329.

*Figure 2.3* *The digital creation of value*

Should an idea be based upon, for example, dealing in used photo cameras in a Digital Marketplace on the internet (founder's point of view), there is a typical way in which value can be digitally created (see Figure 2.3). This value creation is directly reflected in the resulting added value for the user (customer view) and refers centrally to, in the example presented here, the overview, selection and mediation functions. An example is that a supplier would be prepared to pay especially for the mediation function, whereas the customer would be eventually willing to pay a fee for the overview function. In order to realize this creation of value, companies use the value chain to identify particularly those value activities that form the core of value creation (see Figure 2.3). In order to do this, information on the object must be first collected; second, the location and the seller of the used camera must be determined and, in the third step, systematically stored in a database. Using this database, information is then offered to the potential buyers who can formulate a query using appropriate search mechanisms. If a match is found through the query process, then the accompanying information pertinent to the request is exchanged. If all of this occurs, the final product is a transaction. The digital process of creating value, from the company's point of view, is thus collecting information, processing and transferring it.

**The Digital Value Creation Process**

The digital value creation process describes especially those information activities and/or the sequence of information activities, which in total create added value for the customer. This involves both the core and service processes. Core processes hold a true function in the creation of value, whereas service processes support the business processes along the value chain. As a general rule, the digital value chain process begins with the input of information for the digital venture. In order to provide the targeted added value (e.g. overview function), the required information must first be gathered (e.g. who demands what at which level of quality and who offers this?). In the next step, the information is processed internally such that it can then be transferred on to the customer in the desired form as information output and in a way that specifically adds value for that customer. This process can be called the digital value creation process and describes thus the core processes of most digital ventures. When considering digital ventures, it is then possible to formulate a representatively typical digital value creation process (Figure 2.3) (Kollmann, 1998):

- The first step is the acquisition of information, which involves gathering relevant data that serves as information input for the additional creation of value. This results in the collection of useful data stores. This step in the value creation process can also be called information collection.
- The second step involves information processing which means the conversion of the collected data stores into an information product for the customer. This step along the value creation process can also respectively be called information processing.
- The third step involves the information transfer. This means actually implementing the newly acquired or confirmed knowledge obtained from collected, saved, processed and evaluated data for the benefit of the customer. The result is an output of information, which creates value. This step in the value creation can also be described as the information transfer.

It is important to recognize that it is not sufficient to go through the sequence of this – here presented in its most ideal form – digital value creation process just once. Rather, it is the continual process of acquiring, processing and transferring information which is necessary. This is even more essential, when the data – from which information can be drawn – is constantly subject to change. Thus, the data must be continually checked so it remains current. Against this background, several examples of the digital value creation process in the Digital Economy are presented in Figure 2.4.

## ESTABLISHING A COMPANY IN THE DIGITAL ECONOMY

If one takes a closer look at the new companies in the Digital Economy (digital ventures) equipped with digital value chains and digital processes of value creation (Figure 2.4), there are a number of noticeable, common traits with regard to the way the company was established. Most often it is a so-called original company founding, meaning that a completely new company is established without relying on any previously existing or available company structures. Additionally, one observes that these cases were most often so-called independently established companies initiated independently by the company founders seeking self-/full-time employment in the newly established company (Metzger, 2020). Furthermore, establishing the company was a means to securing one's independent, entrepreneurial existence. Finally, it can be seen that established digital ventures were most often innovative companies, that is, not established to imitate an existing company. An innovative start-up presents a situation in which the initiating factors, in the classical sense proposed by Schumpeter (1983), are combined in a new way. This new combination can involve material or immaterial factors. The increasing importance of "information" as a significant factor in the competitive advantage has recently increased particularly the significance of the immaterial factors (e.g. knowledge, know-how, etc.). Due to this, a number of newly formed companies in the Digital Economy are established consistently upon new knowledge-based and conceptually creative factors (the way in which information is dealt with and processed in the context of digital value creation to form a digital product (Figure 2.4).

| | Information Collection | Information Processing | Information Transfer | Value Added |
|---|---|---|---|---|
| **google.com** | Information about Web Sites and Search Queries (=Input) | Matching of search Strings and Web Content | List of appropriate Web Sites (=Output) | Overview Selection |
| **webmiles.de** | Information about Products, Customer, and Web Offers (=Input) | Allocation of incentive Bonus Points for the Usage of Web Content | Bonus Points Status, Exchange Options, Customer Information (=Output) | Transaction Cooperation |
| **delticom.de** | Information about Tires and Customer Requests (=Input) | Matching of Demand and Supply | List of adequate Offers and their Possibility for Online Ordering (=Output) | Overview Selection Transaction |
| **guenstiger.de** | Information about Product Prices and Customer Requests (=Input) | Structuring of Product Prices, matching of Demand, and Supply | Product Information, Price Information, Customer Information (=Output) | Overview Selection Mediation |
| **travelchannel.de** | Facts about Destinations, Online-Booking, and Travel Reports (=Input) | Matching of Demands and Supply, structuring of Travel Offers, and Travel Reports | Travel Offers, Destination Information, Travel Reports (=Output) | Overview Selection Transaction Exchange |

*Source:* Based on Kollman (2006), p. 331.

*Figure 2.4*   *Examples of the digital process supporting the creation of value in the Digital Economy*

In addition to having a digital product when establishing a digital venture, it was and is necessary to have a digital management, that is, members of management who have specific knowledge about the correlating factors within the Digital Economy. In this case, special emphasis is placed on the combination of management and computer science (informatics), to establish the company and guarantee the necessary technical processes. This is particularly important considering that information can change very quickly and along with it the company's basis for the value creation activities in digital data networks. There is a further special characteristic trait of the Digital Economy in addition to the digital value chain – namely that this is a considerably new area of business and lacks the years of experience on which established business sectors can rely. Accordingly, the digital creation of value and the business, which it is based upon, are oriented especially towards future innovations and developments. Furthermore, there is a high level of uncertainty on the customer side with respect to the amount and the timely presence regarding acceptance of innovative information technologies (e.g. internet start-ups' use of Digital Procurement (Kollmann, 2019c). The conditions outlined in such cases as presented here, underline the high level of risk involved with the development of the Digital Economy and the influence this has over investments in this area.

This risk is countered, however, by the fact that the Digital Economy and its underlying technologies represent a central growth sector and are therefore linked to numerous opportunities. This is seen in the continuing, rapid expansion and use of the internet in the USA and Europe. For example, a continuing increase in the dissemination and use of the internet in Germany is still ongoing (Kollmann, 2020). Almost nine out of ten Germans are now connected to the internet. Around 72 percent of these are even on the internet every day, which means that the possibilities of digital business processes have become almost commonplace (Kollmann, 2019a). Similarly, 93 percent of the citizens of the United States make use of the internet, and 77 percent indicate to have a broadband connection at home (Pew Research Center, 2021). Further, the level of investments in information technologies is still quite high, whereby two aspects that are particularly pertinent for new companies become very clear:

- information technologies require a certain amount of capital or funding for the initial development and/or company,
- information technologies are subject to continual change and constant development thus requiring subsequent investments.

In addition to the need for capital to develop the technology, additional investments for the establishment of the new company in the Digital Economy are necessary (e.g. personnel, organization, establishing a brand, sales, production, etc.).

This concludes the description of the basic conditions and requirements for establishing a company in the Digital Economy. In particular, four central characteristic traits can be identified that clearly distinguish the process of establishing a business in the Digital Economy from the "classical" company establishment in the Real Economy (see Figure 2.5):

- type of company established: a digital venture is often an independent, original and innovative company established within the Digital Economy.
- establishing environment: a digital venture is characterized by enormous growth potential and, yet, is also marked by uncertainty of its future development concerning the true success of its information technology – technology that requires significant investments.
- reference for establishing the company: a digital venture is based on a business idea that is first made possible through the use of innovative, information technologies. The idea itself focuses strongly on "information" as a competitive factor within the Digital Economy.
- basis for establishing the company: a digital venture is based upon a business concept that involves the digital creation of customer value offered on a digital platform of the Digital Economy. It requires continual, further development and administration.

In view of these conclusions and based on the circumstances, the following questions arise from the company founder's point of view: what information do I need in order to create value for a customer? What type of platform should I use to present this information? How can I guarantee that my information product will remain attractive for the customer also in future? How do I achieve this in a way so that my innovative company can grow independently? Due to these questions, companies established in the Digital Economy tend to be heterogeneous and more complex. They differ from companies established in the Real Economy in many aspects. This justifies an isolated and separate approach to researching how companies are

| | Type of establishing the Company | Environment of establishing the Company |
|---|---|---|
| **Establishing the Company** | Original Independent Innovative | Growth Potential Risk Capital |

| | Reference for establishing the Company | Basis for establishing the Company |
|---|---|---|
| **Digital Economy** | Information Technology Information Economy Digital Economy | Digital Value Creation (Concept) Digital Platform (Realization) Digital Management (Operation) |

| Establishing the Company in the Digital Economy (Digital Entrepreneurship / Digital Venture) |
|---|

*Source:* Based on Kollman (2006), p. 333.

*Figure 2.5    The distinguishing characteristics of companies in the Digital Economy*

established in the Digital Economy (digital venture). Against this background, the term "Digital Entrepreneurship" can be defined as follows (based on Kollmann 2006, p. 333):

> Digital Entrepreneurship refers to establishing a new company with an innovative business idea within the Digital Economy, which, using a digital platform (also referred to as electronic platform) in data networks, offers its products and/or services based upon a purely digital creation of value. Essential is the fact that this value offer was only made possible through the development of information technology.

**The Success Factors**

A number of studies have shown that, at first glance, success factors for establishing a company in the Digital Economy do not particularly differ from those in the Real Economy, although, one does find specific differences in the realization of and development of these success factors that are directly dependent upon the particular conditions in the Digital Economy. These differences will be presented in the following section and cover the areas of management, product, market access, process, and finance.

The building block "Management" (see Figure 2.6) places emphasis on founders of the company, who, through their personality and motivation, strongly determine the activities of a digital venture. Studies on the influence of technical, social, and methodical skills and capabilities possessed by business founders determined that these have a positive influence on the successful realization of the activities involved with establishing a company (Bingham et al., 2019). This also holds true with respect to the motivation of the founder or the team of founders. A high stress limit, pressure to succeed, self-confidence and awareness of risk, influence and characterize the actions during the sustainable phase of conception and thereafter in the realization phase. Whereas creativity, on the one hand, and analytical and conceptual thinking, on the other, dominate the first development phases of a new company, experience in the digital industry, knowledge of the interrelated aspects of the Digital Economy and real experience in operative management are increasingly the points that truly matter when establishing a digital venture. In view of this, establishing a company in the Digital Economy is very complex and the knowledge required to achieve this must be drawn similarly from the areas of computer science, information management (study of information systems), business administration, and entrepreneurship. Accordingly, the founders must possess competence and know-how in all three of the following areas to a certain extent. This involves the following aspects:

- Computer Science – the technological aspect of the Digital Economy makes it necessary to have a substantial understanding and knowledge of technologies, systems, databases, programming, and the architecture of the internet.
- Information Management – the technological basis, provided by computer science, must be assessable with respect to its content and relevance for business issues. For this reason, it is important to have knowledge in the areas of management information systems, IT security, data warehousing and data mining or even digital payment systems. It is just as important to understand fundamental platforms in the Digital Economy, as it is to have a sound overview of current existing business models and possibilities of creating value digitally.
- Business Administration – at the business administration level, it is essential to have a solid business knowledge. Topics which should be especially emphasized in connection with this, include marketing, business organization, management, financing, or investments.

Seldom does one person possess all of these skills such that it is more often the case that a digital venture was established by a team of founders (Kollmann, Hensellek et al., 2020; Kollmann, Jung et al., 2020).

The building block "Product" (see Figure 2.6) refers to the configuration of the services and offers of a digital venture. In this respect the digital product and/or service offered must be specified and communicated based upon its digital added value. Thus, the essential question is whether the customer needs the digital offer/service provided by the digital ventures based on IT and, if so, is the customer willing to pay? Further, it is the aim of the company to achieve added value for the customer through the realized output with digitally created value. At the same time, it is also the company's aim to assure its offer possesses a unique characteristic, which differentiates it from the other competitors. In addition to this, most digital ventures are dealing in new forms of business ideas and/or business models. From the customer side, initially it takes some time to get acquainted or to acknowledge the effect provided as value added that results from such new ideas and models. For this reason, a regular reconnection with customers and users must take place because it is, in the end, customer acceptance that determines if the digital business idea is a success or not (Kollmann, 2019c). Establishing a business in the Digital Economy is, apart from the aforementioned, singled out by the fact that a digital venture and its digital business idea must not only satisfy a need but also do this in a superior way compared to existing solutions in the Real Economy. Thus, the need for books is already fulfilled through real book shops, however, Amazon.com, with its Digital Shop, can offer overview, selection and transaction functions creating additional digital value in the marketspace (Figure 2.4).

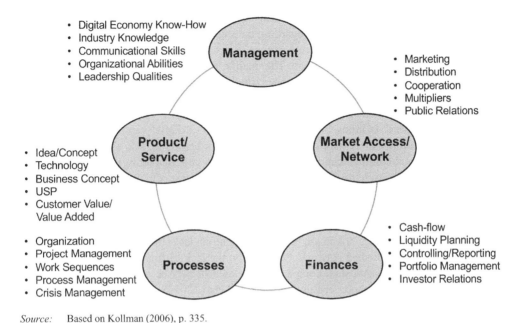

- Digital Economy Know-How
- Industry Knowledge
- Communicational Skills
- Organizational Abilities
- Leadership Qualities

**Management**

- Marketing
- Distribution
- Cooperation
- Multipliers
- Public Relations

**Product/ Service**

- Idea/Concept
- Technology
- Business Concept
- USP
- Customer Value/ Value Added

**Market Access/ Network**

- Organization
- Project Management
- Work Sequences
- Process Management
- Crisis Management

**Processes**

**Finances**

- Cash-flow
- Liquidity Planning
- Controlling/Reporting
- Portfolio Management
- Investor Relations

*Source:*     Based on Kollman (2006), p. 335.

*Figure 2.6*     *Success factors of establishing a company in the Digital Economy*

The building block "Processes" (Figure 2.6) refers particularly to the need for a newly established company to quickly move out of that critical stage where its activities are informal and uncontrolled. This applies especially to work, finance, and organizational processes, which form a solid operative foundation in a newly established company. This essentially means that core processes must be firmly established and harmonize with the evolving company organization. Further, in this context it is also important that not too many activities are initiated simultaneously. Otherwise, there is an ensuing danger that some of these activities may not receive the full attention they require. Therefore, it is necessary to have a logical and effective project and process management. When dealing with a digital venture, sophisticated development and presentation of concrete workflows should be based on a model example of the value creation process that was previously determined (Figure 2.3). The company's business processes can then be conceptualized in parallel to the digital process of value creation. These business processes should be understood as activity bundles necessary for realizing the value offer. They can be described as those targeted activities which are performed in a timely and logical sequence and whose aim is directly determined by the company strategy (Hammer & Champy, 1993). Business processes thus describe the realization of the digital process of creating value with the help of digital resources within a digital venture.

Particularly in the Digital Economy, which is characterized by a high degree of virtualization, the knowledge of concrete process flows is extremely important. Many business models in the Digital Economy are based upon taking advantage of the "effects of economies of scale." This is possible only when a large number of users can be serviced by either very few or even with just one basic process (e.g. at online auction houses). The complexity of value creation, especially if the creation of this value involves the participation of multiple companies, requires reducing the process down to the most essential steps. Weaknesses in core processes can then be more easily recognized. Especially regarding the steps of the process which are digital and thus automatic, mistakes can significantly impact the success of a company. Moreover, the process is externally visible to customers. The quality of process flows influences, therefore, the customer's use behavior. Supported by the virtual quality of information products, process flows become representatives of the quality image. The customer rates a company based upon the functionality and security of its processes.

The "Market access" building block (see Figure 2.6) in a digital venture means not only assuring market entrance and establishing a product and/or brand, but also means reaching the customer via a digital communication channel (e.g. online/viral marketing). The focus here is the question: how do I reach the customer with my information product? Hereby, it is possible to achieve market access through company-initiated marketing and sales activities. However, this seems to pose a signification problem considering the lack of resources of start-up companies. Market entrance in the Digital Economy is – in most cases – characterized by the fact that most digital ventures are unknown, have limited capital, lack, for the most part, resources, and do not have an established network. Particularly, the lack of financial means often leads to deficits for a newly established company in the area of service or product performance, communication/sales and market positioning (Senyard et al., 2014). In order to eliminate these deficits, especially when dealing with digital ventures, potential cooperation plays an elementary role in supporting the market entrance and positively steering the company's further development (Kollmann et al., 2021). In view of the current state of the internet's development and other online media, the idea of capturing a market alone with the existing limitation is unfathomable. Examples of such cooperation are the so-called "affiliate programmers," which have developed alongside the establishment of digital ventures. This is predominantly understood to be marketing and sales concepts that are directly based upon a partnership-like relationship and profit-scheme compensation. The digital venture (merchant) concludes an advertisement and/or sales agreement with a cooperation partner (affiliate), who in turn integrates the merchant's service/product offer on their internet presence or website. If this results in a successful transaction, the affiliate receives a commission on sales which is normally somewhere between 5 and 15 percent (Rayport & Jaworski, 2002). In this way, a newly established company can reach, from the very beginning, a wide range of customer segments and establish a comprehensive sales network.

The building block "Finance" (Figure 2.6) is concerned with guaranteeing the activities from a liquidity point of view. There are two essential aspects which are of importance here. On the one hand, there is a significant need for investing in technology and in establishing the company in the beginning phase; whereby, on the other hand, the free-cash-flow cannot be too negatively influenced. The financing and cash planning is often a significant weak point at companies in the Digital Economy. Often there is a lack of necessary realism, if investors or financers are to be convinced by euphoric turnover forecasts or make decisions based upon underestimated investment requirement (Kollmann & Kuckertz, 2003a). Hence, there should be a continually updated finance planning that can provide, at any given point in time, a realistic estimate of the financial situation of the company and also present the actual financing requirement. The financing of a company in this case becomes increasingly a mixture of equity (own capital) and various forms of participations. In situations such as these, risk capital should be strategically used for investments (e.g. sales), that is, for generating cash flow. The financing of the company furthermore requires proof of a solid controlling especially of the cost-side of the business (Kollmann & Kuckertz, 2003b). A further aspect concerns the communication with investors (Investor Relations), who want to be informed on a regular basis about the development of the company (Kollmann, 2019c).

According to a set of experts, the majority of failed start-ups in the Digital Economy have failed not so much due to a lack of business potential as to inadequate and short-sighted implementation (Fischl et al., 2019). Where the focus used to be on an Initial Public Offering (IPO) in the near future, the focus needs to shift to the gradual development and expansion of products, services and customer bases (Kollmann, 2020). The American venture capitalist Arthur Rock, who among other investments financed Apple Computer at its founding, puts this in a simple formula: "Strategy is simple, implementation is difficult." Against this background, the present has produced enough examples of successful and unsuccessful implementation of start-up ideas in the Digital Economy (Kollmann, 2020). Conclusions can be drawn from each individual case for the necessary building blocks of a successful company foundation in the Digital Economy (Kollmann, 2003).

**The Phases of Development**

The future development of a company in the Digital Economy can be outlined by just one simple question: what will happen to the idea with the passing of time? At the very core, when a new company is to be founded, there is an idea for a possible business concept. This idea must first be discerned and then assessed for its probability and potential for success (phase of idea finding). In a subsequent step, the idea must be transferred to a plausible and sustainable foundation and a corresponding business plan for the idea must be prepared (phase of idea formulation). This must be done in order to actually realize the idea in the next step (phase of idea realization). Success of the digital venture is, however, not only dependent upon the initial realization of the business model, but especially depends upon the continued development and appropriate adjustment to market demands (phase of idea intensification). Finally, the idea must be capable of continually growing with the market and developing into a long-term business (phase of idea continuation). In each of these phases, it is essential that certain tasks along the previously outlined building blocks for establishing a company are fulfilled (Figure 2.7). The individual phases and specific questions, which are of significant importance throughout the development of a company in the Digital Economy, will be described in more detail in the following section (see also Ruhnka & Young, 1987).

The phases of finding, formulating and realizing the idea are considered, in the context of the financing of a new company or start-up, to be the early stage. Generally, they are divided up into the pre-seed, seed and a start-up phase. In the pre-seed and seed-phase the company has not yet been founded. These phases reflect more specifically the time in which the future founders of a company are searching for the idea (Kollmann & Kuckertz, 2005) and planning the realization of their business model (Figure 2.7). Even if there is no company and no marketable product in existence at this phase, there is nevertheless a need for capital as, for instance, market studies or acceptance and feasibility studies must be performed (costs for preparation). If the company is to be established based upon a business plan (idea formulation), then the start-up phase begins, in which production capacities are established, personnel are sought, and the market entrance is prepared. For a digital venture, this most often means the programming of the internet platform and its functionalities (development costs). When a successful online start can take place and the product/service offer is introduced into the market, the start-up phase ends. Following this comes the time when the idea must be intensified and the expansion stage begins. Especially during the "early stage," the building blocks "Product" and "Management" play an essential role as there will surely be no further progress without them.

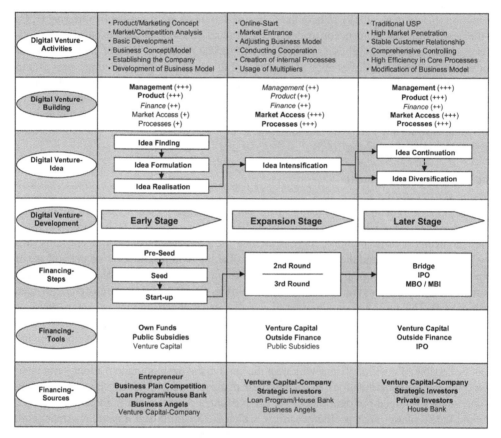

*Note:*    Most important aspects for the respective phase in bold; "+"-signs represent degree of importance in more fine-grained gradation.
*Source:*    Based on Kollman (2006), p. 338.

*Figure 2.7    Building blocks and phases of development for companies in the Digital Economy*

If the start-up phase is completed, then the actual online-start of the digital venture can occur with a market introduction or launch of the product or service (Figure 2.7). Beginning here, one of the central, strategic targets of the company is to expand the presence of its product/service on the market and achieve constant turnover growth. The newly formed company then enters the expansion stage and the first stable income is earned. In this phase, it is absolutely necessary to expand production and sales capacities. In order to achieve this, it is possible to form cooperation. As a general rule, the further expansion of the company cannot be solely financed through its cash-flow. The company is thus confronted with additional capital requirements. At this stage, potential investors can be offered far more security for their investment as compared to the early phase of the business development. Considering this, the management is nevertheless challenged then by an entirely new problem of properly steering the growth of the company. This is the point where internal processes must be established. Within the expansion stage, the building blocks of "Market access" and "Processes" are particularly important as – without them – further growth can most certainly not be achieved.

As soon as a company can rely upon an ever-increasing growth rate and guaranteed business income, the later stage of the company's development has been achieved. From a turnover perspective, the company is stable in its business development and there is eventually the opportunity to consider a diversification of the original idea (Figure 2.7). The company has established unique selling aspects for its product or service that separate it from the competitors and has achieved a significant market penetration. This means that even the future growth of the digital venture can be calculated, and risks can be much better defined than in the previous phases of the business development. When there is a significantly high level of growth potential, the break-even point can be achieved through "bridge financing" or possibly an IPO can be prepared. Investors from the previous financing rounds also have the option of a "trade sale" to a strategic investor as well as selling their shares back to the founders or the management in a management buy-out, or respectively a management buy-in. During the later stage, all of the building blocks play a significant role due to the fact that, generally, growth can only be obtained when all of these elements are functioning seamlessly.

## CONCLUSION

The creation of new ventures plays a decisive role for the social and economic development of every country. This is due to the fact that with each new venture created a market participant comes into existence which potentially stimulates the competition and drives the economy further. The formation of new companies within the Digital Economy (Digital Entrepreneurship) is therefore a key topic for every national industry. Consequently, digital business must not be ignored by decision makers; its technological advantages are obvious and therefore will most certainly lead to new business processes and business concepts as well. Technological innovations will continue to shape the way firms not only collect and distribute data and thus information, but also how they store them (Kollmann, 2020).

Moreover, the possibility of connecting various digital devices (e.g. computers, interactive television, smartphones, tablets, smart watches, or wearables) will continue to shape data collection. Furthermore, there are more and more precise possibilities to evaluate and use the collected data in a targeted manner. The internet also enables the consideration of individual customer needs by providing personalized content and context-related information.

Whether e-commerce for the retail trade, artificial intelligence for business processes, online marketplaces for craftsmen, 3D printing for the printing industry, social media platforms for customer acquisition or electronic geodata for agriculture – the digital transformation of the economy, production and customer relationships continues to be a key challenge. Not least the coronavirus crisis has once again shown how important the digital 3P with products, processes and platforms for information, communication and transaction via the internet have become and where strengths, but also weaknesses lie in dealing with this topic.

Digitization is characterized in particular by digital transformation and digital innovation, since it is not just a matter of digitizing existing business processes and associated models (this can and should also be done innovatively), but also of developing new business processes and models and successfully anchoring them in the network economy of the internet:

- Digital transformation power of existing companies (corporates/SMEs) via the innovative use of digital technologies to adapt and expand existing business processes and models to digital competition (aspect: digital intrapreneurship).
- Digital innovation power of new companies (start-ups) via the innovative use of digital technologies to develop new business processes/models for digital competition (aspect: digital entrepreneurship).
- Digital synergy power between existing (corporates/SMEs) and new companies (start-ups) for the joint development and operation (cooperation, spin-offs, etc.) of digital technologies to develop new business processes and models for digital competition (aspect: digital intrapreneurship).

Because of those circumstances there will be a solid basis for new venture creation within the Digital Economy in the future, too. As this chapter has argued, the competent processing of information has to be the foundation of such entrepreneurial attempts. The digital value chain and the value-oriented processing of information thus serve as the starting point for every Digital Economy venture.

At the same time, against this background, digital entrepreneurship can be interpreted as an integral part of these developments. What this chapter also has shown in its special structure with the deliberate reference to the origin (Kollmann, 2006) is that despite a modern and often interpreted novelty in the terminology, the roots lie in the past and the already elaborated contents and theoretical foundations, which were developed under other names of this topic (e.g. e-entrepreneurship), have not lost their validity and must also be considered by the new generation of researchers as well. Every child also has parents and so it is here, too.

## REFERENCES

Amit, R., & Zott, C. (2001). Value creation in e-business. *Strategic Management Journal*, *22*(6–7), 493–520. https://doi.org/10.1002/smj.187

Beliaeva, T., Ferasso, M., Kraus, S., & Damke, E. J. (2019). Dynamics of digital entrepreneurship and the innovation ecosystem: A multilevel perspective. *International Journal of Entrepreneurial Behaviour and Research*, *26*(2), 266–284. https://doi.org/10.1108/IJEBR-06-2019-0397

Bingham, C. B., Howell, T., & Ott, T. E. (2019). Capability creation: Heuristics as microfoundations. *Strategic Entrepreneurship Journal*, *13*(2), 121–153. https://doi.org/10.1002/sej.1312

BITKOM. (2020). *ITK-Märkte*. https://www.bitkom.org/Marktdaten/ITK-Konjunktur/ITK-Markt-Deutschland.html

Bundesministerium für Wirtschaft und Energie. (2018). *Monitoring-Report Wirtschaft DIGITAL 2018. Der IKT-Standort Deutschland und seine Position im internationalen Vergleich*. https://www.bmwi.de/Redaktion/DE/Publikationen/Digitale-Welt/monitoring-report-wirtschaft-digital-2018-ikt-standort-deutschland.pdf?__blob=publicationFile&v=24

Evans, P. B., & Wurster, T. S. (1997). Strategy and the new economics of information. *Harvard Business Review*, *75*(5), 71–82

Fischl, B., Hartl, M., & Wagner, S. (2019). *Der Businessplan*. https://www.starting-up.de/gruenden/businessplan.html

Ghezzi, A., & Cavallo, A. (2020). Agile business model innovation in digital entrepreneurship: Lean startup approaches. *Journal of Business Research, 110,* 519–537. https://doi.org/10.1016/j.jbusres.2018.06.013

Hagel, J., & Singer, M. (1997). *Net Gain: Expanding Markets through Virtual Communities.* Harvard Business School Press

Hammer, M., & Champy, J. (1993). *Reengineering The Corporation: A Manifesto for Business Revolution.* Harper

Jelassi, T., & Enders, A. (2005). *Strategies for e-Business. Creating Value through Electronic and Mobile Commerce.* Prentice Hall

Jones, A. B., Butler, B. S., Scott, S. V, & Xu, S. X. (2021). Next-generation information systems theorizing: A call-to-action. *MIS Quarterly,* 1–20

Keil, T., Autio, E., & George, G. (2008). Corporate venture capital, disembodied experimentation and capability development. *Journal of Management Studies, 45*(8), 1475–1505. https://doi.org/10.1111/j.1467-6486.2008.00806.x

Kirzner, I. M. (1973). *Competition and Entrepreneurship.* University of Chicago Press

Kollmann, T. (1998). *Akzeptanz innovativer Nutzungsgüter und -systeme: Konsequenzen für die Einführung von Telekommunikations- und Multimediasystemen.* Gabler

Kollmann, T. (2001). Measuring the acceptance of electronic marketplaces: A study based on a used-car trading site. *Journal of Computer-Mediated Communication, 6*(2). https://doi.org/10.1111/j.1083-6101.2001.tb00118.x

Kollmann, T. (2003). Reifeprüfung für das Geschäftsmodell. *Harvard Business Manager, 25*(1), 59–66

Kollmann, T. (2006). What is e-entrepreneurship? – Fundamentals of company founding in the net economy. *International Journal of Technology Management, 33*(4), 322–340. https://doi.org/10.4337/9781781951828.00012

Kollmann, T. (2009/2014). What is e-entrepreneurship? – Fundamentals of company founding in the net economy. In: F. Thérin (Ed.), *Handbook of Research on Techno-Entrepreneurship* (pp. 201–218). Cheltenham, UK and Northampton, MA, USA: Edward Elgar Publishing

Kollmann, T. (2019a). *E-Business: Grundlagen elektronischer Geschäftsprozesse in der Digitalen Wirtschaft* (7th ed.). Springer Gabler

Kollmann, T. (2019b). *E-Business kompakt: Grundlagen elektronischer Geschäftsprozesse in der Digitalen Wirtschaft mit über 70 Fallbeispielen.* Springer Gabler

Kollmann, T. (2019c). *E-Entrepeneurship: Grundlagen der Unternehmensgründung in der Digitalen Wirtschaft* (7th ed.). Springer Gabler. https://doi.org/10.1007/978-3-658-27429-0

Kollmann, T. (2020). Digital Entrepeneurship – Unternehmensgründung in der Digitalen Wirtschaft. In: K. Hölzl, V. Tiberius, & H. Surrey (Eds.), *Perspektiven des Entrepreneurships: Unternehmerische Konzepte zwischen Theorie und Praxis* (pp. 331–342). Schäffer Poeschel

Kollmann, T., Hensellek, S., Stöckmann, C., Kensbock, J. M., & Peschl, A. (2020). How management teams foster the transactive memory system–entrepreneurial orientation link: A domino effect model of positive team processes. *Strategic Entrepreneurship Journal.* https://doi.org/https://doi.org/10.1002/sej.1365

Kollmann, T., Jung, P. B., Kleine-Stegemann, L., Ataee, J., & de Cruppe, K. (2020). *Deutscher Startup Monitor 2020.* https://deutscherstartupmonitor.de/wp-content/uploads/2020/09/dsm_2020.pdf

Kollmann, T., & Kuckertz, A. (2003a). *E-Venture-Capital: Unternehmensfinanzierung in der Net Economy – Grundlagen und Fallstudien.* Springer Gabler

Kollmann, T., & Kuckertz, A. (2003b). Shareholder-Value-Ansatz als Basis für das Controlling bei Start-up-Unternehmen. In: A.-K. Achleitner & A. Bassen (Eds.), *Controlling von jungen Unternehmen* (pp. 199–220). Schäffer-Poeschel

Kollmann, T., & Kuckertz, A. (2005). Rahmenbedingungen der Unternehmensgründung – Eine Analyse des "Entrepreneurial Events" im internationalen Vergleich. *Betriebswirtschaftliche Forschung Und Praxis, 57*(4), 307–318

Kollmann, T., Stöckmann, C., Hensellek, S., & Kensbock, J. (2016). European startup monitor 2016. *Bundesverband Deutsche Startups.* http://europeanstartupmonitor.com/fileadmin/esm_2016/report/ESM_2016.pdf

Kollmann, T., Stöckmann, C., Niemand, T., Hensellek, S., & de Cruppe, K. (2021). A configurational approach to entrepreneurial orientation and cooperation explaining product/service innovation in digital vs. non-digital startups. *Journal of Business Research, 125*(3), 508–519. https://doi.org/10 .1016/j.jbusres.2019.09.041

Kraus, S., Palmer, C., Kailer, N., Kallinger, F. L., & Spitzer, J. (2019). Digital entrepreneurship: A research agenda on new business models for the twenty-first century. *International Journal of Entrepreneurial Behaviour and Research, 25*(2), 353–375. https://doi.org/10.1108/IJEBR-06-2018 -0425

Kraus, S., Roig-Tierno, N., & Bouncken, R. B. (2019). Digital innovation and venturing: An introduction into the digitalization of entrepreneurship. *Review of Managerial Science, 13*(3), 519–528. https://doi .org/10.1007/s11846-019-00333-8

Lumpkin, G. T., & Dess, G. G. (2004). E-business strategies and internet business models: How the internet adds value. *Organizational Dynamics, 33*(2), 161–173. https://doi.org/10.1016/j.orgdyn.2004 .01.004

Matlay, H. (2004). E-entrepreneurship and small e-business development: Towards a comparative research agenda. *Journal of Small Business and Enterprise Development, 11*(3), 408–414. https://doi .org/10.1108/14626000410551663

Metzger, G. (2020). KfW-Gründungsmonitor 2020. *KfW Research.* https://www.kfw.de/PDF/Download -Center/Konzernthemen/Research/PDF-Dokumente-Gründungsmonitor/KfW-Gruendungsmonitor -2020.pdf

Meyer, C. (2001). The second generation of speed. *Harvard Business Review, 79*(4), 24–26

Nambisan, S. (2017). Digital entrepreneurship: Toward a digital technology perspective of entrepreneur-ship. *Entrepreneurship: Theory and Practice, 41*(6), 1029–1055. https://doi.org/10.1111/etap.12254

Pew Research Center. (2021). *Internet/broadband fact sheet.* https://www.pewresearch.org/internet/fact -sheet/internet-broadband/

Porter, M. E. (1985). *Competitive Advantage: Creating and Sustaining Superior.* The Free Press.

Porter, M. E., & Millar, V. E. (1985). How information gives you competitive advantage. *Harvard Business Review, 63*(4), 149–160

Pruden, H. O. (1978). The Kondratieff wave. *Journal of Marketing, 42*(2), 63–70

Rayport, J. F., & Jaworski, B. J. (2002). *Introduction to E-commerce.* McGraw-Hill

Ruhnka, J. C., & Young, J. E. (1987). A venture capital model of the development process for new ventures. *Journal of Business Venturing, 2*(2), 167–184

Schumpeter, J. A. (1983). *The Theory of Economic Development: An Inquiry Into Profits, Capital, Credit, Interest, and the Business Cycle.* Transaction Publishers

Senyard, J., Baker, T., Steffens, P., & Davidsson, P. (2014). Bricolage as a path to innovativeness for resource-constrained new firms. *Journal of Product Innovation Management, 31*(2), 211–230. https:// doi.org/10.1111/jpim.12091

Stalk, G. J. (1988). Time – the next source of competitive advantage. *Harvard Business Review, 66*(4), 28–60

Tapscott, D. (1996). *The Digital Economy. Promise and Peril in the Age of Networked Intelligence.* McGraw-Hill

Taylor, M., & Murphy, A. (2004). SMEs and e-business. *Journal of Small Business and Enterprise Development, 11*(3), 280–289. https://doi.org/10.1108/14626000410551546

Weiber, R., & Kollmann, T. (1998). Competitive advantages in virtual markets – perspectives of "information-based marketing" in cyberspace. *European Journal of Marketing, 32*(7/8), 603–615. https://doi.org/10.1108/03090569810224010

Zwass, V. (2003). Electronic commerce and organizational innovation: Aspects and opportunities. *International Journal of Electronic Commerce, 7*(3), 7–37

# 3. Eras of digital entrepreneurship: connecting the past, present, and future[1]

*Tobias Kollmann, Lucas Kleine-Stegemann, Katharina de Cruppe and Christina Strauss*

## INTRODUCTION

Since the mid-1990s, the steady development of digital technologies has enabled not only the creation but also the scaling of so-called digital ventures, whose business models are based on generating value through electronic information via data networks (Kollmann, 2006). Against this background, the field of digital entrepreneurship[2] describes the dovetailing of digital technologies and entrepreneurship (Nambisan, 2017). Digital technologies comprise "products or services that are either embodied in information and communication technologies or enabled by them" (Lyytinen et al., 2016, p. 49). Today, the field of digital entrepreneurship has become increasingly important and is a topical issue in both practice and research (Ghezzi & Cavallo, 2020; Kraus et al., 2019; Nambisan, 2017). In practice, software-based businesses (Alt et al., 2020) using digital technologies as the core of their business models, such as Google, Amazon, Facebook, Apple, and Microsoft (GAFAM), have become the most valuable firms in the world in terms of brand value and market capitalization (Murphy et al., 2020; Swant, 2020), underlining the importance of data and information as critical success factors (Kraus et al., 2019; Weiber & Kollmann, 1998). Inspired by practical developments, such as the increasing value of the GAFAM firms, the relevance of the field of digital entrepreneurship also continues to grow in research, as shown by the number and quality of publications in highly ranked entrepreneurship and information systems journals (Block et al., 2020; Nambisan et al., 2019; e.g., Ojala, 2016; Smith et al., 2017; Srinivasan & Venkatraman, 2018).

However, while there has been a pronounced interest in literature on the topic of digital entrepreneurship today, this area has its origin in the emergence of internet technology as the first relevant enabler of digital venture creation (Kollmann, 1998; Kollmann et al., 2009). Early developments in internet technology prompted conceptual and empirical research into digital ventures (Kollmann, 1998; e.g., Poon & Swatman, 1997). In this context, previous literature features several terms, including "internet entrepreneurship," "e-entrepreneurship," and "techno-entrepreneurship," which have often been used as synonyms for "digital entrepreneurship," leading to confusion over the years (Zaheer et al., 2019). Nevertheless, most studies attempting to characterize this research field have overlooked the longitudinal evolution of terminology and focused on digital entrepreneurship in isolation, referring to it as if it were an emergent and barely researched field (e.g., Grégoire & Shepherd, 2012; Kraus et al., 2019). This chapter problematizes the in-house assumption[3] that digital entrepreneurship is a new phenomenon (Alvesson & Sandberg, 2011, 2014; Sandberg & Alvesson, 2011) and explores its evolution. Accordingly, this study seeks to answer the following questions: (1) What is the terminological history of digital entrepreneurship and what role do digital technologies play in it? (2) How are the different terms in the field of research on digital entrepreneurship connected? (3) How have the definitions in the field of digital entrepreneurship changed over time? (4) What are the possible avenues for future research in digital entrepreneurship based on digital technologies?

Building on a scoping literature review (Templier & Paré, 2015), we challenge the implication in the existing literature that digital entrepreneurship is a new phenomenon (e.g., Grégoire & Shepherd, 2012; Kraus et al., 2019). In the process, we demonstrate how the different terms around digital entrepreneurship have developed over time, enabled by innovative digital technologies and influenced by certain practical events since the early 1990s. We illustrate the role of digital technologies in entrepreneurship (Shen et al., 2018) and show how the different terms are connected by analyzing cross-mentions among publications. Furthermore, we demonstrate how the phenomenon can be defined with reference to the terms used. We then illustrate whether and why these definitions have changed over time. Finally, we identify critical digital technologies that could be sources of new terms and thus enable future eras of digital entrepreneurship research.

We contribute to the literature on digital entrepreneurship in multiple ways (Block et al., 2020; e.g., Davidson & Vaast, 2010; Nambisan, 2017; Sussan & Acs, 2017). First, we provide new insights into the history of today's digital entrepreneurship terminology based on the specific number of publications per term and year. We show that the publications that did most to drive the development of research on digital entrepreneurship appeared from the early 1990s, following the development and spread of relevant technologies, such as internet technology. Second, we outline the intensity of the connections among the different terms used most frequently within the field. We show that most publications rarely mention other terms, and only two pairs of terms mention each other slightly more often. In addition to exploring the use of terms, we delve deeper into their understanding, showing that they can be interpreted synonymously. Third, we show that some preliminary definitions have evolved over time, leading to the assumption that they reflected the same understanding over time. Therefore, we try to establish box-changing research, motivating other scholars to "reach [...] outwards for new ideas, theories, and methods" (Alvesson & Sandberg, 2014, p. 980) and integrate further terms into their research. Fourth, we provide new insights into the future of digital entrepreneurship research. Specifically, we demonstrate that, among others, artificial intelligence, blockchain technology, and big data analytics might be future digital technologies capable of facilitating numerous new research opportunities and shaping the terms used in the research field of digital entrepreneurship.

## METHOD

This study uses a scoping literature review to identify the full extent, range, and nature of the available literature on the topic (Paré et al., 2015; Schryen et al., 2020). The process thus illuminates the historical development of the field of digital entrepreneurship and its terminology. Drawing on the methodological strategy of Arksey and O'Malley (2005) and Templier and Paré (2015), this scoping literature review can be divided into three overarching phases in terms of (1) planning, (2) conducting, and (3) reporting. The method is intended to ensure transparency and reproducibility (Fisch & Block, 2018; Keding, 2021), which are the most important elements of a trustworthy literature review (Cram et al., 2020). The three steps are described below.

First, as different terms have been used synonymously to describe digital entrepreneurship, resulting in confusion (Matlay, 2004; Zaheer et al., 2019), we ensured our analysis included multiple search terms so as to cover the entire field. Several pilot searches and exploratory readings revealed the most important terms in the field of digital entrepreneurship to be "e-entrepreneurship," "digital entrepreneurship," "virtual entrepreneurship," "online entrepreneurship," "cyber entrepreneurship," "internet entrepreneurship," "IT entrepreneurship," "e-commerce entrepreneurship," and "techno-entrepreneurship."

Second, we obtained our data by focusing on the most important databases in the entrepreneurship literature, such as Business Source Premier via EBSCO host and Scopus (Kraus et al., 2020). To ensure we identified every publication that used any of the aforementioned terms in the field of digital entrepreneurship, we considered different spellings and abbreviations. Table 3.1 illustrates the search terms applied to the titles, abstracts, keywords, and/or subjects of the publications. Using asterisks, we included words that contained not only the term "entrepreneur" but also "entrepreneurial" or "entrepreneurship," as these words also covered the topic. This search led to a total of 1,723 publications. Unlike more traditional systematic literature reviews (e.g., Kraus et al., 2019; Zaheer et al., 2019), our scoping literature review focuses on the breadth of the literature rather than the depth of coverage (Paré et al., 2015). Therefore, our dataset includes all types of publications (e.g., articles, conference papers, book chapters, reviews, and interviews) that used any of the aforementioned terms regardless of the publication's focus and any quality assessment, such as journal ranking (Anderson et al., 2008). We filtered those publications according to criteria that should ensure the trustworthiness of the dataset and its relevance to the research questions (Cram et al., 2020; Templier & Paré, 2015). In particular, we analyzed how prominent a term is in research during a particular period to determine trends in the historical development of digital entrepreneurship. Subsequently, we excluded all publications that were not written in English or published before 1970 because the underlying internet technology that represents one of the cornerstones of digital entrepreneurship did not exist prior to that date (Schatz & Hardin, 1994). That process led to 1,684 remaining publications. Then, we excluded all existing duplicates for the different terms, leaving a total of 1,531 publications. Finally, two authors scanned all titles, abstracts, keywords, and subjects independently to establish the correct use of the terms mentioned above (Paré et al., 2015). They reviewed whether the search terms were mentioned at least once in every publication and referred to the overarching topic of digital entrepreneurship. That review encompassed, for example, ensuring that the term "it entrepreneur*" referred to "information technology" in combination with "entrepreneurship," rather than a random combination of the words "it" and "entrepreneurship" in general. The final sample comprises 1,354 publications produced between 1990[4] and 2020. Table 3.1 illustrates the steps undertaken and the precise number of publications connected to each keyword after the consecutive analysis steps.

Third, we focused on analyzing and synthesizing the data (Templier & Paré, 2015) to present new insights into the history of digital entrepreneurship in a meaningful way (Jesson et al., 2011). We examined the number of publications for each term per year from 1990 to 2020 to understand in which period a specific term was particularly important. Likewise, we identified digital technologies that took on the specific role of enablers for the field of digital entrepreneurship, as well as important practical events that influenced the number of publications. We then matched the number of publications per term with such digital technologies and practical events to show the historical development of digital entrepreneurship along a timeline (see Figure 3.1). We also created a net with bubbles positioned chronologically to represent the

*Table 3.1*     *Number of publications per keyword*

| Terms | Database | Number of Publications After Each Filtering Step | | | |
|---|---|---|---|---|---|
| | | Term in the Titles, Abstracts, Keywords, and/or Subjects | Language: English; Timeframe: 1970–2020 | Exclusion of Duplicates | Scanning of Titles, Abstracts, Keywords, and/or Subjects |
| "e-entrepreneur*" OR "electronic entrepreneur*" | EBSCO and Scopus | 185 | 181 | 167 | 86 |
| "digital entrepreneur*" | EBSCO and Scopus | 383 | 363 | 311 | 306 |
| "virtual entrepreneur*" | EBSCO and Scopus | 42 | 39 | 34 | 33 |
| "online entrepreneur*" | EBSCO and Scopus | 129 | 128 | 110 | 101 |
| "cyber entrepreneur*" OR "cyberentrepreneur*" OR "cyberpreneur*" | EBSCO and Scopus | 35 | 35 | 32 | 25 |
| "internet entrepreneur*" OR "net entrepreneur*" | EBSCO and Scopus | 489 | 486 | 465 | 454 |
| "it entrepreneur*" | EBSCO and Scopus | 147 | 145 | 133 | 93 |
| "e-commerce entrepreneur*" | EBSCO and Scopus | 68 | 68 | 59 | 49 |
| "techno-entrepreneur*" OR "technopreneur*" | EBSCO and Scopus | 245 | 239 | 220 | 207 |
| **Final Sample** | | 1,723 | 1,684 | 1,531 | **1,354** |

relevant terms and to illustrate when most publications containing them appeared by year. The size of the bubbles reflects the total number of citations of the respective term field to convey the relevance of those terms to research (Massaro et al., 2016). That number of citations was based on Google Scholar, which offered the only means of identifying up-to-date citations for all articles (Stewart & Cotton, 2013). Next, we counted how often publications using one term (e.g., "digital entrepreneurship") mentioned other terms (e.g., "e-entrepreneurship") within their titles, abstracts, keywords, subjects, and/or references. We show how the different terms in the field of digital entrepreneurship are connected using arrows between the bubbles, with the size of the arrowheads reflecting on the number of cross-mentions (see Figure 3.2).

Furthermore, we attempted to generate further insights into the understanding of the phenomenon over time. Accordingly, we selected the top ten publications per term with the most Google Scholar citations, as this allowed us to generate actuality and comprehensiveness (Stewart & Cotton, 2013) and assume that these articles were the most relevant in the respective periods (Massaro et al., 2016). We chose ten publications for each term because we wanted to equally cover every term and include every possible understanding of the phenomenon. The number ten was chosen to encompass publications cited more than 100 times, leading to a sub-set that covers more than half of all citations of the entire dataset (67 percent). We then scanned each of those publications for definitions of the phenomenon, checked whether the terms could be interpreted synonymously with regard to their definition of digital entrepreneurship, and then sorted them chronologically. As many articles did not provide any definitions, our set of articles was reduced by half. Subsequently, we arranged seven of the top definitions as examples to explain the historical development of the understanding of digital entrepreneurship. We chose the seven definitions because they had the most citations on Google Scholar and covered 20 percent of the total citations of our sample while being representative of the definitions during their time. Building on this, we identified links to the number of publications over time and also cross-mentions to provide a distinctive but comprehensive assessment of the understanding of the phenomenon.

Finally, we examined how the research field of digital entrepreneurship might evolve in the future based on the current literature (Recker et al., 2019; Schryen, 2013). To do so, we analyzed relevant calls for papers and special issues (Berger et al., 2021; Block et al., 2020), as well as articles with suggestions for future research in the field of digital entrepreneurship (Recker & von Briel, 2019; von Briel et al., 2021). We identified, among others, three major developments – artificial intelligence, blockchain technology, and big data analytics – that might lead to new research opportunities and could influence the terms used in future digital entrepreneurship research. For this reason, we searched top-tier journals in the fields of information systems, entrepreneurship, and general/strategic management[5] for the following word combinations (Steininger, 2019): "artificial intelligence" AND "entrepreneur*," "blockchain" AND "entrepreneur*," and "big data analytics" AND "entrepreneur*." We considered articles published only since 2016 to accord with the starting point of the last identified era in this chapter – the Expansion-Era – and thus the beginning of future digital entrepreneurship research. We checked all articles for content fit and identified 37 articles, providing important insights into possible future eras of digital entrepreneurship.

## ERAS OF DIGITAL ENTREPRENEURSHIP: HISTORICAL DEVELOPMENT

Nambisan (2017) states that digital entrepreneurship describes "the intersection between digital technologies and entrepreneurship" (p. 1029) and addresses the creation and scaling of digital ventures, whose business model is based on generating value through electronic information via data networks (Kollmann, 2006). Accordingly, it is a field instigated by the advent of internet technology and has a long history. This study identifies three eras in the historical development of digital entrepreneurship: the Seed-Era (1990–2000), the Startup-Era (2001–2015), and the Expansion-Era (2016–20xx). Every identified era is enabled by innovations in digital technologies and influenced by particular practical events that can explain certain peaks in the number of publications within an era. Figure 3.1 summarizes the number of publications per term matched with the respective digital technologies and practical events.

### The Seed-Era (1990–2000)

The Seed-Era marks the beginning of historical development in the field of digital entrepreneurship and is primarily characterized by the establishment of internet technology. After about 20 years of development, this technology was finally accessible to the general populace in 1993 (Schatz & Hardin, 1994). The fundamental advantages of internet technology, especially in terms of efficiency and effectiveness (Weiber & Kollmann, 1998), enabled a wide range of entrepreneurial opportunities through "doing business electronically" (European Commission, 1997, p. 2). The first developments in the field of the "internet economy" (Feindt et al., 2002, p. 51) were accompanied by emerging research on these topics (Kollmann, 1998). The first terms to describe the impact of internet technology on the field of entrepreneurship were "virtual entrepreneurship," used in the publications of Henricks in 1993 (1993a, 1993b), and "digital entrepreneurship," used by Rosenbaum and Cronin (1993). Other terms, such as

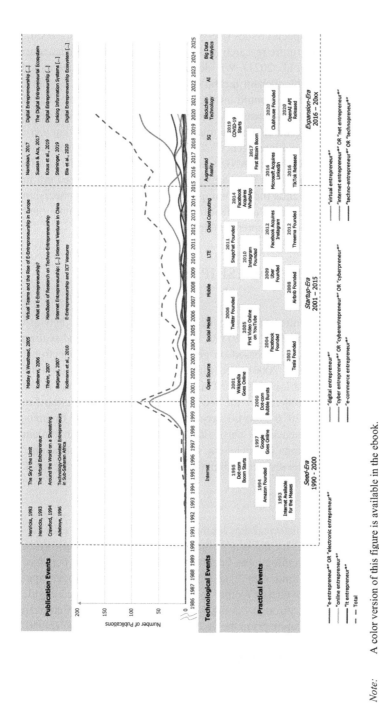

*Note:*   A color version of this figure is available in the ebook.
*Source:*  All references can be found in the original article, Kollmann et al. (2022).

*Figure 3.1*   *The history of digital entrepreneurship*

"internet entrepreneurship" (e.g., Crawford, 1994) and "technopreneurship" (e.g., Adeboye, 1996), were also used. The appearance of those terms shows that certain pioneers planted the seed – giving this era its name – for this field of research. However, during this period, no term could acquire far-reaching acceptance.

By the late 1990s, the initial opportunities provided by the internet had been explored, and new business opportunities had emerged (Kollmann, 1998). Both practitioners and theorists were confident then, referring to the start of a "promising revolution" (Kollmann, 1998, p. 44). Therefore, the *new economy* was defined by the emergence of ever more companies creating electronic value through information via data networks (Amit & Zott, 2000; Kollmann et al., 2016; Shapiro et al., 1999; Weiber & Kollmann, 1998) including Amazon and Google by the late 1990s. Rather than relying on business models built on traditional value chains (Porter, 2001), these companies understood at an early stage the potential of business models built on electronic value (Amit & Zott, 2001), leading to the so-called dot-com boom (Ofek & Richardson, 2003; Senn, 2000).

However, in 2000, the dot-com bubble burst (McFedries, 2002), causing investors to lose the money they had staked on the share prices of internet companies continuing to rise (Zook, 2008). In research, the overall peak of publications was reached during the same year with a total of 89 publications, 67 of which used the term "internet entrepreneurship" (see Figure 3.1). This peak also marked the end of the Seed-Era as the number of publications reached a turning point. The most frequently used term during the Seed-Era was "internet entrepreneurship" (in 115 out of 163 publications), corresponding to the availability of internet technology that made research in this field possible in the first place. This finding further reinforces how internet technology shaped this era.

## The Startup-Era (2001–2015)

The Startup-Era is one of transition that saw the emergence of many new ways of using internet technology. Examples include new digital technologies, such as open source, social media platforms, mobile, LTE, and cloud computing. After a short recovery period following the bursting of the dot-com bubble, users quickly accepted the new market developments, while new platforms offered them not only more ways to interact with one another via electronic data networks (Cormode & Krishnamurthy, 2008; Kollmann et al., 2016) but also the option to take a more active part in the internet and share almost all forms of data (Richter et al., 2017).

In research, the beginning of the Startup-Era was initially characterized by a significant reduction in publications, most likely owing to the collapse of the dot-com bubble. During the entire era, the number of publications increased only very slowly, and the publication peak of 89 publications in 2000 was never achieved. The analysis of terms used during this second era (15 years in total) shows that the term "internet entrepreneurship" remained the most used (mentioned in 274 out of 631 publications in total); however, other terms, such as "technopreneurship" (88 publications) and "e-entrepreneurship" (59 publications), were gaining traction. Such usage of multiple terms during the era, in the sense of an identification phase, reflects the status quo in practice.

The various terms used in publications in the Startup-Era (e.g., "internet entrepreneurship," "e-entrepreneurship," or "technopreneurship") mainly focused on the digitalization of business processes (e.g., value chains), business models (e.g., Veit et al., 2014), and business environments (Kollmann, 2006; Thérin, 2007). In this context, research increasingly considered the interconnectivity and networks between actors (Batjargal, 2007; Gruber & Henkel, 2006; Häsel et al., 2010; e.g., Matlay & Westhead, 2005; Steinberg, 2006). This also reflected a development in practice – the increase in the involvement of users with the internet (Provost & Fawcett, 2013).

Compared to the Seed-Era, the Startup-Era was characterized by a partial rethinking. In research, discourse on the role of new opportunities, such as open-source software based on internet technology, especially in the field of entrepreneurship, slowly increased. An example was Gruber and Henkel (2006) reflecting on how the domain of open-source software would affect new venture creation processes. Other studies addressed similar aspects (von Kortzfleisch et al., 2010; e.g., Zutshi et al., 2006). However, research on the impact of digital technologies and the new possibilities they engendered remained scarce. Even highly ranked academic journals did not publish articles dealing with this topic, which is why studies increasingly appeared in practice-oriented handbooks (Kollmann et al., 2010; e.g., Thérin, 2007).

While the Seed-Era was marked by the domination of the term "internet entrepreneurship," there was no such clearly dominant term during the Startup-Era. This result corresponds with the finding that internet technology and its various emerging opportunities remained the focus, evidenced by no other single outstanding digital technology emerging to enable a new research direction in this era. In addition, after the dot-com crash at the beginning of this era, no further practical event catalyzed any extraordinary increase or decrease in the number of publications during the Startup-Era.

**The Expansion-Era (2016–20xx)**

The last era from 2016 to 20xx is characterized by a turbulent turnaround and the arrival of many new digital technologies that are penetrating the global market (Kollmann, 2020; Rippa & Secundo, 2019). These technologies introduce digitalization into every aspect of people's lives. In this context, the processing of large amounts of data (i.e., big data), now underpins many new digital technologies (Dhar et al., 2014; Kollmann, 2019), as is particularly evident in the power of the five GAFAM firms, which dominate the collection, processing, and transfer of large amounts of electronic information (Marr, 2016).

Similar disrupting developments have also been reflected in research. Although the number of publications initially declined from 78 in 2015 to 62 in 2016, 2017 saw an increase to 88. Interestingly, and yet differing from the previous eras, the frequency of publications focusing on the term "internet entrepreneurship" decreased steadily, whereas publications using the term "digital entrepreneurship" increased (see Figure 3.1). This can be identified as a result of the emergence of new digital technologies during this era.

At the same time, research is again subject to reappraisal. The growing popularity of emerging digital technologies has caused scholars to focus on the link between digital technologies and entrepreneurship under the guise of the term "digital entrepreneurship," and to recognize that "digital technologies are not merely a context in studying entrepreneurship" (Zaheer et al., 2019, p. 2) but "serve as an active ingredient" (Nambisan et al., 2019, p. 2). An increasing number of publications place digital technologies center stage by integrating them into a framework encapsulating digital entrepreneurship (Recker & von Briel, 2019) and even creating digital entrepreneurship ecosystems (Elia et al., 2020; Sussan & Acs, 2017).

As it turns out, the field of digital entrepreneurship is increasingly being seen as a holistic research domain in its own right. In this holistic system, in which digital technologies are con-

*Table 3.2*     *Cross-mentions among publications*

| | Appearance in Publications | EE | DE | VE | OE | CE | IE | ITE | ECE | TE |
|---|---|---|---|---|---|---|---|---|---|---|
| **Term** | Using ... | | | | | | | | | |
| "e-entrepreneur*" OR "electronic entrepreneur*" | | | 21 | 2 | 6 | 4 | 4 | 0 | 1 | 1 |
| "digital entrepreneur*" | | 7 | | 1 | 5 | 3 | 1 | 0 | 0 | 1 |
| "virtual entrepreneur*" | | 2 | 5 | | 2 | 0 | 1 | 0 | 0 | 0 |
| "online entrepreneur*" | | 4 | 4 | 2 | | 2 | 8 | 3 | 3 | 0 |
| "cyber entrepreneur*" OR "cyberentrepreneur*" OR "cyberpreneur*" | | 3 | 8 | 0 | 2 | | 2 | 0 | 0 | 2 |
| "internet entrepreneur*" OR "net entrepreneur*" | | 6 | 10 | 0 | 10 | 1 | | 1 | 1 | 1 |
| "it entrepreneur*" | | 1 | 6 | 0 | 1 | 0 | 3 | | 0 | 0 |
| "e-commerce entrepreneur*" | | 2 | 1 | 0 | 3 | 0 | 1 | 0 | | 0 |
| "techno-entrepreneur*" OR "technopreneur*" | | 0 | 2 | 0 | 0 | 1 | 0 | 3 | 1 | |

sidered ubiquitous (Steininger, 2019, p. 381), scholars acknowledge the growing popularity of digital technologies and attempt to include every aspect of them and explore entrepreneurship in a digital context (Nambisan, 2017). There is as yet no sign of that approach abating. At the same time, since 2020 the emphasis on digital technologies has been fueled by the COVID-19 pandemic. While the resulting economic crash reached levels unseen since the great depression of the 1930s, the use of digital technologies and internet traffic increased by about 60 percent (Soto-Acosta, 2020). The global pandemic has also affected research and led to conferences and workshops adopting virtual formats (e.g., van der Aalst et al., 2020). However, the boundaries of entrepreneurship are increasingly blurred, as reflected in a trend for digital technologies facilitating what has been termed "everyday everyone entrepreneurship" (van Gelderen et al., 2021, p. 1260), allowing each individual to exploit opportunities and be an entrepreneur. That development has, in turn, led to an evolution of the entrepreneurship phenomenon as a whole.

## IN-DEPTH ANALYSIS OF DIGITAL ENTREPRENEURSHIP

This study now moves on from outlining the historical development of individual terms throughout the three eras to analyze the phenomenon of digital entrepreneurship in greater depth. The aim is to provide an overview of how the different terms are connected and how the understanding of digital entrepreneurship has developed over time. From this, we will present some ideas on the future of digital entrepreneurship research based on relevant digital technologies.

**Cross-Mentions of the Different Terms in the Field of Digital Entrepreneurship**

Given that all the described terms are used interchangeably (e.g., Zaheer et al., 2019), we assume that publications using these different terms frequently refer to one another. We thus examined so-called cross-mentions, that is, how often one term (e.g., "e-entrepreneurship") appeared in publications that used another term (e.g., "digital entrepreneurship"). Our analysis reveals that publications utilizing one term mention other terms only 168 times in the entire dataset ($n = 1,354$). Nevertheless, all terms are mentioned at least once by publications that use another term (see Table 3.2).

The frequency with which the various terms appear in publications utilizing another term varies (from 0 to 21 times), resulting in distinct levels of connectivity. Figure 3.2 illustrates the strength of connections among the different terms (bubbles) by the size of the arrowhead, which is based on the frequency of cross-mentions.

Our results show that most mentions occur bilaterally, whereas only eight mentions occur unilaterally. The majority of all mentions occur only in the references (116 times) and far less often in titles, abstracts, and keywords (52 times). Based on the strength of connections, two particularly stand out: the link between "online entrepreneurship" and "internet entrepreneurship" and that between "e-entrepreneurship" and "digital entrepreneurship." While most cross-mentions between other fields appear only between one and five times, these terms are mentioned between seven and 21 times in the field of the other term. Consequently, we investigate these in terms of quantity, content, and time.

It is evident that the connection among publications using the terms "digital entrepreneurship" and "e-entrepreneurship" is stronger but also more asymmetrical; that is, publications dealing with "digital entrepreneurship" mention the term "e-entrepreneurship" three times more often than vice versa (see Table 3.2). Second, our results indicate that the forms of the mentions are different. "Online entrepreneurship" and "internet entrepreneurship" are often used in titles, abstracts, and keywords (13 times) and rarely appear in the references (five times). In contrast, the terms "e-entrepreneurship" and "digital entrepreneurship" are mostly used only in the references (24 times) and rarely appear in titles, abstracts, and keywords (four times). Moreover, while the terms "internet entrepreneurship" and "online entrepreneurship" are often used synonymously (Dai et al., 2018; e.g., Dobbs & Buelow, 2000; Peng & Chen, 2012), publications dealing with "digital entrepreneurship" use the term "e-entrepreneurship" to establish demarcation, that is, to actively present the term "digital entrepreneurship" as a new area of research. The only publication that actively uses this term in the abstract calls "digital entrepreneurship" a further development of "e-entrepreneurship" (Gagan et al., 2018),

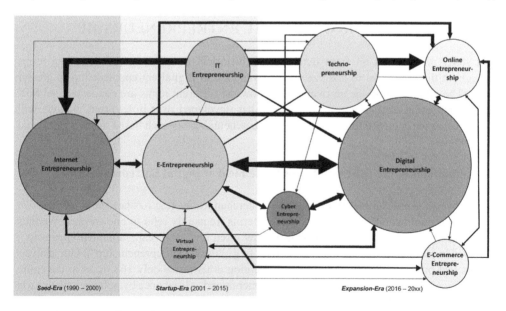

*Figure 3.2    Analysis of cross-mentions*

contradicting the existing otherwise interchangeable usage. Third, the number of mentions among the terms regarding the era in which they are mentioned differs. In the term field of "online entrepreneurship," the most mentions by publications dealing with "internet entrepreneurship" appear in the Expansion-Era (five times) and the Startup-Era (four times) and vice versa (four times in the Startup-Era and three times in the Expansion-Era). The comparable number of mentions in these eras could be explained by the largely synonymous use of these terms.

In contrast, publications on "digital entrepreneurship" mention the term "e-entrepreneurship" most often in the Expansion-Era (16 out of 21 times) and vice versa (five out of seven times). These results show that "e-entrepreneurship," which belongs to the Startup-Era, is still frequently mentioned in the Expansion-Era. This finding indicates that "e-entrepreneurship" or other terms used in previous eras enrich other terms used today and are therefore highly relevant when investigating the topic of digital entrepreneurship.

**Defining Digital Entrepreneurship Over Time**

The eras of digital entrepreneurship and the cross-mentions confirm that research in this field has been conducted since 1990. However, other terms dominated before the term "digital entrepreneurship" gained traction in current studies, which supports our problematization (Alvesson & Sandberg, 2011, 2014; Sandberg & Alvesson, 2011) that digital entrepreneurship is not a new phenomenon. To advance the "dialectical interrogation" (Alvesson & Sandberg, 2011, p. 252), we need to determine how digital entrepreneurship has been understood over time. The definition changing significantly, for example, would justify it being designated a new phenomenon. Accordingly, we examined the most-cited articles for all nine terms to identify definitions reflecting the understanding of digital entrepreneurship.

To enhance the understanding of how digital entrepreneurship evolved, we initially considered all terms together and analyzed definitions irrespective of the terms used. We found that the majority of publications assumed the term was well known and thus did not define it (Batjargal, 2007; e.g., Gould & Zhao, 2006). When definitions appeared, they might be implicit, as in the work of Bolton and Thompson (2004) that defined both "entrepreneurship" and "internet business" but did not combine the two into a single definition, such as one for "internet entrepreneurship." The remaining articles that defined the field of digital entrepreneurship (Davidson & Vaast, 2010; Hull et al., 2007; Kollmann, 2006; Nambisan, 2017; Sussan & Acs, 2017) reveal that the phenomenon is often understood similarly, even if a certain development over time can be identified. The point is exemplified by the seven example definitions listed in Table 3.3. First, we found some general definitions, which were mostly published in the Startup-Era. These were rather general and universal. They claimed that some or even all transactions had to be shifted to the digital sphere (Gruber & Henkel, 2006; Hull et al., 2007; e.g., Matlay & Westhead, 2005) and assumed a "purely electronic creation of value" (Kollmann, 2006, p. 333). In this context, all authors explicitly mention the relevance of the internet as an enabling technology. Second, we identified some expanded definitions, most of which were published in the Expansion-Era. These were not only cited more often (e.g., Nambisan, 2017; Sussan & Acs, 2017), but they also provided more fine-grained definitions. Davidson and Vaast (2010), for example, define digital entrepreneurship as the "pursuit of opportunities based on the use of digital media and other information and communication technologies" (p. 2), which thus matches the main characteristics of entrepreneurship (Bolton

*Table 3.3*      *Definitions of digital entrepreneurship over time*

| | Author(s) | Definitions |
|---|---|---|
| *General Definitions* | Matlay and Westhead (2005) | "Recent research has established that e-entrepreneurs differ from their traditional counterparts in **that all of their economic transactions take place online, via the Internet** (Chulikavit & Rose, 2003; Matlay, 2003a, 2003b)." (p. 282) |
| | Kollmann (2006) | "E-entrepreneurship refers to establishing a new company with an innovative business idea within the **net economy**, which, using an electronic platform in data networks, offers its products and/or services based upon a **purely electronic creation of value**. Essential is the fact that this value offer was only made possible through the development of **information technology**." (p. 333) |
| | Gruber and Henkel (2006) | "The term "e-entrepreneurship" has been coined to address the **discovery and exploitation of business opportunities in the internet economy**." (p. 1) |
| | Hull et al. (2007) | "Digital entrepreneurship is a subcategory of entrepreneurship in which **some or all of what would be physical in a traditional organization has been digitized** [...]. This entrepreneurial activity relies on **information technology** to create, market, distribute, transform or provide the product." (p. 293) |
| *Expanded Definitions* | Davidson and Vaast (2010) | "We refer to digital entrepreneurship as the **pursuit of opportunities based on the use of digital media and other information and communication technologies**. Digital entrepreneurs rely upon the characteristics of digital media and IT to pursue opportunities [...]. The term digital entrepreneurship encompasses the diverse opportunities generated by the Internet, World Wide Web, mobile technologies, and new media." (p. 2) |
| | Sussan and Acs (2017) | "[Digital entrepreneurship] is the combination of **digital infrastructure and entrepreneurial agents within the context of both ecosystems**. [...]" (p. 66) |
| | Nambisan (2017) | "In recent years, the infusion of new digital technologies [...] into various aspects of innovation and entrepreneurship has transformed the nature of uncertainty inherent in entrepreneurial processes and outcomes as well as the ways of dealing with such uncertainty. In turn, this has opened up a host of important research questions at **the intersection of digital technologies and entrepreneurship** – on digital entrepreneurship." (p. 1029) |

& Thompson, 2004) with digital technologies. Other scholars have followed this dichotomy, such as Sussan and Acs (2017) and Nambisan (2017), who call digital entrepreneurship "the intersection of digital technologies and entrepreneurship" (p. 1029).

We next analyzed all definitions within the context of their term field to show the possible differences between terms. Our analysis supports the findings by Zaheer et al. (2019) that these terms can be understood synonymously.[6] Nevertheless, the varying degrees of mentions of other terms are also noticeable in the definitions. With regard to the term field of "e-entrepreneurship," for example, Matlay and Westhead (2005) refer to earlier, and not directly associated, sources and even admit that the related "term [...] 'e-Economy' [was] often used interchangeably with 'Digital Economy'" (p. 280). Gruber and Henkel (2006) use references dealing with digital phenomena in the 1990s (i.e., Weiber & Kollmann, 1998) as part of their expanded definition, which is less common in the term field of "digital entrepreneurship." Here, it can be seen that publications mostly try to establish their own definitions without mentioning prior work (e.g., Davidson & Vaast, 2010), even if their definitions are often similar to earlier ones from publications on, for example, "e-entrepreneurship." Some recent research publications do refer to earlier works but either build upon definitions from the same term field (e.g., Kraus et al., 2019) or refer to earlier works published using the same term (e.g., Dy et al., 2017).

Overall, it is evident that digital entrepreneurship has been understood in very similar ways, not only within the framework of the various terms but also over time. However, after some general definitions were provided that offered a basis for future work, there was a shift toward redefining the phenomenon rather than referring to older definitions. This process was accompanied by an increasingly differentiated examination of the phenomenon itself. While initially the internet – the dominating technology of the time – was assumed to be the sole source of digital entrepreneurship, today, the understanding is far more multifaceted, and not only in terms of the technology itself. Some studies now differentiate digital entrepreneurship in relation to digital technologies according to the former's roles or functions. Steininger et al. (2019) create categories based on digital technology serving as a facilitator, mediator, outcome, or ubiquity. In contrast, Sahut et al. (2019) differentiate between a function as an enabler and the function as both an output and enabler of digital entrepreneurship. Other scholars have established new subcategories that shape the phenomenon, including Nambisan (2017) who proposes a division between digital artifacts, platforms, and infrastructures, which are interrelated but have different implications for digital entrepreneurship. Giones and Brem (2017) identify further subcategories of the phenomenon itself depending on the digital technologies used, stating that "[w]e have reached a consolidation stage in technology entrepreneurship research" (p. 44). Now that the preliminary work to define digital entrepreneurship is complete, it is often more a matter of refining an existing field or unveiling new aspects than of redefining the phenomenon.

**The Future of Digital Entrepreneurship Research**

This study reveals that digital entrepreneurship has a longer and more eventful history than is often assumed. The findings indicate that digital technologies are particularly productive sources of new terms and eras in the research field of digital entrepreneurship. An examination of current research (Recker et al., 2019; Schryen, 2013) helps identify artificial intelligence, blockchain technology, and big data analytics as decisive digital technologies that enable the future of digital entrepreneurship research (see Method). Table 3.4 presents potential future research directions in the field of digital entrepreneurship based on illustrative studies within each digital technology in the entrepreneurship context.

First, the advance of artificial intelligence is one of the greatest technological revolutions of our time (Makridakis, 2017). Understanding how algorithms perform tasks or resolve complex problems, traditionally solved by human intelligence, might lead to disruptive changes in various disciplines, such as economics (e.g., Brynjolfsson & Mitchell, 2017), policy (e.g., Agrawal et al., 2019), management (e.g., Keding, 2021), innovation (e.g., Aghion et al., 2017), and psychology (e.g., Glikson & Woolley, 2020). Against this backdrop, scholars have recently begun to consider the interplay between artificial intelligence and entrepreneurship on a conceptual and empirical basis (Chalmers et al., 2020; e.g., Obschonka & Audretsch,

*Table 3.4*     *The future of digital entrepreneurship and possible research opportunities*

| The Future of Digital Entrepreneurship | Possible Research Directions | Illustrative Studies |
|---|---|---|
| *AI-Entrepreneurship* | Artificial intelligence and…<br>• entrepreneurial opportunities<br>• entrepreneurial decision making<br>• future business models<br>• (team) processes<br>• entrepreneurial rewards<br>• entrepreneurial ecosystems<br>• entrepreneurial financing<br>• entrepreneurial research/education | (Chalmers et al., 2020; Elia et al., 2020; Fossen & Sorgner, 2021; Garbuio & Lin, 2019; Hannigan et al., 2021; Korzynski et al., 2021; Liebregts et al., 2020; Obschonka et al., 2020; Obschonka & Audretsch, 2020; Palmié et al., 2020; Prüfer & Prüfer, 2020; Robledo et al., 2021) |
| *Blockchain-Enabled/ Supported Entrepreneurship* | Blockchain technology and…<br>• entrepreneurial financing (e.g., ICOs)<br>• cryptocurrencies (e.g., Bitcoin)<br>• compliance standards and contracts<br>• business models<br>• electronic marketplaces<br>• innovation (e.g., intellectual property)<br>• transaction costs | (Ahluwalia et al., 2020; Allen et al., 2020; Bellavitis et al., 2020; Block et al., 2021; Bogusz et al., 2020; Chalmers et al., 2020, 2021; Chang et al., 2020; de Soto, 2017; Fisch, 2019; Huang et al., 2020; Islam et al., 2021; Kher et al., 2021; Kollmann et al., 2020; Masiak et al., 2020; Meier & Sannajust, 2021; Momtaz, 2020; Schückes & Gutmann, 2021; Toufaily et al., 2021; Zanella et al., 2021; Zheng et al., 2021) |
| *Data-Driven Entrepreneurship* | Big data analytics and…<br>• business model innovation<br>• entrepreneurial opportunity evaluation<br>• strategic orientation<br>• innovation analytics | (Çanakoğlu et al., 2018; Ciampi et al., 2021; Lévesque & Joglekar, 2018; Lin & Kunnathur, 2019; Mariani & Nambisan, 2021) |

2020). Researchers anticipate that the automation ability of artificial intelligence and its predictive capabilities will affect opportunity recognition, evaluation, and exploitation (Shane & Venkataraman, 2000) at all stages of the entrepreneurial process (Fossen & Sorgner, 2021; Garbuio & Lin, 2019). Artificial intelligence could also change current or future business models (Chalmers et al., 2020) and affect future entrepreneurial decision-making (Liebregts et al., 2020) and the entrepreneurial ecosystem as a whole (Elia et al., 2020). Consequently, we anticipate that improvements in artificial intelligence could define one of the forthcoming eras in the field of digital entrepreneurship, for example, by using the term "AI-entrepreneurship" (Chalmers et al., 2020).

Second, developments in blockchain technology might reveal new opportunities for future digital entrepreneurship (Nambisan et al., 2019; e.g., Nofer et al., 2017; Rippa & Secundo, 2019). For example, artificial intelligence–blockchain hybrid platforms could help new ventures address the challenges that they typically face in their early development stages, such as managing financial accounting, compliance standards, and legal work (Chalmers et al., 2020). Cryptocurrencies, such as Bitcoin or Ethereum, and the associated blockchain technology might provide new payment options for digital products and services (e.g., Kher et al., 2021; Masiak et al., 2020; Momtaz, 2020). Cryptocurrency might also open access to external capital for digital ventures in the form of an initial coin offering (Ahluwalia et al., 2020; Bogusz et al., 2020; e.g., Fisch, 2019; Huang et al., 2020). Blockchain technology might spur new digital business models (Bellavitis et al., 2020), for instance, by replacing typical intermediaries in electronic marketplaces (Kollmann et al., 2020). Therefore, blockchain technology might act as an external enabler of future digital entrepreneurship, leading to "blockchain-enabled entrepreneurship" or "blockchain-supported entrepreneurship" (Chalmers et al., 2021).

Third, having access to big data and being able to analyze them could become increasingly important to entrepreneurs and their ventures (Berg et al., 2018; Kleine-Stegemann, 2021). The development of big data analytics capabilities, considered as a "company's abilities to leverage on technology and talent to exploit big data" (Ciampi et al., 2021, p. 2) – could therefore be critical for entrepreneurial actors to compete in highly dynamic and digitalized markets. Individuals and organizations with big data analytics capabilities are the most likely to exploit the potential to reduce entrepreneurial risks and uncertainties (Çanakoğlu et al., 2018), inform entrepreneurial decisions (Lévesque & Joglekar, 2018), and improve venture innovation performance (Mariani & Nambisan, 2021), for instance. We expect the large amount of data and the burgeoning options to analyze them might lead to "data-driven entrepreneurship," where data-driven techniques and technologies shape the elements of the entrepreneurial process (Çanakoğlu et al., 2018).

## DISCUSSION

Although research in the field of digital entrepreneurship is of paramount importance in today's entrepreneurship literature (Block et al., 2020; e.g., Nambisan, 2017; von Briel et al., 2018), the terminological history of the field is often overlooked. The present study follows the methodological approach of Alvesson and Sandberg (2011, 2014; 2011) to problematize the in-house assumption that digital entrepreneurship is a new phenomenon. We have reviewed the origins of the terms used in the field of digital entrepreneurship and their growth in popularity. Our findings indicate that innovative digital technologies enabled that growth in terms relating to the field of digital entrepreneurship in certain eras. Relevant practical events influenced the number of publications within those identified eras. Moreover, even when terms are used interchangeably, they rarely reference each other, as illustrated by examining the evolution of the definitions, ultimately indicating a very similar understanding of the phenomenon. Our findings support four decisive contributions to theory.

First, our study extends prior findings by Zaheer et al. (2019) by identifying three relevant eras based on our publications analysis per term and year: the Seed-Era (1990–2000), the Startup-Era (2001–2015), and the Expansion-Era (2016–20xx). Distinguishing these three eras allows us to highlight the scientific dependence of entrepreneurship research on key technological developments. While other academic terminologies seem to be driven by regulatory factors, digital entrepreneurship terms are still rooted in practical phenomena (i.e., the development and spread of digital technologies). Accordingly, we add to the scientific debate by demonstrating the relevance of temporal contingencies to the emergence of new research topics and terminologies. This insight might support future studies attempting to bridge the gap between practice and research (Shen et al., 2018) and predict future evolutions in research. Therefore, researchers should always remain abreast of new digital technologies and maintain connections with practice.

Second, our study generates new knowledge on the connections among the different terms of today's digital entrepreneurship by analyzing how often publications using a certain term (e.g., "e-entrepreneurship") mention another one (e.g., "digital entrepreneurship"). Surprisingly, our findings reveal that researchers using one term rarely mention another in their published work;

if they do so, it is likely to be only in the references. This omission of historical terms could be explained as follows: It could be that at the time of publication researchers were not yet able to generate a deeper understanding of the phenomenon and thus could not recognize that other terms, such as "e-entrepreneurship" and "internet entrepreneurship," also describe the phenomenon of digital entrepreneurship. Therefore, they unintentionally excluded other terms from their studies. Another reason could be that researchers were aware of the history of the research field, but chose to stick with one term because they considered all other terms to be synonyms (e.g., Elia et al., 2020).

Moreover, some studies might simply not search for historical terms or simply ignore them as an element of a demarcation strategy (e.g., Gagan et al., 2018). Our results indicate that the term "digital entrepreneurship" continues to dominate new publications, which we suggest is a consequence of researchers seeking novelty and uniqueness by establishing a terminological distance from other longer-established terms.

Third, this study reveals new insights into the evolution of the understanding of digital entrepreneurship (e.g., Steininger, 2019; Zaheer et al., 2019). We show that despite some changes prompted by the ongoing integration of digital technologies into our lives, the basic understanding has remained consistent. Accordingly, we add to the scientific discourse (Elia et al., 2020; e.g., Nambisan, 2017; Shen et al., 2018; Steininger, 2019; Sussan & Acs, 2017) holding that contingency over time is also highly relevant when considering the content of the phenomenon and that the enabling role of digital technologies is reflected in the basic understanding of it. The current research thus extends previous research, such as that of Giones and Brem (2017) and Sahut et al. (2019), who put a content-based division of digital entrepreneurship center stage.

Fourth, we generate new knowledge about what future research on digital entrepreneurship might look like (e.g., van Gelderen et al., 2021). We identify artificial intelligence (Chalmers et al., 2020), blockchain technology (Chen & Bellavitis, 2020; Kollmann et al., 2020), and big data analytics (Çanakoğlu et al., 2018) as potentially groundbreaking digital technologies, thus offering other research topics that subsequent studies might explore. We also apply our findings to the terminological evolution of terms and suggest future terms for digital entrepreneurship based on the underlying digital technologies used.

## LIMITATIONS

Despite the study's contributions, we must acknowledge several limitations regarding the generalizability of our statements. First, we used a large dataset ($n = 1,354$). Although this large dataset with few exclusion criteria is typical of scoping literature reviews (Paré et al., 2015), future studies could validate or extend our findings with more traditional systematic literature reviews. For instance, studies could conduct in-depth content analyses only in highly ranked academic journals to generate an even deeper understanding of the history of digital entrepreneurship (Anderson et al., 2008).

Second, we only excluded duplicates within one term field (i.e., if a single publication using "e-entrepreneurship" is listed more than once in the term field of "e-entrepreneurship") and not between term fields (i.e., if a single publication using "e-entrepreneurship" is listed more than once between the term fields of "e-entrepreneurship" and "digital entrepreneurship"). The approach was dictated by there being no objective decision criteria on which to assign a publication to just one term field when it is mentioned in multiple term fields. The situation means that publications mentioning various terms in their titles, abstracts, keywords, and/or subjects could have appeared in multiple term fields and thus more than once in our overall dataset. Further research could extend our findings by controlling for the possible effects of multiple occurrences of publications between the term fields.

Third, we identify the connections among the different terms of digital entrepreneurship based on the cross-mentions between the publications within titles, abstracts, keywords, subjects, and/or references. Future studies could extend these results by searching for cross-mentions also in the main body of the study or using explorative quantitative methods, such as searching for networks and graph representations of citations between the documents via bibliometric (Zupic & Čater, 2015) or network analysis (Bhupatiraju et al., 2012).

Fourth, we have expanded the understanding of digital entrepreneurship based on given definitions. We did not search all publications for definitions but only the top ten per term (which nevertheless covered 67 percent of all citations of the entire dataset). Subsequent studies might consider additional definitions to expand our findings. Furthermore, the understanding of a phenomenon is often reflected in both the definitions employed and other parts of the publication. Future research could include more than just the stated definitions (e.g., the content of the abstract or the body text) to obtain more detailed information on the basic understanding of the publications.

Finally, we determine the future of digital entrepreneurship research based on current calls for papers and future research direction sections within articles in the field of digital entrepreneurship. While our approach facilitates a prediction of the future based on the literature (Recker et al., 2019; Schryen, 2013), future research might employ other methods, such as the Delphi method that offers a systematic and multilevel estimation procedure to predict future events (van Gelderen et al., 2021).

## ACKNOWLEDGMENT

This chapter is a reprint of Kollmann, T., Kleine-Stegemann, L., de Cruppe, K., & Then-Bergh, C. (2022). Eras of digital entrepreneurship. *Business & Information Systems Engineering*, *64*(1), 15–31. https://doi.org/10.1007/s12599-021-00728-6. Since this article was first published, Christina Then-Bergh's name has changed to Christina Strauss. We have updated her name in this chapter.

## NOTES

1.  This chapter is available for free as Open Access from the individual project page at www.elgaronline.com under a Creative Commons AttributionNonCommercial-NoDerivatives 4.0 Unported (https://creativecommons.org/licenses/by-nc-nd/4.0/) license.
2.  In our study, we distinguish between the overall field of research on digital entrepreneurship (i.e., "the field of research on digital entrepreneurship") and the term "digital entrepreneurship" itself (i.e., "digital entrepreneurship").
3.  Problematization challenges "the assumptions that underlie not only others' but also one's own theoretical position and, based on that, to construct novel research questions" (Alvesson & Sandberg, 2011, S. 252). In-house assumptions are those that "exist within a particular school of thought in the

sense that they are shared and accepted as unproblematic by its advocates" (Alvesson & Sandberg, 2011, S. 254).

4.    Although internet technology was introduced as early as 1970, it did not become fully accessible to the general population until the early 1990s. This appears to explain why despite searching from 1970 we did not find the first publications until 1990.

5.    We included only articles from peer-reviewed journals having the minimum VHB-Jourqual 3 rating of "B." Jourqual 3 is a magazine ranking published by the German Academic Association for Business Research. It can be accessed online at http://www.vhbonline.org (retrieved on September 9, 2021).

6.    Interestingly, we could also not find any major differences in the understanding between the research fields (i.e., entrepreneurship, technology, and innovation). What was evident, however, was a slightly stronger focus on the technological side of digital entrepreneurship in technology journals (e.g., Giones & Brem, 2017).

# REFERENCES

Adeboye, T. (1996). Technology–oriented entrepreneurs in sub-Saharan Africa: Who are they and how are they involved in development and industrialization in Africa? *Entrepreneurship & Regional Development*, *8*(4), 297–320. https://doi.org/10.1080/08985629600000017

Aghion, P., Jones, B. F., & Jones, C. I. (2017). Artificial intelligence and economic growth. In *National Bureau of Economic Research* (Nr. 23928). https://doi.org/10.3386/w23928

Agrawal, A. K., Gans, J. S., & Goldfarb, A. (2019). Economic policy for artificial intelligence. *Innovation Policy and the Economy*, *19*(1), 139–159. https://doi.org/10.1086/699935

Ahluwalia, S., Mahto, R. V, & Guerrero, M. (2020). Blockchain technology and startup financing: A transaction cost economics perspective. *Technological Forecasting and Social Change*, *151*. https://doi.org/10.1016/j.techfore.2019.119854

Allen, D. W. E., Berg, C., Markey-Towler, B., Novak, M., & Potts, J. (2020). Blockchain and the evolution of institutional technologies: Implications for innovation policy. *Research Policy*, *49*(1). https://doi.org/10.1016/j.respol.2019.103865

Alt, R., Leimeister, J. M., Priemuth, T., Sachse, S., Urbach, N., & Wunderlich, N. (2020). Software-defined business: Implications for IT management. *Business and Information Systems Engineering*, *62*(6), 609–621. https://doi.org/10.1007/s12599-020-00669-6

Alvesson, M., & Sandberg, J. (2011). Generating research questions through problematization. *Academy of Management Review*, *36*(2), 247–271. https://doi.org/10.5465/amr.2009.0188

Alvesson, M., & Sandberg, J. (2014). Habitat and habitus: Boxed-in versus box-breaking research. *Organization Studies*, *35*(7), 967–987. https://doi.org/10.1177/0170840614530916

Amit, R., & Zott, C. (2000). *Value Drivers of E-commerce Business Models*. Wiley Online Library.

Amit, R., & Zott, C. (2001). Value creation in e-business. *Strategic Management Journal*, *22*(6–7), 493–520. https://doi.org/10.1002/smj.187

Anderson, S., Allen, P., Peckham, S., & Goodwin, N. (2008). Asking the right questions: Scoping studies in the commissioning of research on the organisation and delivery of health services. *Health Research Policy and Systems*, *6*, 1–12. https://doi.org/10.1186/1478-4505-6-7

Arksey, H., & O'Malley, L. (2005). Scoping studies: Towards a methodological framework. *International Journal of Social Research Methodology*, *8*(1), 19–32. https://doi.org/10.1080/1364557032000119616

Batjargal, B. (2007). Internet entrepreneurship: Social capital, human capital, and performance of internet ventures in China. *Research Policy*, *36*(5), 605–618. https://doi.org/10.1016/j.respol.2006.09.029

Bellavitis, C., Cumming, D., & Vanacker, T. (2020). Ban, boom, and echo! Entrepreneurship and initial coin offerings. *Entrepreneurship Theory and Practice*. https://doi.org/10.1177/1042258720940114

Berg, V., Birkeland, J., Pappas, I. O., & Jaccheri, L. (2018). The role of data analytics in startup companies: Exploring challenges and barriers. In S. A. Al-Sharhan, A. C. Simintiras, Y. K. Dwivedi, M. Janssen, M. Mäntymäki, L. Tahat, I. Moughrabi, T. M. Ali, & N. P. Rana (Eds.), *Conference on E-Business, E-Service and E-Society* (pp. 205–216). Springer. https://doi.org/10.1007/978-3-030-02131-3_19

Berger, E. S. C., von Briel, F., Davidsson, P., & Kuckertz, A. (2021). Digital or not – The future of entrepreneurship and innovation. *Journal of Business Research, 125*(March 2021), 436–442. https://doi.org/10.1016/j.jbusres.2019.12.020

Bhupatiraju, S., Nomaler, Ö., Triulzi, G., & Verspagen, B. (2012). Knowledge flows – Analyzing the core literature of innovation, entrepreneurship and science and technology studies. *Research Policy, 41*(7), 1205–1218. https://doi.org/10.1016/j.respol.2012.03.011

Block, J. H., Brohman, K., & Steininger, D. M. (2020). Digital entrepreneurship: Opportunities, challenges, and impacts. *Business & Information Systems Engineering, 62*, 397–399. https://doi.org/10.1007/s12599-020-00651-2

Block, J. H., Groh, A., Hornuf, L., Vanacker, T., & Vismara, S. (2021). The entrepreneurial finance markets of the future: A comparison of crowdfunding and initial coin offerings. *Small Business Economics, 57*(2), 865–882. https://doi.org/10.1007/s11187-020-00330-2

Bogusz, C. I., Laurell, C., & Sandström, C. (2020). Tracking the digital evolution of entrepreneurial finance: The interplay between crowdfunding, blockchain technologies, cryptocurrencies, and initial coin offerings. *IEEE Transactions on Engineering Management, 67*(4), 1099–1108. https://doi.org/10.1109/TEM.2020.2984032

Bolton, B., & Thompson, J. (2004). *Entrepreneurs: Talent, temperament and opportunity* (2nd ed.). Elsevier Butterworth-Heinemann.

Brynjolfsson, E., & Mitchell, T. (2017). What can machine learning do? Workforce implications. *Science, 358*(6370), 1530–1534. https://doi.org/10.1126/science.aap8062

Çanakoğlu, E., Erzurumlu, S. S., & Erzurumlu, Y. O. (2018). How data-driven entrepreneur analyzes imperfect information for business opportunity evaluation. *IEEE Transactions on Engineering Management, 65*(4), 604–617. https://doi.org/10.1109/TEM.2018.2826983

Chalmers, D., MacKenzie, N. G., & Carter, S. (2020). Artificial intelligence and entrepreneurship: Implications for venture creation in the fourth industrial revolution. *Entrepreneurship Theory and Practice, 45*(5), 1028–1053. https://doi.org/10.1177/1042258720934581

Chalmers, D., Matthews, R., & Hyslop, A. (2021). Blockchain as an external enabler of new venture ideas: Digital entrepreneurs and the disintermediation of the global music industry. *Journal of Business Research, 125*(December 2018), 577–591. https://doi.org/10.1016/j.jbusres.2019.09.002

Chang, V., Baudier, P., Zhang, H., Xu, Q., Zhang, J., & Arami, M. (2020). How blockchain can impact financial services – The overview, challenges and recommendations from expert interviewees. *Technological Forecasting and Social Change, 158*. https://doi.org/10.1016/j.techfore.2020.120166

Chen, Y., & Bellavitis, C. (2020). Blockchain disruption and decentralized finance: The rise of decentralized business models. *Journal of Business Venturing Insights, 13*. https://doi.org/10.1016/j.jbvi.2019.e00151

Chulikavit, K., & Rose, J. (2003). E-commerce and the internationalization of SMEs. In H. Etemad & R. Wright (Eds.), *Globalization and Entrepreneurship: Policy and Strategy Perspectives* (pp. 205–222). Cheltenham, UK and Northampton, MA, USA: Edward Elgar Publishing. https://doi.org/10.4337/9781843767084.00020

Ciampi, F., Demi, S., Magrini, A., Marzi, G., & Papa, A. (2021). Exploring the impact of big data analytics capabilities on business model innovation: The mediating role of entrepreneurial orientation. *Journal of Business Research, 123*, 1–13. https://doi.org/10.1016/j.jbusres.2020.09.023

Cormode, G., & Krishnamurthy, B. (2008). Key differences between web 1.0 and web 2.0. *First Monday, 13*(6). https://doi.org/10.5210/fm.v13i6.2125

Cram, W. A., Templier, M., & Paré, G. (2020). (Re)considering the concept of literature review reproducibility. *Journal of the Association for Information Systems, 21*(5), 1103–1114. https://doi.org/10.17705/1jais.00630

Crawford, M. (1994). Around the world on a shoestring. *Canadian Business, 67*(12), 83.

Dai, H., Yin, J., Wang, K., Tsai, S.-B., Zhou, B., & Lin, W.-P. (2018). Trust building in dynamic process of internet entrepreneurial social network. *IEEE Access, 6*, 79138–79150. https://doi.org/10.1109/ACCESS.2018.2883755

Davidson, E., & Vaast, E. (2010). Digital entrepreneurship and its sociomaterial enactment. *Proceedings of the 43rd Hawaii International Conference on System Sciences, USA*, 1–10. https://doi.org/10.1109/HICSS.2010.150

de Soto, H. (2017). A tale of two civilizations in the era of facebook and blockchain. *Small Business Economics*, *49*(4), 729–739. https://doi.org/10.1007/s11187-017-9949-4

Dhar, V., Jarke, M., & Laartz, J. (2014). Big data. *Business and Information Systems Engineering*, *6*(5), 257–259. https://doi.org/10.1007/s12599-014-0338-0

Dobbs, K., & Buelow, A. (2000). Online entrepreneurs. *Training*, *37*(12), 38.

Dy, A. M., Marlow, S., & Martin, L. (2017). A Web of opportunity or the same old story? Women digital entrepreneurs and intersectionality theory. *Human Relations*, *70*(3), 286–311. https://doi.org/10.1177/0018726716650730

Elia, G., Margherita, A., & Passiante, G. (2020). Digital entrepreneurship ecosystem: How digital technologies and collective intelligence are reshaping the entrepreneurial process. *Technological Forecasting and Social Change*, *150*(1). https://doi.org/10.1016/j.techfore.2019.119791

European Commission. (1997). *A European Initiative in Electronic Commerce*. https://eur-lex.europa.eu/LexUriServ/LexUriServ.do?uri=COM:1997:0157:FIN:EN:PDF

Feindt, S., Jeffcoate, J., & Chappell, C. (2002). Identifying success factors for rapid growth in SME e-commerce. *Small business economics*, *19*(1), 51–62. https://doi.org/10.1023/A:1016165825476

Fisch, C. (2019). Initial coin offerings (ICOs) to finance new ventures. *Journal of Business Venturing*, *34*(1), 1–22. https://doi.org/10.1016/j.jbusvent.2018.09.007

Fisch, C., & Block, J. H. (2018). Six tips for your (systematic) literature review in business and management research. *Management Review Quarterly*, *68*(2), 103–106. https://doi.org/10.1007/s11301-018-0142-x

Fossen, F. M., & Sorgner, A. (2021). Digitalization of work and entry into entrepreneurship. *Journal of Business Research*, *125*(4), 548–563. https://doi.org/10.1016/j.jbusres.2019.09.019

Gagan, K., Majumdar, S. K., & Menon, S. (2018). Manoeuvre of electronic entrepreneurial ecosystem to contemporary indicator of techno business leadership in industry 4.0: Digital entrepreneurship. *Global Journal of Enterprise Information System*, *10*(3), 25–33. https://www.gjeis.com/index.php/GJEIS/article/view/247

Garbuio, M., & Lin, N. (2019). Artificial intelligence as a growth engine for health care startups: Emerging business models. *California Management Review*, *61*(2), 59–83. https://doi.org/10.1177/0008125618811931

Ghezzi, A., & Cavallo, A. (2020). Agile business model innovation in digital entrepreneurship: Lean startup approaches. *Journal of Business Research*, *110*, 519–537. https://doi.org/https://doi.org/10.1016/j.jbusres.2018.06.013

Giones, F., & Brem, A. (2017). Digital technology entrepreneurship: A definition and research agenda. *Technology Innovation Management Review*, *7*(5), 44–51. https://doi.org/10.22215/timreview1076

Glikson, E., & Woolley, A. W. (2020). Human trust in artificial intelligence: Review of empirical research. *Academy of Management Annals*, *14*(2), 627–660. https://doi.org/10.5465/annals.2018.0057

Gould, C., & Zhao, F. (2006). Online information privacy and its implications for e-entrepreneurship and e-business ethics. In F. Zhao (Ed.), *Entrepreneurship and Innovations in E-business: An Integrative Perspective* (pp. 200–222). IGI Global.

Grégoire, D. A., & Shepherd, D. A. (2012). Technology-market combinations and the identification of entrepreneurial opportunities: An investigation of the opportunity-individual nexus. *Academy of Management Journal*, *55*(4), 753–785. https://doi.org/10.5465/amj.2011.0126

Gruber, M., & Henkel, J. (2006). New ventures based on open innovation: An empirical analysis of start-up firms in embedded Linux. *International Journal of Technology Management*, *33*(4), 356–372. https://doi.org/10.1504/IJTM.2006.009249

Hannigan, T. R., Briggs, A. R., Valadao, R., Seidel, M.-D. L., & Jennings, P. D. (2021). A new tool for policymakers: Mapping cultural possibilities in an emerging AI entrepreneurial ecosystem. *Research Policy*. https://doi.org/10.1016/j.respol.2021.104315

Häsel, M., Kollmann, T., & Breugst, N. (2010). IT competence in internet founder teams. *Business & Information Systems Engineering*, *2*(4), 209–217. https://doi.org/10.1007/s12599-010-0109-5

Henricks, M. (1993a, June). The virtual entrepreneur. *Success*, 41–44.

Henricks, M. (1993b, July). The sky's the limit. *Entrepreneur*, 38–40.

Huang, W., Meoli, M., & Vismara, S. (2020). The geography of initial coin offerings. *Small Business Economics*, *55*(1), 77–102. https://doi.org/10.1007/s11187-019-00135-y

Hull, C. E., Hung, Y.-T. C., Hair, N., Perotti, V., & DeMartino, R. (2007). Taking advantage of digital opportunities: A typology of digital entrepreneurship. *International Journal of Networking and Virtual Organisations*, *4*(3), 290–303. https://doi.org/10.1504/IJNVO.2007.015166

Islam, N., Marinakis, Y., Olson, S., White, R., & Walsh, S. (2021). Is blockchain mining profitable in the long run? *IEEE Transactions on Engineering Management*. https://doi.org/10.1109/TEM.2020.3045774

Jesson, J., Matheson, L., & Lacey, F. M. (2011). *Doing your Literature Review: Traditional and Systematic Techniques*. Sage Publications.

Keding, C. (2021). Understanding the interplay of artificial intelligence and strategic management: Four decades of research in review. *Management Review Quarterly*, *71*(1), 91–134. https://doi.org/10.1007/s11301-020-00181-x

Kher, R., Terjesen, S., & Liu, C. (2021). Blockchain, bitcoin, and ICOs: A review and research agenda. *Small Business Economics*, *56*, 1699–1720. https://doi.org/10.1007/s11187-019-00286-y

Kleine-Stegemann, L. (2021). Lean Analytics: Ein Vorgehensmodell zur Nutzung von Data Analytics in Startups der Digitalen Wirtschaft. In T. Kollmann (Ed.), *Handbuch Digitale Wirtschaft*. Springer Reference. Online first. https://doi.org/https://doi.org/10.1007/978-3-658-17345-6_91-1

Kollmann, T. (1998). The information triple jump as the measure of success in electronic commerce. *Electronic Markets*, *8*(4), 44–49.

Kollmann, T. (2006). What is e-entrepreneurship? Fundamentals of company founding in the net economy. *International Journal of Technology Management*, *33*(4), 322–340. https://doi.org/10.1504/IJTM.2006.009247

Kollmann, T. (2019). *E-Business – Grundlagen elektronischer Geschäftsprozesse in der Digitalen Wirtschaft* (7th ed.). Springer.

Kollmann, T. (2020). Digital entrepreneurship – Unternehmensgründung in der digitalen Wirtschaft. In K. Hölzle, V. Tiberius, & H. Surrey (Eds.), *Perspektiven des Entrepreneurships: Unternehmerische Konzepte zwischen Theorie und Praxis* (1st edn, pp. 331–342). Schäffer-Poeschel.

Kollmann, T., Häsel, M., & Breugst, N. (2009). Competence of IT professionals in e-business venture teams: The effect of experience and expertise on preference structure. *Journal of Management Information Systems*, *25*(4), 51–80. https://doi.org/10.2753/MIS0742-1222250402

Kollmann, T., Hensellek, S., de Cruppe, K., & Sirges, A. (2020). Toward a renaissance of cooperatives fostered by blockchain on electronic marketplaces: A theory-driven case study approach. *Electronic Markets*, *30*(2), 273–284. https://doi.org/10.1007/s12525-019-00369-4

Kollmann, T., Kleine-Stegemann, L., de Cruppe, K., & Then-Bergh, C. (2022). Eras of digital entrepreneurship. *Business & Information Systems Engineering*, *64*(1), 15–31.

Kollmann, T., Kuckertz, A., & Stöckmann, C. (2010). *E-Entrepreneurship and ICT Ventures: Strategy, Organization and Technology*. IGI Global. http://services.igi-global.com/resolvedoi/resolve.aspx?doi=10.4018/978-1-61520-597-4

Kollmann, T., Lomberg, C., & Peschl, A. (2016). Web 1.0, web 2.0, and web 3.0. In I. Lee (Ed.), *Encyclopedia of E-commerce Development, Implementation, and Management* (pp. 1139–1148). IGI Global. https://doi.org/10.4018/978-1-4666-9787-4.ch081

Korzynski, P., Haenlein, M., & Rautiainen, M. (2021). Impression management techniques in crowdfunding: An analysis of kickstarter videos using artificial intelligence. *European Management Journal*. https://doi.org/10.1016/j.emj.2021.01.001

Kraus, S., Breier, M., & Dasí-Rodríguez, S. (2020). The art of crafting a systematic literature review in entrepreneurship research. *International Entrepreneurship and Management Journal*, *16*(3), 1023–1042. https://doi.org/10.1007/s11365-020-00635-4

Kraus, S., Palmer, C., Kailer, N., Kallinger, F. L., & Spitzer, J. (2019). Digital entrepreneurship: A research agenda on new business models for the twenty-first century. *International Journal of Entrepreneurial Behaviour and Research*, *25*(2), 353–375. https://doi.org/10.1108/IJEBR-06-2018-0425

Lévesque, M., & Joglekar, N. (2018). Guest editorial resource, routine, reputation, or regulation shortages: Can data- and analytics-driven capabilities inform tech entrepreneur decisions. *IEEE Transactions on Engineering Management*, *65*(4), 537–544. https://doi.org/10.1109/TEM.2018.2869183

Liebregts, W., Darnihamedani, P., Postma, E., & Atzmueller, M. (2020). The promise of social signal processing for research on decision-making in entrepreneurial contexts. *Small Business Economics*, *55*(3), 589–605. https://doi.org/10.1007/s11187-019-00205-1

Lin, C., & Kunnathur, A. (2019). Strategic orientations, developmental culture, and big data capability. *Journal of Business Research*, *105*, 49–60. https://doi.org/10.1016/j.jbusres.2019.07.016

Lyytinen, K., Yoo, Y., & Boland, R. J. J. (2016). Digital product innovation within four classes of innovation networks. *Information Systems Journal*, *26*(1), 47–75.

Makridakis, S. (2017). The forthcoming artificial intelligence (AI) revolution: Its impact on society and firms. *Futures*, *90*, 46–60. https://doi.org/10.1016/j.futures.2017.03.006

Mariani, M. M., & Nambisan, S. (2021). Innovation analytics and digital innovation experimentation: The rise of research-driven online review platforms. *Technological Forecasting and Social Change*, *172*. https://doi.org/10.1016/j.techfore.2021.121009

Marr, B. (2016). *Big data in practice: How 45 Successful Companies Used Big Data Analytics to Deliver Extraordinary Results* (1st edn.). John Wiley & Sons.

Masiak, C., Block, J. H., Masiak, T., Neuenkirch, M., & Pielen, K. N. (2020). Initial coin offerings (ICOs): Market cycles and relationship with bitcoin and ether. *Small Business Economics*, *55*(4), 1113–1130. https://doi.org/10.1007/s11187-019-00176-3

Massaro, M., Dumay, J., & Guthrie, J. (2016). On the shoulders of giants: Undertaking a structured literature review in accounting. *Accounting, Auditing and Accountability Journal*, *29*(5), 767–801. https://doi.org/10.1108/AAAJ-01-2015-1939

Matlay, H. (2003a). *e-Babel: In search of a theory of e-everything*. Paper presented at the UCE Business School Research Seminar, Birmingham, 11–13 March.

Matlay, H. (2003b). Small tourism firms in e-Europe: Definitional, conceptual and contextual considerations. In T. Rhodri (Ed.), *Small Firms in Tourism: International Perspectives* (pp. 297–312). Pergamon.

Matlay, H. (2004). E-entrepreneurship and small e-business development: Towards a comparative research agenda. *Journal of Small Business and Enterprise Development*, *11*(3), 408–414. https://doi.org/10.1108/14626000410551663

Matlay, H., & Westhead, P. (2005). Virtual teams and the rise of e-entrepreneurship in Europe. *International Small Business Journal*, *23*(3), 279–302. https://doi.org/10.1177/0266242605052074

McFedries, P. (2002). Tall poppy syndrome dot-com. *IEEE Spectrum*, *39*(12), 68–68. https://doi.org/10.1109/MSPEC.2002.1088460

Meier, O., & Sannajust, A. (2021). The smart contract revolution: A solution for the holdup problem? *Small Business Economics*, *57*(2), 1073–1088. https://doi.org/10.1007/s11187-020-00339-7

Momtaz, P. P. (2020). Entrepreneurial finance and moral hazard: Evidence from token offerings. *Journal of Business Venturing*, *36*(5). https://doi.org/10.1016/j.jbusvent.2020.106001

Murphy, A., Tucker, H., Coyne, M., & Touryalai, H. (2020). *GLOBAL 2000 – the world's largest public companies*. https://www.forbes.com/global2000/#7acf271f335d

Nambisan, S. (2017). Digital entrepreneurship: Toward a digital technology perspective of entrepreneurship. *Entrepreneurship Theory and Practice*, *41*(6), 1029–1055. https://doi.org/10.1111/etap.12254

Nambisan, S., Wright, M., & Feldman, M. (2019). The digital transformation of innovation and entrepreneurship: Progress, challenges and key themes. *Research Policy*, *48*(8). https://doi.org/10.1016/j.respol.2019.03.018

Nofer, M., Gomber, P., Hinz, O., & Schiereck, D. (2017). Blockchain. *Business and Information Systems Engineering*, *59*(3), 183–187. https://doi.org/10.1007/s12599-017-0467-3

Obschonka, M., & Audretsch, D. B. (2020). Artificial intelligence and big data in entrepreneurship: A new era has begun. *Small Business Economics*, *55*(3), 529–539. https://doi.org/https://doi.org/10.1007/s11187-019-00202-4

Obschonka, M., Lee, N., Rodríguez-Pose, A., Eichstaedt, J. C., & Ebert, T. (2020). Big data methods, social media, and the psychology of entrepreneurial regions: Capturing cross-county personality traits and their impact on entrepreneurship in the USA. *Small Business Economics*, *55*(3), 567–588. https://doi.org/10.1007/s11187-019-00204-2

Ofek, E., & Richardson, M. (2003). Dotcom mania: The rise and fall of internet stock prices. *The Journal of Finance*, *58*(3), 1113–1137. https://doi.org/10.1111/1540-6261.00560

Ojala, A. (2016). Business models and opportunity creation: How IT entrepreneurs create and develop business models under uncertainty. *Information Systems Journal, 26*(5), 451–476. https://doi.org/10.1111/isj.12078

Palmié, M., Wincent, J., Parida, V., & Caglar, U. (2020). The evolution of the financial technology ecosystem: An introduction and agenda for future research on disruptive innovations in ecosystems. *Technological Forecasting and Social Change, 151.* https://doi.org/10.1016/j.techfore.2019.119779

Paré, G., Trudel, M.-C., Jaana, M., & Kitsiou, S. (2015). Synthesizing information systems knowledge: A typology of literature reviews. *Information and Management, 52*(2), 183–199. https://doi.org/10.1016/j.im.2014.08.008

Peng, W.-B., & Chen, X.-H. (2012). Study on the optimization of undergraduates' internet entrepreneurship environment in China. *2012 International Conference on Management Science & Engineering 19th Annual Conference Proceedings*, 896–905. https://doi.org/https://doi.org/10.1109/ICMSE20219.2012

Poon, S., & Swatman, P. M. C. (1997). Small business use of the internet: Findings from Australian case studies. *International Marketing Review, 14*(5), 385–402. https://doi.org/10.1108/02651339710184343

Porter, M. E. (2001). The value chain and competitive advantage. In D. Barnes (Ed.), *Understanding Business: Processes* (pp. 50–66). Routledge in association with the Open University.

Provost, F., & Fawcett, T. (2013). Data science and its relationship to big data and data-driven decision making. *Big Data, 1*(1), 51–59. https://doi.org/10.1089/big.2013.1508

Prüfer, J., & Prüfer, P. (2020). Data science for entrepreneurship research: Studying demand dynamics for entrepreneurial skills in the Netherlands. *Small Business Economics, 55*(3), 651–672. https://doi.org/10.1007/s11187-019-00208-y

Recker, J., Indulska, M., Green, P. F., Burton-Jones, A., & Weber, R. (2019). Information systems as representations: A review of the theory and evidence. *Journal of the Association for Information Systems, 20*(6), 735–786. https://doi.org/10.17705/1jais.00550

Recker, J., & von Briel, F. (2019). The future of digital entrepreneurship research: Existing and emerging opportunities. In H. Krcmar, J. Fedorowicz, W. F. Boh, J. M. Leimeister, & S. Wattal (Eds.), *40th International Conference on Information Systems, ICIS 2019.*

Richter, C., Kraus, S., Brem, A., Durst, S., & Giselbrecht, C. (2017). Digital entrepreneurship: Innovative business models for the sharing economy. *Creativity and Innovation Management, 26*(3), 300–310. https://doi.org/10.1111/caim.12227

Rippa, P., & Secundo, G. (2019). Digital academic entrepreneurship: The potential of digital technologies on academic entrepreneurship. *Technological Forecasting and Social Change, 146*, 900–911. https://doi.org/10.1016/j.techfore.2018.07.013

Robledo, S., Grisales Aguirre, A. M., Hughes, M., & Eggers, F. (2021). "Hasta la vista, baby" – Will machine learning terminate human literature reviews in entrepreneurship? *Journal of Small Business Management*, 1–30. https://doi.org/10.1080/00472778.2021.1955125

Rosenbaum, H., & Cronin, B. (1993). Digital entrepreneurship: Doing business on the information superhighway. *International Journal of Information Management, 16*(3), 461–463. https://doi.org/10.1016/0268-4012(93)90062-9

Sahut, J.-M., Iandoli, L., & Teulon, F. (2019). The age of digital entrepreneurship. *Small Business Economics, 56*(3), 1159–1169. https://doi.org/10.1007/s11187-019-00260-8

Sandberg, J., & Alvesson, M. (2011). Ways of constructing research questions: Gap-spotting or problematization? *Organization, 18*(1), 23–44. https://doi.org/10.1177/1350508410372151

Schatz, B. R., & Hardin, J. B. (1994). NCSA mosaic and the world wide web: Global hypermedia protocols for the internet. *Science, 265*(5174), 895–901.

Schryen, G. (2013). Revisiting IS business value research: What we already know, what we still need to know, and how we can get there. *European Journal of Information Systems, 22*(2), 139–169. https://doi.org/10.1057/ejis.2012.45

Schryen, G., Wagner, G., Benlian, A., & Paré, G. (2020). A knowledge development perspective on literature reviews: Validation of a new typology in the IS field. *Communications of the Association for Information Systems, 46*(1), 134–186. https://doi.org/10.17705/1CAIS.04607

Schückes, M., & Gutmann, T. (2021). Why do startups pursue initial coin offerings (ICOs)? The role of economic drivers and social identity on funding choice. *Small Business Economics, 57*(2), 1027–1052. https://doi.org/10.1007/s11187-020-00337-9

Senn, J. A. (2000). Electronic commerce beyond the "dot com" boom. *National Tax Journal*, *53*(3), 373–383. https://doi.org/10.17310/ntj.2000.3.04

Shane, S., & Venkataraman, S. (2000). The promise of entrepreneurship as a field of research. *Academy of Management Review*, *25*(1), 217–226. https://doi.org/10.2307/259271

Shapiro, C., Carl, S., & Varian, H. R. (1999). *Information Rules: A Strategic Guide to the Network Economy* (1st edn.). Harvard Business Review Press.

Shen, K. N., Lindsay, V., & Xu, Y. (Calvin). (2018). Digital entrepreneurship. *Information Systems Journal*, *28*(6), 1125–1128. https://doi.org/10.1111/isj.12219

Smith, C., Smith, J. B., & Shaw, E. (2017). Embracing digital networks: Entrepreneurs' social capital online. *Journal of Business Venturing*, *32*(1), 18–34. https://doi.org/10.1016/j.jbusvent.2016.10.003

Soto-Acosta, P. (2020). COVID-19 pandemic: Shifting digital transformation to a high-speed gear. *Information Systems Management*, *37*(4), 260–266. https://doi.org/10.1080/10580530.2020.1814461

Srinivasan, A., & Venkatraman, N. (2018). Entrepreneurship in digital platforms: A network-centric view. *Strategic Entrepreneurship Journal*, *12*(1), 54–71. https://doi.org/10.1002/sej.1272

Steinberg, A. (2006). Exploring rhizomic becomings in post dot-com crash networks: A Deleuzian approach to emergent knowledge dynamics. In F. Zhao (Ed.), *Entrepreneurship and Innovations in E-business: An Integrative Perspective* (pp. 18–40). IGI Global. https://doi.org/10.4018/978-1-59140-920-5.ch002

Steininger, D. M. (2019). Linking information systems and entrepreneurship: A review and agenda for IT-associated and digital entrepreneurship research. *Information Systems Journal*, *29*(2), 363–407. https://doi.org/10.1111/isj.12206

Stewart, A., & Cotton, J. (2013). Making sense of entrepreneurship journals: Journal rankings and policy choices. *International Journal of Entrepreneurial Behaviour and Research*, *19*(3), 303–323. https://doi.org/10.1108/13552551311330192

Sussan, F., & Acs, Z. J. (2017). The digital entrepreneurial ecosystem. *Small Business Economics*, *49*(1), 55–73. https://doi.org/10.1007/s11187-017-9867-5

Swant, M. (2020). *The 2020 world's most valuable brands*. Forbes. https://www.forbes.com/the-worlds-most-valuable-brands/#25d22340119c

Templier, M., & Paré, G. (2015). A framework for guiding and evaluating literature reviews. *Communications of the Association for Information Systems*, *37*, 112–137. https://doi.org/10.17705/1cais.03706

Thérin, F. (2007). *Handbook of Research on Techno-Entrepreneurship* (1st ed.). Cheltenham, UK and Northampton, MA, USA: Edward Elgar Publishing. https://doi.org/10.4337/9781847205551

Toufaily, E., Zalan, T., & Dhaou, S. Ben. (2021). A framework of blockchain technology adoption: An investigation of challenges and expected value. *Information and Management*, *58*(3), 103444. https://doi.org/10.1016/j.im.2021.103444

van der Aalst, W., Hinz, O., & Weinhardt, C. (2020). Impact of COVID-19 on BISE research and education. *Business and Information Systems Engineering*, *62*(6), 463–466. https://doi.org/10.1007/s12599-020-00666-9

van Gelderen, M., Wiklund, J., & McMullen, J. S. (2021). Entrepreneurship in the future: A delphi study of ETP and JBV editorial board members. *Entrepreneurship Theory and Practice*. https://doi.org/10.1177/10422587211010503

Veit, D., Clemons, E., Benlian, A., Buxmann, P., Hess, T., Kundisch, D., Leimeister, J. M., Loos, P., & Spann, M. (2014). Business models: An information systems research agenda. *Business and Information Systems Engineering*, *6*(1), 45–53. https://doi.org/10.1007/s12599-013-0308-y

von Briel, F., Davidsson, P., & Recker, J. (2018). Digital technologies as external enablers of new venture creation in the IT hardware sector. *Entrepreneurship Theory and Practice*, *42*(1), 47–69. https://doi.org/10.1177/1042258717732779

von Briel, F., Recker, J., Selander, L., Jarvenpaa, S. L., Hukal, P., Yoo, Y., Lehmann, J., Chan, Y., Rothe, H., Alpar, P., Fürstenau, D., & Wurm, B. (2021). Researching digital entrepreneurship: Current issues and suggestions for future directions. *Communications of the Association for Information Systems*, *48*(September 2020), 284–304. https://doi.org/10.17705/1CAIS.04833

von Kortzfleisch, H., Schaarschmidt, M., & Magin, P. (2010). Open scientific entrepreneurship: How the open source paradigm can foster entrepreneurial activities in scientific institutions.

*International Journal of Open Source Software and Processes*, *2*, 48–66. https://doi.org/10.4018/IJOSSP.2010100104

Weiber, R., & Kollmann, T. (1998). Competitive advantages in virtual markets – perspectives of "information-based marketing" in cyberspace. *European Journal of Marketing*, *32*(7/8), 603–615. https://doi.org/10.1108/03090569810224010

Zaheer, H., Breyer, Y., & Dumay, J. (2019). Digital entrepreneurship: An interdisciplinary structured literature review and research agenda. *Technological Forecasting and Social Change*, *148*. https://doi.org/10.1016/j.techfore.2019.119735

Zanella, G., Liu, C. Z., & Choo, K. K. R. (2021). Understanding the trends in blockchain domain through an unsupervised systematic patent analysis. *IEEE Transactions on Engineering Management*. https://doi.org/10.1109/TEM.2021.3074310

Zheng, L. J., Xiong, C., Chen, X., & Li, C. S. (2021). Product innovation in entrepreneurial firms: How business model design influences disruptive and adoptive innovation. *Technological Forecasting and Social Change*, *170*. https://doi.org/10.1016/j.techfore.2021.120894

Zook, M. (2008). *The Geography of the Internet Industry: Venture Capital, Dot-coms, and Local Knowledge* (1st edn.). John Wiley & Sons.

Zupic, I., & Čater, T. (2015). Bibliometric methods in management and organization. *Organizational Research Methods*, *18*(3), 429–472. https://doi.org/10.1177/1094428114562629

Zutshi, A., Zutshi, S., & Sohal, A. (2006). How e-entrepreneurs operate in the context of open source software. In F. Zhao (Ed.), *Entrepreneurship and Innovations in E-business: An Integrative Perspective* (pp. 62–88). IGI Global. https://doi.org/10.4018/978-1-59140-920-5.ch004

# 4. Exploring the field of digital entrepreneurship: a bibliometric analysis

*Eusebio Scornavacca, Tobias Kollmann, Stefano Za, Lucas Kleine-Stegemann and Christina Strauss*

## 1. INTRODUCTION

The digital revolution has transformed many aspects of society, such as social relationships, education, and work (Agarwal et al., 2010; Collins & Halverson, 2018; Majchrzak et al., 2016). It has also affected many aspects of business, such as value creation, innovation, company valuation, and internationalization (Bharadwaj et al., 2013; Vial, 2019; Weiber & Kollmann, 1998).

The pervasive advancement has also transformed many aspects of entrepreneurial activity (Elia et al., 2020; Nambisan, 2017). Some of these aspects are related to the entrepreneurial opportunities that could arise due to new technologies, digitalization of products and services, as well as business model innovation (Autio et al., 2018; Kollmann & Jung, Chapter 2 in this handbook; Nambisan et al., 2018). The overlay between the incentivization and acceleration of entrepreneurial activities—due to its potential contribution to economic development and social transformation (Malecki, 2018)—and the growing impact of the digital revolution, has resulted in the emergence of the research field of digital entrepreneurship.[1]

While some studies criticize the lack of research in the field of digital entrepreneurship (Nambisan, 2017; Steininger, 2019), articles in this area have increased significantly in recent years, underlining its ever-growing importance (e.g., Elia et al., 2020; Ghezzi & Cavallo, 2020; Orlandi et al., 2021). Nevertheless, while the term "digital entrepreneurship" is relatively new and has recently become a buzzword, the study of the underlying phenomena is not new. Following the technological advancements in digital technologies in the past couple of decades, the terminology used to describe "digital entrepreneurship" has evolved through time. Terms such as "online entrepreneurship," "e-entrepreneurship," and "techno-entrepreneurship" have been often used as synonyms to "digital entrepreneurship" in previous literature (Kollmann et al., Chapter 3 in this handbook; Zaheer, Breyer, & Dumay, 2019).

Since this set of historically evolved terms describe the same phenomena, they must be considered as a whole to describe the emergence of digital entrepreneurship as a field of research. Yet, most previous studies attempting to characterize this research field have failed to acknowledge this longitudinal evolution of terminology and have focused on "digital entrepreneurship" in isolation as a new emergent field. As a result, the goal of this study is to characterize the development of this research stream by exploring the evolution of the terminology used in the scholarly debate on digital entrepreneurship. In order to achieve this goal, this research develops a bibliometric analysis following Lamboglia et al. (2020).

This chapter is structured as follows: The next sections describe the research methodology and the literature search protocol. This is followed by a presentation of the results of the descriptive analysis and an exploration of the main topic emerging from the dataset. The last section presents a summary of the results, conclusions, limitations, and avenues for future research.

## 2.   METHOD

In this study, we analyzed the literature based on a bibliometric approach adapted from Lamboglia et al. (2020). Bibliometric analysis uses a quantitative approach to describe, evaluate, and monitor published research. It provides the potential for introducing a systematic, transparent, and reproducible review process to improve review quality. Bibliometric methods serve as a useful tool when conducting literature reviews, even prior to the start of reading, by directing researchers to highly influential pieces and mapping the field of research with minimal subjective bias (Zupic & Čater, 2015). Bibliometric methods have two major applications: performance analysis and science mapping (Cobo et al., 2011). While the first investigates the publication and research output of both individuals and institutions, the second focuses structures and dynamics within the field under study (Zupic & Čater, 2015).

We performed a co-word analysis to provide a complete picture of the current body of research and to discover key clusters (Za et al., 2020). Co-word analysis allows the discovery of the main concepts addressed by the field and represents a valuable technique to detect and describe the relationships between different areas of research (Cobo et al., 2011). It involves using the co-occurrence of a pair of concepts in a given number of articles. Thereby, the co-occurrence of two words in the same paper is an indicator of the relationship between these two (Cambrosio et al., 1993). Co-word analysis is unique as it uses the actual content of articles to build a measure of similarity, whereas other methods indirectly associate papers on the basis of citations or joint authorships (Zupic & Čater, 2015).

In bibliometric studies, the selection of literature is a crucial element in assuring validity and consistency. In order to choose the relevant body of literature and perform the analysis of the findings, we define the process with three steps (see Figure 4.1). First, we chose a database that included bibliometric elements and filtered out the main document set. Second, we refined

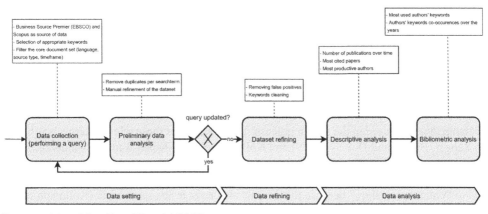

*Source:*   Adapted from Za and Braccini (2017).

*Figure 4.1*      *Research protocol*

the document set by revising the keywords and preparing it for further analysis. Third, the data was analyzed in the following two phases (Lamboglia et al., 2020):

A. Analyzing the descriptive performance indicators (descriptive analysis);
B. Analyzing the conceptual structure of the corpus of data, examining the major topics under discussion through a co-word analysis using SNA tools (bibliometric analysis).

The bibliometric analysis was performed using R and the bibliometrix package (Aria & Cuccurullo, 2017; Cuccurullo et al., 2016).

The selection of the sample involved an all-inclusive search through an extensive research query on two major databases: Business Source Premier (EBSCO) and Scopus (Figure 4.2). The selection of Scopus and EBSCO is based on the fact that the two databases have a far-reaching coverage of peer-reviewed journals (Meho & Yang, 2007). They offer a substantial and high-impact collection of data. In addition, they are often recognized as the most reliable database for research of this nature (Meho & Yang, 2007).

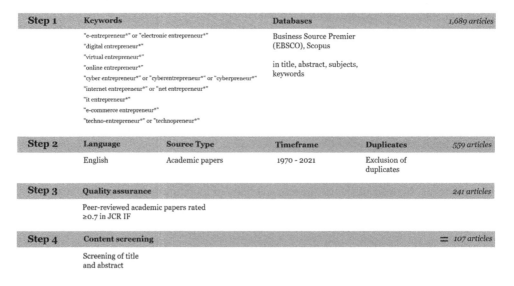

| Step 1 | Keywords | | Databases | | 1,689 articles |
|---|---|---|---|---|---|
| | "e-entrepreneur*" or "electronic entrepreneur*" | | Business Source Premier | | |
| | "digital entrepreneur*" | | (EBSCO), Scopus | | |
| | "virtual entrepreneur*" | | | | |
| | "online entrepreneur*" | | in title, abstract, subjects, | | |
| | "cyber entrepreneur*" or "cyberentrepreneur*" or "cyberpreneur*" | | keywords | | |
| | "internet entrepreneur*" or "net entrepreneur*" | | | | |
| | "it entrepreneur*" | | | | |
| | "e-commerce entrepreneur*" | | | | |
| | "techno-entrepreneur*" or "technopreneur*" | | | | |

| Step 2 | Language | Source Type | Timeframe | Duplicates | 559 articles |
|---|---|---|---|---|---|
| | English | Academic papers | 1970 - 2021 | Exclusion of duplicates | |

| Step 3 | Quality assurance | | | | 241 articles |
|---|---|---|---|---|---|
| | Peer-reviewed academic papers rated ≥0.7 in JCR IF | | | | |

| Step 4 | Content screening | | | | = 107 articles |
|---|---|---|---|---|---|
| | Screening of title and abstract | | | | |

*Figure 4.2    Systematic approach to article selection*

The process related to the selection of the research query is based on Lamboglia et al. (2020) and began with a literature review of the cornerstone papers related to digital entrepreneurship (Caputo et al., 2018). We have identified nine relevant terms in the field of digital entrepreneurship that were used in the search process. The selection of these relevant terms was based on Zaheer, Breyer and Dumay (2019) and Kollmann et al. (Chapter 3 in this handbook). The resulting terms used in the query are shown in the first step of Figure 4.2. Through the use of asterisks, we also included words containing not just "entrepreneur," but also "entrepreneurial" or "entrepreneurship," because these terms also refer to the same topic (Kollmann et al., Chapter 3 in this handbook). Both databases are searched individually with the selected terms previously indicated. We performed a full search of the selected terms in titles, abstracts, subjects, and keywords. This step generated a total of 1,689 papers.

The second step consisted of restricting the search considering articles published in English between 1970 and 2021 and excluding duplicates per term. The third step focused on quality assurance. Following Bouncken et al. (2015), only peer-reviewed articles rated higher than 0.7 in JCR impact factor passed through the next phase of analysis. This choice was motivated by the quality control of search results due to the peer review process. As a result, the sample was narrowed down to 241 articles.

In order to ensure that all out-of-topic papers were identified, we performed a manual refinement of the dataset by reading the title and abstract of the 241 papers. In this selection, we followed the two-level methodology proposed by Keupp et al. (2012) and Denyer and Neely (2004) to reduce subjective biases, encourage transparency, and improve the validity of the method. The authors carried out this analysis independently of each other by agreeing in advance on the inclusion and exclusion criteria (Tranfield et al., 2003). In particular, we excluded the papers focused solely on entrepreneurship or technology, without any reference to the link between them. This means that we only included articles that, on the one hand, did not focus exclusively on entrepreneurship topics, and used technological terms such as "online" in this context, and, on the other hand, were not purely technology papers that used the term "entrepreneur*." Instead, we explicitly made sure that the publications were dealing with startups from the digital economy. To maximize inter-rater reliability, two groups of authors independently flagged articles for exclusion based on these criteria. In case of divergence or doubt, the authors read the respective articles more closely and discussed them until an agreement was reached. At the end of this process, the sample was composed of 107 articles.

In order to proceed to the data analysis phase, the dataset had to be cleaned. This process consisted of homogenizing authors' keywords used in the articles (e.g., using only a plural or singular form). As a result, all the keywords that indicated the same topic were replaced with a unique word. The keyword analysis was performed separately by two separate groups of researchers within the research team and the results were then compared. In case of divergences or doubts, a discussion with the five members of the research team was used to reach an agreement (Za et al., 2018).

## 3.   DESCRIPTIVE ANALYSIS

The descriptive analysis is adapted from Lamboglia et al. (2020) and presented in three subsections: (1) the trend of the number of publications over time, (2) the most cited papers, and (3) the most productive authors.

### 3.1   Number of Publications Over Time

As shown in Figure 4.3, papers investigating the relationship between digital technologies and entrepreneurship first appeared in the research literature 25 years ago (the first paper was published in 1996). The publication trend had a small peak in 2006 following the popularization of e-commerce. From 2007 to 2014, the publication's trend appears rather irregular. However, starting in 2016, we identify a significant and sharp increase in the volume of publications reaching more than 30 papers in 2019 as a reflection of the overwhelming popularization of interest in the research community on the relevance of digitalization for entrepreneurship (Nambisan, 2017; Steininger, 2019).

PUBLICATIONS TREND

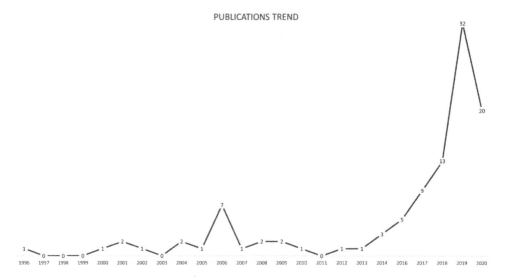

*Figure 4.3     Number of publications over time in full years 1996–2020*

## 3.2    Most Cited Papers

By analyzing the number of citations, one can achieve an accurate picture of the documents published in a specific discipline (Baier-Fuentes et al., 2019; Merigó & Yang, 2017). The number of citations shows the popularity and influence of the paper in the scientific community. Table 4.1 presents the most cited articles in the sample, receiving at least 50 citations. The most cited paper is Venkataraman (2004), which has 586 citations and used the term "technopreneurship." While analyzing the most cited articles in our dataset, it is possible to clearly identify groups of papers using different terms, such as "e-entrepreneurship" through time. The most cited papers for "e-entrepreneurship" were Matlay and Westhead (2005), Gruber and Henkel (2006), and Kollmann (2006). It is also interesting to observe the quick gain of popularity of recent papers on the term "digital entrepreneurship," such as Nambisan (2017) and Sussan and Acs (2017). Furthermore, it can be seen that the various terms were used at different times. While "digital entrepreneurship" was used in more recent publications, "e-entrepreneurship," "technopreneurship," or "internet entrepreneurship" were used much earlier, more precisely in the first decade of the 2000s.

## 3.3    Most Productive Authors

Table 4.2 shows the authors' production over the time in sole or co-authorship and the associate sum of citations for their articles for every term. In the analysis, we included the 19 authors with at least two publications in the dataset. In terms of the total number of articles, A. Ghezzi contributed with five papers, followed by A. Cavallo with three publications. Although these authors have published more articles, it is interesting to see that the authors with the highest accumulated impact are S. Nambisan, S. Venkataraman, and B. Batjargal.

*Table 4.1*    Most cited papers

| # | Article | Term | Total Citations |
|---|---------|------|-----------------|
| 1. | Venkataraman, S. (2004). Regional transformation through technological entrepreneurship. *Journal of Business venturing, 19*(1), 153–167. | Technopreneurship | 586 |
| 2. | Nambisan, S. (2017). Digital entrepreneurship: Toward a digital technology perspective of entrepreneurship. *Entrepreneurship Theory and Practice, 41*(6), 1029–1055. | Digital Entrepreneurship | 573 |
| 3. | Batjargal, B. (2007). Internet entrepreneurship: Social capital, human capital, and performance of Internet ventures in China. *Research Policy, 36*(5), 605–618. | Internet Entrepreneurship | 307 |
| 4. | Matlay, H., & Westhead, P. (2005). Virtual teams and the rise of e-entrepreneurship in Europe. *International Small Business Journal, 23*(3), 279–302. | E-Entrepreneurship | 249 |
| 5. | Gruber, M., & Henkel, J. (2006). New ventures based on open innovation—An empirical analysis of start-up firms in embedded Linux. *International Journal of Technology Management, 33*(4), 356–372. | E-Entrepreneurship | 230 |
| 6. | Sussan, F., & Acs, Z. J. (2017). The digital entrepreneurial ecosystem. *Small Business Economics, 49*(1), 55–73. | Digital Entrepreneurship | 226 |
| 7. | Kollmann, T. (2006). What is e-entrepreneurship? Fundamentals of company founding in the net economy. *International Journal of Technology Management, 33*(4), 322–340. | E-Entrepreneurship | 164 |
| 8. | Colombo, M. G., & Delmastro, M. (2001). Technology-based entrepreneurs: does Internet make a difference? *Small Business Economics, 16*(3), 177–190. | Internet Entrepreneurship | 157 |
| 9. | Li, L., Su, F., Zhang, W., & Mao, J. Y. (2018). Digital transformation by SME entrepreneurs: A capability perspective. *Information Systems Journal, 28*(6), 1129–1157. | Digital Entrepreneurship | 141 |
| 10. | Dy, A. M., Marlow, S., & Martin, L. (2017). A Web of opportunity or the same old story? Women digital entrepreneurs and intersectionality theory. *Human Relations, 70*(3), 286–311. | Digital Entrepreneurship & Online Entrepreneurship | 138 |
| 11. | Ghezzi, A., & Cavallo, A. (2020). Agile business model innovation in digital entrepreneurship: Lean startup approaches. *Journal of Business Research, 110*, 519–537. | Digital Entrepreneurship | 130 |
| 12. | Sebora, T. C., Lee, S. M., & Sukasame, N. (2009). Critical success factors for e-commerce entrepreneurship: an empirical study of Thailand. *Small Business Economics, 32*(3), 303–316. | E-Commerce Entrepreneurship | 124 |
| 13. | Richter, C., Kraus, S., Brem, A., Durst, S., & Giselbrecht, C. (2017). Digital entrepreneurship: Innovative business models for the sharing economy. *Creativity and Innovation Management, 26*(3), 300–310. | Digital Entrepreneurship | 116 |
| 14. | Carrier, C., Raymond, L., & Eltaief, A. (2004). Cyberentrepreneurship: A multiple case study. *International Journal of Entrepreneurial Behavior & Research, 10*(5), 349–363. | Cyber Entrepreneurship | 104 |
| 15. | Lakomaa, E., & Kallberg, J. (2013). Open data as a foundation for innovation: The enabling effect of free public sector information for entrepreneurs. *IEEE Access, 1*, 558–563. | IT-Entrepreneurship | 98 |

| # | Article | Term | Total Citations |
|---|---------|------|-----------------|
| 16. | Ojala, A. (2016). Business models and opportunity creation: How IT entrepreneurs create and develop business models under uncertainty. *Information Systems Journal, 26*(5), 451–476. | IT-Entrepreneurship | 96 |
| 17. | Batjargal, B. (2010). Network dynamics and new ventures in China: A longitudinal study. *Entrepreneurship and Regional Development, 22*(2), 139–153. | Internet Entrepreneurship | 79 |
| 18. | Srinivasan, A., & Venkatraman, N. (2018). Entrepreneurship in digital platforms: A network-centric view. *Strategic Entrepreneurship Journal, 12*(1), 54–71. | Digital Entrepreneurship | 66 |
| 19. | Kickul, J., & Walters, J. (2002). Recognizing new opportunities and innovations. *International Journal of Entrepreneurial Behavior & Research, 8*(6), 292–308. | Internet Entrepreneurship | 57 |
| 20. | Steininger, D. M. (2019). Linking information systems and entrepreneurship: A review and agenda for IT-associated and digital entrepreneurship research. *Information Systems Journal, 29*(2), 363–407. | Digital Entrepreneurship | 53 |

*Table 4.2    Most productive authors*

| Author | No. of publications | Total citations | Most cited digital entrepreneurship publication |
|---|---|---|---|
| Ghezzi, Antonio (Politecnico di Milano, Italy) | 5 | 226 | Ghezzi, A., & Cavallo, A. (2020). Agile business model innovation in digital entrepreneurship: Lean startup approaches. *Journal of Business Research, 110*, 519–537. |
| Cavallo, Angelo (Politecnico di Milano, Italy) | 3 | 179 | Ghezzi, A., & Cavallo, A. (2020). Agile business model innovation in digital entrepreneurship: Lean startup approaches. *Journal of Business Research, 110*, 519–537. |
| Batjargal, Bat (Oklahoma State University, USA) | 2 | 386 | Batjargal, B. (2007). Internet entrepreneurship: Social capital, human capital, and performance of Internet ventures in China. *Research Policy, 36*(5), 605–618. |
| Sebora, Terrence C. (University of Nebraska – Lincoln, USA) | 2 | 134 | Sebora, T.C., Lee, A.M., & Sukasame, N. (2009). Critical success factors for e-commerce entrepreneurship: An empirical study of Thailand. *Small Business Economics, 32*(3), 303–316. |
| McAdam, Maura (Dublin City University – DCU Business School, Ireland) | 2 | 26 | McAdam, M., Crowley, C., & Harrison, R.T. (2019). "To boldly go where no [man] has gone before" – Institutional voids and the development of women's digital entrepreneurship. *Technological Forecasting and Social Change, 146*, 912–922. |
| Brem, Alexander (Universität Stuttgart, Germany) | 2 | 121 | Richter, C., Kraus, S., Brem, A., Durst, S., & Giselbrecht, C. (2017). Digital entrepreneurship: Innovative business models for the sharing economy. *Creativity and Innovation Management, 26*(3), 300–310. |
| Wang, Yi-Shun (National Changhua University of Education, Taiwan) | 2 | 22 | Wang, Y.-S., Lin, S.-J., Yeh, C.-H., Li, C.-R., & Li, H.-T. (2016). What drives students' cyber entrepreneurial intention: The moderating role of disciplinary difference. *Thinking Skills and Creativity, 22*, 22–35. |
| Breyer, Yvonne Alexandra (Macquarie University, Australia) | 2 | 49 | Zaheer, H., Breyer, Y.A., Dumay, J.C., & Enjeti, M. (2019). Straight from the horse's mouth: Founders' perspectives on achieving 'traction' in digital start-ups. *Computers in Human Behavior, 95*, 262–274. |
| Harrison, Richard T. (University of Edinburgh Business School, United Kingdom) | 2 | 26 | McAdam, M., Crowley, C., & Harrison, R.T. (2019). "To boldly go where no [man] has gone before" – Institutional voids and the development of women's digital entrepreneurship. *Technological Forecasting and Social Change, 146*, 912–922. |
| Mourmant, Gaëtan (IÉSEG School of Management, France) | 2 | 54 | Mourmant, G., Gallivan, M.J., & Kalika, M. (2009). Another road to IT turnover: The entrepreneurial path. *European Journal of Information Systems, 18*(5), 498–521. |
| Bican, Peter M. (Friedrich-Alexander Universität Erlangen-Nürnberg, Germany) | 2 | 5 | Bican, P.M., & Brem, A. (2020). Digital business model, digital transformation, digital entrepreneurship: Is there a sustainable "digital"? *Sustainability (Switzerland), 12*(13). |

| Author | No. of publications | Total citations | Most cited digital entrepreneurship publication |
|---|---|---|---|
| Nambisan, Satish (Weatherhead School of Management, Case Western Reserve University, USA) | 2 | 590 | Nambisan, S. (2017). Digital entrepreneurship: Toward a digital technology perspective of entrepreneurship. *Entrepreneurship Theory and Practice, 41*(6), 1029–1055. |
| Salimath, Manjula S. (G. Brint Ryan College of Business, University of North Texas, USA) | 2 | 38 | Chandna, V., & Salimath, M.S. (2018). Peer-to-peer selling in online platforms: A salient business model for virtual entrepreneurship. *Journal of Business Research, 84*, 162–174. |
| Chandna, Vallari (School of Business, University of Wisconsin – Green Bay, USA) | 2 | 38 | Chandna, V., & Salimath, M.S. (2018). Peer-to-peer selling in online platforms: A salient business model for virtual entrepreneurship. *Journal of Business Research, 84*, 162–174. |
| Sukasame, Nittana (Bangkok University, Thailand) | 2 | 134 | Sebora, T.C., Lee, S.M., & Sukasame, N. (2009). Critical success factors for e-commerce entrepreneurship: An empirical study of Thailand. *Small Business Economics, 32*(3), 303–316. |
| Crowley, Caren (Maastricht School of Management, Netherlands) | 2 | 26 | McAdam, M., Crowley, C., & Harrison, R.T. (2019). "To boldly go where no [man] has gone before" – Institutional voids and the development of women's digital entrepreneurship. *Technological Forecasting and Social Change, 146*, 912–922. |
| Zaheer, Hasnain (Macquarie University, Australia) | 2 | 49 | Zaheer, H., Breyer, Y.A., Dumay, J.C., & Enjeti, M. (2019). Straight from the horse's mouth: Founders' perspectives on achieving 'traction' in digital start-ups. *Computers in Human Behavior, 95*, 262–274. |
| Dumay, John C. (Macquarie University, Australia) | 2 | 49 | Zaheer, H., Breyer, Y.A., Dumay, J.C., & Enjeti, M. (2019). Straight from the horse's mouth: Founders' perspectives on achieving 'traction' in digital start-ups. *Computers in Human Behavior, 95*, 262–274. |
| Kraus, Sascha (Free University of Bozen-Bolzano, Italy) | 2 | 134 | Richter, C., Kraus, S., Brem, A., Durst, S., & Giselbrecht, C. (2017). Digital entrepreneurship: Innovative business models for the sharing economy. *Creativity and Innovation Management, 26*(3), 300–310. |

## 4.    BIBLIOMETRIC ANALYSIS

In order to explore the most relevant topic discussed in our dataset, we analyzed the most recurring keywords used by authors. The analysis of the keywords provides some insights regarding the content and the main issues in the field of digital entrepreneurship discussed in the 107 papers of our dataset.

In our chapter the topic analysis is articulated in the two parts:

1. The trend of the top 21 (every keyword with more than 5 occurrences) most used keywords;
2. Authors keywords co-occurrences across the years.

## 4.1    Most Used Authors' Keywords

The keyword analysis started with the distribution over the years of the 21 most used keywords defined by the authors (with at least six occurrences) (Figure 4.4). "Digital entrepreneurship" is the most frequent keyword with 45 occurrences, followed by "entrepreneurship" with 28 occurrences and "information technology" with 14 occurrences.

It is interesting to observe the longitudinal distribution of different keywords used to describe "digital entrepreneurship" following the technological advancements of digital technologies. For example, "digital entrepreneurship" gained popularity in the past six years along with keywords, such as "start-up" and "digital innovation and transformation." Similarly, "e-entrepreneurship" appears in the early 2000s alongside keywords, such as "internet" and "e-commerce." Finally, "techno-entrepreneurship" appears in the late 1990s to early 2000s before the popularization of e-commerce. It can be seen that the terms "technopreneurship" and "e-entrepreneurship" appeared even before the term "digital entrepreneurship" and therefore laid the foundation for later work. The distribution of keywords also suggests that the terms "technopreneurship," which later disappeared altogether, and "e-entrepreneurship" were replaced subsequently by "digital entrepreneurship." This can also be concluded from the strong dominance of this term in recent years and is in line with the findings of other studies dealing with the history/eras of the digital entrepreneurship terminology (Kollmann et al., Chapter 3 in this handbook).

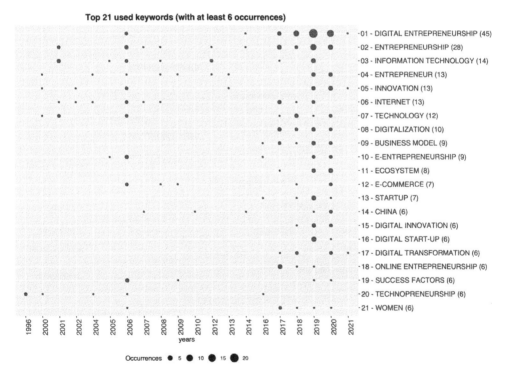

*Figure 4.4      The main 21 keywords used in the dataset over the years*

## 4.2      Authors' Keywords Co-Occurrences over the Years

The analysis of the connections among the main topics discussed in our dataset can provide further insights about the "digital entrepreneurship" discourse. Starting from the 36 most recurring authors' keywords (with at least three occurrences), the co-occurrences network was created (Figure 4.5). In the graph, the keywords are the nodes (the size represents the median of citations for each keyword), and there is a tie among two of them if mentioned together in the same publication (co-occurrence); the thickness reflects the number of contributions in which the pair appears. The darkness of the grey-tones represents the temporal indication of the most occurrences (dark if the median of total mentions ran towards 2004 and light if it ran towards 2020). Finally, some of the most recurring keywords are not mentioned since the isolated nodes (without any connections with the nodes in the same graph) are deleted.

On the basis of their connections, it is possible to recognize the temporal evolution of the terminology used in this area of study. Our results provide evidence for the more recent use of "digital entrepreneurship" and the keywords like "start-up," "digital innovation," and "platforms.". Similarly, "e-entrepreneurship" and "techno entrepreneurship" appear in the early to mid-2000s alongside keywords like "internet," "information technology," and "e-commerce." Furthermore, it can be seen that not only terms of the same time appear together, but also older terms are mentioned with newer ones, suggesting that older terms were picked up by studies that used newer terms. For example, terms like "e-commerce" or "e-entrepreneurship" show that there is a connection between them and popular ones today, such as "digital entrepreneurship" or "digitalization."

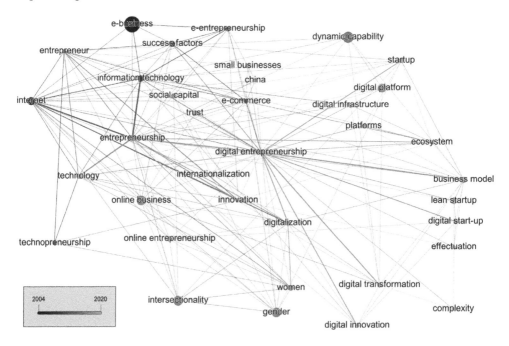

*Figure 4.5      Co-occurrences of keywords used in different times*

## 5. CONCLUSION

In this chapter, we examined existing literature in the field of digital entrepreneurship by conducting a literature analysis of 107 articles. This analysis consisted of two parts: First, we conducted a descriptive analysis; second, we used a bibliometric analysis to identify the main topics in our dataset.

The results show that interest in the field of digital entrepreneurship has been growing in the last years. This can be supported by the fact that the number of publications has continuously been increasing over time. Still, it is important to notice the longitudinal evolution of the terminology surrounding the "digital entrepreneurship" phenomena and the relevance of work developed using terms, such as "technopreneurship" or "e-entrepreneurship." In this vein, we demonstrate that there were already highly influential publications on the topic of digital entrepreneurship several years ago that laid the foundations for the current state of research (e.g., Batjargal, 2007, Venkataraman, 2004).

To get deeper insights into the topic of digital entrepreneurship, we analyzed the most used authors' keywords in the dataset. In this context, we find out that the 21 most occurring keywords appear with different frequencies over time. While terms such as "technopreneurship" or "e-entrepreneurship" were popular some time ago, "digital entrepreneurship" is mostly used in recent years. The use of different terms across time comes with the challenge that some authors may fail to acknowledge the contribution of earlier works and limit their literature review to the use of current terminology (e.g., "digital entrepreneurship"). Our work aims to assist current digital entrepreneurship researchers to not overlook the contributions that have been published under other terms.

This study has both theoretical and practical implications. From a theoretical perspective, we contribute to the research field of digital entrepreneurship (e.g., Elia et al., 2020; Kollmann et al., Chapter 3 in this handbook; Nambisan, 2017; Sussan & Acs, 2017) by giving descriptive insights about the current literature and how the terms used by the different studies are connected to each other over time. In more detail, we identify a body of literature that has been published long before the term "digital entrepreneurship" received much attention. In addition, we offer guidance for future research that seeks to shed further light on this topic in several ways. First, by listing the most cited articles in this research area, we create a starting point from which further analysis can be conducted. Second, by demonstrating the time course of authors' keywords and their associations, we give researchers the opportunity to increase their visibility by using the right keywords for their own work.

From a practical perspective, our research provides an overview of the current digital entrepreneurship field. With this overview, founders and members of startups can better navigate the most important publications, the most cited authors, and the most relevant terminology in relation to digital entrepreneurship.

There are also limitations to be noted. We only analyzed papers published in scientific journals available on EBSCO or Scopus which were ranked with a JCR IF. Although this ensures a high quality of the publications studied (Bouncken et al., 2015; Kraus et al., 2018), it might be useful for further research to consider other sources such as handbooks or conference proceedings, as many publications in this field are published there. This could, for example, provide insights into whether a broader dataset can confirm our findings. Furthermore, we only examined co-occurrences of authors' keywords. Although this allows conclusions to be drawn about the extent to which terms occurred together, no influences of the terms on each other can be detected. Therefore, our study could be extended to include a cross-citation analysis (i.e., which sources cite each other) to better identify influences of topics and authors on each other.

## NOTE

1.  Within our study, we differentiate between the overall field of research on digital entrepreneurship (i.e., "the field of research on digital entrepreneurship") and the term of digital entrepreneurship itself (i.e., "digital entrepreneurship").

## REFERENCES

Agarwal, R., Gao, G., DesRoches, C., & Jha, A. K. (2010). Research commentary—The digital transformation of healthcare: Current status and the road ahead. *Information Systems Research*, *21*(4), 796–809. https://doi.org/10.1287/isre.1100.0327

Aria, M., & Cuccurullo, C. (2017). Bibliometrix: An R-tool for comprehensive science mapping analysis. *Journal of Informetrics*, *11*(4), 959–975. https://doi.org/10.1016/j.joi.2017.08.007

Autio, E., Nambisan, S., Thomas, L. D. W. W., & Wright, M. (2018). Digital affordances, spatial affordances, and the genesis of entrepreneurial ecosystems. *Strategic Entrepreneurship Journal*, *12*(1), 72–95. https://doi.org/10.1002/sej.1266

Baier-Fuentes, H., Merigó, J. M., Amorós, J. E., & Gaviria-Marín, M. (2019). International entrepreneurship: A bibliometric overview. *International Entrepreneurship and Management Journal*, *15*(2), 385–429. https://doi.org/10.1007/s11365-017-0487-y

Batjargal, B. (2007). Internet entrepreneurship: Social capital, human capital, and performance of Internet ventures in China. *Research Policy*, *36*(5), 605–618. https://doi.org/10.1016/j.respol.2006.09.029

Batjargal, B. (2010). Network dynamics and new ventures in China: A longitudinal study. *Entrepreneurship and Regional Development*, *22*(2), 139–153. https://doi.org/10.1080/08985620802628864

Bharadwaj, A., El Sawy, O. A., Pavlou, P. A., & Venkatraman, N. (2013). Digital business strategy: Toward a next generation of insights. *MIS Quarterly*, 471–482.

Bican, P. M., & Brem, A. (2020). Digital Business Model, Digital Transformation, Digital Entrepreneurship: Is there a sustainable "digital"? *Sustainability (Switzerland)*, *12*(13), 1–15. https://doi.org/10.3390/su12135239

Bouncken, R. B., Gast, J., Kraus, S., & Bogers, M. (2015). Coopetition: A systematic review, synthesis, and future research directions. *Review of Managerial Science*, *9*(3), 577–601. https://doi.org/10.1007/s11846-015-0168-6

Cambrosio, A., Limoges, C., Courtial, J., & Laville, F. (1993). Historical scientometrics? Mapping over 70 years of biological safety research with coword analysis. *Scientometrics*, *27*(2), 119–143. https://doi.org/10.1007/BF02016546

Caputo, A., Marzi, G., Pellegrini, M., & Rialti, R. (2018). Conflict management in family businesses: A bibliometric analysis and systematic literature review. *International Journal of Conflict Management*, *29*(4), 519–542. https://doi.org/10.1108/IJCMA-02-2018-0027

Carrier, C., Raymond, L., & Eltaief, A. (2004). Cyberentrepreneurship: A multiple case study. *International Journal of Entrepreneurial Behaviour & Research*, *10*(5), 349–363. https://doi.org/10.1108/13552550410554320

Chandna, V., & Salimath, M. S. (2018). Peer-to-peer selling in online platforms: A salient business model for virtual entrepreneurship. *Journal of Business Research*, *84*(November 2017), 162–174. https://doi.org/10.1016/j.jbusres.2017.11.019

Cobo, M. J., López-Herrera, A. G., Herrera-Viedma, E., & Herrera, F. (2011). Science mapping software tools: Review, analysis, and cooperative study among tools. *Journal of the American Society for Information Science and Technology*, *62*(7), 1382–1402. https://doi.org/10.1002/asi.21525

Collins, A., & Halverson, R. (2018). *Rethinking education in the age of technology: The digital revolution and schooling in America.* Teachers College Press.

Colombo, M. G., & Delmastro, M. (2001). Technology-based entrepreneurs: Does internet make a difference? *Small Business Economics, 16*(3), 177–190. https://doi.org/10.1023/A:1011127205758

Cuccurullo, C., Aria, M., & Sarto, F. (2016). Foundations and trends in performance management: A twenty-five years bibliometric analysis in business and public administration domains. *Scientometrics, 108*(2), 595–611. https://doi.org/10.1007/s11192-016-1948-8

Denyer, D., & Neely, A. (2004). Introduction to special issue: Innovation and productivity performance in the UK. *International Journal of Management Reviews, 5–6*(3–4), 131–135. https://doi.org/10.1111/j.1460-8545.2004.00100.x

Dy, A. M., Marlow, S., & Martin, L. (2017). A Web of opportunity or the same old story? Women digital entrepreneurs and intersectionality theory. *Human Relations, 70*(3), 286–311. https://doi.org/10.1177/0018726716650730

Elia, G., Margherita, A., & Passiante, G. (2020). Digital entrepreneurship ecosystem: How digital technologies and collective intelligence are reshaping the entrepreneurial process. *Technological Forecasting and Social Change, 150*, Article 119791. https://doi.org/10.1016/j.techfore.2019.119791

Ghezzi, A., & Cavallo, A. (2020). Agile business model innovation in digital entrepreneurship: Lean startup approaches. *Journal of Business Research, 110*, 519–537. https://doi.org/10.1016/j.jbusres.2018.06.013

Gruber, M., & Henkel, J. (2006). New ventures based on open innovation—An empirical analysis of start-up firms in embedded Linux. *International Journal of Technology Management, 33*(4), 356–372. https://doi.org/10.1504/IJTM.2006.009249

Keupp, M. M., Palmié, M., & Gassmann, O. (2012). The strategic management of innovation: A systematic review and paths for future research. *International Journal of Management Reviews, 14*(4), 367–390. https://doi.org/10.1111/j.1468-2370.2011.00321.x

Kickul, J., & Walters, J. (2002). Recognizing new opportunities and innovations: The role of strategic orientation and proactivity in Internet firms. *International Journal of Entrepreneurial Behaviour & Research, 8*(6), 292–308. https://doi.org/10.1108/13552550210448375

Kollmann, T. (2006). What is e-entrepreneurship?—Fundamentals of company founding in the net economy. *International Journal of Technology Management, 33*(4), 322–340. https://doi.org/10.1504/IJTM.2006.009247

Kraus, S., Palmer, C., Kailer, N., Kallinger, F. L., & Spitzer, J. (2018). Digital entrepreneurship: A research agenda on new business models for the twenty-first century. *International Journal of Entrepreneurial Behaviour and Research, 25*(2), 353–375. https://doi.org/10.1108/IJEBR-06-2018-0425

Lakomaa, E., & Kallberg, J. (2013). Open data as a foundation for innovation: The enabling effect of free public sector information for entrepreneurs. *IEEE Access, 1*, 558–563. https://doi.org/10.1109/ACCESS.2013.2279164

Lamboglia, R., Lavorato, D., Scornavacca, E., & Za, S. (2020). Exploring the relationship between audit and technology. A bibliometric analysis. *Meditari Accountancy Research.* https://doi.org/10.1108/MEDAR-03-2020-0836

Li, L., Su, F., Zhang, W., & Mao, J. Y. (2018). Digital transformation by SME entrepreneurs: A capability perspective. *Information Systems Journal, 28*(6), 1129–1157. https://doi.org/10.1111/isj.12153

Majchrzak, A., Markus, M. L., & Wareham, J. (2016). Designing for digital transformation: Lessons for information systems research from the study of ICT and societal challenges. *MIS Quarterly, 40*(2), 267–277.

Malecki, E. J. (2018). Entrepreneurship and entrepreneurial ecosystems. *Geography Compass, 12*(3), Article e12359. https://doi.org/10.1111/gec3.12359

Matlay, H., & Westhead, P. (2005). Virtual teams and the rise of e-entrepreneurship in Europe. *International Small Business Journal, 23*(3), 279–302. https://doi.org/10.1177/0266242605052074

McAdam, M., Crowley, C., & Harrison, R. T. (2019). "To boldly go where no [man] has gone before" – Institutional voids and the development of women's digital entrepreneurship. *Technological Forecasting and Social Change, 146*(December 2017), 912–922. https://doi.org/10.1016/j.techfore.2018.07.051

Meho, L. I., & Yang, K. (2007). Impact of data sources on citation counts and rankings of LIS faculty: Web of Science versus Scopus and Google Scholar. *Journal of the American Society for Information Science and Technology, 58*(13), 2105–2125. https://doi.org/10.1002/asi.20677

Merigó, J. M., & Yang, J.-B. (2017). A bibliometric analysis of operations research and management science. *Omega, 73*, 37–48. https://doi.org/10.1016/j.omega.2016.12.004

Mourmant, G., Gallivan, M. J., & Kalika, M. (2009). Another road to IT turnover: The entrepreneurial path. *European Journal of Information Systems, 18*(5), 498–521. https://doi.org/10.1057/ejis.2009.37

Nambisan, S. (2017). Digital entrepreneurship: Toward a digital technology perspective of entrepreneurship. *Entrepreneurship: Theory and Practice, 41*(6), 1029–1055. https://doi.org/10.1111/etap.12254

Nambisan, S., Siegel, D., & Kenney, M. (2018). On open innovation, platforms, and entrepreneurship. *Strategic Entrepreneurship Journal, 12*(3), 354–368. https://doi.org/10.1002/sej.1300

Ojala, A. (2016). Business models and opportunity creation: How IT entrepreneurs create and develop business models under uncertainty. *Information Systems Journal, 26*(5), 451–476. https://doi.org/10.1111/isj.12078

Orlandi, L. B., Zardini, A., & Rossignoli, C. (2021). Highway to hell: Cultural propensity and digital infrastructure gap as recipe to entrepreneurial death. *Journal of Business Research, 123*, 188–195. https://doi.org/10.1016/j.jbusres.2020.09.047

Richter, C., Kraus, S., Brem, A., Durst, S., & Giselbrecht, C. (2017). Digital entrepreneurship: Innovative business models for the sharing economy. *Creativity and Innovation Management, 26*(3), 300–310. https://doi.org/10.1111/caim.12227

Sebora, T. C., Lee, S. M., & Sukasame, N. (2009). Critical success factors for e-commerce entrepreneurship: An empirical study of Thailand. *Small Business Economics, 32*(3), 303–316. https://doi.org/10.1007/s11187-007-9091-9

Srinivasan, A., & Venkatraman, N. (2018). Entrepreneurship in digital platforms: A network-centric view. *Strategic Entrepreneurship Journal, 12*(1), 54–71. https://doi.org/10.1002/sej.1272

Steininger, D. M. (2019). Linking information systems and entrepreneurship: A review and agenda for IT-associated and digital entrepreneurship research. *Information Systems Journal, 29*(2), 363–407. https://doi.org/10.1111/isj.12206

Sussan, F., & Acs, Z. J. (2017). The digital entrepreneurial ecosystem. *Small Business Economics, 49*(1), 55–73. https://doi.org/10.1007/s11187-017-9867-5

Tranfield, D., Denyer, D., & Smart, P. (2003). Towards a methodology for developing evidence-informed management knowledge by means of systematic review. *British Journal of Management, 14*(3), 207–222. https://doi.org/10.1111/1467-8551.00375

Venkataraman, S. (2004). Regional transformation through technological entrepreneurship. *Journal of Business Venturing, 19*(1), 153–167. https://doi.org/10.1016/j.jbusvent.2003.04.001

Vial, G. (2019). Understanding digital transformation: A review and a research agenda. *The Journal of Strategic Information Systems, 28*(2), 118–144. https://doi.org/10.1016/j.jsis.2019.01.003

Wang, Y. S., Lin, S. J., Yeh, C. H., Li, C. R., & Li, H. T. (2016). What drives students' cyber entrepreneurial intention: The moderating role of disciplinary difference. *Thinking Skills and Creativity, 22*, 22–35. https://doi.org/10.1016/j.tsc.2016.08.003

Weiber, R., & Kollmann, T. (1998). Competitive advantages in virtual markets – perspectives of "information-based marketing" in cyberspace. *European Journal of Marketing, 32*(7/8), 603–615. https://doi.org/10.1108/03090569810224010

Za, S., & Braccini, A. M. (2017). Tracing the roots of the organizational benefits of IT services. *IESS*, 3–11. https://doi.org/10.1007/978-3-319-56925-3_1

Za, S., Pallud, J., Agrifoglio, R., & Metallo, C. (2020). Value co-creation in online communities: A preliminary literature analysis. In A. Lazazzara, F. Ricciardi, & S. Za (Eds.), *Exploring Digital Ecosystems* (pp. 33–46). Springer. https://doi.org/10.1007/978-3-030-23665-6_4

Za, S., Spagnoletti, P., Winter, R., & Mettler, T. (2018). Exploring foundations for using simulations in IS research. *Communications of the Association for Information Systems, 42*(1), 10. https://doi.org/10.17705/1CAIS.04210

Zaheer, H., Breyer, Y., & Dumay, J. (2019). Digital entrepreneurship: An interdisciplinary structured literature review and research agenda. *Technological Forecasting and Social Change, 148*, Article 119735. https://doi.org/10.1016/j.techfore.2019.119735

Zaheer, H., Breyer, Y., Dumay, J., & Enjeti, M. (2019). Straight from the horse's mouth: Founders' perspectives on achieving 'traction' in digital start-ups. *Computers in Human Behavior*, *95*, 262–274. https://doi.org/10.1016/j.chb.2018.03.002

Zupic, I., & Čater, T. (2015). Bibliometric methods in management and organization. *Organizational Research Methods*, *18*(3), 429–472. https://doi.org/10.1177/1094428114562629

# PART III

# DIGITAL ENTREPRENEURSHIP ECOSYSTEMS

# 5.   Measuring the digital platform economy

## Zoltan J. Acs, László Szerb, Abraham K. Song, Esteban Lafuente and Éva Komlósi

## INTRODUCTION

In one of the most interesting articles on the Information-Technology Revolution (ITR), Hobijn and Jovanovic (2001) argued that the arrival of the ITR in the 1970s created the need for new firms to emerge.[1] Technology breakthroughs favor new firm formation for three reasons: awareness and skills; vintage capital; and vested interests. The stock market incumbents of the day were not ready to implement the new digital technologies and it took new firms to bring the technology to market after the mid-1980s. Stock prices of incumbents fell immediately. New capital flowed via venture capital to startups in the United States that built the new industries but not in Europe (Gompers and Lerner, 2001). Between 1980 and 2020 the US stock market raised thirty fold. The five most valuable public companies in the United States in 2020 – that is, Apple, Amazon, Microsoft, Facebook and Google – are valued at or near $1 trillion each.[2] Many of them are *Matchmaker* businesses whose core competency is the ability to match one group of users with another by reducing transaction costs.

The ITR is about digital technology and the representation of information in bits (Shannon, 1948). Information in bits reduces the cost of storage, computation and transmission of data. *Digital economics* examines whether and how digital technology changes economic activity (Goldfarb and Tucker, 2019). Digital technologies reduce five types of distinct costs that affect economic activities; search, replication, transportation, tracking and verification. The reduction of search costs leads to more matching and peer to peer platforms that increase the efficiency of trade. Most of the major technology firms can be seen as platform-based businesses. There are two main reasons why digital markets give rise to platforms (Jullien, 2012). First, platforms facilitate matching because they provide a structure that can take advantage of low search costs to create efficient matches. Second, platforms increase the efficiency of trade. They do this through lower search costs, lower reproduction costs and lower verification costs (Goldfarb and Tucker, 2019, p. 13). While the literature on digital economics has examined how digital technology changes economic activity, less has been written about how it affects the platform economy.

Entrepreneurship ecosystem (EE) is another line of evolving research examining the entrepreneurship components not in isolation but from the viewpoint of mutually interconnected factors (Isenberg, 2011; Acs et al., 2017; Cavallo, Ghezzi, and Balocco, 2018). The creation of new, high value added startups, as a sign of properly functioning ecosystem, is a central tenet of EE exploration (Stam, 2015; Szerb et al., 2019). With the emergence of digital technologies, the focus of research has shifted to a combined approach of entrepreneurship and digital ecosystems (Sussan and Acs 2017, Autio et al., 2018a; Elia, Margherita, and Passiante, 2020). Parallel to the conceptual developments, the dominant type of new ventures emerging out of the digital ecosystem has also changed. While e-entrepreneurship in the late 1990s and early 2000s was typically a business using some digital components or the internet, later the fully digital and internet-based startups, nowadays platform businesses become dominant (Kollmann 2006, Song 2019).

The purpose of this chapter is to create a framework to better understand the platform economy, multi-sided platforms and the platform-based ecosystems and to provide an appropriate country-level measure of it. The term 'Digital Platform Economy' was coined by Kenney and Zysman (2016, p.62) as, "…a more neutral term that encompasses a growing number of digitally enabled activities in business, politics, and social interaction.[3] If the industrial revolution was organized around the factory, today's changes are organized around these digital platforms, loosely defined." The advancements in information and communication technologies (ICT) opened a pathway for these businesses. More specifically, platforms are enabled by technological openness (architectural interface specification) and organizational openness (governance) both of which are mediated by the platform owner. This rise of digital *multi-sided platforms* as avenues for value creation, appropriation, and innovation is commonly known as *platformization*.

While Kenny and Zysman (2016) focused on the nature of work, this study focuses on the changing structure of the economy. In the platform economy costs are reduced not by management but via digital platforms – technology. Therefore, one of the hallmarks of the platform economy is the creation of markets where they did not exist through increased matching and the spread of platform-based businesses (Cusumano, Gawer and Yoffie, 2019). A question that has received less attention is how the ITR has affected the organization of the firm. In other words, "How do lower search costs affect firm organization?" The reduction in search costs and verification costs has also led to a new form of organization – *the platform-based ecosystem*.

This chapter makes two contributions to the literature. First, we provide a concept-based measure of the Digital Platform Economy consisting of twelve pillars and four quadrants: Digital Multi-sided Platforms, Digital User Citizenship, Digital Technology Entrepreneurship and Digital Technology Infrastructure. These four quadrants include the key economic, business, social and policy issues: competition, privacy, innovation and security, respectively (Sussan and Acs, 2017, Song, 2019). Building on the National Systems of Entrepreneurship methodology (Acs, Autio and Szerb, 2014) we calculate the DPE index for 116 countries. A major advantage of our index is that it allows us to make international comparisons about digital efficiency across countries and over time.

Second, we examine the European Union's platform economy dilemma using the new measure of the DPE index. The EU platformization lag stems from the fact that incumbent firms in Europe have not introduced new technologies in sufficient volume and startups have remained small and not scalable (Kollmann et al., 2016; Naudé, 2016).

## THE CONCEPT OF PLATFORM-BASED ECOSYSTEM: THE DIGITAL PLATFORM ECONOMY

One of the main institutional differences, if not the most significant, between the managed economy and the platform economy is the role of the *platform-based ecosystem*. While a large literature has now developed on entrepreneurial ecosystems this literature can be misleading in some ways. Entrepreneurial ecosystems appear to be a regional or local phenomenon as many have argued (Stam, 2015).[4] However, when one compares entrepreneurial ecosystems with *platform-based ecosystems* and includes the role of digital technology the *platform-based ecosystem* is immediately global in nature with billions of users and millions of agents (Sussan and Acs, 2017). The *platform-based ecosystems* are developed and nurtured not by regions or governments but by platform organizations. Ecosystem governance, the rules for who gets on a platform and what the rules of good behavior, are determined by the owners of the platform firms.

Among the first to recognize this shortcoming in the ecosystem literature was Sussan and Acs (2017). They observed that *a significant gap exists in the conceptualization of entrepreneurship in the digital age precisely because it ignored the fundamental role of knowledge as a resource in the economy*. To address this gap Sussan and Acs proposed a novel framework for the *platform-based ecosystem* also known as the Digital Entrepreneurial Ecosystem (DEE) integrating two separate but related literatures on ecosystems, namely, the digital ecosystem and the entrepreneurial ecosystem literature. This new framework situates the platform-based ecosystem in the broader context of users, agents, infrastructure and institutions, such that two biotic entities (users and agents) actuate individual agency, whereas two abiotic components (digital technology and digital institutions) form the external environment. Song (2019) further refined the DEE framework and expanded it to multi-sided platforms.

The DPE framework consists of four concepts: (1) Digital User Citizenship (DUC) includes users on the demand-side and the supply-side; (2) Digital Technology Entrepreneurship (DTE) includes app developers and various agents that contribute to entrepreneurial innovation, experimentation and value creation on platforms; (3) Digital Multi-sided Platforms (DMP) that orchestrate social and economic activities between users and agents; and (4) Digital Technology Infrastructure (DTI) pertains to all regulations that govern technical, social and economic activities of the digital technology.

First, users' privacy protection is critical for a healthy and active *Digital User Citizenship*. If public trust becomes eroded, the sustainability of the DEE suffers. Erosion of trust in platforms can lead to a decline in user activities or membership. For example, Facebook's scandal involving Cambridge Analytica exposed millions of users and served as a watershed moment that prompted more government regulation of the internet to protect consumer privacy. Since then, Facebook has experienced a steady decline of daily active users in Europe. The policy response to the growing need to protect consumer privacy was best represented by the passing of the General Data Protection Regulation (GDPR). Adopted into the European Union law in 2016, the regulation contains various provisions and requirements related to processing personal data of individuals and enterprises. GDPR marked a watershed moment to regulation on data protection and became a model for many national laws outside the EU, including UK, Turkey, Mauritius, Chile, Japan, Brazil, South Korea, Argentina and Kenya. Even the California Consumer Privacy Act (CCPA), adopted in 2018, had many similarities with the GDPR.

Second, *Digital Technology Entrepreneurship* brings forth entrepreneurial innovation and thereby increases platform efficiency. The larger the user base, the larger the market segments and niches. A good platform sponsor provides boundary resources to ease the entrepreneurial innovation process and offers a fair profit-share plan. Over the years, some critics have complained about Apple's high developer commissions and fierce control over its App store. While it may be true that commissions have become a new added cost to entrepreneurs, Marc Andreessen, a renowned venture capitalist claims that overall entry costs to digital entrepre-

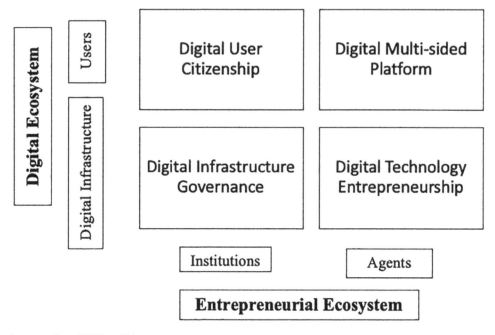

*Source:*    Song (2019), p. 576.

*Figure 5.1    The platform-based ecosystem*

neurship have declined. He states, "In the 90s, if you wanted to build an Internet company, you needed to buy Sun servers, Cisco networking gear, Oracle databases, and EMC storage systems… The new start-ups today… [are] paying somewhere between 100x and 1000x [less] per unit of compute, per unit of storage, per unit of networking."[5] In many ways, Apples' App store and Google Play platforms have dramatically decreased the cost and increased experimentation, entrepreneurial innovation, and value creation.

Third, *Digital Multi-sided platforms* are the key organizational innovation of the ITR (Rochet and Tirole, 2003, 2006; Gawer, 2009; Evans and Schmalensee, 2007, 2016). Saadatmand, Lindgren and Shultze (2019) describe, "digital platforms as an emergent organizational form characterized by technology and social processes." The network effects that drive *Digital Multi-sided Platforms* often result in winner-take-all outcomes. The monopolistic behavior of digital platforms will stifle competition, innovation, and entrepreneurial activities, which results in a welfare loss for consumers and the society as a whole. Arguably the most influential publication on the topic of platform monopolies is Lina Khan's "Amazon's Antitrust Paradox." She observes that Amazon has become the titan of twenty-first century commerce. It is no longer just a retailer but now "… a marketing platform, a delivery and logistics network, a payment service, a credit lender, an auction house, a major book publisher, a producer of television and films, a fashion designer, a hardware manufacturer, and a leading host of cloud server space" (Khan, 2017, p. 710). Although now nearly a two trillion dollar company, it generates relatively meager profits and has heretofore avoided the antitrust scrutiny in large part because of antiquated antitrust laws that have simply become outdated to measure market power of digital platforms. She argues that the potential harms to competition posed by Amazon's dominance cannot be properly accounted for if we measure competition primarily through price and output. The traditional antitrust laws underappreciate the risks to predatory pricing or how the integration across business lines can prove anticompetitive. The economics of platforms driven by network effects incentivizes firms to pursue growth over profits; this strategy justifies predatory pricing. Online platforms act as major critical intermediaries on which rivals depend but also often exploit information collected on companies and consumers using its services to undermine them as competitors.

One of the major contributors to the emergence of the platform-based ecosystem is the rapid migration and evolution of digital finance. Digital finance, which is a broad term to include everything from digital finance (e.g., online banking) among users and buyers to private equity flowing into digital entrepreneurship, is the adhesive that sustains and enables the platform-based ecosystem.

Secure and reliable digital technologies are necessary preconditions for the flourishing of the online financial transactions. A migration to a cashless society is a necessary first step, which users will be inclined to take only if there are tangible benefits. One such benefit is the reduction of transaction costs – the seamless payment experience between users and agents. In the digital age, digital finance has transformed capital markets too. One rather remarkable trend is the emergence of crowdfunding as an alternative method to raising capital. Similar to the way knowledge commons is a concerted effort of sourcing knowledge online, crowdfunding is a concerted effort of sourcing funding online.

Fourth, *digital technology infrastructure* enables the platform economy to operate. Digital infrastructure represents the technology of the digital age along with the rules and regulations that govern its use. This technological infrastructure is crucial to the smooth working of the DPE that is also responsible for keeping the digital economy open and secure. Over the years, the Chinese government strategically pursued its digital protectionism by blocking major US technology platforms from entering its market. The so-called Facebook, Amazon, Apple, and Google (FAANG), with a notable exception of Apple, ran into the "Great Firewall." In the absence of these technology platforms, China was able to incubate its own digital platforms, namely BATs (Baidu, Alibaba and Tencent). This policy stands in stark contrast to the laissez faire approach of the European Union or most of other countries where US technology platforms quickly established market dominance. But the global competition amongst FAANG and BATs for digital supremacy is not simply about market competition but also a national security and national competitiveness issue. Huawei has been accused of being controlled by the Chinese government, and its equipment spying on companies and countries. These allegations on the issues of control, ownership, and fraud have raised questions as to whether the Chinese smartphone and telecommunication giant should be allowed to build the world's 5G mobile infrastructure. While Huawei has defended itself as an open, transparent and trustworthy company, it remains to be seen how global users and governments will respond.

Another important trend is the rise of digital platforms, many of which are unicorns. Startups are reaching $1 billion or even $10 valuation (e.g., decacorns) at faster pace. The average time for a US technology company to go public has gone down from eleven years in 1999 to four years in 2011. The formation of mega funds, such as the Softbank's $100 billion Vision Fund, and the availability of venture capital funds increasingly leave little incentive for platform startups to go public. Part of this decision-making is that demand-side driven businesses tend to take a long time to develop a sustainable revenue model and going public

*Table 5.1*      *Keys to building a sustainable digital platform economy*

| Digital User Citizenship | Digital Multi-sided Platform |
|---|---|
| For a sustainable DPE, terms of user privacy should be clearly laid out and upheld by a social contract since public trust is a prerequisite to user participation in the digital economy. | For a sustainable DPE, digital platforms should be kept in check from partaking in monopolistic behavior that stifles market competition, innovation, and entrepreneurial activities. |
| Key word: "Privacy" | Key word: "Competition" |
| Example: Facebook | Example: Amazon |
| Digital Technology Infrastructure | Digital Technology Entrepreneurship |
| For a sustainable DPE, governments are responsible for enacting and enforcing rules and regulations that discourage destructive activities that undermine data security and encourage productive activities. | For a sustainable DPE, third-party agents engage in entrepreneurial innovation and knowledge exchange that close the gap between supply opportunity and demand need within platforms that increase platform efficiency. |
| Key word: "Security" | Key word: "Efficiency" |
| Example: Huawei | Example: Apple |

would subject it to scrutiny and pressure that tends to drive down the value. In short, finding a sustained long-term growth remains elusive.

## FROM CONCEPT TO MEASUREMENT: THE TWELVE PILLARS AND THEIR MEASUREMENT

While ecosystem theories and concepts have a relatively long history for both entrepreneurial ecosystems (Acs, Stam, Audretsch and O'Connor, 2017) and digital ecosystems (Li, Badr and Biennier, 2012; Weill and Woerner, 2015), the concepts of a digital entrepreneurship ecosystem and platform-based economy has been emerging only recently (Nambisan, 2017; Sahut, Iandoli, and Teulon, 2019; Elia, Margherita, and Passiante, 2020). However, measurements have been lagging behind conceptual developments. Some argue that all ecosystems are unique and have their own component structure, strengths and weaknesses. Consequently, case studies rather than simple or composite indicators are more appropriate to describe the ecosystem phenomenon (Isenberg, 2010; Spigel, 2017). While we can agree that the specifics of each ecosystem can be viewed under a microscope, a birds-eye view can identify some common structures and features (Szerb et al., 2019). Accurate measurement is vital because of three reasons. First, one can recognize the relative development of a particular unit by comparing with other units based on rankings and index scores. Second, ecosystem strengths and weaknesses can be identified from a benchmarking perspective. Third, solid policy recommendations should ideally be based on appropriate measures.

While digital ecosystem and entrepreneurship ecosystem measures have been available for a longer time, there is only one country-level digital entrepreneurship ecosystem index, known as the European Index of Digital Entrepreneurship Systems (EIDES), that we are aware of (Autio et al., 2018b, 2019). EIDES has its theoretical roots in the entrepreneurship ecosystem concept, where entrepreneurship ecosystem pillars are contextualized by their digital counterpart. This notion reflects the general-purpose use of digitalization, in particular of digital technologies. Our suggested DPE index is different from this because EIDES conceptualizes the entrepreneurship ecosystem based on the three business development stages (stand-up, start-up, and scale-up), while the DPE index is designed to focus on the context of users, agents, digital technology, and institutions to capture fully the systemic developments as identified by Jovanovic (1982, 2001). Second, our DPE index is centered around platformization and not solely on the use or the application of digital technologies. Moreover, EIDES is only for the EU member countries while DPE makes it possible to compare EU countries to other nations.[6]

The new DPE index proposed in this study attempts to measure the Digital Platform Economy at the country-level. Figure 5.1 pictures the structure of the DPE index showing the four frameworks, called sub-indices. All four frameworks include three constituents reflecting the most important aspects of Digital Technology Infrastructure, Digital User Citizenship, Digital Multi-sided Platforms, and Digital Technology Entrepreneurship. All pillars have two types of components, called variables (Figure 5.2). For example, the Digital rights pillar has an Institutions and a User's component; and the Digital adoption pillar consists of a Digital technology and an Agent variable.

*Digital Technology Infrastructure* (DTI) "…addresses the coordination and governance needed to establish a set of institutional standards…" (Sussan and Acs 2017, p. 64) that are related to digital technology.

- *Digital openness* reflects to how well a country's institutions support the reach and the use of digital technology. The digital technology part is proxied by the percentage of individuals and households having access to the internet. The institutions side is measured by an indicator reflecting the laws relating to ICT and a more complex indicator, the Global Cyberlaw Tracker.
- *Digital freedom* reflects how the government and their institutions are able to give enough freedom to digital technology development. The infrastructure part is measured by three indicators. The Freedom House two indices, the Freedom of the press, and the Freedom of the world reflects to the overall freedom of a country. The internet and telephone competition from the WEF Network Readiness Index measure the potential monopolization of the digital technology. The associated counterpart from the digital technology is measured by the number of internet domains from the Global Innovation Index, and Webhosting, standardized by the size of population.
- *Digital protection* captures the degree to which law and regulation protect from piracy and cybercrime. The infrastructure part is measured by the Legal sub index of the Global Security Index and the Corruption Perception Index from Transparency International. The digital part is proxied by the WEF Network Readiness Index software piracy rate.

*Digital User Citizenship* "…addresses the explicit legitimization and implicit social norms that enable users to participate in digital society" (Sussan and Acs, 2017, p. 64).

- *Digital literacy* refers to the abilities of the citizens necessary to use computers, the digital technology and digital platforms. From the user side we use two indicators: one is the level of digital skills amongst the population from WEF and the other is the number of search users in a country as reported by Bloom Consulting. From the institutional part, we use two educational indicators, the quality of education and the internet access to schools, and both are from WEF.
- *Digital access* refers to the level of access citizens have to the digital technology including computers and the internet. The institutional part of Digital access is captured by two proxy indicators: the technical and organizational sub-index from the Global Cybersecurity

| Sub-Indexes | Pillars | Variables (entrepreneurship/*digital*) |
|---|---|---|
| **Digital Technology Infrastructure** | Digital access | **Digital access Institutions** |
| | | *Digital access Digital technology* |
| | Digital freedom | **Digital Freedom Institutions** |
| | | *Digital Freedom Digital technology* |
| | Digital protection | **Digital protection Institutions** |
| | | *Digital protection Digital technology* |
| **Digital User Citizenship** | Digital literacy | **Digital literacy Institutions** |
| | | *Digital literacy Users* |
| | Digital openness | **Digital Openness Institutions** |
| | | *Digital openness Digital technology* |
| | Digital rights | **Digital rights Institutions** |
| | | *Digital rights Digital technology* |
| **Digital Multi-sided Platform** | Networking | **Networking Agents** |
| | | *Networking Users* |
| | Matchmaking | **Matchmaking Agents** |
| | | *Matchmaking Users* |
| | Financial facilitation | **Financial facilitation Agents** |
| | | *Financial facilitation Users* |
| **Digital Technology Entrepreneurship** | Digital adaptation | **Digital adoption Agents** |
| | | *Digital adoption Digital technology* |
| | Technology absorption | **Technology absorption Agents** |
| | | *Technology absorption Digital technology* |
| | Technology transfer | **Technology transfer Agents** |
| | | *Technology transfer Digital technology* |

*(Sub-indexes grouped under the vertical heading* **DIGITAL PLATFORM ECONOMY**.*)*

*Figure 5.2    The structure of the DPE index*

Index. The user part includes three indicators as fixed broadband internet subscriptions, international internet bandwidth, and the percentage of individuals using a computer.

- *Digital rights* reflect those human and legal rights that make it possible for citizens to use the digital technology and protect their privacy at the same time. The institutional part of Digital Rights is captured by personal rights – from the Global Talent Competitiveness

Index, by fundamental rights – from the Rule of Law index, and by property rights – from the Property Rights Alliance. The digital part is proxied by a Kaspersky-based variable that is the net infection rate and the internet censorship and surveillance data from Wikipedia.

*Digital Multi-sided Platforms* are where users of the digital technology and agent of the entrepreneurship ecosystem meet. DMSP serve as an "…intermediary for transaction of goods and services, and also a medium for knowledge exchanges that enables and facilitates experimentation, entrepreneurial innovation, and value creation" (Song 2019, p. 4).

- The *Networking* pillar aims to grasp the network and other externality effect of MSP. We apply three, partially overlapping, indicators from the users' side: the use of virtual social networks (ITU), social media penetration (Hootsuite), and the use of virtual professional networks (WEF). From the agent side, we apply two WEF related indicators that are the ICT use of business-to-business transactions and the business-to-customer internet use.
- *Matchmaking* component aims to capture the multi-sided platform model effect. From the user side, the active participation effect captured by two indicators from INSEAD that are the Wikipedia yearly edits, and the video uploads on YouTube. From the agent side we use the number of professional developers as a percentage of population and as a logarithmic of the country share. This later indicator is supposed to grasp the size effect.
- *Financial facilitation* reflects the various aspects of finance that fuel matchmaking start-ups, make possible financial transactions via the internet as well as provide platforms for financial source providers and users. From the user side, we apply four World Bank related indicators as debit/credit card average, used the internet to pay bills or to buy something online, used a mobile phone or the internet to access a financial institution account, and made or received digital payments. For the agent side we rely on three indicators, the depth of capital market sub-index score from the venture capital and private equity country attractiveness index, the standardized number of fintech companies based on deal room data, and venture capital availability from WEF.

*Digital Technology Entrepreneurship* "…is comprised of various third-party agents that partake in experimentation, entrepreneurial innovation, and value creation using hardware/ software to build products that connect to platforms" (Song 2019, p. 9).

- *Digital adaptation* aims to detect the basic capabilities of entrepreneurial agents to use digital technologies. From the agent side, we use two proxies, one for measuring the level of digitalization by computer software spending and another for the quantifying the basic talents in the country (skills of the workforce).
- The *Digital Absorption* pillar involves the advanced capabilities of the agents to be able to build new business models and/or digital products/services based on the opportunities provided by the digital technology. The digital technology component is captured by two indicators: The number of data centers from the Data Centers catalog and the availability of latest technology from WEF. The agent component is measured by a complex variable that is the knowledge absorption capacity sub-index and by two indicators reflecting the effect of ICT on new business and organizational models. All data are from the Global Innovation Index.
- The *Technology Transfer* pillar includes the knowledge spillover effect when agents are working on the discovery, evaluation, and exploitation of new opportunities brought about

by evolving technologies. From the agent side, the tech transfer capability is proxied by a startup ranking based indicator that is the number of startups. The skill component is measured by the High-level skills which is a complex sub-index from the Global Talent Competitiveness Report. From the digital technology part, we use two components one is from the Global Innovation index that is the Knowledge and technology output and a similar component from the Global Competitiveness Index that is the Innovation capacity.

The full description of the applied 61 indicators and their sources can be found in the Appendix.

## MEASUREMENT – CALCULATING THE DPE INDEX AND ITS COMPONENT SCORES

According to the model pictured in Figure 5.1, and detailed out in Figure 5.2, we suggest a five-level composite indicator building following as (1) indicators, (2) variables, (3) pillars, (4) sub-indices, and (5) the super-index. The super index is called the Digital Platform Economy index and its sub-indices are the four frameworks. The twelve components are called pillars. Pillars are the most important constituents of the model. Pillars are comprised from 24 variables, representing digital ecosystem (12) and entrepreneurship ecosystem (12). Variables are built from 61 indicators that are the elementary building blocks of DPE index.

Indicator selection was based on three criteria:

1. Relevance of the indicator for the phenomenon we aim to measure.
2. Specificity of the variable to the phenomenon it represents.
3. Potentially flawless and clear interpretation of the indicator.

We also aimed to have the indicator available for at least 90% of all countries, but in five cases, we could not reach this goal. For 85 countries more than 95.1%, for 23 countries 90.1–95.0%, and for 8 countries 80.1–90.0% of the indicators are available. The results for these eight countries – Benin, Burundi, Hong Kong, Jamaica, Macedonia, Madagascar, Namibia, Taiwan – should be viewed with precaution. Variables were calculated from normalized indicator scores. Following the Global Entrepreneurship Index building methodology we provide the most important steps of calculation (Acs et al., 2014).

All pillars contain two types of variables: one representing the Digital Ecosystem (Digital technology and Users) and the other representing the Entrepreneurship Ecosystem (Institutions and Agents). The overall influence of these two types of variables is captured by multiplying the two components:

$$DPE\_pillar_{i,j} = DE\_variable_{i,j} * EE\_variable_{i,j}. \tag{5.1}$$

where

i = 1 ......n, the number of countries
$DPE\_pillar_{i,j}$ represents the digital entrepreneurship ecosystem pillars, j = 1 ,.....12
$DE\_pillar_{i,j}$ represents the digital ecosystem pillars, j = 1 ,.....12
$EE\_pillar_{i,j}$ represents the entrepreneurship ecosystem pillars, j = 1 ,.....12

After the calculation of the raw pillar scores we normalized them using the distance methodology.

When we calculate the normalized averages of the twelve pillars for the 116 countries, it ranges from 0.153 (Matchmaking) to 0.525 (Digital rights) with 0.361 overall average value. The different averages of the normalized values of the pillars imply that reaching the same pillar values requires different efforts and resources. Consequently, the effect of additional resources to achieve the same marginal improvement of the pillar values is different and it is problematic for using the pillar values to public policy purposes. The average pillar adjustment methodology developed by Acs, Autio and Szerb (2014) reduces but not fully eliminates this problem.

After these transformations, the penalty for bottleneck methodology was used to create pillar-adjusted PFB values. A bottleneck is defined as the worst performing pillar or a limiting constraint in a particular country's digital entrepreneurship system. Here, bottleneck is defined as the lowest level of a particular pillar, relative to other pillars in a particular country. This notion of a bottleneck is important for policy purposes considering the systemic nature of DEE. The system perspective means that that pillars have an effect to one another. This interaction should be included in the calculation of the pillar, the sub-index and the DPE index scores. We consider the system being optimal if all the average adjusted pillar scores are the same for the particular country. Differences imply non-optimal use of the resources. Practically it means that after equalizing the pillar averages, the value of each pillar of a country is penalized by linking it to the score of the pillar with the weakest scores in that country. This simulates the notion of a bottleneck; if the weakest pillar were improved, the whole DPE Index would show a significant improvement.

We define our penalty function following as:

$$DPE\_penalized_{(i),j} = 100*\min DPE\_pillar(equal)_{(i),j} + \left(1 - e^{-\left(y_{(i)j} - \min DPE\_pillar(equal)_{(i),j}\right)}\right). \quad (5.2)$$

where $DPE\_penalized_{i,j}$ is the modified, post-penalty value of pillar j in country i

$DPE\_pillar(equal)_{i,j}$ is the normalized value of index component j in country i

$DPE\_pillar(equal)_{min}$ is the lowest value of $y_{i,j}$ for country i.

i = 1, 2,......116 = the number of countries

j = 1, 2,.......12 = the number of pillars

Note that the multiplication by 100 is purely practical to get a 0–100 point scale instead of the 0–1 range. Sub-index calculation is simple, just taking the arithmetic average of its PFB-adjusted pillars for that sub-index.

Finally, the Digital Platform Economy index (DPE) score is calculated as the simple arithmetic average of the four sub-indices.

$$DPE_i = \frac{1}{4}\left(DIG_i + DUC_i + DMSP_i + DTE_i\right) \quad (5.3)$$

Where $DIG_i$ = Digital Technology Infrastructure score for country i

$DUC_i$ = Digital User Citizenship score for country i
$DMSP_i$ = Digital Multi-sided Platform score for country i, and
$DTE_i$ = Digital Technology Entrepreneurship score for country i
$DPE_i$ is the Digital Platform Economy index score for country i.

We have done the basic tests for consistency of the composite indicator components. The Cronbach alpha values for the four sub-indices are in an acceptable range; for DUC=0.93, for DIG=0.84 for DMSP=0.92 for DTE=0.93.

## ANALYSIS – COUNTRY RANKINGS, CLUSTERING, AND PILLAR BASED EVALUATION

In this section, we provide a basic analysis of the DPE index and their components for 116 countries from all continents and all development stages. We highlight some European countries to present the real varieties of DEE.

First, we present the DPE Index scores ranking of the 116 countries. According to Table 5.2, the United States leads the DPE Index 2020 ranking with a score of 85.0 followed by the United Kingdom (82.7), and the Netherlands (82.4). In the first ten countries there are two from North America (US and Canada), seven from Europe (UK, Netherlands, Sweden, Switzerland, Norway, Denmark and Finland) and there is only one Asian country, the ninth ranked Australia. The second ten countries, ranked in the 11–20 spots, show a similar regional distribution: Besides eight European countries – Ireland, Luxemburg, Germany, France, Iceland, Belgium, Estonia, and Austria there are New Zealand and Hong Kong. All of these countries are highly developed, innovation driven economies. In contrast, in the last ten places (107–116) there are low developed, resource driven countries mainly from the African continent with the exception of Cambodia.

Table 5.2 provides us with a look at the global position of the EU versus the rest of the world. Scandinavian countries (Sweden, Norway, Denmark and Finland) as well as Switzerland are stronger than the large European countries; however, they are small in terms of population and output. While there are four EU member countries in the first ten countries, Europe's large countries, Germany, France, Italy and Spain are clearly in the second cohort of ranking. The difference between the first three leading countries is marginal. However, the US DPE Index score is higher than that of the 14th ranked Germany by more than 20 DPE Index scores, by almost 25%.

There is a close connection between development and DPE Index scores: The Pearson correlation coefficient is 0.66, without the oil-rich countries, and countries with higher than 65 000 inter. $ per capita GDP. The third-degree trend line shows even closer connection as pictured in Figure 5.3.

The third-degree adjusted curve explains around 90% of the variation between development (measured by the per capita GDP) and digital platform-based ecosystem (DPE Index). Note that it is not implying a causal relationship; we simply refer to the strong connection between development and digital entrepreneurship ecosystem. Examining a particular country's position being below or above the development implied trend line is more appropriate than simply comparing differently developed nations. For example, the United States has the highest DPE Index score, 85.0, and is above the trend line as is the United Kingdom, the Netherlands, and

*Table 5.2   The DPE index ranking of the countries, 2020*

| Rank | Country | DPE 2020 | GDP 2017 | Rank | Country | DPE 2020 | GDP 2017 | Rank | Country | DPE 2020 | GDP 2017 |
|---|---|---|---|---|---|---|---|---|---|---|---|
| 1 | United States | 85,0 | 54225 | 40 | **Slovakia** | **40,5** | **30155** | 79 | Ecuador | 21,3 | 10582 |
| 2 | United Kingdom | 82,7 | 39753 | 41 | **Hungary** | **38,4** | **26778** | 80 | Tunisia | 21,1 | 10849 |
| 3 | **Netherlands** | **82,4** | **48473** | 42 | Uruguay | 36,3 | 20551 | 81 | Albania | 20,5 | 11803 |
| 4 | Canada | 78,2 | 44018 | 43 | **Greece** | **35,9** | **24574** | 82 | Vietnam | 20,3 | 6172 |
| 5 | **Sweden** | **76,8** | **46949** | 44 | **Bulgaria** | **35,0** | **18563** | 83 | Dominican Republic | 19,8 | 14601 |
| 6 | Switzerland | 76,3 | 57410 | 45 | **Croatia** | **34,8** | **22670** | 84 | Jamaica | 19,7 | 8194 |
| 7 | Norway | 74,4 | 64800 | 46 | Costa Rica | 34,1 | 15525 | 85 | Egypt | 19,5 | 10550 |
| 8 | **Denmark** | **71,1** | **46683** | 47 | **Romania** | **33,0** | **23313** | 86 | Iran | 19,5 | 19083 |
| 9 | Australia | 69,3 | 44649 | 48 | Russia | 32,7 | 24766 | 87 | Botswana | 19,5 | 15807 |
| 10 | **Finland** | **68,9** | **40586** | 49 | Turkey | 32,3 | 25129 | 88 | Namibia | 18,3 | 9542 |
| 11 | **Ireland** | **66,0** | **67335** | 50 | Mauritius | 32,0 | 20293 | 89 | Sri Lanka | 18,3 | 11669 |
| 12 | **Luxembourg** | **65,6** | **94278** | 51 | Brazil | 31,2 | 14103 | 90 | Lebanon | 17,6 | 13368 |
| 13 | New Zealand | 65,3 | 36086 | 52 | Argentina | 30,4 | 18934 | 91 | Kenya | 17,5 | 2993 |
| 14 | **Germany** | **64,4** | **45229** | 53 | Mexico | 29,4 | 17336 | 92 | Mongolia | 17,3 | 11841 |
| 15 | **France** | **63,6** | **38606** | 54 | Ukraine | 29,3 | 7894 | 93 | El Salvador | 16,7 | 7292 |
| 16 | Iceland | 62,6 | 46483 | 55 | Saudi Arabia | 29,3 | 49045 | 94 | Paraguay | 15,6 | 8827 |
| 17 | **Belgium** | **62,5** | **42659** | 56 | Oman | 28,8 | 37961 | 95 | Guatemala | 15,0 | 7424 |
| 18 | **Estonia** | **60,0** | **29481** | 57 | Montenegro | 28,5 | 16409 | 96 | Senegal | 14,5 | 2471 |
| 19 | Hong Kong | 58,5 | 56055 | 58 | **China** | **28,1** | **15309** | 97 | Pakistan | 14,0 | 5035 |
| 20 | **Austria** | **57,0** | **45437** | 59 | Colombia | 28,0 | 13255 | 98 | Honduras | 13,9 | 4542 |
| 21 | Japan | 56,8 | 39002 | 60 | Panama | 28,0 | 22267 | 99 | Nigeria | 13,7 | 5338 |
| 22 | South Korea | 56,4 | 35938 | 61 | Bahrain | 27,6 | 43291 | 100 | Zambia | 13,4 | 3689 |
| 23 | Israel | 56,2 | 33132 | 62 | Serbia | 27,5 | 14049 | 101 | Algeria | 12,5 | 13914 |
| 24 | Singapore | 55,8 | 85535 | 63 | Thailand | 27,2 | 16278 | 102 | Rwanda | 11,9 | 1854 |
| 25 | **Spain** | **53,5** | **34272** | 64 | Georgia | 26,5 | 9745 | 103 | Nepal | 11,6 | 2443 |
| 26 | **Malta** | **53,4** | **36513** | 65 | South Africa | 26,4 | 12295 | 104 | Kyrgyzstan | 11,5 | 3393 |
| 27 | **Portugal** | **50,8** | **27937** | 66 | Macedonia | 25,3 | 13111 | 105 | Bangladesh | 11,2 | 3524 |
| 28 | **Czech Republic** | **48,9** | **32606** | 67 | Jordan | 25,0 | 8337 | 106 | Uganda | 11,0 | 1698 |
| 29 | Taiwan | 47,1 | 50294 | 68 | Armenia | 25,0 | 8788 | 107 | Cameroon | 10,8 | 3365 |
| 30 | **Italy** | **46,1** | **35220** | 69 | Moldova | 24,4 | 5190 | 108 | Mali | 10,4 | 2014 |
| 31 | **Slovenia** | **45,1** | **31401** | 70 | Morocco | 24,4 | 7485 | 109 | Zimbabwe | 10,0 | 1900 |
| 32 | **Lithuania** | **44,3** | **29524** | 71 | Philippines | 24,3 | 7599 | 110 | Cambodia | 9,8 | 3645 |

| Rank | Country | DPE 2020 | GDP 2017 | Rank | Country | DPE 2020 | GDP 2017 | Rank | Country | DPE 2020 | GDP 2017 |
|---|---|---|---|---|---|---|---|---|---|---|---|
| **33** | **Cyprus** | **44,3** | **32415** | 72 | Azerbaijan | 23,9 | 15847 | 111 | Tanzania | 9,8 | 2683 |
| 34 | United Arab Emirates | 43,1 | 67293 | 73 | India | 23,8 | 6427 | 112 | Malawi | 9,8 | 1095 |
| **35** | **Latvia** | **42,8** | **25064** | 74 | Peru | 23,6 | 12237 | 113 | Benin | 9,6 | 2064 |
| 36 | Malaysia | 42,1 | 26808 | 75 | Kazakhstan | 23,5 | 24056 | 114 | Madagascar | 7,3 | 1416 |
| 37 | Qatar | 40,7 | 116936 | 76 | Indonesia | 23,1 | 11189 | 115 | Burundi | 6,9 | 702 |
| 38 | Chile | 40,6 | 22767 | 77 | Kuwait | 22,8 | 65531 | 116 | Ethiopia | 6,0 | 1730 |
| **39** | **Poland** | **40,6** | **27216** | 78 | Bosnia and Herzegovina | 21,4 | 11714 | | | | |

*Note:*     DPE INDEX: Digital Platform Economy index score; European Union countries are **bold**.
*Source:*   The per capita GDP of the country in purchasing power parity, 2017 from the World Bank (https://data.worldbank.org/indicator/NY.GDP.PCAP.PP.KD).

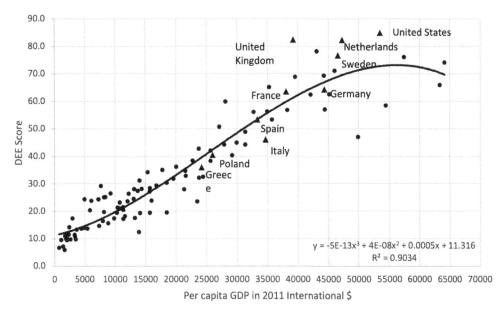

*Note:* Trend line is calculated without countries over 65 000 inter. $ per capital GDP and without oil-based economies of Bahrain, Kuwait, Oman, Qatar, Saudi Arabia, United Arab Emirates.

*Figure 5.3*     *The connection between development and the DPE Index scores (third-degree polynomial adjustment)*

Sweden. Out of the large EU countries, only France and Spain are on or above the trend line. Germany and Italy both have lower DPE Index scores than implied by the trend line. Poorer EU countries like Poland or Greece have much lower DPE Index scores and they are below the trend-line.

While DPE Index score is useful to evaluate the digital platform-based ecosystem performance of a country as compared to other nations, it does not tell us anything about the strengths and weaknesses of this country. For viewing it, we need to decompose the DPE Index into its components. Table 5.3 presents the four sub-index scores and rankings of the first 25 countries.

The United States is first in the DMSP and the DTE sub-indices but sixth in DUC and second in DIG. The US best sub-index score is 92.3 (DTE) and the worst is 73.3 (DUC) a 20.6% difference. The United Kingdom's performance is even more balanced ranging from the first (DUC=84.8) to the fourth (DIG=81.3). Some other countries show higher variations. For example, the 9th ranked Australia is 7th in DIG=78.2 score but only the 18th in DTE=57.0, a 27.1% difference. Looking at the EU member countries, various imbalances can be seen. While Netherlands is first in DTI (DIG=90.5) it is only the fourth in DUC (DUC=74.1) with significantly lower score (18% difference). Germany has its major weaknesses in DMSP, while France and Spain are more balanced.

Figure 5.4 shows the grouping of the 116 countries into four quadrants. On the horizontal axis is the difference between the DPE Index trend-line and the actual DPE Index score in

*Table 5.3    The four sub-index scores and ranking of the first 25 countries*

| DPE Ranking | Country | DIG score | DIG ranking | DUC score | DUC ranking | DMSP score | DMSP ranking | DTE score | DTE ranking | DPE Score |
|---|---|---|---|---|---|---|---|---|---|---|
| 1 | United States | 80,7 | 3 | 79,0 | 3 | 87,4 | 1 | 92,2 | 1 | 84,8 |
| 2 | United Kingdom | 80,1 | 4 | 83,5 | 1 | 84,8 | 3 | 81,3 | 3 | 82,4 |
| 3 | **Netherlands** | **89,5** | **1** | **74,3** | **7** | **86,3** | **2** | **78,6** | **4** | **82,2** |
| 4 | Canada | 75,4 | 8 | 81,3 | 2 | 78,8 | 5 | 77,1 | 5 | 78,2 |
| 5 | **Sweden** | **78,3** | **5** | **74,2** | **8** | **79,5** | **4** | **74,3** | **6** | **76,6** |
| 6 | Switzerland | 75,5 | 7 | 74,6 | 6 | 69,3 | 9 | 84,8 | 2 | 76,1 |
| 7 | Norway | 84,4 | 2 | 75,0 | 5 | 73,5 | 6 | 63,7 | 12 | 74,1 |
| 8 | **Denmark** | **78,2** | **6** | **68,4** | **11** | **73,3** | **7** | **64,3** | **11** | **71,1** |
| 9 | Australia | 73,7 | 9 | 77,3 | 4 | 69,2 | 10 | 56,9 | 18 | 69,3 |
| 10 | **Finland** | **71,5** | **11** | **70,9** | **9** | **67,1** | **11** | **66,0** | **8** | **68,9** |
| 11 | **Ireland** | **66,0** | **15** | **63,2** | **17** | **65,3** | **14** | **69,5** | **7** | **66,0** |
| 12 | **Luxembourg** | **73,6** | **10** | **65,5** | **14** | **60,3** | **17** | **62,9** | **14** | **65,5** |
| 13 | New Zealand | 69,4 | 13 | 66,0 | 13 | 70,3 | 8 | 54,9 | 23 | 65,1 |
| 14 | **Germany** | **67,6** | **14** | **70,3** | **10** | **56,3** | **23** | **63,1** | **13** | **64,3** |
| 15 | **France** | **63,5** | **18** | **64,9** | **15** | **60,3** | **16** | **65,3** | **9** | **63,5** |
| 16 | Iceland | 70,7 | 12 | 48,7 | 28 | 65,6 | 13 | 65,3 | 10 | 62,6 |
| 17 | **Belgium** | **65,8** | **16** | **59,8** | **18** | **64,9** | **15** | **59,5** | **17** | **62,5** |
| 18 | **Estonia** | **63,1** | **19** | **64,0** | **16** | **57,4** | **22** | **55,1** | **21** | **59,9** |
| 19 | Hong Kong | 62,0 | 20 | 56,1 | 20 | 58,7 | 20 | 56,9 | 19 | 58,4 |
| 20 | **Austria** | **63,7** | **17** | **57,6** | **19** | **50,0** | **28** | **56,6** | **20** | **57,0** |
| 21 | Japan | 61,0 | 21 | 68,2 | 12 | 44,2 | 34 | 53,7 | 24 | 56,8 |
| 22 | Korea | 57,9 | 22 | 54,6 | 22 | 59,5 | 18 | 53,2 | 26 | 56,3 |
| 23 | Israel | 48,2 | 31 | 48,5 | 29 | 66,9 | 12 | 60,9 | 16 | 56,1 |
| 24 | Singapore | 55,1 | 24 | 47,7 | 30 | 58,5 | 21 | 61,2 | 15 | 55,6 |
| 25 | **Spain** | **54,0** | **25** | **53,1** | **23** | **52,5** | **25** | **53,7** | **25** | **53,3** |

*Note:*    DIG: Digital Infrastructure Governance; DUC: Digital User Citizenship; DMSP: Digital Multi-Sided Platform; DTE: Digital Technology Entrepreneurship; EU member countries are **bold**.

percentages. The DPE Index trend-line calculation is based on the per capita GDP. The DPE Index trend-line represents the best fit power function according to the following equation:

$$GDP\ per\ capita = -5E\ (-13)*DPE\ Index^3 + 4E\ (-08)DPE\ Index^2 + 0.0005*DPE\ Index + 11.34 \quad (5.4)$$

Countries above zero have higher digital entrepreneurship ecosystem development than implied by its per capita GDP (I and IV quadrants). Countries below zero have lower digital entrepreneurship ecosystem development than implied by the trend-line (II and III quadrants). For countries significantly below the trend-line (by rule of thumb the 10% threshold is selected) is suggested to increase more on the development of the digital entrepreneurship ecosystem. Caution is advised if the DE is somewhere between the 5–10% range.

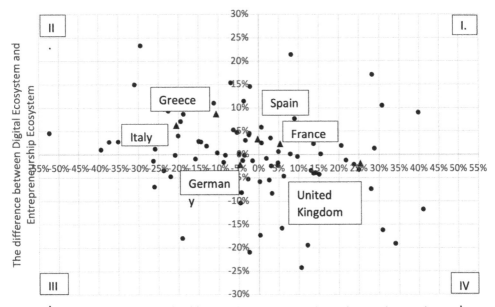

*Figure 5.4*　　*The four groups of countries based on the difference between DE and EE scores and the deviation from development implied trend-line*

On the vertical axis, there is the difference between the digital ecosystem (DE) and the Entrepreneurship Ecosystem (EE) scores. Countries in quadrants I and II have higher DE than EE score. In quadrants III and IV, countries have higher EE than DE scores. For a balanced development, DE and EE scores should be about the same. If the difference is higher than 10%, resources should be redirected to harmonize the digital and the entrepreneurship ecosystems. If the difference is between 5% and 10%, some resource allocation seems to be reasonable to balance the two ecosystems. So, for countries in quadrants I and II entrepreneurship ecosystem development is suggested. For countries in quadrants III and IV digital ecosystem development is more fruitful. Countries where the DPE Index-DPE Index trend difference is positive and they are within the 10% DE–EE difference range are suggested to maintain the balance between DE and EE.

According to Figure 5.4 the countries in the [-10%; 10%] range of DE and EE difference and have lower than -10% value in the DPE Index-DPE Index trend difference are considered to be optimal implying that no extra spending for DPE Index development is necessary and their DE–EE balance is roughly fine. Germany, France and Spain all belong to this group together with many innovation-driven, developed countries and with some efficiency driven, developing countries. For the second cohort, Chile is an example.

Another group of mainly lower developed countries have positive deviation from the development implied trend line and significantly higher DE score (quadrant I). For example, Morocco has a low DPE Index score but it is higher than implied by its development. At the same time, the country's digital ecosystem is much higher than the entrepreneurship ecosystem. None of our examined countries belong to this group.

Quadrant IV countries' overall DPE Index level is sufficient; however, their digital component is relatively underdeveloped as compared to the entrepreneurship components. For example, China can be found here. China's DPE Index score is higher than implied by the trend line but its EE score is higher than its DE score (by 11.3%). Consequently, further effort is suggested to improve China's digital ecosystem. The United Kingdom, being second in the DPE Index ranking is also here, but its digital and entrepreneurship components are in balance. In fact, the positive 25% deviation from the development implied trend-line implies that UK's digital entrepreneurship ecosystem is an important factor of its growth.

There are many countries that have lower DPE Index scores than implied by the trend line and have imbalances in the DE–EE context in favor of digital ecosystem development (quadrant II). Note that we maximized the deviation up to -55% in Figure 5.5. Our highlighted examples are Italy and Greece. Their overall DPE Index development is well below what we could expect from these developed countries. Moreover, their digital ecosystem is more advanced than their entrepreneurship component. Though, this imbalance is below the critical 10% threshold.

In quadrant III there are nations that spend too little on DPE Index development and their digital ecosystem is also lacking as compared to their entrepreneurship ecosystem. For example, some poorer African countries belong to this quadrant.

Table 5.4 provides further details about policy suggestions in terms of DEE and the DE/EE mix based on Figure 5.4 data. The recommendations are based on the deviation from the DPE Index trend-line and the difference between DE and EE scores. As is clearly seen, most countries (41) and most EU member countries (15) belong to the balanced category where DEE development should follow the development of the country with keeping the balance between DE and EE. The second largest group (19) with two EU member countries, where the DE and EE are balanced but the country is well below the development implied trend-line. Eleven countries belong to the cohort where DEE level fits to development, but the digital ecosystem requires significant improvement. Eight countries have proper DEE levels but their entrepreneurship ecosystems are at a low level. Seven countries' DPE Index scores are somewhat below the trend-line and the DE and the EE are in balance. Four EU member countries can be found here. All the other groups contain less than seven countries. Note that only five EU member countries – Austria, Cyprus, Greece, Italy, and Slovakia require substantial DEE development. It is also important to add, that the trend-line is about the average performance. So if the EU wants to step ahead in the digital entrepreneurship ecosystem then the proper benchmarks are the United States, the United Kingdom, and the Netherlands.

*Table 5.4*   Suggested policy recommendation with respect to DPE Index trend-line deviation, and Digital Ecosystem/Entrepreneurship Ecosystem mix

| | Strong DE development (DE–EE difference is below -10%) | Some DE development (DE–EE difference is between (-5%, -10%) | Keep balance between DE and EE (DE–EE difference is between (-5%, 5%) | Some EE development (DE–EE difference is between 5%, 10%) | Strong EE development (DE–EE difference is above 10%) |
|---|---|---|---|---|---|
| **Keep DEE development with GDP** | Albania, Bosnia and Herzegovina, Colombia, Honduras, India, Indonesia, Peru, Philippines, Senegal, Ukraine, Vietnam | China, **Finland**, Jordan, Pakistan, South Africa, Switzerland, | Argentina, Armenia, Australia, Bahrain, **Belgium**, Brazil, **Bulgaria**, Canada, Chile, Costa Rica, **Croatia**, **Czech Republic**, **Denmark**, Ecuador, Egypt, **Estonia**, **France**, **Germany**, Israel, Jamaica, Kenya, Korea, **Lithuania**, **Luxembourg**, Malaysia, Mexico, Montenegro, **Netherlands**, New Zealand, Norway, **Poland**, **Portugal**, Qatar, Singapore, **Spain**, **Sweden**, Tunisia, United Arab Emirates, United Kingdom, United States, Zambia | Kuwait, **Latvia**, Moldova, Saudi Arabia, Thailand | Georgia, Macedonia, Mauritius, Morocco, Oman, Rwanda, Serbia, Uruguay |
| **Some DEE development (deviation from trend-line is 5%–10%)** | - | **Malta** | El Salvador, **Hungary**, Iceland, **Ireland**, Nepal, **Romania**, **Slovenia** | Japan, Namibia | - |
| **Overall DEE development (deviation from trend-line is over 10%)** | Madagascar, Sri Lanka | **Austria**, Dominican Republic | Azerbaijan, Botswana, Burundi, Cambodia, Cameroon, **Cyprus**, Ethiopia, Guatemala, Hong Kong, Kazakhstan, Kyrgyzstan, Lebanon, Malawi, Mali, Nigeria, Panama, **Slovakia**, Taiwan, Turkey | Bangladesh, **Greece**, **Italy**, Mongolia, Paraguay, Russia | Algeria, Benin, Iran, Tanzania, Uganda, Zimbabwe |

*Note:*   EU member countries are **bold**.

## SUMMARY AND CONCLUSION

The recent digital and information technology revolution has had a major impact on entre-preneurship. In particular, platform based developments contribute to drastically decreasing transaction costs and the appearance of new business models. However, digital entrepreneurs require a different environmental context as compared to non-digital ones. If a country builds out its *digital ecosystem* there is no guarantee it will be implemented by existing firms. In the same vein, if a country builds out its *entrepreneurial ecosystem* there is no guarantee startups will introduce new technologies. For technology to be successfully introduced, both the *digital ecosystem* and the *entrepreneurial ecosystem* need to be developed simultaneously. The digital entrepreneurship ecosystem theory developed by Sussan and Acs (2017) and amended by Song (2019), integrates the entrepreneurship ecosystem and the digital ecosystem concepts.

This chapter builds on the DEE concept and provides a measurement of it. The Digital Platform Economy Index consists of four sub-indices (i.e., *Digital User Citizenship, Digital Technology Infrastructure, Digital Multi-sided Platform* and *Digital Technology Entrepreneurship*), twelve pillars (i.e., *Digital Access, Digital Freedom, Digital Protection, Digital Literacy, Digital Openness, Digital Rights, Networking, Matchmaking, Financial Facilitation, Digital Adoption, Technology Absorption*, and *Technology Transfer*), and 61 indices.

The DPE index is aiming to provide a suitable, comprehensive tool for policy makers and researchers as well as platform economy participants on how to pinpoint bottlenecks in the operation of the country's digital entrepreneurship ecosystem, to identify imbalances between the digital and entrepreneurship components, and to improve the weakest components of operation. While digital technology-based innovations are accelerating, many people face difficulties in using them. The DPE index makes it possible to find out these potentially crucial barriers either on the infrastructure or on the human side that limit digital development. The DPE index provides suitable, tailor-made policy recommendations at the country level. However, DPE index-based policies can be formulated at a larger scale, something like the European Union. At the global scale, developed Anglo-Saxon and Nordic nations lead the DPE ranking followed by other European, Asian as well as Oceania (i.e., Australia and New Zealand) prosperous countries. Many mid-developed countries from Europe, Asia and Latin America together with some oil-rich countries (i.e., Bahrain, Oman, Qatar, Saudi Arabia, and United Arab Emirates) report below average DPE index scores. The group of poor performing countries, in terms of the DPE index, includes underdeveloped African and Asian countries as well as some developing European and Latin American nations. The specific analysis for the EU reveals that for most countries (22 out of 27), they are on or above the development implied trend-line; however, they are far from the DPE top performing countries (US and UK), with the exception of the Netherlands. The gap between the US and the large EU member countries like Germany and France is significant, around 25%. Spain, Italy and Poland lag behind the US by more than 35%. It seems that the EU's institutional setup supports more the self-employment type of small business than fast growing billion dollar businesses, that is, the unicorns. Recent regulations, like the General Data Protection Regulation or GDPR, focusing on ensuring that users know, understand, and consent to the data collected about them, are not really helpful and limit not only the existing non-EU businesses but also weaken EU based startups. Other EU investigations against Microsoft, Alphabet/Google or Facebook and other digital giants could only provide temporal protection for EU-based platform businesses. If the

EU is to survive and prosper, the EU needs to rebalance its digital entrepreneurial ecosystem policy to promote technology innovation, platform companies and create a sustainable platform economy.

Besides policy makers, our DPE index can be useful for researchers intending to examine digital entrepreneurship ecosystems and their influence. In that respect, economic growth as well as income distribution and poverty effects can also be important.

## ACKNOWLEDGMENT

Project no. TKP2020-IKA-08 has been implemented with the support provided from the National Research, Development and Innovation Fund of Hungary, financed under the 2020-4.1.1-TKP2020 funding scheme.

## NOTES

1. Also see Greenwood and Jovanovic (1999).
2. https://www.androidcentral.com/alphabet-becomes-fourth-trillion-dollar-company (accessed 2/14/2020).
3. Also see Peitz and Waldfogel (2012).
4. Malecki (2018) emphasized the regional aspect of entrepreneurial ecosystems and Cavallo, Ghezzi and Balocco (2018) focused on the present debates and future directions.
5. https://www.wsj.com/articles/SB10001424052702303640604579298330921690014.
6. For other entrepreneurship ecosystem measures see the Global Entrepreneurship Index, its regional counterpart the regional Entrepreneurship and Development index, Kauffmann's entrepreneurship ecosystem and the Startup Genome's Global Startup Ecosystem model. Digital measures can be divided into maturity/readiness, transformation, and complex indices. The most well-known composite digital index is the European Union's Digital Economy and Transformation Index (DESI). Beside it, there are the Mastercard and the Fletcher School at Tufts University's Digital Evolution Index, and the Economic Intelligence Unit's Inclusive Internet Index.

## BIBLIOGRAPHY

Acs, Z. J., Autio, E., & Szerb, L. (2014). National systems of entrepreneurship: Measurement issues and policy implications. *Research Policy*, *43*(3), 476–494. https://doi.org/10.1016/j.respol.2013.08.016

Acs, Z. J., Stam, E., Audretsch, D. B., & O'Connor, A. (2017). The lineages of the entrepreneurial ecosystem approach. *Small Business Economics*, *49*(1), 1–10. https://doi.org/10.1007/s11187-017-9864-8

Autio, E., Nambisan, S., Thomas, L. D., & Wright, M. (2018a). Digital affordances, spatial affordances, and the genesis of entrepreneurial ecosystems. *Strategic Entrepreneurship Journal*, *12*(1), 72–95.

Autio, E., Szerb, L., Komlosi, E., & Tiszberger, M. (2018b). The European index of digital entrepreneurship systems. Publications Office of the European Union (Ed.), *JRC Technical Reports*, *153*.

Autio, E., Szerb, L., Komlosi, E., & Tiszberger, M. (2019). *EIDES 2019: The European Index of Digital Entrepreneurship Systems* (No. JRC117495). Joint Research Centre (Seville site).

Cavallo, A., Ghezzi, A., & Balocco, R. (2018). Entrepreneurial ecosystem research: Present debates and future directions. *International Entrepreneurship and Management Journal*. https://doi.org/10.1007/s11365-018-0526-3

Cusumano, M. A., Gawer, A., & Yoffie, D. B. (2019). *The business of platforms: Strategy in the age of digital competition, innovation, and power*. New York: HarperCollins.

Elia, G., Margherita, A., & Passiante, G. (2020). Digital entrepreneurship ecosystem: How digital technologies and collective intelligence are reshaping the entrepreneurial process. *Technological Forecasting and Social Change, 150*, 119791.

Evans, D., & Schmalensee, R. (2007). *The catalyst code: The strategies behind the world's most dynamic companies.* Boston, MA: Harvard Business School Press.

Evans, D. S., & Schmalensee, R. (2016). *Matchmakers: The new economics of multi-sided platforms.* Boston, MA: Harvard Business Review Press.

Ferguson, N. (2019). *The square and the tower: Networks and power, from the Freemasons to Facebook.* London: Penguin Books.

Gawer, A. (Ed.) (2009). *Platforms, markets, and innovation.* Cheltenham, UK and Northampton, MA, USA: Edward Elgar Publishing.

Goldfarb, A., & Tucker, C. (2019). Digital economics. *Journal of Economic Literature, 57*(1), 3–43.

Gompers, P., & Lerner, J. (2001). The venture capital revolution. *Journal of Economic Perspectives, 15*(2), 145–168.

Greenwood, J., & Jovanovic, B. (1999). The information-technology revolution and the stock market. *American Economic Review, 89*(2), 116–122. DOI: 10.1257/aer.89.2.116

Hobijn, B., & Jovanovic, B. (2001). The information-technology revolution and the stock market: Evidence. *American Economic Review, 91*(5), 1203–1220. https://doi.org/10.1257/aer.91.5.1203

Isenberg, D. J. (2010). How to start an entrepreneurial revolution. *Harvard Business Review, 88*(6), 40–50.

Isenberg, D. (2011). The entrepreneurship ecosystem strategy as a new paradigm for economic policy: Principles for cultivating entrepreneurship. *Presentation at the Institute of International and European Affairs, 1*(781), 1–13.

Jovanovic, B. (1982). Selection and the evolution of industry. *Econometrica, 50*(3), 649–670. https://doi.org/10.2307/1912606

Jovanovic, B. (2001). New technology and the small firm. *Small Business Economics, 16*(1), 53–56. https://doi.org/10.1023/A:1011132809150

Jullien, B. (2012). Two-sided B to B platforms. In *The Oxford Handbook of the Digital Economy*, edited by Martin Peitz and Joel Waldfogel, 161–185. Oxford and New York: Oxford University Press.

Kenney, M., & Zysman, J. (2016). The rise of the platform economy. *Issues in Science and Technology, 32*(3), 61–69.

Khan, L. M. (2017). Amazon's antitrust paradox. *Yale Law Journal, 126*(3), 710–805.

Kollmann, T. (2006). What is e-entrepreneurship? Fundamentals of company founding in the net economy. *International Journal of Technology Management, 33*(4), 322–340.

Kollmann, T., Stöckmann, C., Hensellek, S., & Kensbock, J. (2016). *European startup monitor 2016.* Universität Duisburg-Essen Lehrstuhl für E-Business.

Li, W., Badr, Y., & Biennier, F. (2012). Digital ecosystems: Challenges and prospects. In *Proceedings of the International Conference on Management of Emergent Digital EcoSystems*, pp. 117–122. New York: Machinery.

Malecki, E. J. (2018). Entrepreneurship and entrepreneurial ecosystems. *Geography Compass, 12*(3). https://doi.org/10.1111/gec3.12359

Nambisan, S. (2017). Digital entrepreneurship: Toward a digital technology perspective of entrepreneurship. *Entrepreneurship Theory and Practice, 41*(6), 1029–1055. https://doi.org/10.1111/etap.12254

Naudé, W. (2016). Is European entrepreneurship in crisis? *IZA Working Paper, DP* 9817.

Peitz, M., & Waldfogel, J. (Eds.) (2012). *The Oxford handbook of the digital economy.* Oxford: Oxford University Press.

Rochet, J. C., & Tirole, J. (2003). Platform competition in two-sided markets. *Journal of the European Economic Association, 1*(4), 990–1029. https://doi.org/10.1162/154247603322493212

Rochet, J.-C., & Tirole, J. (2006). Two-sided markets: A progress report. *The RAND Journal of Economics, 37*(3), 645–667. https://doi.org/10.1111/j.1756-2171.2006.tb00036.x

Root, H.L. (2020) *Network origins of the global economy.* Cambridge: Cambridge University Press.

Saadatmand, F., Lindgren, R., & Schultze, U. (2019). Configurations of platform organizations: Implications for complementor engagement. *Research Policy, 48*(8), 103770. https://doi.org/10.1016/j.respol.2019.03.015

Sahut, J.-M., Iandoli, L., & Teulon, F. (2019). The age of digital entrepreneurship. *Small Business Economics*. https://doi.org/10.1007/s11187-019-00260-8

Shannon, C. (1948). A mathematical theory of communication, *Bell Systems Technical Journal, 27*(3), 379–423.

Song, A. K. (2019). The digital entrepreneurial ecosystem: A critique and reconfiguration. *Small Business Economics, 53*(3), 569–590. https://doi.org/10.1007/s11187-019-00232-y

Spigel, B. (2017). The relational organization of entrepreneurial ecosystems. *Entrepreneurship Theory and Practice, 41*(1), 49–72.

Stam, E. (2015). Entrepreneurial ecosystems and regional policy: A sympathetic critique. *European Planning Studies, 23*(9), 1759–1769. https://doi.org/10.1080/09654313.2015.1061484

Sussan, F., & Acs, Z. J. (2017). The digital entrepreneurial ecosystem. *Small Business Economics, 49*(1), 55–73. https://doi.org/10.1007/s11187-017-9867-5

Szerb, L., Lafuente, E., Horváth, K., & Páger, B. (2019). The relevance of quantity and quality entrepreneurship for regional performance: the moderating role of the entrepreneurial ecosystem. *Regional Studies, 53*(9), 1308–1320.

Weill, P., & Woerner, S. L. (2015). Thriving in an increasingly digital ecosystem. *MIT Sloan Management Review, 56*(4), 27.

# THE APPLIED INDICATORS IN THE DIGITAL ENTREPRENEURSHIP INDEX

*Table 5A.1    The applied indicators of DTI sub-index*

| | | |
|---|---|---|
| **DIG_P1_I1** | *Laws relating to ICTs, 1–7 (best)* <br> World Economic Forum, Executive Opinion Survey, 2014 and 2015 editions <br> Digital Openness – Institutions | How developed are your country's laws relating to the use of ICTs (e.g., e-commerce, digital signatures, consumer protection)? [1 = not developed at all; 7 = extremely well developed] |
| **DIG_P1_I2** | *Global Cyberlaw Tracker* <br> UNCTAD, 19/12/2017 <br> Digital Openness – Institutions | It tracks the state of e-commerce legislation in the field of e-transactions, consumer protection, data protection/privacy and cybercrime adoption in the 194 UNCTAD member states. It indicates whether or not a given country has adopted legislation, or has a draft law pending adoption. In some instances where information about a country's legislation adoption was not readily available, 'no data' is indicated. |
| **DIG_P1_I3** | *Percentage of Individuals using the internet* <br> World Telecommunication/ICT Indicators Database, 2018 (2016 data) <br> Digital Openness – Digital technology | Percentage of Individuals using the internet |
| **DIG_P1_I4** | *Percentage of households with internet access at home* <br> World Telecommunication/ICT Indicators Database, 2018 (2017 data) <br> Digital Openness – Digital technology | Percentage of households with internet access at home |
| **DIG_P2_I1** | *Business freedom* <br> Index of Economic Freedom, 2018 (data 2016, 2017) <br> Digital Freedom – Institutions | Business freedom is an overall indicator of the efficiency of government regulation of business. The quantitative score is derived from an array of measurements of the difficulty of starting, operating, and closing a business. |
| **DIG_P2_I2** | *Freedom of the Press* <br> Freedom House, 2017 (data 2016) <br> Digital Freedom – Institutions | Annual report on media independence around the world, assesses the degree of print, broadcast, and digital media freedom in 199 countries and territories |
| | *Freedom in the World* <br> Freedom House, 2018 (data 2017) <br> Digital Freedom – Institutions | Freedom in the World is an annual global report on political rights and civil liberties, composed of numerical ratings and descriptive texts for each country and a select group of territories. The 2018 edition covers developments in 195 countries and 14 territories from January 1, 2017, through December 31, 2017. It uses a three-tiered system consisting of scores, ratings, and status. The complete list of the questions used in the scoring process, and the tables for converting scores to ratings and ratings to status, appear at the end of this chapter. |
| **DIG_P2_I3** | *Internet & telephony competition/ Global Cyberlaw Tracker* <br> ICT Regualtory Tracker, ITU, 2017 <br> Digital Freedom – Digital technology | Competition framework for the ICT sector (level of competition in the main market segments). |

| | | |
|---|---|---|
| **DIG_P2_I4** | ***Generic top-level domains (gTLDs)*** <br> Global Innovation Index, 2017 (data 2016) <br> Digital Freedom – Digital technology | Generic top-level domains (gTLDs) (per thousand population 15–69 years old). |
| | ***Internet domains / 1000 population*** <br> Webhosting, 2015 <br> Digital Freedom – Digital technology | Number of active internet domain registrations per 1000 number of population. |
| **DIG_P3_I1** | ***Software piracy rate, % software installed*** <br> WEF Network Readiness Index, 2013 data <br> Digital Protection – Digital technology | Unlicensed software units as a percentage of total software units installed. This measure covers piracy of all packaged software that runs on personal computers (PCs), including desktops, laptops, and ultra-portables, including netbooks. This includes operating systems; systems software such as databases and security packages; business applications; and consumer applications such as games, personal finance, and reference software. The study does not include software that runs on servers or mainframes, or software loaded onto tablets or smartphones. |
| **DIG_P3_I2** | ***Secure internet servers/million pop.*** <br> WEF Network Readiness Index 2016 report (2014 data) <br> Digital Protection – Digital technology | Secure internet servers per million population. |
| **DIG_P3_I3** | ***Corruption Perception Index*** <br> Corruption Perception Index (CPI), 2017 (data 2016-2018) <br> Digital Protection – Institutions | The index, which ranks 180 countries and territories by their perceived levels of public sector corruption according to experts and businesspeople, uses a scale of 0 to 100, where 0 is highly corrupt and 100 is very clean. |
| **DIG_P3_I4** | ***Global Cybersecurity Index legal subindex (GCI), 2017*** <br> Digital Protection – Institutions | The GCI revolves around the ITU Global Cybersecurity Agenda (GCA) and its five pillars (legal, technical, organizational, capacity building and cooperation). For each of these pillars, questions were developed to assess commitment. Legal component is based on the existence of legal institutions and frameworks dealing with cybersecurity and cybercrime. |

*Table 5A.2    The applied indicators of the DUC sub-index*

| | | |
|---|---|---|
| **DUC_P1_I1** | ***Digital skills among population*** <br> Global Competitiveness Index, 2017, WEF <br> Digital literacy – Users | Executive Opinion Survey: "In your country, to what extent does the active population possess sufficient digital skills (e.g., computer skills, basic coding, digital reading)? (1= not at all, 7= to a great extent)" |
| **DUC_P1_I2** | ***Number of searches by users in a country*** <br> The Digital Country Index, 2017 <br> Digital literacy – Users | First presented in 2015, the Digital Country Index tracks the number of searches performed by all worldwide citizens toward any given country, in connection with six topic areas: tourism, investment, exports, talent and national prominence. |
| **DUC_P1_I3** | ***Quality of the education system, 1–7 (best)*** <br> Global Competitiveness Index, 2017–2018 (data 2015–2016 average) <br> Digital Literacy – Institutions | In your country, how well does the education system meet the needs of a competitive economy? [1 = not well at all; 7 = extremely well] |
| **DUC_P1_I4** | ***Internet access in schools, 1–7 (best)*** <br> Global Competitiveness Index, 2017–2018 (data 2015–2016 average) <br> Digital Literacy – Institutions | In your country, to what extent is the internet used in schools for learning purposes? [1 = not at all; 7 = to a great extent] |

| DUC_P2_I1 | *Fixed broadband internet subscriptions/100 pop.* Global Competitiveness Index, 2017–2018 (2016 or most recent data) Digital access – Users | Fixed-broadband internet subscriptions per 100 population |
| | *Int'l internet bandwidth, kb/s per user* Global Competitiveness Index, 2017–2018 (2016 data) Digital access – Users | International internet bandwidth (kb/s) per internet user |
| DUC_P2_I2 | *Percentage of households equipped with a personal computer* World Telecommunication/ICT Indicators Database, 4 January 2018 (2017 data) Digital access – Users | Percentage of households equipped with a personal computer |
| | **Percentage of individuals using a computer** World Telecommunication/ICT Indicators Database, 4 January 2018 (2017 data) Digital access – Users | Percentage of individuals using a computer |
| DUC_P2_I3 | *Global Cybersecurity Index technical sub-index* ITU, 2017 Digital access – Institution | Technical: Measured based on the existence of technical institutions and frameworks dealing with cybersecurity. |
| DUC_P2_I4 | *Global Cybersecurity Index technical sub-index* ITU, 2017 Digital access – Institution | Organizational: Measured based on the existence of policy coordination institutions and strategies for cybersecurity development at the national level. |
| DUC_P3_I1 | *Net infection ratio* Securelist statistics, Kaspersky, Download: 17/03/2018 (monthly data) Digital Rights – Users | The map shows the percentages of users on whose devices Kaspersky Lab products intercepted local infections in the last 24 hours. KL products' users are always protected from all – even the very latest – threats. |
| DUC_P3_I2 | *Internet censorship and surveillance* Wikipedia, 2018 Digital Rights – Users | Detailed country by country information on internet censorship and surveillance is provided in the Freedom on the Net reports from Freedom House, by the OpenNet Initiative, by Reporters Without Borders, and in the Country Reports on Human Rights Practices from the U.S. State Department Bureau of Democracy, Human Rights, and Labor. The ratings produced by several of these organizations are summarized below as well as in the Censorship by country article. Four category rating: 1: pervasive; 2: selective; 3: substantial; 4: little or none. |

| DUC_P3_I3 | *Personal rights* | Personal Rights are a component in the Opportunity Dimension of the Social |
|---|---|---|
| | The Global Talent Competitiveness | Progress Index. This component is based on five variables: Political rights, |
| | Report, 2018 (2016 data) | Freedom of speech, Freedom of assembly/association, Freedom of movement, |
| | Digital Rights – Institution | and Private property rights. |
| | *Fundamental rights* | Equal treatment and absence of discrimination |
| | Rule of Law Index, World Justice | 4.2 The right to life and security of the person is effectively guaranteed |
| | Project, 2017–2018 | 4.3 Due process of law and rights of the accused |
| | Digital Rights – Institution | 4.4 Freedom of opinion and expression is effectively guaranteed |
| | | 4.5 Freedom of belief and religion is effectively guaranteed |
| | | 4.6 Freedom from arbitrary interference with privacy is effectively guaranteed |
| | | 4.7 Freedom of assembly and association is effectively guaranteed |
| | | 4.8 Fundamental labor rights are effectively guaranteed. |
| | *Property rights* | The average of the two sub-indexes as Physical property rights and |
| | International Property Rights Index, | Intellectual property rights from International Property Rights Index. |
| | Property Rights Alliance, 2013 | |
| | Digital Rights – Institution | |

*Table 5A.3*    *The applied indicators of the DMSP sub-index*

| DMSP_P1_I1 | *Use of virtual social networks, 1–7 (best)* | In your country, how widely are virtual social networks used (e.g., |
|---|---|---|
| | WEF Network Readiness Index, 2016 | Facebook, Twitter, LinkedIn)? [1 = not at all used; 7 = used extensively] |
| | (2014–2015 average data) | |
| | Networking – Users | |
| DMSP_P1_I2 | *Social media penetration* | Active social media users, penetration (%). |
| | 2017 DIGITAL YEARBOOK | |
| | INTERNET, SOCIAL MEDIA, AND | |
| | MOBILE DATA FOR | |
| | Networking – Users | |
| DMSP_P1_I3 | *Use of virtual professional networks* | LinkedIn users refers to the number of registered LinkedIn accounts per |
| | The Global Talent Competitiveness | 1,000 labor force (15–64 years old). |
| | Report, 2018 (2015 data) | |
| | Networking – Users | |
| DMSP_P1_I4 | *ICT use for business-to-business* | In your country, to what extent do businesses use ICTs for transactions |
| | *transactions, 1–7 (best)* | with other businesses? [1 = not at all; 7 = to a great extent] |
| | WEF Network Readiness Index, 2016 | |
| | (2014–2015 average data) | |
| | Networking – Agent | |
| DMSP_P1_I5 | *Business-to-consumer internet use, 1–7* | In your country, to what extent do businesses use the internet for selling |
| | *(best)* | their goods and services to consumers? [1 = not at all; 7 = to a great |
| | WEF Network Readiness Index, 2016 | extent] |
| | (2014–2015 average data) | |
| | Networking – Agent | |

**DMSP_P2_I1**  *Wikipedia yearly edits*
Global Innovation Index, 2017 (2016 data)
Matchmaking – Users

Wikipedia yearly edits by country (per million population 15–69 years old) | 2014
Data extracted from Wikimedia Foundation's internal data sources. For every country with more than 100,000 edit counts in 2016, the data from 2016 are used. For all other countries, the data from 2014 are utilized. The data excludes bot contributions to the extent that is identifiable in the data sources. Data are reported per million population 15–69 years old.

**DMSP_P2_I2**  *Video uploads on YouTube*
Global Innovation Index, 2017 (2016 data)
Matchmaking – Users

Number of video uploads on YouTube (scaled by population 15–69 years old) | 2015
Total number of video uploads on YouTube, per country, scaled by population
15–69 years old. The raw data are survey based: the country of affiliation is chosen by each user on the basis of a multi-choice selection. This metric counts all video upload events by users. For confidentiality reasons, only normalized values are reported; while relative positions are preserved, magnitudes are not.

**DMSP_P2_I3**  *Number of professional developers / population*
*Developer Survey Results, 2017 (2016 data)*
Matchmaking – Agent

Ratio of professional developers.

**DMSP_P3_I1**  *Credit card (% age 15+)*
World Bank Global Financial Inclusion, 2017
Financial facilitation – Users

Denotes the percentage of respondents who report having a credit card (% age 15+) [ts: data are available for multiple waves].

*Debit card (% age 15+)*
World Bank Global Financial Inclusion, 2017
Financial facilitation – Users

Denotes the percentage of respondents who report having a debit card (% age 15+) [ts: data are available for multiple waves].

**DMSP_P3_I2**  *Used the internet to pay bills or to buy something online in the past year (% age 15+)*
World Bank Global Financial Inclusion, 2017
Financial facilitation – Users

Denotes the percentage of respondents who report paying bills or making purchases online using the internet in the past 12 months (% age 15+) [w2: data are available for wave 2].

**DMSP_P3_I3**  *Used a mobile phone or the internet to access a financial institution account in the past year (% age 15+)*
World Bank Global Financial Inclusion, 2017
Financial facilitation – Users

Denotes the percentage of respondents who used a mobile phone or the internet to access a financial institution account in the past year (% with an account, age 15+) [w2: data are available for wave 2].

**DMSP_P3_I4**  *Made or received digital payments in the past year (% age 15+)*
Financial facilitation – Users

Denotes the percentage of respondents who report making or receiving digital payments in the past 12 months (% age 15+).

**DMSP_P3_I5**  *Depth of Capital Market Sub-Index Score (US 2016=100)*
World Bank Global Financial Inclusion, 2017 (data 2016)
Financial facilitation – Agent

The Depth of Capital Market is one of the six sub-indices of the Venture Capital and Private Equity index. This variable is a complex measure of the size and liquidity of the stock market, level of IPO, M&A and debt and credit market activity.

| DMSP_P3_I6 | *Fintech business* | The number of financial technology businesses standardized by the |
|---|---|---|
| | dealroom, 26/03/2018 | number of population 2018, own calculation. |
| | Financial facilitation – Agent | |
| DMSP_P3_I7 | *Venture capital availability* | Answers to the question: In your country, how easy is it for |
| | Global Competitiveness Index, | entrepreneurs with innovative but risky projects to find venture capital? |
| | 2017–2018 (2016–2017 average data) | [1 = extremely difficult; 7 = extremely easy] (World Economic Forum |
| | Financial facilitation – Agent | dataset). |

*Table 5A.4*    *The applied indicators of DTE sub-index*

| DTE_P1_I1 | *Quality of electricity supply, 1–7 (best)* | In your country, how reliable is the electricity supply (lack of |
|---|---|---|
| | Global Competitiveness Index, 2017.2018 | interruptions and lack of voltage fluctuations)? [1 = extremely |
| | (2016–2017 average data) | unreliable; 7 = extremely reliable] |
| | Digital adoption – Digital technology | |
| | *Electricity production, kWh/capita* | Electricity production (kWh) per capita. |
| | WEF Network Readiness Index, 2016 | |
| | (2013 data) | |
| | Digital adoption – Digital technology | |
| DTE_P1_I2 | *Fixed telephone lines/100 pop.* | Number of fixed-telephone lines per 100 population. |
| | Global Competitiveness Index, 2017.2018 | |
| | (2016-2017 average data) | |
| | Digital adoption – Digital technology | |
| DTE_P1_I3 | *Mobile telephone subscriptions/100 pop.* * | Number of mobile-cellular telephone subscriptions per 100 population. |
| | Global Competitiveness Index, 2017.2018 | |
| | (2016–2017 average data) | |
| | Digital adoption – Digital technology | |
| DTE_P1_I4 | *Mobile network coverage, % pop.* | Percentage of total population covered by a mobile network signal. |
| | WEF Network Readiness Index, 2016 | |
| | (2014 data) | |
| | Digital adoption – Digital technology | |
| DTE_P1_I5 | *Computer software spending* | Total computer software spending (% of GDP). |
| | Global Innovation Index, 2018 (2016 data) | |
| | Digital adoption – Agent | |
| DTE_P1_I6 | *Skills of workforce* | Skills, a pillar of GCI, consist of two parts, skills of current workforce |
| | Global Innovation Index, 2018 | and skills of future workforce. |
| | Digital adoption – Agent | |
| DTE_P2_I1 | *Data centers* | Combined data centers number and density based on population. |
| | Data Centers Catalog, 2019 | |
| | Technology absorption – Digital | |
| | technology | |
| DTE_P2_I2 | *Availability of latest technologies, 1–7 (best)* | In your country, to what extent are the latest technologies available? [1 = |
| | Global Competitiveness Index, 2017–2018 | not at all; 7 = to a great extent] |
| | (2016–2017 average data) | |
| | Digital technology absorption – | |
| | Technology absorption – Digital | |
| | technology | |

**DTE_P2_I3**  *Knowledge absorption (sub-index in GII)*   It reveals how good economies are at absorbing knowledge. A complex
Global Innovation Index, 2017 (data 2016)   variable from GII consisting of five indicators as: Intellectual property
Digital technology absorption –   payments, High-tech.
Technology absorption – Agent

**DTE_P2_I4**  *Impact of ICTs on business models, 1–7*   Average answer to the question: In your country, to what extent do ICTs
*(best)*   enable new business models? [1=not at all; 7=to a great extent]
Global Innovation Index, 2017 (2016 data)
Technology absorption – Agent

*Impact of ICTs on new organizational*   Average answer to the question: In your country, to what extent do ICTs
*models, 1–7 (best)*   enable new organizational models?
Global Innovation Index, 2017 (2016 data)
Technology absorption – Agent

**DTE_P3_I1**  *Knowledge and technology outputs (GII)*   A sub-index of GII consisting of three part, knowledge creation,
The Global Innovation Index, 2017 (2016   knowledge impact and knowledge diffusion.
data)
Technology transfer – Digital technology

**DTE_P1_I2**  *Capacity for innovation*   In your country, to what extent do companies have the capacity to
Global Competitiveness Index, 2007–2017   innovate? [1 = not at all; 7 = to a great extent]
Technology transfer – Digital technology

**DTE_P2_I3**  *High level skills ( GTCI)*   The average of six indicators as Workforce with tertiary education,
The Global Talent Competitiveness Report,   Population with tertiary education, Professionals, Researchers, Senior
2018 (data 2015)   officials and managers, Availability of scientists and engineers.
Technology transfer – Agent

**DTE_P2_I4**  *Startups*   Number of startups, a normalized average of the population standardized
Startup ranking, 2018   startups and the log of startups in the country.
Technology transfer – Agent

# 6. The regional impacts of digitalization of work on entrepreneurship in the United States

*Frank M. Fossen, Trevor McLemore and Alina Sorgner*

## 1. INTRODUCTION

Research on digital entrepreneurial ecosystems has emerged with an aim to enhance our understanding of entrepreneurship in the digital economy (Sussan and Acs, 2017; Elia et al., 2020; Du et al., 2018; Acs et al., Chapter 5 in this handbook). A common aspect of studies on digital entrepreneurial ecosystems is that they emphasize the importance of the regional environment for entrepreneurship, even though digital technologies are global. For instance, Sussan and Acs (2017) discuss digital ecosystem elements such as digital infrastructure, which includes digital technologies and users with access to these technologies. According to these authors, digital ecosystem elements play an important role as determinants of productive entrepreneurship in a region. Thus, digital ecosystem elements add to traditional elements of entrepreneurial ecosystems, such as institutions and entrepreneurial agents (Spigel, 2015).

This chapter adds to the literature on digital entrepreneurial ecosystems by showing for the case of the United States that the occupational structure of regional labor markets constitutes, together with the exposure of occupations to new digital technologies such as artificial intelligence (AI), an important element of a regional digital entrepreneurial ecosystem. As the world of labor is becoming increasingly digitalized, many occupations are facing significant changes. Potential effects of new digital technologies on labor markets have received a lot of attention among academics, policymakers, and the general public. The debate tends to focus on the perceived threat that large numbers of workers are at risk of losing their jobs due to automation, although digitalization may also benefit employees in certain occupations by making them more productive (Fossen and Sorgner, 2019, 2022). Entrepreneurship scholars have emphasized the role of digital technologies as accelerators of entrepreneurship (Nambisan, 2017), although digitalization can have adverse impacts on entrepreneurs that can be entrepreneurship inhibiting as well (Fossen and Sorgner, 2021).

While digital technologies are a global phenomenon, they can be applied to local labor markets because the occupational structure is very specific to the location and varies significantly across regions. This is, for instance, due to differences in the industrial composition of the regional economies and the availability of human capital in a region. Moreover, digital technologies may affect labor markets in different ways. Fossen and Sorgner (2021), who investigate the effects of digitalization of occupations on individual entry into entrepreneurship in the United States, distinguish between transformative and destructive new digital technologies according to their impacts on occupations, which can be labor-augmenting or labor-replacing. Fossen and Sorgner (2022) provide empirical evidence that workers in occupations facing destructive digitalization have a high risk of being displaced by digital machines. The risk of job loss due to destructive effects of digitalization leads to an increase in the likelihood of entrepreneurship with unincorporated businesses (Fossen and Sorgner, 2021), which are more often started out of unemployment due to necessity motives (Fossen, 2021) and are less likely to be innovative than incorporated businesses (Levine and Rubinstein, 2017). In contrast, transformative digitalization augments working processes through new digital technologies that lead to a stronger interaction between humans and digital machines.[1] Fossen and Sorgner (2021) demonstrate that transformative effects of digitalization likely lead to the emergence of new entrepreneurial opportunities in occupations, which is reflected in a higher likelihood of entrepreneurship with incorporated businesses. This type of entrepreneurship is associated with innovative and opportunity-driven entrepreneurship, as well as digital entrepreneurship.

Therefore, when translating these insights to the level of regions, one can expect the effects of new digital technologies on regional labor markets to depend strongly on the occupational structure of regional labor markets. The exposure of regional labor markets to different types of digital technologies – transformative and destructive – is expected to affect the level and the type of entrepreneurship (e.g., opportunity- vs. necessity-driven, and digital entrepreneurship) that prevails in a region.

This chapter's contributions are as follows. First, we document the extent to which regional labor markets in the United States are affected by transformative and destructive digitalization, using four measures of different types of new digital technologies' impacts on occupations. Second, we provide rankings of states and heat maps of regions defined at the level of states and, where possible, counties, to illustrate the regional impact of digitalization on more ambitious versus less ambitious types of entrepreneurship, which we operationalize with incorporated and unincorporated self-employment following the literature (Levine and Rubinstein, 2017).[2]

The results clearly demonstrate that impacts of digitalization on regional labor markets is an important element of regional digital entrepreneurial ecosystems. The results reveal that entrepreneurs in urban areas tend to be more affected by advances in AI than entrepreneurs in rural areas, although there are many exceptions to this rule. This AI occupational impact is likely to transform occupations and to stimulate more ambitious, opportunity-driven entrepreneurship. In turn, regions will likely see higher levels of less ambitious or even necessity-driven entrepreneurship if their labor markets are impacted by destructive digitalization that displaces human workers. In addition to enhancing our understanding of regional digital entrepreneurial ecosystems, the results of this chapter are useful for policymakers and practitioners in order to prepare for the challenges and opportunities that entrepreneurs are beginning to encounter in different regions due to digitalization.

The chapter proceeds as follows. Section 2 describes the data and methods used in this chapter. Section 3 presents the results of the regional analysis. We provide rankings and heat maps of US states and regions showing the impacts of different digital technologies on regional labor markets and entrepreneurship with incorporated and unincorporated businesses. Section 4 concludes the analysis.

## 2.     DATA

### 2.1     Measures of Digitalization of Occupations

Following Fossen and Sorgner (2021, 2022), we use four measures of different new digital technologies' impacts on occupations. The first measure is provided by Frey and Osborne

(2017). These authors develop a measure of the computerization probability of occupations, which captures the predicted risk of displacement of human workers by computer-controlled equipment. More precisely, Frey and Osborne (2017) estimate computerization probabilities for the next 10–20 years (as viewed from the publication year of the working paper in 2013) based on expert judgments and selected characteristics of occupations. The authors first asked an expert group of machine learning or robotics researchers to identify occupations that would be fully automatable, or not at all, in the near future. The experts classified 37 occupations with very high and 34 with very low susceptibility to automation. Then Frey and Osborne (2017) identified nine occupational skills that arguably represent automation bottlenecks in the O*NET database of occupations compiled by the US Department of Labor.[3] The authors combined the expert judgments with these occupational skills to construct a training dataset. This training dataset indicates how the experts' susceptibility to automation classification of the 71 categorized occupations relates to the levels of the bottleneck abilities required for these occupations. Based on these training data, the authors then used machine learning techniques to predict computerization probabilities for 702 occupations using the O*NET bottleneck skills. Since this measure was constructed to indicate displacement risks of workers due to potential future digital automation, it is straightforward to use this measure as an indicator of destructive entrepreneurship. Consistent with this, Fossen and Sorgner (2022) confirm that a higher computerization probability in an occupation increases the risk of unemployment and is associated with declining wage growth.

The second measure we use is the AI Occupational Impact (AIOI) score estimated by Felten et al. (2018, 2019). In contrast to the other three measures we use, the approach of these authors does not rely on experts' predictions of the future. Instead, the authors estimate progress slopes for nine categories of AI[4] based on past advances of these technologies (in 2010–2015) as reported by the AI Progress Measurement dataset provided by the Electronic Frontier Foundation. Then the authors link the advances in the AI categories to 52 distinct abilities that the O*NET database uses to describe job requirements. This allows the authors to estimate progress slopes in AI performance at the level of occupations. Using occupation-level data, Felten et al. (2019) find that higher AIOI scores are associated with positive growth in occupational employment and wages in high-income occupations, and Fossen and Sorgner (2022) show that AIOI increases job stability and wages based on individual-level data. Thus, AIOI can be characterized as a measure of transformative digitalization.

We adopt the third and fourth measures from Brynjolfsson et al. (2018), who study how machine learning techniques can be used to automate job tasks.[5] Specifically, our third measure of the impact of digitalization on occupations is the suitability for machine learning (SML) as estimated by Brynjolfsson and Mitchell (2017) and Brynjolfsson et al. (2018). The authors first assess the suitability of 2,069 narrowly defined work activities for machine learning via surveys conducted on the crowdsourcing platform CrowdFlower. To ensure the quality of the data, only respondents with industry-specific experience and understanding of a specific task were approached. The measure of SML was then aggregated to the level of tasks and then to the level of occupations. Since the assessment of the work activities for the suitability for machine learning focused on automation, this measure of SML captures potentially destructive digital technologies. Brynjolfsson et al. (2018) also calculate the standard deviation of the SML scores of the tasks within each occupation (sdSML). This is our fourth measure of the exposure of occupations to digitalization. Brynjolfsson et al. (2018) argue that occupations that include both, tasks that can be automated and tasks that cannot be automated, are likely to be reorganized rather than lost for human workers. Thus, the sdSML measure is likely to reflect transformative digitalization.[6]

The four measures capture different types of new digital technologies that are expected to have different impacts on occupations. Indeed, the computerization probability, one of our two measures of destructive digitalization, is strongly negatively correlated with AIOI, one of our two measures of transformative digitalization. The scatter plot in Figure 6.1 shows the relationship between the computerization risk and the AIOI scores. Each bubble represents one occupation, with the size of the bubble reflecting total employment in this occupation in the United States. The largest occupations are labeled and listed in Table 6.1.[7]

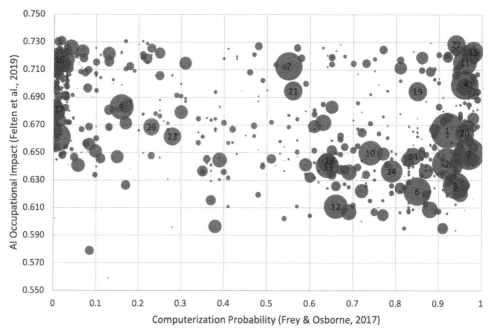

*Notes:*    Each bubble represents an occupation. The size of the bubbles reflects total US employment in the occupations (Bureau of Labor Statistics, 2018). The largest 25 occupations are labeled in Table 6.1.
*Source:*    Fossen and Sorgner (2019), updated by using the Occupational Impact scores from Felten et al. (2019).

*Figure 6.1    Computerization probabilities of occupations and AI Occupational Impact scores*

## 2.2    Individual-level Data from the American Community Survey

To create rankings and heat maps of states and regions within the US, we use the American Community Survey (ACS) from 2017. The ACS is a representative survey of households in the United States provided by the Census Bureau. We use IPUMS-USA (Ruggles et al., 2020) for access to the ACS individual-level data. The ACS is suitable for fine-grained regional analysis within the United States due to a very large sample size and because the survey is sent to random addresses, not individuals, to ensure representativeness at a more narrowly defined level of regions.

*Table 6.1*    *Impact of digitalization on the largest occupations*

| No. in Figure 6.1 | SOC 2010 Code | Occupation | Employment in the US | Comput. prob. | AI Occ. Impact | Mean SML | Std. dev. SML |
|---|---|---|---|---|---|---|---|
| 1 | 41-2031 | Retail Salespersons | 4,448,120 | 0.92 | 0.666 | 3.574 | 0.486 |
| 2 | 35-3021 | Combined Food Preparation & Serving Workers, Including Fast Food | 3,676,180 | 0.92 | 0.642 | 3.451 | 0.593 |
| 3 | 41-2011 | Cashiers | 3,635,550 | 0.97 | 0.649 | 3.670 | 0.465 |
| 4 | 43-9061 | Office Clerks, General | 2,972,930 | 0.96 | 0.699 | 3.613 | 0.574 |
| 5 | 29-1141 | Registered Nurses | 2,951,960 | 0.009 | 0.661 | 3.428 | 0.556 |
| 6 | 53-7062 | Laborers & Freight, Stock, & Material Movers, Hand | 2,893,180 | 0.85 | 0.622 | 3.314 | 0.627 |
| 7 | 43-4051 | Customer Service Representatives | 2,871,400 | 0.55 | 0.713 | 3.597 | 0.558 |
| 8 | 35-3031 | Waiters & Waitresses | 2,582,410 | 0.94 | 0.626 | 3.447 | 0.703 |
| 9 | 11-1021 | General & Operations Managers | 2,289,770 | 0.16 | 0.683 | 3.473 | 0.508 |
| 10 | 39-9021 | Personal Care Aides | 2,211,950 | 0.74 | 0.650 | 3.483 | 0.510 |
| 11 | 43-6014 | Secretaries & Administrative Assistants, Except Legal, Medical, & Executive | 2,165,310 | 0.96 | 0.715 | 3.659 | 0.613 |
| 12 | 37-2011 | Janitors & Cleaners, Except Maids & Housekeeping Cleaners | 2,156,270 | 0.66 | 0.611 | 3.376 | 0.654 |
| 13 | 43-5081 | Stock Clerks & Order Fillers | 2,056,030 | 0.64 | 0.640 | n.a. | n.a. |
| 14 | 53-3032 | Heavy & Tractor-Trailer Truck Drivers | 1,800,330 | 0.79 | 0.636 | 3.405 | 0.676 |
| 15 | 43-3031 | Bookkeeping, Accounting, & Auditing Clerks | 1,530,430 | 0.98 | 0.723 | 3.723 | 0.605 |
| 16 | 43-1011 | First-Line Supervisors of Office & Administrative Support Workers | 1,477,560 | 0.014 | 0.717 | 3.576 | 0.631 |
| 17 | 25-2021 | Elementary School Teachers, Except Special Education | 1,410,970 | 0.0044 | 0.681 | 3.488 | 0.606 |
| 18 | 49-9071 | Maintenance & Repair Workers, General | 1,384,240 | 0.64 | 0.643 | 3.468 | 0.509 |
| 19 | 41-4012 | Sales Representatives, Wholesale & Manufacturing, Except Techn. & Sci. Products | 1,350,180 | 0.85 | 0.694 | 3.621 | 0.469 |
| 20 | 35-2014 | Cooks, Restaurant | 1,340,810 | 0.96 | 0.664 | 3.353 | 0.620 |
| 21 | 25-9041 | Teacher Assistants | 1,331,560 | 0.56 | 0.695 | 3.448 | 0.710 |
| 22 | 13-2011 | Accountants & Auditors | 1,259,930 | 0.94 | 0.728 | n.a. | n.a. |
| 23 | 41-1011 | First-Line Supervisors of Retail Sales Workers | 1,181,530 | 0.28 | 0.662 | 3.410 | 0.537 |
| 24 | 33-9032 | Security Guards | 1,114,380 | 0.84 | 0.647 | 3.565 | 0.582 |
| 25 | 13-1199 | Business Operations Specialists, All Oth. | 1,060,580 | 0.23 | 0.669 | n.a. | n.a. |
| Average over all occupations weighted by employment | | | | 0.573 | 0.670 | 3.487 | 0.589 |

*Notes:*    The table lists the 25 occupations that have the largest employment numbers in the United States (Bureau of Labor Statistics, 2018). For reference, the last row shows the average over all 750 occupations, weighted by US employment in the occupation. The computerization probabilities are adopted from Frey and Osborne (2017), the AI Occupational Impact scores from Felten et al. (2019), and the mean suitability for machine learning of tasks in an occupation (SML) and its within–occupation standard deviation (sdSML) from Brynjolfsson et al. (2018). For three occupations in the table, SML and sdSML are not available.

*Source:*    Similar to Fossen and Sorgner (2019).

For our regional analysis, we use information on the location of residence of each respondent. The ACS provides the county and state of residence of each respondent. For data protection reasons, counties with small population numbers are unidentified in the ACS to prevent potential re-identification of individual respondents. This is regularly the case in rural counties. While there are more than 3,000 counties in the United States, the ACS only identifies 589 counties, mostly intersecting metropolitan areas. Most observations that are missing county information still list the state. In order to visualize information for less populated counties on maps, we average the unreported counties within each state. Thus, this average usually combines the rural counties within each state. For instance, in Missouri, we have county level data on Boone, Franklin, Greene, Jackson, Jefferson, St. Charles, St. Louis, and St. Louis City, so we display results for these counties separately. The over 100 remaining counties in Missouri are averaged.

Table 6.2 provides descriptive statistics for the samples of paid employees and entrepreneurs with unincorporated and incorporated businesses.[8] Among the entrepreneurs, we distinguish between rural and urban areas based on whether the entrepreneur lives in a metropolitan area or not. The majority of the entrepreneurs, in particular of those with incorporated businesses, are male; this gender gap is even larger in rural than in urban areas. Entrepreneurs are also older on average than paid employees. Entrepreneurs in urban areas have a college degree more often than entrepreneurs in rural areas, and those with incorporated businesses more often than those with unincorporated businesses. Black Americans are underrepresented among entrepreneurs: Their share among both types of entrepreneurs is lower than their share among paid employees.

The lower panel of the table shows the distribution of occupation groups among each sample. Employment in management occupations is reported by 24–27% of the entrepreneurs with incorporated businesses, in comparison to 10% among the paid employees. Entrepreneurs with unincorporated businesses often work in personal care and service occupations or construction trades, whereas entrepreneurs with incorporated businesses are disproportionately often professionals working as financial specialists, in legal occupations, or as healthcare practitioners.

The exposure of entrepreneurs to different digital technologies through their occupations, as captured by the four digitalization measures, differs from the exposure of paid employees, and also differs between the two types of entrepreneurs. Entrepreneurs are less exposed to computerization risk of their occupations in comparison to paid employees, especially entrepreneurs with incorporated businesses. Entrepreneurs with incorporated businesses benefit more, but those with unincorporated businesses less from AI occupational impact than employees. The occupations of entrepreneurs are less suitable for machine learning than the occupations of employees. At the same time, the variation of the suitability of tasks for machine learning within an occupation is larger for entrepreneurs than for paid employees, except for entrepreneurs with incorporated businesses in rural areas. This indicates that the occupations of entrepreneurs will more often be transformed rather than displaced by machines in comparison to employees.

*Table 6.2*   *Mean characteristics by type of worker*

| | All Areas | Urban Areas | | Rural Areas | |
|---|---|---|---|---|---|
| | Paid employees | Entrepreneurs, unincorporated | Entrepreneurs, incorporated | Entrepreneurs, unincorporated | Entrepreneurs, incorporated |
| *Digitalization of occupations:* | | | | | |
| Computerization Risk | 0.4992 | 0.4750 | 0.3828 | 0.4637 | 0.4252 |
| AI Occupational Impact | 0.6751 | 0.6696 | 0.6872 | 0.6610 | 0.6780 |
| Suitability for machine learning (SML) | 3.4843 | 3.4501 | 3.4601 | 3.4424 | 3.4618 |
| Within-occ. std. dev. of SML (sdSML) | 0.5927 | 0.5942 | 0.5931 | 0.5962 | 0.5916 |
| *Socio-demographic variables:* | | | | | |
| Male | 0.5086 | 0.5747 | 0.6835 | 0.6570 | 0.7128 |
| Age | 42.6 | 50.1 | 51.5 | 51.2 | 52.6 |
| Married | 0.5491 | 0.6270 | 0.7538 | 0.6993 | 0.7946 |
| Less than high school | 0.0802 | 0.1150 | 0.0593 | 0.1041 | 0.0592 |
| High school degree | 0.2375 | 0.2258 | 0.1729 | 0.3548 | 0.2994 |
| Some college | 0.3199 | 0.2818 | 0.2614 | 0.3238 | 0.3269 |
| College degree | 0.3625 | 0.3773 | 0.5064 | 0.2173 | 0.3146 |
| White | 0.7735 | 0.7956 | 0.8300 | 0.9406 | 0.9533 |
| Black | 0.0932 | 0.0623 | 0.0433 | 0.0191 | 0.0123 |
| Asian | 0.0608 | 0.0638 | 0.0810 | 0.0071 | 0.0086 |
| Other race | 0.0725 | 0.0784 | 0.0458 | 0.0332 | 0.0258 |
| Hispanic | 0.1414 | 0.1720 | 0.1068 | 0.0401 | 0.0221 |
| *Major occupation groups:* | | | | | |
| Management Occ. | 0.1035 | 0.1026 | 0.2413 | 0.2228 | 0.2708 |
| Business Operations Specialists | 0.0279 | 0.0314 | 0.0414 | 0.0123 | 0.0180 |
| Financial Specialists | 0.0231 | 0.0269 | 0.0322 | 0.0135 | 0.0248 |
| Computer & Mathematical Occ. | 0.0331 | 0.0143 | 0.0173 | 0.0074 | 0.0105 |
| Architecture & Engineering Occ. | 0.0206 | 0.0095 | 0.0148 | 0.0051 | 0.0096 |
| Life, Physical, & Social Science Occ. | 0.0097 | 0.0110 | 0.0079 | 0.0053 | 0.0039 |
| Community & Social Service Occ. | 0.0195 | 0.0115 | 0.0087 | 0.0093 | 0.0080 |
| Legal Occ. | 0.0103 | 0.0267 | 0.0391 | 0.0111 | 0.0180 |
| Education, Training, & Library Occ. | 0.0708 | 0.0279 | 0.0110 | 0.0101 | 0.0061 |
| Arts, Design, Entert., Sports, & Media Occ. | 0.0163 | 0.0853 | 0.0481 | 0.0401 | 0.0219 |

| | All Areas | Urban Areas | | Rural Areas | |
|---|---|---|---|---|---|
| | Paid employees | Entrepreneurs, unincorporated | Entrepreneurs, incorporated | Entrepreneurs, unincorporated | Entrepreneurs, incorporated |
| Healthcare Practitioners & Technical Occ. | 0.0654 | 0.0313 | 0.0692 | 0.0195 | 0.0506 |
| Healthcare Support Occ. | 0.0222 | 0.0138 | 0.0062 | 0.0131 | 0.0070 |
| Protective Service Occ. | 0.0231 | 0.0018 | 0.0017 | 0.0012 | 0.0010 |
| Food Preparation & Serving Related Occ. | 0.0551 | 0.0093 | 0.0139 | 0.0103 | 0.0145 |
| Building, Grounds Cleaning & Maint. Occ. | 0.0318 | 0.0893 | 0.0337 | 0.0769 | 0.0287 |
| Personal Care & Service Occ. | 0.0300 | 0.1197 | 0.0432 | 0.1064 | 0.0348 |
| Sales & Related Occ. | 0.0949 | 0.1261 | 0.1632 | 0.0915 | 0.1562 |
| Office & Admin. Support Occ. | 0.1386 | 0.0354 | 0.0525 | 0.0314 | 0.0728 |
| Farming, Fishing, & Forestry Occ. | 0.0070 | 0.0046 | 0.0028 | 0.0305 | 0.0238 |
| Construction Trades | 0.0392 | 0.1098 | 0.0698 | 0.1443 | 0.0881 |
| Extraction Workers | 0.0013 | 0.0003 | 0.0002 | 0.0011 | 0.0014 |
| Installation, Mainten., & Repair Workers | 0.0305 | 0.0319 | 0.0242 | 0.0421 | 0.0369 |
| Production Occ. | 0.0599 | 0.0248 | 0.0197 | 0.0379 | 0.0305 |
| Transportation & Material Moving Occ. | 0.0622 | 0.0548 | 0.0378 | 0.0566 | 0.0623 |
| Observations | 1,336,063 | 68,240 | 46,935 | 11,049 | 5121 |

*Notes:*    The table shows mean characteristics for paid employees and entrepreneurs with unincorporated and incorporated businesses. Urban denotes metropolitan areas and rural denotes non-metropolitan areas.
*Source:*    Authors' calculations based on the 2017 ACS.

## 3.  COMPARISON OF REGIONS

### 3.1  Ranking of States with Respect to the Digitalization Impacts

Table 6.3 provides the average scores of the four digitalization measures for the 50 states and Washington, DC, for the full sample. The average values are calculated over individual observations in the states in the representative ACS. The digitalization measures capture the impacts of digitalization on occupations, so the average scores reflect the exposure of states to different types of digitalization due to the occupation structures within the states. The table provides also the ranks (R.) of the states with respect to each of the digitalization measures and the rates of entrepreneurship with incorporated and unincorporated businesses. Figure 6.2 further illustrates the impacts of transformative and destructive digital technologies on regional labor markets in the states.

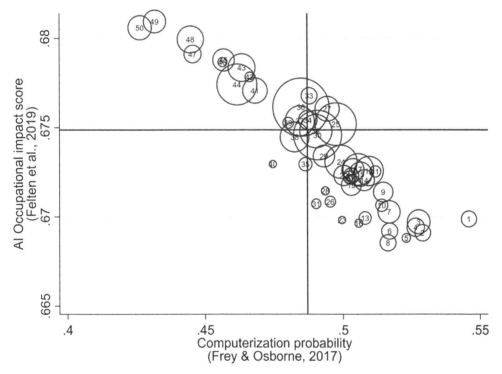

*Notes:*     Each bubble represents a US state. The size of the bubbles reflects the state population numbers in 2017, as provided by the US Census Bureau. The numbers in the bubbles correspond to each state's rank of computerization probability, as indicated in Table 6.3. Washington, DC demonstrates the highest value for the AIOI and is not shown in the chart for better data visualization. The horizontal and vertical lines correspond to the average values of both digitalization measures.

*Figure 6.2     Impacts of new digital technologies on US states*

The computerization probability, which reflects the risk of workers to be displaced by digital machines in the near future, is highest for Nevada and Iowa and lowest for Washington

*Table 6.3*   *Digitalization on states for the full population*

| State | Comput. Risk | | AI Occ. Impact | | SML | | sdSML | | Uninc. entrep. | | Inc. entrep. | | N |
|---|---|---|---|---|---|---|---|---|---|---|---|---|---|
| | Prob. | R. | Score | R. | Mean | R. | Std. Dev. | R. | Rate | R. | Rate | R. | |
| Nevada | 0.5459 | 1 | 0.66987 | 43 | 3.48512 | 32 | 0.59212 | 39 | 0.0499 | 40 | 0.0310 | 37 | 11959 |
| Iowa | 0.5289 | 2 | 0.66909 | 49 | 3.48370 | 36 | 0.59253 | 33 | 0.0622 | 16 | 0.0301 | 43 | 14734 |
| Indiana | 0.5274 | 3 | 0.66971 | 45 | 3.48648 | 18 | 0.59245 | 35 | 0.0439 | 47 | 0.0276 | 46 | 28374 |
| Oklahoma | 0.5263 | 4 | 0.66940 | 47 | 3.48325 | 39 | 0.59365 | 16 | 0.0626 | 14 | 0.0346 | 28 | 14394 |
| South Dakota | 0.5228 | 5 | 0.66880 | 50 | 3.48637 | 19 | 0.59285 | 24 | 0.0819 | 5 | 0.0350 | 25 | 3963 |
| Arkansas | 0.5168 | 6 | 0.66919 | 48 | 3.48152 | 48 | 0.59335 | 19 | 0.0583 | 24 | 0.0331 | 31 | 11331 |
| Wisconsin | 0.5166 | 7 | 0.67027 | 41 | 3.48579 | 25 | 0.59166 | 49 | 0.0606 | 19 | 0.0368 | 19 | 26519 |
| Mississippi | 0.5162 | 8 | 0.66853 | 51 | 3.48297 | 42 | 0.59234 | 37 | 0.0516 | 35 | 0.0295 | 45 | 10157 |
| Kentucky | 0.5145 | 9 | 0.67138 | 37 | 3.48708 | 14 | 0.59188 | 45 | 0.0479 | 43 | 0.0305 | 40 | 17874 |
| Idaho | 0.5140 | 10 | 0.67064 | 40 | 3.48292 | 43 | 0.59239 | 36 | 0.0667 | 8 | 0.0525 | 4 | 6452 |
| Hawaii | 0.5117 | 11 | 0.67253 | 29 | 3.48340 | 38 | 0.59604 | 4 | 0.0594 | 21 | 0.0330 | 32 | 6019 |
| Michigan | 0.5094 | 12 | 0.67256 | 28 | 3.48875 | 4 | 0.59272 | 28 | 0.0512 | 36 | 0.0348 | 27 | 40598 |
| West Virginia | 0.5080 | 13 | 0.66993 | 42 | 3.48263 | 44 | 0.59188 | 46 | 0.0437 | 48 | 0.0207 | 51 | 6424 |
| South Carolina | 0.5077 | 14 | 0.67204 | 34 | 3.48667 | 16 | 0.59098 | 51 | 0.0505 | 37 | 0.0342 | 29 | 19326 |
| Tennessee | 0.5063 | 15 | 0.67238 | 30 | 3.48722 | 12 | 0.59187 | 47 | 0.0659 | 10 | 0.0249 | 49 | 27729 |
| North Dakota | 0.5057 | 16 | 0.66964 | 46 | 3.48363 | 37 | 0.59420 | 11 | 0.0833 | 4 | 0.0390 | 14 | 3950 |
| Ohio | 0.5055 | 17 | 0.67265 | 26 | 3.48538 | 28 | 0.59298 | 22 | 0.0452 | 44 | 0.0266 | 47 | 50769 |
| Missouri | 0.5036 | 18 | 0.67262 | 27 | 3.48532 | 29 | 0.59260 | 31 | 0.0549 | 27 | 0.0309 | 38 | 26179 |
| Alabama | 0.5030 | 19 | 0.67177 | 35 | 3.48606 | 23 | 0.59213 | 38 | 0.0520 | 34 | 0.0330 | 33 | 17566 |
| Kansas | 0.5029 | 20 | 0.67228 | 32 | 3.48634 | 20 | 0.59393 | 13 | 0.0619 | 17 | 0.0311 | 36 | 13039 |
| Nebraska | 0.5024 | 21 | 0.67220 | 33 | 3.48629 | 21 | 0.59366 | 15 | 0.0611 | 18 | 0.0352 | 23 | 9116 |
| Louisiana | 0.5002 | 22 | 0.67231 | 31 | 3.48255 | 45 | 0.59338 | 18 | 0.0587 | 23 | 0.0360 | 22 | 17066 |
| Wyoming | 0.4996 | 23 | 0.66982 | 44 | 3.47572 | 51 | 0.59781 | 2 | 0.0664 | 9 | 0.0420 | 10 | 2584 |
| Pennsylvania | 0.4993 | 24 | 0.67308 | 23 | 3.48438 | 34 | 0.59287 | 23 | 0.0503 | 38 | 0.0303 | 41 | 54759 |
| Florida | 0.4974 | 25 | 0.67519 | 18 | 3.48747 | 11 | 0.59130 | 50 | 0.0540 | 28 | 0.0618 | 2 | 78784 |
| Maine | 0.4954 | 26 | 0.67085 | 38 | 3.48181 | 46 | 0.59364 | 17 | 0.0844 | 3 | 0.0425 | 9 | 5185 |
| Arizona | 0.4943 | 27 | 0.67605 | 13 | 3.48775 | 9 | 0.59262 | 30 | 0.0533 | 30 | 0.0371 | 17 | 26355 |
| Alaska | 0.4936 | 28 | 0.67145 | 36 | 3.48177 | 47 | 0.59400 | 12 | 0.0632 | 13 | 0.0258 | 48 | 2651 |
| Minnesota | 0.4931 | 29 | 0.67340 | 22 | 3.48780 | 8 | 0.59202 | 42 | 0.0624 | 15 | 0.0437 | 7 | 26048 |
| Texas | 0.4908 | 30 | 0.67458 | 20 | 3.48576 | 27 | 0.59176 | 48 | 0.0653 | 12 | 0.0314 | 34 | 111112 |
| Montana | 0.4903 | 31 | 0.67073 | 39 | 3.48063 | 50 | 0.59625 | 3 | 0.0940 | 2 | 0.0687 | 1 | 4231 |

| State | Comput. Risk | | AI Occ. Impact | | SML | | sdSML | | Uninc. entrep. | | Inc. entrep. | | |
|---|---|---|---|---|---|---|---|---|---|---|---|---|---|
| Illinois | 0.4902 | 32 | 0.67480 | 19 | 3.48748 | 10 | 0.59195 | 43 | 0.0440 | 46 | 0.0351 | 24 | 55116 |
| Utah | 0.4878 | 33 | 0.67678 | 12 | 3.48889 | 3 | 0.59247 | 34 | 0.0492 | 42 | 0.0459 | 6 | 13413 |
| Oregon | 0.4873 | 34 | 0.67542 | 15 | 3.48488 | 33 | 0.59272 | 27 | 0.0657 | 11 | 0.0431 | 8 | 17906 |
| **Average** | **0.4871** | | **0.67487** | | **3.48624** | | **0.59271** | | **0.0566** | | **0.0367** | | **25887** |
| New Mexico | 0.4864 | 35 | 0.67294 | 25 | 3.48305 | 41 | 0.59560 | 5 | 0.0596 | 20 | 0.0311 | 35 | 7034 |
| California | 0.4848 | 36 | 0.67614 | 13 | 3.48684 | 15 | 0.59211 | 40 | 0.0733 | 6 | 0.0361 | 21 | 159229 |
| Georgia | 0.4844 | 37 | 0.67537 | 16 | 3.48618 | 22 | 0.59195 | 44 | 0.0524 | 32 | 0.0414 | 11 | 41245 |
| North Carolina | 0.4825 | 38 | 0.67447 | 21 | 3.48532 | 30 | 0.59203 | 41 | 0.0524 | 33 | 0.0374 | 16 | 41596 |
| New Hampshire | 0.4802 | 39 | 0.67526 | 17 | 3.48667 | 17 | 0.59259 | 32 | 0.0689 | 7 | 0.0308 | 39 | 6226 |
| Vermont | 0.4745 | 40 | 0.67295 | 24 | 3.48113 | 49 | 0.59523 | 6 | 0.0962 | 1 | 0.0500 | 5 | 2870 |
| Washington | 0.4681 | 41 | 0.67707 | 11 | 3.48310 | 40 | 0.59282 | 25 | 0.0555 | 26 | 0.0412 | 12 | 31545 |
| Rhode Island | 0.4662 | 42 | 0.67784 | 9 | 3.48845 | 5 | 0.59509 | 7 | 0.0524 | 31 | 0.0303 | 42 | 4498 |
| New Jersey | 0.4633 | 43 | 0.67836 | 8 | 3.49004 | 1 | 0.59313 | 20 | 0.0423 | 50 | 0.0404 | 13 | 35355 |
| New York | 0.4616 | 44 | 0.67741 | 10 | 3.48780 | 7 | 0.59474 | 8 | 0.0534 | 29 | 0.0381 | 15 | 88383 |
| Colorado | 0.4568 | 45 | 0.67879 | 6 | 3.48521 | 31 | 0.59305 | 21 | 0.0591 | 22 | 0.0528 | 3 | 25356 |
| Delaware | 0.4564 | 46 | 0.67867 | 7 | 3.48431 | 35 | 0.59267 | 29 | 0.0429 | 49 | 0.0370 | 18 | 3674 |
| Connecticut | 0.4456 | 47 | 0.67912 | 5 | 3.48826 | 6 | 0.59386 | 14 | 0.0567 | 25 | 0.0364 | 20 | 15539 |
| Virginia | 0.4448 | 48 | 0.67994 | 4 | 3.48584 | 24 | 0.59278 | 26 | 0.0440 | 45 | 0.0337 | 30 | 36556 |
| Maryland | 0.4319 | 49 | 0.68095 | 2 | 3.48713 | 13 | 0.59452 | 9 | 0.0499 | 41 | 0.0349 | 26 | 24902 |
| Massachusetts | 0.4265 | 50 | 0.68060 | 3 | 3.48576 | 26 | 0.59423 | 10 | 0.0502 | 39 | 0.0298 | 44 | 32647 |
| DC | 0.3307 | 51 | 0.69588 | 1 | 3.48927 | 2 | 0.60273 | 1 | 0.0287 | 51 | 0.0225 | 50 | 7801 |

*Notes:*    The table shows the average digitalization measures across the full population in each state. R. is the rank of the states according to each measure. The table also provides the shares of entrepreneurs with unincorporated and incorporated businesses in the states and the corresponding rankings.

DC and the northeastern states. States like Nevada and Iowa may face an increase in the levels of necessity entrepreneurship in the future. Figures 6.1 and 6.2 show that the AIOI score, a measure of transformative digitalization, is strongly inversely correlated with the computerization risk. The top AIOI scores are in northeastern states and the bottom scores in Midwestern and southern states. This may indicate a high potential for the emergence of new entrepreneurial opportunities for ambitious entrepreneurship in the northeastern states. Vermont is a state with below-average impacts of both transformative and destructive digitalization, which suggests that this regional labor market is relatively well protected from labor-replacing automation and, at the same time, is less likely to benefit from labor-augmenting digital technologies. In addition, the table shows that the suitability for machine learning metrics do not show pronounced region-specific patterns and have less variation than the computerization probabilities or AIOI. The states that have the lowest SML are rural such as Wyoming, Montana, Vermont, Arkansas, and Alaska.

Washington DC is an interesting case as it is densely populated, urban and with a small area size compared to the states. Its averages tend to be extremes. DC has the lowest computerization risk, the highest AIOI score, the second highest mean SML, and the highest within-occupation standard deviation of SML (sdSML). The results with respect to the computerization risk, AIOI and sdSML suggest that urban areas benefit more from transformative digitalization and are less exposed to destructive digitalization than rural areas, although the high mean SML score does not fit into this picture. The share of the population that are incorporated entrepreneurs is the second lowest in Washington DC when ranked against the states and the share of unincorporated entrepreneurs is the lowest.

## 3.2    Regional Rates of Entrepreneurship

To examine the current geographical distribution of different types of entrepreneurial activities in the United States, we distinguish between entrepreneurship with unincorporated businesses (Figure 6.3) and entrepreneurship with incorporated businesses (Figure 6.4). As discussed in the introduction, incorporated entrepreneurship is more likely to be innovative and opportunity-oriented than unincorporated entrepreneurship, which is more often associated with necessity entrepreneurship.

Rates of both unincorporated and incorporated entrepreneurship are high in Montana, North Dakota, and Maine. Apart from these states, the distributions of the two types of entrepreneurship are often very different. Incorporated entrepreneurship is high in many urban areas such as the Bay Area and low in many rural areas. The urban-rural contrast is often the opposite for unincorporated entrepreneurship, with high rates in many rural and low rates in many urban areas. These urban-rural patterns for incorporated and unincorporated entrepreneurship are clearly visible in Texas, for example.

## 3.3    Regional Exposure of Entrepreneurs to New Digital Technologies

To analyze the regional exposure of entrepreneurs to new digital technologies, we focus on the computerization probability as a measure of destructive digitalization and on the AI Occupational Impact as a measure of transformative digitalization. We calculate the scores as averages over the individuals in the ACS who live in each region and report being self-employed, using their occupational codes. As before, we distinguish between entrepre-

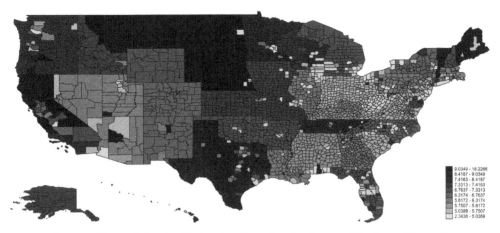

*Notes:*   Percent of the population that falls into the self-employed, unincorporated category. We provide within-state averages for rural counties with a low population size because these counties are unidentified in the ACS for data protection reasons.

*Figure 6.3*   *Share of unincorporated entrepreneurs in the population*

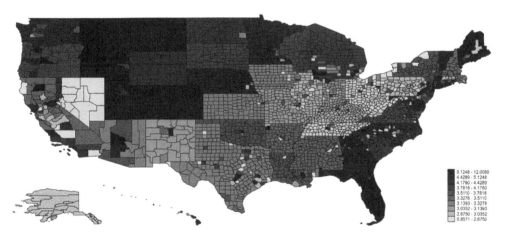

*Notes:*   Percent of the population that falls into the self-employed, incorporated category. We provide within-state averages for rural counties with a low population size because these counties are unidentified in the ACS for data protection reasons.

*Figure 6.4*   *Share of incorporated entrepreneurs in the population*

neurs with unincorporated and incorporated businesses. For each of the two digitalization measures, we first define a scale for the color coding of the maps as 10 intervals with equal width spanning from the minimum average score to the maximum average score in a region when pooling both types of entrepreneurs. Then we adjust the bottom interval to start at the minimum regional average score for each entrepreneurship type and the top interval to end at the maximum for each type. This way, we use the same scales for both types of entrepreneurs except for the outer limits of the top and bottom intervals.

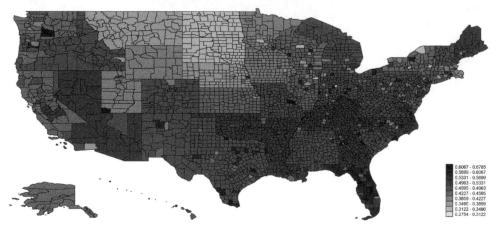

*Notes:*    Computerization probability of occupations averaged over entrepreneurs with unincorporated businesses in each region. We provide within-state averages for rural counties with a low population size because these counties are unidentified in the ACS for data protection reasons.

*Figure 6.5*    *Exposure of unincorporate entrepreneurs to computerization risk*

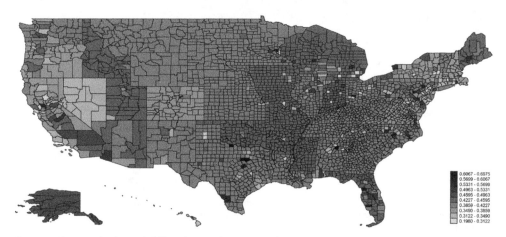

*Notes:*    Computerization probability of occupations averaged over entrepreneurs with incorporated businesses in each region. We provide within-state averages for rural counties with a low population size because these counties are unidentified in the ACS for data protection reasons.

*Figure 6.6*    *Exposure of incorporated entrepreneurs to computerization risk*

Figures 6.5 and 6.6 illustrate the regional exposure of entrepreneurs to computerization risk, the measure of destructive digitalization, through the occupations they are working in. Entrepreneurs with unincorporated businesses are clearly more exposed to the risk of automation of their occupations than entrepreneurs with incorporated businesses. Exposure to computerization risk is especially large for unincorporated entrepreneurs in Florida, but small in North and South Dakota.

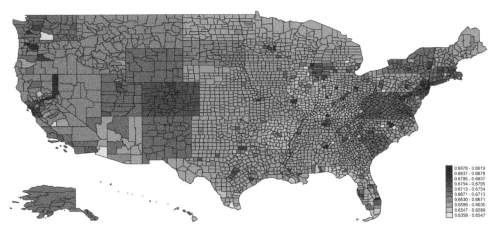

*Notes:*    AI Occupational Impact scores averaged over entrepreneurs with unincorporated businesses in each region. We provide within-state averages for rural counties with a low population size because these counties are unidentified in the ACS for data protection reasons.

*Figure 6.7*    *Exposure of unincorporated entrepreneurs to AI Occupational Impact*

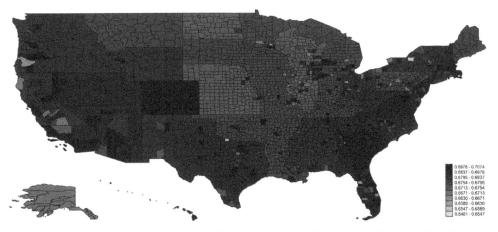

*Notes:*    AI Occupational Impact scores averaged over entrepreneurs with incorporated businesses in each region. We provide within-state averages for rural counties with a low population size because these counties are unidentified in the ACS for data protection reasons.

*Figure 6.8*    *Exposure of incorporated entrepreneurs to AI Occupational Impact*

Figures 6.7 and 6.8 show the regional exposure of entrepreneurs to AI Occupational Impact, the measure of transformative digitalization. In contrast to the finding concerning computerization risk, incorporated entrepreneurs are clearly more exposed to AIOI than unincorporated entrepreneurs. This indicates that entrepreneurs with incorporated businesses are more likely to benefit from new opportunities brought about by AI technologies. Furthermore, for both types of entrepreneurs, exposure to transformative AI is generally stronger in larger cities than in rural areas (for example, the Bay Area, extending via Sacramento to Reno in Nevada, versus the Central Valley in California). This suggests that entrepreneurs in cities work in occupations that are transformed more by AI, likely in a productivity enhancing way, in comparison to entrepreneurs in rural areas (including self-employed farmers).

## 4.     CONCLUSIONS

While digital technologies are global, entrepreneurship remains a phenomenon rooted in regions. Therefore, emerging literature on digital entrepreneurial ecosystems calls for a better understanding of different elements of regional ecosystems that impact entrepreneurship in the digital economy. This chapter provides rankings and heat maps of the states and regions within the United States showing the impact of new digital technologies on entrepreneurship with incorporated and unincorporated businesses. We show that the existing occupational structure of regional labor markets determines how new digital technologies will likely affect different types of entrepreneurship in a region.

In general, the results indicate that entrepreneurs in urban areas are most likely to benefit from advances in AI (Felten et al., 2019), which seem to transform rather than replace occupations. Entrepreneurs in rural areas tend to be more affected by destructive digitalization as captured by computerization probabilities (Frey and Osborne, 2017). However, the heat maps also reveal that there are many exceptions to these general patterns, thus emphasizing the importance of the regional environment for digital entrepreneurial ecosystems. Therefore, a closer look into specific regions and at different types of entrepreneurs is crucial before deriving any recommendations for local policymaking, as our findings suggest that there might be other region-specific factors at play that influence the relationship between new digital technologies and entrepreneurship. These factors could be, for instance, other elements of digital entrepreneurial ecosystems, such as the quality of digital infrastructure and accessibility of digital technologies by users (Sussan and Acs, 2017).

There are several important considerations for regional policymaking. Entrepreneurship, in particular with unincorporated businesses, can be an escape route for current employees who are at risk of being displaced by new digital technologies. Therefore, regional policy should avoid imposing barriers to entrepreneurial entry. Furthermore, digitalization may exacerbate already existing inequalities in entrepreneurial growth potential between different regions in the near future. Potential ways to mitigate these trends could include provision of broadband internet in rural areas, although more research on the effectiveness of such policies is needed. However, the most important takeaway from this analysis is that there is no one-size-fits-all prescription for regional policymakers when it comes to digitalization and entrepreneurship. Even when comparing areas with similar population densities, the impacts of digitalization can be very heterogeneous, depending on the regional occupation structures. Thus, regional data must be analyzed and carefully interpreted before developing tailored local policies toward entrepreneurship during the digital transformation of the labor markets.

One implication of our results for practitioners is that the emergence of entrepreneurial opportunities in the digital age is region-specific. This goes far beyond a simple distinction between rural and urban areas, albeit the latter are more likely to be breeding grounds for entrepreneurship during the digital transformation. One source of entrepreneurial opportunities is related to applications of new digital technologies such as AI in the context of occupations.

In sum, regional differences in occupational exposure to digitalization reflect the ability of regions to benefit from digitalization by means of entrepreneurship. Regions with high susceptibility to destructive digitalization and low potential for transformative digitalization might see a lower number of entrepreneurial opportunities emerge in the future, which could potentially lead to regional inequalities.

## ACKNOWLEDGMENTS

We thank the participants at the virtual OECD International Conference on Artificial Intelligence in Work, Innovation, Productivity and Skills in January 2021 for valuable comments. Frank Fossen thanks the Ewing Marion Kauffman Foundation for financial support of the research project RG-201802-3798. The contents of this publication are solely the responsibility of the authors.

## NOTES

1. Note that we use the terms "destructive" and "transformative" to denote effects of digitalization on individuals' current occupations. The first term is intuitive from the point of view of workers whose current occupations are affected by destructive digitalization, which puts them at risk of losing their current job due to automation. However, the terms are not supposed to describe effects on the firm or the economy as a whole or to imply value judgments.
2. Levine and Rubinstein (2017) show that entrepreneurs with incorporated businesses tend to be more innovative and growth-oriented than entrepreneurs with unincorporated businesses. Unincorporated businesses are more often (but of course not always) associated with necessity entrepreneurship (Fossen, 2021).
3. These bottleneck skills are: Perception and manipulation (finger dexterity, manual dexterity, and cramped work space or awkward positions), creative intelligence (originality, fine arts, and social perceptiveness), and social intelligence (negotiation, persuasion, and assisting and caring for others).
4. These categories of AI are: image recognition, visual question answering, image generation, reading comprehension, language modeling, translation, speech recognition, abstract strategy games, and real-time video games.
5. Their findings suggest that most occupations include at least some tasks that are suitable for machine learning, but few occupations consist exclusively of tasks that are suitable for machine learning. The authors point out that the automation impacts of machine learning will strongly depend on the reorganization of jobs, and in particular, on the potential to disentangle tasks that are suitable for machine learning from those that are not.
6. We include the SML and sdSML measures in our tables, but not in our maps, as they show only limited regional variation.
7. To give some further examples, occupations such as pilots, surgeons, biochemists and architects have high AIOI exposure, but face low risks of computerization. These occupations are being

transformed by AI technologies, but employees are not displaced by automation, so they do not face destructive digitalization. In contrast, hand sewers, tax preparers and library technicians have high computerization probabilities and are thus exposed to destructive digitalization. They are at high risk of being displaced by digital machines.

8.   The definition of entrepreneurs used in this chapter includes self-employed farmers.

# REFERENCES

Brynjolfsson, E. & Mitchell, T. (2017). What Can Machine Learning Do? Workforce Implications. *Science, 358*(6370), 1530–1534.

Brynjolfsson, E., Mitchell, T., & Rock, D. (2018). What Can Machines Learn, and What Does It Mean for Occupations and the Economy? *American Economic Association Papers and Proceedings, 108,* 43–47.

Bureau of Labor Statistics (2018). Occupational Employment Statistics, May 2018 Data, https://www.bls.gov/oes/home.htm.

Du, E., Pan, S.L., Zhou, N., & Ouyang, T. (2018). From a Marketplace of Electronics to a Digital Entrepreneurial Ecosystem (DEE): The Emergence of a Meta-organization in Zhongguancun, China. *Information Systems Journal, 28*(6), 1158–1175.

Elia, G., Margherita, A., & Passiante, G. (2020). Digital Entrepreneurship Ecosystem: How Digital Technologies and Collective Intelligence are Reshaping the Entrepreneurial Process. *Technological Forecasting and Social Change, 150,* 119791. https://doi.org/10.1016/j.techfore.2019.119791.

Felten, E.W., Raj, M., & Seamans, R. (2018). A Method to Link Advances in Artificial Intelligence to Occupational Abilities. *American Economic Association Papers and Proceedings, 108,* 54–57.

Felten, E.W., Raj, M., & Seamans, R. (2019). *The Occupational Impact of Artificial Intelligence: Labor, Skills, and Polarization.* Working Paper. SSRN: http://dx.doi.org/10.2139/ssrn.3368605.

Fossen, F.M. (2021). Self-employment Over the Business Cycle in the USA: a Decomposition. *Small Business Economics, 57,* 1837–1855. https://doi.org/10.1007/s11187-020-00375-3.

Fossen, F.M. & Sorgner, A. (2019). Mapping the Future of Occupations: Transformative and Destructive Effects of New Digital Technologies on Jobs. *Foresight and STI Governance, 13*(2), 10–18.

Fossen, F.M. & Sorgner, A. (2021). Digitalization of Work and Entry into Entrepreneurship. *Journal of Business Research, 125,* 548–563.

Fossen, F.M. & Sorgner, A. (2022). New Digital Technologies and Heterogeneous Employment and Wage Dynamics in the United States: Evidence from Individual-level Data. *Technological Forecasting and Social Change, 175,* 121381. https://doi.org/10.1016/j.techfore.2021.121381.

Frey, C.B. & Osborne, M.A. (2017). The Future of Employment: How Susceptible are Jobs to Computerization? *Technological Forecasting and Social Change, 114,* 254–280.

Levine, R. & Rubinstein, Y. (2017). Smart and Illicit: Who Becomes an Entrepreneur and Does It Pay? *Quarterly Journal of Economics, 132*(2), 963–1018.

Nambisan, S. (2017). Digital Entrepreneurship: Toward a Digital Technology Perspective of Entrepreneurship. *Entrepreneurship Theory and Practice, 41*(6), 1029–1055.

Ruggles, S., Flood, S., Goeken, R., Grover, J., Meyer, E., Pacas, J., & Sobek, M. (2020). IPUMS USA: Version 10.0 [dataset]. Minneapolis, MN, https://doi.org/10.18128/D010.V10.0.

Spigel, B. (2015). The Relational Organization of Entrepreneurial Ecosystems. *Entrepreneurship Theory and Practice, 41*(1), 49–72.

Sussan, F. & Acs Z.J. (2017). The Digital Entrepreneurial Ecosystem. *Small Business Economics, 49,* 55–73.

# PART IV

# DIGITAL ENTREPRENEURSHIP
# TECHNOLOGIES

# 7. Startup stacks: understanding the new landscape of digital entrepreneurship technology

*Mohammad Keyhani*

## INTRODUCTION

Digital technologies are fundamentally changing the nature of entrepreneurship (Nambisan, 2017). And as with many other instances of technological change, the impact of technology on entrepreneurship has followed an exponential pattern: a slow start that has suddenly turned into a huge wave bringing dramatic change to the entrepreneurship landscape only recently (Christensen, 1997). Most of the technological tools in widespread use today among startups did not exist just a few years ago.

The rapidly increasing importance of the phenomenon of digital entrepreneurship, and the correspondingly increasing scholarly interest, begets the need to recognize the technologies of entrepreneurship as an important category of technologies, and the need to study and understand this category. I define "entrepreneurship technology" as the application of technological tools to support, improve and transform the process of starting and running a new venture. These tools are typically digital, information technology-enabled and web-based systems, and impact the entire spectrum of entrepreneurial processes from the early stages of idea and team formation all the way to the growth and exit of the firm. By allowing startups to outsource these support technologies to specialized SaaS providers, entrepreneurship technology is reducing costs, increasing speed and agility, allowing for increasingly lean teams and organization structures. A list of how a startup today may outsource a number of business processes was provided by Varian (2019), and here we present a revised and updated version. A typical startup today may employ the following stack of SaaS tools:

- Fund your project on Kickstarter or IndieGogo (reward-based crowdfunding) or AngelList or Fundable (equity-based crowdfunding) or issue an Initial Coin Offering (Keyhani et al., Chapter 1 in this handbook).
- Build a quick landing page or full-fledged website with Carrd, Weebly or SquareSpace.
- Set up payments with Gumroad, PayPal or Stripe.
- Use cloud computing and networking resources from Google Cloud, Amazon Web Services, or Microsoft Azure.
- Use open- source software like Linux, Python, TensorFlow, and so forth.
- Manage your software development processes using GitHub or Jira.
- Become a micromultinational and hire programmers from abroad using international contracting services like Deel (LetsDeel.com) or hire virtual assistants and freelancers from around the world using Upwork.com, Fiverr.com, Piralto.com, FacnyHands.com, and TimeEtc.com.

- Set up an open innovation and crowdsourcing competitions on Kaggle, Innocentive, OpenIdeo, or Amazon Mechanical Turk.
- Use Skype, Hangouts, Zoom, and others for team communication.
- Use Google Docs, Notion, or Coda for collaborative documents.
- Use Nolo, Athennian, or DocuSign for legal documents and contracts.
- Use QuickBooks, Xero or Wave for accounting.
- Use AdWords, Bing, or Facebook for marketing.
- Use ZenDesk, HootDesk or FreshDesk for user support.
- Use HubSpot, Zoho or Salesforce for customer relationship management.
- And many more…

Most scholarship around business technology has evolved around the study of enterprise technology to the neglect of entrepreneurship technology. This may have been partly justified due to the comparatively narrow range and lower complexity of the technological tools available to, and used by entrepreneurs and startups. But the rapid rise of digital technologies that support, improve or transform entrepreneurship has completely undermined this justification. There are now entire categories of such tools (often developed by a corresponding nascent and rapidly evolving micro-industry of companies) for everything from brainstorming and testing ideas, identifying trends and market research, building prototypes, choosing a name and slogan, designing a logo, practicing a pitch, writing a business plan, finding co-founders, borrowing money, registering a corporation, raising funds, building a website or product launch page, accepting payments, accounting and invoicing, packaging and delivery, and more.

This chapter aims to take a first step in understanding entrepreneurship technology as a category by attempting to map the current landscape, that is, by investigating directories that catalogue and categorize the variety of technological tools supporting the entrepreneurship process that are available to today's entrepreneurs. Practitioners refer to these directories to discover tools they can use to build their "startup stacks" as they are sometimes referred to (mostly in the software industry). The chapter proceeds with some background on the concept of digital entrepreneurship technology, why it has emerged, why it matters, and why business scholars have largely missed it so far.

## DIGITAL ENTREPRENEURSHIP AND ENTREPRENEURSHIP TECHNOLOGY: A NOTE ON TERMINOLOGY

The recent literature studying the impact of technology on entrepreneurship has largely coalesced under the label of "Digital Entrepreneurship" as an organizing label (Davidson & Vaast, 2010; Giones & Brem, 2017; Nambisan, 2017; Richter, Kraus, Brem, Durst, & Giselbrecht, 2017). I emphasize the importance of a sister concept that can be titled "Entrepreneurship Technology" for the following reasons:

First, the term "digital entrepreneurship" grammatically implies that it is a sub-type of entrepreneurship, and specifically a sub-type of technology entrepreneurship. This is a notion that can be challenged because all entrepreneurship – even low tech or non-tech entrepreneurship – is to varying degrees technology-assisted (Hull, Hung, Hair, Perotti, & DeMartino, 2007). The label "digital entrepreneurship" may imply that it has nothing to do with low tech mom-and-pop shops that can benefit from many digital technologies of entrepreneurship.

In fact, the advancement of digital entrepreneurship technology has resulted in the com-modification of many technological components of new businesses, to the extent that some ventures previously considered "high-tech" are no longer always necessarily so. For example, a two-sided marketplace platform is typically considered a high-tech business, but today using Marketplace-as-a-Service tools such as Sharetribe.com and Near-Me.com, the entire techno-logical infrastructure of a marketplace platform can be purchased as a service, requiring no programming skills from the entrepreneur or startup. As another example software built with complex natural language models is no longer only the domain of computer scientists who are experts in machine learning, artificial intelligence, and natural language processing if language models like GPT-3 and GPT-J are easily available through APIs (Keyhani et al., Chapter 1 in this handbook).

Second, the digital entrepreneurship label unnecessarily excludes the role of non-digital technology in supporting, improving and changing the nature of entrepreneurship. Examples of non-digital entrepreneurship technology include the shipping container (Levinson, 2016) and physical makerspaces (Van Holm, 2015). It also downplays the role of non-digital techno-logical components in technologies that have both digital and non-digital components, such as 3D printers and their non-digital material technologies (Laplume, Petersen, & Pearce, 2016), as well as autonomous drones and the hardware and cooling technologies behind server farms.

Having said that, I agree that the recent rapid evolution and profusion of entrepreneurship technology is chiefly due to digital technologies, and thus an emphasis on the digital is needed to better understand the more recent aspects of the phenomenon that are resulting in more radical change compared to non-digital forms of entrepreneurship technology. In fact, even the "digital" label does not do it justice, because technologies like accounting software, spreadsheets and word processing that entrepreneurs have been using for decades are also "digital." What is important here is not necessarily "digital" per se, but how the amalgamation of a number of internet-based technologies such as cloud computing, Software as a Service (SaaS), open source, platforms, social media, and Application Programming Interfaces (APIs) have enabled the flourishing of a new and rapidly evolving landscape of technologies that support, improve and transform the nature of entrepreneurship. This is the type of technology we are referring to in the remainder of this chapter when we talk about digital entrepreneurship technology.

## REDUCING BARRIERS: TECHNOLOGY AS AN ENABLER OF ENTREPRENEURING

All economies – even the most entrepreneurial and efficient "free" markets – see countless opportunities unexploited and gone to waste: otherwise entrepreneurial people do not take action on them because of the various barriers to entry such as lack of resources and time, the prospect of legal and regulatory hurdles, and a lack of access to the right people and networks. This results in entrepreneurship often being perceived as a herculean endeavor, involving unreasonable risk, more the forte of the already privileged who have the support mechanisms in place and can afford the risks (Levine & Rubinstein, 2017). Recognizing this, the Kauffman foundation has recently started an initiative promoting a "zero barriers" movement,[1] to pave the road for a broader range of entrepreneurial activity, by a broader range of entrepreneurs.

Overall, industry experts have estimated that the cost of launching a product has reduced significantly in recent years, especially in the technology sector. Consider the case of ProductHunt, a website for discovering and ranking new products, that was recently acquired by AngelList for about 20 million dollars.[2] In a blog post,[3] Ryan Hoover, founder of ProductHunt, described how he leveraged technology to build a quick Minimum Viable Product (MVP) version of ProductHunt in just 20 minutes on November 6, 2013, and how the full product was up and running by the end of the same month. This is not to diminish the valuable and hard work of many startups that actually need to put in large amounts of time and resources, but it highlights the new possibilities that technology brings for many cases where much less time and resources are now needed.

Upfront Ventures, a venture capital investment firm, estimates a 99% reduction of costs of tech entrepreneurs launching a product, from $5 million in 1995 to just $5 thousand in 2014. Some of the key technology drivers of this cost reduction can be identified as follows:

(1) The increasing availability of high quality open source and free software solutions that provide an alternative to otherwise costly components of a startup's toolkit. Examples include Linux, WordPress, Apache, MySQL, Magento, GnuCash, Audacity, GIMP, 7-Zip and VLC Media Player.

(2) The rise of cloud computing, and the availability of Amazon Web Services which significantly reduces the infrastructure costs of deploying and managing a web or mobile application on a large scale.

(3) The economics of digital products with network effects and zero marginal costs, results in cutthroat competition in many segments (Shapiro & Varian, 1999; Varian, 2001), leading to heavy price drops or even free or freemium products and services.

(4) A new wave of web startups that build on the reduced costs of creating and running a company to launch products that target the increasing number of startups that arise from such lower entry barriers. In other words, the technology-driven cost reduction of launching a startup increases both the supply and demand of the phenomenon commonly referred to as "startups for startups," and this two-sided synergy leads to exponential growth and hence the rapid increase in the technological tools available for entrepreneurs in recent years. Paul Graham, founder of YCombinator, explicitly referred to "startups for startups" as an attractive investment category in a 2008 memo.[4]

(5) The internet and modern computing technology have enabled an era of automated and computer-mediated transactions (Varian, 2010). Many costly but routine human tasks can now be easily automated, thereby significantly reducing the costs entrepreneurs incur in accomplishing them. For example, much of the day to day accounting activities of small businesses are automated through software tools such as Intuit QuickBooks and Wave. Sequences of mass customized emails can now be sent to a large number of users automatically, subject to prompts and if-then rules with tools such as MailChimp, Drip, and Mixmax.

(6) In addition to allowing increasing automation of a variety of tasks, computer-mediated transactions have also enabled much more efficient human-to-human transactions, allowing much more efficient matching of supply and demand, contracting, new business models, and general reduction of transaction costs. This has given rise to the four intertwined phenomena of outsourcing, crowdsourcing, the freelancer economy,

and the sharing economy/collaborative consumption, all of which have had enormous cost-saving and barrier-reducing effects on entrepreneurship and startups.

(7)    Many of these tools are allowing entrepreneurs who are not computer programmers to build and ship software with no-code technology such as Bubble.io and Adalo.com. This has prompted me to begin researching "No-Code Entrepreneurship" and the ways in which it changes the game (Keyhani, 2021b).

(8)    Some ways in which no-code entrepreneurship is disrupting digital entrepreneurship is that it is giving rise to a new breed of single-person software companies (a.k.a. "solopreneurs") who often follow the "build in public" and "indie hacker" movements and document every step of their journey on social media (yummy data for us researchers!). Often these projects are small scope software tools known as "MicroSaaS" products and these have given rise to a new market for "micro-acquisitions" (see TinyAcquisitions. com and MicroAcquire.com) especially by proponents of the "passive income movement." Overall, the trend is toward a democratization of wealth and access to scalable opportunities.

Take the example of Voxifier, an early stage startup that provides phonetically correct name pronunciation in different languages as a service. The founders have been able to save significant amounts of money by taking advantage of open source technology, cloud solutions, and freelancers. The founders report that using WordPress for the design and deployment of their website resulted in a tenfold cost saving. They used an open source Linux library (FFmpeg) to write the code to automatically create videos of each name pronunciation, and they use YouTube to freely host their videos on the cloud. In addition, for a variety of tasks including logo design, development of a mobile app, phonetic transcription, voice recording of thousands of names, and development of Salesforce integration, they have been able to get the job done by hiring freelancers with cost savings ranging from 75% to 90% compared to what they were quoted by local programmers and service providers (source: personal correspondence).

An important barrier to entrepreneurship is finding the right co-founders and early team to work with (Der Foo, Wong, & Ong, 2005; Eisenhardt & Schoonhoven, 1990). An entrepreneur typically has to look for qualities and expertise in other people that complement his or her own. Once such people are identified, the entrepreneur faces a substantial barrier in convincing them to join their effort, typically with little or no guaranteed pay. If the entrepreneur decides to pay them as an employee, a salary expense is typically a huge cost item for a new venture. The increasing availability and commodification of tools for many support functions in entrepreneurship (accounting, marketing, etc.) means that entrepreneurs can increasingly substitute co-founders with tools, especially when it comes to the skills and capabilities needed in support functions. Thus entrepreneurs are less constrained in the necessity and choice of early co-founders and team members.

It is true that most entrepreneurship technologies today are supplied by SaaS Startups and much of them are in turn targeted to other SaaS startups and app developers, but this should not reinforce the mistaken idea that entrepreneurship technology is only for technology entrepreneurship. In fact, where entrepreneurship technology is likely to have its greatest impact is for low technology entrepreneurship, because for every one global high tech startup or venture capital darling out there, hundreds if not thousands of local, low tech, mom-and-pop shops exist, and they bring employment and economic development for their founders and communities. Thus the main economic impact of entrepreneurship technology will be felt when it moves beyond the techies and comes into widespread use by the everyday "common" entrepreneur. In fact, entrepreneurship technology will enable many otherwise non-entrepreneurs to cross the bridge into entrepreneurship.

Entrepreneurship technology is also broader than just an enabler of for-profit entrepreneurship. In a broader sense, it can be thought of as "entrepreneuring technology" meaning the application of technological tools to support, improve and transform the process of bringing about "new economic, social, institutional, and cultural environments through the actions of an individual or group" (Rindova, Barry, & Ketchen, 2009, p. 477). In this sense, different research foci are required to study categories such as social entrepreneurship technology, institutional entrepreneurship technology, political entrepreneurship technology, environmental entrepreneurship technology, academic entrepreneurship technology, and so on.

## WHY DIGITAL ENTREPRENEURSHIP TECHNOLOGY REMAINS UNDERSTUDIED

Most business schools around the world have a specific area of research and teaching typically under the title of Information Systems (IS) or Business Technology. So if such a field exists, why has entrepreneurship technology gone under the radar? Why is entrepreneurship technology missing from most business school courses and why is there no textbook on the subject? This omission can be attributed to three main factors:

(i)    IS research to date has mainly focused on applications of information technology (IT) in established organizations, largely ignoring the process of organization formation itself (i.e. entrepreneurship). Startups and smaller organizations have traditionally been viewed as less complex systems not in need of sophisticated information technology solutions. Although some researchers began studying information technology in small firms in the 1990s, most of the technologies studied in this line of work were similar to technologies used in larger organizations and were not representative of the full range of the new breed of technologies that is changing the process of entrepreneurship itself (even before firm formation) today (see for example, Cragg & King, 1993; Cragg & Zinatelli, 1995; Igbaria, Zinatelli, Cragg, & Cavaye, 1997).

(ii)   Digital entrepreneurship technology as a real world phenomenon is relatively recent and rapidly evolving. As a testament to how recent the major growth in entrepreneurship technology has been, many of the tools listed in the tables of this chapter did not exist five years ago, and many of them may no longer be operational five years from now. Large academic institutions are typically cumbersome and move slowly in response to change as they have to bargain with multiple stakeholders and deal with bureaucratic processes. Research is slow to move forward as well, since it takes considerable time for scholars to study a phenomenon rigorously, collect data, write papers, and go through the peer-review process (Keyhani et al., Chapter 1 in this handbook).

(iii)  Entrepreneurship itself has only recently been getting traction as an independent field of research and a distinct area in the structure of business schools, previously having been considered mostly a sub-area of strategic management (Keyhani, 2021a). The major paper that argued for the existence of entrepreneurship as a distinct domain was published as recently as 2000 (Shane & Venkataraman, 2000). Many business schools hesitated to invest heavily in entrepreneurship because entrepreneurship education was seen to be not in line with the needs of the large corporations that typically hire business school graduates. This is while many top strategy thinkers have consistently noted that the most interesting strategies are observed in new ventures and entrepreneurial firms (Porter, 1996; Rumelt, 2011). With the newly revived interest of large organizations in entrepreneurial thinking (Dewald, 2016) and the renewed realization of policy makers that healthy economies need healthy entrepreneurial ecosystems, entrepreneurship education is becoming an increasingly important function of business schools.

## METHOD AND DATA

While many technologies of entrepreneurship are useful in any industry and for any startup, web based businesses are at the forefront of leveraging these technologies. They routinely use entrepreneurship technology as part of their overall set of technological tools, commonly referred to as their software "stack." Web-based directories of the latest technologies of entrepreneurship are highly popular in startup communities around the world. On the popular ProductHunt platform where many of these software tools are promoted, the most upvoted product of all time is a directory of software tools for entrepreneurs called Startup Stash. Similar directories are available with names such as Stacklist, Growth Supply, The Starter Kit, Entrepreneur Tools, and Startup Resources. The world's top startup incubators such as YCombinator and 500Startups routinely encourage the teams in their programs to take advantage of the latest entrepreneurship technologies, and companies such as Siftery, Datanyze, StackShare, and BuiltWith have started to track and catalogue which technologies are used by which companies.

I systematically review several of the most popular and most comprehensive directories of entrepreneurship technology that are currently used by entrepreneurs and startup communities around the world. The aim is to understand the landscape of entrepreneurship technology by studying efforts to catalogue and organize its components. I investigated five directories for the core of our data: Siftery (Siftery.com), StackList (StackList.com), Startup Stash (StartupStash.com), Startup Resources (StartupResources.io), and compared these with the "Entrepreneur Tools" directory (Entrepreneur-tools.zeef.com) which I had curated myself as an educational tool.

Among these, Siftery is the most comprehensive directory with more than ten thousand tools catalogued, but it is also the only one that does not explicitly brand itself as mainly targeted for startups and entrepreneurs. However, due to its comprehensiveness and the fact that most of the tools listed in the other directories are also listed on Siftery, I decided to include this directory in the analysis. Comparing the entrepreneurship-specific lists with Siftery helps us examine ways in which the scope of entrepreneurship technology can be delineated within the broader scope of general enterprise or business technology.

In addition, I also looked at data from other popular directories for some analyses, but did not include them in our core data because they targeted more narrow audiences or categories of tools. These narrower directories include The Makers (themakers.io/tools/), Growth Supply (growthsupply.com/free), Design for Startup (DesignForStartup.net), and Marketing Stack (MarketingStack.io). I did not include Datanyze because it is based on automated data collection from website source codes and many of the tools of interest to us do not leave a trace in website code.

For data collection, I used a web scraping tool (webscraper.io) to create sitemaps of each of the directories. Using this sitemap, the web scraper followed a hierarchical path through each sub-section of the directories and assigned parent child relationships to each tier. This data was then exported to excel and cleaned to remove unnecessary data, errors and duplicate entries. Once complete, the data from all the directories were combined and analyzed for patterns and insight into the breadth of the entrepreneurship technology landscape. Data collection was conducted in 2018.

I was particularly interested in how directories categorize the tools, the wording used, the breadth of areas considered, which tools show up in multiple categories, and how categorization of the same tool differs across directories. In the case of Siftery, additional data was available on the number of companies tracked by Siftery that use any given tool. This allowed me to identify the most popular tools in each category, at least according to Siftery data. However, I acknowledge that due to the fast-changing nature of the entrepreneurship technology landscape, the data is likely to be somewhat dated by the time it is published and read.

# RESULTS

## Delineating the Scope of Digital Entrepreneurship Technology

Table 7.1 provides a list of some examples of digital entrepreneurship technology. As the list shows, it is challenging to attempt a clear delineation of the scope of this category. While some of the tools are very specific to entrepreneurship (e.g., tools for finding co-founders), others are equally useful for established organizations, even large ones (e.g., social media analytics). Some of them are tools used by startups and large incumbents alike in the exact same form (e.g., online payment technologies), while other tools have taken technologies previously used by larger enterprises and customized it for small businesses and new ventures (e.g., lightweight customer relationship management systems or CRMs). Rare but existing, is a category of tools created initially for entrepreneurs specifically, but increasingly being used also by larger organizations as well (e.g., crowdfunding platforms, see Grell, Marom, and Swart (2015) and Ashjari (Chapter 11 in this handbook)). Some tools are used temporarily and are specific to certain phases in the entrepreneurial process (e.g., tools for designing a logo, pitching, or legal registration), while others may be used throughout all stages of venturing and growth (e.g., tools for managing teams and communication).

Given the above complexities, how might one decide whether a given tool falls under the label of digital entrepreneurship technology? I suggest the following criteria. A tool falls within the scope of digital entrepreneurship technology, if any of the following apply:

1.  The tool's functionality specifically addresses a task or need that is an important part of the entrepreneurial process (e.g., pitching, finding co-founders, raising capital, etc.).
2.  The tool's provider specifically markets it to entrepreneurs and startups. Although its functionality may suit other purposes as well, the tool is marketed as applying particularly well to the startup context (e.g., while there are many website building tools, some like LeanSites.io specifically market themselves to startups). Typically, such tools also have

*Table 7.1      Examples of digital entrepreneurship technologies*

| Technology category | Sample functions | Sample tools |
|---|---|---|
| Brainstorming and Ideation | Sketch out ideas visually using lists, mind maps, etc. Collaborate with others on idea development via co-editing, commenting, etc. Social ranking and voting on ideas | Ideator.com Exobrain.co Viima.com Pengloo.com Codigital.com Stormboard.com |
| Finding and Matching Cofounders | Online profiled and job posting Professional networking community Matching services based on location, profiles and qualifications Forums and Q&A on professional topics | FounderDating.com CodeArmy.com Founders-Nation.com StartupMatcher.com CoFoundersLab.com |
| Pitching | Templates for different types of pitches Timing practice and pitch structuring Managing communication of pitch documents | Pitcherific.com Attach.io DocSend.com |
| Crowdfunding Platforms | Funding through mass micro-investments or pre-payments Circumvent due diligence and red tape Online campaign creation and hosting Analytics and optimization Social sharing and engagement | Kickstarter.com Indiegogo.com Fundable.com Krowdster.co Selfstarter.us Crowdfunder.com |
| Designing a Logo | Logo templates Pre-designed logos Artificial intelligence tools for automated logo design Drag and drop tools for manual logo design based on pre-existing design elements | TailorBrands.com GraphicSprings.com Logoshi.com Logaster.com Withoomph.com |
| Choosing a Name and Branding | Check availability of URL domain and social media accounts matching a given name Suggest alternative names and wordplay on names with association, rhyming, puns, etc. Provision of pre-registered packages of brand names, logos and domains | Namechk.com Naminum.com WerdMerge.com WikiRhymer.com BrandBucket.com NameSmith.io |
| Legal Services | Legal document templates Automated legal document generation Lawyer matching services based on needs and qualifications Legal service price auctions Fast-track legal registration over the web | Lawdepot.com Joincontractclub.com Clerky.com RocketLawyer.com Lawtrades.com Docracy.com Upcounsel.com |
| Growth Marketing / Growth Hacking | Automation of marketing and sales processes Managing and automation of promotions, referral systems and incentive programs Managing and automation of social media engagement Automated experiments, data and analytics to support marketing campaign strategy and design | Anygrowth.com Untorch.com Sumome.com Intercom.io Optimizely.com Introbar.com Hellobar.com |

| Technology category | Sample functions | Sample tools |
|---|---|---|
| Accounting and Invoicing | Provision of accounting software catering to the needs of new ventures and SMEs<br>Online invoicing and payment processing<br>Automation of recurrent billing<br>Computer supported payroll systems<br>Computer supported tax reporting<br>Bookkeeping and storage of accounting documents<br>Accountant matching services | Waveapps.com<br>Freshbooks.com<br>Invoicely.com<br>InvoicePlane.com<br>InvoiceOcean.com<br>ClearBooks.co.uk<br>Chargify.com<br>Countup.io<br>FinancialsOnTap.co |
| Group Collaboration and Teamwork | Instant messaging, voice/video conferencing, and screen sharing<br>Shared virtual workspaces and file sharing<br>Collaborative editing and commenting on documents and notes<br>Simplified project management, task management and scheduling | Slack.com<br>Trello.com<br>Asana.com<br>Teamweek.com<br>Ryver.com<br>Join.me<br>GoToMeeting.com |
| Testing Ideas, Polling and Feedback | Online poll creation and design<br>Participant recruitment and survey deployment<br>A/B testing and product usage analytics<br>Collection of feedback from existing and new users through surveys, written and video reviews<br>Design of questions to elicit useful information from customers | Erlibird.com<br>UserTesting.com<br>Proved.co<br>Validately.com<br>Worthix.com<br>Splitforce.com<br>Survicate.com |

pricing models that are specifically attractive to entrepreneurs (e.g., MailChimp and many other email management services have pricing models that become more expensive only when the startup has enough of an audience to make it worthwhile).
3. Even if the tool provider does not explicitly market the tool to entrepreneurs, in some cases the tool's functionality and features are such that among other tools with similar functionality, it serves the startup and entrepreneurship context particularly well (e.g., various tools that are "lightweight" versions of enterprise software such as CRMs help startups avoid overkill technologies that could slow down organizational processes).
4. Finally, and pragmatically speaking, any tool that becomes widely used among entrepreneurs and startups, will be considered *de facto* entrepreneurship technology.

**The Breadth of Digital Entrepreneurship Technology**

In order to get a better picture of the breadth of entrepreneurship technology, we looked at all the category structures and category labels of the five main directories (Siftery, StackList, Startup Stash, Startup Resources, and Entrepreneur Tools). Table 7.2 showcases the full category lists of all of these directories except Siftery, whose categories are listed in Table 7.3. Siftery also had a lower level of classification which included hundreds of subcategories, not reproduced here.

*Table 7.2*   *Lists of categories from four popular entrepreneurship technology directories*

**Stack List (Stacklist.com)**

| | | | |
|---|---|---|---|
| Accounting Firms & Services | Customer Service | Find Freelancers | Payroll |
| Applicant Tracking Software | Design | Find Interns | Payroll for Salaried Employees |
| BI / Analytics | Ecommerce | Hiring | Productivity |
| Billing & Invoicing | Email Marketing | HR | Project Management |
| Candidate Assessment | Expense Reports | Internal Communication | Recurring Payments |
| Cap Table Management | File Sharing | Office Space | Social Media Management |
| Content Marketing | Finance & Accounting | Online Accounting Suites | Suites |
| Credit Card Processing | Find Designers | Other | |
| CRM | Find Developers | Paying Contractors | |

**Startup Stash (StartupStash.com)**

| | | | |
|---|---|---|---|
| Analytics | Domain names | Learning | Payments |
| Articles | Early users | Legal | Presentations |
| Blogs | Feedback & Bug tracking | Market research | Product demo |
| Books | Finance | Marketing | Productivity |
| Collaboration & Communication | Forms & Surveys | Mobile (app) analytics | Project management |
| CRM | Hosting | Mockups & Wire framing | Raising capital |
| Customer support | HR | MVP | Sales |
| Deployment | Idea generation | Naming | Shop |
| Design | Investor relations | Newsletters | Social tools |
| Development | Launching | Outsourcing | Videos |

**Startup Resources (StartupResources.io)**

| | | | |
|---|---|---|---|
| A/B Testing | Espionage | Marketing | Schedulers |
| Advertising | File Transfer | Misc | SEO |
| Advice | Financial | Mockups | Site Builders |
| Affiliate | Forms | Monitoring | Site Support |
| Analytics | Fundraising | Networking | Social Media |
| Automation | Graphics | Newslettering | Stock Photos |
| Billing | Growth Hacking | Organization | Swag |

| | | | |
|---|---|---|---|
| Blogging | Help Desks | Outreach | Telecom Systems |
| Books | Hiring | Payment Solutions | Templates |
| Contests | Hosting | Podcasts | Traction |
| Conversion | Leads | Pop Ups | User Chat |
| CRM | Legal | Pre-Launch Traction | Video |
| Customer Discovery | List Apps | Productivity | Virtual Assistants |
| Development | List Building | Research | Webinars |
| Domains | Listing Services | Sales | Writing Tools |
| Email Tools | Logos | Sales Funnels | |

## Entrepreneur Tools (Entrepreneur-tools.zeef.com)

| | | | |
|---|---|---|---|
| Accounting & Invoicing | Freelancers & Task Economy | Market Research | Social Media Management |
| Advice & Mentorship | Fulfillment, Shipping & Delivery | Marketplace Creation | Spreadsheet & Database Management |
| App & Mobile Analytics | Funding & Investor Relations | Media Monitoring & Social Listening | Startup & Tech News |
| App & Tool Discovery | Game Development Tools | Meeting Management & Organization | Startup Community |
| App & Website Prototyping & Design | Group Collaboration & Teamwork | Mindmapping Tools | Startup Tool Packages & Deals |
| App Development Resources | Growth Hacking | Naming & Domains | Stock Photos & Design Assets |
| App Development Tools | Helpdesk & Customer Support | Networking | Surveys & Forms |
| App Monetization & Mobile Advertising | Hiring & Recruiting | Online Stores & Shopping Carts | Systems Engineering & Product Management |
| Audio Assets & Tools | Hosted Website Building | Payment Solutions & Card Swipe | Telephony & Call Management |
| Bots & Workflow Automation | Ideation | Personal Branding & Reputation | Testing & Feedback |
| Business Planning & Product Roadmaps | Image Editing & Graphic Design | Physical Promo Material & Swag | Translation & Localization |
| Content Curation | Insurance | Physical Prototyping & 3D Printing | Trends |
| Crowdfunding | International Trade | Pitching | User Onboarding & Engagement |
| Customer Relationship Management | Keyword Research | Polling | Video & Animation Tools |
| Decision Tools | Learning Entrepreneurship | Press & Public Relations | Video Advertising |
| Email Management & Newsletters | Legal & Contracts | Product Launch & Landing Pages | Video Assets |
| e-signatures | Link Curation | Productivity & Time Management | Web Analytics & Market Intelligence |
| Event Management & Ticketing | Lists by Others | Project Management | Website Analytics & Optimization |
| Explainer Videos | Loans & Borrowing | Scheduling & Booking | Website Maintenance |
| Finding Co-Founders | Logo Design | Screen Capture & Screencasting | Work Spaces |
| Franchising | Managing Humans / HRM | Search Engine Optimization | Working with Startups |

Based on the data on the categories and the tools listed in each category by each directory, we can make some observations on the breadth of what is included in directories of entrepreneurship technology:

- Directories often include learning resources such as articles and books alongside software tools. These learning resources, however, do not fall within the definition of entrepreneurship technology.
- In some subcategories, it is common to include specific service providers rather than software tools. For example, in video creation it is common to link to video production companies and in legal services it is sometimes linked to specific law offices. These service providers again are not "tools" that would qualify as entrepreneurship technology.
- Directories sometimes use different words for similar concepts (e.g., mock-ups vs. prototyping).
- Directories often have a miscellaneous or other category, which is often large, reflecting the fast paced growth and evolution of the landscape of entrepreneurship technology, and the difficulty of classifying such a rapidly evolving structure.
- Some categories are specifically directed at developers or other specialists such as designers. However, often tools can be found in these categories whose purpose is to render those specialist tasks easy for the non-specialist. The fact that many directories list such tools is indicative of the need for entrepreneurs to often handle multiple roles and specialties at the same time (Churchill & Lewis, 1983).
- The pervasiveness of the lean startup approach (Blank, 2013; Ries, 2011) is evident in the directories of entrepreneurship technology with key concepts in that methodology often referred to in category labels, especially the terms testing, feedback, and minimum viable product (MVP).

**The Leaders of Digital Entrepreneurship Technology**

We used two approaches to identify some of the leading digital tools of entrepreneurship technology. First, we used Siftery's data on the number of companies they track that use each tool to identify the most popular tools in each category. These are listed in Table 7.3. However, there are two caveats here:

First, we have to be careful that what's already popular is not always indicative of what is most significant or has the highest future potential. This is why in addition to efforts in cataloging and categorizing tools, another important type of effort is identifying the trending, hot, or fast growing tools. Siftery dedicates a specific section of their website to "trending" tools and another section to "stories" about how certain tools are gaining traction. Example of a trending tool is Zapier which is rapidly turning into a widely used tool, but is not yet popular enough to rank high in Siftery's usage index. Another example is the database subcategory on Siftery where the top tools are mostly dominant incumbents who have been leading this category for years. However, under the "API and Developer Tools" subcategory, there is a third-level category called "Spreadsheets as a backend" where tools such as Airtable, X-Author, and Fieldbook are changing the way startups are managing their database infrastructure with much lighter and easy to use solutions.

Second, Siftery's data is not based on a representative sample, and although geared toward the new developments of the software landscape, the top tools on sifter are not necessarily the

*Table 7.3*   *First and second level categories in Siftery with top tools in each*

| Category / Subcategory | Top Tools According to Siftery |
|---|---|
| **Analytics and Data Science** | |
| Analytics and Business Intelligence | Google Analytics, Mixpanel, Quantcast Measure, Hotjar, Optimizely, CrazeEgg |
| Data Infrastructure | Pusher, Realtime Framework, PubNub, Socket |
| Data Science | Segment, Mixpanel, Amplitude, Apache Hadoop |
| **Customer Support and Success** | |
| Community | Fuel Cycle, vBulletin, Liferay |
| Support | Zendesk, Intercom, UserVoice, LivePerson, Olark |
| User Engagement and Feedback | Gravity Forms, Intercom, SurveyMonkey, Olark, OptinMonster, Wufoo |
| **Developer** | |
| API and Developer Tools | Bolts, Google Custom Search, Google Translate API, OpenSearch, Google Could Vision API |
| Databases | MySQL, MongoDB, PostgreSQL, Redis, Microsoft SQL Server, Oracle |
| Languages and Frameworks | HTML5, PHP, JavaScript, Java, Ruby on Rails, Python, Node.js, Django |
| Mobile Development | Apache Cordova, Bolts, Appcelerator, Stetho |
| Software Development | jQuery, Bootstrap, Google Maps, Modernizr, Adobe Flash, Microsoft .NET |
| **DevOps and IT** | |
| Application Maintenance and Monitoring | Nagios, Crashlytics, Pingdom, Cedexis Radar |
| Content Management System (CMS) | WordPress, Vimeo, Facebook Comments, Gravatar, Disqus |
| DevOps | Plesk, Atlassian Jira, Chef |
| Hosting | GoDaddy, Amazon Route 53, Cloudflare, MarkMonitor, Akamai |
| PaaS, IaaS and Containers | Amazon EC2. Google Compute Engine, Microsoft Azure, Rackspace, DigitalOcean |
| Security | Comodo SSL, reCAPTCHA, GeoTrust SSL, GoDaddy SSL, DigiCert, GlobalSign |
| Servers, Networks and Storage | Apache Web Server, nginx, Microsoft IIS, Plesk, Amazon S3 |
| **Finance and Accounting** | |
| Accounting | Intuit QuickBooks, Xero, Recurly, FreshBooks |
| Finance | SAP ERP, Oracle Hyperion, Expensify, NetSuite ERP |
| Payments | Google Wallet, Square, Stripe, PayPal, Amazon Payments, Braintree |
| **Human Resources** | |
| Hiring | AngelList Jobs, iCIMS, Oracle Taleo, Greenhouse, Jobvite, SuccessFactors, Workable |
| Workforce Management | SuccessFactors, Workable, Workday |
| **Marketing** | |
| Ad Tech | Google DoubleClick, The Trade Desk, StreamRail, Rubicon, PageFair, Signal |

| Category / Subcategory | Top Tools According to Siftery |
|---|---|
| Content Marketing | VigLink, Taboola, SharePoint, Outbrain, Embedly, MailMunch |
| Demand Generation | LinkedIn Ads, Demandbase, Yotpo, Infusionsoft, Privy |
| Email Marketing | Mandrill, SendGrid, Criteo, Mailgun, Amazon SES, Market, Postmark, Campaign Monitor |
| Marketing Intelligence | Buxton, Moat, App Annie, Alexa |
| Mobile Marketing | Google AdMob, Privy, Urban Airship, OneSignal |
| SEO and Search Marketing | Siteimprove, Trustpilot, Unbounce |
| Social Media | Google Sign-in, Twitter Sign-In, Facebook Login, Refersion, Buffer, Gigya |
| **Product and Design** | |
| Design | Google Fonts, Adobe Typekit, Fonts.com, HubSpot, Shopify, WooCommerce |
| Product Management | Trello, Hive, Asana |
| **Productivity and Operations** | |
| BPM and Workflow | KiSSFLOW, Appian, Intellect |
| Collaboration | Google Drive, Loom, Slack, SharePoint, Hive, InVision |
| Communications | Skype for Business, Loom, Slack, NextPlane, Webex |
| Ecommerce | Fluid, Magento, Shopify, WooCommerce, Beeketing |
| Email Hosting and Tools | G Suite by Google, Microsoft Outlook, GoDaddy, Clearbit Connect, Mimecast Gateway |
| Legal | OutsideGC, Brudge US |
| Operations | Airba, Jolt, GrowSumo |
| Productivity | G Suite by Google, Microsoft Office 365, Google Drive, Loom, Dropbox, DocuSign, Evernote |
| Vertical Software | Google Fit SDK, Edmodo, iubenda |
| **Sales and BD** | |
| CRM | Clearbit Connect, HubSpot CRM, Batchbook |
| Sales | Clearbit Connect, Salesforce, Oracle Service Cloud, ClearSlide, Base CRM |

best options for very small and cash-strapped bootstrapping startups. For example MailChimp is very popular with startups, and has a startup-friendly pricing model that starts free and increases as the business grows. While it is not considered popular by Siftery, it is a commonly listed tool in other directories.

This points us toward a second method for identifying some of the leading tools in entrepreneurship technology, which is to look for tools that are mentioned in multiple directories. While this method produces a list that is too long to include here, in Table 7.4 I have attempted to provide a small selection of these leaders. The table also indicates the variety of category labels used to describe each tool, in order to showcase the level of agreement or disagreement among different directories in categorizing various tools.

## DISCUSSION AND CONCLUDING REMARKS

In this chapter, we have argued that the study of information systems in management research has largely focused on enterprise technologies and the technological needs and practices of large firms, to the neglect of a rapidly evolving category of technological tools and practices that support, improve, and transform the process of entrepreneuring. We argued that this category of technologies needs to be better recognized and studied, and in order to take a first step we labeled it "entrepreneurship technology" and provided a definition. It remains to be seen whether this suggested new term will gain widespread use within the ebb and flow of terminology in the field of digital entrepreneurship (Kollmann & Jung, Chapter 2, Kollmann, Kleine-Stegemann, de Cruppe, & Then-Bergh, Chapter 3, and Scornavacca, Kollmann, Za, Kleine-Stegemann, & Then-Bergh, Chapter 4 in this handbook).

Furthermore, we have taken initial steps to understand the landscape of entrepreneurship technology by investigating existing directories of software tools for entrepreneurs and startups. Since almost all of the tools listed in these directories that we investigated were digital in nature, our focus has been on digital entrepreneurship technologies. Our analysis sheds light on the scope of what can and cannot be labeled "digital entrepreneurship technology," the breadth of this category, and some of the currently leading tools within it.

**Entrepreneurship Technology and Entrepreneurial Ecosystems: Implications for Policy**

It is true that the average entrepreneurial firm typically deals with a smaller scale of employees, revenue, and resources than a large corporation. In fact, entrepreneurship regularly involves dealing with severe resource constraints (hence the common reference to "bootstrapping" in the startup community). But precisely because of these conditions, technological tools that provide even minor improvements in efficiency, effectiveness and productivity of new and nascent ventures that allow entrepreneurs to do more with less, are likely to have significant impact on reducing entry barriers, increasing survival rates, and increasing the overall positive impact (and positive spillover effects) of entrepreneurship in the broader economy. Technology that improves the productivity of thousands of potential entrepreneurs may have even a larger socioeconomic impact than technology that improves the productivity of a handful of large corporations.

At the ecosystem or industry level, the tools and technologies of interest are an important part of a broader technological infrastructure of entrepreneurship, and so we may expect that

*Table 7.4   Selection of entrepreneurship technology software tools commonly listed across directories, and category labels used to describe them*

| Tool | Description | Category Labels |
| --- | --- | --- |
| 1Password | Single login service. Saves all log in information and accesses them for you. | DevOps and IT, Security, Password Management, Productivity, Utility |
| Adobe TypeKit | Provides database of fonts from designers around the world. Eliminates licensing hurdles for users. | Product and Design, Design, Web Fonts and Design Assets |
| Amazon Web Services | Massive web services, hosting, analytics, develop, etc., platform providing 45+ other tools also listed among the directories, in duplicate at times. | Hosting, Other, Mobile analytics, Web Hosting, Media Transcoding, Big Data Infrastructure, Analytics and Data Science, Developer, Productivity, Servers, Networks and Storage, Databases, API Management etc. |
| AngelList | Startup ecosystem job board and investment portal. | Hiring, Raising Capital, Product News & Startups, Startup and Tech News, HR, Job Board, Startup Community |
| Asana | Productivity and project management hub SaaS. Expanded to enterprise scale as well in 2013. | Product and Design, Product Management, Project Management, Task Management, CRMs, Organization, Collaboration |
| Balsamiq | Mockup and wireframe service for GUIs and websites. | Product and Design, Design, Mockups, Wireframing and Prototyping, Mockups & Wireframing, Prototypes |
| Basecamp | Web based project management tool. | Product Management, Project Management, Collaboration, Product and Design |
| Buffer | Social media hub, provides content management and account management and linking. | Marketing, Social Media, Social Media Data, Social Media Management, Social tools, Social |
| Dribbble | Designer marketplace, content discovery and sharing hub. Supports team, and freelance designers. | HR, Product and Design, Hiring, Find Designers, Find Freelancers, Design, Design Marketplace, Job Boards |
| Evernote | Cloud storage service for documents, notes, images, files etc. Enables searching images and documents for text as well as content sharing. | Productivity and Operations, GTD and Personal Organizers, Web Clipping and Bookmarking, Collaboration. Other, Project Collaboration/Task Management |
| HipChat | Business focussed video calling, file sharing, screen sharing, team chat, instant messaging and searching within everything previous. | Productivity and Operations, File Sharing and Backup, Internal Communication, Project Collaboration/Task Management, Instant Messaging |
| HootSuite | Social media hub that aides or performs, marketing, content management, collaboration, scheduling and analytics. | Social Media Management, Social tools, Social, media Monitoring & Social Listening |
| InVision | Collaborative design and project management suite. Provides, collaborative editing, file sharing, version control, feedback and workflow organization. | Collaborative Design and Prototyping, Mockups, Wireframing and Prototyping, Team Collaboration, Design, Project Management |
| Join.me | Web based video and audio conferencing software. Also enables screen and file sharing. | Audio Conferencing, Screen Sharing, Web and Video Conferencing, Internal Communication, Collaboration & Communication, Productivity and Operations |
| Mailchimp | Email marketing support, enables linking websites and products to emails, provides reporting, integrated Facebook advertising and email automation. | Useful Tools, Email Marketing, Email Management & Newsletters, Email |

| Tool | Description | Category Labels |
|---|---|---|
| Pitcherific | Business pitch preparation aid. Provides, pitch templates, video and audio rehearsals, teleprompter practice and pitch coaching. | Useful Tools, Pitch, Pitching |
| Segment | Business intelligence and analytics centralization and distribution hub. Integrates with 180+ other services to collect and share data. | Data Integration, Data Science, Analytics and Data Science, BI/Analytics, Analytics |
| Sidekick | Email tracking service that allows user to know when emails are opened, email recipient's email history. | Productivity, Sales, Email Management & Newsletters |
| Sketch | Vector based design, mockup, prototype and graphic design suite. | Design, Graphic Design Software, prototypes, App & website Prototyping & Design, Image Editing & Graphic Design |
| Slack | Multi-platform team collaboration platform. Provides chat, file sharing, calling, archive searching, as well as a robust suite of extensions and integrations to other services. | Productivity and operations, Collaboration, Communications, Instant Messaging, Team Collaboration, Internal Communication, Group Collaboration & Teamwork |
| Strikingly | Catering to low tech users, provides, templates and website building, hosting and analytics. | Design, Site Builder, MVP, Website Builder, Product and Design |
| Stripe | Multiplatform payment processing services. | Payments, Payments Processing, Recurring Billing and Payments, Credit Card Processing, Ecommerce, Payment Solutions & Card Swipe |
| Trello | Workflow, internal communication and project management platform with mobile support. | Kanban Boards, Product Management, Task Management, Project Management, Collaboration, Organization, Group Collaboration & Teamwork |
| Tweetdeck | Real time analytics and management for Twitter. | Marketing, Social Media, Twitter Marketing, Other, Social, Social Media Management, Media Monitoring & Social Listening |
| Untorch | Fully automated referral software for email signups. | Pre-Launch Traction, MVP, Growth Hacking |
| Upwork | Freelancer job board. Employers/Project managers post jobs and freelancers apply. Hiring, collaboration, file sharing, chat and invoicing occur internally. | Find Designers, Find Freelancers, Hiring, Outsourcing, Freelancers & Task Economy |
| Wave | Accounting web platform that provides accounting, invoicing, payroll, receipts, etc. | Finance, Accounting, Bookkeeping and Accounting, Payroll Management, Online Accounting Suites |
| Zapier | Automation web services integrates apps, over 750, creates automated workflows, connects data and files between apps. | Integrations Marketplace, Other, Useful Tools, utility, Automation, Bots & Workflow Automation |
| Zendesk | Customer relationship management web services. Provides CRM data, chat, support, ticketing contact, etc. | Customer Support and Success, Support, Help Desk and Ticketing |
| Zuora | Subscription billing services with accounting, payments, taxes and other applications built in. | Finance and Accounting, Payments, Recurring Billing and Payments |

countries and regions in which these tools are more easily accessible or more widely adopted will experience a significant improvement in the quantity and quality of entrepreneurial activity. Thus beyond competitive advantage for startups, entrepreneurship technology may soon become a crucial determinant of the competitive advantage of cities, regions and nations (Fossen, McLemore, & Sorgner, Chapter 6 and Gerli & Whalley, Chapter 15 in this handbook).

One mechanism through which entrepreneurship technology has benefits on a societal level is that through the systematization and commodification of technology for various support functions of entrepreneurship, the locus of competitive advantage moves increasingly away from these support functions and shifts toward core functions, including the actual value created by the offering for customers. The shift in the locus of competitive advantage in turn results in a shift in the locus of competition. When the ability to access high quality support functions becomes ubiquitous, competition among new ventures intensifies over their core value propositions.

Entrepreneurial activity is such a widely pursued policy objective that policy makers have by now tried a plethora of levers and initiatives such as loans, grants, tax benefits, legal exemptions, training programs, advisory services, and so on to spark the entrepreneurial fire. These initiatives however, are often criticized for putting the government in a position of "picking winners" (Shane, 2009). Empowering budding entrepreneurs with access to technology may be a less intrusive way for governments to cradle the entrepreneurial fire. Evidence suggests that ease of startup is a strong predictor of startup activity in an industry, even more so than the success rate of startups in that industry (Shane, 2008, 2009). Thus policy makers may benefit from viewing entrepreneurship technology as a form of infrastructure underlying economic activity and an essential component of an entrepreneurial ecosystem. In fact, differences in the extent to which the new digital technologies of entrepreneurship are embraced around the world are likely to lead to a new and important aspect of the technology gap among nations (Fagerberg, 1987).

**Future Directions**

Important avenues for future research include systematic testing of adoption rates of various technologies and testing the relationship between usage of various technological tools and portfolios of tools on the performance, survival, and growth of startups. Furthermore, the impact of these tools on the organizational processes, managerial issues, and team dynamics may be of interest to entrepreneurship scholars, as well as how these technologies impact social entrepreneurship and in general forms of entrepreneuring other than purely for-profit ventures.

Furthermore, studies of entrepreneurship technology as an infrastructure at the city, state, country and regional levels are yet to be conducted. It is important to see if the data supports the idea that differences in access to new digital entrepreneurship technologies is indeed widening the technology gap among nations or not.

Investigating these and other questions in such a rapidly evolving landscape is unquestionably difficult, but not doing so can risk entrepreneurship research falling far behind entrepreneurship practice and losing relevance. I'm optimistic that the community of entrepreneurship scholars can rise to the challenge.

# ACKNOWLEDGMENTS

This chapter has benefited from the feedback of participants in the 2017 annual conference of the Canadian Council for Small Business and Entrepreneurship (CCSBE) in Quebec City, and reviewers of the 2018 Annual Interdisciplinary Conference on Entrepreneurship, Innovation and SMEs (G-Forum) in the University of Hohenheim.

# NOTES

1. https://www.entrepreneurship.org/zero-barriers.
2. https://techcrunch.com/2016/12/01/angelhunt/.
3. http://ryanhoover.me/post/69599262875/product-hunt-began-as-an-email-list.
4. http://old.ycombinator.com/ideas.html.

# REFERENCES

Blank, S. (2013). Why the lean start-up changes everything. *Harvard Business Review, 91*(5), 65–72.
Christensen, C. M. (1997). *The innovator's dilemma: when new technologies cause great firms to fail.* Boston, MA: Harvard Business School Press.
Churchill, N. C., & Lewis, V. L. (1983). The five stages of small business growth. *Harvard Business Review, 61*(3), 30–50.
Cragg, P. B., & King, M. (1993). Small-firm computing: motivators and inhibitors. *Mis Quarterly*, 47–60.
Cragg, P. B., & Zinatelli, N. (1995). The evolution of information systems in small firms. *Information & Management, 29*(1), 1–8.
Davidson, E., & Vaast, E. (2010). *Digital entrepreneurship and its sociomaterial enactment.* Paper presented at the 43rd Hawaii International Conference on System Sciences (HICSS).
Der Foo, M., Wong, P. K., & Ong, A. (2005). Do others think you have a viable business idea? Team diversity and judges' evaluation of ideas in a business plan competition. *Journal of Business Venturing, 20*(3), 385–402.
Dewald, J. R. (2016). *Achieving longevity: how great firms prosper through entrepreneurial thinking.* Toronto: University of Toronto Press.
Eisenhardt, K. M., & Schoonhoven, C. B. (1990). Organizational growth: Linking founding team, strategy, environment, and growth among US semiconductor ventures, 1978–1988. *Administrative Science Quarterly*, 504–529.
Fagerberg, J. (1987). A technology gap approach to why growth rates differ. *Research Policy, 16*(2–4), 87–99.
Giones, F., & Brem, A. (2017). Digital technology entrepreneurship: A definition and research agenda. *Technology Innovation Management Review, 7*(5), 44–51.
Grell, K. B., Marom, D., & Swart, R. (2015). *Crowdfunding: the corporate era.* London: Elliott and Thompson.
Hull, C. E., Hung, Y.-T. C., Hair, N., Perotti, V., & DeMartino, R. (2007). Taking advantage of digital opportunities: a typology of digital entrepreneurship. *International Journal of Networking and Virtual Organisations, 4*(3), 290–303.
Igbaria, M., Zinatelli, N., Cragg, P., & Cavaye, A. L. (1997). Personal computing acceptance factors in small firms: a structural equation model. *Mis Quarterly*, 279–305.
Keyhani, M. (2021a). The logic of strategic entrepreneurship. *Strategic Organization.* doi:https://doi.org/10.1177%2F14761270211057571.
Keyhani, M. (2021b). *The rise of no-code entrepreneurship.* University of Calgary.

Laplume, A. O., Petersen, B., & Pearce, J. M. (2016). Global value chains from a 3D printing perspective. *Journal of International Business Studies, 47*(5), 595–609.

Levine, R., & Rubinstein, Y. (2017). Smart and illicit: who becomes an entrepreneur and do they earn more?. *The Quarterly Journal of Economics, 132*(2), 963–1018.

Levinson, M. (2016). *The box: how the shipping container made the world smaller and the world economy bigger.* Princeton, NJ: Princeton University Press.

Nambisan, S. (2017). Digital entrepreneurship: Toward a digital technology perspective of entrepreneurship. *Entrepreneurship Theory and Practice, 41*(6), 1029–1055.

Porter, M. E. (1996). What is strategy? *Harvard Business Review, 74*(6), 61–78.

Richter, C., Kraus, S., Brem, A., Durst, S., & Giselbrecht, C. (2017). Digital entrepreneurship: Innovative business models for the sharing economy. *Creativity and Innovation Management, 26*(3), 300–310.

Ries, E. (2011). *The lean startup: how today's entrepreneurs use continuous innovation to create radically successful businesses* (1st ed.). New York: Crown Business.

Rindova, V., Barry, D., & Ketchen, D. J. (2009). Entrepreneuring as emancipation. *Academy of Management Review, 34*(3), 477–491.

Rumelt, R. P. (2011). *Good strategy, bad strategy: the difference and why it matters* (1st ed.). New York: Crown Business.

Shane, S. A. (2008). *The illusions of entrepreneurship: the costly myths that entrepreneurs, investors, and policy makers live by.* New Haven: Yale University Press.

Shane, S. A. (2009). Why encouraging more people to become entrepreneurs is bad public policy. *Small Business Economics, 33*(2), 141–149.

Shane, S. A., & Venkataraman, S. (2000). The promise of entrepreneurship as a field of research. *Academy of Management Review, 25*(1), 217–226.

Shapiro, C., & Varian, H. R. (1999). *Information rules: a strategic guide to the network economy.* Boston, MA: Harvard Business School Press.

Van Holm, E. J. (2015). Makerspaces and contributions to entrepreneurship. *Procedia-Social and Behavioral Sciences, 195*, 24–31.

Varian, H. R. (2001). High-technology industries and market structure. http://people.ischool.berkeley.edu/~hal/Papers/structure.pdf.

Varian, H. R. (2010). Computer mediated transactions. *The American Economic Review, 100*(2), 1–10.

Varian, H. R. (2019). Artificial intelligence, economics, and industrial organization. In A. Agrawal, J. Gans, & A. Goldfarb (Eds.), *The Economics of Artificial Intelligence: An Agenda* (pp. 399–419). Chicago: University of Chicago Press.

# 8.   Digital product-assisted learning: transforming entrepreneurial learning with product usage analytics

*Varun Nagaraj*

## INTRODUCTION

Digitization – the adoption of digital technologies to conceive or reimagine new products, core business processes, and business models (Bughin, 2017; Venkatraman, 2017) – is transforming the practice of entrepreneurship and altering the boundaries of core entrepreneurial processes and agency (Berger, von Briel, Davidsson, & Kuckertz, 2019; Nambisan, 2017). This chapter introduces a specific type of digital technology – *product usage analytics tools* – and examines its impact on the entrepreneurial learning process.

### Product Usage Analytics Tools

Product Collective (see http://www.productcollective.com), a leading industry forum for digital product innovators with over 30,000 registered members, defines product usage analytics as a set of tools that allows digital product teams to instrument product features, measure users' real-time in-use interaction with those features, and assess the overall digital experience offered to the user (Khayaglou, 2021). The user interacting with the features may be human, accessing the product's features through a user interface (UI) or the user may be a computational machine consuming the feature through an application program interface (API).

Product usage analytics tools typically consist of software components (also called tags or agents) that product engineers embed into the product's UI or API code, and a cloud-based analysis and dashboard software that the embedded code connects to in real-time. The embedded software captures how human or machine users navigate each feature offered by the product: whether they use it or not, how frequently they access it, how long they take to consume that feature, how they come to that feature, where they go next, and so on. The cloud-based software collects this quantitative usage data (also called clickstreams or events), from millions of deployed products, and summarizes user journeys (if human user), API sequences (if machine user) and feature usage patterns (for both human and machine users) for the product team, thus giving voice to the product. The embedded software may additionally prompt human users to provide qualitative inputs on specific features or on the whole product, such as through a "what do you think" input box placed next to the feature. The set of product usage analytics tools also include tools for providing different feature variants to different human users (referred to as A/B testing) so as to understand user preferences (Hynninen & Kauppinen, 2014; Kohavi & Longbotham, 2017).

Product usage analytics tools are widely available in the market and are routinely used by digital product development teams. G2, an industry resource used by digital product innovators to select software technologies, lists and rates tens of companies offering product usage analytics tools (see https://www.g2.com/categories/product-analytics), the category is an active area for venture capital investing (Miller, 2019), and as of 2018, adoption was more than 60% (Nagaraj, 2019).

**Digital Product-Assisted Learning**

Building on the literature and a qualitative field study of two digital startups deploying product usage analytics tools, the chapter outlines a normative process model for the digital product-assisted learning that emerges from using such tools. The transformative effects of digital technology often manifest in significant and simultaneous changes to the scale, scope, and speed of business strategies and processes (Bharadwaj, El Sawy, Pavlou, & Venkatraman, 2013; Venkatraman, 2017), and we discover similar effects of digitization on the scale, scope, and speed of entrepreneurial learning.

However, while the impact on scale is broadly consistent with digital's observed positive effects on scale in other contexts (Venkatraman, 2017; Verhoef et al., 2021; Vial, 2019), the results on scope and speed are nuanced. Economies of scope stem from the surprising ambidexterity of the digital product-assisted learning process – the process produces both exploitative learning (required to improve the usability of an existing feature of the product) and exploratory learning (required to identify new opportunities). Such ambidexterity or versatility within one process challenges generally accepted management thinking that exploration and exploitation merit distinct organizational forms, work structures, and processes (Benner & Tushman, 2003; O'Reilly & Tushman, 2013). We also identify an interaction between speed and scope: realized economies of speed may be contingent upon the type of learning.

The scalable, fast, versatile, and ultimately cost-effective nature of digital product-assisted learning suggests that digital entrepreneurs should prioritize and master this particular form of learning (noting its limitations) as they construct a streamlined repertoire of approaches to create required learning within their organizations. To that end, the proposed process reference model can serve as a normative implementation template for practitioners.

The rest of the chapter is organized as follows: We first draw upon the entrepreneurial learning and lean startup methodology literatures to theoretically frame digital product-assisted learning as a particular variant of the general entrepreneurial learning process. Following a brief description of the research method deployed for the field study, we present findings in the form of a process reference model for digital product-assisted learning. We then discuss how digitization impacts the scale, speed, and scope of entrepreneurial learning, and conclude by outlining implications for practice and research.

## THEORETICAL FRAMING

Learning is central to entrepreneurship (Cope, 2005; Smilor, 1997), and given the importance of the team in new venture creation and innovation in digital contexts, team learning is especially critical (El-Awad, Gabrielsson, & Politis, 2017; Kamm, Shuman, Seeger, & Nurick, 1990; Nagaraj, 2019). In this section, we first outline the general entrepreneurial team learning process, and subsequently describe the more specific 'product-assisted' variant.

Entrepreneurial learning is a dynamic experiential process (Cope, 2005) that creates knowledge required to explore and exploit opportunities (Wang & Chugh, 2014) during new venture or product creation (Nogueira, 2019). The process encompasses the acquisition of experiences and their subsequent transformation into applicable knowledge (Corbett, 2005; Kolb, 2014; Politis, 2005).

Experiences can be acquired by leveraging team members' a priori experiences (Rerup, 2005) or by creating new personal or shared experiences. The continuous creation of new experiences is critically important in digital entrepreneurship where markets and technologies are dynamic, and are thus not easily comprehended based on past experiences alone (Nagaraj, 2019). New experiences may result (1) from everyday actions taken in the context of the entrepreneurial venture (Lumpkin & Lichtenstein, 2005), (2) through purposeful experimentation (Thomke, 2001) and reflection (Fust, Jenert, & Winkler, 2017); and (3) by seeking and internalizing the experiences of others (Lévesque, Minniti, & Shepherd, 2009; Myers, 2018).

Transforming experiences into applicable team knowledge follows many of the steps of team-level sensemaking (Akgün, Keskin, Lynn, & Dogan, 2012; Maitlis & Christianson, 2014; Nagaraj, Boland, & Lyytinen, 2017; Weick, Sutcliffe, & Obstfeld, 2005; Wright, Manning, Farmer, & Gilbreath, 2000). These steps create an understanding of what the team's accumulated experiences (historic and new) mean in the context of the specific opportunity or challenge facing the team. Specifically, the team (1) adds context to each experience (Turpin & du Plooy, 2004), (2) connects the dots and creates shared frames (Raffaelli, Glynn, & Tushman, 2019; Seidl & Werle, 2018), (3) triangulates and integrates them with divergent sources of information (Berente, Vandenbosch, & Aubert, 2009; Overby, Bharadwaj, & Sambamurthy, 2006), and (4) engages in vigorous deliberation and discourse to interpret the information and identify the best course of going-forward action (Lyytinen & Hirschheim, 1988; Nagaraj et al., 2017; Weick & Meader, 1993).

Entrepreneurial learning aims to create two distinct types of knowledge – exploratory and exploitative (Wang & Chugh, 2014) – that are both critical but can often conflict with or contradict each other (March, 1991; Siren, Kohtamäki, & Kuckertz, 2012). Knowledge required for exploration or discovering opportunities involves a wide search space that can generate enough variations, whereas knowledge necessary for exploitation or seeking advantage requires a narrower search that limits variety, focuses on and refines initial insights, thus building team confidence and commitment to action (Lumpkin & Lichtenstein, 2005; March, 1991; Wang & Chugh, 2014). In addition, exploration and exploitation often require distinct processes, organizational separation and distinct governance rules (Benner & Tushman, 2003; O'Reilly & Tushman, 2013). However, given the characteristics that distinguish entrepreneurship such as proactivity, urgency, risk-taking, and limited resources (Blank, 2013; Covin & Wales, 2012; Dess & Lumpkin, 2005; Lumpkin & Dess, 1996; Michaelis, Carr, Scheaf, & Pollack, 2020; Ries, 2011), entrepreneurial ventures must achieve such ambidexterity more efficiently than traditional large organizations. Thus entrepreneurial learning requires the construction of a streamlined and cost-effective repertoire of learning process variants that can collectively create both exploitative and exploratory knowledge.

Product-assisted learning is a specialized variant of the general entrepreneurial learning process in which the product plays a leading role in the creation of new experiences that trigger the learning cycle. Entrepreneurial teams build new experiences as they interact with their environment, such as by engaging with or observing customers, suppliers, competitors, employees, and associates (Smilor, 1997). These interactions could be in the context of taking every day action (Lumpkin & Lichtenstein, 2005), purposeful experimentation (Thomke, 2001), or consciously seeking the experience of others (Lévesque et al., 2009). In product-assisted learning, the team's products serve as boundary objects or probes that facilitate such interactions and trigger feedback (Bechky, 2003; Brown & Eisenhardt, 1997; Carlile, 2002; Eisenhardt & Tabrizi, 1995). For example, a restauranteur who solicits feedback from patrons trying a new dessert item and iterates the recipe daily until they rate it highly is practicing product-assisted learning.

Product-assisted learning is exemplified in the lean startup methodology (Blank, 2013; Ries, 2011) – an approach favored by startups that operate in dynamic environments. Product-assisted learning in lean startups is implemented as an iterative three-stage "Build-Measure-Learn" (BML) process that creates new experiences and transformation of experiences into knowledge. The product development team quickly *builds* and deploys the product to purposefully test certain product and business assumptions with stakeholders. Deployed products generate feedback from the product's many users, and the team *measures* this feedback, thus internalizing the users' (vicarious) experiences. The team then interprets, transforms, and *learns* from these experiences, either validating their original assumptions or creating new insights. Finally, the team acts on its new insights by modifying the product's features, which not only improves product–market fit, but also triggers the next cycle of learning (Olsen, 2015). In sum, the product-assisted learning process variant, as outlined by the BML model, particularizes the general experiential entrepreneurial learning process in two ways: (1) the product triggers the creation of new experiences, and (2) the process is closed loop and iterative.

While there is nothing inherently digital about the product-assisted learning process and the BML model per se, as illustrated by the example of the restauranteur, digital startups are particularly enthusiastic proponents of product-assisted learning. This is because unlike conventional products, digital products are more than just static and inanimate boundary objects used in the learning process; they are vocal, malleable, and generative anthromorphic participants (Orlikowski, 2009) in the creation of new experiences. Digital products are vocal – they can continuously and remotely communicate with the product team after deployment (Joglekar & Nagaraj, 2017; Porter & Heppelmann, 2015), effectively providing vicarious 'in-use' observations from the field. Digital products are also malleable – post deployment, in response to emergent learning, their functionality and behavior can be reconfigured or reprogrammed rapidly and remotely by the product team (Joglekar & Nagaraj, 2017; Yoo, 2012; Yoo, Boland Jr, Lyytinen, & Majchrzak, 2012) to trigger the next cycle of experiences and learning. Therefore, digital product-assisted learning can be viewed as a more generative form of product-assisted learning that is afforded to digital product development teams.

Product usage analytics tools enable and enhance the BML loop in digital product development. Specifically, the embedded component of the product analytics tool is incorporated into the product during the build stage, the cloud-based collection component of the product analytics tool automates the ongoing measurement of the digital trace data produced as the product is used (Fabijan, Olsson, & Bosch, 2015; Joglekar & Nagaraj, 2017), and the dashboards that consolidate and display the collected information help guide discussions and deliberations during the learning stage.

While digitizing the product-assisted learning process with product usage analytics tools is now common practice, our theoretical understanding of the dynamics of this phenomenon is incomplete. Certainly, scholars have highlighted individual aspects of the digital product-assisted learning process. For example, Fabijan, Dmitriev, Olsson, and Bosch (2017) and Fagerholm, Guinea, Mäenpää, and Münch (2017) examine continuous and purposeful product-based experimentation by lean-agile software teams, while Robinson (2006), Robinson and Fickas (2009), and Souza, Lapouchnian, Robinson, and Mylopoulos (2013) examine how product requirements monitoring helps software developers know if a feature is indeed satisfying its intended requirement. However, the empirical literature with some exceptions (see Werder et al. (2020) for a case study of digital product-assisted learning in video game development) is muted about how teams transform such measurements at scale into applied knowledge, and whether such knowledge is explorative or exploitative. In sum, we lack a holistic, integrated, and empirically grounded process-based view of the emergence and characteristics of digital product-assisted learning.

# METHODS

## Sample and Data Collection

In order to understand how learning emerges in teams that deploy product usage analytics tools in product development, the author engaged with two fast-growing and venture capital funded B2B2C Software-as-a-Service companies with $10M to $50M annual revenues. EnergyEfficiencyCo (EE) is based in Silicon Valley, California, while GiftCardCo (GC) is based in Bangalore, India. EE's product is used by electric and gas utilities to engage with their approximately 20 million customers by providing personalized energy efficiency-related insights and recommendations. GC provides a software platform that powers an on-line and off-line gifting ecosystem of retail brands, gift card resellers, corporates, and individuals. More than 400 retailers, resellers, and corporates build on the platform and provide gift cards and related services to their millions of customers. Both companies regard themselves as lean startups, use agile development processes, and deploy commercial product usage analytics tools.

The author spent approximately 20 hours at each company, holding semi-structured discussions with each company's Chief Technology Officer (CTO), Chief Product Officer (CPO), and Product Management staff, singly and in groups. The discussions used the critical incident technique (Cope & Watts, 2000; Flanagan, 1954) and focused on memorable episodes of how the teams transformed feedback triggered by product features into insights that they subsequently acted upon. The use of a recording device was prohibited by both companies, and therefore, the author made notes in real-time during interactions and added to them subsequently through recollection. Eight episodes of digital product-assisted learning – three drawn from EE and five from GC – were subsequently summarized (see Table 8.1).

## Process Reference Modelling

The eight episodes were then used to develop a process reference model for digital product-assisted learning (see Figure 8.1). A process reference model is an abstraction or a blueprint of a complex management process that identifies and links the diverse information flows and activities that constitute the process (Fettke & Loos, 2006). A reference model attempts to provide a generalizable, complete, understandable, flexible, and usable explanation of the focal process (Matook & Indulska, 2009) and thus contributes to theory and practice – it provides an integrating context to researchers exploring various dimensions of an emerging phenomenon, and also serves as the basis for process implementation, benchmarking, and ongoing improvement by practitioners (Stewart, 1997). A process reference model can be developed either by adapting or extending an existing process model to address new requirements, or by inductively abstracting observations from several cases (Otto & Ofner, 2010). In this chapter, the BML model for product-assisted learning (Blank, 2013; Ries, 2011) provided the basic framework, which was then extended with the specific information flows and activities derived from the eight summarized episodes.

## FINDINGS

First, the interviews validate the importance of the digital product in the learning process. As noted by the CPO of GC: "Our biggest and boldest ideas may have originated from our strategic vision and conviction. But hard to know if you are right or wrong until you put a product in front of customers." More specifically, the findings unpack "how" learning emerges when a digital product is placed in front of customers (see Table 8.1).

The episodes illuminate several aspects of digital product-assisted learning – human interactions through graphical user interfaces (UIs), machine interactions through application programming interfaces (APIs), planned experimentation, anomaly based detection, information triangulation, synchronous and asynchronous decision making, incremental feature improvements, and white space identification. Collectively, they provide the empirical foundation for the process reference model outlined in Figure 8.1.

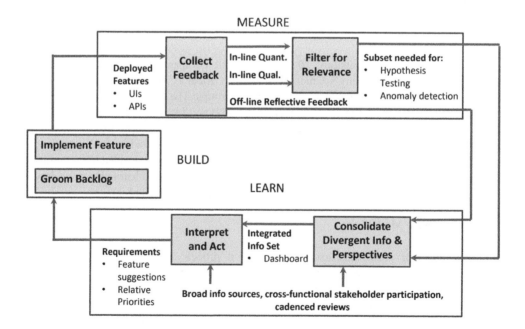

*Figure 8.1    Digital product-assisted-learning process reference model*

*Table 8.1*   Digital product-assisted learning episodes

| Episode ID | Learning Outcomes | Learning Process |
|---|---|---|
| EE1: The "High Bill Analysis" feature for customer service rep desktop | Identified feature modifications required to improve service rep experience | The feature is used by the service rep in the call center to quickly resolve customer billing complaints. In addition to click sequence, the team collected instantaneous on-line feedback from the rep at the end of each call and also interviewed the reps after a month. Input was discussed at the monthly executive product review and feature enhancements identified. |
| EE2: Anomaly based high-usage customer notification and recommendations | Kicked off new core algorithm to improve relevance of notifications | Open rates of the notification and thumbs up/down inputs did not indicate customer dissatisfaction, but the team noticed an unexpectedly high number of on-line comments from users complaining that the recommendations presented to them were too generic. The monthly executive product review identified the need to improve the recommendation algorithm. |
| EE3: Drop in monthly summary email open rate | Decided to roll back new changes that caused drop in user engagement | Anomaly was detected in a routinely tracked monthly metric – the open rates of emails generated by the EE platform fell dramatically one month. The anomaly was immediately investigated by the cross-functional product team. The implementation sub-team discovered that the customer had changed the "From" field before the emails were sent, resulting in many emails being ensnared in customers' spam filters. Issue was fixed before next monthly executive review. |
| GC1: APIs for on-boarding retailer onto the GC platform | Identified features modifications to improve integrator experience | Learning cycle was triggered by an offline observation from an integrator noting that the onboarding process was clumsy. The PM and engineers dug into the API event logs to understand why and identified a "lean" set of APIs that could be packaged together to reduce the number of steps. The priority of this feature improvement versus other development alternatives was debated at the monthly executive meeting and was greenlighted. |
| GC2: APIs for developing new retailer programs | Identified new "product buy-back" opportunity and features required | Dashboard showed a sudden drop in API performance at major retailer. Analysis of logs showed an unfamiliar API call sequence that was compromising performance. A live discussion with the programmers at the retailer revealed that the retailer had introduced a new use case around product buy backs that had nothing to do with gift cards. Discussion at monthly executive review concluded that this could be a common new use case across retailers and commissioned a multi-sprint project to create the features that would support this requirement. |
| GC3: Reports package | Optimized migration of reports feature from old platform to new platform | An upcoming platform change required that the (bloated) reports package be rewritten for the new platform. An analysis of which reports were most popular based on filters applied by users identified the smallest number of reports that could satisfy the largest number of users – these reports could be rewritten to be performance-optimized. The insights derived from usage data were also validated with a few live customer interviews. |

| Episode ID | Learning Outcomes | Learning Process |
|---|---|---|
| GC4: Self-gifting on consumer portal | Identified "self-gifting" as a new business opportunity | The gifting features were initially designed based on customer interviews that indicated they wanted more personalization. Analyzing click stream data, it emerged that many users were using it to "self-gift" cards to themselves and that personalization was not as relevant for this use case. Executive team deliberated on this surprising information and greenlighted a new project focused on this unexpected new use case. |
| GC5: Gift card trading on consumer portal | Learned how to improve intent-to-transaction conversion | The team introduced new features to facilitate trading of gift cards on the platform and analyzed click stream. Data indicated that many users were starting but not completing the transaction, dropping off at the step that asked for personal information. Team also looked at offline support tickets opened by irate customers and spotted comments on this topic. In the next sprint, the team moved the personal information collection step to later in the sequence based on hypothesis that they needed to gain the customer's trust before asking for personal information. New clickstream data showed a big reduction in the drop-off rate. |

## Build

Both EE and GS followed a standard agile build methodology for all their projects – grooming their feature backlog and modifying or developing features in 2-week sprint cycles (Cockburn, 2006; Dingsøyr, Nerur, Balijepally, & Moe, 2012; Inayat, Salim, Marczak, Daneva, & Shamshirband, 2015; Olsson, Alahyari, & Bosch, 2012). Both EE and GC selected commercially available product usage analytics tools and mandated their development engineers to instrument all features with embedded analytics code so that usage events (feedback) would be recorded upon feature exercise. In six of the eight cases (EE1, EE2, EE3, GC3, GC4, GC5), the feature was meant to be used by a human user and was exposed through a UI, and in two cases (GC1 and GC2), the feature was exposed as an API to be called by a machine user. Features were developed over one or multiple sprint cycles depending on the complexity of the feature. Not all the developed UI features were instantaneously released to end consumers in the field upon sprint completion as is common in B2C contexts; instead, given that EE and GC are B2B2C companies, end consumer UI features only went "live" when EE and GC's business customers decided to expose them to the end consumers.

## Measure – Collect Feedback

EE and GC collected three types of product-assisted feedback. (1) In all eight cases, "in-line quantitative" usage event data was produced and logged in real-time as the UIs (EE1, EE2, EE3, GC3, GC4, GC5) and APIs (GC1, GC2) associated with the released features were exercised by human and machine users. (2) In two of the six UI cases (EE1 and EE2), the teams explicitly sought qualitative user inputs through a "what do you think" input box placed next to a new feature. Such "in-line qualitative" input generated in real time was used to provide context to the in-line quantitative usage event stream. (3) Six of eight cases (EE1, EE3, GC1, GC2, GC3, and GC4) also involved "offline reflective" feedback sometime after product use or exposure. This form of feedback captured the "voice of the customer" through more traditional and labor-intensive interactions (see Griffin and Hauser (1993) and others) between EE and GC and their business customers. These interactions were sometimes initiated by the customer (GC1), or more generally they were proactively solicited by EE and GC (EE1, EE3, GC2, GC3, and GC4).

## Measure – Filter for Relevance

Using a "just-in-case" mindset, EE and GC instrumented all their features to produce and collect vast amounts of in-line quantitative feedback. Also, the product stimulated additional in-line qualitative feedback and off-line reflective feedback in some cases. When confronted with voluminous information, deciding what to pay attention to becomes critical (Ocasio, 2011). The teams attended to the subset of feedback data that met the following criteria. (1) The data was required to build an understanding of a use case of interest and to define a new feature (GC3). (2) The data was relevant to an explicit experiment being run to validate assumptions regarding a specific new feature being introduced (Fabijan et al., 2017; Fagerholm et al., 2017) as in EE1 and GC5. (3) The data was associated with an anomaly (EE2, EE3, GC1, GC2, and GC4). Unlike explicit experimentation on specific new features, anomaly detection was based on routine monitoring of all deployed features, with anomalies being flagged when measured values did not match expectations (Robinson, 2006; Robinson & Fickas, 2009; Silva Souza, Lapouchnian, Robinson, & Mylopoulos, 2011).

**Learn – Consolidate Divergent Information and Perspectives**

The teams recognized the value of integrating divergent data points to better understand the customer situation confronting them (Overby et al., 2006; Turpin & du Plooy, 2004; Vandenbosch & Huff, 1997; Werder et al., 2020) and took the following steps to create a consolidated view. (1) In seven of eight cases (with the exception of GC5), the team mindfully blended the filtered and relevant in-line feedback with reflective off-line feedback generated post-use. As noted by a product manager (PM) at GC: "I don't know how any API analysis can give you context. It needs other inputs like the sales guy coming in and telling what the customer wants to do." But the various types of feedback were not always congruent and additive. For example, discussing GC4, the PM explained: "The actual digital usage data contradicted what the users had told us about why they wanted personalization features while gifting." (2) In-line and off-line feedback was further sharpened by bringing in other perspectives and information sources. For example, the PMs at EE routinely initiated internal discussion threads inviting employees to provide their experience-based inputs on ambiguous product-generated feedback. The CTO of GC similarly said: "Understanding what that anomaly is requires business discussions. An anomaly draws attention to an issue and brings in those that may know something." EE also used additional data such as demographic and seasonality information to add context to in-line and off-line feedback. (3) Both companies implemented an integrated dashboard – the "source of truth" as described by the CTO of GC – that coded and blended various forms of feedback to create a starting point for subsequent discourse. The CTO of GC stated: "We use our new integrated metrics dashboard regularly – it helps us quickly identify issues that we might otherwise miss if we were looking at each piece of the puzzle separately." Similarly, the CTO of EE said: "We've made a big investment in developing and enhancing our integrated dashboard – we need a single source of truth."

**Learn – Interpret and Act**

EE and GC relied on a few common principles of constructive discourse (Boland Jr & Tenkasi, 1995; Lyytinen & Hirschheim, 1988; Weick & Meader, 1993) as they reviewed the consolidated information, derived customer needs, considered potential responses, evaluated implications to the team and company's own goals and resources, and decided whether to and how to modify the product. (1) They used a structured and cadenced process to interpret and act, consistent with scholarship that thoughtful pacing and cadence facilitate convergence and change in dynamic contexts more effectively than reacting instantaneously (Brown & Eisenhardt, 1997; Gersick, 1994). The CPO of EE noted: "Our regular metrics reviews may tell us what to do, but it's our monthly meeting where we discuss if something is worth doing. Sometimes it triggers a product action, sometimes it triggers further study." (2) Participation in the process was cross-functional: the PMs at GC appreciatively recollected the roles played by the marketing and customer support executives in prioritizing roadmap changes based on the implications of various alternatives to their functional areas. (3) Cross-functional and cadenced deliberation around the consolidated information resulted in decisions regarding whether to and how to modify various product features, what new features to offer, and their relative priorities. These feature requirements were then placed into the feature backlog that the product team considered and groomed in their bi-weekly sprint (build) planning in order to determine what features to implement in the next BML cycle.

## Emergent Nature of Learning

The digital product-assisted learning cycle is initiated when you "put a product in front of customers," to use the words of the CPO of GC. The subsequent process is dynamic – as product-triggered feedback traverses the BML loop, the learning that emerges is contingent. For example, consider the interaction between in-line product feedback and other information sources and perspectives. (1) In EE2, EE3, GC2, and GC5, in-line feedback acted as the primary source of information that drove learning. (2) In EE1, GC1, and GC3, in-line feedback played a supporting role in the learning process, confirming primary insights derived from other sources of information such as the off-line voice of the customers and team members' own prior experiences and intuitions. (3) In GC4, the observed in-line usage data contradicted the initial insights that were based on traditional voice-of-the-customer techniques, and the dichotomy re-directed the learning: the PM for GC4 succinctly noted the contingent and unpredictable nature of learning: "In this case, we went with the usage data."

Having outlined a dynamic process-centric view of digital product-assisted learning, we next discuss how digitization transforms entrepreneurial learning.

# DISCUSSION

There are several ways of characterizing a redesigned or enhanced process and its output. In traditional business process management contexts, processes are often described along dimensions of time, cost, quality, and flexibility (Kaplan, Murdock, & Ostroff, 1991; Mansar & Reijers, 2007; Reijers & Mansar, 2005). However, processes may also be described in terms of their strategic and economic characteristics. For example, recent digital scholarship posits that the effects of digital transformation are profound and manifest themselves as significant and higher-order changes in the scale, scope, and speed of the business, its underlying economics, and its enabling structures and processes (Bharadwaj et al., 2013; Matt, Hess, & Benlian, 2015; Verhoef et al., 2021; Vial, 2019). In this section, we adopt the digital transformation lens and discuss the digital product-assisted learning process in terms of its economic characteristics – specifically its economies of scale, scope, and speed (Chandler, 1990; Morris, 2008; Panzar & Willig, 1981; Petrick & Maitland, 2007).

## Economies of Scale

Economies of scale are savings that accrue when the cost of producing a unit of output falls as volume expands (Morris, 2008). That is, a process that has positive economies of scale can increase its output without a proportional increase in cost. The digital product-assisted learning process outputs usage data during the Measure step of the BML loop. Two components drive the volume of such output – the amount of usage data generated per user and the number of users that the product is deployed to.

After their initial investment in adopting product usage analytics tools, both EC and GC easily scaled up the amount of information generated per user by routinely instrumenting every newly added product feature to create usage trace data. Instrumenting a new feature simply involved adding pre-tested and well understood code to the feature and developers became facile at this task over time. Furthermore, there was no explicit setup cost associated with turning on a new user after the product had been deployed to that user – deployed products automatically came on-line and began providing feedback. Unit costs associated with storing and processing feedback data also fell due to volume-pricing contracts from their cloud providers like Amazon Web Services (AWS). The economies of scale exhibited by digital product-assisted learning is in stark contrast to the near-linear scaling associated with traditional labor-intensive product-assisted learning techniques such as interviewing customers to capture their voices (Burchill & Brodie, 1997; Griffin & Hauser, 1993) or working with lead users (Franke, Von Hippel, & Schreier, 2006; Von Hippel, 1986).

**Economies of Scope**

Economies of scope are the cost savings realized when the same process is used in the production of different, but related, outputs (Morris, 2008; Panzar & Willig, 1981). That is, the cost of producing multiple distinct outputs using the same process is less than the cost of producing each output individually with distinct processes. While economies of scale are a volume-related effect, economies of scope are variety-related: when Amazon uses the same infrastructure and customer base to sell both books and apparel, it is realizing economies of scope. Entrepreneurial learning seeks to produce two distinct outputs: exploitative knowledge (identifying how to improve the usability and overall desirability of a feature) and exploratory learning (identifying an opportunity to implement a new feature that may support a new use case and thus draw in new users and expand the product's addressable market). Characterizing the digital product-assisted learning process' economies of scope requires assessing whether the process is capable of producing both exploitative and exploratory knowledge.

Two of the eight cases (GC2 and GC4) demonstrated exploratory knowledge creation, while the other six showcased exploitative knowledge production. In GC2, the usage data indicated that one specific retailer was using the GC platform's APIs in a peculiar manner, not to create gift cards for their customers (the intended use case) but to support a product buy-back program with their customers (a use case that the GC team was unaware of until this point). The anomalous usage revealed an untapped opportunity for GC to create a product buy-back API package to target retailers that would previously not have considered GC as a supplier because they were not interested in GC's core gift card features. In GC4, the team identified a peculiar usage pattern – a set of consumers were using the features intended for gifting cards to others to instead "self-gift" to avail of the discount. Anomalous usage forced GC to reconsider their previous perspective on their target market of gifting, by pointing to new opportunities in the pre-paid wallet business.

The theme of anomaly driven discovery observed in GC2 and GC4 is present in the many case examples vividly chronicled in *The Power of Customer Misbehaviour* by Fisher, Abbott, and Lyytinen (2014). (1) Anomalous usage patterns observed on eBay's collectibles trading application led to the realization that some users were using that application to sell real cars (and not toy car collectibles), which then led to the launch of a new set of features called eBay Motors that targeted the used car market. (2) Intuit created a crowdsourced advice product called Live Community based on how Intuit's TurboTax users often asked esoteric on-line questions that were outside the scope of Intuit's automated advice database. (3) Facebook created new features to support groups and events (areas that Facebook had not considered in its initial product concept) based on how its users were hacking together groups and events by (mis)using Facebook's standard personal networking features in ways that Facebook had not intended. In their detailed case study of product-assisted learning at Ubisoft (a leading producer of video games), Werder et al. (2020) highlight how the team responsible for the popular game *Ghost Recon Wildlands* analyzed feature usage data to not only refine features to better meet customer expectations (i.e. exploitation) but to also look for patterns and anomalies that might inspire the creation of novel player experiences that could change the nature of the game (i.e. exploration). An example of such exploration: usage data indicated a growing group of players looking to cooperate on missions, and this led to the development of a mode called *Ghost War* that greatly extended the possibilities for cooperation and was suitable for military team training exercises (new use case).

Digital product-assisted learning exhibits economies of scope, creating both exploitative and exploratory knowledge from the vast amounts of usage data. Such ambidexterity or versatility within one process is surprising and runs counter to generally accepted management thinking that exploration and exploitation merit distinct organizational forms, work structures, and processes (Benner & Tushman, 2003; O'Reilly & Tushman, 2013).

## Economies of Speed

Speedy decision-making and action are critical, especially in fast-moving environments that typify digital entrepreneurship (Bharadwaj et al., 2013; Brown & Eisenhardt, 1997; Baum & Wally, 2003; Stalk Jr & Hout, 1990). Economies of speed are savings that are realized when faster decisions and actions result in greater throughput and utilization of the underlying process, thereby reducing the unit cost of producing output (Ito & Rose, 2004; Laine & Vepsäläinen, 1994; Petrick & Maitland, 2007). The final outputs of the digital product-assisted learning process are the exploratory and exploitative knowledge that lead to decisions and actions related to new feature development. The throughput of such knowledge production is paced by the speed of the BML cycle.

In the case of EE and GC, the learning that led to top-level decisions regarding the relative priorities on what features to build next and what opportunities to investigate further was created on a monthly cadence, while feature grooming and feature initiation were paced by the bi-weekly sprint cycle. These cycle times of two and four weeks are remarkably shorter than typical product development metrics (see Markham and Lee (2013) for benchmarks for different types of products). Furthermore, product development teams are increasingly implementing an even more aggressive form of agile development called "continuous integration / continuous delivery" (CI/CD) that can result in the entire BML cycle (feature release, feedback review, and feature modification) being completed in a day rather than in weeks (Rossel, 2017). However, CI/CD may increase economies of speed only conditionally: throughput may improve in straightforward cases of exploitative learning and subsequent feature refinement, but may be stagnant in exploratory contexts that require reflective and deliberative human activities such as interpretation and commitment building.

## CONCLUSIONS

Organizations must possess an appropriate repertoire of routines or processes in order to pursue their business objectives (Becker, 2004; Pentland, Feldman, Becker, & Liu, 2012). Continuous and fast learning is central to entrepreneurship (Cope, 2005; Smilor, 1997) and entrepreneurial ventures must accordingly construct a portfolio of processes that rapidly creates the learning required for both exploitation and exploration (Politis, 2005; Wang & Chugh, 2014). However, entrepreneurship is characterized by limited resources and frugality (Michaelis et al., 2020) and thus such a portfolio must also be parsimonious, and each variant within that portfolio must be cost-effective. The digital product-assisted learning process variant, with its economies of scale, scope, and speed can play an essential role in such a learning process portfolio. The reference model proposed in this chapter can serve as a pragmatic template for entrepreneurial product teams looking to implement, manage, and improve this mode of learning. But practitioners should proceed with some caution.

Given the modest field study with just eight cases, our claims regarding economies of scale, scope, and speed should be viewed as preliminary. For example, only two of the cases (GC2 and GC4) chronicle exploratory learning and support our claim of economies of scope (that the process produces both exploitative and exploratory knowledge). We therefore introduce several other well-recognized examples of product-assisted exploratory learning at companies such as Facebook, eBay, Intuit, and Ubisoft to supplement this aspect of the field study. However, even considering this expanded set of exploratory learning examples; one could question whether they are *sufficiently* exploratory in nature because the resultant discoveries are anchored to some extent by the initial intent of the product.

Our proposed process model substantively extends the BML model, but lacks the level of detail typically associated with mature process reference models that guide practice (for an example, see Stewart (1997)). Thus, practitioners adopting this model will need to flesh out the model further.

Finally, like with other emerging and hyped 'best practices' for innovation like design thinking where a knowledge of boundary conditions and contextual applicability is critical (Nagaraj, Berente, Lyytinen, & Gaskin, 2020), product teams should be cognizant of the limitations of digital product-assisted learning as well. Specifically, teams wishing to explore specific opportunities that are very distinct from their core business should not rely exclusively on this method. Also, there are limits to the cost-effectiveness of this process variant: improving the speed of learning and realizing expected economies of speed may be difficult in unfamiliar and exploratory contexts where anomalies must be detected and interpreted. The detection of anomalies could potentially be automated and accelerated as upcoming versions of product usage analytics tools add this capability to their toolsets, but the deliberate and cadenced human activities of interpretation and commitment building are likely to become bottlenecks that are presently outside the charter of these tools.

A potential path to resolving the human bottleneck is to reconsider conjoint human–AI agency in the socio-technical learning process (Murray, Rhymer, & Sirmon, 2021; Orlikowski, 2009). AI technology may be incorporated in design processes with varying levels of autonomy (Seidel et al., 2020). As Seidel et al. (2020) note, autonomous AI agents can act independently and indeed make decisions that cannot be anticipated, but ultimately they are still part of a control system – their decision making depends on inputs from their human peers and from signals that come from the environment after they enact their decision. In the context of digital product-assisted learning, autonomous AI agents could be entrusted with interpretation and sensemaking and rapidly identifying both exploitative and exploratory feature ideas, using product usage data to adjust their next cycle of decision making. The idea of fully autonomous agents is an abstraction at this time, but the digital product-assisted learning process may represent a fruitful context to study such conjoint agency as new AI tools are invented and deployed to further increase its economies of scope and speed.

Product-assisted learning, which is being transformed by "here-and-now" technologies such as product usage analytics tools, has emerged as a critical enabler of digital entrepreneurship. While inspiration for innovation may come from several sources, as the CPO of GC noted, it is "hard to know if you are right or wrong until you put a product in front of customers." Furthermore, the importance of digital product-assisted learning is only likely to grow in the future as AI technologies are increasingly used to automate and augment learning, and are eventually deployed to create and act on learning autonomously. Describing his vision of how the entrepreneurial learning and innovation process would morph over time, the CTO of EE noted: "In the medium term, I can see products identifying anomalies themselves and suggesting changes to the product manager. In the future, we will send a product to the wild. A year later it would've changed itself as customer preferences change." Understanding and harnessing this unfolding digital transformation phenomenon is critical for entrepreneurship.

# REFERENCES

Akgün, A. E., Keskin, H., Lynn, G., & Dogan, D. (2012). Antecedents and consequences of team sensemaking capability in product development projects. *R&D Management, 42*(5), 473–493.

Baum, J. R., & Wally, S. (2003). Strategic decision speed and firm performance. *Strategic Management Journal, 24*(11), 1107–1129.

Bechky, B. A. (2003). Sharing meaning across occupational communities: The transformation of understanding on a production floor. *Organization Science, 14*(3), 312–330.

Becker, M. C. (2004). Organizational routines: a review of the literature. *Industrial and Corporate Change, 13*(4), 643–678.

Benner, M. J., & Tushman, M. L. (2003). Exploitation, exploration, and process management: The productivity dilemma revisited. *Academy of Management Review, 28*(2), 238–256.

Berente, N., Vandenbosch, B., & Aubert, B. (2009). Information flows and business process integration. *Business Process Management Journal, 15*(1), 119–141.

Berger, E. S., von Briel, F., Davidsson, P., & Kuckertz, A. (2019). Digital or not: The future of entrepreneurship and innovation: Introduction to the special issue. *Journal of Business Research, 125*(March), 436–442.

Bharadwaj, A., El Sawy, O. A., Pavlou, P. A., & Venkatraman, N. V. (2013). Digital business strategy: Toward a next generation of insights. *MIS Quarterly, 37*(2), 471–482.

Blank, S. (2013). Why the lean start-up changes everything. *Harvard Business Review, 91*(5), 63–72.

Boland Jr, R. J., & Tenkasi, R. V. (1995). Perspective making and perspective taking in communities of knowing. *Organization Science, 6*(4), 350–372.

Brown, S. L., & Eisenhardt, K. M. (1997). The art of continuous change: Linking complexity theory and time-paced evolution in relentlessly shifting organizations. *Administrative Science Quarterly*, 1–34.

Bughin, J. (2017). The best response to digital disruption. *MIT Sloan Management Review, 58*(4).

Burchill, G., & Brodie, C. H. (1997). *Voices into choices: Acting on the voice of the customer*. Oriel Incorporated.

Carlile, P. R. (2002). A pragmatic view of knowledge and boundaries: Boundary objects in new product development. *Organization Science, 13*(4), 442–455.

Chandler, A. D. (1990). *Scale and scope: The dynamics of industrial capitalism*. Harvard University Press.

Cockburn, A. (2006). *Agile software development: the cooperative game.* Pearson Education.
Cope, J. (2005). Toward a dynamic learning perspective of entrepreneurship. *Entrepreneurship Theory and Practice, 29*(4), 373–397.
Cope, J., & Watts, G. (2000). Learning by doing: An exploration of experience, critical incidents and reflection in entrepreneurial learning. *International Journal of Entrepreneurial Behavior & Research, 6*(3), 104–124.
Corbett, A. C. (2005). Experiential learning within the process of opportunity identification and exploitation. *Entrepreneurship Theory and Practice, 29*(4), 473–491.
Covin, J. G., & Wales, W. J. (2012). The measurement of entrepreneurial orientation. *Entrepreneurship Theory and Practice, 36*(4), 677–702.
Dess, G. G., & Lumpkin, G. T. (2005). The role of entrepreneurial orientation in stimulating effective corporate entrepreneurship. *Academy of Management Perspectives, 19*(1), 147–156.
Dingsøyr, T., Nerur, S., Balijepally, V., & Moe, N. B. (2012). A decade of agile methodologies: Towards explaining agile software development. *Journal of Systems and Software, 85*, 1213–1221.
Eisenhardt, K. M., & Tabrizi, B. N. (1995). Accelerating adaptive processes: Product innovation in the global computer industry. *Administrative Science Quarterly*, 84–110.
El-Awad, Z., Gabrielsson, J., & Politis, D. (2017). Entrepreneurial learning and innovation. *International Journal of Entrepreneurial Behavior & Research, 23*(3), 381–405.
Fabijan, A., Dmitriev, P., Olsson, H. H., & Bosch, J. (2017). *The evolution of continuous experimentation in software product development: From data to a data-driven organization at scale.* Paper presented at the Proceedings of the 39th International Conference on Software Engineering.
Fabijan, A., Olsson, H. H., & Bosch, J. (2015). *Customer feedback and data collection techniques in software R&D: a literature review.* Paper presented at the International Conference of Software Business.
Fagerholm, F., Guinea, A. S., Mäenpää, H., & Münch, J. (2017). The RIGHT model for continuous experimentation. *Journal of Systems and Software, 123*, 292–305.
Fettke, P., & Loos, P. (2006). *Reference modeling for business systems analysis.* IGI Global.
Fisher, M., Abbott, M., & Lyytinen, K. (2014). *The power of customer misbehavior: drive growth and innovation by learning from your customers.* Palgrave Macmillan.
Flanagan, J. C. (1954). The critical incident technique. *Psychological Bulletin, 51*(4), 327.
Franke, N., Von Hippel, E., & Schreier, M. (2006). Finding commercially attractive user innovations: A test of lead-user theory. *Journal of Product Innovation Management, 23*(4), 301–315.
Fust, A. P., Jenert, T., & Winkler, C. (2017). Experiential or self-regulated learning: A critical reflection of entrepreneurial learning processes. *Entrepreneurship Research Journal, 8*(2).
Gersick, C. J. (1994). Pacing strategic change: The case of a new venture. *Academy of Management Journal, 37*(1), 9–45.
Griffin, A., & Hauser, J. R. (1993). The voice of the customer. *Marketing Science, 12*(1), 1–27.
Hynninen, P., & Kauppinen, M. (2014). *A/B testing: A promising tool for customer value evaluation.* Paper presented at the 2014 IEEE 1st International Workshop on Requirements Engineering and Testing (RET).
Inayat, I., Salim, S. S., Marczak, S., Daneva, M., & Shamshirband, S. (2015). A systematic literature review on agile requirements engineering practices and challenges. *Computers in Human Behavior, 51*, 915–929.
Ito, K., & Rose, E. L. (2004). An emerging structure of corporations. *Multinational Business Review, 12*(3), 63–83.
Joglekar, N., and Nagaraj, V. (2017). *Digital product management thinking: Integrating analytics, business model, coordination and design thinking.* SenseShaping Ventures.
Kamm, J. B., Shuman, J. C., Seeger, J. A., & Nurick, A. J. (1990). Entrepreneurial teams in new venture creation: A research agenda. *Entrepreneurship Theory and Practice, 14*(4), 7–17.
Kaplan, R. B., Murdock, L., & Ostroff, F. (1991). Core process redesign. *The McKinsey Quarterly*, (2), 27–44.
Khayaglou, D. (2021). Top 10 product analytics tools for product managers. Retrieved from https://productcollective.com/top-10-product-analytics-tools-for-product-managers/.
Kohavi, R., & Longbotham, R. (2017). Online controlled experiments and a/b testing. In C. Sammut & G. I. Webb (Eds.), *Encyclopedia of machine learning and data mining* (pp. 922–929): Springer.

Kolb, D. A. (2014). *Experiential learning: Experience as the source of learning and development*. FT press.

Laine, J. T., & Vepsäläinen, A. P. (1994). Economies of speed in sea transportation. *International Journal of Physical Distribution & Logistics Management, 24*(8), 33–41.

Lévesque, M., Minniti, M., & Shepherd, D. (2009). Entrepreneurs' decisions on timing of entry: Learning from participation and from the experiences of others. *Entrepreneurship Theory and Practice, 33*(2), 547–570.

Lumpkin, G. T., & Dess, G. G. (1996). Clarifying the entrepreneurial orientation construct and linking it to performance. *Academy of Management Review, 21*(1), 135–172.

Lumpkin, G. T., & Lichtenstein, B. B. (2005). The role of organizational learning in the opportunity–recognition process. *Entrepreneurship Theory and Practice, 29*(4), 451–472.

Lyytinen, K., & Hirschheim, R. (1988). Information systems as rational discourse: An application of Habermas's theory of communicative action. *Scandinavian Journal of Management, 4*(1), 19–30.

Maitlis, S., & Christianson, M. (2014). Sensemaking in organizations: Taking stock and moving forward. *The Academy of Management Annals, 8*(1), 57–125.

Mansar, S. L., & Reijers, H. A. (2007). Best practices in business process redesign: Use and impact. *Business Process Management Journal, 13*(2), 193–212.

March, J. G. (1991). Exploration and exploitation in organizational learning. *Organization Science, 2*(1), 71–87.

Markham, S. K., & Lee, H. (2013). Product development and management association's 2012 comparative performance assessment study. *Journal of Product Innovation Management, 30*(3), 408–429.

Matook, S., & Indulska, M. (2009). Improving the quality of process reference models: A quality function deployment-based approach. *Decision Support Systems, 47*(1), 60–71.

Matt, C., Hess, T., & Benlian, A. (2015). Digital transformation strategies. *Business & Information Systems Engineering, 57*(5), 339–343.

Michaelis, T. L., Carr, J. C., Scheaf, D. J., & Pollack, J. M. (2020). The frugal entrepreneur: A self-regulatory perspective of resourceful entrepreneurial behavior. *Journal of Business Venturing, 35*(4), 105969.

Miller, R. (2019, October 17). Pendo scores $100M Series-E investment on $1B valuation. Retrieved from https://techcrunch.com/2019/10/17/pendo-scores-100m-series-e-on-1-billion-valuation/.

Morris, D. (2008). Economies of scale and scope in e-learning. *Studies in Higher Education, 33*(3), 331–343.

Murray, A., Rhymer, J., & Sirmon, D. G. (2021). Humans and technology: Forms of conjoined agency in organizations. *Academy of Management Review, 46*(3), 552–571.

Myers, C. G. (2018). Coactive vicarious learning: Toward a relational theory of vicarious learning in organizations. *Academy of Management Review, 43*(4), 610–634.

Nagaraj, V. (2019). *Emergent learning in digital product teams*. ProQuest Dissertations Publishing.

Nagaraj, V., Berente, N., Lyytinen, K., & Gaskin, J. (2020). Team design thinking, product innovativeness, and the moderating role of problem unfamiliarity. *Journal of Product Innovation Management, 37*(4), 297–323.

Nagaraj, V., Boland, R. J., and Lyytinen, K. (2017). Senseshaping: The dynamics of sensemaking and sensegiving in high velocity product innovation. *Academy of Management Proceedings*. doi: 10.5465/AMBPP.2017.13314abstract.

Nambisan, S. (2017). Digital entrepreneurship: Toward a digital technology perspective of entrepreneurship. *Entrepreneurship Theory and Practice, 41*(6), 1029–1055.

Nogueira, T. F. (2019). Entrepreneurial learning: what do we mean by it? *The Learning Organization, 26*(6), 560–573.

O'Reilly, C. A., & Tushman, M. L. (2013). Organizational ambidexterity: Past, present, and future. *The Academy of Management Perspectives, 27*(4), 324–338.

Ocasio, W. (2011). Attention to attention. *Organization Science, 22*(5), 1286–1296.

Olsen, D. (2015). *The lean product playbook: How to innovate with minimum viable products and rapid customer feedback*. John Wiley & Sons.

Olsson, H. H., Alahyari, H., & Bosch, J. (2012). *Climbing the "Stairway to Heaven"—a multiple-case study exploring barriers in the transition from agile development towards continuous deployment of software*. Paper presented at the 38th EUROMICRO Conference on Software Engineering and Advanced Applications (SEAA).

Orlikowski, W. J. (2009). The sociomateriality of organisational life: Considering technology in management research. *Cambridge Journal of Economics, 34*(1), 125–141.

Otto, B., & Ofner, M. H. (2010). Towards a process reference model for information supply chain management. *ECIS 2010 Proceedings, 75*.

Overby, E., Bharadwaj, A., & Sambamurthy, V. (2006). Enterprise agility and the enabling role of information technology. *European Journal of Information Systems, 15*(2), 120–131.

Panzar, J. C., & Willig, R. D. (1981). Economies of scope. *The American Economic Review, 71*(2), 268–272.

Pentland, B. T., Feldman, M. S., Becker, M. C., & Liu, P. (2012). Dynamics of organizational routines: A generative model. *Journal of Management Studies, 49*(8), 1484–1508.

Petrick, I. J., & Maitland, C. (2007). Economies of speed: a conceptual framework to describe network effectiveness. In G. I. Susman (Ed.), *Small and medium-sized enterprises and the global economy* (pp. 61–77). Cheltenham, UK and Northampton, MA, USA: Edward Elgar Publishing.

Politis, D. (2005). The process of entrepreneurial learning: A conceptual framework. *Entrepreneurship Theory and Practice, 29*(4), 399–424.

Porter, M. E., & Heppelmann, J. E. (2015). How smart, connected products are transforming companies. *Harvard Business Review, 93*(10), 96–114.

Raffaelli, R., Glynn, M. A., & Tushman, M. (2019). Frame flexibility: The role of cognitive and emotional framing in innovation adoption by incumbent firms. *Strategic Management Journal, 40*(7), 1013–1039.

Reijers, H. A., & Mansar, S. L. (2005). Best practices in business process redesign: An overview and qualitative evaluation of successful redesign heuristics. *Omega, 33*(4), 283–306.

Rerup, C. (2005). Learning from past experience: Footnotes on mindfulness and habitual entrepreneurship. *Scandinavian Journal of Management, 21*(4), 451–472.

Ries, E. (2011). *The lean startup: How today's entrepreneurs use continuous innovation to create radically successful businesses*. Crown Books.

Robinson, W. N. (2006). A requirements monitoring framework for enterprise systems. *Requirements Engineering, 11*(1), 17–41.

Robinson, W. N., & Fickas, S. (2009). Designs can talk: A case of feedback for design evolution in assistive technology. In K. Lyytinen, P., Loucopoulos, J., Mylopoulos, & B. Robinson (Eds.), *Design requirements engineering: A ten-year perspective*. Lecture Notes in Business Information Processing, vol 14. Springer. https://doi.org/10.1007/978-3-540-92966-6_12.

Rossel, S. (2017). *Continuous integration, delivery, and deployment: Reliable and faster software releases with automating builds, tests, and deployment*. Packt Publishing.

Seidel, S., Berente, N., Lindberg, A., Lyytinen, K., Martinez, B., & Nickerson, J. V. (2020). Artificial intelligence and video game creation: A framework for the new logic of autonomous design. *Journal of Digital Social Research, 2*(3), 126–157.

Seidl, D., & Werle, F. (2018). Inter-organizational sensemaking in the face of strategic meta-problems: Requisite variety and dynamics of participation. *Strategic Management Journal, 39*(3), 830–858.

Silva Souza, V. E., Lapouchnian, A., Robinson, W. N., & Mylopoulos, J. (2011). *Awareness requirements for adaptive systems*. Paper presented at the Proceedings of the 6th international symposium on software engineering for adaptive and self-managing systems.

Siren, C. A., Kohtamäki, M., & Kuckertz, A. (2012). Exploration and exploitation strategies, profit performance, and the mediating role of strategic learning: Escaping the exploitation trap. *Strategic Entrepreneurship Journal, 6*(1), 18–41.

Smilor, R. W. (1997). Entrepreneurship: Reflections on a subversive activity. *Journal of Business Venturing, 12*(5), 341–346.

Souza, V. E. S., Lapouchnian, A., Robinson, W. N., & Mylopoulos, J. (2013). Awareness requirements. In R. de Lemos, H. Giese, H. A, Müller, & M. Shaw (Eds.), *Software engineering for self-adaptive systems II*. Lecture Notes in Computer Science, vol 7475. Springer. https://doi.org/10.1007/978-3-642-35813-5_6

Stalk Jr, G., & Hout, T. M. (1990). Competing against time. *Research-Technology Management, 33*(2), 19–24.

Stewart, G. (1997). Supply-chain operations reference model (SCOR): The first cross-industry framework for integrated supply-chain management. *Logistics Information Management, 10*(2), 62–67.

Thomke, S. (2001). Enlightened experimentation: The new imperative for innovation. *Harvard Business Review, 79*(2), 66–75.

Turpin, M., & du Plooy, N. (2004). *Decision-making biases and information systems.* Paper presented at the Proceedings of the 2004 IFIP International Conference on Decision Support Systems (DSS2004): Decision Support in an Uncertain World. Prato, Tuscany.

Vandenbosch, B., & Huff, S. L. (1997). Searching and scanning: how executives obtain information from executive information systems. *MIS Quarterly*, 81–107.

Venkatraman, V. (2017). *The digital matrix: New rules for business transformation through technology.* Lifetree Media.

Verhoef, P. C., Broekhuizen, T., Bart, Y., Bhattacharya, A., Dong, J. Q., Fabian, N., & Haenlein, M. (2021). Digital transformation: A multidisciplinary reflection and research agenda. *Journal of Business Research, 122*, 889–901.

Vial, G. (2019). Understanding digital transformation: A review and a research agenda. *The Journal of Strategic Information Systems, 28*(2), 118–144.

Von Hippel, E. (1986). Lead users: a source of novel product concepts. *Management Science, 32*(7), 791–805.

Wang, C. L., & Chugh, H. (2014). Entrepreneurial learning: past research and future challenges. *International Journal of Management Reviews, 16*(1), 24–61.

Weick, K., & Meader, D. (1993). Sensemaking and group support systems. In J. V. L. Jessup (Ed.), *Group support systems: New perspectives.* Macmillan, pp. 230–252.

Weick, K. E., Sutcliffe, K. M., & Obstfeld, D. (2005). Organizing and the process of sensemaking. *Organization Science, 16*(4), 409–421.

Werder, K., Seidel, S., Recker, J., Berente, N., Gibbs, J., Abboud, N., & Benzeghadi, Y. (2020). Data-driven, data-informed, data-augmented: How Ubisoft's ghost recon wildlands live unit uses data for continuous product innovation. *California Management Review, 62*(3), 86–102.

Wright, C. R., Manning, M. R., Farmer, B., & Gilbreath, B. (2000). Resourceful sensemaking in product development teams. *Organization Studies, 21*(4), 807–825.

Yoo, Y. (2012). *Digital materiality and the emergence of an evolutionary science of the artificial.* Oxford University Press.

Yoo, Y., Boland Jr, R. J., Lyytinen, K., & Majchrzak, A. (2012). Organizing for innovation in the digitized world. *Organization Science, 23*(5), 1398–1408.

# PART V

# DIGITAL ENTREPRENEURSHIP ADOPTION AND OUTCOMES

# 9. Punching above their weight class: assessing how digital technologies enhance new and small firm survival and competitiveness

*Franz T. Lohrke, Alexander B. Hamrick and Qiongrui (Missy) Yao*

New ventures (NVs) and small- to medium-sized enterprises (SMEs) often face myriad competitive challenges based on their newness and/or size. For example, when first launching NVs, entrepreneurs must overcome both their firms' lack of legitimacy with external stakeholders and absence of established internal routines (i.e., "liabilities of newness" (LoN)), which can threaten nascent firms' survival (Stinchcombe, 1965). SMEs, even well-established ones, face on-going size disadvantages (i.e., "liabilities of smallness" (LoS)), which can include difficulties in developing economies of scale or competing with larger firms for human resource talent and/or customer attention (Aldrich & Auster, 1986). Given that these liabilities can reduce both the performance of and even survival chances for these firms, research has frequently investigated whether and how entrepreneurs can overcome them (Aldrich & Fiol, 1994; Fariborzi & Keyhani, 2018; Shepherd & Zacharakis, 2003; Überbacher, 2014).[1]

Despite these challenges, being new and/or small may also provide important strategic advantages relative to larger, more established firms (Carayannopoulos, 2009). For example, the long-held Schumpterian view of entrepreneurship proposes that NVs employ new technologies to enter industries and usurp established firms, suggesting these firms also may enjoy some competitive advantages rather than just suffer from liabilities relative to incumbent firms (Tripsas, 1997). Other research suggests that NVs actually may enjoy "assets of newness" (AoN), and SMEs may be able to avoid organizational inertia, resulting in potential competitive advantages for both types of firms (Chen & Hambrick, 1995; Choi & Shepherd, 2005).

We posit that the rise of digital technologies (DTs) may also affect LoN, LoS, and AoN by enhancing some NV and SME advantages and at least partially mitigating various disadvantages. For example, compared to the formidable competitive and resource acquisition barriers they have historically faced, these firms can now raise capital via crowdfunding, competitively differentiate themselves on social media sites, rapidly prototype products with 3D printing, reduce computer software costs through cloud computing, and access human resources worldwide on digital labor platforms. In effect, DTs may allow NVs and SMEs to "punch above their weight class" in accessing important resources and competing with larger, more established firms (e.g., Courtney, Dutta, & Li, 2017; Fischer & Reuber, 2014; Keyhani, Chapter 7 in this handbook).

These developments suggest the need to reassess extant LoN, LoS, and AoN research and establish a future research agenda in the digital entrepreneurship (DE) age. Scholars have increasingly noted that key assumptions underlying theoretical frameworks employed in organizational research may not fully account for the rise of DTs (Coviello, Kano, & Liesch, 2017; Hui, 2014), and we suggest this issue also exists in NV and SME research. Not only have these technologies spawned new products and industries, they have fundamentally affected how entrepreneurial firms launch, organize, and compete (Kollman & Jung, Chapter 2 in this handbook; Morse, Fowler, & Lawrence, 2007). Specifically, they can impact the entire entrepreneurial process by removing constraints to how, when, and where different stages of the process occur, as well as by whom they can be completed (Nambisan, 2017). In turn, these changes suggest a need to examine important theoretical perspectives employed in extant research to study challenges entrepreneurs face during venture founding and growth.

Accordingly, employing a DE perspective, we will first briefly review extant LoN, LoS, and AoN research. We then examine how DTs (i.e., artifacts, platforms, and infrastructures, Nambisan, 2017) can help entrepreneurial firms alleviate liabilities and/or maximize advantages related to newness and smallness. We, thus, contribute to the nascent but growing DE literature by noting important topics that have been examined, to date. In addition, we discuss DTs' potential impact on the entrepreneurial process, in general (e.g., Shepherd & Zacharakis, 2003), as well as studying important topics such as how specific DTs may help overcome important resource challenges like raising capital (e.g., Courtney et al., 2017) and managing geographically dispersed operations (e.g., Nambisan, Zahra, & Luo, 2019). We conclude by suggesting some future DE research avenues related to these issues.

## COMPETITIVE LIABILITIES AND ASSETS IN ENTREPRENEURIAL FIRMS

New and small firm liabilities arise, in part, based on two foundational entrepreneurship concepts, environmental uncertainty and information asymmetry (Shepherd, Douglas, & Shanley, 2000). First, resource providers (e.g., potential funders, suppliers, customers, and employees) must decide whether to invest time and resources in firms while facing considerable uncertainty about their ability to function as reliable exchange partners (Aldrich & Auster, 1986) or even survive (Shepherd et al., 2000). Second, resource providers face information asymmetry risks arising from entrepreneurs' unwillingness or inability to fully communicate information about their firms' competitive advantages (Venkatraman, 1997), which contribute to high "adverse selection" hazards (Akerlof, 1970). Thus, unless entrepreneurs find mechanisms to signal their firms' legitimacy and long-term competitive viability, resource providers may withhold resources, endangering firms' growth and survival (Shepherd & Zacharakis, 2003).

To address these challenges, entrepreneurs must successfully resolve three general (i.e., entrepreneurial, engineering, and administrative) problems (Miles & Snow, 1978). Addressing the entrepreneurial problem involves enlisting stakeholder support and determining what product/market domain a firm will serve (Choi & Shepherd, 2005). Solving the engineering problem requires deciding what technologies a firm should use to transform inputs into outputs as well as how it will develop organizational routines. Resolving the administrative problem involves establishing a firm's boundaries (Katz & Gartner, 1988) and signaling to potential stakeholders that a firm adheres to widely accepted business norms (Hannan & Freeman, 1984).

Extant LoN and LoS research suggests that resolving these problems can be daunting. For example, founders must establish and learn new organizational roles, develop trust among founding team members, and build resource linkages (e.g., accessing funding and building supplier relationships) with external stakeholders (Stinchcombe, 1965). As a result, NVs face both internal efficiencies and external resource acquisition challenges, which entrepreneurs must overcome while simultaneously competing against established firms (Shepherd et al., 2000).

SMEs also face myriad competitive challenges including contending with high supplier bargaining power, recruiting top human resource talent, and difficulty accessing external financing (Aldrich & Auster, 1986; Beck, Demirgc-Kunt, & Maksimovic, 2008). In addition, they may face internal difficulties like overcoming production scale disadvantages (Strotmann, 2007). Given the critical impact both LoN and LoS can have on firm performance, and even survival, scholars have examined how entrepreneurs can remedy these challenges for several decades (Lohrke & Landström, 2016).

Some scholars note, however, that rather than being just a liability, newness and smallness may provide competitive advantages. First, if these firms offer innovative products, then stakeholders may support them based on an emotional attraction to (i.e., "affective congruence" with) their products (Choi & Shepherd, 2005). In addition, these firms may capitalize on their "youthfulness" and/or smaller size to avoid inertia that can plague larger, established rivals (Chen & Hambrick, 1995).

When studying LoN, LoS, and AoN issues, scholars have often drawn from several theoretical frameworks including legitimacy (e.g., Überbacher, 2014), reputation (Fischer & Reuber, 2014), trust (Aldrich & Fiol, 1994), internationalization (Fariborzi & Keyhani, 2018), organizational routines (Morse et al., 2007), and affective congruence (Choi & Shepherd, 2005). Thus, we will employ these and other theoretical foundations in our discussion below examining how DTs impact challenges entrepreneurs face during venture founding and growth.

## THE IMPACT OF DIGITAL TECHNOLOGIES ON VENTURE FOUNDING AND GROWTH

DTs have presented numerous opportunities to entrepreneurs. Growth in these technologies has made the entrepreneurship process less bounded by time and space as well as more fluid in terms of who is involved and when different actors participate in the process (Nambisan, 2017). As a result, these technologies have had both disruptive and efficiency-enhancing effects (Fossen & Sogner, 2021). For example, DLPs (e.g., Uber and Lyft) have disrupted some industries (e.g., taxis), providing entrepreneurial opportunities to NVs and competitive challenges to incumbents. The ability to locate and employ underutilized assets (e.g., idle labor) via electronic marketplaces (e.g., Upwork and Freelancer.com) also has provided firms access to specialized labor and aspiring entrepreneurs with opportunities for self-employment. In addition, digital platforms' ability to cut out (i.e., "disintermediate") the middleman in some industries has created opportunities to launch online services (e.g., Stripe and Venmo) that reduce costs and time required for different business (e.g., financial) transactions.

DTs can be examined in terms of three related but distinct elements: artifacts, platforms, and infrastructures (Nambisan, 2017). Artifacts include stand-alone software (e.g., apps) or hardware (e.g., internet-connected devices), which can create customer value and entrepreneurial opportunities in multiple ways, based on having varying combinations of physical, information storage, and internet-connected attributes (Porter & Heppelmann, 2015). These artifacts have generated numerous entrepreneurial opportunities ranging from enhancing customer interactions to redefining industry boundaries. Platforms are defined as common sets of shared services and architecture that host complementary offerings, including artifacts (Nambisan, 2017). They include digital products, services, and ecosystems ranging from smartphone operating systems to online marketplaces (Tiwana, Konsynski, & Bush, 2010). They also include on-line labor platforms, which provide access to human resources that heretofore may have been prohibitively difficult to access. Infrastructures include tools and systems that "offer communications, collaboration, or computing capabilities to support innovation and entrepreneurship" (Nambisan, 2017, p. 1032). Thus, they can include technologies like 3D printing and cloud computing, as well as financing (e.g., crowdfunding), innovation (e.g., crowdsourcing) and marketing (e.g., social media) websites that expand entrepreneurial firms' opportunities and strategic capabilities (Breznitz, Forman, & Wen, 2018; Eckhardt, Ciuchta, & Carpenter, 2018; Fischer & Reuber, 2014).

Building on Davidsson's (2015) entrepreneurial opportunity framework, Nambisan (2017) noted that both artifacts and platforms can serve as a business idea that individual entrepreneurs can use to found NVs. Infrastructures, in contrast, often serve as external enablers that can facilitate the entrepreneurial process. Continued innovation across all three elements suggests that DTs may help both reduce LoN and LoS as well as enhance AoN. To examine these issues, we will build on theoretical frameworks employed in extant entrepreneurship research and discuss how these technologies can enhance entrepreneurs' abilities to address entrepreneurial, engineering, and administrative problems facing entrepreneurial firms (see Table 9.1).

## THE ENTREPRENEURIAL PROBLEM

To address the entrepreneurial problem, entrepreneurs first need to develop a business model that offers an attractive value proposition to potential customers. In addition, they also must address two important questions, "How can we convince stakeholders to provide our firm with resources?" and "What product/market domain(s) will our company serve?" (Choi & Shepherd, 2005).

### Enlisting Stakeholder Support

To acquire the resources needed to start and grow a firm, entrepreneurs often need to enlist external stakeholders. Lack of external ties, however, represents a fundamental LoN challenge for NVs (Stinchcombe, 1965), and low bargaining power can subject SMEs to higher resource costs or prevent access all together (Beck et al., 2008). These firms also often struggle to inform potential stakeholders about their value propositions as an overture to accessing resources or enlisting potential customers (Shepherd & Zacharakis, 2003).

Digital artifacts, platforms, and infrastructures help alleviate these challenges by providing entrepreneurs with conduits to funding and other critical resources. In addition, they can use DTs to build a firm's competitive assets, including its business network and reputation. We next focus on two digital infrastructures, crowdfunding and social media sites, that have received significant attention in extant research.

Crowdfunding, defined as "an open call, mostly through the Internet, for the provision of financial resources…to support initiatives for specific purposes" (Belleflamme, Lambert, & Schwienbacher, 2014, p. 588), provides entrepreneurs a way to both increase stakeholder awareness and build support for their ventures. In crowdfunding, the entrepreneur solicits

*Table 9.1*  Resolving entrepreneurial, engineering and administrative problems faced by new and small firms in the digital entrepreneurship age

| Problems / Issues | Entrepreneurial | Engineering | Administrative |
|---|---|---|---|
| **Key Questions** | How do entrepreneurs build stakeholder support?<br><br>What product/market domain does a firm serve? | How does the firm transform inputs into outputs?<br><br>How does the firm develop routines to produce a product/service consistently? | Where should entrepreneurs establish a firm's boundaries?<br><br>How does a firm demonstrate accountability to key stakeholders? |
| **Examples of LoN and LoS challenges that need to be solved and AoN advantages that might be exploited** | External LoN<br>• Lack of external ties needed to acquire funding, raw materials, and other key inputs<br>• Low customer awareness about firm's value proposition<br><br>External LoS<br>• High financing costs<br>• Low bargaining power with suppliers and customers<br>• Lack of reputation and other resources needed to expand to new markets<br><br>External AoN<br>• Ability to market to early adopters attracted to a venture's "youthfulness" | External LoN<br>• Lack of internal routines needed to establish legitimacy with and trust from external stakeholders<br><br>Internal LoN<br>• Lack of internal routines needed to achieve efficiency<br><br>Internal LoS<br>• Inability to attain economies of scale<br>• Lack of resources needed to prototype new products<br><br>Internal AoN<br>• Ability to employ the latest information and production technologies to enhance competitiveness | External LoN<br>• Inability to demonstrate accountability to external stakeholders<br><br>External LoS<br>• Potential exposure to partner exploitation based on the need to outsource key business functions<br><br>Internal AoN<br>• Ability to adapt quickly to changing competitive environments |
| **Examples of digital artifacts, platforms, or infrastructures that can help address the problem** | Crowdfunding sites<br>Digital supply and distribution chains<br>Social media sites | 3D printing<br>Cloud computing<br>Networked production | Digital labor platforms<br>Open innovation platforms<br>Blockchain-based technologies |

| Problems | Entrepreneurial | Engineering | Administrative |
| --- | --- | --- | --- |
| **Issues** | | | |
| **Research topics** | Acquiring legitimacy | Establishing routines | Establishing company boundaries |
| | Building reputation | Acquiring legitimacy | Spanning company boundaries |
| | Leveraging affect | Building trust | Establishing routines |
| | Building trust | Achieving scale economies | Building trust |
| | Growing the firm | | Demonstrating accountability |
| **Theoretical perspectives** | Signaling | Signaling | Signaling |
| | Social capital | Network effects | Governance |
| | Resource-based view | Embeddedness | Trust |
| | Network theory | | Resource dependency |
| | Affective congruence | | |
| | International new ventures | | |
| **Exemplar studies** | Courtney et al., 2017; Davis et al., 2017; Moss et al., 2015; Reuber & Fischer, 2011; Schaupp & Bélanger, 2014; Smith et al., 2017; Taeuscher, 2019 | Beltagui et al., 2020; Breznitz et al., 2018; Browder et al., 2019; Fazli et al., 2018; Morse et al., 2007 | Coviello et al., 2017; Duggan et al., 2020; Eckhardt et al., 2018; Lehdonvirta et al., 2019; Liu et al., 2017; Schierstedt et al., Chapter 13 in this handbook |

*Note:*   LoN = liabilities of newness, LoS = liabilities of smallness, AoN = Assets of newness.

to a large population ("the crowd"), often via websites (e.g., Kickstarter, Indiegogo, or Crowdcube). Funding can take several forms including offering funders early products or perks (i.e., "reward-based"), an ownership stake (i.e., "equity-based"), promises to repay funds (i.e., "debt-based") or simply gratitude (i.e., "donation-based" funding) in exchange for financially supporting the firm (Li & Wang, 2019).

Because of its digital footprint, crowdfunding, unlike other sources of funding (e.g., venture capital), provides a digital infrastructure to combat many issues NVs and SMEs face. Extant research has focused on how firms signal attractive characteristics and behavioral intentions to attain stakeholder support (Ashjari, Chapter 11 in this handbook). For example, studies have investigated the importance of communicating a firm's autonomy, competitive aggressiveness, and risk-taking (Sahaym, Datta, & Brooks, 2021), as well as results in progress and accomplishment narratives (Allison et al., 2015) to potential funders to achieve crowdfunding success.

Along with its ability to help entrepreneurial firms overcome financial resource constraints, crowdfunding offers an avenue for potential stakeholders (e.g., customers) to learn about firms. Thus, entrepreneurs do not need to limit crowdfunding goals to raising capital; they can also use these infrastructures to raise awareness about their firms (Mollick, 2014). Several studies have focused on a signaling perspective of crowdfunding (Ahlers et al., 2015; Moss, Neubaum, & Meyskens, 2015). Because information asymmetry is high for potential funders and websites are crowded with numerous firms seeking funds, signaling can be paramount to help increase awareness of and support for a firm (Courtney et al., 2017).

Indeed, Ahlers et al. (2015) argued that three major signals (i.e., human, social, and intellectual capital) can help stakeholders learn about entrepreneurs and their firms. For example, extant research has found that entrepreneurs' prior crowdfunding experience can enhance NVs' reputations (Butticè, Colombo, & Wright, 2017). Specifically, a founder's social capital (based on factors like follower base, reputation, and online social ties) can help increase crowd engagement and trigger "herding behavior" (Herzenstein, Dholakia, & Andrews, 2011; Liu, Chen, & Fan, 2021). In addition, Fisher et al. (2017) suggested that the crowd tends to adhere to community norms, so entrepreneurs can increase their firms' legitimacy by highlighting previous contributions to a particular funding community.

Crowdfunding can also have substantial implications for building stakeholder support, particularly when firms offer novel products or services. Specifically, unlike traditional funding routes where firm or product uniqueness may hinder attaining legitimacy (Shepherd et al., 2000), distinctiveness can actually enhance firm legitimacy when seeking funding from "novelty-expecting audiences," like crowdfunders (Taeuscher, Bouncken, & Pesch, 2021). For example, employing affective events theory, Davis, Hmieleski, Webb, and Coombs (2017) demonstrated that perceived product creativity was positively related to potential funders' affective reaction to a campaign, and, in turn, its ultimate success. These results highlight the role that positive affect, a key AoN component, has in a crowdfunding context.

Social media sites (SMS) represent another digital infrastructure that can help firms overcome newness and size challenges. Research has long recognized the important role that entrepreneurs' social networks play in their ability to accumulate resources for their firms (Granovetter, 1973). To date, however, many studies have not incorporated SMS' novel characteristics, which might affect key assumptions underlying social network analysis theory (Smith & Smith, 2021).

Entrepreneurs can employ SMS for multiple business functions including enhancing their own social capital as well as enhancing their firms' competitiveness and expanding the markets they serve (Schaupp & Bélanger, 2014). First, entrepreneurs can develop their own social capital, which can be important throughout the entrepreneurship process, including helping them identify and exploit opportunities as well as gain access to external resources (Davidsson & Honig, 2003; Masiello & Izzo, 2019). For example, important SMS characteristics, such as the ability to signal expertise via one's user profile and postings, piggyback on other members' social networks, and quickly transmit information to multiple receivers, provide different ways for enhancing social capital relative to what is possible in face-to-face settings (Smith, Smith, & Shaw, 2017). SMS also provide a platform for entrepreneurs to connect and collaborate with as well as exhibit altruistic behaviors toward potential stakeholders, providing additional opportunities for enhancing entrepreneurs' social capital (Drummond, McGrath, & O'Toole, 2017).

Second, SMS can help entrepreneurs enhance their firms' competitive differentiation. In contrast to relying exclusively on traditional (and often prohibitively expensive) advertising routes like print, television, or other forms of "paid media," entrepreneurs can employ social media to build their firms' brand recognition (Schaupp & Bélanger, 2014). Research has shown that this "earned media" can create additional utility for customers by providing them opportunities to socialize around firms' products (Lovett & Staelin, 2016). In addition, Fischer and Reuber (2014) found that entrepreneurs enhanced their firms' growth prospects and differentiation vis-à-vis competitors by maintaining high-volume, "multidimensional" communication streams on SMS that focused on signaling quality, relational orientation, distinctiveness, and positive affect.

**Serving a Product/Market Domain**

Both NVs and SMEs face resource constraints, which may limit the number of products they can offer and markets they can serve. DTs, however, provide opportunities for entrepreneurs to fundamentally rethink their business models (Amit & Han, 2017; Kollman & Jung, Chapter 2 in this handbook), which, in turn, may allow them to expand their firms' product offerings and market reach.

First, if firms offer digital products, they can capitalize on unique product features that can help them overcome newness and size liabilities. Specifically, these products are "non-rival," meaning they are not "used up" in consumption like physical ones are. In addition, they can be produced and distributed, even over large distances, at near zero marginal costs, and customers often incur lower search costs relative to physical goods when finding them (Lambrecht et al., 2014). Internet-connected products and services, even minimally viable ones first introduced when NVs launch, can be updated virtually, greatly reducing the costs of new product introductions and enabling companies to continuously offer added value to customers (Hui, 2014). Marketing on digital platforms (e.g., in an app store) can also provide entrepreneurs with critical customer feedback that can be used to introduce additional product features or even change their firms' overall business model over time (Eckhardt et al., 2018).

Second, the rise of DTs has also provided entrepreneurs with ways to serve increasingly distant geographic markets by providing a channel for entrepreneurs to monitor innovations, assess competitors, recruit suppliers, and source capital from outside their firms' immediate geographic area (Nambisan et al., 2019; Zhang, Sarkar, & Sarker, 2013). SMS also allow firms to build reputations in new markets, which enhances firms' trustworthiness with potential customers outside their immediate geographic area (Reuber & Fischer, 2011).

Indeed, DTs can allow firms, even new and small ones, to serve customers around the world, a strategic move that in an increasingly global economy can produce legitimacy benefits (Fariborzi & Keyhani, 2018). Firms may still face traditional international adoption barriers, like cultural and economic differences, but the more digital their product or service, the more firms can surmount these barriers through methods like engaging potential customers in the product co-creation process (Shaheer & Li, 2020). Thus, these technologies can accelerate the propensity for firms to be "born global" (Oviatt & McDougall, 1994), rather than progressing through the traditional (e.g., Uppsala) internationalization model whereby they grow within their home market for years before offering their products to overseas customers (Coviello et al., 2017).

## THE ENGINEERING PROBLEM

To tackle the engineering problem, entrepreneurs must establish operational systems to produce and market their products or services (Miles & Snow, 1978). They also must address two critical questions, "What technologies should their firms employ to transform inputs into outputs?" and "How can firms develop organization routines to overcome LoN and/or LoS?"

### Transforming Inputs to Outputs

To produce products or services, entrepreneurs need to select appropriate technologies and establish operational routines (Choi & Shepherd, 2005). Small size and resource constraints often limit SMEs' ability to purchase important operating equipment, and a dearth of established routines represents a fundamental LoN challenge for NVs. In addition, facing unknown demand for their new products or services, entrepreneurs often face uncertainty regarding how much equipment to purchase. All these issues affect firms' internal efficiency and/or external legitimacy (Shepherd et al., 2000; Stinchcombe, 1965).

DTs, however, have increasingly provided firms with lower-cost, flexible access to equipment and technologies that heretofore were only available to large, established firms (Beltagui, Rosli, & Candi, 2020). Temporary resource access can be useful, particularly when entrepreneurs first develop a new product. For example, these firms often must produce a prototype to show potential customers and investors, a process that historically has involved a long and expensive process as entrepreneurs searched for and then paid engineering firms with prototyping capabilities. Increased access to 3D printing and other digital infrastructures enabled by trends such as the rise of the "maker movement," however, have allowed many entrepreneurial firms to both speed up and reduce costs of prototyping and other steps in the entrepreneurship process (Browder, Aldrich, & Bradley, 2019). These technologies also have the potential to transform supply chains as entrepreneurial firms move from relying on remote to operating local manufacturing, giving rise to more agile production while simultaneously reducing transportation costs (Kyriakou, Nickerson, & Sabnis, 2017).

Digitization also has increasingly provided entrepreneurial firms access to heretofore prohibitively expensive resources on a long-term basis. For example, infrastructures like cloud computing services have reduced up-front information technology (IT) expenses, relative to what firms would pay to purchase on-premises software (Keyhani, Chapter 7 in this handbook; Zhang, Nan, & Tan, 2020). By accessing these shared services, entrepreneurs can employ the most current software to help run their firms, thus gaining previously unattainable efficiencies. In addition, cloud computing provides firms facing uncertain product demand with flexibility by giving them the ability to "autoscale" up or down on their computational IT load, depending on realized demand (Fazli, Sayedi, & Shulman, 2018).

Widespread adoption of these services has also provided entrepreneurial opportunities to "cloud-native" firms (e.g., Salesforce.com) to grow rapidly by providing cost-effective software solutions to other companies (Benlian et al., 2018). As a result, venture capitalists have increasingly funded entrepreneurial firms providing cloud-based IT solutions, leading to high growth in this digital infrastructure (Breznitz et al., 2018).

**Establishing Routines**

Establishing routines represents a critical step to overcoming LoN and LoS because it allows firms to both gain efficiencies and demonstrate reliability to outside stakeholders. Routines represent "regular and predictable behavior patterns of firms" (Nelson & Winter, 1982, p. 14) and exist throughout a firm, ranging from functional (e.g., R&D processes) to normative (e.g., group interactions) processes. Routines improve efficiency by reducing time needed to execute business activities, and they can enhance a firm's legitimacy by signaling that firms can produce highly consistent products or services (Choi & Shepherd, 2005). Entrepreneurs face challenges, however, because routines remain both time- and path-dependent to develop (Nelson & Winter, 1982).

DTs may provide a way for NVs to quickly access routines by reducing search costs for external partners, who can provide necessary services. These technologies provide a way for these firms to form ties with external partners, such as by joining digital supply chains. This "virtual embeddedness" not only provides legitimacy benefits that help address the entrepreneurial problem noted above, but also allows firms to quickly access or even learn established routines from partners (Morse et al., 2007).

## THE ADMINISTRATIVE PROBLEM

To successfully address the administrative problem, entrepreneurs need to decide which value chain activities to perform within a firm and which ones to outsource. To do so, they must address two fundamental questions, "Where should entrepreneurs establish their firms' boundaries?" and "How does a firm demonstrate accountability to potential stakeholders?" (Choi & Shepherd, 2005; Katz & Gartner, 1988).

**Establishing a Firm's Boundaries**

Firms can control critical resources and perform important activities in-house or they can rely on outside partners (Amit & Han, 2017). Given their resource constraints, NVs and SMEs are often forced to take the latter option to perform critical primary (e.g., manufacturing) and support (e.g., accounting) functions. Although outsourcing provides access to partners' expertise and helps firms overcome resource constraints, it also exposes them to transaction cost (e.g., partner opportunism) risks (Kaul, 2013).

DTs, however, have enabled firms to fundamentally rethink their business models, including how and whether to perform value chain functions in-house (Amit & Han, 2017; Liu, Hull, & Hung, 2017). One important development has been the rise of DLPs. Employing these platforms, entrepreneurs can access human resource talent outside their immediate vicinity (e.g., via LinkedIn or Monster.com) or even outsource necessary tasks (e.g., via Fiverr or Upwork) globally (Lehdonvirta et al., 2019). In addition, the rise of these platforms has allowed entrepreneurs to launch NVs and grow rapidly by leveraging underutilized assets owned by outside parties (Duggan et al., 2020).

First, DLPs provide firms with access to a worldwide labor pool. A surge of solo self-employment in a digital world has changed the composition of the workforce globally during the past two decades (Boeri et al., 2020). Many "platform-dependent entrepreneurs" (PDEs) operate on their own and may even eschew opportunities for local employment in favor of platform work. Built and maintained by profit-driven firms, DLPs match PDEs with clients to meet labor needs globally (Kuhn & Maleki, 2017).

DLPs provide NVs and SMEs ways to access professional, consulting, and other human resource skills beyond their organizational boundaries. Given DLPs' global footprints, low entry barriers, affordable pricing, and institutional safeguards, firms can outsource routine and nonroutine projects to PDEs with spare time (e.g., on Amazon Mechanical Turk) and/or strong technical skills (e.g., via Freelancer.com) on "crowdwork" platforms (Duggan et al., 2020).

Second, DLPs provide entrepreneurs with opportunities to disrupt existing industries by launching ventures that enlist underutilized assets owned by people outside their firms. Building a national hotel company, for example, historically took decades, given both the resource and management demands required to construct numerous hotels across a vast market (cf. Penrose, 1959). Entrepreneurs traditionally have overcome these resource constraints employing growth strategies like franchising, which required franchisors, who buy a company's business model, to invest their own time and money to build local outlets (Shane, 1996). The advent of DTs, however, has provided entrepreneurs with the means to launch and grow NVs even more quickly by both reducing search costs for and simplifying the enlistment of assets not directly controlled by their firms. Specifically, by building either "capital" (e.g., Airbnb or Drivy) or "app-work" (e.g., Uber or Grubhub) DLPs, these NVs can facilitate economic exchanges between PDEs and clients as well as collect a percentage of PDEs' revenues, even without having a physical market presence (Duggan et al., 2020).

## Demonstrating Accountability

NVs and SMEs often face challenges enlisting support because stakeholders face high uncertainty and information asymmetry about firms' internal decision making and resource allocation processes (Choi & Shepherd, 2005). As highlighted above, establishing routines (e.g., via "virtual embeddedness" in digital supply chains) provides one way for firms to signal that they can reliably offer products and services. DTs, however, can also help signal a firm's accountability, viz., its adherence to widely acceptable decision and behavioral norms, to potential stakeholders (cf. Hannan & Freeman, 1984).

First, these technologies provide mechanisms for signaling firms' accountability and, in turn, building their legitimacy through transparency and certification. For example, crowdfunding platforms provide entrepreneurs with channels to communicate with potential and current funders (e.g., via project updates), which help firms demonstrate operational transparency (Mejia, Urrea, & Pedraza-Martinez, 2019). In addition, DLPs have multiple mechanisms, including PDE- (e.g., self-reported skills), customer- (e.g., rating systems), and platform-generated (e.g., cumulative completed projects) certifications, which provide PDEs with means to signal accountability to potential customers (Lehdonvirta et al., 2019).

Second, with the rise of blockchain-based technologies, firms' need to demonstrate accountability through their own actions has declined because these infrastructures provide assurances to all parties in a transaction (Schierstedt, Göttel, & Klever, Chapter 13 in this handbook). Through their ability to "chronologically capture and store transactional data in a standardized and tamperproof format that is transparent to all stakeholders" (Chong et al., 2019, p. 1380), blockchain-based technologies help enforce accountability by having a "distributed ledger" of transactions (e.g., for cryptocurrencies), distributed market (e.g., in peer-to-peer exchanges), or automatic transaction execution (e.g., for "smart contracts"; Gaur & Gaiha, 2020). Hence, blockchain has removed the need for (and related costs of) third-party verification by banks, rating agencies, and other firms that have historically reduced transaction cost risks in business exchanges (Allen et al., 2020). Products now can be tracked and verified as authentic within a supply chain, contracts guaranteed and executed automatically, and cryptocurrency exchanged regardless of firms' home country currency volatility, all employing blockchain-based technologies.

In terms of DE, blockchain technologies also provide entrepreneurs with opportunities to launch and grow firms based on innovative business models (Chong et al., 2019). In addition, they may reduce LoN and LoS for existing firms. Specifically, in contrast to other DTs we have reviewed, which help firms build legitimacy and reputation with external stakeholders by demonstrating various characteristics, blockchain technologies may make these firm characteristics largely (or completely) irrelevant, at least in terms of needing to demonstrate accountability, because the infrastructure provides this accountability during transactions (Chalmers, Matthews, & Hyslop, 2021). As a result, these technologies may help reduce governance costs at both the firm and transaction level (Chod et al., 2020).

## FUTURE RESEARCH

Although we have reviewed a wide range of research examining how DTs may help NVs and SMEs overcome some of their biggest challenges related to newness and size, future research opportunities also exist. We suggest several potentially fruitful future areas of study within the framework of entrepreneurial, engineering, and administrative issues.

In terms of addressing the entrepreneurial problem, future research should continue to focus on how DTs allow NVs and SMEs to expand product/market offerings and overcome resource constraints. For example, questions such as how they can engage additional stakeholders (e.g., third-party developers) to help expand digital product offerings (e.g., by developing complementary products) and employ data generated via digital interactions with stakeholders (e.g., on an SMS) to enhance their value propositions remain important future DE research issues (Porter & Hepplemann, 2015; Srinivasan & Venkatraman, 2018).

In addition, extant research has examined how these firms can employ DTs like crowdfunding to overcome financial constraints. Building on this research, we suggest four other potential future crowdfunding research avenues. First, because trust plays a pivotal role in the investor-entrepreneur relationship, especially within the digital environment (Moysidou & Hausberg, 2020), research has started investigating the importance of trust and trust management in crowdfunding contexts (Mejia et al., 2019). Thus, future research could examine how different types of trust, including competence- (i.e., the expectation that the entrepreneur can fulfill his or her requirements) and integrity-based (i.e., perceptions surrounding the entrepreneur's values) trust (Connelly et al., 2018), impact the success of crowdfunding campaigns as well as how DTs can assist in developing this trust.

Second, research has focused on the important role human capital characteristics (e.g., crowdfunding experience) can play in crowdfunding success (Courtney et al., 2017). However, because entrepreneurs might seek funding from a variety of sources (e.g., venture capitalists, angel investors, and crowdfunders) over time, how previous funding sources employed by entrepreneurs impact future investor decision-making remains important. For example, "Does previous crowdfunding success improve future funding probabilities from private equity sources?" or, conversely, "Does previous use of venture capital send an adverse signal to crowdfunders that an entrepreneur is only seeking crowdfunding investments because venture capitalists rejected the current project?" represent interesting future research questions.

Third, research has focused on how online campaign design elements like product, social, and new venture narratives impact campaign success (Allison et al., 2015), which can be useful for combatting high information asymmetry surrounding crowdfunding (Moss et al., 2015). Future research, however, could investigate other information asymmetry issues. For example, interesting questions include, "Do thorough and cognitive-based descriptions that reduce information asymmetry or do simple affective descriptions targeting the crowd's emotions foster more funding, even in the presence of high information asymmetry?" (cf. Bergh et al., 2019). Future research could examine these and other related questions using policy-capturing experiments and/or content analysis-based designs.

Fourth, future research could examine potential problems that can arise from employing crowdfunding. For example, crowdfunding success helps address entrepreneurial problems related to resource constraints and firm reputation, but too much success actually could create engineering problems. For example, if a firm's production technology is insufficient to keep up with campaign-generated product demand, the crowdfunding campaign could succeed, but the firm could ultimately fail (Pala, 2018). Although extensive research exists on crowdfunding success, few studies, to date, have investigated how "too much success" can create conflicts among entrepreneurial, engineering, and/or administrative issues.

In terms of tackling the engineering problem, future research can focus on advantages that DTs provide firms (e.g., the ability to autoscale using cloud computing based on realized demand), but studies should also focus on possible downsides. For example, cyberattack vulnerability increases when firms manage their key resources and activities on-line via DTs. Although a significant amount of research on cyberattacks targeting large firms exists, much less has focused on NV and SME vulnerabilities (Zhang, Nan, & Tan, 2020). These firms, however, often make attractive targets because they possess valuable (e.g., customer financial) information but often employ fewer cyber defenses than large firms.

In terms of addressing the administrative problem, future research can continue focusing on where entrepreneurs should establish firms' boundaries. In terms of investigating this issue, DLPs represent one promising future research avenue. For example, studies could consider entrepreneurial opportunities presented by DLP diffusion, such as whether entrepreneurs should build their own DLPs or launch complementary services for existing platforms.

In addition, studies can examine the internationalization process, where multiple relationships between a DLP firm, PDEs, clients, and other stakeholders constitute a network/community. For example, existing stocks of information, knowledge, experience, and commitment allow network members to learn, create new knowledge, and build trust (Johanson & Vahlne, 2009). Thus, questions such as "Can DLP-based firms progressively transition to large open-source communities coordinated by trust?" and "If so, what kinds of trust strengthen the coordinating mechanisms?" represent interesting questions (Kost, Fieseler, & Wong, 2020).

In terms of limitations, although DTs provide some remedies for newness and size limitations, they may not help entrepreneurs overcome all these issues. For example, contrary to the general assumption that entrepreneurs employ their networks to successfully access critical resources, Smith and Smith (2021) recently found entrepreneurs were sometimes reluctant to employ virtual networks to seek funding or physical resources. The authors posited that entrepreneurs feared social judgement about their firms' resource deficiencies on a publicly visible SMS. These findings reinforce the need for developing new theory for how DTs affect the entrepreneurship process relative to traditional face-to-face interactions.

In addition, we focus on the impact that DTs have on the entrepreneurial process by examining artifacts and platforms, which serve as venture-level factors, as well as infrastructures, which serve as macro-environmental enablers to the entrepreneurship process. Davidsson (2015), however, also examined "opportunity confidence" as a key component of entrepreneurial opportunities. Defined as "the result of an actor's evaluation of a stimulus…as a basis for the creation of new economic activity" (Davidsson, 2015, p. 683), opportunity confidence represents an individual-level factor encompassing how individual entrepreneurs assess the potential created by external enablers or inherent in a new venture idea. Thus, some interesting research questions exist around the role that DTs have on an entrepreneur's confidence in his/her ability to overcome LoN and LoS or create AoN when founding their new ventures.

## CONCLUSION

Scholars have noted that key assumptions underlying theoretical frameworks employed in organizational research may not fully account for the rise of DTs, and we suggest this issue also exists in NV and SME research. Specifically, in this chapter, we posit that the advent and dissemination of digital artifacts, platforms, and infrastructures can impact LoN, and LoS challenges faced by NVs and SMEs by helping these firms overcome the formidable competitive and resource acquisition barriers they have historically faced. In addition, we note how DTs may enhance some of the benefits (e.g., AoN and strategic flexibility) that these firms can enjoy.

To examine these ideas, we have reviewed extant research investigating issues related to entrepreneurship, engineering, and administrative problems these firms must address. This examination suggests that entrepreneurs' abilities to increasingly leverage DTs as they start and grow their firms raise important questions about the extent to which these challenges still exist, given these technologies may enhance some NV and SME advantages and at least partially mitigate some disadvantages. Despite their benefits, we do not suggest these technologies can remedy all the issues faced by these firms, which, for example, still have to develop time-dependent routines internally and acquire resources externally. We hope, however, that by examining extant research and suggesting future research avenues, this chapter prompts additional research on how DTs affect important issues that entrepreneurs face during venture startup and growth.

## NOTE

1. Although definitions vary, practitioners have often described NVs employing definitions such as "a temporary organization designed to search for a repeatable and scalable business model" (Blank, 2013), and entrepreneurship scholars have often empirically defined them as firms seven years old or younger (e.g., Boeker & Wiltbank, 2005). The U.S. Small Business Administration and European Commission's standards for SMEs are often based on firm size (500 or 250 employees, respectively) or sales level (Eurostat, 2021; Small Business Administration, 2021). Based on these definitions, most NVs also start out as SMEs, and, thus, face liabilities of newness and smallness.

## REFERENCES

Ahlers, G., Cumming, D., Günther, C., & Schweizer, D. (2015). Signaling in equity crowdfunding. *Entrepreneurship Theory and Practice*, *39*, 955–80.

Akerlof, G. (1970). The market for "lemons": Quality uncertainty and the market mechanism. *Quarterly Journal of Economics*, *84*, 488–500.

Aldrich, H., & Auster, E. (1986). Even dwarfs started small: Liabilities of age and size and their strategic implications. *Research in Organizational Behavior*, *8*, 165–98.

Aldrich, H., & Fiol, C. (1994). Fools rush in: The institutional context of industry creation. *Academy of Management Review*, *19*, 645–67.

Allen, D., Berg, C., Markey-Towler, B., Novak, M., & Potts, J. (2020). Blockchain and the evolution of institutional technologies: Implications for innovation policy. *Research Policy*, *49*, 1–8.

Allison, T., Davis, B., Short, J., & Webb, J. (2015). Crowdfunding in a prosocial microlending environment: Examining the role of intrinsic versus extrinsic cues. *Entrepreneurship Theory and Practice*, *39*, 53–73.

Amit, R., & Han, X. (2017). Value creation through novel resource configurations in a digitally enabled world. *Strategic Entrepreneurship Journal*, *11*, 228–42.

Beck, T., Demirgc-Kunt, A., & Maksimovic, V. (2008). Financing patterns around the world: Are small firms different? *Journal of Financial Economics*, *89*, 467–87.

Beltagui, A., Rosli, A., & Candi, M. (2020). Exaptation in a digital innovation ecosystem: The disruptive impacts of 3D printing. *Research Policy*, *49*, 1–16.

Belleflamme, P., Lambert, T., & Schwienbacher, A. (2014). Crowdfunding: Tapping the right crowd. *Journal of Business Venturing*, *29*, 585–609.

Benlian, A., Kettinger, W., Sunyaey, A., & Winkler, T. (2018). The transformative value of cloud computing: A decoupling, platformization, and recombination theoretical framework. *Journal of Management Information Systems*, *35*, 719–39.

Bergh, D., Ketchen, D., Orlandi, I., Heugens, P., & Boyd, B. (2019). Information asymmetry in management research: Past accomplishments and future opportunities. *Journal of Management*, *45*, 122–58.

Blank, S. (2013). Why the lean startup changes everything. *Harvard Business Review*, *91(5)*, 63–72.

Boeker, W., & Wiltbank, R. (2005). New venture evolution and managerial capabilities. *Organization Science*, *16*, 123–33.

Boeri, T., Giupponi, G., Krueger, A., & Machin, S. (2020). Solo self-employment and alternative work arrangements: A cross-country perspective on the changing composition of jobs. *Journal of Economic Perspectives*, *34*, 170–95.

Breznitz, D., Forman, C., & Wen, W. (2018). The role of venture capital in the formation of a new technological ecosystem: Evidence from the cloud. *MIS Quarterly*, *42*, 1143–69.

Browder, R., Aldrich, H., & Bradley, S. (2019). The emergence of the maker movement: Implications for entrepreneurship research. *Journal of Business Venturing, 34*, 459–76.

Butticè, V., Colombo, M., & Wright, M. (2017). Serial crowdfunding, social capital, and project success. *Entrepreneurship Theory and Practice, 4*, 183–207.

Carayannopoulos, S. (2009). How technology-based new firms leverage newness and smallness to commercialize disruptive technologies. *Entrepreneurship Theory & Practice, 33*, 419–38.

Chalmers, D., Matthews, R., & Hyslop, A. (2021). Blockchain as an external enabler of new venture ideas: Digital entrepreneurs and the disintermediation of the global music industry. *Journal of Business Research, 125*, 577–91.

Chen, M.-J., & Hambrick, D. (1995). Speed, stealth, and selective attack: How small firms differ from large firms in competitive behavior. *Academy of Management Journal, 38*, 453–82.

Chod, J., Trichakis, N., Tsoukalas, G., Aspegren, H., & Weber, M. (2020). On the financing benefits of supply chain transparency and blockchain adoption. *Management Science, 66*, 4378–96.

Choi, Y., & Shepherd, D. (2005). Stakeholder perceptions of age and other dimensions of newness. *Journal of Management, 31*, 573–96.

Chong, A., Lim, E., Hua, X., Zheng, S., & Tan, C.-W. (2019). Business on chain: A comparative case study of five blockchain-inspired business models. *Journal of the Association for Information Systems, 20*, 1310–39.

Connelly, B., Crook, T., Combs, J., Ketchen, D., & Aguinis, H. (2018). Competence- and integrity-based trust in interorganizational relationships: Which matters more? *Journal of Management, 44*, 919–45.

Courtney, C., Dutta, S., & Li, Y. (2017). Resolving information asymmetry: Signaling, endorsement, and crowdfunding success. *Entrepreneurship Theory & Practice, 41*, 265–90.

Coviello, N., Kano, L., & Liesch, P. (2017). Adapting the Uppsala model to a modern world: Macro-context and micro-foundations. *Journal of International Business Studies, 48*, 1151–64.

Davidsson, P. (2015). Entrepreneurial opportunities and the entrepreneurship nexus: A re-conceptualization. *Journal of Business Venturing, 30*, 674–95.

Davidsson, P., & Honig, B. (2003). The role of social and human capital among nascent entrepreneurs. *Journal of Business Venturing, 18*, 301–31.

Davis, B., Hmieleski, K., Webb, J., & Coombs, J. (2017). Funders' positive affective reactions to entrepreneurs' crowdfunding pitches: The influence of perceived product creativity and entrepreneurial passion. *Journal of Business Venturing, 32*, 90–106.

Drummond, C., McGrath, H., & O'Toole, T. (2017). The impact of social media on resource mobilisation in entrepreneurial firms. *Industrial Marketing Management, 70*, 68–89.

Duggan, J., Sherman, U., Carbery, R., & McDonnell, A. (2020). Algorithmic management and app-work in the gig economy: A research agenda for employment relations and HRM. *Human Resource Management Journal, 30*, 114–32.

Eckhardt, J., Ciuchta, M., & Carpenter, M. (2018). Open innovation, information, and entrepreneurship within platform ecosystems. *Strategic Entrepreneurship Journal, 12*, 369–91.

Eurostat. (2021). Small and medium-sized enterprises (SMEs) https://ec.europa.eu/eurostat/web/structural-business-statistics/small-and-medium-sized-enterprises. Accessed June 24, 2021.

Fariborzi, H., & Keyhani, M. (2018). Internationalize to live: A study of the post-internationalization survival of new ventures. *Small Business Economics, 50*, 607–24.

Fazli, A., Sayedi, A., & Shulman, J. (2018). The effects of autoscaling in cloud computing. *Management Science, 64*, 5149–63.

Fischer, E., & Reuber, A. (2014). Online entrepreneurial communication: Mitigating uncertainty and increasing differentiation via Twitter. *Journal of Business Venturing, 29*, 565–83.

Fisher, G., Kuratko, D., Bloodgood, J., & Hornsby, J. (2017). Legitimate to whom? The challenge of audience diversity and new venture legitimacy. *Journal of Business Venturing, 32*, 52–71.

Fossen, F., & Sogner, A. (2021). Digitalization of work and entry into entrepreneurship. *Journal of Business Research, 125*, 548–63.

Gaur, V., & Gaiha, A. (2020). Building a transparent supply chain. *Harvard Business Review, 98(3)*, 94–103.

Granovetter, M. (1973). The strength of weak ties. *American Journal of Sociology, 78*, 1360–80.

Hannan, M., & Freeman, J. (1984). Structural inertia and organizational change. *American Sociological Review, 49*, 149–64.

Herzenstein, M., Dholakia, U., & Andrews, R. (2011). Strategic herding behavior in peer-to-peer loan auctions. *Journal of Interactive Marketing*, *25*, 27–36.

Hui, G. (2014). How the Internet of Things changes business models. *Harvard Business Review*, July 29, 2–5.

Johanson, J., & Vahlne, J.-E. (2009). The Uppsala internationalization process model revisited: From liability of foreignness to liability of outsidership. *Journal of International Business Studies*, *40*, 1411–31.

Katz, J., & Gartner. W. (1988). Properties of emerging organizations. *Academy of Management Review*, *13*, 429–41.

Kaul, A. (2013). Entrepreneurial action, unique assets, and appropriate risk: Firms as a means of appropriating profit from capability creation. *Organization Science*, *24*, 1765–81.

Kost, D., Fieseler, C., & Wong, S. I. (2020). Boundaryless careers in the gig economy: An oxymoron? *Human Resource Management Journal*, *30*, 100–13.

Kuhn, K., & Maleki, A. (2017). Micro-entrepreneurs, dependent contractors, and instaserfs: Understanding online labor platform workforces. *Academy of Management Perspectives*, *31*, 183–200.

Kyriakou, H., Nickerson, J., & Sabnis, G. (2017). Knowledge reuse for customization: Metamodels in an open design community for 3D printing. *MIS Quarterly*, *41*, 315–32.

Lambrecht, A., Goldfarb, A., Bonatti, A., Ghose, A., Goldstein, D., Lewis, R., Rao, A., Sahni, N., & Yao, S. (2014). How do firms make money selling digital goods online? *Marketing Letters*, *25*, 331–41.

Lehdonvirta, V., Kassi, O., Hjorth, I., Barnard, H., & Graham, M. (2019). The global platform economy: A new offshoring institution enabling emerging-economy microproviders. *Journal of Management*, *45*, 567–99.

Li, G., & Wang, J. (2019). Threshold effects on backer motivations in reward-based crowdfunding. *Journal of Management Information Systems*, *36*, 546–73.

Liu, M., Hull, C., & Hung, Y.-T. (2017). Starting open source collaborative innovation: The antecedents of network formation in community sources. *Information Systems Journal*, *27*, 643–70.

Liu, Y., Chen, Y., & Fan, Z. (2021). Do social network crowds help fundraising campaigns? Effects of social influence on crowdfunding performance. *Journal of Business Research*, *122*, 97–108.

Lohrke, F., & Landström, H. (2016). Young, small, and imprintable: Assessing progress and exploring future directions in new venture and small business research. *Group & Organization Management*, *41*, 703–16.

Lovett, M., & Staelin, R. (2016). The role of paid, earned, and owned media in building entertainment brands: Reminding, informing, and enhancing enjoyment. *Marketing Science*, *35*, 142–57.

Masiello, B., & Izzo, F. (2019). Interpersonal social networks and internationalization of traditional SMEs. *Journal of Small Business Management*, *57*, 658–91.

Mejia, J., Urrea, G., & Pedraza-Martinez, A. (2019). Operational transparency on crowdfunding platforms: Effect on donations for emergency response. *Production and Operations Management*, *28*, 1773–91.

Miles, R., & Snow, C. (1978). *Organizational Strategy, Structure, and Process*. McGraw-Hill.

Mollick, E. (2014). The dynamics of crowdfunding: An exploratory study. *Journal of Business Venturing*, *29*, 1–16.

Morse, E. Fowler, S., & Lawrence, T. (2007). The impact of virtual embeddedness on new venture survival: Overcoming the liabilities of newness. *Entrepreneurship Theory and Practice*, *31*, 139–59.

Moss, T., Neubaum, D., & Meyskens, M. (2015). The effect of virtuous and entrepreneurial orientations on microfinance lending and repayment: A signaling theory perspective. *Entrepreneurship Theory and Practice*, *39*, 27–52.

Moysidou, K., & Hausberg, J. (2020). In crowdfunding we trust: A trust-building model in lending crowdfunding. *Journal of Small Business Management*, *58*, 511–43.

Nambisan, S. (2017). Digital entrepreneurship: Toward a digital technology perspective of entrepreneurship. *Entrepreneurship Theory and Practice*, *41*, 1029–55.

Nambisan, S., Zahra, S., & Luo, Y. (2019). Global platforms and ecosystems: Implications for international business theories. *Journal of International Business Studies*, *50*, 1464–86.

Nelson, R., & Winter, S. (1982). *An Evolutionary Theory of Economic Change*. Harvard University Press.

Oviatt, B., & McDougall, P. (1994). Toward a theory of International New Ventures. *Journal of International Business Studies, 25*, 45–64.

Pala, S. (2018). 3 lessons from failed startups with highly successful crowdfunding campaigns. *Inc.* May 30. https://www.inc.com/serhat-pala/3-lessons-from-failed-startups-with-highly-successful -crowdfunding-campaigns.html. Accessed February 13, 2021.

Penrose, E. (1959). *The Theory of the Growth of the Firm.* Oxford University Press.

Porter, M., & Heppelmann, J. (2015). How smart, connected products are transforming companies. *Harvard Business Review, 93(10)*, 96–114.

Reuber, A., & Fischer, E. (2011). International entrepreneurship in internet-enabled markets. *Journal of Business Venturing, 26*, 660–79.

Sahaym, A., Datta, A., & Brooks, S. (2021). Crowdfunding success through social media: Going beyond entrepreneurial orientation in the context of small and medium-sized enterprises. *Journal of Business Research, 125*, 483–94.

Schaupp, L., & Bélanger, F. (2014). The value of social media for small businesses. *Journal of Information Systems, 28*, 187–207.

Shaheer, N., & Li, S. (2020). The CAGE around cyberspace? How digital innovations internationalize in a virtual world. *Journal of Business Venturing, 35*, 1–19.

Shane, S. (1996). Hybrid organizational arrangements and their implications for firm growth and survival: A study of new franchisors. *Academy of Management Journal, 39*, 216–34.

Shepherd, D., Douglas, E., & Shanley, M. (2000). New venture survival: Ignorance, external shocks, and risk reduction strategies. *Journal of Business Venturing, 15*, 393–410.

Shepherd, D., & Zacharakis, A. (2003). A new venture's cognitive legitimacy: An assessment by customers. *Journal of Small Business Management, 41*, 148–67.

Small Business Administration. (2021). Size standards. https://www.sba.gov/federal-contracting/ contracting-guide/size-standards. Accessed June 24, 2021.

Smith, C., & Smith, J. (2021). Founders' uses of digital networks for resource acquisition: Extending network theory online. *Journal of Business Research, 125*, 466–82.

Smith, C., Smith, J., & Shaw, E. (2017). Embracing digital networks: Entrepreneurs' social capital online. *Journal of Business Venturing, 32*, 18–34.

Srinivasan, A., & Venkatraman, N. (2018). Entrepreneurship in digital platforms: A network-centric view. *Strategic Entrepreneurship Journal, 12*, 54–71.

Stinchcombe, A. (1965). Social structure and organizations. In J. March (Ed.), *Handbook of Organizations* (pp. 142–93). Rand McNally.

Strotmann, H. (2007). Entrepreneurial survival. *Small Business Economics, 28*, 87–104.

Taeuscher, K. (2019). Reputation and new venture performance in online markets: The moderating role of market crowding. *Journal of Business Venturing, 34*, 1–17.

Taeuscher, K., Bouncken, R., & Pesch, R. (2021). Gaining legitimacy by being different: Optimal distinctiveness in crowdfunding platforms. *Academy of Management Journal, 64*, 149–79.

Tiwana, A., Konsynski, B., & Bush, A. (2010). Platform evolution: Coevolution of platform architecture, governance, and environmental dynamics. *Information Systems Research, 21*, 675–87.

Tripsas, M. (1997). Unraveling the process of creative destruction: Complementary assets and incumbent survival in the typesetting industry. *Strategic Management Journal, 18*, 119–42.

Überbacher, F. (2014). Legitimation of new ventures: A review and research programme. *Journal of Management Studies, 51*, 667–98.

Venkatraman, S. (1997). The distinctive domain of entrepreneurship research: An editor's perspective. In J. Katz & R. Brockhaus (Eds.), *Advances in Entrepreneurship, Firm Emergence, and Growth* (pp. 119–28). JAI Press.

Zhang, Z., Nan, G., & Tan, Y. (2020). Cloud services vs. on-premises software: Competition under security risk and product customization. *Information Systems Research, 31*, 848–64.

Zhang, M., Sarker, S., & Sarker, S. (2013). Drivers and export performance impacts of IT capability in 'born-global' firms: A cross-national study. *Information Systems Journal, 23*, 419–43.

# 10. Digital adoption in micro and small enterprise clusters: a dependency theory study in Kenya

*Ben Mkalama, Giacomo Ciambotti and Bitange Ndemo*

## INTRODUCTION

The adoption of digital technology is phenomenally sweeping across different industries and countries in the world (Ndemo & Weiss, 2017; Friederici, 2018; Valdeolmillos, Mezquita, Gonzalez-Briones, Prieto, & Corchado, 2019), and entrepreneurs across different spheres of life have extensively embraced the use of technology (Ndemo & Weiss, 2017). While many nations consider digital adoption as the highway to achieving some of their prosperity goals (World Bank, 2018), there is still a need to validate its effects across the micro and small enterprises segment (MSEs). This need is valid in the context of developing and emerging nations (Nambisan, 2017; Sydow, Sunny, & Coffman, 2020; Sottini, Ciambotti & Littlewood, 2022; Gerli & Whalley, Chapter 15 in this handbook). As Africa debuts into the digital space, the more dominant digital economies are expected to adopt, adapt, create, and disperse technological innovations across the various societies (Ndemo & Weiss, 2017). The use of digital technology ranges from the formal to the informal sector (Sydow et al., 2020) and straddles different industries in the economy (Graham, 2019). The adoption of digital technology has ranged from opportunity identification, idea generation, marketing and goes as far as the final payment of sales proceeds (Nambisan, 2017; van der Westhuizen & Goyayi, 2020). Has the adoption of digital technology delivered the expected dividends in Africa?

Comparative statistics estimate that the highest offline population is in Africa, with a penetration rate of 28.2% against the global online penetration rate of 53.6%. While developing countries have an online penetration rate of 47.0%, this compares to 86.6% in developed countries (ITU, 2020). This low penetration rate essentially demonstrates that there is still some work to be done on coverage. Most of the recent growth in internet capacity in Africa has been through mobile phones. Recent global trends have been such that mobile signals and handsets are no longer seen as prosperity symbols but ubiquitous convenience tools (Donner & Locke, 2019). Indeed, Donner and Locke further suggested that these disparities insinuate a need for perspectives of power and exclusion into the broader discourse on technology and development. Hitherto, scholars like Ndemo and Weiss (2017) opined that digital transformation was a mere extension of Africa's colonial past, whereby African economies continued to try to catch up with the rest of the dominant world. In its Digital Dividend Report, the World Bank (2016) was cautiously optimistic that, whereas efforts to address poverty reduction can be made, there was a need to understand the full ramifications of digital adoption. A view by Mann (2017) posited that existing pathological dependencies were reproduced and remained dictated by powerful elites, multinational corporations, and other transnational agencies. In turn, Juma (2017) went further and challenged the notion that a digital revolution without an accompanying industrial base was sufficient for economic growth. Juma, therefore, argued that industrial development needed to go hand in hand with digital growth. We adopt a techno-optimist approach that identifies technologically enabled business models as the panacea to social and economic development (Ndemo & Weiss, 2017).

Scholars have widely acknowledged that digitization has set into motion vigorous economic activity in both analog and digital markets (Ndemo & Weiss, 2017; Acs et al., Chapter 5 in this handbook). However, entrepreneurs choose between adoption and non-adoption of technology based on distinct justification of the net revenue return. Often, this has led to a bias towards e-commerce technologies that focus on receipt and payment of funds. The ascendancy of the mobile revolution in Africa largely drove digital adoption and gave hope to many that African economic development had come of age. Further to this, some previous empirical work like Mkalama, Ndemo, and Maalu (2020) has shown that technology adoption is very limited in the small enterprise sectors in some developing countries. The focus of this research would then lead to a better understanding of the impact of digital adoption on MSE organizations in Kenya.

We define digital adoption as the progressive state of acquiring an ability to use new digital tools and processes against their initial design. The adoption of digital technology is consistent with Rogers' theory of diffusion of innovation and is affected by many factors (Talwar, Talwar, Kaur, & Dhir, 2020). However, MSEs operate under different circumstances, and therefore their adoption of innovation varies. Roger's theory postulates that innovation diffuses once individuals go through a series of self-reflection steps. These include, the perceived value innovation and constant communication with other innovators within the social network of the individuals (Rogers, 2003). According to the theory, a typical diffusion takes time initiated by early adopters, then matures progressively before innovation laggards finally pick it up. Generally, MSEs have unique characteristics that would allow them to benefit from digital adoption.

Despite MSEs' importance in national economies, there has been limited but growing scholarly discourse on insights on digital adoption in MSEs (Hossain & Kauranen, 2016; Sottini et al., 2022). For example, Yun, Zhao, Park, and Shi (2020) posited that Alibaba became a top global eCommerce company within a short time after adopting and applying creative eCommerce business models. The key driver to this growth was an innovation-friendly culture and feedback loop system that created an enabling environment. In addition, some scholars have demonstrated that digital footprints may be affected across different social groups (Marina, Lutz, & Buchi, 2018). These examples stimulate the natural curiosity of the policymakers on what makes digital adoption influence the growth of micro and small enterprises. Heeding this evidence, we argue that a research question that we seek to address is *whether digital adoption has happened to MSEs in Africa*. Whereas there is increasing discourse on the actual impact of digitization across all sectors of the economy (Friederici, 2018), numerous studies have shown that there are bottlenecks in the digital adoption of enterprises (Friederici, Wahome, & Graham, 2020). Therefore, a second question that is still little explored would be *what are the implications and patterns of digital adoption in MSEs in Africa?*

To address such questions, we then applied the generally accepted definition of MSEs as firms with annualized sales turnover of less than US\$ 50,000 and individually employed less than 50 people (Ndemo & Weiss, 2017). Such definition is also very pertinent with the local Kenyan ecosystem, where Micro, Small, and Medium Enterprises (MSME) accounted for over 33% of the country's Gross Domestic Product (GDP). The local MSMEs similarly employed over 15 million individuals, out of which 81% were employed by the micro sector (KNBS, 2016). Kenya National Bureau of Statistics (KNBS) estimated that over 99% of the estimated 7.5 million business establishments were MSEs. KNBS further estimated that in 2019, wholesale and retail trade, hotels, and restaurants had approximately 9 million employees, followed by 3 million employees in the manufacturing sector (KNBS, 2020a). In addition, Kenya has a large informal sector covering mainly semi-organized and unregulated activities and has been growing progressively. Thus, the MSE sector includes both formal and informal enterprises (KNBS, 2016). The informal sector employs 5.3 million employees in urban areas, whereas there are 9.7 million employees in rural areas.

This study seeks to add to the compendium of knowledge on the studies on digital adoption in MSEs that has so far been generally low. The chapter proceeds as follows. First, we document recent theoretical developments and present our theoretical framework. We next illustrate the research methodology and proceed with the findings. Finally, we discuss our results, highlighting contributions and offering future avenues for research.

## LITERATURE REVIEW

Even though scholars have extensively studied the growth of technological innovation and subsequent adoption, it is increasingly apparent that other emerging areas like the macro-level socio-economic implications have not been exhaustively discussed (Yoo, Henfridsson, & Lyytinen, 2010; Nan, 2019). Astonishingly, the excitement about exponentially growing technology permeating across all facets of our lives does not transform itself in an equally exponential manner (Chesbrough, 2020). Chesbrough (2020) coined the term exponential paradox to explain the puzzle around rapid technological growth unaccompanied by productivity growth. Indeed, Helsper (2017) posited that theorization and empirical research on digital inequalities could benefit alternative approaches by considering contextual and social settings into existing discourse. Furthermore, Marina et al. (2018) opined that those digital footprints that originate from active content creation, passive participation, and platform-generated data are important social differentiators. Thus, there is a need to look at digital adoption for alternative approaches critically.

### Theory of Technological Affordances and Constraints

Technological Affordances and Constraints Theory (TACT) is a recent view in the Information Systems (IS) literature that seeks to understand technology use and its consequences (Wang, Carte, & Schwarzkopf, 2015). It originated from the seminal work of James Gibson, who, in his affordance perspective work in 1977, defined affordance as what the environment provides or furnishes the animal (Greeno, 1994; Wang et al., 2015). Markus and Silver (2008, p. 622) further defined functional affordances as "possibilities for goal-oriented action afforded to specific user groups by technical objects." A technology affordance (or constraint) is a relational construct that depends on the interaction between technology features and individual goals (Strong et al., 2014; Wang et al., 2015). We consider TACT as appropriate for this study because digital gadgets come in various shapes and forms. The convenience offered by digital gadgets similarly varies.

Globally, all Information Communication Technology (ICT) indicators have been positive, with the growth in internet usage influenced by increased investments in data storage, processing power, and innovation ecosystem (ITU, 2019). Platform launches across Africa to complement the growth of digital innovation have continued to grow (Smit, Johnson, Hunter, Dunn, & van Vuuren, 2019), thereby offering various conveniences to different users. Indeed, Kenya has recorded one of the fastest growth rates of platform hubs across the continent on the back of optimism of a significant impact of social-economic status by digital adoption (Ng'weno & Porteous, 2018; Smit et al., 2019).

There are still questions on the rate and consequences of digital adoption. Additionally, discussions amongst scholars on the measurement of technology affordances are still incomplete. As a result of which Wang et al., 2015 recommended that researchers develop their measurement of technology affordances for each specific context through review of existing literature, conducting qualitative research, and in some cases, mixed-method approaches.

**Theory of Socio-materiality**

A second important theoretical aspect being considered is related to the Theory of Socio-materiality (TSM). This emerging theory within the information system (IS) field has ongoing conversations that border on uncertainties on conceptually and analytically discussing socio-materiality (Parmigianni & Mikalsen, 2013). TSM brought together the fields of organizational studies and technology. The desire for researchers to focus on the social (organization and its attendant processes) and the material (technology and other physical objects used in the organization like computers, machinery, and buildings) further developed TSM. The seminal and subsequent work of Wanda Orlikowski (Orlikowski, 1991, 2007) that showed technology as an essential amplifier for rejuvenating organizations was the genesis of TSM. Socio-materiality is popular because it brings together the previous conceptual distinctions between organizations, work, and technology (Parmigianni & Mikalsen, 2013).

We consider TSM as appropriate for this study because it explores the relationship between enterprises and their use of beneficial digital communication gadgets. In their systematic literature review, Parmigianni and Mikalsen (2013) opined that the research around socio-materiality revolved around three vital resulting facets, mutuality, performativity, and multidimensionality. These facets address the nature of *what, how, when*, and *where questions* of socio-material assemblage. Such questions are best addressed through qualitative studies.

**Exploring the Infrastructure and Access Context in Kenya**

Kenya is acknowledged as one of Africa's digital powerhouses (GSMA, 2020). Its digital adoption has primarily been driven by mobile phone technology, whose mobile cellular subscription was 114 per 100 inhabitants (KNBS, 2020a). According to the International Telecommunications Union (ITU), as of 2019, Kenya had a mobile cellular network coverage of 97% (ITU, 2020). Furthermore, in 2019, the population covered by at least a 3G network in Kenya was 93% compared to an average coverage of 77.1% in Africa and a global average of 93.2%. As of 2019, the total utilized bandwidth in the country stood at 2.7 million megabits per second (KNBS, 2020a).

ITU (2020) estimated that as at 2019, 23% of Kenyan individuals were actively using the internet (from any location via gadgets like computer, mobile phone, personal digital assistant, games machine, or digital TV). Further to this, the households with internet access were estimated at 18%. The use, which is estimated to have grown with the onset of the COVID-19 pandemic appears inconsistent with infrastructural access indices. Figure 10.1 presents a comparison of similar measures.

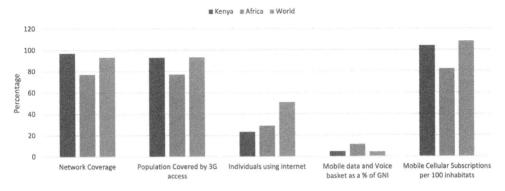

*Source:*   ITU (2019).

*Figure 10.1*    *Comparison of infrastructure and access – Kenya, Africa and the World (ITU, 2019)*

From the comparison, we note that the range of disparities across the different demographic groups is also huge. Comparatively, 30% of the youth aged between 15 and 24 years use the internet compared to 24% of the population between 25 and 74 years of age. Less than 2% of the other age bands use the internet. The distinction in coverage in rural versus urban areas is even more pronounced in all indices, with the rural areas having significant gaps in coverage. For example, households with internet access at home in urban areas are 56% against a paltry 15% for rural areas. Additionally, the gender parity index for the use of the internet in Kenya was at 0.8 in 2019, indicating that women were less likely to use the internet than men. This measure compared to 0.54 for Africa and a global parity of 0.87 over the same period. No data has been maintained in Kenya on ICT skills either at the basic, standard or advanced level.

The previous data shows that Kenya's basic infrastructure compares favorably well with the global picture. However, we see signs of inequities in the distribution across different demographic and geographical parameters.

**Towards Digital Enterprise in Kenya**

The growth of ICT-enabled enterprises in Kenya has seen leaps and bounds since the landing of the underground cables in Kenya (Ndemo & Mkalama, 2019). This phenomenon has primarily been due to the growth of mobile money and has been predominantly driven by MSEs. The focus of growth in MSEs has mainly been in the space of eCommerce. As of 2010, 39% of private enterprises in Kenya were engaged in eCommerce (KNBS & CCK, 2016). Between 2016 and 2019, the number and value of mobile commerce transactions in Kenya grew by close to 128% and 300%, respectively (KNBS, 2020a). A potential market of close to 50 million people, high mobile cellular subscription rate, balanced gender population, and burgeoning youth points to an underlying potential for a robust digital ecosystem in Kenya (Friederici et al., 2020).

Nairobi, the capital and commercial city of Kenya, acts as a hub to many regional and global offices of international institutions. As a result of this, it also hosts many diplomatic experts and economic migrants. It also has a significant presence of immigrant tech start-up founders. Although according to (Friederici et al., 2020), this is a large enough market for many start-up entrepreneurs, their impact has not been as outstanding as expected from the level of continuous activities. The available data indicates some disparities in eCommerce transactions across different genders and demographics at the macro level.

Digital adoption in MSEs has predominantly been affected by the environment in which the MSEs operate. To further spur digital adoption, the Kenyan government, through its Digital Economy Blueprint (GOK, 2019), developed a comprehensive framework and identified a set of policies for implementation. The plan acknowledged that the need for a digital economy was motivated by socio-cultural, political, and economic factors. The following four pillars anchored the plan: digital government, digital business, infrastructure innovation-driven entrepreneurship, and digital skills and values. The implementation of the different pillars is at various stages and, in some cases, reasonably nascent.

KNBS (2020a) estimated that the 2019 uptake of the new digital economy (NDE) in the industry stood at 39.7%. NDE forms accounted for included robotics, artificial intelligence, the internet of things, cloud computing, big data analytics, digital payment systems, three-dimensional printing, drones, and blockchains. Furthermore, KNBS estimated that 25.4% of industries in Kenya engaged in eCommerce activities with intra-sectoral variations on their usage. Thus, after a period of conscious policy reforms for more than 10 years, the expectation would be that the entire population would have fully adopted eCommerce. However, despite the impressive statistics, we contend that the conversation is incomplete and that some areas still require attention.

**Building the Theoretical Framework for Digital Adoption**

Given the recent theoretical developments, this study investigated antecedents of digital adoption within the MSEs in a developing context such as Kenya. Much earlier, Tsatsou (2011) recommended additional research on digital divides, intending to clarify the essential role of socio-cultural and decision-making dynamics in structuring digital adoption. Tsatsou further posited that research should go beyond access and usage indicators and have additional measures on quality of use and variations in usage, thereby avoiding simplistic linear explanations. From our review, research on digital adoption in MSEs is relatively nascent and requires supplementary conceptualization. This study will seek to bridge the gap in the conceptualization of digital adoption in small enterprises with a specific focus on MSEs. Based on TACT and TSM, we adopted three core anchors to our discussion. These anchors included the psycho-social, socio-economic factors, and technological capability as affecting digital adoption.

According to Vizzotto, de Oliveira, Elkis, Cordeiro, and Buchain (2013), psycho-social factors describe the influence of an individual's social and cultural environment on their mental health and behavior. Scholars have identified these factors as cognitions, emotions, motivations, attitudes, personality characteristics, and intelligence (Fried, 2017; Roberts, Flin, Millar, & Corradi, 2021). The limited nature of research on digital adoption on MSEs allows for exploratory research on the implications of psycho-social factors on digital adoption. For instance, the current overwhelming wave of digitization lends credence to the view that MSEs should be flexible and quickly adopt the technology. Nevertheless, as demonstrated by Roberts et al. (2021), an underlying psychological barrier needs to be overcome before they can quickly adopt. Rogers' theory articulates that the diffusion of innovation will percolate based on psycho-social factors such as personality characteristics, attitudes, social norms, and predictability. This view resonates with the fact that a dominant individual makes decision-making within the MSE firm. We opine that those decisions on digital adoption are made on the basis that the dominant individual is comfortable with the change. The underlying logic behind such decisions would have been that the individual perceives benefits and security in the proposed change. On this basis, we adopt the Psychological Technological Adoption framework (PTAF) by Roberts et al. (2021) to carry out our assessment.

Socio-economic factors are derived from the general well-being of individuals, and the determining factors include employment or income source, education, and health. Examination of socio-economic indicators shows that access to resources, privilege, and power is often skewed. The positive effects of digital innovation on the socio-economic development of the different countries in Africa are well enumerated (Nan, 2019). There have also been previous studies on the progress and opportunities available for technology in Africa (Ponelis & Holmner, 2015). Disparate socio-economic factors nevertheless lead to digital inequalities across different societies, thereby creating the term digital margins. Rather than emphasizing developing nations as compared to developed nations, the study focuses on global margins, defined as those individuals, places, and activities at the periphery of transnational networks of production and value addition (Graham, 2019). Scholars have argued a linkage between socio-economic inequality and the ability to leverage digital innovation (Robinson et al., 2015; Cinnamon, 2020). Our approach is to disaggregate the socio-economic factors that dissuade digital adoption in the global margins focusing on Africa.

We consider technological capability as the inherent ability to absorb, create and utilize technological knowledge (Kang, Baek, & Lee, 2017; Poudel, Carter, & Lonial, 2019). Cinnamon (2020) posited that access to technological opportunities initially determined digital inclusion and subsequent adoption. Additionally, Cinnamon posited that there might be further differentiation in technological skills and usage and even how the technology was applied at a subsequent level. Finally, this determined who could make use of and derive definite benefits from the technology use. Therefore, our study approach is to explore the extent and state of technological capabilities that influence digital adoption.

We seek to answer a critical research question in determining the factors that influence digital adoption in micro and small enterprises. As a result of this, we develop our conceptual model, as shown in Figure 10.2.

Our conceptual framework tries to explain that digital adoption is affected by the psycho-social factors, socio-economic factors, and the technological capability of the micro and small enterprises, as we develop this through the findings.

## METHODOLOGY

Given the exploratory nature of this study, we decided to undertake qualitative research through case studies (Eisenhardt, 1989; Gehman et al., 2018) which are preferred as they provided the three basic principles of describing, understanding and explaining a phenomenon as recommended by Harrison, Birks, Franklin, and Mills (2017). Furthermore, this methodology is particularly relevant for research that focuses on "why" and "how" in relatively new

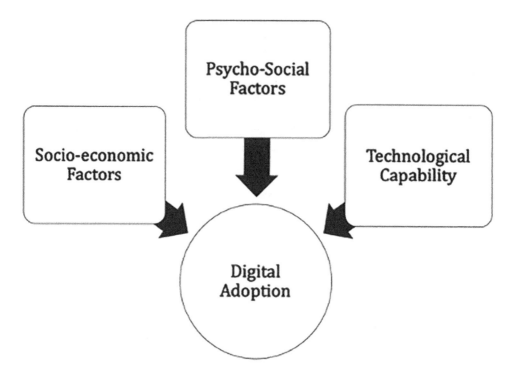

*Figure 10.2      Conceptual framework*

and undiscovered areas (Yin, 2009), for process inquiries such as our research question and when we collect data in an uncertain environment, such as our research setting (Eisenhardt & Graebner, 2007).

We conducted our research on both formal and informal MSEs in Kenya, which is appropriate to address the research question. In fact, as one of the most promising emerging economies in East Africa with recent attention also of scholars from research in management and entrepreneurship (George, Corbishley, Khayesi, Haas, & Tihanyi, 2016; Ciambotti & Pedrini, 2021), Kenya is primarily recognized as a fruitful field for investigating the informal economy aspects and resources' mobilization activities by institutions and local actors (Zoogah, Peng, & Woldu, 2015; Sydow et al., 2020; Sottini et al., 2022).

We collected primary data through a multiple instrumental case design approach that involved entrepreneurs in busy MSE markets in Nairobi as the primary units of study. As the key respondents, we conducted semi-structured interviews with 30 MSE entrepreneurs who have been in business for at least three years. We identified the cases through a multi-stage replication process. In the first instance, we biased the case selection towards the manufacturing and general trade sector, which were stratified based on the activities of the firms. We chose these sectors as they employ the most significant number of people at a national level. Subsequently, we identified some cases from each of these identified clusters. Finally, we purposively determined the cases as entrepreneurs who were likely to enrich the information sought. As a prerequisite, all the respondents interviewed had exposure to digital technology, which we defined as mobile phones, computers, or any relevant electronic gadgets within

*Table 10.1      Sectoral distribution of cases studied*

|  | Frequency | Percent | Cumulative Percent |
|---|---|---|---|
| Textile and Apparel | 4 | 13.3 | 13.3 |
| Fabricated Metal Products | 5 | 16.7 | 30.0 |
| Furniture | 4 | 13.3 | 43.3 |
| Wood and Products of Wood and Cork | 2 | 6.7 | 50.0 |
| Chemicals and their Products | 4 | 13.3 | 63.3 |
| Plastics | 1 | 3.3 | 66.7 |
| General Merchandise Trade | 3 | 10.0 | 76.7 |
| Other – Leather | 1 | 3.3 | 80.0 |
| Food Products | 6 | 20.0 | 100.0 |
| Total | 30 | 100.0 |  |

*Table 10.2      Descriptive analysis of firm profiles and cost of internet*

|  | N | | Mean | Std. Deviation | CV |
|---|---|---|---|---|---|
|  | Valid | Missing |  |  |  |
| Age of the primary owner | 30 | 0 | 43.17 | 11.277 | 26% |
| Years of Operation | 30 | 0 | 8.93 | 6.507 | 73% |
| No. of regular employees | 29 | 1 | 4.00 | 2.619 | 65% |
| The proportion of internet cost to total expenditure | 30 | 0 | 4.34% | 4.6164 | 106% |

the business. We excluded all entrepreneurs who did not use any digital technology from the survey. Table 10.1 presents a summary of the choice of the sectors.

Research rigor in the qualitative part of the study was maintained by abiding to the four principles recommended by Yin (2009). These principles included collection and incorporation into the analysis of additional secondary evidence where available; consideration and critical review of all rival interpretations of the findings; consideration of the most significant aspects of the cases and finally, the use of the researchers' *prior* knowledge.

We addressed potential common method biases by advising the respondents on the study's purpose, encouraging them to provide objective evidence, and assuring them, where applicable, of our utmost confidentiality (Podsakoff, Mackenzie, Lee, & Podsakoff, 2003). To ensure that the responses are honest and consistent, the interviewers spent time clarifying the study's objectives with a focus on explanation building and rival explanations in an iterative manner. Upon the completion of the interviews, we transcribed the interview notes and analyzed outcomes for content. During the qualitative data analysis, we comprehensively challenged all observed and explained phenomena using alternative logic to the point of saturation. This analysis allowed the researchers to tease out the derived themes.

## FINDINGS

The cases were geographically well-distributed across Nairobi. Furthermore, 70% of the interviewed cases were single owners, with the rest having invited additional shareholders into their businesses. The firms were generally small, and over 75% of them had less than five staff members. At 97%, nearly all the business owners rented their business premises. This latter fact reflects micro and small enterprises, which are often inadequately capitalized and do not

*Table 10.3    Descriptive analysis of profiles of interviewed firms and their owners*

| Profile | | Gender | | Total |
|---|---|---|---|---|
| | | Male | Female | |
| Age Band of Primary Owner | Equal or below 30 | 4 | 1 | 5 |
| | Between 30 and less than 40 | 4 | 5 | 9 |
| | Between 40 and less than 50 | 6 | 2 | 8 |
| | Between 50 and less than 60 | 6 | 0 | 6 |
| | Equal to or more than 60 | 2 | 0 | 2 |
| | Total | 22 | 8 | 30 |
| Years of Operation | Less than 5 years | 6 | 5 | 11 |
| | Between 5 and less than 10 years | 8 | 1 | 9 |
| | Between 10 and less than 15 years | 3 | 1 | 4 |
| | More than 15 years | 5 | 1 | 6 |
| | Total | 22 | 8 | 30 |
| Number of Regular Employees | Less than 5 employees | 15 | 8 | 23 |
| | More than 5 employees | 6 | 0 | 6 |
| | Total | 21 | 8 | 29 |
| Level of Education | Secondary | 9 | 4 | 13 |
| | Tertiary | 7 | 3 | 10 |
| | Graduate | 2 | 1 | 3 |
| | Postgraduate | 0 | 1 | 1 |
| | Total | 18 | 9 | 27 |

have enough assets to support external borrowing. We provide a descriptive summary of these profiles of the cases in Table 10.2.

From Table 10.2, the mean age of owners is 43.17 ($SD = 11.277$, $CV = 26\%$) with the firms having been in operation averagely for over 8 years ($SD = 6.507$, $CV = 73\%$). These are predominantly firms that employ on average less than five employees ($SD = 2.619$, $CV = 65\%$). The study also sought the respondents on the amount of money they spent on internet cost as a proportion of their total expenditure. This measure was arrived at by comparing the actual amount every month spent on internet bundles as a proportion of the business' cost of total expenditure. The study findings showed that the respondents estimated the mode of the amount they spent on the internet was between 2% and 5% of their total expenses. The mean proportionate cost of expenditure on internet was 4.34% ($SD = 4.6164$, $CV = 106\%$). However, the coefficient of variation for these findings was pretty high, as shown in Table 10.2. This variation meant that there were some outliers in some of the opinions provided by the respondents. This measure on proportionate cost compares favorably well with the ITU estimates of 4.8% for the country mobile cellular basket as percentage of Gross National Income (GNI) (ITU, 2019). We provide a descriptive summary of the additional profiles of the cases in Table 10.3.

The findings in Table 10.3 show that the age band of the primary business owner was evenly distributed. Similarly, the number of years in which the businesses have been in existence was generally evenly distributed. However, we noted that of the interviewed people, 73% were male, and as such, the respondent selection was biased against the female gender. In addition,

*Table 10.4    Perceived cost of internet*

|  | Frequency | Percent | Valid Percent |
|---|---|---|---|
| Affordable | 13 | 43.3 | 43.3 |
| Slightly affordable | 5 | 16.7 | 16.7 |
| Neither affordable nor unaffordable | 6 | 20.0 | 20.0 |
| Slightly unaffordable | 4 | 13.3 | 13.3 |
| Not Affordable | 2 | 6.7 | 6.7 |
| **Total** | **30** | **100.0** | **100.0** |

less than 15% of the respondents had a university level of education, with most having a secondary and tertiary level of education.

Through a rigorous process of data analysis, we were able to map out the integration of digital innovation into the business practices of the entrepreneurs to provide the findings of the research. Our findings traced the flow of value chains of the various products in the market. Due to the multi-case nature of the study, the range of products and raw materials was extensively diverse. The raw materials were sourced from both local and international sources. They underwent a process for refinement, after which the finished products were offered for sale and predominantly for the local markets.

We noted that the network coverage in Nairobi was relatively extensive, and therefore, access to the internet was generally predicated by individual circumstances rather than general infrastructural conditions. During the study, we tested our observations that access to the internet was affected by its perceived affordability, thereby affecting digital adoption. We present their responses in Table 10.4.

According to the survey, 60% of the respondents felt that the internet was affordable, whereas 20% felt that the internet was generally unaffordable. Further, some businesses felt that the internet was not affordable with some specific mobile network operators. The businesses that stated this mainly were the smaller businesses in profile. Furthermore, these businesses felt that ancillary infrastructure like access to computers and internet stability was similarly unaffordable.

The survey also sought to establish the entrepreneur's opinion on whether there was a noticeable growth in business due to the adoption of digital technologies. Closed questions that required the respondent to state whether there had been a growth, no growth or decline in business over the past three years were asked. Growth was defined as a progressive increase in sales turnover over the prior year, whereas decline was defined as a drop in the prior year's sales turnover. Where the growth was more significant than 20%, this was deemed to be an increased growth in business, whereas if it was between 5% and 20%, then it was deemed to be a slight growth. On the converse, if the decline was more significant than 5% but less than 20%, then it was deemed to be a slight decline, whereas if it was greater than 20%, then it was deemed to be a declined growth in business. Finally, if the deviation over the prior periods was less than 5%, then the growth was neither an increase nor a decline in business. We present these findings in Table 10.5.

The findings overwhelmingly suggested that the influence of digital technology positively affected the business. Furthermore, more than 93% of the respondents felt that the digital technology that they had used led to increased business.

The qualitative discussions revealed that the entrepreneurs used digital technology for various reasons. This use ranged from opportunity identification, idea generation, receipt, and

*Table 10.5      Impact on business*

|  | Frequency | Percent | Valid Percent |
|---|---|---|---|
| Increased business | 21 | 70.0 | 70.0 |
| Slightly increased business | 7 | 23.3 | 23.3 |
| Neither increased nor declined business | 2 | 6.7 | 6.7 |
| **Total** | **30** | **100.0** | **100.0** |

the making of payments. We further observed that market opportunities were similarly availed based on digital technology. At least 50% of the firms explained using digital technology to search for opportunities and generate new ideas. In addition, at least 70% of the respondents acknowledged that they used digital technology for advertising their businesses due to the changing market dynamics. To market their businesses, twelve of the respondents had business accounts on social media sites, including Facebook, WhatsApp, Instagram, and YouTube channels.

Additionally, 33% of the interviewed firms used digital technology to source raw materials and new markets for their products. Furthermore, all the respondents acknowledged that they used communication technology due to its convenience, thereby not physically meeting their business partners. The findings suggested that due to digital innovation, MSEs obtain different ideas and are aware of different opportunities, which they leverage to improve their businesses. For instance, technology allowed the firms to preview their products through images before they committed to purchases.

The back-end processes in the firms also adopted digital technology. For instance, some respondents explained that they used it to monitor their businesses and ensure the safety of the stocks through CCTV installation whose signal was streamed onto their phones. Additionally, market intelligence and research were enabled by the use of computers on the premises. Some firms had computerized their finance and accounting functions, thereby projecting the firms' performance easily. All the respondents used digital technology to make and receive payments predominantly through M-Pesa – the dominant mobile money payment system in the country. Digital technology was also used in back-end logistics as some of the firms used technology to track their international shipments to delivery.

The awareness of the expansive range of IT-based platforms was found to be limited in the studied cases. The most commonly used eCommerce channel was the M-Pesa payments platform being used by all respondents. At least 76% of the respondents did not use other digital platforms. The reason for single platform use ranged from not being aware of the existence of other platforms to not knowing how to use them. A number of the respondents also claimed that the other platforms were too expensive to use or that they did not trust them. Some respondents observed that for an online business to succeed, one needed a constant flow of online customer inquiries on the platforms, and therefore much marketing. This requirement, they felt, was discouraging for some of them as small-scale businesses and was only beneficial to the platform owners. In addition, some firms were unhappy about the applicable terms and conditions for use by different platform sites. There were cases whereby some platforms forcibly subscribed firms to premium sites if they wanted their advertisements to feature on business pages, thereby increasing the operational expenses with no guarantees of recovery to the investments.

Inconsistent quality of products and unassured warranties of the products was also found as an issue. Similarly, untimely and unreliable deliveries also eroded confidence in

*Table 10.6*   *Mapping of psychological technological adoption framework*

| Respondent statements | Emerging themes | Category |
| --- | --- | --- |
| • Looking forward to buying a smartphone to market products through WhatsApp | Innovativeness | Personality factors |
| • Marketing and advertising of products through developing more unique content which is eye-catching to the target audience | | |
| • The online market is flooded with imported products from China which makes me remain offline and look for customers who are mainly from referrals | Risk Aversion | |
| • Looking forward to using solar panels as a source of power because electricity seems to be expensive | Personal Incentive | Motivation factors |
| • Opening a website from where customers can reach our products and for any communications | | |
| • Sometimes there is a problem with network overload, maybe because we are worlds apart | Fear of Technology | |
| • There are times when M-Pesa services aren't available during maintenance which can delay your payments more so when clients have come to pick their products | Failure | |
| • Sometimes there is a power outage which makes it hard to charge the phones for further cash transactions | Technology attitudes | Attitude factors |
| • Some technologies can be incorporated in only large enterprises because of high maintenance costs | | |
| • Some people don't believe in your work as they think that we exaggerate the adverts thus shy away | Trust | |
| • Sometimes I don't trust these online markets since you can order for something and they bring you something sub-standard from what you saw in the advert | | |
| • Like with M-Pesa when sending money, you might miss some digits and end up sending money to the wrong persons who might withdraw immediately thus losing the cash | Risk Perception | Cognitive factors |
| • The same applies to the operation of a computer where I might not keep orders well when my employee who is responsible for its operation isn't there since I am not so good at internet | | |
| • Sometimes I am not so good at the internet, so when one of my workers who is good at that is not there and I want to check something, I have to wait which can lead to loss of opportunity or delayed orders from clients | Technical knowledge | |
| • Lack of technical skills in operating the website like posting products | | |
| • Getting counterfeit raw materials when we order online | Perceptions of certainty | |
| • Being delivered with different goods from the one ordered | | |
| • After doing intense marketing on social media and getting referrals from existing the business experienced a boom after which the business grew | Social influence | Social Factors |
| • Lack of bundles to connect to the internet | | |
| • Online platforms can derail you from the main course of business and it disturbs you a lot | Subjective norms | |

| Respondent statements | Emerging themes | Category |
|---|---|---|
| • To track materials, for instance, know how the stocks are being depleted and know when to replenish | Leadership | Organizational factors |
| • I also find it easy to advertise my products since most people aren't ready to come for products for fear of COVID-19. This helps me reach other markets than the walk-ins | | |
| • I have received support in the provision of the machines that were brought and installed by some donors | Collaborative culture | |
| • I wish to embrace technology like getting good mixing machines (computers) but they are expensive. They require heavy capital to invest | Technology Adoption Culture | |
| • I do sometimes get to check if at all there are new technologies for making our works better | | |

*Table 10.7     Socio-economic factor mapping*

| Factor | Theme |
|---|---|
| Employment/Income | Low-income enterprises – less than Kes. 5 million annualized turnovers. |
| | High infrastructural expenditures |
| | Macroeconomy – multidimensional Poverty index of 24% of the population in Nairobi, Kenya 2021 |
| Education | 85% of respondents secondary and tertiary level of education. Only 15% had a university level of education |
| | None of the respondents had formal training in information technology |
| | Macroeconomy – multidimensional poverty index of 24% of the population in Nairobi, Kenya 2021 |

platform-originated businesses. Aside from the digital platforms, the respondents identified network availability and reliability and lack of knowledge on the use of technology as also hindering the use of digital technology in running their businesses. Furthermore, occasionally infrastructural needs like inconsistent and unaffordable electricity supply affected their use of technological gadgets. Based on the data collected and analyzed, insights were subsequently developed.

The PTAF approach by Roberts et al. (2021) was adopted to map out the psychological factors that influenced digital adoption by the MSEs. The framework was mapped against the emerging themes by the statements from the respondents. We present some of the mapped statements in Table 10.6.

The empirical data obtained indicated that personality, motivational, attitudinal, cognitive, social, and organizational factors played a significant role in deciding on digital adoption in the studied MSEs.

As a measure of the socio-economic status, KNBS (2020b), assessed the multidimensional poverty index in Nairobi at 27%. The multidimensional index was derived from several measures that included defined standards in nutrition, education, economic activity, information, water, sanitation, and housing. Two measures were used in this study to determine the construct of socio-economic factors. These included the education and employment of the respondents. Unfortunately, this study could not assess the third measurement of health due to the unavailability of relevant data. We further noted that the access to privilege and power was skewed against the respondents as they were based in informal micro and small enterprise markets that are often not privileged in basic market infrastructure. These measures were mapped against various data obtained from the respondents, and we present them in Table 10.7.

From the mapping indicated in Table 10.7, the level of socio-economic status in the micro-enterprise cluster was adjudged as being below the average in the Nairobi urban area. In the study, the opinion of the MSEs on the cost of access to the internet and other digital platforms was widely varied, which influenced the adoption and application of digital technology by the MSEs. These variances were consistent with other surveys that were carried out on a global scene. For example, the State of Mobile Internet Connectivity Report, 2020 (GSMA, 2020), estimated that more than half of the global population were not using mobile-based internet. The reasons hereof included a lack of mobile broadband coverage, lack of awareness, unaffordability, and lack of literacy and digital skills. We opine that this pattern was demonstrated in our research.

In the context of this research, technological capability, therefore, is considered the blended fusion of access to digital opportunities and the skills, application, and utilization of digital technology. Skills and technical expertise are harnessed through tertiary education and work experience. We presented a summary of the level of education and experience in Table 10.3, which shows that 33% of the respondents had tertiary education. The findings also show that 63% of the respondents had more than five years of experience in their respective lines of business. The findings suggest that the respondents were reasonably well-versed with their respective businesses. We were, however, not able to categorize the findings into industry-specific nuances as the industry sub-samples were too small for generalization.

## DISCUSSIONS

The adoption of digital technology in developing countries has democratized the available information on material, resources, and product availability, and market awareness (George et al., 2016; Sydow et al., 2020). This convenience has been enabled by using various digital applications and platforms (Ng'weno & Porteous, 2018; Donner & Locke, 2019; Acs et al., Chapter 5 in this handbook). The study sought to address the question of whether digital adoption has happened to MSEs in Africa. It also sought to assess the implications and patterns of digital adoption in MSEs of Africa. As a result of these overarching questions, the study aimed to establish the extent of the adoption of digital technology in MSEs. It also studied how MSEs, through technology, run their businesses, accessed their raw materials, and offered products for sale to their respective markets.

The study tested extant theory against our observations that digital adoption in MSEs was not as widespread as has been found in the medium and corporate enterprises. From the earlier analysis, it was demonstrated that psychological factors determined the adoption of digital technology. Different aspects of digitization were adopted, and the choice was predominantly determined by the owners' comfort with the available knowledge and the sense of security around the respective digital aspect. Previous studies like Ng'weno and Porteous (2018) demonstrated that the adoption of digital technology allowed manufacturing entrepreneurs to source raw materials remotely. Ng'weno and Porteous (2018) also showed that digitalization allowed entrepreneurs to expand their operations and operate from multiple locations. Our study, however, found that MSEs did not fully harness the available opportunities on the digital eCommerce platforms. The study also showed that digital adoption was limited in scale in MSEs and varied individually. Even though more than 90% of the respondents attributed digitization to increased business, the adoption across MSEs was varied.

Digital adoption likewise facilitated quick and convenient settlement of payments (Smit et al., 2019). Our study findings confirmed this view, and only a tiny proportion of the respondents felt that the cost of digitalization was unaffordable. The study further established from the respondents that the average cost of an internet bundle as a proportion of expenditure was 4.3%. However, this is far more expensive than a comparative rate of less than 1% for a similar measure for developed countries. Furthermore, the available poverty indices across the country revealed evidence of significant inequalities in purchasing power. Such pricing and purchasing power portend inequities in digital adoption and thereby limit development (Cinnamon, 2020). Scholars such as Eggers (2020) argued that small enterprises were vulnerable to external forces that affected their markets and subsequent ability to adapt to new changes due to a lack of financial resources. This phenomenon is particularly relevant in Kenya, with severe resource constraints (Ciambotti & Pedrini, 2021). We argue that by considering the contextual challenges, we found that MSEs in Kenya were much smaller and faced challenges in identifying suitable markets due to financial resource limitations. This finding placates our view that socio-economic circumstances play a crucial role in digital adoption.

Our findings further indicated that the MSEs obtained information about new technologies from a myriad of sources. They, in turn, shared their experience on these technologies with other firms. However, the study also observed that MSEs were primarily ignorant of new advances in technologies and efficiencies of production. As a result of this, they are competitively disadvantaged and therefore not able to increase their productivity. This disadvantage could have a detrimental impact on the local industries, whose products are perceived as low quality and expensive to most customers. However, some MSEs confirmed that they sourced raw materials from different markets but predominantly sold their finished products in the local markets. Consistent with Eggers (2020), the rate of adoption of digital technology was based on enabling external environmental circumstances. Leveraging on the arguments of the socio-materiality theory (Orlikowski, 1991, 2007), the study also argues that most of the reasons for digital adoption identified bordered on the socio-economic circumstances of the firms.

By applying the theory of technology affordances and constraints (Strong et al., 2014; Wang et al., 2015), this study argues that a combination of socio-economic and psycho-social factors placed certain restrictions on the local entrepreneurs, thereby affecting their digital adoption. For instance, the study findings showed a general positive increase in business due to the use of the technology and that the entrepreneurs considered the cost of the internet as low. An expectation for this would be that the level of adoption of digital technology would be higher and well distributed across the different sectors. However, paradoxically, the study established that the digital adoption was neither high nor well distributed in MSEs. From our study, many MSEs were neither aware of the availability nor the functionality of the different digital technologies. We consider this as an attribute of psycho-social awareness, which hampered the digital adoption by the MSEs. Using James Gibson's affordance approach (Greeno, 1994), the MSEs interviewed in the micro-enterprise market clusters operate in an environment not endowed with infrastructural and financial resources. Therefore, their approach to adoption reflects their psycho-biases based on their previous experience and preferences.

The study also identified potential ramifications of digital adoption. In doing so, we complement extant studies by revealing that this impact could be varied due to the uneven adoption of digital technology. The findings suggested that their unfamiliarity and discomfort hampered the use of new technology by the MSEs. It is worth noting that the education profile of the entrepreneurs was of average education, with few of them having gone beyond secondary school. Insights also showed that post-school education varied based on the individual effort by the MSE owners. The lack of technical training in information technology skills further limited their versatility in making choices on digital adoption. Consistent with Rogers' theory, they will only adopt technology they were sure about (Talwar et al., 2020).

It is not enough that digital technology is availed to all stakeholders without an ancillary public policy that spurs adoption; otherwise, there is skewed adoption and a resultant decline in general productivity (Andrews, Criscuolo, & Gal, 2016). Studies have shown that many entrepreneurs rely on easily available products in the digital space (Sydow et al., 2020). Institutional reforms that enabled the transformation of digital innovation in Kenya and Africa at large are well documented (Ndemo & Weiss, 2017; Graham, 2019). The impact of these reforms is an area that requires further redress. Whereas Kenya has been globally acclaimed as increasingly embracing digital innovation (ITU, 2019; 2020), trade statistics indicate that its balance of payments has been progressively deteriorating (CBK, 2021). This disparity suggests that the adoption of digital technology has not necessarily delivered the expected dividends in Africa.

Paradoxically, the import trade volumes in Kenya due to eCommerce platforms have also grown exponentially (UNCTAD, 2018). Thus, we postulate that the foreign producers often have a competitive advantage that allows them to ship into the developing countries products that would be comparatively cheaper than locally produced goods. Whereas this would seem acceptable from the economic efficiency point of view, it flies against local expectations of economic development, which out of necessity requires a shift towards industrial production capabilities. Ultimately, there is now a general dependence on imported products and a manifestation of the dependency theory.

## CONCLUSIONS, LIMITATIONS, AND FUTURE RESEARCH

The study sought to determine whether digital adoption has occurred and to understand its implications and patterns in MSEs of a developing country and specifically to Kenya. Using the three anchor factors of the study, namely, psycho-social, socio-economic, and technological capability, we postulate that digital adoption is enabled once all these factors are in place. The study complements the existing conceptualization around socio-materiality theory and theory of technology affordances and constraints. It demonstrates that both human and non-human factors affect the uptake of digital innovation. Unfortunately, the desire for development through wide-scale digital adoption has not been met. Consistent with the dependency theory may be an action of retrogression if the inequalities are not addressed.

Whereas it has been assumed that the digital dividend percolates all sectors, our research shows that this is not always the case. From our research, digital adoption is slow in the micro and small enterprises and more so in areas at the digital margins. The MSEs form the critical masses that would allow adequate technology adoption; however, they are often said to be at the digital margins and for which digital innovation would be a great panacea to some of their challenges. This adoption can be done by leveraging technology such as big data and the internet of things. Our techno-optimism approach posits that there are positive scale opportunities if digital adoption were to be adopted at the margins.

A recommendation of this research to the applications platform designers is that their focus needs to go beyond the urban, formal market type of entrepreneurs. Second, we emphasize that policies that encourage digital innovation should also be aware of the local entrepreneurs at the margins of technology. In particular, a holistic approach that ensures infrastructural support and affordable and stable internet should be considered. Third, the development of digital infrastructure needs to be accompanied by enhanced MSE training and ICT investor funding to influence their perspectives about digitization. Finally, MSEs need to leverage networking opportunities that would allow them to share business development services that include skills, knowledge, experience from other MSEs. These networks could facilitate the development of platforms that integrate value chain activities.

The study was not without its limitations. Additional research is required to empirically validate our results with larger sample sizes and different sectoral and geographical settings. Additionally, the identified concepts of psycho-social, socio-economic and technological capability have been analyzed independently. Future research can move from this limitation by deep diving into the inter-relations among the constructs to better understand their outcomes and impact on digital adoption.

With our work, we tried to open the black box of digital adoption in MSEs. We argued that digital adoption was influenced by the presence of socio-economic, psycho-social, and technological capability factors. We hope to have stimulated sufficient interest in additional empirical research in digital adoption in MSEs in developing countries.

## ACKNOWLEDGMENTS

We acknowledge the effort by Wesley Onsongo, Esther Guto, and Kenneth Mwanga during the field research.

## REFERENCES

Andrews, D., Criscuolo, C., & Gal, P. (2016). *The Best versus the Rest: The Global Productivity Slowdown, Divergence across Firms and the Role of Public Policy.* Paris: OECD Publishing.

CBK. (2021). *Central Bank of Kenya.* Retrieved March 2021, from Balance of Payments Statistics, December 2020: www.centralbank.go.ke.

Chesbrough, H. (2020). *Open Innovation Results. Going Beyond the Hype, and Getting Down to Business.* Oxford: Oxford University Press: DOI: 10.1093/oso/9780198841906.001.0001.

Ciambotti, G., & Pedrini, M. (2021). Hybrid harvesting strategies to overcome resource constraints: Evidence from social enterprises in Kenya. *Journal of Business Ethics, 168*(3), 631–650.

Cinnamon, J. (2020). Data inequalities and why they matter for development. *Information Technology for Development, 26*(2), 214–233.

Donner, J., & Locke, C. (2019). Platforms at the Margins. In M. Graham (ed.), *Digital Economies at Global Margins* (pp. 39–41). Cambridge, M.A.: MIT Press/International Development Research Centre: ISBN 978-1-55250-600-4 (IDRC e-book).

Eggers, F. (2020). Masters of disasters? Challenges and opportunities for SMEs in times of crisis. *Journal of Business Research, 116*, 199–208.

Eisenhardt, K. (1989). Building theories from case study research. *Academy of Management Review, 14*(4), 532–550.

Eisenhardt, K., & Graebner, M. (2007). Theory building from cases: Opportunities and challenges. *Academy of Management Journal, 50*(1), 25–32.

Fried, E. (2017). What are psychological constructs? On the nature and statistical modelling of emotions, intelligence, personality traits and mental disorders. *Health Psychology Review, 11*(2), 130–134.

Friederici, N. (2018). Grounding the dream of African innovation hubs: Two cases in Kigali. *Journal of Development Entrepreneurship, 23*(2), 1–22.

Friederici, N., Wahome, M., & Graham, M. (2020). *Digital Entrepreneurship in Africa: How a Continent is Escaping Silicon Valley's Long Shadow.* Cambridge, MA: MIT Press.

Gehman, J., Glaser, V. L., Eisenhardt, K. M., Gioia, D., Langley, A., & Corley, K. G. (2018). Finding theory–method fit: A comparison of three qualitative approaches to theory building. *Journal of Management Inquiry, 27*(3), 284–300.

George, G., Corbishley, C., Khayesi, J., Haas, M., & Tihanyi, L. (2016). Bringing Africa in: Promising directions for management research. *Academy of Management Journal, 59*(2), 377–393.

GOK. (2019). *Digital Economy Blueprint: Powering Kenya's Transformation*. Nairobi: Republic of Kenya.

Graham, M. (ed.) (2019). *Digital Economies at Global Margins*. Cambridge, MA: MIT Press/ International Development Research Centre: ISBN 978-1-55250-600-4 (IDRC e-book).

Greeno, J. (1994). Gibson's affordances. *Psychological Review, 101*(2), 336–342.

GSMA. (2020). *The State of Mobile Internet Connectivity Report 2020*. GSM Association. GSMA Intelligence.

Harrison, H., Birks, M., Franklin, R., & Mills, J. (2017). Case study research: Foundations and methodological orientations. *Forum: Qualitative Social Research, 18*(1), Article 19.

Helsper, E. (2017). The social relativity of digital exclusion: Applying relative deprivation theory to digital inequalities. *Communication Theory*, 1–31.

Hossain, M., & Kauranen, I. (2016). Open innovation in SMEs: A systematic literature review. *Journal of Strategy and Management, 9*(1), 58–73.

ITU. (2019). *Global and Regional ICT Data*. Retrieved July 2020, from International Telecommunications Union: www.itu.int/itu-d/itu-d ict statistics.

ITU. (2020). *Measuring Digital Development: Facts and Figures 2020*. ITU Telecommunication Development Bureau. International Telecommunication Union.

Juma, C. (2017). Leapfrogging for progress: The misplaced promise of Africa's mobile revolution. *The Breakthrough Journal* (blog). Summer 2017

Kang, T., Baek, C., & Lee, J. (2017). The persistence and volatility of the firm R&D investment: Revisted from the perspective of technological capability. *Research Policy, 46*, 1570–1579.

KNBS & CCK. (2016). *National ICT Survey Report*. Nairobi: Kenya National Bureau of Statistics & Communications Commission of Kenya.

KNBS. (2016). *Micro, Small and Medium Establishment (MSME) Survey: Basic Report*. Nairobi: Kenya National Bureau of Statistics. GOK.

KNBS. (2020a). *Economic Survey 2020*. Nairobi: Kenya National Bureau of Statistics.

KNBS. (2020b). *Comprehensive Poverty Report*. Nairobi: Kenya National Bureau of Statistics.

Mann, L. (2017). Left to other peoples' devices? A political economy perspective on the big data revolution in development. *Development and Change*. ISSN 0012-155X

Marina, M., Lutz, C., & Buchi, M. (2018). Digital footprints: An emerging dimension of digital inequality. *Journal of Information, Communication and Ethics in Society, 16*(3), 242–251.

Markus, M., & Silver, M. (2008). A foundation for the study of IT effects: A new look at Desanctis and Poole's concepts of structural features and spirit. *Journal of the Association for Information Systems, 9*(10), 609–632.

Mkalama, B., Ndemo, B., & Maalu, J. (2020). The antecedents of innovativeness in manufacturing small and medium entreprises: A qualitative approach. *African Journal of Business And Management, 6*(1), 90–117.

Nambisan, S. (2017). Digital entrepreneurship: Towards a digital technology perspective of entrepreneurship. *Entrepreneurship Theory and Practise, 41*(6), 1029–1055.

Nan, W. (2019). Mobile money and socioeconomic development: A cross-country investigation in sub-Saharan Africa. *Journal of International Technology and Information Management, 27*(4 Article 3), 36–65.

Ndemo, B., & Mkalama, B. (2019). Micro, small and medium enterprises in Kenya: Current state opportunities and challenges. In T. Tambunan (ed.), *Development of MSMEs in Developing Countries: Stories from Asia, Africa and Latin America* (pp. 236–250). New Delhi, India: AkiNik Publications.

Ndemo, B., & Weiss, T. (2017). Making sense of Africa's emerging digital transformation and its many futures. *Africa Journal of Management, 3*(3–4), 328–347.

Ng'weno, A., & Porteous, D. (2018). *Let's be real: The informal sector and the gig economy are the future, and the present, of work in Africa*. Centre for Global Development.

Orlikowski, W. (1991). Integrated information environment or matrix of control? The contradictory implications of information technology. *Accounting, Management and Information Technologies, 1*(1), 9–42.

Orlikowski, W. (2007). Sociomaterial practices: exploring technology at work. *Organization Studies, 28*(9), 1435–1448.

Parmigianni, E., & Mikalsen, M. (2013). The facets of sociomateriality: A systematic mapping of emerging concepts and definitions. In M. Aanestad, & T. Bratteteig (eds.), *Nordic Contributions in IS Research, Lecture Notes in Business Information Processing* (pp. 87–103). Berlin Heidelberg: Springer: http://link.springer.com/chapter/10.1007/978-3-642- 39832-2_6.

Podsakoff, P., Mackenzie, S., Lee, Y., & Podsakoff, N. (2003). Common method biases in behavioural research: A critical review of the literature and the recommended remedies. *Journal of Applied Psychology, 88*(5), 879–903.

Ponelis, S., & Holmner, M. (2015). ICT in Africa: Enabling a better life for all [Editorial]. *Information Technology for Development, 21*(1), 1–11.

Poudel, K., Carter, R., & Lonial, S. (2019). The impact of entrepreneurial orientation, technological capability and consumer attitude on firm performance: A multi theory perspective. *Journal of Small Business Management, 57*(Supp 2), 268–295.

Roberts, R., Flin, R., Millar, D., & Corradi, L. (2021). Psychological factors influencing technology adoption: A case study from the oil and gas industry. *Technovation, 102*(102219).

Robinson, L., Cotten, S., Ono, H., Quan-Haase, A., Mesch, G., Chen, W., ... Stern, M. (2015). Digital inequalities and why they matter. *Information, Communication & Society, 18*(5), 569–582.

Rogers, E. (2003). *Diffusion of Innovations, 5th Edition*. New York: Simon & Schuster, 0743258231, 9780743258234.

Smit, H., Johnson, C., Hunter, R., Dunn, M., & van Vuuren, P. (2019). *Africa's Digital Platforms and Financial Services: An Eight-Country Overview*. Johannesburg: Insight2impact.

Sottini, A., Ciambotti, G., & Littlewood, D. (2022). Engaging symbiotic ecosystems to build community centred business models for the BoP: Evidence from small social enterprises in East Africa. *International Small Business Journal*. Online first.

Strong, D., Volkoff, O., Johnson, S., Pelletier, L., Tulu, B., Bar-On, I., ... Garber, L. (2014). A theory of organization-EHR affordance actualization. *Journal of the Association for Information Systems, 15*(2), 53–85.

Sydow, A., Sunny, S., & Coffman, C. (2020). Leveraging blockchain's potential: The paradox of centrally legitimate, decentralized solutions to institutional challenges in Kenya. *Journal of Business Venturing Insights, 14*. Online first.

Talwar, S., Talwar, M., Kaur, P., & Dhir, A. (2020). Consumers' resistance to digital innovations: A systematic review and framework development. *Australian Marketing Journal, 28*, 286–299.

Tsatsou, P. (2011). Digital divides revisited: What is new about divides and their research? *Media, Culture & Society, 33*(2), 317–331.

UNCTAD. (2018). *UNCTAD Estimates of Global E-Commerce 2018*. United Nations Conference on Trade And Development.

Valdeolmillos, D., Mezquita, Y., Gonzalez-Briones, A., Prieto, J., & Corchado, J. (2019). Blockchain technology: A review of the current challenges of cryptocurrency. *International Congress of Blockchain and Applications – June 2019* (pp. 153–160). Cham: Springer.

van der Westhuizen, T., & Goyayi, M. (2020). The influence of technology on entrepreneurial self efficacy development for online business start-up in developing nations. *The International Journal of Entrepreneurship and Innovation, 21*(3), 168–177.

Vizzotto, A., de Oliveira, A., Elkis, H., Cordeiro, Q., & Buchain, P. (2013). Psycho-social characteristics. In M. Gellman, & J. Turner (eds.), *Encyclopedia of Behavioural Medicine*. New York, NY: Springer: https://doi.org/10.1007/978-1-4419-1005-9_918.

Wang, N., Carte, T., & Schwarzkopf, A. (2015). How should technology affordances be measured? An initial comparison of two approaches. *Twenty-first Americas Conference on Information Systems* (pp. 1–14). Puerto Rico: Emergent Research Forum.

World Bank. (2016). *World Development Report 2016: Digital Dividends*. Washington: The World Bank. DOI: 10.1596/978-1-4648-0671-1.

World Bank. (2018). *The World Bank. In Search of Fiscal Space: Kenya Economic Update 2018*. Retrieved from: http://documents.worldbank.org/curated/en/766271538749794576/pdf/Kenya-Economic-Update-18-FINAL.pdf.

Yin, R. (2009). *Case Studies Research: Design and Methods* (4th edition). Los Angeles, CA: Sage.

Yoo, Y., Henfridsson, O., & Lyytinen, K. (2010). Research commentary – the new organizing logic of digital innovation: An agenda for information systems research. *Information Systems Research, 21*(4), 724–735.

Yun, J., Zhao, X., Park, K., & Shi, L. (2020). Sustainability condition of open innovation: Dynamic growth of Alibaba from SME to large enterprise. *Sustainability, 12*(4379), 1–24.

Zoogah, D., Peng, M., & Woldu, H. (2015). Institutions, resources and organizational effectiveness in Africa. *Academy of Management Perspectives, 29*(1), 7–31.

# PART VI

# DIGITAL ENTREPRENEURSHIP AND FINANCING

# 11. Crowdfunding: a competency framework for creators

*Andishe Ashjari*

## INTRODUCTION

The continuous evolution of new digital tools and technologies provides a fertile foundation for new forms of entrepreneurship. Consequently, the concept of "digital entrepreneurship" has recently emerged in academic discourse to address the rising interest in understanding our increasingly digital world. Early work on digital entrepreneurship contends that digital technologies have "transformed the nature of uncertainty inherent in entrepreneurial processes and outcomes as well as the ways of dealing with such uncertainty" (Nambisan, 2017, p. 1029) and subsequently altered our extant understanding of entrepreneurial processes and outcomes. This alteration introduces a collection of important research questions on digital entrepreneurship that demand "careful consideration of digital technologies and their unique characteristics in shaping entrepreneurial pursuits" (Nambisan, 2017, p. 1029). Digital infrastructures, that is, "digital technology tools and systems that offer communication, collaboration, and/or computing capabilities to support innovation and entrepreneurship," are a distinct element of digital technologies (Nambisan, 2017, p. 1030). Hence, understanding the dynamics around digital infrastructures' facilitation of entrepreneurial activity is a fundamental part of understanding how entrepreneurship evolves in the digital age.

A crowdfunding platform is an example of digital infrastructures that support (digital) entrepreneurs in their entrepreneurial pursuit. In the current decade, the number of crowdfunding platforms has increased rapidly from dozens in 2009 to more than a thousand worldwide in 2015 (Massolution, 2015). The World Bank estimated that the global crowdfunding market is expected to reach 93$ billion by 2025, while some venture capital professionals predicted it could grow to 300$ billion (Global i Ventures, 2015). Following its rising popularity, a growing number of entrepreneurs are adopting crowdfunding tools as part of their entrepreneurial journeys (Haas et al., 2014). Moreover, the number of entrepreneurs who return to crowdfunding platforms to raise funds for their projects has also increased rapidly in recent years (Butticè et al., 2017).

Because of this multi-directional growth of the crowdfunding market and its potential in assisting entrepreneurs to transform their creative ideas into economically viable entities (Baumol, 2010), a significant body of entrepreneurship literature is dedicated to understanding the dynamics of crowdfunding platforms and factors that contribute to the success of crowdfunding campaigns (Agrawal et al., 2014; Colombo et al., 2015; Mollick, 2014). However, to the best of this author's knowledge, no attempt has yet been made to answer the question, "what does an individual need to become a capable crowdfunder?" The answer to this question can contribute to research on digital entrepreneurship by providing a theoretical framework for tackling the more general question of "why are some entrepreneurs more successful than others in acquiring entrepreneurial resources through digital crowdfunding systems?"

(Nambisan, 2017, p. 1030). Nambisan (2017) suggests that scholars should explicitly theorize about digital technologies and their characteristics considering the consolidation of existing theories and concepts in entrepreneurship with such digital theories to find a valid and reliable answer to the latter question.

In this conceptual chapter – following Nambisan's suggestion – I theorize about digital crowdfunding and its characteristics, particularly the similarity between the digital crowdfunding process and the entrepreneurship process, and integrating this perspective with existing theories and concepts in entrepreneurship, specifically the literature on entrepreneurial competency, in order to introduce a competency framework for creators of crowdfunding projects.

In the following sections, first, I review the entrepreneurship literature intending to answer the question of "who is a capable entrepreneur?" Subsequently, I discuss the nature of the crowdfunding process and its similarity with the entrepreneurship process and then propose a holistic framework for being a capable crowdfunder. The chapter closes with a discussion section and suggested avenues for future studies.

## WHO IS A CAPABLE ENTREPRENEUR?

Definition of entrepreneurship has been a source of debate in the literature for a long time. Entrepreneurship involves the nexus of two phenomena, the existence of profitable opportunities and the presence of enterprising individuals. Early research on entrepreneurship focused on investigating the characteristics and traits that potential entrepreneurs possess, whereas, for the past two decades, scholars have redirected their attention to the concept of opportunity. While some scholars argue that opportunities exist independent of the entrepreneur and thus available to all (Kirzner, 1979), others contend that the entrepreneur creates opportunities and opportunities cannot exist apart from the actor (Knight, 1921). In line with these observations, the field of entrepreneurship involves studying sources of opportunities, the process of discovery/creation, evaluation and exploitation of opportunities, and the set of individuals who discover/create, evaluate and exploit them (Shane & Venkataraman, 2000).

Notwithstanding the complexity and elusiveness of a definition for entrepreneurship, it is evident that there is no entrepreneurship without an entrepreneur. Not all people become an entrepreneur, and not all entrepreneurs become successful and competent. Scholars need to distinguish between two seemingly similar questions: "who does become an entrepreneur?" and "who becomes a capable entrepreneur?" The former's answer is expected to be partially present in answer to the latter because becoming an entrepreneur precedes becoming a capable entrepreneur. When we determine the characteristics of an individual to become an entrepreneur, we differentiate entrepreneurs from non-entrepreneurs. Conversely, in the case of capable entrepreneurs, we seek characteristics that differentiate successful entrepreneurs from average entrepreneurs. Whereas the literature on entrepreneurial intention and motivation seeks answers to the first question, a significant body of literature searching for answers to the second question has been dedicated to studying entrepreneurial competencies.

Following the early research on entrepreneurship, one research stream trying to identify sources of entrepreneurial success focuses on entrepreneurs' personality traits and cognitive styles. The center of attention in this stream of research, the temperament traits, mainly has been represented by five-factor model (FFM) system (Openness, Conscientiousness, Extraversion, Agreeableness, and Neuroticism) either directly or by traits equivalent to one of the five factors located in the FFM-system (Zhao et al., 2010; Zhao & Seibert, 2006). Some traits can also be represented as equivalent to a weighted composite of several FFM dimensions (Brandstätter, 2011). Innovativeness and proactive personality are examples of such traits that have been studied as drivers of success in an entrepreneurial endeavor (Rauch & Frese, 2007).

Many scholars argue that this research stream has been inconclusive, in the sense that very few entrepreneurs had all these traits and attributes recognized by the literature (Mitchelmore & Rowley, 2010). These characteristics are hard to identify, measure and develop as the concept of personality and personality traits are rather fuzzy. Moreover, one may view personality traits as biologically (genetically) based structures that originate and regulate the way people act and experience. Though being aware of one's personality structure could be helpful for counseling and self-reflection and also increase the efficiency of business support for entrepreneurs (Brandstätter, 2011), one can argue that personality traits are less suitable for training and development purposes. In other words, personality structures are useful but not sufficient information for training successful entrepreneurs.

Therefore, stakeholders, both academics and practitioners, were dissatisfied with this line of research, demanding a more comprehensive, testable and actionable perspective. Consequently, entrepreneurship research has recently changed direction towards theories of competencies due to discussed limitations.

## A COMPETENCY APPROACH TO ENTREPRENEURIAL SUCCESS

The notion of entrepreneurial competency lies at the intersection of the competency literature and the entrepreneurship literature. The literature on competencies is quite different from early entrepreneurial research on personality traits and cognitive styles. In general, competencies have been defined as combined and integrated components of *knowledge*, *skills*, and *attitudes*. As such, competencies are changeable, learnable and attainable through experience, training or mentoring (Volery et al., 2015). Hence, competencies play an important role in successful entrepreneurship. According to Bird (1995), entrepreneurial competencies are defined as an individual's traits – such as specific knowledge, motives, features, self-images, social roles – and abilities that result in a venture's success. She also points out a difference between competence as a "baseline standard" for planning and launching a venture and competency as a higher standard for achieving success. In other words, she distinguishes between two groups of entrepreneurs. While an average entrepreneur discovers/creates, evaluates and decides to exploit an opportunity, a capable entrepreneur goes beyond the decision and becomes a successful entrepreneur by achieving sustainability and growth. These definitions imply that different stages of entrepreneurship (venture start-up and growth) require different competencies. Several researchers also pointed out this argument (Chandler & Hanks, 1994; Chandler & Jansen, 1992; Man et al., 2002; Rasmussen et al., 2011). As noted by Ghoshal (1997), three categories of entrepreneurial competencies are attitudes/traits, knowledge/experience, and skills/abilities. In the past two decades, several scholars have attempted to observe/identify entrepreneurial competencies and/or demonstrate an association between observed/identified competencies and venture success. Next, I will briefly discuss some of the entrepreneurial competencies recognized by previous research.

*Table 11.1*    *Entrepreneurial competency areas identified by the literature*

| Competency Area | Behavioral focus |
| --- | --- |
| Opportunity[a] | Competencies related to recognizing and developing market opportunities through various means |
| Relationship[a,c] | Competencies related to person-to-person or individual-to-group-based interactions, e.g., building a context of cooperation and trust, using contacts and connections, persuasive ability, communication and interpersonal skill |
| Conceptual[a] | Competencies related to different conceptual abilities, which are reflected in the behaviors of the entrepreneur, e.g., decision skills, absorbing and understanding complex information, and risk-taking, and innovativeness |
| Organizing[a] | Competencies related to the organization of different internal and external human, physical, financial and technological resources, including team-building, leading employees, training, and controlling |
| Strategic[a] | Competencies related to setting, evaluating and implementing strategies |
| Commitment[a] | Competencies that drive the entrepreneur to move ahead with the business |
| Ethical[b] | Competencies related to being honest and transparent in business dealings and take responsibility and be accountable for own actions |

*Notes:*    a) Adopted from Man et al. (2002); b) Adopted from Ahmad (2007); c) Familism is defined as "identify and seek help from employees that can be trusted, get support and advice from family and close associates, share knowledge and resources with others" which is conceptually covered by relationship competency area.

Chandler and Jansen (1992) cluster the entrepreneurs' competencies based on three fundamental roles: technical, entrepreneurial, and managerial. According to the authors, a successful entrepreneur should demonstrate high proficiency in all three roles. Man et al. (2002) take a process/behavioral approach and indicate six clusters of entrepreneurs' competencies based on a review of prior empirical studies: opportunity, conceptual, relationship, commitment, strategic, and organizing competencies. Bergevoet and Woerkum (2006), almost similar to Man and colleagues' work, categorize entrepreneurial competencies into five domains: opportunity, conceptual, strategy, organizing, and relationship competencies. Ahmad (2007) added ethical and familism competency domains to Man et al.'s (2002) framework. A summary of competency areas introduced by literature is shown in Table 11.1.

Morris et al. (2013) adopt a competency-based lens and identified thirteen entrepreneurial competencies: opportunity recognition, opportunity assessment, risk management/mitigation, conveying a compelling vision, tenacity/perseverance, creative problem solving/imaginativeness, resource leveraging, guerilla skills, value creation, maintain focus yet adapt, resilience, self-efficacy, and building and using networks. Reviewing the extant literature, Kyndt and Baert (2015) also propose twelve entrepreneurial competencies: perseverance, self-knowledge, learning orientation, insight into the market, seeing opportunities, ability to persuade, building networks, decisiveness, awareness of potential returns on investment, planning for the future, independence, and social and environmentally conscious conduct. These entrepreneurial competencies play an essential role in venture success, with a variety of studies reporting significant positive relationships (Mitchelmore & Rowley, 2013). Table 11.2 summarizes these competencies (not competency areas) and what they refer to. Furthermore, a stream of research also explores the antecedents of entrepreneurial competencies such as situational, demographic, environmental and historical factors (e.g., see Autio et al., 2011; Capaldo et al., 2004; Colombo & Grilli, 2005).

Several points could be identified by looking into the past two decades of research on entrepreneurial competencies. First, reflecting on the fact that literature on entrepreneurial competencies follows Boyatzis' (1982) work in determining managerial competencies,

*Table 11.2      Entrepreneurial competencies identified by the literature*

| Entrepreneurial Competency | Definition |
| --- | --- |
| Opportunity Recognition [b] (Seeing Opportunities) | The capacity to perceive changed conditions or overlooked possibilities in the environment that represent potential sources of profit or return to a venture |
| Opportunity Assessment [b] (Awareness of Potential ROI) | Ability to evaluate the content structure of opportunities to determine their relative attractiveness accurately |
| Risk Management/Mitigation | The taking of actions that reduce the probability of a risk occurring or reduce the potential impact if the risk were to occur |
| Conveying a Compelling Vision | The ability to conceive an image of a future organizational state and to articulate that image in a manner that empowers followers to enact it |
| Tenacity/Perseverance [b] | Ability to sustain goal-directed action and energy when confronting difficulties and obstacles that impede goal achievement |
| Creative Problem Solving/ Imaginativeness | The ability to relate previously unrelated objects or variables to produce novel and appropriate outcomes |
| Resource Leveraging | Skills at accessing resources one does not necessarily own or control to accomplish personal ends |
| Guerrilla Skills | The capacity to take advantage of one's surroundings, employ unconventional, low-cost tactics not recognized by others, and do more with less |
| Value Creation | Capabilities of developing new products, services, and/or business models that generate revenues exceeding their costs and produce sufficient user benefits to bring about a fair return |
| Maintain Focus yet Adapt [b] (Planning for the future) | Ability to balance an emphasis on goal achievement and the strategic direction of the organization while addressing the need to identify and pursue actions to improve the fit between an organization and developments in the external environment |
| Resilience | Ability to cope with stresses and disturbances such that one remains well, recovers, or even thrives in the face of adversity |
| Self-Efficacy [b] (Self-knowledge) | Ability to maintain a sense of self-confidence regarding one's ability to accomplish a particular task or attain a level of performance |
| Building and Using Networks [b] | Social interaction skills that enable an individual to establish, develop and maintain sets of relationships with others who assist them in advancing their work or career |
| Orientation towards learning [a] | Ability and wish to keep on learning and search for new knowledge and skills to deal with new challenges such as technical and economic changes and innovations |
| Decisiveness [a] | Ability to draw conclusions based on different sources of information and recommendations offered, for example, by experts, consultants, and colleagues, to advance the organization. They dare to make decisions even when not everyone agrees with them, and the outcome is not entirely predictable |
| Independence [a] | Ability to decide and determine for oneself what to do. It also entails trust in oneself as well as taking responsibility for one's actions |
| Ability to Persuade [a] | It enables entrepreneurs to convince others of their point of view, plan or product |
| Insight into the market [a] | Ability to know their current and future competitors and how they are positioned within the continuously evolving market |
| Social and environmentally conscious conduct [a] | Ability to conduct oneself and the business at hand in a social and environmentally conscious manner |

*Notes:*     a) Adopted from Kyndt and Baert (2015); b) Identified in both studies and terms in parentheses show Kyndt and Baert's (2015) labels.
*Source:*     Kyndt and Baert (2015); Morris et al. (2013).

unsurprisingly, several competencies similar to those identified by literature on managerial competencies are proposed here. This finding is consistent with the argument that entrepreneurs need different competencies in different stages of the entrepreneurship process, namely, venture start-up and venture growth. Scholars frequently translate entrepreneurial success into venture growth and competitiveness, and this assumption becomes the core of competency frameworks. This representation of entrepreneurial success only recognizes entrepreneurs who stay within the venture during the growth process. When it comes to entrepreneurs who exit early to start another entrepreneurial activity and transfer the managerial role to professional managers, entrepreneurial competencies literature implicitly excludes them from its theoretical framework. It is crucial to accentuate that though entrepreneurship is often associated with new venture creation and small business management (Gibb, 1996), not all owner-managers can be regarded as entrepreneurs, nor are all small businesses entrepreneurial. As Shane and Venkataraman (2000) argue, entrepreneurship is the process of discovering, evaluating, and exploiting opportunities. The crucial question here is, is venture growth a necessary part of successful opportunity exploitation? In this author's view, the answer to this question is no. Venture growth is a *potential outcome* of successful opportunity exploitation, and opportunity exploitation may also occur via value creation (even within an established firm). Therefore, the literature on entrepreneurial competencies demands new theoretical perspectives to address this gap.

Second, most of the early entrepreneurship research findings concerning successful entrepreneurs' personality traits and cognitive styles have been incorporated into competency frameworks under the traits/attributes/attitudes category of competency. Hence, a competency-based perspective is a more appealing approach for answering what it takes to be a capable entrepreneur. Finally, finding a conclusive answer to this question is a herculean task considering entrepreneurial competencies' eclectic nature. Competency areas (e.g., Man et al., 2002), though comprehensive and adaptable to various contexts, are hard to quantify. On the other hand, applying the exact competencies approach (e.g., Morris et al., 2013), though it helps to measure competencies, lacks contextual coverage (e.g., Kyndt and Baert (2015) find only two statistically significant competencies in predicting entrepreneurship).

## WHAT DOES IT TAKE TO BECOME A CAPABLE CROWDFUNDER?

Crowdfunding is a new label for an activity with a long history in many domains (Ordanini et al., 2011). For instance:

> Mozart and Beethoven financed concerts and new music compositions with money from interested patrons. The Statue of Liberty in New York was funded by small donations from the American and French people, a human rights organization is trying to raise money to buy a communications satellite to provide Internet access to people in third world countries. (Kuppuswamy & Bayus, 2018)

Today, in our digitalized world, hundreds of online platforms exist to match up consumer-investors with initiatives that they wish to help fund. This form of crowdfunding, enabled by Web 2.0 and facilitated by the rise of the platform economy, is termed "digital crowdfunding." Since almost all crowdfunding activity today is digital, we simply use the term "crowdfunding." Focusing too literally on what the term implies, crowdfunding may be viewed as part of the entrepreneurial process referred to as entrepreneurial finance. However, consistent with the literature (Mollick & Kuppuswamy, 2014), creating and running a crowdfunding campaign encompasses a much broader range of entrepreneurial activity. For this reason, in my view, the crowdfunding process resembles the entrepreneurship process of value creation.

Crowdfunders – who turn to the crowd to raise money for their entrepreneurial endeavors, initially discover and evaluate a *valuable* (i.e. contain a financial or non-financial value for others or themselves) *idea*, decide to implement the idea and launch a campaign to raise funds for the implementation. In exchange for investment, they offer a sort of reward. This reward can take monetary, tangible but non-monetary or intangible forms. If their campaign becomes successful, they will take the money and make a promise (formal or informal) to deliver the reward based on *ex ante* terms. Deciding to launch a campaign, having a successful campaign and finally keeping the promise of reward by executing the project resemble the entrepreneur's decision to exploit the opportunity for value creation and carrying it out.

In this framework, a crowdfunder is not regarded as only a fundraiser. There are other elements of interest in crowdfunding that make the experience different for crowdfunders. In addition to financial gain, crowdfunders utilize crowdfunding platforms to raise awareness, build community or a fan base, obtain individual (consumer or not) feedback, and/or estimate demand. Therefore, their interest in crowdfunding is not limited to the campaign. They may want to keep their connection with backers to expand the community, make sure of rewards delivery, utilize their potential for promoting their product, ask for feedback, or tap into the crowd's potential for the next campaign. Thus, finding success in a crowdfunding campaign is not necessarily the end of the line for the crowdfunder. In line with the above observations, I suggest that a *capable crowdfunder* should be defined as *"someone who finds success in meeting the campaign's financial goal, fulfils her/his promise to deliver the rewards to backers in a timely and profitable fashion, builds a community and takes advantage of it for feedback or future marketing and sales."*

A crowdfunder could be an individual, a team, a new venture or even an established firm. In this study, for identifying characteristics of a capable crowdfunder, I treat all types of crowdfunders as single entities in need of those characteristics either in a collective form or individual form. Given the discussed similarity between crowdfunding and entrepreneurship activity, and the fact that crowdfunding is an external enabler (digital infrastructure) for entrepreneurial pursuit, applying the entrepreneurial competency framework to answer "what does it take for an individual to become a capable crowdfunder?" seems a reasonable path to pursue.

## TOWARDS A CROWDFUNDING COMPETENCY FRAMEWORK

As demonstrated in Table 11.3, in the present study, I propose eight competency areas for crowdfunding. The following section will discuss these competency areas in more detail and explain how they can be mapped into a crowdfunding process.

Crowdfunding can be thought of as encompassing three phases: pre-campaign, in-campaign and post-campaign. The pre-campaign period involves both ideation and preparation. Having a valuable idea is the first step for going to platforms to start the campaign. This idea could be valuable to crowdfunders themselves or other stakeholders, whereas this value ranges from pure altruistic to pure egocentric. The quality of the idea and the nature of its value play an essential role in triggering backers' motivation to participate and subsequently in the campaign's success. The process of ideation bears a resemblance to opportunity discovery and evaluation in the entrepreneurship process. Therefore, I propose *opportunity competency* as the first competency area for a capable crowdfunder. This competency refers to the ability to recognize/create and evaluate opportunities/ideas through various means. The fit between

*Table 11.3*    *Crowdfunding competency framework proposed for this study*

| Crowdfunding Competency Area | Definition | Examples of Specific Competencies for Crowdfunders |
|---|---|---|
| Opportunity Competency | Competencies related to recognizing and evaluating ideas through various means | Idea recognition<br>Idea value assessment<br>Idea/Crowdfunder fitness assessment |
| Strategic Competency | Competencies related to planning, evaluating, monitoring, implementing and adjusting strategies | Goal Setting<br>Adaptation (maintain focus yet adapt)<br>Visioning (conveying a compelling vision) |
| Organizing Competency | Competencies related to carrying out the functional roles of an entrepreneur such as accounting, budgeting and production | Leadership<br>Team building<br>Financial literacy |
| Relational Competency | Competencies related to crowdfunder's interactions with individuals, groups or crowd | Networking<br>Interpersonal skills<br>Ability to persuade |
| Conceptual Competency | Competencies related to conceptual abilities, which are reflected in the behaviors of crowdfunders | Creative problem solving<br>Orientation towards learning<br>Ability to absorb and understand complex information |
| Ethical Competency | Competencies that a crowdfunder requires to act ethically, accept responsibility for his/her actions and make required adjustments, and fulfill his/her commitments | Socially and environmentally conscious conduct<br>Honesty and transparency<br>Self-accountability |
| Digital Competency | Competencies required for a crowdfunder to efficiently and proactively use digital technologies or digital infrastructures that are helpful for their endeavor, including the crowdfunding platform itself | Digital communication skills<br>Data management and analysis<br>Technical skills (e.g., Search Engine Optimization (SEO)) |
| Narrative Competency | Competencies related to crowdfunder's ability to identify, listen to, understand and tell the stories that she/he is exposed to | Storytelling skills<br>Content creation skills<br>Linguistic skills |

crowdfunder and idea is also crucial as it could communicate a signal of quality to the crowd (Ahlers et al., 2015). Then it comes to the preparation stage, in which crowdfunders plan their way for the realization of their idea. In this stage, crowdfunders, depending on the projects' nature, may build prototypes, look for the appropriate crowdfunding platform, estimate the cost, create a business plan, calculate risk and design their campaign. These activities resemble the pre-launch stage of the entrepreneurial endeavor. Therefore, I propose *strategic* and *organizing competency* areas as two required competency areas for capable crowdfunders. Whereas strategic competency refers to knowledge/experience, ability/skills, or traits/attitudes required for setting goals, planning to achieve them and monitoring the process for adaptations, organizing competency refers to competencies required for carrying out the functional roles of an entrepreneur such as accounting, budgeting and production. The organizing competency area is also crucial for in-campaign and post-campaign operations.

In the next phase, the crowdfunder launches the campaign for a pre-determined period to attract backers. During this time, he/she needs to broadcast and promote his/her campaign through every available medium to increase its reach. Moreover, the crowdfunder should continuously communicate with the crowd, answer their questions, update the project webpage, build community, and monitor their feedback to make potential improvements in his/her idea or execution plan. As the crowdfunding literature repeatedly suggests, crowdfunder's social capital plays an important role in his/her campaign's success. The *relational competency* area is what enables a crowdfunder to carry out these activities with quality.

After having a successful campaign, an idea finds legitimacy outside the crowdfunder's mind through the crowd's support. In the post-campaign phase, a crowdfunder should commit to their project and fulfill his/her obligation to backers. I propose a new competency area for a capable crowdfunder to not only fulfill his/her commitment but also remain ethical and responsible during the entire process. *Ethical competency* area is an overarching term for competencies that make a crowdfunder act ethically, accept responsibility for his/her actions and make required adjustments, and fulfill his/her commitments. It should be pointed out that the ethical competency I proposed is a conceptual combination of commitment competency identified by Man et al. (2002) and ethical competency introduced by Ahmad (2007). A capable crowdfunder should stay alert about learning opportunities, complex information and unforeseen problems coming directly or indirectly from the crowd (e.g., crowd's feedback, comments and choice of rewards). Thus, I also incorporate a *Conceptual competency* area in the proposed framework to indicate conceptual abilities that crowdfunders reflect in their behaviors. This area includes competencies required for a crowdfunder to learn from various sources via various means, learn proactively, effectively apply learned knowledge to make decisions, devise creative solutions, taking risks and obtain analytical expertise.

Furthermore, it should be noted that the crowdfunding process happens through digital infrastructure. Hence, an inherently digital component in crowdfunding demands a particular competency area, *Digital competency*. A capable crowdfunder may possess a valuable idea, a perfect business plan, and a great team to execute the plan. Without digital competencies, an individual cannot tap into crowdfunding platforms' full capacity, and it is more likely to end up with an unsuccessful campaign. Improving campaign design, digital content creation, and building online social networks are examples of digital activities embedded in crowdfunding. The primary digital-oriented stage of the crowdfunding process is the in-campaign phase. This stage happens through a dialogue between crowdfunder and the crowd via a digital intermediary, the crowdfunding platform. In addition to digital communication, data generation via online feedback, backers' participation, traffic monitoring, and media presence and reactions may also happen during the in-campaign and post-campaign stages. Obtaining and managing the data and translating them into actionable information demand specific digital competencies.

Digital competence is not user-dependent but tools-dependent. For instance, performing a task with an iPhone could form an experience quite different from one when performing the same task with an Android phone. Hence, they may demand different competencies. Following this line of reasoning, I suggest that understanding the digital competencies required for a capable crowdfunder is impossible without in-depth knowledge about the crowdfunding platform he/she intends to use. However, some general areas of digital competence have been identified in the literature: *creation of content and knowledge, communication and sharing, information management, collaboration, technical operations, ethics and responsibility*, and *evaluation and problem-solving* (Ferrari et al., 2012).

Finally, I propose an entirely new competency area crucial to crowdfunding campaign success: *Narrative competency*. Crowdfunding platforms are internet-based entities that bring together different types of individuals with various roles (creators, backers, interested visitors

*Table 11.4*    *Competency framework for crowdfunders over the crowdfunding process*

| Phases | Pre-Campaign | In-Campaign | Post-Campaign |
|---|---|---|---|
| **Competency Areas** | **Opportunity** | **Digital/Relational/Narrative** | **Ethical** |
| | Organizing/Strategic/Conceptual/ Ethical/Relational/Digital/Narrative | Organizing/Strategic/Ethical/ Conceptual | Organizing/Strategic/Conceptual/ Digital/Relational/Narrative |

or a combination of those) through online broadcasting of narratives about creators, projects (ideas) and potential stakeholders in the form of proposals for attracting financial resources. Recently, a growing number of studies have highlighted the crucial role of the narrative's language, content and style in crowdfunding campaign success in different contexts. Gorbatai and Nelson (2015) find that crowdfunders' language affects crowdfunding campaigns' performance by rewarding the linguistic style of women. Anglin et al. report a significant relationship between narcissistic (2018) and charismatic rhetoric (2014) and crowdfunding performance. Allison et al. (2015) highlighted the significant effect of framing on crowdfunding outcomes in the context of prosocial microlending, comparing "venture as a business opportunity" framing against "venture as an opportunity to help others." Cappa et al. (2021) investigate how the success of reward-based crowdfunding is affected by narrative styles. Therefore, in addition to content, framing and language also play an essential role in crowdfunders' success. Since crowdfunding platforms are rather standardized in the presentation of projects, crowdfunders can apply other websites, social media or traditional media channels (meetings, events, newspapers, etc.) to present their narratives with an individualized and personal design. Though most of the channels utilized by crowdfunders to present their narratives are considered digital channels, traditional non-digital channels are still available for crowdfunders to exploit. Thus crowdfunders need to obtain competencies beyond what they can find in the digital competency area to create content, frame it and broadcast their story. Crowdfunders also can interact with others through various channels, listen to their stories or feedback, and reflect on them to optimize their narrative and consequently improve the contribution rate. Hence, the narrative competency area includes competencies related to a crowdfunder's ability to identify, listen to, understand and tell the stories that she/he is exposed to including their own stories.

## DISCUSSION

In this chapter, I discussed the similarities between a crowdfunding project and the process of entrepreneurship, taking a value creation approach to reflect on the entrepreneurial competency literature to answer the question, "what does it take for an individual to become a capable crowdfunder?" In doing so, I regarded crowdfunding as an example of a value creation process. This process encompasses three stages: pre-campaign, in-campaign, and post-campaign. Eight areas of competency are proposed to cover the entire crowdfunding process. Table 11.4 summarizes the proposed competency framework for crowdfunders based on different phases of the crowdfunding process.

Some competency areas (marked in bold) play a fundamental role in each phase of the crowdfunding process. While a crowdfunder does not need to achieve high levels in all competency areas to be successful, it is very unlikely to succeed in the relevant stages of the crowdfunding process without those critical competency areas. Moreover, it should be noted that the bundle of competencies that constitute each competency area at any particular phase does not necessarily remain the same. For instance, organizing competencies required in the post-campaign stage are not necessarily the same as the organizing competencies required in the pre-campaign stage. (While production and distribution management skills are essential for post-campaign success and irrelevant for pre-campaign success, financial literacy and risk calculation skills are the exact opposite.)

All competency areas except "opportunity" are shared among different phases of crowdfunding. The opportunity competency area revolves around idea creation/discovery and evaluation. Once a crowdfunder starts the idea realization process, they do not need to engage in the ideation process anymore. Nevertheless, they can continue the ideation process to stay alert to forthcoming opportunities, but when they decide to make changes to the initial idea, they must return to the pre-campaign stage again and start a new process from the beginning to ensure that all previous assumptions, calculations and decisions still hold. In doing so, they reinitiate another crowdfunding process with the opportunity competency area playing a critical role in the pre-campaign stage again.

To build a stepping stone in the path to answer the question of who is a capable crowdfunder/creator, I took a holistic view of the crowdfunding process to develop a framework adaptable to different crowdfunding platforms (i.e. reward-based, equity-based, donation-based or lending-based). As discussed earlier, each crowdfunding competency area in the framework includes specific, measurable competencies. These particular competencies can vary according to the stages of the crowdfunding process and the types of crowdfunding platforms. Future studies should identify these competencies for different platforms and empirically test their influence on crowdfunders' success, both in a particular stage and overall process. In addition to variation among the relative importance of specific competencies belonging to a single competency area during different stages of the crowdfunding process, the relative importance of those specific competencies in crowdfunders' success is also expected to vary according to crowdfunding platforms. Crowdfunding platforms can differ in several elements, such as business model, campaign strategy, offering type (e.g., intangible reward, equity, profit sharing, product/service, donation), campaign design elements, target crowd, location and industry. Considering these differentiations, crowdfunders can look into a host of platforms to find a good fit for their idea/project.

Viewing crowdfunding as a three stage process that includes but is not limited to the campaign itself is an element that differentiated this study from extant literature examining factors contributing to crowdfunding success. A significant body of crowdfunding literature focuses on the in-campaign stage of the crowdfunding process and ignores the before and after stages. In that one-dimensional perspective, crowdfunding is a new (digital) tool for entrepreneurial finance that sometimes offers additional benefits at close to zero cost (e.g., market research, community building and raising product awareness).

In the present chapter, I proposed two new competency areas, digital competency as well as narrative competency, which, to the extent of my knowledge, are also new to entrepreneurial competency literature. Future studies can empirically investigate the validity of these competencies in the broader field of entrepreneurial competency. Particularly, introducing the digital competency area into the entrepreneurial competency frameworks could extend these frameworks' conceptual boundaries by providing insight for tackling the narrower question, what does it take for an individual to be a capable "digital entrepreneur?" As Nambisan (2017) argued, some implicit assumptions of extant entrepreneurship literature do not hold in our digitalized environment. Hence, the relatively old literature on entrepreneurial competency demands a fresh perspective.

Why are some entrepreneurs more successful than others? It is a very general question that we cannot explicitly answer unless we specify the context of success. However, regardless of context, we can contend that variations in outcomes come from variations in processes, actors or both. Entrepreneur, as an actor, has agency over some of the variations in processes and actors. Hence, the variations with entrepreneur as the locus of agency constitute a segment of the ultimate answer. When we put the initial question into the digital crowdfunding context, the question takes the form of "why are some entrepreneurs more successful than others in acquiring entrepreneurial resources through digital crowdfunding?" The crowdfunding competency framework offers a partial answer to this question by answering who is a capable crowdfunder, focusing on the factors over which crowdfunders have agency. In contrast, aspects that reside outside the boundaries of crowdfunders' agency (e.g., gender, ethnicity, parents' education, environmental uncertainty) have been neglected by the proposed framework. Future scholars should investigate the factors in which the locus of agency lies outside the crowdfunders and the interactions between factors with and without crowdfunders' agency to improve the framework proposed in the present study.

Finally, it can be inferred from the crowdfunding competency framework that non-individual crowdfunders (either teams or organizations) are more likely than individual crowdfunders to become capable crowdfunders. Since non-individual crowdfunders are collective entities constituted of distinct individuals with various degrees and combinations of (crowdfunding) competencies, when collaborating, their collective entity is more likely than an individual to encompass higher degrees of or more variety of (crowdfunding) competencies. Hence, non-individuals are more likely than individuals to become capable crowdfunders. However, this argument's validity depends on the frictionless collaboration assumption, which is a relatively strong assumption. In a frictionless collaboration, for each competency, the level of competency for a collective entity is equal to or greater than the maximum level of that competency among individual members. Future studies should empirically examine the abovementioned conclusion.

# REFERENCES

Agrawal, A., Catalini, C., & Goldfarb, A. (2014). Some simple economics of crowdfunding. *Innovation Policy and the Economy, 14*(1), 63–97.

Ahlers, G. K., Cumming, D., Günther, C., & Schweizer, D. (2015). Signaling in equity crowdfunding. *Entrepreneurship Theory and Practice, 39*(4), 955–980.

Ahmad, N. H. (2007). *A cross cultural study of entrepreneurial competencies and entrepreneurial success in SMEs in Australia and Malaysia* [Ph.D. Dissertation]. University of Adelaide.

Allison, T. H., Davis, B. C., Short, J. C., & Webb, J. W. (2015). Crowdfunding in a prosocial microlending environment: Examining the role of intrinsic versus extrinsic cues. *Entrepreneurship Theory and Practice, 39*(1), 53–73. https://doi.org/10.1111/etap.12108

Anglin, A. H., Allison, T. H., McKenny, A. F., & Busenitz, L. W. (2014). The role of charismatic rhetoric in crowdfunding: An examination with computer-aided text analysis. In J. Short (Ed.), *Research Methodology in Strategy and Management* (Vol. 9, pp. 19–48). Emerald Group Publishing. https://doi.org/10.1108/S1479-838720140000009010

Anglin, A. H., Wolfe, M. T., Short, J. C., McKenny, A. F., & Pidduck, R. J. (2018). Narcissistic rhetoric and crowdfunding performance: A social role theory perspective. *Journal of Business Venturing, 33*(6), 780–812. https://doi.org/10.1016/j.jbusvent.2018.04.004

Autio, E., George, G., & Alexy, O. (2011). International entrepreneurship and capability development: Qualitative evidence and future research directions. *Entrepreneurship Theory and Practice*, *35*(1), 11–37. https://doi.org/10.1111/j.1540-6520.2010.00421.x

Baumol, W. J. (2010). *The Microtheory of Innovative Entrepreneurship*. Princeton University Press. https://doi.org/10.2307/j.ctt21668j9

Bergevoet, R. H. M., & Woerkum, C. V. (2006). Improving the entrepreneurial competencies of Dutch dairy farmers through the use of study groups. *The Journal of Agricultural Education and Extension*, *12*(1), 25–39. https://doi.org/10.1080/13892240600740852

Bird, B. (1995). Toward a theory of entrepreneurial competency. In J. A. Katz & A. C. Corbet (Eds.), *Seminal Ideas for the Next Twenty-Five Years of Advances* (Vol. 21, pp. 115–131). Emerald Publishing. https://doi.org/10.1108/S1074-754020190000021011

Boyatzis, R. E. (1982). *The Competent Manager: A Model for Effective Performance*. Wiley.

Brandstätter, H. (2011). Personality aspects of entrepreneurship: A look at five meta-analyses. *Personality and Individual Differences*, *51*(3), 222–230. https://doi.org/10.1016/j.paid.2010.07.007

Butticè, V., Colombo, M. G., & Wright, M. (2017). Serial crowdfunding, social capital, and project success. *Entrepreneurship Theory and Practice*, *41*(2), 183–207. https://doi.org/10.1111/etap.12271

Capaldo, G., Iandoli, L., & Ponsiglione, C. (2004). Entrepreneurial competencies and training needs of small firms: A methodological approach. *14th Annual IntEnt Conference, Napoli*, 606.

Cappa, F., Pinelli, M., Maiolini, R., & Leone, M. I. (2021). "Pledge" me your ears! The role of narratives and narrator experience in explaining crowdfunding success. *Small Business Economics*, *57*(2), 953–973. https://doi.org/10.1007/s11187-020-00334-y

Chandler, G. N., & Hanks, S. H. (1994). Founder competence, the environment, and venture performance. *Entrepreneurship Theory and Practice*, *18*(3), 77–89. https://doi.org/10.1177/104225879401800306

Chandler, G. N., & Jansen, E. (1992). The founder's self-assessed competence and venture performance. *Journal of Business Venturing*, *7*(3), 223–236. https://doi.org/10.1016/0883-9026(92)90028-P

Colombo, M. G., Franzoni, C., & Rossi–Lamastra, C. (2015). Internal social capital and the attraction of early contributions in crowdfunding. *Entrepreneurship Theory and Practice*, *39*(1), 75–100.

Colombo, M. G., & Grilli, L. (2005). Start-up size: The role of external financing. *Economics Letters*, *88*(2), 243–250. https://doi.org/10.1016/j.econlet.2005.02.018

Ferrari, A., Punie, Y., & Redecker, C. (2012). Understanding digital competence in the 21st century: An analysis of current frameworks. *21st Century Learning for 21st Century Skills*, 79–92.

Ghoshal, S. (1997). The individualized corporation: An interview with Sumantra Ghoshal. *European Management Journal*, *15*(6), 625–632.

Gibb, A. A. (1996). Entrepreneurship and small business management: Can we afford to neglect them in the twenty-first century business school? *British Journal of Management*, *7*(4), 309–321.

Global i Ventures. (2015). *Ten things you need to know before engaging in accredited crowdfunding*. http://www.globaliventures .com/ten-things-you-need-to-know-before-engaging-in-accredited-crowdfunding/

Gorbatai, A. D., & Nelson, L. (2015). Gender and the language of crowdfunding. *Academy of Management Proceedings*, *2015*(1), 15785. https://doi.org/10.5465/ambpp.2015.15785abstract

Haas, P., Blohm, I., & Leimeister, J. (2014). An empirical taxonomy of crowdfunding intermediaries. *ICIS 2014 Proceedings*. https://aisel.aisnet.org/icis2014/proceedings/SocialMedia/13

Kirzner, I. M. (1979). Producer, entrepreneur, and the right to property. In Kirzner, I. *Perception, Opportunity, and Profit* (pp. 185–199). University of Chicago Press.

Knight, F. H. (1921). *Risk, Uncertainty and Profit*. Hart, Schaffner & Marx.

Kuppuswamy, V., & Bayus, B. L. (2018). Crowdfunding creative ideas: The dynamics of project backers. In D. Cumming & L. Hornuf (Eds.), *The Economics of Crowdfunding: Startups, Portals and Investor Behavior* (pp. 151–182). Springer International Publishing. https://doi.org/10.1007/978-3-319-66119-3_8

Kyndt, E., & Baert, H. (2015). Entrepreneurial competencies: Assessment and predictive value for entrepreneurship. *Journal of Vocational Behavior*, *90*, 13–25. https://doi.org/10.1016/j.jvb.2015.07.002

Man, T. W. Y., Lau, T., & Chan, K. F. (2002). The competitiveness of small and medium enterprises: A conceptualization with focus on entrepreneurial competencies. *Journal of Business Venturing*, *17*(2), 123–142. https://doi.org/10.1016/S0883-9026(00)00058-6

Massolution. (2015). *The Crowdfunding Industry Report*. http://reports. crowdsourcing. org/index. php.

Mitchelmore, S., & Rowley, J. (2010). Entrepreneurial competencies: A literature review and development agenda. *International Journal of Entrepreneurial Behavior & Research, 16*(2), 92–111. https://doi.org/10.1108/13552551011026995

Mitchelmore, S., & Rowley, J. (2013). Entrepreneurial competencies of women entrepreneurs pursuing business growth. *Journal of Small Business and Enterprise Development, 20*(1), 125–142. https://doi.org/10.1108/14626001311298448

Mollick, E. (2014). The dynamics of crowdfunding: An exploratory study. *Journal of Business Venturing, 29*(1), 1–16. https://doi.org/10.1016/j.jbusvent.2013.06.005

Mollick, E., & Kuppuswamy, V. (2014). After the campaign: Outcomes of crowdfunding. *SSRN Electronic Journal*. https://doi.org/10.2139/ssrn.2376997

Morris, M. H., Webb, J. W., Fu, J., & Singhal, S. (2013). A competency-based perspective on entrepreneurship education: Conceptual and empirical insights. *Journal of Small Business Management, 51*(3), 352–369. https://doi.org/10.1111/jsbm.12023

Nambisan, S. (2017). Digital entrepreneurship: Toward a digital technology perspective of entrepreneurship. *Entrepreneurship Theory and Practice, 41*(6), 1029–1055. https://doi.org/10.1111/etap.12254

Ordanini, A., Miceli, L., Pizzetti, M., & Parasuraman, A. (2011). Crowd-funding: Transforming customers into investors through innovative service platforms. *Journal of Service Management, 22*(4), 443–470. https://doi.org/10.1108/09564231111155079

Rasmussen, E., Mosey, S., & Wright, M. (2011). The evolution of entrepreneurial competencies: A longitudinal study of university spin-off venture emergence. *Journal of Management Studies, 48*(6), 1314–1345. https://doi.org/10.1111/j.1467-6486.2010.00995.x

Rauch, A., & Frese, M. (2007). Let's put the person back into entrepreneurship research: A meta-analysis on the relationship between business owners' personality traits, business creation, and success. *European Journal of Work and Organizational Psychology, 16*(4), 353–385. https://doi.org/10.1080/13594320701595438

Shane, S., & Venkataraman, S. (2000). The promise of entrepreneurship as a field of research. *Academy of Management Review, 25*(1), 217–226.

Volery, T., Mueller, S., & von Siemens, B. (2015). Entrepreneur ambidexterity: A study of entrepreneur behaviours and competencies in growth-oriented small and medium-sized enterprises. *International Small Business Journal, 33*(2), 109–129. https://doi.org/10.1177/0266242613484777

Zhao, H., & Seibert, S. E. (2006). The big five personality dimensions and entrepreneurial status: A meta-analytical review. *Journal of Applied Psychology, 91*(2), 259.

Zhao, H., Seibert, S. E., & Lumpkin, G. T. (2010). The relationship of personality to entrepreneurial intentions and performance: A meta-analytic review. *Journal of Management, 36*(2), 381–404.

# 12. Backers: consumers or investors? Crowdfunding vs. traditional financing as an optimal security design problem

*Anton Miglo*

## 1 INTRODUCTION

Under digital entrepreneurship the entrepreneurial venture takes place digitally (some parts or all of it) in contrast to more traditional forms of entrepreneurship (Hull, Baroody and Payne (2007a)). It is a growing area of interest in practice and research. The financial aspects of digital entrepreneurship are closely related to the development of FinTech that represents a revolutionary development in the finance industry according to many experts (see e.g. Alt, Beck and Smits (2018), Das (2019)). The comparison of digital entrepreneurship and traditional entrepreneurship is an interesting line of research that has been extensively studied in recent years (see e.g. Hair, Wetsch, Hull, Perotti and Hung (2012), Hull, Hung, Yu-T, Hair, Perotti and DeMartino (2007b)). Among the issues of interest note the following: the advantages and disadvantages of digital entrepreneurship vs. traditional entrepreneurship (Hull et al (2007b)); what factors determine the entrepreneurs' choice between digital form of entrepreneurship and the traditional one (Fossen and Sorgner (2021)); the effect of digital entrepreneurship on product innovation (see e.g. Liao, Hull and Murthy (2013)) and so on.

Crowdfunding has been one of the most popular parts of digital entrepreneurship in the last 10–15 years (Tajedin, Madhok and Keyhani (2019)). It is a highly growing area of interest among practitioners and theorists.[1] The number of theoretical papers is quickly growing while the structure of this research area or its main directions are not quite established yet.[2] Crowdfunding is also often considered as a part of FinTech that refers to various financial technologies used to automate process in the financial sector (Das (2019), Thakor (2019)). It is a form of online fundraising where firms raise funds from a large number of investors/funders (see e.g. Ahlers, Cumming, Guenther and Schweizer (2015), Belleflamme, Omrani and Peitz (2015), Estrin et al (2018)).

The choice between traditional entrepreneurship and digital entrepreneurship can be analyzed from different points of view. The one we are focused on in this chapter is the choice between new digital ways of financing (that includes crowdfunding) and traditional financing (e.g. bank financing). Some examples related to this line of research include Schwienbacher (2018), Babich, Marinesi and Tsoukalas (2019), Fairchild, Liu and Yao (2017) and Miglo (2021). When analyzing this problem existing papers usually take parameters of contracts/ securities as given. We look at this problem from a more general perspective where optimal types of contracts/securities emerge from the model internally. An analogy is the security design problem as compared to a more traditional debt/equity choice problem where contracts/ securities (e.g. debt and equity) are given. One of the reasons for why such a more general approach can be useful is that crowdfunding campaigns have a lot of interesting and yet not very well understood features. Second, crowdfunding regulation that affects the features of crowdfunding campaigns and their consequences for different participants is still in the process of development (see e.g. Sadzius and Sadzius (2017)). Finally, existing theoretical literature on reward-based crowdfunding usually models backers' behavior using traditional demand functions, however the costs and benefits for backers for a large variety of practical situations related to crowdfunding may include different types of financial costs and benefits (see e.g. Appio, Leone, Platania and Schiavone (2020), Dobrynskaya and Grebennikova (2020), Bakri, Soleh and Radzai (2021)) so their objective function is rather multidimensional.

In this chapter we analyze a model of financing where the choice of financing is affected by the moral hazard problem regarding the choice of production scale, by asymmetric information about firm quality and by the uncertainty about consumer valuation of the product. The moral hazard problem is related to the difficulties of writing complete contracts between investors and entrepreneurs where all actions of entrepreneurs can be described or at least creating an environment where these actions can not only be observable by investors but also verifiable and ultimately enforceable (see e.g. Jensen and Meckling (1976) or Myers (1977)). Financing contracts affect the entrepreneur's incentives selecting the firm production scale (Brander and Lewis (1986)), the amount of investments (Myers (1977)) and the level of effort (Jensen and Meckling (1976)) so the providers of capital should rationally anticipate these decisions when designing or negotiating financing contracts because these decisions ultimately affect the investors' payoffs.[3] Asymmetric information on the other hand means that investors do not possess the same amount of information about a firm's projects and their qualities as compared to entrepreneurs (Myers and Majluf (1984)). This creates difficulties for investors to correctly estimate the value of securities issued by the firm. Although the famous Modigliani and Miller (1958) proposition suggested that firm financing is irrelevant, empirical literature and finance text books usually do not confirm this result (see e.g. Brealey, Myers and Allen (2016)). This is because this proposition can only be applied to perfect markets (i.e. markets without asymmetric information or moral hazard problems as well as without other market imperfections) while real financial markets are imperfect. The area of optimal financing (or capital structure choice) remains one of the most controversial areas in finance (see e.g. Graham and Harvey (2001)) but most experts agree that moral hazard and asymmetric information problems are important factors when conducting an analysis in this area (see e.g. Harris and Raviv (1991)). This holds for traditional financing (see e.g. Innes (1990), Nachman and Noe (1994)) as well as for crowdfunding (Strausz (2017), Miglo and Miglo (2019), Kleinert, Volkmann and Grünhagen (2020)). Traditional entrepreneurs seeking traditional finance usually face a lot of asymmetric information problems when trying to convince potential providers of capital in high quality of their projects which often leads to such problems as markets failure, credit rationing and so on (see e.g. Stiglitz and Weiss (1981) where entrepreneurs are not able to receive financing even if their projects have positive net present value). In empirical literature on crowdfunding the importance of asymmetric information is also well recognized. Usually this literature finds that entrepreneurs should try to find ways to improve information about their projects. It usually increases the likelihood of campaign success that suggests that informational problems play an important role in crowdfunding (see e.g. Mollick (2014)). Finally note that uncertainty about market demand (the third important feature of our model) is a relatively new phenomenon in theoretical literature related to firm financing decisions. It's been recognized in the literature on crowdfunding (both theoretical and empirical) that this factor plays an important role in crowdfunding (see e.g. Chemla and Tinn (2019)). For many entrepreneurs one of the main objectives of conducting a crowdfunding campaign is to receive a market feedback about the demand for their products/services.[4]

Our model predicts that in a perfect market the firm has multiple choices that lead to an optimal outcome that is consistent with the spirit of Modigliani and Miller (1958). Next we show that under moral hazard, but when information about market valuation and firm quality is symmetric, a large variety of contracts exist (although smaller than in the previous case) that generate optimal outcome. The main difference with the previous case is that the solution should contain a non-decreasing function of payoff for both entrepreneur and investor (otherwise the entrepreneur has no incentive to improve his effort). When information about firm quality is asymmetric but market valuation is common knowledge, an optimal contract is similar to traditional debt that is consistent with traditional asymmetric information literature (Nachman and Noe (1994), Leland and Pyle (1977) etc.). This is because debt contract in its nature (fixed payments) is less sensitive to informational problems as compared to other contracts. Next we analyze the case where information about firm quality is symmetric but the entrepreneur does not know the market valuation of the product. An optimal contract is a two-stage financing with crowdfunding at stage 1 and mixed financing at stage 2. Finally we analyze our main case where both information about firm quality is asymmetric as well as the market valuation of the product is unknown. An optimal contract is a two-stage financing where at stage 1 crowdfunding is used (small size) and a debt financing is used at stage 2. Although there are no direct tests of this result in existing literature, some papers provide evidence consistent with these results. For example, the following papers illustrate that crowdfunding followed by a subsequent financing is a quite frequent and seemingly growing phenomenon (Vanacker, Vismara, Walthoff-Born (2018), Xu (2018), Drover et al. (2017), Colombo and Shafi (2016), Roma, Petruzzelli and Perrone (2017) and Roma, Gal-Or and Chen (2018)). Our chapter determines optimal financing for different situations (asymmetric information, moral hazard, market uncertainty etc.) and helps entrepreneurs select optimal financing depending on the dominant type of environment they are facing. Our results also imply that digital and traditional entrepreneurship can complement each other: digital financing in the first stage and traditional financing in the second stage can often be optimal. Some empirical research finds the results that are consistent with the spirit of this prediction, for example that crowdfunding plays a positive role for subsequent financing. For example, Colombo and Shafi (2016) find that crowdfunding improves subsequent bank financing opportunities. In a similar spirit, crowdfunding platform Ulule provides good conditions for participating entrepreneurs for obtaining bank loans in addition to funds received from crowdfunding.[5,6]

The rest of the chapter is organized as follows. Section 2 contains a literature review. Section 3 presents the basic model and its main results. Section 4 analyzes the main case with asymmetric information and demand uncertainty. Section 5 presents the model's implications and its consistency with empirical evidence. Section 6 discusses the model's robustness and extensions and Section 7 concludes.

## 2    LITERATURE REVIEW

### 2.1    Security Design

Nachman and Noe (1994) analyze optimal security design in a one-period environment with asymmetric information. Information asymmetries are characterized by one entity having more information than another. Insiders may have private (exclusive) information about a firm that is unavailable to outsiders. Brennan and Kraus (1987) show that in these conditions a perfect signaling by a good firm is impossible. Myers and Majluf (1984) suggested that a good firm should always rely on retained earnings to finance new projects to avoid an underpricing of securities issued by the firm externally. In their absence they will issue debt and only as a last resort will issue equity (so called pecking order). Risky debt also suffers from asymmetric information problems (for example in the form of higher interest rates for firms) but not to the same degree as equity underpricing. This was proven in a more general (security design) setting by Nachman and Noe (1994). A similar result was obtained by Innes (1993).

In previously mentioned papers feasible contracts (securities) are characterized by monotonic payoff functions. Koufopoulos, Kozhan and Trigilia (2019) consider a model of financing under asymmetric information by relaxing a traditional assumption regarding monotonic securities. They characterize the optimal contract when entrepreneurs can misreport their earnings by some amount. Straight debt is often suboptimal and never uniquely optimal. The optimal contract is non-monotonic and involves profit manipulation in equilibrium. It can be implemented either including performance-based bonuses, or via milestone payments (as in venture capital).

Malenko and Tsoy (2018) study optimal security design by an informed issuer when the investor demands robustness and evaluates each security by the worst-case distribution at which she could justify it being offered by the issuer. They show that both standard outside equity and standard risky debt arise as equilibrium securities. Also they argue that the equilibrium security differs depending on the degree of uncertainty and on whether private information concerns assets in place or the new project. If private information concerns the new project and uncertainty is sufficiently high, standard equity arises as the unique equilibrium security. When uncertainty is sufficiently small, the equilibrium typically features risky debt. In the intermediate case, both risky debt and standard equity arise in equilibrium. In contrast, if private information concerns assets in place, standard equity is never issued in equilibrium, irrespective of the level of uncertainty, and the equilibrium security is (usually) risky debt.

Miglo (2020a) considers a security design problem under asymmetric information when cash flow from the project is divisible. It includes the case considered by Brennan and Kraus (1987) when the total cash flows of different types of firm can be ranked by the first-order dominance condition but not necessarily separate projects, that is, one firm can have a better project than another firm but the second project may not necessarily be better. It is shown that if the firms are allowed to issue securities with projects' cash flows contingent on payoffs, a separating equilibrium may exist even if the firms' total cash flows are ordered by the first-order dominance condition. A number of applications including financing with non-recourse debt, project financing, asset-backed securities and sukuk bonds are discussed.

Several papers analyze optimal contracts in a principal-agent setting based on moral hazard issues (see e.g. Innes (1990), Dewatripont, Legros and Matthews (2003), Gottlieb and Moreira (2017)).

In addition/in contrast to the literature mentioned above, in our model the payments to investors can be made in cash as well as using goods produced by the firm (payment-in-kind or PIK).

## 2.2    Crowdfunding Under Asymmetric Information and Moral Hazard

Miglo and Miglo (2019) argue that under asymmetric information between entrepreneurs and potential investors (funders) regarding the quality of a firm's projects, high-quality firms are not able to signal their quality by choosing a particular crowdfunding method when a one-period setting is considered (one-campaign setting). Low-quality firms will always mimic high-quality firms (similar to the traditional market for lemons idea in Akerlof (1970)). Additional assumptions should then be made in the basic setup that will allow for signaling opportunities to exist. Miglo and Miglo (2019) consider a situation with two consecutive rounds of financing and argue that reward-based crowdfunding can be used as a signal of quality when there is asymmetric information concerning either the cost of production or product quality. Low-quality firms may not be interested in mimicking high-quality firms when the latter use AON (all-or-nothing) campaigns because the risk of their projects failing may be too high, which can be costly in the second period.[7] Alternatively, Belleflamme et al. (2014) add non-monetary benefits (social benefits for funders from participating in crowdfunding) in the basic set-up and argue that equity-based crowdfunding can provide a slightly higher value to an entrepreneur under asymmetric information than it can under symmetric information. They also argue that asymmetric information reduces the value of reward-based crowdfunding to entrepreneurs. Chakraborty and Swinney (2019) consider a crowdfunding model where product quality is known to the entrepreneur but not to some contributors. They find that a larger campaign target can be used by high-quality firms as a signaling device.

Schwienbacher (2018) analyzes the role of entrepreneurial moral hazard in the choice between crowdfunding (AON) and venture capital and also its role in the choice of crowdfunding method and the choice of threshold. The author finds that under AON, sensible strategies for the firm are either to establish a high threshold and provide a high level of effort or to establish a low threshold and a low effort. The entrepreneur prefers the former if the effort cost is relatively low or when the demand uncertainty is high. Also the entrepreneur prefers crowdfunding to venture capital if the effort cost is low or when the demand in low-demand scenario is very small. This is because continuation happens under venture capital more often than under AON, however this continuation may be inefficient in a low-demand scenario if the demand is very low in this case. Schwienbacher (2018) also argues that entrepreneurs raise more money to minimize project discontinuation. This effect is exacerbated when there is a risk that the idea is quickly replicated by others, leading to even higher fundraising goals but also to fewer projects offered on platforms. Conversely, the presence of professional investors (business angels, venture capitalists) reduces the entrepreneurs' incentives in their crowdfunding campaign, which leads to more but on average smaller crowdfunding campaigns. The overall impact on crowdfunding volume is unclear. Despite this effect on campaigns, professional investors lower the entrepreneur's risk-taking, supporting the notion that crowdfunding can complement rather than substitute existing investors.

Babich, Marinesi and Tsoukalas (2019) study an optimal financing strategy for a start-up that includes a mix of crowdfunding as well as venture capital (VC) and bank financing. They model a bargaining game, with a moral-hazard problem between an entrepreneur, a bank and a VC. Similar to the spirit of analysis above when designing a crowdfunding campaign, the entrepreneur considers opportunities to get VC or bank financing after concluding the crowdfunding campaign. In some cases crowdfunding is not beneficial when the probability of project success is too high prior to bargaining with VC or when the amount of funds raised during a campaign is too large (overfunded project) that can exacerbate competition from banks and worsen the position of VC and ultimately the outcome of bargaining as well. The finding that VC can walk away after a successful crowdfunding campaign is consistent with Ryu, Kim and Hahn (2019). Babich et al. (2019) also find that projects that may not be beneficial if crowdfunding succeeds are likely to be ones with relatively low external capital required.

Miglo and Miglo (2019) find that pricing and production strategies of firms that use crowdfunding are affected by moral hazard issues. Especially with regard to equity-based crowdfunding because under equity-based crowdfunding the fraction of shares owned by the entrepreneur is reduced (in the spirit of Jensen and Meckling (1976)). In particular, prices can be higher and quantity produced can be lower under equity-based crowdfunding. This is consistent with Paakkarinen (2016) who noted that in contrast to reward-based crowdfunding, equity-based crowdfunding may have fewer customers, but higher margins. More broadly, the point that moral hazard issues related to the entrepreneurial cost of effort and the reduced equity stake are more important under equity-based crowdfunding is consistent with Gabison (2015) and Paakkarinen (2016), which noted that equity-based crowdfunding is much more constricted in comparison to other forms of crowdfunding.

Strausz (2017) studies entrepreneurs' interactions with customers before investment using the mechanism design approach. Under aggregate demand uncertainty, crowdfunding improves the screening of potential customers. However entrepreneurial moral hazard can reduce the value of this benefit. Studying the subsequent trade-off between screening and moral hazard, the paper characterizes optimal mechanisms. Efficiency is sustainable only if returns exceed investment costs by a margin reflecting the degree of moral hazard. Constrained efficient mechanisms exhibit underinvestment.

Chemla and Tinn (2019) consider a model where an entrepreneur has an ability to divert funds collected during crowdfunding. They argue that a higher amount of funds raised during crowdfunding mitigates the chance that funds will be diverted by the entrepreneur.

Ellman and Hurkens (2017) provide a simple example of a crowdfunding design that raises profit and welfare by tolerating some fraud risk. This shows how cross-subsidizing between cost states relaxes the most restrictive moral hazard constraints and generates better outcomes. They also characterize the optimal mechanism in the case of one consumer and two cost states. In general, this must hide information, including prices, from consumers. So crowdfunding cannot implement these optima. Belavina, Marinesi and Tsoukalas (2020) analyze the choice between reward-based crowdfunding and bank financing by focusing on two risks: entrepreneurs may run away with backers' money and product specifications may be misrepresented. They show that each of these risks can amplify their individual adverse effects. Belavina et al. (2020) analyze a total of ten different mechanisms and show that two of them dominate: the early stopping mechanism, and the escrow mechanism with mandatory ex-post verification.

Our contribution to this literature is that first we combine asymmetric information and moral hazard issues. Also we do not take the features of a crowdfunding campaign as given but derive them internally.

# 3    THE MODEL AND BASIC RESULTS

## 3.1    Model Description

An entrepreneurial firm designs a financing campaign for the production of its innovative product or service. The production is denoted by $q$. The cost of production is $K = cq^2/2$.[8] The firm has no initial resources available. To finance the production cost the firm needs to raise funds from an infinite number of potential investors. Investors are identical. The value of the product to investors equals $v$. The market price of the product after the project completion is also $v$. During the campaign, the firm raises an amount $F$. The firm is owned by an entrepreneur. After the completion of production the firm amount of cash equals $C = F - K$ and the total value of the firm assets equals $X = F - K + vq$. In contrast to traditional financing/security design models where payments to investors are made in cash here the firm can use two kinds of payments: in cash or PIK. Another important feature of the model is that the firm's main decision ($q$) is non-contractible. Financing contract is $(F, q_0, P(X))$. Here $q_0$ is the number of items promised to be paid (delivered) to investors (in contrast to $q$, $q_0$ can be verifiable/contractible), and $P(X)$ is cash payment to investors, where $X = C + v(q - q_0)$. Everybody is risk-neutral and the risk-free interest rate is zero. Investors provide funds as long as their expected payoff covers investment cost.

$c$ and $v$ are unknown in the beginning. At the beginning of a campaign, the entrepreneur learns $c$ and investors learn $v$. The entrepreneur offers a contract $(F, q_0, P(X))$ to investors. Investors can accept or reject the contract. If the latter is the case, payoff is zero for both entrepreneur and investors. If the former is the case investors provide financing $F$ and the entrepreneur selects $q$. After the production completion payments are made according to the contract. The timing of events is present in Figure 12.1.

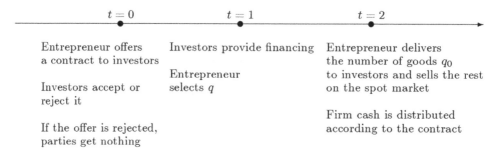

Figure 12.1    *The sequence of events*

## 3.2    Perfect Market

First consider a perfect market case (in the spirit of Modigliani and Miller (1958)). Suppose that $v$ and $c$ are common knowledge and no moral hazard problem exists, that is, $q$ can be contracted. Financing contract is $(q, F, q_0, P(X))$. Investors will provide funds if

$vq_0 + P\left(F - cq^2/2 + v(q - q_0)\right) \geq F$. Here $vq_0$ is the value of the goods to investors and $P\left(F - cq^2/2 + v(q - q_0)\right)$ is their cash payment. The entrepreneur maximizes $v(q - q_0) - cq^2/2 + F - P\left(v(q - q_0) - cq^2/2 + F\right)$ under conditions that $vq_0 + P\left(v(q - q_0) - cq^2/2 + F\right) \geq F$ and $F \geq cq^2/2$.

*Lemma 1. Under perfect market any contract is optimal such as:* $q = v/c$, $q_0 \leq v/c$, $F = v^2/2c$ *and* $P\left(v(v/c - q_0)\right) = v^2/2 - vq_0$.

*Proof.* First note that socially optimal $q$ (that maximizes total surplus) maximizes $vq - cq^2/2$. So optimal $q = v/c$.

Consider the following contract: $q = v/c$, $q_0 \leq v/c$, $F = v^2/2c$ and

$$P\left(v\left(\frac{v}{c} - q_0\right)\right) = \frac{v^2}{2c} - vq_0.$$

The entrepreneur's profit in this case equals

$$v(q - q_0) - \frac{v^2}{2c} + F - P\left(F - \frac{v^2}{2c} + v(q - q_0)\right) = v(q - q_0) - P\left(v\left(\frac{v}{c} - q_0\right)\right) = \frac{v^2}{c} - v^2/2c = v^2/2c.$$ Investor's payoff

equals: $vq_0 + P\left(F - cq^2/2 + v(q - q_0)\right) = vq_0 + P\left(v(q - q_0)\right) = v^2/2c$. So investors will

agree to provide an amount of financing $F$ that equals $v^2/2c$.

Similar to the spirit of the Modigliani and Miller (1958) proposition, under perfect market, a large variety of financing strategies exist that can be optimal. For example it can be a contract with $q_0 = 0$ and $P(X) = v^2/2c$, $\forall X \geq 0$ or one with $q_0 = v/c$ and $P(X) = 0$, $\forall X \geq 0$.

Now consider the case with moral hazard when $q$ is non-contractible.

### 3.3 Moral Hazard Problem Under Symmetric Information

Financing contract is $(F, q_0, P(X))$.

*Lemma 2. Under moral hazard and perfect information about c and v any contract is optimal such as:* $q_0 \leq v/c$, $F = v^2/2c$, $vq_0 + P\left(v(q - q_0)\right) = v^2/2c$ *and* $0 \leq P'(X) \leq 1, \forall X \geq 0$.

*Proof.* Consider the following contract: $q_0 \leq v/c$, $F = v^2/2c$, $vq_0 + P\left(v(q - q_0)\right) = v^2/2c$ and $0 \leq P'(X) \leq 1$, $\forall X \geq 0$. If it is accepted, the entrepreneur will select $q$ that maximizes

$$v(q - q_0) - cq^2/2 + F - P\left(F - cq^2/2 + v(q - q_0)\right) = v(q - q_0) - cq^2/2 + \frac{v^2}{2c} - P\left(\frac{v^2}{2c} - cq^2/2 + v(q - q_0)\right)$$

under condition that $q \geq q_0$ and $F = v^2/2c - cq^2/2$. Optimal $q$ is determined by the following condition: $v - qc - (v - qc)P'\left(v^2/2c - cq^2/2 + v(q - q_0)\right) = 0$. This is a first-order optimality condition (FOC) for two reasons. First the second-order condition (SOC) is satisfied because $P'(X) \leq 1$. Second, $F \geq c(v/c)^2/2$ or $F \geq v^2/2c$. It means that the amount of financing covers the production of optimal quantity of goods $q$ that (according to FOC) equals $q = v/c$. The entrepreneur's profit in this case equals $vq - vq_0 - cq^2/2 + v^2/2c - P\left(v^2/2c - cq^2/2 + v(q - q_0)\right) = v^2/c - v^2/2c = v^2/2c$.

Investors' payoff equals: $vq_0 + P\left(F - cq^2/2 + v(q - q_0)\right) = vq_0 + P\left(v(q - q_0)\right) = v^2/2c$. So the investors will agree to provide an amount of financing $F$ that equals $v^2/2c$.

Although Lemma 2 provides a closed-form solution to the optimal financing contract under moral hazard, it is difficult to find a practical interpretation of this result except perhaps the condition $0 \leq P'(X) \leq 1$ that implies monotonicity for both entrepreneur's and investors' cash payment. All known securities satisfy this condition and it has been well described in previous literature as discussed in Section 2.

## 3.4    Asymmetric Information About Cost

This case assumes a moral hazard problem and, in addition, that $c$ is privately known by the entrepreneur. So we have a game with incomplete information where investors face multiple types of the firm (depending on the cost $c$). An equilibrium is a situation where no type of firm has an incentive to deviate. We will show that a perfect signaling equilibrium exists, that is, an equilibrium where the different types of firm select different strategies.

Lemma 3. *There exists a separating equilibrium where an entrepreneur of type c uses the following contract:* $q_0 = 0$, $F = v^2/2c$ *and* $P(X) = v^2/2c$, $\forall X \geq 0$.

*Proof.* Consider an equilibrium where an entrepreneur of type $c$ selects the following contract: $q_0 = 0$, $F = v^2/2c$ and $P(X) = v^2/2c$, $\forall X \geq 0$. First consider the choice of $q$ in case the contract is accepted. The entrepreneur maximizes $v(q - q_0) - cq^2/2 + F - P\left(F - cq^2/2 + v(q - q_0)\right) = vq - cq^2/2 + v^2/2c - v^2/2c$ under condition that $F = v^2/2c - cq^2/2$. Optimal $q$ is determined by the following condition: $v - qc = 0$ that implies $q = v/c$. Also entrepreneurs with different $c$ have no incentive to mimic each other. Indeed suppose an entrepreneur with $c > c'$ decides to mimic an entrepreneur with $c'$. Equilibrium payoff of entrepreneur $c$ equals $v^2/2c$. If he decides to mimic an entrepreneur with $c'$, the choice of $q$ will be the same as his equilibrium choice (only the fixed part of objective function changes, that is, the values of $F$ and $P$ while the funds raised $(F')$ are sufficient to cover the production of $q = v/c$ because $F' = v^2/2c' > F = v^2/2c$ because in turn $c' < c$). And the entrepreneur's payoff is the same as in equilibrium because $F' = P'$. Now suppose an entrepreneur with $c < c'$ decides to mimic an entrepreneur with $c'$. First $F' = v^2/2c' < v^2/2c$ so the entrepreneur will not be able to produce $q = v/c$. Since the derivative of the entrepreneur's objective function is positive in $q$ for any $q < v/c$, the entre-

preneur will produce the maximal feasible quantity of goods $\sqrt{\dfrac{2F}{c}} = \dfrac{v}{\sqrt{cc'}}$. The entrepre-

neur's profit in this case equals: $v(q - q_0) - \dfrac{cq^2}{2} + F - P\left(F - \dfrac{cq^2}{2} + v(q - q_0)\right)$

$$= \frac{v^2}{\sqrt{cc'}} - \frac{v^2}{2c'} + \frac{v^2}{2c'} - \frac{v^2}{2c'} = \frac{v^2}{\sqrt{cc'}} - \frac{v^2}{2c'}.$$ This is less than $v/2c$. Indeed we have

$$\frac{v}{2c} - \frac{v^2}{\sqrt{cc'}} + \frac{v^2}{2c'} = \frac{v^2\left(\sqrt{c'} - \sqrt{c}\right)^2}{2cc'} > 0.$$

A possible interpretation of Lemma 3 is debt financing because the cash payment to investors does not depend on the firm value/the amount of cash available. This is consistent with the spirit of traditional asymmetric information theories of capital structure (Myers and Majluf (1984) or Leland and Pyle (1977)).

## 3.5   Uncertain Demand

Now consider the case when $v$ is unknown by the entrepreneur while $c$ is common knowledge. First we will argue that contracts described above (we will call them traditional contracts) do not lead to an optimal outcome (as described in Lemma 2: i.e. when the entrepreneur's profit equals $v^2/2c$).

Lemma 4. *No traditional contract leads to an optimal outcome.*

*Proof.* First note that the only signal that the entrepreneur can receive from investors is whether they accept or reject the contract. A contract that leads to an optimal outcome should not be rejected in any case (i.e. for any value of $v$). Otherwise the expected payoff of the entrepreneur will be less than $v^2/2c$. The reason is that under optimal contract the entrepreneur's payoff is strictly equal to $v^2/2c$ for any value of $v$. If the investors accept the contract and the entrepreneur makes more than $v^2/2c$, such a contract should not be accepted by investors because in this case they make less than $v^2/2c$. This is because the optimal amount of surplus does not exceed $v^2/c$ (and equals it when $q$ is socially optimal as was shown previously). So if the contract is accepted the entrepreneur makes not more than $v^2/2c$. However if it is rejected he makes 0 so if the contract is rejected with a positive probability, the entrepreneur's expected payoff is less than optimal. So the contract should be accepted by investors with any value of $v$. It implies that signaling by investors is not possible and therefore when selecting $q$ (assuming that investors accept the contract), the entrepreneur maximizes

$$E\left(v(q-q_0) - cq^2/2 + F - P\left(F - cq^2/2 + v(q-q_0)\right)\right) = Ev(q-q_0) - cq^2/2 + F - EP\left(F - cq^2/2 + v(q-q_0)\right),$$

where $E$ denotes the expected value. Optimal $q$ is determined by the following condition: $Ev - q_c - EP'\left(v^2/2c - cq^2/2 + v(q-q_0)\right) = 0$. If it holds for any $v$, then we have $Ev - v - EP'\left(v^2/c - vq_0\right) = 0$. But this implies that $P(X)$ should depend on $v$ which is impossible because the entrepreneur does not know $v$.

We then consider a new class of contracts namely we add a two-stage financing where in stage 1 the entrepreneur offers a menu of contracts $\left(F_1(q_{01}), P_1(X)\right)$, and the investors can select themselves a contract (i.e. the value of $q_{01}$ and respectively $F_1(q_{01})$ that is most profitable for them). And at stage 2 (negotiations about it are conducted after the stage 1 financing is completed) the entrepreneur offers $\left(q_{02}, F_2, P_2(X)\right)$. Production takes place after both stages of financing are completed.

Proposition 1. *The following contract is optimal:* $P_1(X)=0$, $F_1(q_{01})=ncq_{01}^2/2$, $q_{02} \le v/c$, $F_2 = v^2/2c - F_1$, $vq_{02} + P_2(v(q-q_{02}-q_{01})) = v^2/2c$ *and* $0 \le P_2'(X) \le 1$.

*Proof.* Consider the following contract $P_1(X)=0$, $F_1(q_{01})=ncq_{01}^2/2$, $q_{02} \le v/c$, $F_2 = v^2/2c - F_1$, $vq_{02} + P_2(v(q-q_{02}-q_{01})) = v^2/2c$ and $0 \le P_2'(X) \le 1$. First as we will show below, at the end of stage 1 the entrepreneur will learn $v$. So during production the entrepreneur maximizes $v(q-q_{01}-q_{02})-cq^2/2+F_1+F_2-P_2(v(q-q_{01}-q_{02})-cq^2/2+F_1+F_2)$ under condition that $q \ge q_{01}+q_{02}$. We have $F = F_1 + F_2 = F_1 + v^2/2c - F_1 = v^2/2c$. Since $v^2/2c \ge c(v/c)^2/2$ optimal $q = v/c$. Now consider stage 1 financing. After the entrepreneur offers $P_1(X)=0$, the only possible payoff for investors are goods. The investors will select a contract that maximizes $vq_{01}-F_1$, where $F_1 = ncq_{01}^2/2$. So $q_{01}=v/nc$ and $F_1 = v^2/2cn$. The investor (stage 1) payoff equals $vq_{01}=v^2/nc$ that is greater than their total investment $v^2/2cn$. So stage 1 financing will be accepted and the investor will select $q_{01} = v/nc$. At stage 2, the investor payoff equals $vq_{02} + P_2(v(q-q_{01}-q_{02})) = v^2/2c$ so stage 2 financing will be accepted too. The entrepreneur's payoff equals: $v(q-q_{01}-q_{02})-cq^2/2+F_1+F_2-P_2(v(q-q_{01}-q_{02})-cq^2/2+F_1+F_2)=v^2/2c-v^2/nc+v^2/2cn$ that will approach $v^2/2c$ as $n$ increases.

The interpretation of this result is that optimal financing for the entrepreneur under demand uncertainty is crowdfunding at stage 1 and mixed financing (crowdfunding campaign and traditional financing) at stage 2.

## 4   ASYMMETRIC INFORMATION ABOUT COST AND UNCERTAIN DEMAND

Now consider the case when v is unknown by the entrepreneur and c is the entrepreneur's private information.

Proposition 2. *There exists a separating equilibrium where an entrepreneur of type c uses the following contract:* $P_1(X)=0$, $q_{02}=0$, $P_1(X)=F_2=F_1=ncq^2/2$.

*Proof.* First as we will show below, at the end of stage 1 the entrepreneur will learn $v$. So the entrepreneur maximizes $v(q-q_{01})-cq^2/2+F_1+F_2$ under condition that $q \ge q_{01}$. Since $vq_{01} \ge c(v/c)^2/2$ or $q_{01} \ge v/2c$ optimal $q = v/c$. Second, suppose that the market believes the entrepreneur's message when observing stage 1 offer and realized the value of $c$. Since $P_1(v)=0$, the only possible payoff for the investor is PIK. If the investors select $F_1$ then $q_{01} = \sqrt{2F_1/nc}$ goods to be received. The investor will select a contract that maximizes $vq_{01}-F_1$, where $F_1 = ncq_{01}^2/2$. So $q_{01}=v/nc$. Indeed they will not "order" less since it leads to a negative payoff for them and they cannot order more since this contract will be unfeasible.

Finally no type has an incentive to mimic another type (so the entrepreneur's message is credible). Indeed suppose an entrepreneur with $c > c'$ decides to mimic an entrepreneur with $c'$. Equilibrium payoff of entrepreneur $c$ equals $v^2 / 2c - \dfrac{v^2}{nc} + \dfrac{v^2}{2cn}$. If he decides to mimic an entrepreneur with $c'$, the choice of $q$ will be the same as his equilibrium choice (only fixed part of objective function changes, that is, the values of $F_1$ and $F_2$ while the funds raised $(F_1' + F_2')$ are sufficient to cover the production of $q = v/c$ because $F'_1 + F'_2 = v^2 / c' > F_1 + F_2 = v^2 / c$ because $c' < c$). And the payoff is smaller than that in equilibrium because $v(q - q'_{01}) - \dfrac{cq^2}{2} + F_1' + F_2' - \dfrac{v^2}{nc'} + \dfrac{v^2}{2c'n} < v(q - q_0) - cq^2 / 2 + F_1 + F_2 - \dfrac{v^2}{nc} + \dfrac{v^2}{2cn}$. Indeed this is equivalent to $\dfrac{(2n-1)v^2}{2nc'} > \dfrac{(2n-1)v^2}{2nc}$ that holds because $c' < c$.
Now if an entrepreneur with $c < c'$ decides to mimic an entrepreneur with $c'$, then his choice $q = v/c < q' = v/c'$ so he produces less and profits are smaller.

A possible interpretation of the result in Proposition 2 is that under demand uncertainty, asymmetric information and moral hazard, an optimal financing for the firm is crowdfunding at stage 1 and debt at stage 2.

## 5  MODEL IMPLICATIONS

Our chapter has several implications for an entrepreneurial firm's choice of optimal financing.

Proposition 1 has several implications. First, optimal financing is a two-stage financing because any one-stage financing does not lead to an optimal outcome. Empirical research shows that a growing number of firms after conducting a crowdfunding campaign organize the second round of fundraising that in most cases is different from crowdfunding (see, for example, Tuo, Feng, Sarpong and Wang (2019)). Second, it implies that crowdfunding followed by a second-stage financing is preferred to traditional financing if the market uncertainty increases. Although this prediction has not been tested directly it is consistent with the spirit of Chemla and Tinn (2019) and Xu (2018). Chemla and Tinn (2019) present data that support their results based on the comparison of crowdfunding campaigns by technology firms (with a higher degree of demand uncertainty) and theatre firms. It is also consistent with the spirit of findings in Xu (2018).

Proposition 1 also implies that crowdfunding campaign size at stage 1 should be sufficiently small. This is consistent with empirical findings in Mollick (2014).

Lemma 3 implies that debt financing is preferred when information about firm quality is asymmetric.

Proposition 2 implies that optimal financing when the model has entrepreneur's private information about firm's quality and market valuation of the product is uncertain is crowdfunding at stage 1 and debt financing at stage 2. Crowdfunding campaigns are small compared to the size of traditional financing. The second part has not been tested so far.

# 6    MODEL EXTENSIONS AND ROBUSTNESS

*Other types of moral hazard.* In our model, the moral hazard takes place because, for example, the entrepreneur's stake in the firm's earnings is not 100% while the production is costly and this cost is not shared. This approach is very common in financing literature (starting with Jensen and Meckling (1976)) and typically creates an agency cost of financing. There are many different ways to analyze moral hazard issues, for example, to explicitly assume that the entrepreneurs can "steal" money from the firm. In this case the entrepreneur trades-off private benefits from "inefficient" investments and the cost incurred in the case of the firm's bankruptcy. The entrepreneur's objective function can be made more complicated by including, for example, some bonuses from "good" investments. At this point, however, we do not see which parts of our ideas can be affected qualitatively without significantly complicating the model's solutions so we leave it for future research.

*Cost of production.* Suppose that the fixed costs of launching production equals $I > 0$. The financing campaign needs to then cover these costs along with the variable cost of production. The analysis of this extension is pretty much identical to the main analysis of the model. The only interesting conclusion is that if $I$ is large enough the firm will not be able to use crowdfunding. This is consistent in general with the spirit of Belleflamme et al. (2014) and Miglo and Miglo (2019) where reward-based crowdfunding cannot be used if $I$ is large enough. Similarly one can extend the model by introducing a variable cost of production $c$ per item during operational stage. Main results do not change qualitatively.

*Bankruptcy costs.* One can further extend the model by including bankruptcy cost. Although intuitively it can be important because the value of the product may not be known to the firm and in some scenarios it will not able to make promised cash payment to investors or deliver promised amount of goods but the existence of perfect signaling equilibrium mitigates this issue. Since a signaling equilibrium exists, the true value of the product and the cost of production will be common knowledge in equilibrium. Therefore bankruptcy should not occur in equilibrium. One can change the model by adding, for example, a "variance" in the production function. In this case even if the product valuation is common knowledge the campaign fails in some cases. At this point we do not see how it may significantly change the model's results qualitatively (similarly to the introduction of risky debt in Modigliani-Miller analysis that would not change its main predictions (Stiglitz (1969)) or the introduction of risky debt in the pecking-order theory (Nachman and Noe (1994)) etc.) while complicating the technical part so we leave it to further research.

# 7    CONCLUSION

This chapter is the first one that analyzes the choice between crowdfunding and traditional financing as a security design problem. We analyze a model of financing where the investors' objective function includes benefits from consuming a good as well as purely financial benefits; where a set of possible contracts is larger than in traditional security design and crowdfunding literature and includes different types of contracts (financial contracts) including possible PIK (payments-in-kind); and where the choice of financing is affected by moral hazard problem regarding the choice of production scale, by asymmetric information about firm quality, and by the uncertainty about consumer valuation of the product and so on. We argue that a two-stage financing where the first stage has small size and delivers goods to investors while the second stage financing has a fixed monetary payment is an optimal solution for entrepreneurs. This combination corresponds to reward-based crowdfunding followed by bank financing.

With regard to digital entrepreneurship the chapter contributes to discussions about entrepreneur's choice between digital entrepreneurship and traditional entrepreneurship. Our chapter provides several suggestions and recommendations for entrepreneurs selecting their strategy of financing that may include traditional financing (e.g. bank loans), digital financing (e.g. crowdfunding) or a mix of both. First, the chapter results suggest that the crowdfunding is more likely to be selected when the uncertainty about market demand for firm products/ services is high. Indeed when comparing the results of our analysis in Sections 3–4, crowdfunding emerges as an optimal financing at stage 1 in sections 3.5 and 4 where the demand is unknown. This also contributes to another question mentioned in the Introduction, namely the effect of digital entrepreneurship on product innovation. Indeed crowdfunding (especially reward-based crowdfunding) is usually used by firms to finance innovative products such as 3-D printers, smart watches, drones and so on. In contrast to traditional products, the demand for this type of product is highly risky/uncertain so using crowdfunding (i.e. in the model PIK financing) is optimal. It is consistent with Kozinets (2002) and Hair et al. (2012) who state that an increasingly popular tool available to the digital entrepreneur is electronic communities that permit the rapid exchange of innovative ideas between customers and the organization.

Second, we argue that in many cases the entrepreneur should select a two-stage financing where crowdfunding should be followed by a second stage financing. The following papers illustrate that crowdfunding is often followed by a subsequent financing: Vanacker et al. (2018), Xu (2018), Drover et al. (2017), Colombo and Shafi (2016), Roma et al. (2017), Roma et al. (2018), Tuo et al. (2019). Further, some research finds that crowdfunding plays a positive role for subsequent financing so that indirectly confirms that two-stage financing is good. For example, Colombo and Shafi (2016) find that crowdfunding improves subsequent bank financing opportunities.

Third, we argue that digital ways of raising funds via crowdfunding should be optimal for mostly small size campaigns. This is consistent with observed evidence on crowdfunding that crowdfunding campaigns are typically small (see e.g. Bernardino and Santos (2020)). This is also consistent with the spirit of Belleflamme et al. (2014) and Miglo and Miglo (2019) in that large projects should not use crowdfunding. An indirect evidence that is consistent with this phenomenon is that there is a negative correlation between the campaign size and its degree of success (see e.g. Mollick (2014)). This is also consistent with Keyhani, Neyshabouri and Amereii (2020) who found that crowdfunding is mostly used by small theatrical projects.

Fourth, the chapter suggests that digital entrepreneurship and traditional entrepreneurship do not have to be substitutes and can compliment each other. This contributes to the literature that discusses if crowdfunding and bank financing are substitutes or complements (see e.g. De Buysere, Gajda, Kleverlaan and Marom (2012), Xu (2018), Blaseg and Koetter (2016), Miglo (2021)). An indirect evidence consistent with this idea is, for example, previously mentioned crowdfunding platform Ulule that offers entrepreneurs good opportunities to raise bank loans in addition to funds raised with crowdfunding.

Fifth, the chapter suggests that when the market demand is uncertain, the firm should offer a menu of contracts to potential investors (optimal contracts in sections 3.5 and 4) which can be interpreted as the price menu when the firm opens a crowdfunding campaign (Hu, Li and

Shi (2015), De Lange (2018)). Some entrepreneurs think that an opportunity to offer different combinations of price–reward was a great tool they used during their crowdfunding campaign.[9]

Finally, more transparent firms (e.g. section 3.5 considers an environment without asymmetric information) could select crowdfunding at stage 2 while with asymmetric information (Section 4), debt financing at stage 2 is optimal. This result has potential policy implications. It can help regulators who are responsible for developing/promoting the number of innovations in the economy including innovative ways of financing such as crowdfunding. Some of our previous points (such as that crowdfunding is more likely to emerge in industries with high degree of market demand uncertainty; that crowdfunding helps entrepreneurs developing innovative products; or that crowdfunding will more likely be optimal for small size campaigns) should also help regulators dealing with crowdfunding.

The chapter also contributes to the literature that analyzes the choice of financing and security design under asymmetric information. Usually this literature argues that bank financing serves as a signal of a firm's quality as compared to, for example, equity financing (see e.g. Nachman and Noe (1994), Leland and Pyle (1977) and Ross (1977)). In the spirit of this literature our model predicts that when asymmetric information is present but there are no moral hazard problems and no uncertainty about demand exists, debt is optimal financing. However in addition to traditional literature we add two other factors and argue that when asymmetric information coexists with these factors, optimal financing consists of a mix of crowdfunding and bank financing. Note also that empirical evidence regarding the signaling effect of debt vs. equity is mixed.[10] Other papers argue that high-quality firms can use crowdfunding to signal their quality and further seek traditional finance provided by banks or other large investors (Roma et al. (2017), Roma et al. (2018) and Babich et al. (2019)). This literature mostly focuses on crowdfunding followed by venture capital finance. In our paper crowdfunding should be followed by a contract with fixed payment which can be bank financing. Mollick (2014) argues that high-quality entrepreneurs use reward-based crowdfunding to signal their quality in a similar way to using other financing tools. In Miglo and Miglo (2019) high-quality firms use reward-based crowdfunding as a signal. In Fairchild et al. (2017) there is a non-monotonic relationship between a firm's quality and its choice between crowdfunding and venture capital finance.[11] Our contribution to this literature is that we argue that crowdfunding can be a part of separating equilibrium in a model where in addition to asymmetric information there are other market imperfections. In this case the signal is not just the fact of selecting crowdfunding but, for example, the choice of crowdfunding prices that signals information about the firm.

Our chapter suggests that bank financing should be part of an optimal financing mix selected by firms. This is consistent with observed evidence that in practice bank loans are still widely used by small-medium-size enterprises (SMEs).[12] The vast majority of these firms rely on bank loans in their financing strategy despite traditional difficulties with obtaining bank loans.[13]

Also our chapter explains how reward-based crowdfunding emerges as an optimal financing in an environment where the investor's objective function is multidimensional and includes both financial and "consumption" elements. As we argue the primary reason is the uncertainty about market demand when the entrepreneur optimally uses PIK (i.e. crowdfunding) and offers a menu of contracts (i.e. different prices) to potential investors to receive information. Based on the result in sections 3.5 and 4 an optimal contract includes PIK and zero fixed payment in the first stage that suggests that in equilibrium the consumption element should dominate and reward-based crowdfunding emerges as an optimal financing.

# ACKNOWLEDGEMENTS

I am grateful to Vincent Crawford, Gary Dushnitsky, Geoffrey Hodgson, Todd Kaplan, Peter Klein, Claire Leitch, Victor Miglo, Simon C Parker, Mark Taylor, Deborah Trask, the seminar participants at University of Sussex, University of West England Bristol, Ulster University and London South Bank University for their helpful comments and editing assistance.

# NOTES

1. For a review of literature on digital entrepreneurship see e.g. Keyhani et al. (Chapter 1 in this handbook). For a review on crowdfunding see, for example, Moritz and Block (2014), Ahlstrom, Cumming and Vismara (2018), Estrin, Gozman and Khavul (2018), Mochkabadi and Volkmann (2018) and Miglo (2020b).
2. Miglo (2020b).
3. Appio et al. (2020) argue that the entrepreneur's bad decisions and often fraud are behind the reasons why many crowdfunding campaigns fail to deliver products and rewards to their backers. Bakri et al. (2021) argue that the entrepreneur's effort and performance expectancy affect the backers' decision-making.
4. Martin Kallstrom, CEO of Memoto company that used Kickstarter to conduct a crowdfunding campaign, argues that one the most important objectives of campaign success is to get feedback from market participants. He said: "Crowdfunding is the perfect entrepreneurial launch tool - for us it meant an opportunity to do a market estimation (or at least validate product demand)" (https://djksar.wordpress.com/2012/11/14/kickstarter-campaigns-interview-with-martin-kallstrom-ceo-of-memoto/).
5. See e.g. https://lenderkit.com/blog/banks-and-crowdfunding/.
6. Another example is the UK-based platform Zopa, that created its own bank that allows entrepreneurs to rely both on funds originated directly by online deposits, as well as on other traditional banking sources of funding (Navaretti, Calzolari and Pozzolo (2018)).
7. The AON model involves the entrepreneurial firm setting a fundraising goal and keeping nothing unless the goal is achieved. This contrasts the "Keep-It-All" (KIA) model, which involves the entrepreneurial firm setting a fundraising goal and keeping the entire amount raised, regardless of whether or not they meet their goal.
8. Section 6 discusses model extensions and robustness with regard to different assumptions made.
9. See e.g. an interview with Ebony Love, CEO of LoveBuz. https://mariapeaglerdigital.com/how-to-run-a-successful-crowdfunding-campaign-interview- with-ebony-love-lovebug-studios/.
10. The empirical studies typically find a negative relation between profitability and leverage (Titman and Wessels (1988), Rajan and Zingales (1995), Fama and French (2002) and Frank and Goyal (2009)). Eckbo (1986) and Antweiler and Frank (2006) find insignificant changes in stock prices in response to straight corporate debt issues.
11. See also Chakraborty and Swinney (2019).
12. See e.g. https://www.british-business-bank.co.uk/research/sbfm/ or Durkin et al. (2016).
13. See, e.g. Stiglitz and Weiss (1981), Jaffee and Russell (1976), Watson (1984), Bhattacharya and Thakor (1993), Parker (2002), Arnold and Riley (2009) and Su and Zhang (2017).

# REFERENCES

Ahlers, G., Cumming, D., Guenther, C., & Schweizer, D. (2015). Signaling in equity crowdfunding. *Entrepreneurship Theory and Practice*, 39(4), 955–980.

Ahlstrom, D., Cumming, D., & Vismara, S. (2018). New methods of entrepreneurial firm financing: fintech, crowdfunding and corporate governance implications. *Corporate Governance – An International Review*, 26(5), 310–313.

Akerlof, G. (1970). The market for lemons: quality uncertainty and the market mechanism. *Quarterly Review of Economics*, 74, 488–500. 10.2307/1879431

Alt, R., Beck, R., & Smits, M. T. (2018). FinTech and the transformation of the financial industry. *Electronic Markets*, 28, 235–243.

Antweiler, W., Frank, M. (2006). Do U.S. stock markets typically overreact to corporate news stories? Working Paper, University of British Columbia and University of Minnesota.

Appio, F. P., Leone, D., Platania, F., & Schiavone, F. (2020). Why are rewards not delivered on time in rewards-based crowdfunding campaigns? An empirical exploration. *Technological Forecasting and Social Change*, 157(C).

Arnold, L. G., Riley, J. G. (2009). On the possibility of credit rationing in the Stiglitz–Weiss model. *American Economic Review*, 99(5), 2012–2021.

Babich, V., Marinesi, S., & Tsoukalas, G. (2019). Does crowdfunding benefit entrepreneurs and venture capital investors? *Manufacturing & Service Operations Management*. https://ssrn.com/abstract= 2971685or http://dx.doi.org/10.2139/ssrn.2971685

Bakri, M. H., Soleh, M., & Radzai, M. D. (2021). Technology acceptance in crowdfunding among retailers. *Studies of Applied Economics*, 39(5),1–12. DOI: 10.25115/eea.v39i5.4818.

Belavina, E., Marinesi, S., & Tsoukalas, G. (2020). Rethinking crowdfunding platform design: mechanisms to deter misconduct and improve efficiency. *Management Science*. https://ssrn.com/abstract= 3093437 or http://dx.doi.org/10.2139/ssrn.3093437

Belleflamme, P., Lambert, T., & Schwienbacher, A. (2014). Crowdfunding: tapping the right crowd. *Journal of Business Venturing*, 29(5), 585–609.

Belleflamme, P., Omrani, N., & Peitz, M. (2015). The economics of crowdfunding platforms. *Information Economics and Policy*, 33(C), 11–28.

Bernardino, S., Santos, J. F. (2020). Crowdfunding: an exploratory study on knowledge, benefits and barriers perceived by young potential entrepreneurs. *Journal of Risk and Financial Management*, 13(4), 81. DOI: 10.3390/jrfm13040081.

Bhattacharya S., Thakor A., (1993). Contemporary banking theory. *Journal of Financial Intermediation*, 3, 2–50.

Blaseg, D., Koetter, M. (2016). Crowdfunding and bank stress. In Paolo Tasca, Tomaso Aste, Loriana Pelizzon, & Nicolas Perony (Eds.), *Banking Beyond Banks and Money* (pp. 17–54). Springer. https://www.springer.com/gp/book/9783319424460

Brander, J., Lewis, T. (1986). Oligopoly and financial structure: the limited liability effect. *American Economic Review*, 76(5), 956–70. https://EconPapers.repec.org/RePEc:aea:aecrev:v:76:y:1986:i:5: p:956-70

Brealey, R., Myers, S., & Allen, F. (2016). *Principles of Corporate Finance*. McGraw-Hill Education; 12th edition.

Brennan, M., Kraus, A. 1987. Efficient financing under asymmetric information. *Journal of Finance*, 42(5), 1225–1243.

Chakraborty, S., Swinney, R. (2019). Signalling to the crowd: private quality information and rewards-based crowdfunding. *Manufacturing and Service Operations Management*. http://dx.doi.org/ 10.2139/ssrn.2885457.

Chemla, G., Tinn, K. (2019). Learning through crowdfunding. *Management Science*. https://doi.org/10 .1287/mnsc.2018.3278. https://ssrn.com/abstract=2796435

Colombo, M., Shafi, K. (2016). When does reward-based crowdfunding help firms obtain external financing? *Business*. https://www.semanticscholar.org/paper/When-Does-Reward-Based -Crowdfunding-Help-Firms-Colombo-Shafi/f73c213288809600f93e9f621644f6e17319b220. DOI: 10.2139/SSRN.2785538.

Das, S. (2019). The future of FinTech. *Financial Management*, 48(4), 981–1007.

De Buysere, K., Gajda, O., Kleverlaan, R., & Marom, D. (2012). A framework for European crowdfunding. *European Crowdfunding Network (ECN)*. www.europecrowdfunding.org/european _crowdfunding_framework (accessed on 15 February 2020).

De Lange, R. (2018). The influence of a price menu strategy on crowdfunding campaigns, Erasmus School of Economics. Weblink: file:///C:/Users/Baseo/Downloads/Lange-R.B.G.M.-de-435690rl-.pdf

Dewatripont, M., Legros, P., & Matthews, S. (2003). Moral hazard and capital structure dynamics. *Journal of European Economic Association*, 1(4), 890–930. https://doi.org/10.1162/154247603322493186

Dobrynskaya, V., Grebennikova, J. (2020). Financial returns in reward-based crowdfunding. Working paper. SSRN: https://ssrn.com/abstract=3582141

Drover, W., Wood, M. S., & Zacharakis, A. (2017). Attributes of angel and crowdfunded investments as determinants of VC screening decisions. *Entrepreneurship Theory and Practice*, 41(3), 323–347.

Durkin, M., Laffey, D., Gandy, A., Cummins, D., & Fearon, C. (2016). The SME–bank relationship: exploring the impact of crowdfunding at start-up. A research study by Ulster University Business School, Kent Business School and the London Institute of Banking and Finance. https://www.ulster.ac.uk/__data/assets/pdf_file/0009/168417/crowdfunding.pdf

Eckbo, E. (1986). Valuation effects of corporate debt offerings. *Journal of Financial Economics*, 15, 119–151.

Ellman, M., Hurkens, J.P.M. (2017). A theory of crowdfunding a mechanism design approach with demand uncertainty and moral hazard: comment. http://www.iae.csic.es/investigatorsMaterial/a1812160140sp40258.pdf

Estrin, S., Gozman, D., & Khavul, S. (2018). The evolution and adoption of equity crowdfunding: entrepreneur and investor entry into a new market. *Small Business Economics*, 51(2), 425–439. DOI: 10.1007/s11187-018-0009-5.

Fairchild, R., Liu, W., & Yao, Y. (2017). An entrepreneur's choice of crowdfunding or venture capital financing: the effect of entrepreneurial overconfidence and CF-investors' passion. Working paper. SSRN: https://ssrn.com/abstract=2926980

Fama, E., French, K. (2002). Testing trade-off and pecking order predictions about dividends and debt. *Review of Financial Studies*, 15, 1–33.

Fossen, F., Sorgner, A. (2021). Digitalization of work and entry into entrepreneurship. *Journal of Business Research*, 125, issue C, 548–563.

Frank, M., Goyal, V. (2009) Capital structure decisions: which factors are reliably important? *Financial Management*, 38(1), 1–37.

Gabison, G. (2015). Understanding crowdfunding and its regulations. http://publications.jrc.ec.europa.eu/repository/bitstream/JRC92482/lbna26992enn.pdf

Gottlieb, D., Moreira, H. (2017). Simple contracts with adverse selection and moral hazard. The Wharton School Research Paper No. 78. SSRN: https://ssrn.com/abstract=2568271

Graham, J. R., Harvey, C. R. (2001). The theory and practice of corporate finance: evidence from the field. *Journal of Financial Economics*, 60, 187–243.

Hair, N., Wetsch, L.-R., Hull, C.-E., V. Perotti, & Hung, Yu-T. C. (2012). Market orientation in digital entrepreneurship: advantages and challenges in a Web 2.0 networked world. *International Journal of Innovation and Technology Management*, 9(6), 1250045.

Harris, M., Raviv, A. (1991). The theory of capital structure. *Journal of Finance*, 46(1), 297–356.

Hu, M., Li, X., & Shi, M. (2015). Product and pricing decisions in crowdfunding. *Home Marketing Science*, 34(3). https://doi.org/10.1287/mksc.2014.0900

Hull, C. E., Baroody, A. J., & Payne, B. R. (2007a). Supplementing the six facets model of technology management with a modified analytic hierarchic process: The effective evaluation of new technology prior to implementation. *International Journal of Innovation and Technology Management*, 4(1), 1–10.

Hull, C.-E., Hung, Yu-T. C., Hair, N., V. Perotti, & DeMartino, R. (2007b). Taking advantage of digital opportunities: a typology of digital entrepreneurship. *International Journal of Networking and Virtual Organisations*, 4(3), 290–303.

Innes, R. (1990). Limited liability and incentive contracting with ex-ante action choices. *Journal of Economic Theory*, 52, 45–67.

Innes, R. (1993). Financial contracting under risk neutrality, limited liability and ex ante asymmetric information. *Economica*, 60, 27–40.

Jaffee, D., Russell, T. (1976). Imperfect information, uncertainty, and credit rationing. *The Quarterly Journal of Economics*, 90(4), 651–666.

Jensen, M., Meckling, W. (1976). Theory of the firm: managerial behavior, agency costs and ownership structure. *Journal of Financial Economics*, 3, 305–360.

Keyhani, M., Neyshabouri, S. M., & Amereii, A. H. (2020). Crowdfunding Canadian theatre. *Journal of Entrepreneurship and Arts*, 9(1), 99–129.

Kleinert, S., Volkmann, C. & Grünhagen, M. (2020). Third-party signals in equity crowdfunding: the role of prior financing. *Small Business Economics*, 54, 341–365.

Koufopoulos, K., Kozhan, R., & Trigilia, G. (2019). Optimal security design under asymmetric information and profit manipulation. *The Review of Corporate Finance Studies*, 8(1), 146–173. https://doi.org/10.1093/rcfs/cfy008

Kozinets, R. V. (2002). The field behind the screen: Using netnography for marketing research in online communities. *Journal of Marketing Research*, 39(2), 61–72.

Leland, H.E., Pyle, D.H. (1977). Information asymmetries, financial structure, and financial intermediation. *Journal of Finance*, 32, 371–387.

Liao, A., Hull, C., & Murthy, R. (2013). The six facets model of digital business: a study in the digital business industry. *International Journal of Innovation and Technology Management*, 10(4), 1350019-1–1350019-24.

Malenko, A., Tsoy, A. (2018). Asymmetric information and security design under Knightian uncertainty. Working paper.

Miglo, A., Miglo, V. (2019). Market imperfections and crowdfunding. *Small Business Economics*, 53(1), 51–79. DOI: 10.1007/s11187-018-0037-1.

Miglo, A. (2020a). A note on issuing securities and opportunities for efficient signalling. Working paper. https://papers.ssrn.com/sol3/papers.cfm?abstract_id=686462

Miglo, A. (2020b). Theories of crowdfunding and token issues: a review. Working paper.

Miglo, A. (2021). Crowdfunding and bank financing: substitutes or complements? Working paper. https://ssrn.com/abstract=3980652

Mochkabadi, K., Volkmann, C. (2018). Equity crowdfunding: a systematic review of the literature. *Small Business Economics*. https://doi.org/10.1007/s11187-018-0081-x

Modigliani, F., Miller, M. (1958). The cost of capital, corporation finance and the theory of investment. *American Economic Review*, 48 (3), 261–297.

Mollick, E. R. (2014). The dynamics of crowdfunding: an exploratory study. *Journal of Business Venturing*, 29(1), 1–16. SSRN: https://ssrn.com/abstract=2088298.

Moritz, A., Block, J. (2014). Crowdfunding: a literature review and research directions. SSRN: http://ssrn.com/abstract=2554444 or http://dx.doi.org/10.2139/ssrn.2554444. 10.2139/ssrn.2554444

Myers, S. (1977). Determinants of corporate borrowing. *Journal of Financial Economics*, 5–2, 147–175.

Myers, S.C., Majluf, N. (1984). Corporate financing and investment decisions when firms have information that investors do not have. *Journal of Financial Economics*, 13, 187–222.

Nachman, D., Noe, T. (1994). Optimal design of securities under asymmetric information. *The Review of Financial Studies*, Spring 7(1), 1–44.

Navaretti, G. B., Calzolari, G., & Pozzolo, A. F. (2018). FinTech and banks: friends or foes? https://european-economy.eu/wp-content/uploads/2018/01/EE_2.2017-2.pdf

Paakkarinen, P. (2016). Success factors in reward based and equity based crowdfunding in Finland. Master's thesis.

Parker, S. (2002). Do banks ration credit to new enterprises? And should governments intervene? *Scottish Journal of Political Economy*, 49(2), 162–195.

Rajan, R., Zingales L. (1995). What do we know about capital structure: some evidence from international data. *Journal of Finance*, 50, 1421–1460.

Roma, P., Petruzzelli, A. M., & Perrone, G. (2017). From the crowd to the market: the role of reward-based crowdfunding performance in attracting professional investors. *Research Policy*, 46(9), 1606–1628. https://doi.org/10.1016/j.respol.2017.07.012

Roma, P., Gal-Or, E., & Chen, R. R. (2018). Reward-based crowdfunding campaigns: informational value and access to venture capital. *Information Systems Research*, 29, 679–697.

Ross, S. A. (1977). The determination of financial structure: the incentive signaling approach. *Bell Journal of Economics*, 8, 23–40.

Ryu, S., Kim, K., & Hahn, J. (2019). The effect of crowdfunding success on subsequent financing outcomes of start-ups. *Academy of Management Annual Meeting Proceedings.* DOI: 10.5465/AMBPP.2019.17486abstract.

Sadzius, L., Sadzius, T. (2017). Existing legal issues for crowdfunding regulation in European Union member states. *International Journal of Business, Humanities and Technology,* 7(3), 52–62.

Schwienbacher, A. (2018). Entrepreneurial risk-taking in crowdfunding campaigns. *Small Business Economics,* 51(4), 843–859.

Stiglitz, J. (1969). A re-examination of the Modigliani–Miller theorem. *American Economic Review,* 59(5), 784–793.

Stiglitz, J., Weiss, A. (1981). Credit rationing in markets with imperfect information. *American Economic Review,* 73, 93–109. https://www.jstor.org/stable/1802787

Strausz, R. (2017). Crowdfunding, demand uncertainty, and moral hazard – a mechanism design approach. *American Economic Review,* 107(6), 1430–1476.

Su, X., Zhang, L. (2017). A re-examination of credit rationing in the Stiglitz and Weiss model. *Journal of Money, Credit and Banking,* 49(5), 1059–1072.

Tajedin, H., Madhok, A. & Keyhani, M. (2019). A theory of digital firm-designed markets: defying knowledge constraints with crowds and market-places. *Strategy Science,* 4(4), 251–342.

Thakor, A. V. (2019). Fintech and banking: what do we know? *Journal of Financial Intermediation.* https://ssrn.com/abstract=3429223

Titman, S., Wessels, R. (1988). The determinants of capital structure choice, *Journal of Finance,* 43, 1–21.

Tuo, G., Feng, Y., Sarpong, S., & Wang, W. (2019). The second round resource acquisition of entrepreneurial crowdfunded ventures: the relevance of campaign and project implementation performance outcomes. *Entrepreneurship Research Journal.* https://doi.org/10.1515/erj-2018-0123

Vanacker, T., Vismara, S., & Walthoff-Borm, X. (2018), What happens after a crowdfunding campaign? In Hans Landstrom, Annaleena Parhankangas & Colin Mason (Eds.), *Handbook of Research on Crowdfunding* (Chapter 8). Research Handbooks in Business and Management series. Cheltenham, UK and Northampton, MA, USA: Edward Elgar Publishing.

Watson, H. (1984). Credit markets and borrower effort. *Southern Economic Journal,* 50, 802–813.

Xu, T. (2018). Learning from the crowd: the feedback value of crowdfunding. University of British Columbia working paper. https://privpapers.ssrn.com/sol3/papers.cfm?abstract

# 13. Blockchain economy: the challenges and opportunities of initial coin offerings

*Bennet Schierstedt, Vincent Göttel and Lisa Klever*

## 1.  INTRODUCTION

Blockchain technology has the potential to change the world, like personal computers and the internet have done before (Andreessen, 2014). The latter have paved the way for digitisation, which plays a major role in our everyday lives, affecting almost all industries, as well as governments, the public and private lives (Wright & De Filippi, 2015).

Digitisation describes the transformation of analogous data into digital formats and making them accessible for electronic data processing. This has led to all sorts of opportunities for business models, from faster communication to facilitated trading or increased efficiency in producing goods. Furthermore, issues like the treatment of big data, data privacy, data theft or surveillance by governments and big global companies have become important topics. They have given rise to heated discussions and public discontent. The lack of transparency about how data is used and distributed, whether it is by big players like Google or Facebook or institutions like banks or even governments, is a big point of critique (Olleros & Zhegu, 2016).

This is where blockchain technology comes into play. Such technology enables the creation of completely decentralised platforms, where data is stored in a safe, unchangeable manner and with full transparency. Thus, ownership and control over personal data is shifted away from centralised and powerful authorities back towards the users themselves. As a result, blockchain technology will lead to a decreasing need for intermediaries, whose only job is to provide trust. It will introduce a reorganisation of old structures in many areas, from economic to social, humanitarian, political and scientific matters (Swan, 2015; Wright & De Filippi, 2015).

When the first cryptocurrency, Bitcoin, was introduced in 2008, blockchain was merely the technology behind Bitcoin and an element of its business model, enabling the secure and safe use of bitcoins as a digital means of payment (Nakamoto, 2008). Even today, when people hear about blockchain, they might think about Bitcoin or cryptocurrencies, but as an investment to make money rather than as a new means of payment. As of July 2021, all cryptocurrencies account for a combined market capitalisation of over USD 1.3 trillion. Bitcoin accounts for around 47% of this market capitalisation, followed by Ethereum with 18% and Tether with 3% (Coinmarketcap, 2021a). These numbers already demonstrate the enormous relevance and potential of blockchain technology today.

Yet, most people neglect the immense potential and further opportunities for business model development provided by blockchain technology itself (Yli-Huumo, Ko, Choi, Park, & Smolander, 2016). This leads to the paradox that large parts of the public and entrepreneurs do still not know what blockchain technology actually is, while blockchain-based businesses form and grow rapidly all around the world. At the same time, the alleged opportunities, in combination with this high market capitalisation, create an immense hype to which many start-ups and investors have already fallen victim (Cheng, De Franco, Jiang, & Lin, 2019).

Given this hype, so far, there has also been a certain amount of research regarding blockchain from technological, economical, legal and social points of view. Yet, most studies have focused on corporations that are trying to implement blockchain in businesses they are already running. Yet, history has shown that revolutionary technologies and innovations are driven by agile, open and venturesome environments. Oftentimes, mature corporations cannot offer this environment due to long chains of command, immobile resources and rigid hierarchical structures (Freeman & Engel, 2007).

This is why start-ups will play a major role in promoting blockchain technology. Start-ups are often described as the drivers of breakthrough innovations and economic growth. Blockchain, in turn, offers them the opportunities and conditions for such advances (Freeman & Engel, 2007). Despite this great potential, blockchain-based start-ups have so far shown failure rates of around 46% in their first year (Morris, 2018), while failure rates for start-ups in general only reach up to 20% (Picken, 2017). This indicates the particularly challenging environment of blockchain-based start-ups. Therefore, research about the opportunities and challenges of blockchain applications for start-ups is needed to help practitioners prosper, but also to help academics familiarise themselves with this environment.

One prominent application of blockchain technology is the usage of initial coin offerings (ICO), which are also referred to as initial token sales, and are a form of financing, especially for young, blockchain-based companies. In this context, a start-up raises capital by issuing cryptographic, blockchain-based tokens. During a predetermined period of time, the tokens are exchanged for other cryptocurrencies (e.g. Bitcoin, Ether) or for traditional fiat currencies. As part of the ICO, these tokens are publicly sold to a crowd of investors (Fisch, 2019; Momtaz, 2020).

The number of ICOs and the volume of capital raised worldwide has been rapidly increasing over the last years. Between 2013 and 2016, only 69 ICOs with a total volume of USD 300 million had been performed (Diemers, Arslanian, McNamara, Dobrauz, & Wohlgemuth, 2018). According to the ICO rating platform ICObench, this number has increased by 5,728 realised ICO projects, with a total financing volume of more than USD 27 billion, since July 2021 (ICObench, 2021).

In light of the illustrated potential, this book chapter focuses on blockchain-based ICOs. The aim of the chapter is to assess ICOs based on the extant literature, and to highlight the various possible opportunities and associated challenges that should be considered by blockchain-based start-ups.

With this focus in mind, the chapter unfolds into the following parts: In section 2, we introduce blockchain technology as a driver of digital entrepreneurship in general. To do so, we give examples of how that technology can build the basis for innovating existing digital business models. Following up on this, section 3 focuses in more detail on blockchain technology as a particular opportunity for developing new digital business models. Focusing on the financing aspect of this development, we introduce blockchain-related business models based on ICOs and their particularities in section 3.1. We illustrate the specific opportunities and challenges of ICOs in section 3.2. Finally, in our discussion and conclusion in section 4, we balance the illustrated opportunities and challenges, and evaluate the meaning of ICOs for the future of the blockchain economy and digital entrepreneurship.

## 2.    BLOCKCHAIN TECHNOLOGY AS A DRIVER OF DIGITAL ENTREPRENEURSHIP

While it is rather indisputable that the digital economy is consistently on the rise, involving an increasing number of new business ideas and models, blockchain technology has the potential to pave the way for further major innovations. For instance, this appears to be particularly true in one prominent industry for digital entrepreneurs nowadays: the collaborative or sharing economy (Ertz & Boily, 2019).

When thinking of existing, well-known digital platforms of the sharing economy like Airbnb and Uber, but also a broad range of possible future opportunities (e.g. in the areas of peer-to-peer payment systems or digital rights management), scholars in the field have emphasised that blockchain technology is capable of facilitating decentralised sharing economy applications 'that enable individuals to create value by monetising their resources securely' (Ertz & Boily, 2019, p. 88; Baller, Dutta, & Lanvin, 2016; Huckle, Bhattacharya, White, & Beloff, 2016).

While the current companies in these markets act as central intermediaries between workers and customers, ensuring the relevant transactions and pocketing their respective fees for this service, blockchain technology may enable the exchange of services or products without an intermediary – that is, without a platform operated by organisations in the background. If this were to become the case, and the existing intermediaries could be replaced by blockchain technology, it would disrupt the current business models of the sharing economy and create the need for the existing platforms to be adapted and for new market entrants to be developed accordingly. Against this background, in line with Kollmann, Kleine-Stegemann, de Cruppe, & Then-Bergh (Chapter 3 in this handbook), who suggest that blockchain technology has the power to shape terms used in digital entrepreneurship research, other researchers even go as far as to speak of blockchain technology having 'the potential to create a 2.0 sharing economy' (Ertz & Boily, 2019, p. 89; Hawlitschek, Notheisen, & Teubner, 2018; Lundy, 2016).

The aforementioned adaptations the existing platforms would have to make, as well as the new ways of approaching the sharing economy for digital entrepreneurs based on blockchain technology, are certainly worth considering when thinking of the remarkable cost reductions which can result for organisations that use blockchain in general (Huckle & White, 2016; White, 2017). For instance, one could think that blockchain technology brought only disadvantages for the financial services sector since the former has the potential to render intermediaries like banks redundant. Yet, the possible blockchain applications in financial services are manifold, including the areas of securities and commodities exchanges, investment and wealth management as well as trade services and capital markets. With regard to such applications and the related possibility to decommission legacy systems and significantly reduce IT costs, a Santander FinTech study found that blockchain technology could reduce financial services infrastructure cost between $15 billion and $20 billion per year from 2017 to 2022 (PwC, 2017).

Another notable area in which opportunities and business models can result from blockchain technology can also be seen in certain forms of corporate digital entrepreneurship. The social network Facebook, for example, is somewhat outdated in the social media world when compared to TikTok, for instance. In addition to acquiring Instagram to counteract this development and conducting many other business activities, Facebook has developed its own global payment network based on blockchain technology, called Diem (formerly known as Libra) (Coinmarketcap, 2021b; Diem, 2021; Ertz & Boily, 2019).

The aforementioned examples have already shown how blockchain technology can build the basis for innovating existing digital business models in a variety of contexts. Following up on these elaborations, the next section focuses in more detail on blockchain technology as a particular opportunity for developing new digital business models.

## 3.   BLOCKCHAIN TECHNOLOGY AS AN OPPORTUNITY FOR THE DEVELOPMENT OF NEW DIGITAL BUSINESS MODELS

Blockchain technology was first publicly introduced by developers under the pseudonym 'Satoshi Nakamoto' in 2008, when introducing Bitcoin (Nakamoto, 2008). Bitcoin was the first digital cryptocurrency, and blockchain was the technological basis that made its application and business model possible in the first place.

Blockchain is an immutable, distributed-ledger technology for verifying and storing (transaction) data in a decentralised system that uses cryptography to confirm transactions and protect them from being changed or manipulated retrospectively. It consists of a peer-to-peer network in which every member, a so-called node, participates in verifying new data through a consensus algorithm. This stands in contrast to centralised systems in which one person or a small group has the power to make decisions, verify data and even change the transaction history in retrospect. In decentralised systems, the power is equally distributed between all members of the network. Furthermore, 'distributed' means that the whole blockchain, containing the complete transaction history, is stored on every node's computer. Thus, there is no central authority with the power to manipulate or influence transactions, which creates trust and makes the blockchain transparent, as well as fraud and censorship resistant (Drescher, 2017).

In general, there is not 'the one blockchain' or one blockchain business model, but numerous different blockchains with different purposes, currencies, levels of decentralisation and consensus mechanisms (Amsden & Schweizer, 2018). As already mentioned, the Bitcoin blockchain was the first to be introduced to the public in 2008. Bitcoin was developed as the first 'purely peer-to-peer version of electronic cash' that is completely decentralised and does not require trusted third parties like financial institutions to verify and secure online payments (Nakamoto, 2008). Hence, the blockchain was merely a means to enable this form of electronic cash.

The next blockchain to appear was the Ethereum blockchain with the cryptocurrency *ether*, introduced by its creator Vitalik Buterin in 2014 (Buterin, 2014). While Bitcoin is solely a digital currency and its essential function is to store money electronically or enable digital payments, Ethereum's features go beyond its use as a digital currency (Buterin, 2014). Specifically, Ethereum is primarily an open source platform for the development of decentralised applications that support smart contracts (Anwar, Anayat, Butt, Butt, & Saad, 2020). Smart contracts are digital programs or codes containing bi- or multilateral agreements about certain rights and obligations regarding (digital) assets. Stored in the Ethereum blockchain, the non-modifiable smart contracts automatically execute and enforce themselves if pre-defined conditions have been met (Crosby, Pattanayak, Verma, & Kalyanaraman, 2016; Lauslahti,

Mattila, & Seppala, 2017). While the maximum possible number of generated Bitcoins is limited to 21 million to protect them from inflation, the total coin supply of Ethereum has no upper limit. As of July 2021, there are around 18.7 million Bitcoins in circulation, while the total amount of Ethereum coins generated is already over 116.8 million (Coinmarketcap, 2021a). However, mining Ethereum coins is much more efficient than Bitcoins in terms of computing power and energy consumption (Anwar et al., 2020).

Nowadays, there are vast numbers of blockchains and related business models being deployed, but Bitcoin and Ethereum are still the most common ones. While Ethereum accounts for a market capitalisation of around USD 235.63 billion, Bitcoin reached a market capitalisation of around USD 604.20 billion as of July 2021. Tether follows with significantly less but still USD 61.83 billion. Figure 13.1 depicts the top 10 cryptocurrencies according to their market capitalisation as of July 2021.

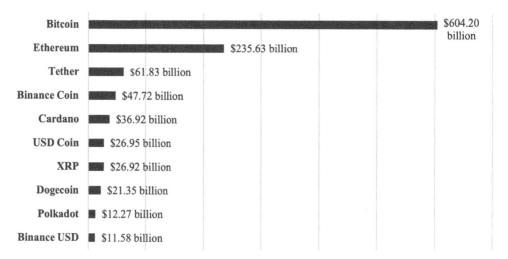

*Figure 13.1    Top 10 cryptocurrencies according to their total market capitalisation*

### 3.1    Blockchain-Related Business Models Based on Initial Coin Offerings and their Particularities

With regard to the financing component of a blockchain-related business model, an initial coin offering (ICO) represents a new and fairly unregulated form of crowd financing by selling tokens to a crowd of investors, especially for early-stage companies with limited access to classical public financing (Fisch, 2019). Specifically, an ICO enables external financing without an intermediary through smart contracts based on the novel blockchain technology (e.g. Fisch & Momtaz, 2020; Howell, Niessner, & Yermack, 2020). In the context of an ICO, underlying smart contracts can automatically execute and enforce themselves when specific, pre-defined and verifiable events have happened, or milestones have been met (Crosby et al., 2016; Lauslahti, Mattila, & Seppala, 2017). Therefore, the combination of the immutable blockchain and the functionality of smart contracts enables direct transactions between investors and token issuers without traditional intermediaries such as notaries, banks or venture capital funds (Momtaz, 2019).

ICOs have become one of the most prominent applications of blockchain technology in the real world so far, besides cryptocurrencies such as Bitcoin or Ether. The number of ICOs and the volume of capital raised by this method worldwide has been continuously increasing over the last years. During an ICO, a company creates digital units, called tokens (token-generating event), on a blockchain, and sells them in an unregulated, public process to private or institutional investors (token sale) (Cappa & Pinelli, 2020). In a token sale, the issuing company can then sell the new tokens in exchange for cryptocurrencies. Investors who want to buy tokens during an ICO have to acquire cryptocurrencies in exchange for fiat money first. These cryptocurrencies can then be sent to the address of the ICO on the blockchain, which triggers the underlying smart contract and thus the issuing of the tokens to the investors (Hahn, 2018).

The main difference between ICOs and traditional initial public offerings (IPO) on a stock exchange is that tokens do not (necessarily) represent equity shares or include shareholder rights for the investor. A company conducting an ICO has more freedom to decide what utilities and rights the token is representing (Hahn, 2018). While IPOs are highly regulated and require conformity with legal requirements for the issuing company, the legal situation for ICOs in their respective countries is often unclear and dependent on the particular token design.

Comparing ICOs with conventional crowdfunding platforms reveals parallels but also significant differences. For example, equity-based crowdfunding platforms (ECF) like Seedmatch also allow a crowd of unsophisticated investors to finance an entrepreneurial venture. However, in ICOs, funds are collected directly from investors without any kind of intermediaries (Chen, 2018). Another major difference is the liquidity of the acquired shares for investors. Unlike in traditional ECF, the tokens are usually fungible and can be traded on digital cryptocurrency exchanges immediately after an ICO has been conducted (Amsden & Schweizer, 2018).

Three broad types of tokens can be distinguished: security, pure currency and utility tokens. While security tokens offer ownership and voting rights similar to those attached to traditional stocks, or rights to participate in the performance of the underlying asset, pure currency tokens can be used as a cryptocurrency such as Bitcoin (Giudici & Adhami, 2019). In most countries, these types of tokens fall under strict regulations and taxation laws due to their financial security or asset character (Momtaz, Rennertseder, & Schröder, 2019). However, the most relevant type of tokens are utility tokens, which offer more flexible use and minimal legislative restrictions. Although they offer virtually no legal investor protection, they account for around 90% of all ICO funds raised so far (Momtaz et al., 2019). Utility tokens function like vouchers that can be redeemed for the ventures' goods and services, often with favourable conditions or exclusive license rights (Giudici & Adhami, 2019; Momtaz et al., 2019). Table 13.1 depicts an overview of three broad types of tokens (i.e., security, currency and utility).

In every ICO, there are certain stages and associated milestones that the issuing company should reach. At first, after deciding to perform an ICO, the start-up will create a so-called *whitepaper* to provide information for potential investors. The *whitepaper* is a voluntary disclosure of information that usually contains a description of the business idea and model, future milestones, the intended use of the raised capital, team members, and further information such as token characteristics and the maximum funding target. The maximum funding target is precisely defined as the *hard cap*, which is complemented by the *soft cap*, defining the minimum number of tokens that must be sold. If the soft cap is not reached during the ICO

*Table 13.1    Overview of token types*

|  | Security Token | Currency Token | Utility Token |
| --- | --- | --- | --- |
| **Short description** | Ownership and voting rights for an underlying asset, comparable to participation in ventures via stocks, bonds etc. | Decentralised currency for digital payments and money storage (e.g. Bitcoin, Tether) | Type of a digital voucher for a service or a product, comparable to reward-based crowdfunding on Kickstarter |
| **Legal situation** | Varies according to country, but usually regulated | Varies according to country, but usually regulated | Still unclear |
| **Investor protection** | Usually high | Usually high | Low to none |
| **Scam risk** | Low | Low | High |

period, funds are usually returned to the investors (Hahn & Naumann, 2014; Ofir & Sadeh, 2020).

Besides formulating the whitepaper, the technology setup and marketing are crucial pre-ICO activities to ensure a successful ICO. The start-up must prepare a digital wallet for the tokens to enable possible investors to participate in the ICO. In addition, the technological infrastructure has to be suitable for the very high transaction flows that can occur during an ICO. However, it is also crucial for the success of the ICO to attract and convince investors in the first place. Hence, one major task for the start-up is to communicate the upcoming ICO in the relevant forums, on websites and social media, in journals and at specialist events (Gusmann & Weisenberger, 2018; Ofir & Sadeh, 2020).

Once the ICO is ended, the post-ICO phase begins. Investors can now decide whether to spend their tokens to purchase goods or services on the new platform or to trade them in exchange for other tokens, coins or fiat money on secondary markets. The start-up, on the other hand, can now focus on and expand its business activities. At this stage, it is important for the start-up to cultivate good investor relations by informing investors about progress, possible setbacks and how the funds are used (Amsden & Schweizer, 2018). We visualise the aforementioned stages and milestones for companies implementing ICOs within a process model in Figure 13.2.

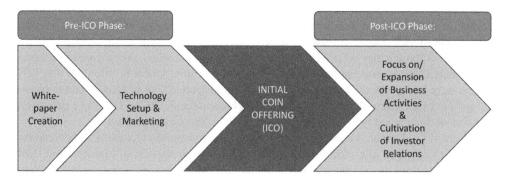

*Figure 13.2    Stages and milestones for companies' implementation of ICOs*

## 3.2 Challenges and Opportunities of Initial Coin Offerings (ICO)

**Challenges**

Now that the basic principles of ICOs are clear, it is evident that the events can offer start-ups great opportunities, but also significant challenges in terms of funding and business model development. Estimations indicate an overall success rate of around 35% to 50% (Fenu, Marchesi, Marchesi, & Tonelli, 2018; Ventures, 2018).

There are multiple possible reasons for an ICO to fail. A major challenge for start-ups that want to conduct ICOs is the unclear legal situation. The applicable laws and regulations are highly dependent on the country that the ICO is hosted in, the specific kinds of tokens and the rights associated with these. All this leads to high levels of uncertainty and risk for start-ups, as well as for the ICO participants and all other stakeholders (Hahn, 2018).

In some countries, like China or South Korea, ICOs have been completely banned since September 2017 (Adhami, Giudici, & Martinazzi, 2018). In the USA and Europe, ICOs are generally allowed but subject to regulations concerning the way they are conducted. For example, the US Securities and Exchange Commission (SEC) declared tokens a security (Howell et al., 2020). Start-ups are therefore obligated to register with the SEC, and are subject to heavy scrutiny and duties. On the one hand, this makes it very complicated for a start-up to conduct an ICO in the USA. On the other hand, even investors and other participants would be at risk of being applicable to SEC sanctions if they participated in unregistered ICOs (SEC, 2021). As these examples suggest, the legal situation for ICOs varies significantly in each case and each country, but does always require effort and scrutiny, and brings levels of uncertainty.

One of the reasons public authorities all over the world are paying such particular attention when it comes to ICOs is that there have been many cases of scams and fraudulent activities in connection with ICOs in the past. Consequently, regulatory bodies like the SEC warn against investing in ICOs on their websites (SEC, 2021). This has led to low trust in ICOs among members of the public and potential investors, which represents a big challenge for start-ups (Fisch & Momtaz, 2020; Hahn, 2018).

In some cases, for example, whitepapers did not include information about the identity, contact address or legal entity of the company conducting the ICO (Howell et al., 2020). Hence, some of the companies did not even exist, and absconded with the funds after their ICOs ended. This happened at the beginning of 2018, when the Vietnamese start-up Pincoin took off with more than USD 660 million after its ICO (Biggs, 2018). In other cases, the funds from the ICO are not invested in the development of the business and product, but embezzled little by little by the managers. ICOs are prone to scams like this, since they usually lack control, information, membership or voting rights. Furthermore, whitepapers are not subject to official audit and verification, which intensifies information asymmetries between capital seekers and investors and therefore the risk of fraudulent actions (Giudici & Adhami, 2019; Zetzsche, Buckley, Arner, & Fohr, 2019). When tokens become worthless, there is more or less no legal protection for investors (Adhami et al., 2018).

Another challenge for the start-up lies in the public disclosure of large parts of the business model, concept and idea, and further information in the whitepaper (Hahn, 2018). Although the token issuer himself can determine the amount of information being published, at the same time there is an immanent pressure to disclose as much information as possible to increase the credibility perceived by potential investors. However, especially for a start-up with innovative products and ideas in early development phases, this creates a high risk of imitation by competitors.

Besides the problem of the anonymity of the token issuer and the accompanying risk of fraudulent actions, there is the problem of investor anonymity for the start-up as well. Since tokens are bought with cryptocurrencies, token buyers can stay anonymous, which could imply the risk of criminal activities like money laundering or terrorist financing. Therefore, public authorities like the European Union (EU) have adopted regulations that are summarised under the umbrella term *know-your-customer requirements* (KYC), which obligate companies to identify their customers precisely before doing business with them (Ostern & Riedel, 2020). In the US, for example, start-ups conducting ICOs should be sensitive to the *Bank Secrecy Act* (BSA), which make them subject to BSA regulation as money transmitters. This would require procedures and internal controls by the start-up to prevent money laundering or terrorist financing by their investors (Nolan, Dartley, Baker, ReVeal, & Rinearson, 2018). Of course, these regulations are legitimate requirements to avoid such criminal activities, but implementing appropriate procedures and internal controls that meet the respective legal requirements also represents further responsibilities and challenges for a start-up.

Besides the external factors that can pose a challenge for a start-up, the marketing and promotion of the ICO is a big challenge and crucial for its success as well. It includes choosing the right channel for promotion, the right timing and the right pricing, as well as suitable and effective advertising campaigns. In comparison to crowdfunding campaigns, which are launched on specific and official crowdfunding-websites like Kickstarter.com (Miglo, Chapter 12 in this handbook), ICOs are usually hosted on companies' own websites (Amsden & Schweizer, 2018).

There are platforms like ICOwatch-list.com or ICOtracker.net informing potential investors about current and future ICOs, but the marketing effort required from the token issuer to reach possible investors is still comparatively high. Hence, the challenge for the start-up is to gain as much positive attention as possible on various channels.

Another major challenge for a start-up during an ICO and afterwards is to provide security and avoid cyberattacks. While regulations such as the *Know-Your-Customer-Requirements* (KYC) in the EU or the *Bank Secrecy Act* (BSA) in the US aim to stop criminal individuals from using the ICO in their interest, it is important for the company to stop hackers from attacking the ICO and stealing funds or tokens. According to the study of EY (2017), examining 372 global projects running ICOs, up to 10% of all funds raised in ICOs are stolen by hackers. Hackers often benefit from the lack of central authorities, incompetent participants, the informational clutter and the irreversibility of transactions. Popular targets for such cyberattacks are unsecure or forged wallets, private keys or coding errors. A very prominent example was the attack during the ICO of a company called The DAO, when hackers stole more than USD 50 million out of USD 140 million total funds raised, due to security flaws and a mistake in the code (Adhami et al., 2018). Therefore, it is of great importance and a major challenge for the start-up to protect itself and the investors from theft and hacker attacks. In addition to the loss of funds, such attacks also put the start-up's reputation with all investors at stake.

Another challenge concerns the possibility that ICOs can trigger big hypes among investors. Oftentimes though, this leads to valuations that are solely based on hype and 'fear of missing-out,' which consequently evokes high volatility and high pressure on the company (Roosenboom, van der Kolk, & de Jong, 2020). As the value of a token is highly dependent on the public perception, small faults or setbacks after the ICO can have a vast impact on the start-up's situation. Moreover, this volatility, in combination with the possibility to trade tokens on exchanges, might attract more speculators who want to trade the tokens right away. Hence, there might be fewer investors who are actually intending to use the tokens on the platform, which is usually a desired side effect of an ICO.

Even though there are multiple challenges for a start-up when conducting an ICO, the rapidly increasing number of ICOs indicates the existence of important opportunities and advantages as well. A selection of these, both financial and non-financial, will be analysed in the following section.

**Opportunities**

A very evident opportunity for a start-up is the acquisition of funds in very early development stages of its business and the development of its products or services, when traditional financing sources like debt financing, equity procurement or even venture capital are less likely to be available (Hahn & Naumann, 2014). The study of EY (2017) observed that over 90% of all companies conducting ICOs do not have a running business yet, and 84% of those are in fact still at the idea stage. They also found that the majority of ICO projects and business models are expected to be launched not later than one year after the ICO, emphasising the growth and development potential for start-ups through early ICO financing.

In terms of the funding volume, ICOs offer enormous potential, and investment sums can be tremendous. For example, the biggest ICOs so far have been conducted by start-ups named Telegram and EOS, raising more than USD 1.7 billion and USD 4.1 billion respectively (Diemers et al., 2018).

Other opportunities for start-ups are the saved costs for transactions and intermediaries and the increased speed of transactions which required the involvement of intermediaries before. Both advantages arise from the fact that ICOs are based on smart contracts, which execute themselves automatically when a certain criterion is fulfilled. During an ICO, this means that the tokens are automatically sent to investors as soon as their investments have arrived at the issuing company. Thus, investors typically send the investment sum directly to the start-up and the immutable smart contract on the underlying blockchain guarantees that investors will receive the tokens in exchange. Hence, intermediaries who ensure that tokens are given out after receiving the investment are not necessary anymore. Consequently, the process is sped up for both, the investor and the token issuer, and transaction costs like underwriting and disclosure fees can be omitted (Adhami et al., 2018; Crosby et al., 2016; Howell et al., 2020).

Besides the financial opportunities of ICOs, there are also non-financial reasons that play a major role for start-ups and should not be neglected. First, ICOs enable start-ups to reach a larger group of investors on a global scale. Business angels, on the other hand, often prefer geographical proximity and crowdfunding can be restricted to certain countries, which reduces the possibilities for start-ups to find investors (Amsden & Schweizer, 2018; Hahn & Naumann, 2014).

Another advantage is the so-called tokenisation of goods and services. This means that a start-up can avoid selling equity or convertible bonds, which is common practice for seed- and A-round financing. Through this, the founders can keep their authority and decision-making power on one hand, and avoid committing to liabilities like long-term debts on the other hand (Hahn, 2018). Instead, the start-up can design the token as coupons that are usable within the new platform or for the new product or service. Theoretically, it is also possible to turn non-fungible assets into tokens. They would then be divided and sold as sub-tokens, each rep-

*Table 13.2      Challenges and opportunities of ICOs*

| Challenges | Opportunities |
|---|---|
| Unclear Legal Situation and Government Regulations | Acquisition of Funds in Early Development Stages |
| Scams/Fraudulent Activities and Warnings of Regulatory Bodies | Enormous Funding Volume Potential |
| Public Disclosure of Business Information and Risk of Imitation by Competitors | Saved Costs for Transactions and Intermediaries |
| Investor Anonymity and Risk of Criminal Activities | Increased Speed of Transactions |
| Marketing and Promotion | Reaching a Larger Group of Investors on a Global Scale |
| Provision of Security and Prevention of Cyberattacks | Tokenisation of Goods and Services |
| Hype-based Valuation and High Volatility | Gauging Product/Market fit and Market Value |
| | Network Effect for Start-ups Using Platform Business Models |

resenting a part of the particular asset. For example, this could be applied to a work of art, real estate or the like. This would make such projects accessible for small and private investors, as it also splits the responsibilities for the maintenance and care of the assets between multiple investors (Hahn & Naumann, 2014).

The fact that utility tokens are usable on the new platform or for the new product or service also includes further opportunities for a start-up. The company has the possibility to gauge the product/market fit of its product, because investors in utility tokens usually tend to only invest in projects when they are actually interested in the projects and in using the tokens on the developing platform or for the new product or service. If too few investors participate in the ICO and the soft cap is not reached, this can be an indicator that the platform or product is abdicable (Hahn, 2018; Howell et al., 2020). Moreover, as in an IPO, the company has the chance to gauge its market value through an ICO, because that value is related to the amount of capital raised (Subrahmanyam & Titman, 1999).

The number of active investors plays another crucial role for a start-up that is developing a new platform, as it positively affects the network effect. Network effects describe the (positive) externality of an increasing number of platform users on the platform value for further customers. The more individuals are participating, the exponentially more attractive it becomes for other individuals to join the network as well. Furthermore, Valente (1996) found that once a critical mass of participants is reached, an exponential increase in participants is likely to follow. This effect raised increasing interest through the emergence of the internet, playing a crucial role for all kinds of platforms: social media platforms like Facebook, sharing economy platforms like Uber, e-commerce platforms like eBay and many more (Evans & Schmalensee, 2010).

In this respect, the network effect is an important opportunity for blockchain-related start-ups using a platform business model as well. Besides raising capital with an ICO, start-ups are simultaneously attracting a crowd of future customers and users, which lays the foundation for reaching the critical mass. This facilitates future business operations and the attraction of further customers once the platform is launched. Table 13.2 summarises the above illustrated challenges and opportunities of ICOs.

## 4.    DISCUSSION AND CONCLUSION

The starting point of this chapter was the paradox between the rapidly growing number of blockchain-related ventures all around the world and a still improvable understanding of blockchain technology and its application in large parts of society, also among entrepreneurs. To help create a better comprehension and emphasise its potential, we initially introduced blockchain technology as a driver of digital entrepreneurship by giving concrete, cutting-edge examples of its potential to revolutionise entire industries (e.g. the sharing and payment industries).

In a next step, we then looked at how the blockchain technology particularly offers opportunities for developing new digital business models and, thereby, focused on the financial component of business model development (Wirtz, Pistoia, Ullrich, & Göttel, 2016). In doing so, we illustrated the possibility to finance blockchain-related start-ups based on ICOs and highlighted the particularities which entrepreneurs would have to consider when choosing this path. As with any innovative but rather unexplored entrepreneurial approach, it is advisable to consider not only the related opportunities, but also potential challenges. Therefore, we also provided a closer look at these two sides of the coin for ICOs.

To summarise this look at the respective challenges and opportunities and to balance which side appears to prevail for entrepreneurs trying to pursue ICOs, initially we can state that there are indeed some serious challenges with which entrepreneurs should deal cautiously when deciding for an ICO. Yet, there are also certain strategies which digital entrepreneurs can apply to cope with those challenges.

For instance, when reconsidering the challenge to create trust and to convince possible investors of a start-up's credibility, there are several possibilities to reduce information asymmetries between capital seekers and investors. In general, no specific type of enterprise is officially prescribed for the implementation of an ICO, which means that this financing instrument is also open to a single private individual. Nevertheless, it is expedient to act as a registered company, providing a signal of security for investors. Besides that, it is beneficial for a start-up to hire personnel with credible track records and reputations to lower the perceived risk of fraudulent actions and thus increase the success prospect for its ICO.

There is also the challenge for start-ups to gain as much positive attention as possible for their ICOs. To reach this goal, the entrepreneurs should be present on various channels like ICO listings, forums, Reddit, Telegram, GitHub, Twitter, start-up events and the like. The start-ups should communicate actively about recent events, operations and future plans and maintain generated business contacts, which requires them to have well-organised marketing departments and make sustained efforts (Howell et al., 2020). A frequently used instrument associated with this issue is the pre-sale of tokens. Tokens are sold to selected investors, often venture capital investors or other institutional investors, before the actual ICO. The start-ups can use the early funds to finance the aforementioned necessary marketing activities. Moreover, early investors with good track records and high reputation can also help to enhance the reputation of the ICO. The downside for the issuers in this case is the lower price that they usually get for their pre-sold tokens, because the investors must be compensated for taking a higher risk (Howell et al., 2020).

In addition, while there is of course always the challenge or risk of having an ICO attacked by hackers, entrepreneurs can prevent such incidents. To do so, it is of highest importance to pay special attention to ensuring the security of the code and the system before the launch of the ICO, in order to create trust among potential investors, but also to continuously monitoring the defence against cyberattacks.

Overall, one has to acknowledge that there are indeed some challenges which entrepreneurs should not neglect when deciding for an ICO, but also actionable strategies to cope with those challenges. Hence, the promising opportunities of ICOs for start-ups, like the access to financing in very early stages, the saved costs for transactions and the increased speed of transactions which required the involvement of intermediaries before, appear to prevail. Thus, ICOs offer attractive ways for digital entrepreneurs to create and develop business models within the blockchain economy. This is particularly the case for blockchain-related start-ups, since they already possess the respective technological infrastructure to conduct ICOs. New ventures which have not used the blockchain technology before should approach an ICO much more cautiously, if at all, since this would entail much more preparation and effort and, thus, pose the question if the ICO would still be worthwhile overall.

# REFERENCES

Adhami, S., Giudici, G., & Martinazzi, S. (2018). Why do businesses go crypto? An empirical analysis of initial coin offerings. *Journal of Economics and Business, 100*, 64–75.

Amsden, R., & Schweizer, D. (2018). Are blockchain crowdsales the new 'gold rush'? Success determinants of initial coin offerings. *SSRN Electronic Journal*. https://doi.org/10.2139/ssrn.3163849.

Andreessen, M. (2014). Why bitcoin matters. *New York Times*. Retrieved from https://dealbook.nytimes.com/2014/01/21/why-bitcoin-matters/

Anwar, S., Anayat, S., Butt, S., Butt, S., & Saad, M. (2020). Generation analysis of blockchain technology: Bitcoin and Ethereum. *International Journal of Information Engineering & Electronic Business, 12*(4), 30–39.

Baller, S., Dutta, S., & Lanvin, B. (2016). *The Global Information Technology Report 2016 – Innovating in the Digital Economy*. Geneva, Switzerland: World Economic Forum.

Biggs, J. (2018). Exit scammers run off with $660 million in ICO earnings. Retrieved from https://techcrunch.com/2018/04/13/exit-scammers-run-off-with-660-million-in-ico-earnings/

Buterin, V. (2014). A next-generation smart contract and decentralized application platform. *White paper, 3*(37), 1–36.

Cappa, F., & Pinelli, M. (2020). Collecting money through blockchain technologies: First insights on the determinants of the return on Initial Coin Offerings. *Information Technology for Development*, 1–18.

Chen, Y. (2018). Blockchain tokens and the potential democratization of entrepreneurship and innovation. *Business Horizons, 61*(4), 567–575.

Cheng, S. F., De Franco, G., Jiang, H., & Lin, P. (2019). Riding the blockchain mania: Public firms' speculative 8-k disclosures. *Management Science, 65*(12), 5901–5913.

Coinmarketcap. (2021a). Retrieved from https://coinmarketcap.com/charts/

Coinmarketcap. (2021b). Retrieved from https://coinmarketcap.com/de/currencies/facebook-libra/

Crosby, M., Pattanayak, P., Verma, S., & Kalyanaraman, V. (2016). Blockchain technology: Beyond bitcoin. *Applied Innovation, 2*(6–10), 71.

Diem. (2021). Retrieved from https://www.diem.com/en-us/

Diemers, D., Arslanian, H., McNamara, G., Dobrauz, G., & Wohlgemuth, L. (2018). Initial coin offerings: A strategic perspective. *Strategy&/PwC*, June, 1–10.

Drescher, D. (2017). *Blockchain Basics: A non-technical introduction in 25 steps* (1st ed.). Frankfurt am Main: Apress.

Ertz, M., & Boily, É. (2019). The rise of the digital economy: Thoughts on blockchain technology and cryptocurrencies for the collaborative economy. *International Journal of Innovation Studies, 3*(4), 84–93.

Evans, D. S., & Schmalensee, R. (2010). Failure to launch: Critical mass in platform businesses. *Review of Network Economics, 9*(4), 1–26.

EY. (2017). *EY research: initial coin offerings (ICOs)*. Retrieved from https://www.ey.com/Publication/vwLUAssets/ey-research-initial-coin-offerings-icos/$File/ey-research-initial-coin-offerings-icos.pdf

Fenu, G., Marchesi, L., Marchesi, M., & Tonelli, R. (2018). *The ICO phenomenon and its relationships with ethereum smart contract environment*. Paper presented at the 2018 International Workshop on Blockchain Oriented Software Engineering (IWBOSE).

Fisch, C. (2019). Initial coin offerings (ICOs) to finance new ventures. *Journal of Business Venturing, 34*(1), 1–22.

Fisch, C., & Momtaz, P. P. (2020). Institutional investors and post-ICO performance: An empirical analysis of investor returns in initial coin offerings (ICOs). *Journal of Corporate Finance, 64*, 101679.

Freeman, J., & Engel, J. S. (2007). Models of innovation: Startups and mature corporations. *California Management Review, 50*(1), 94–119.

Giudici, G., & Adhami, S. (2019). The impact of governance signals on ICO fundraising success. *Journal of Industrial and Business Economics, 46*(2), 283–312.

Gusmann, A., & Weisenberger, F. (2018). Initial coin offerings – Tokens im kontext der shared economy. Retrieved from https://www.bearingpoint.com/files/Initial_Coin_Offerings.pdf?download=0&itemId=517162

Hahn, C. (2018). *Finanzierung von Start-up-Unternehmen: Praxisbuch für erfolgreiche Gründer: Finanzierung, Besteuerung, Investor Relations*: Dordrecht: Springer.

Hahn, C., & Naumann, D. (2014). *Finanzierung und Besteuerung von Start-Up-Unternehmen*. Dordrecht: Springer.

Hawlitschek, F., Notheisen, B., & Teubner, T. (2018). The limits of trust-free systems: A literature review on blockchain technology and trust in the sharing economy. *Electronic Commerce Research and Applications, 29*, 50–63.

Howell, S. T., Niessner, M., & Yermack, D. (2020). Initial coin offerings: Financing growth with cryptocurrency token sales. *The Review of Financial Studies, 33*(9), 3925–3974.

Huckle, S., Bhattacharya, R., White, M., & Beloff, N. (2016). Internet of things, blockchain and shared economy applications. *Procedia Computer Science, 98*, 461–466.

Huckle, S., & White, M. (2016). Socialism and the blockchain. *Future Internet, 8*(4), 49.

ICObench. (2021). Retrieved from www.icobench.com

Lauslahti, K., Mattila, J., & Seppala, T. (2017). Smart contracts–How will blockchain technology affect contractual practices? *ETLA Reports, 68*, 1–30.

Lundy, L. (2016). Blockchain and the sharing economy 2.0: The real potential of blockchain for developers. Retrieved from https://www.ibm.com/developerworks/library/iot-blockchain-sharing-economy/index.html

Momtaz, P. P. (2019). Token sales and initial coin offerings: introduction. *The Journal of Alternative Investments, 21*(4), 7-12.

Momtaz, P. P. (2020). Initial coin offerings. *PloS one, 15*(5), e0233018.

Momtaz, P. P., Rennertseder, K., & Schröder, H. (2019). Token offerings: A revolution in corporate finance? https://dx.doi.org/10.2139/ssrn.33446964

Morris, D. (2018). Nearly half of 2017's cryptocurrency 'ICO'projects have already died. Fortune. Retrieved from https://fortune.com/2018/02/25/cryptocurrency-ico-collapse/

Nakamoto, S. (2008). A peer-to-peer electronic cash system. Retrieved from https://bitcoin.org/bitcoin.pdf

Nolan, A. R., Dartley, E. T., Baker, M. B., ReVeal, J., & Rinearson, J. E. (2018). Initial coin offerings: key US legal considerations for ICO investors and sponsors. *Journal of Investment Compliance, 19*(1), 1–9.

Ofir, M., & Sadeh, I. (2020). ICO vs. IPO: Empirical findings, information asymmetry, and the appropriate regulatory framework. *Vanderbilt Journal of Transnational Law, 53*, 525.

Olleros, F. X., & Zhegu, M. (2016). Digital transformations: an introduction. In F.X. Olleros, & M. Zhegu (Eds.), *Research Handbook on Digital Transformations* (pp. 1–19). Cheltenham, UK and Northampton, MA, USA: Edward Elgar Publishing.

Ostern, N. K., & Riedel, J. (2020). Know-your-customer (KYC) requirements for initial coin offerings. *Business & Information Systems Engineering*, 1–17.

Picken, J. C. (2017). From startup to scalable enterprise: Laying the foundation. *Business Horizons, 60*(5), 587–595.

PwC (2017). Blockchain: A new tool to cut costs. Retrieved from https://www.pwc.com/m1/en/media-centre/2017/articles/max-di-gregorio-me-insurance-review-feb2017.pdf

Roosenboom, P., van der Kolk, T., & de Jong, A. (2020). What determines success in initial coin offerings? *Venture Capital, 22*(2), 161–183.

SEC. (2021). Retrieved from https://www.sec.gov/ICO

Subrahmanyam, A., & Titman, S. (1999). The going-public decision and the development of financial markets. *The Journal of Finance, 54*(3), 1045–1082.

Swan, M. (2015). *Blockchain: Blueprint for a new economy.* O'Reilly Media, Inc.

Valente, T. W. (1996). Network models of the diffusion of innovations. *Computational & Mathematical Organization Theory, 2*(2), 163–164.

Ventures, F. (2018). *TokenData report (2018). The State of the Token Market: A year in review and an outlook for 2018.* Retrieved from https://static1.squarespace.com/static/5a19eca6c027d8615635f801/ t/5a73697bc8302551711523ca/1517513088503/The+State+of+the+Token+Market+Final2.pdf

White, G. R. (2017). Future applications of blockchain in business and management: A Delphi study. *Strategic Change, 26*(5), 439–451.

Wirtz, B. W., Pistoia, A., Ullrich, S., & Göttel, V. (2016). Business models: Origin, development and future research perspectives. *Long Range Planning, 49*(1), 36–54.

Wright, A., & De Filippi, P. (2015). Decentralized blockchain technology and the rise of lex cryptographia. https://dx.doi.org/10.2139/ssrn.2580664

Yli-Huumo, J., Ko, D., Choi, S., Park, S., & Smolander, K. (2016). Where is current research on blockchain technology? A systematic review. *PloS one, 11*(10), e0163477.

Zetzsche, D. A., Buckley, R. P., Arner, D. W., & Fohr, L. (2019). The ICO Gold Rush: It's a scam, it's a bubble, it's a super challenge for regulators. *Harvard International Law Journal, 60*, 267.

# PART VII

# DIGITAL ENTREPRENEURSHIP AND SOCIAL ISSUES

# 14. Agentifying the body algorithmic: digital entrepreneurial agency and accountability gaps

*Angela Martinez Dy*

## INTRODUCTION

This chapter explores the implications of the distribution of entrepreneurial agency across a key set of non-human actors of particular importance to the contemporary digital era: algorithms, and the systems of artificial intelligence (SAI) they drive, the agential activities of which are still under-theorised (Andersen, Lindberg, Lindgren, & Selander, 2016; Klinger & Svensson, 2018). Recent efforts have been made to unify debates in the field of entrepreneurship studies with more detailed attention to the construct of entrepreneurial agency (McMullen, Ingram, & Adams, 2020). McMullen et al. conceptualise entrepreneurial agents as those who 'exercise the *power of transformative capacity*', defined as 'the capability to intervene in worldly events to produce definite outcomes by getting circumstances and others to comply with one's wants' (McMullen et al., 2020, p. 4, original emphasis). However, the implications for understanding entrepreneurial agency from socio-technical, or techno-cultural, perspectives are less clear. Ontological insights suggest that the agency of non-human actors is also vitally important to entrepreneurial processes (Korsgaard, 2011). While algorithmic agency is ontologically dissimilar to human agency, it is not difficult to recognise that, following McMullen et al.'s (2020) definition, SAIs also have the capability to intervene in worldly events and produce definite outcomes – and, if enabled to do so, enforce compliance with the algorithmic equivalent of will.

In this chapter, I conceptualise the accountability gaps that arise as algorithmic agents are given rights without commensurate obligations. I employ a novel transdisciplinary theoretical approach that blends critical anti-racist sociology (Bhattacharyya, 2018), abolitionist feminist science and technology studies (Benjamin, 2019b, 2019a), intersectional feminism (Collins, 2019; Martinez Dy, Martin, & Marlow, 2014) and realist methodology (Archer, 2007; Eckstrom, 1992; Elder-Vass, 2012, 2017; Lawson, 2019) to develop a critique of algorithmic agency in the context of digital entrepreneurial activity. As such, the chapter makes a timely and unique contribution to the emerging digital entrepreneurship literature. It proceeds as follows: first, it expands the notion of entrepreneurial agency in the digital era to include non-human actors, such as SAIs. I consider these algorithmic agents, exerting a type of non-human, synthetic agency with collective effects that are currently emergent. Second, it conceptualises and examines the implications of what I call 'digital entrepreneurial accountability gaps', and theorises, through the construction of four Weberian ideal types (algorithmic agents as oracle, trader, manager, and enforcer), how such gaps may arise as entrepreneurial agency is increasingly digitally distributed. Finally, it considers what might be done to close accountability gaps and reduce potential for emergent harm.

# ENTREPRENEURIAL AGENCY IN A DIGITAL ERA

The field of entrepreneurship studies has continually grappled with questions surrounding the scope and ontology of the phenomenon, spurring debates which have shaped perspectives, boundaries and definitions (Alvarez, Barney, McBride, & Wuebker, 2017; Gartner, 1990, 1989; Garud & Giuliani, 2013; Mole & Mole, 2010; Ramoglou & Tsang, 2016; Sarasvathy, 2001; Shane & Venkataraman, 2000). Academic debate has moved on from early identification of entrepreneurial individuals and personalities, assuming agential meritocracy (Kirzner, 1973; McClelland, 1961; Schumpeter, 2010) to a more nuanced perspective upon not only entrepreneurial actors, but also entrepreneurial behaviours, action, activities, projects, processes and practices (Hjorth, Holt, & Steyaert, 2015; Kautonen, van Gelderen, & Fink, 2015; Kitching & Rouse, 2017; Thompson, Verduijn, & Gartner, 2020; Watson, 2013a). These are now understood to be enacted in a wider context of families, households, teams, places and ecosystems (Cantino, Devalle, Cortese, Ricciardi, & Longo, 2017; Carter, Kuhl, Marlow, & Mwaura, 2017; Matlay & Westhead, 2005; Sussan & Acs, 2017), and shaped by enduring social structures such as gender, race, caste and class (Chrispal, Bapuji, & Zietsma, 2020; Forson, 2013; Martinez Dy & Agwunobi, 2019; Welter, Brush, & de Bruin, 2013). For their projects to succeed, entrepreneurial actors require access to relevant knowledge, networks and resources (Martinez Dy, 2020; Pittaway & Thorpe, 2012; Politis, 2005) through and with which they engage in processes of entrepreneurial agency, learning, working, and mobilising resources towards entrepreneurial ends.

Concepts of agency have been present, even if implicitly, in established literature. For example, Kirzner's notion of 'entrepreneurial alertness' (Kirzner, 1979; Minniti, 2004), and the related concept of opportunity identification (Ucbasaran, Westhead, & Wright, 2009) centre on the individual's capacity to identify, select and pursue an entrepreneurial action pathway. Psychological perspectives on entrepreneurship were typically used to understand the agential aspects of the phenomenon, while economic perspectives attended to the structural (Watson, 2009). Yet although the psychological literature offers interesting insight into entrepreneurial orientation, personality traits and cognition (Baron, 1998; Frese & Gielnik, 2014), results have, on the whole, been critiqued as inconclusive (Jones & Spicer, 2009). A diverse strand of literature has attended closely to entrepreneurship's agential aspects from perspectives beyond the psychological, including economic (Block & Koellinger, 2009), sociological (Martinez Dy & Agwunobi, 2019; Watson, 2013a, 2013b) and ontological perspectives (Korsgaard, 2011; Martinez Dy, 2020). Typically, the agency of entrepreneurial actors tends to be privileged over structure, or the two are conflated (Blundel, 2007; Martinez Dy, 2020). Moreover, the methodological individualism present in such approaches has been critiqued, with calls for further exploration of the ontology of entrepreneurship at the level of practice. This practice-based literature aims to draw such concepts as 'searching' and 'perceiving' down from highly abstract levels of analysis to more tangible everyday activities, such as 'meeting, talking, selling, form-filling and number crunching' (Thompson et al., 2020, p. 247). As such, scholars at the forefront of the field are concerned with unpacking and elaborating highly abstract conceptualisations of entrepreneurial agency, and destabilising assumptions of individualism in the process.

The relationship between entrepreneurship and technology was at one point central to explorations of entrepreneurial agency. The most prominent example is Schumpeter's (2010) notion of 'creative destruction' in which technological innovation is entrepreneurially exploited to create fundamental changes in market conditions and relations. In the contemporary period, how entrepreneurial activity is shaped by technology, and vice versa, has again come to the fore: in the age of digital entrepreneurship, the high-growth, high-value 'billion dollar digital start-ups' (Sahut, Iandoli, & Teulon, 2019, p. 1159) are seen as the epitome of such activity. The definition of digital entrepreneurship (DE) used herein builds on existing definitions (Davidson & Vaast, 2010; Nambisan, 2016) to include not only these so-called 'unicorns' (Brown & Wiles, 2015; McNeill, 2016), but also a wider variety of digital entrepreneurial activities. I conceptualise DE as a socially embedded process by which digital artefacts, platforms and architecture are used to pursue novel sources of value creation through profitable exchange (Martinez Dy, 2022).

Continuous advancements in information and computing technologies (ICTs) have enabled emergent digital affordances, and concomitant entrepreneurial capabilities and capacities, which are still underexplored. Importantly, 'the digital' has impacted the full spectrum of entrepreneurial activity – from providing new platforms and channels for trading existing products, to enabling the development of novel products, services and business models. In this late capitalist era, entrepreneurialism is a taken-for-granted part of the political and cultural economy, celebrated as both an economic driver and personal empowerment pathway (Bhattacharyya, 2018; Calás, Smircich, & Bourne, 2009; Du Gay, 2004; Duffy, 2017). The assumed enabling potential of digital technologies for entrepreneurial activity, especially by marginalised or socially disadvantaged actors, dominated the early conceptual conversation (Fairlie, 2006; Matlay & Westhead, 2005; Thompson Jackson, 2009). More recent empirical work has, in contrast, illustrated the nuanced ways in which entrepreneurial agency may not only be enabled by digital platform usage (McAdam, 2020), but also potentially constrained by enduring social structures and the agential limitations they present (Duffy & Pruchniewska, 2017; Martinez Dy, Marlow, & Martin, 2017; Martinez Dy, Martin, & Marlow, 2018)

Contemporary DE theory notes that the digital has introduced more porous and fluid boundaries to entrepreneurial outcomes, processes, and agency. Nambisan (2016) argues that DE tends to exhibit both less bounded entrepreneurial outcomes – for example features, scope and market reach of an offering – and, significantly for my argument here, a less predefined locus of entrepreneurial agency. Digital transformation of entrepreneurial activity tends to break down the boundaries between entrepreneurial phases, introduce greater unpredictability and non-linearity into processes, alter the nature and degree of openness, and produce new affordances and sources of generativity (Nambisan, 2016; Nambisan, Wright, & Feldman, 2019). The changing locus of agency, which is increasingly distributed, is well illustrated in the enabling of the participation of 'the crowd', or myriad human agents who are able to engage in some aspect of wider entrepreneurial processes. These range from individuals taking on micro-tasks in Amazon's Mechanical Turk online labour market (Ellmer, 2015; Ross & Tomlinson, 2010) to crowdsourced open innovation projects such as those on the platform InnoCentive.com where expert hobby scientists and engineers bid for the opportunity to develop solutions for companies ('InnoCentive takes the incentive: How open innovation boosts R&D', 2005). Often geographically distant from the founding individual or team, these many individuals lend their agency to the entrepreneurial projects of others. From project initiators to task completers, they work along the spectrum of bidding for, designing and executing entrepreneurial projects. A similar issue arises when confronted with the distributed nature of a 'lean' gig economy start-up such as Uber or Deliveroo, in which drivers were not originally conceptualised as employees but rather as self-employed independent contractors. They thus occupy the lower-potential value, lower-prestige end of a spectrum of entrepreneurial activity (Martinez Dy, 2022), with a variety of disruptive organisational formations produced in the move to so-called 'Uberization' (Davis & Sinha, 2021; Faraj & Pachidi, 2021). Independent contractors as entrepreneurial actors are not usually comparable with founders of new digital start-ups, and furthermore, the classification of drivers as self-employed has recently been successfully contested in court (Russon, 2021). Nonetheless, in these settings, it is still assumed that such self-employment offers more agentic power to determine the quantity and frequency of one's labour (Kitching & Marlow, 2013; Martinez Dy et al., 2017), which is a key aspect of human entrepreneurial agency in the digital era.

Yet what remains under-theorised in these scenarios is the fact that an increasing proportion of this distributed digital entrepreneurial agency is enacted not by human actors, but by non-human machines, powered both by human input and what I term *algorithmic agents*. A combination of computing hardware and software enables the execution of sophisticated, complex, and dynamic algorithms, which produce outputs used in increasingly autonomous machines and predictive applications. Systems of Artificial Intelligence (SAI) have been named but not fully ontologised in previous work (Čerka, Grigienė, & Sirbikytė, 2017). They are here conceived of as the input-to-output totality of an artificial intelligence system, including the hardware, software, data inputs, calculating algorithms, and predictive applications and autonomous machines by which their outputs are delivered to human users (Figure 14.1). In this model, algorithmic agents are defined to be the specific programmes used to calculate the outputs of the SAI, which require for their functioning both hardware and software, or machinic and algorithmic components. Take the example of ride-hailing and delivery services: while drivers and users operate at different application faces, it is algorithmic agents producing the day-to-day customer service and management functions with which customers and contractors interact, and which mete out worker penalty and reward based on tracked performance indicators. Socio-technical ontological studies have long pointed out the relevance of non-human actors to worldly events (Elder-Vass, 2017; Latour, 1987). In light of McMullen et al.'s definition of entrepreneurial agents, in a digital age, algorithmic agents as well as humans arguably possess the power of entrepreneurial transformative capacity (McMullen et al., 2020, p. 4), although it varies much in kind and degree. Nevertheless, the impact of such algorithmic agency must form part of the ongoing debate within digital entrepreneurship studies.

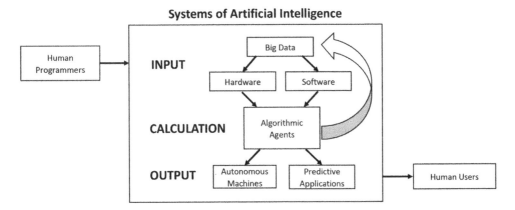

*Figure 14.1    SAI and algorithmic agent model*

The creation and monetisation of digital properties through software and application development is fundamental to the digital entrepreneurial landscape. Emanating from the design thinking methodology that underpins the popular lean start-up model (Balocco, Cavallo, Ghezzi, & Berbegal-Mirabent, 2019; Standing & Mattsson, 2018), a common theme in digital start-up culture is that entrepreneurial opportunities are premised on the 'solving' of particular user problems. Yet, the relationships of rentiership driving the monetisation of many of these so-called solutions often go unrecognised. Rentiership exists when users or clients pay rent for access to an asset owned by another, including digital platforms and properties, where rent is 'income derived from the ownership, possession or control of scarce assets under conditions of limited or no competition' (Christophers, 2019, p. 5; see also Scrambler, 2021). Weber posits that the entrepreneurial function emerges from the relationship between wealth, property, and capital; transferring property between spheres of use – from 'wealth' to 'capital' – is the mechanism that enables entrepreneurship within the propertied class (1968; as cited by Kalber, 2005, p. 152). This is illuminating; however, a slight amendment to this classic sociological theory is necessary when evaluating physical and digital properties. Unlike arable land and valuable buildings, digital properties are not valuable in and of themselves, but are monetised through rentiership to users or advertisers in order to put them to use as capital. To understand this, one needs only look at the myriad digital platform start-ups that failed to attract users to reach a stage known as 'traction' (Zaheer, Breyer, Dumay, & Enjeti, 2018). Such rentier business models, a prominent feature of the contemporary digital economy, often require entrepreneurial founders to develop or employ SAIs to create value and generate profit. Thus, access to software-as-a-service – that is, the use of a particular digital property rented out to users through various business models such as pay-per-use or subscription, and/or to commercial advertisers through the selling of ad space – is a particular type of digital rentiership. Other digital entrepreneurial models rely on algorithmic agents they may or may not control to grow their user base, market share, and revenue. Digital entrepreneurial agency is therefore clearly distributed across, and enacted by, human and algorithmic agents in varying combinations.

SAI comprise the core of the contemporary digital economy, an age in which enormous amounts of data already exist, with more being generated at ever increasing rates – a phenomenon known as 'Big Data' (Feldman, Kenney, & Lissoni, 2015). The amount of data 'created, captured, copied and consumed' globally is expected to reach 74 zettabytes in 2021 (Holst, 2021). This vast amount of data can be fed into SAIs to produce a vast range of outputs, which can either inform human decision making, or the SAI itself can be empowered to use the outputs to make decisions and take action. Each algorithmic agent makes an incomprehensible number of micro-decisions that, overall, produce macro-level processes about key aspects of day-to-day business; of this, scholars of digital and high-tech entrepreneurship should take note. For example, SAI employed in social media and matchmaking platform businesses use big data to make fundamental sales and marketing decisions, such as defining and refining user profiles, categorising and classifying users, and selecting what content or messaging to serve. In other use cases, SAI play a central role in decision making for loan application assessments, semi-autonomous vehicles, and the delegative management of delivery and rideshare platforms (Andersen et al., 2016; Newlands, 2020; Webster, Svalastog, & Allgaier, 2020). Algorithmic agents are continually increasing in both sophistication and complexity, with new breakthroughs occurring regularly in both self-teaching ability and competitiveness with human intelligence (Sample, 2017). Makridakis suggests that in the next two decades, such artificial intelligence may consistently surpass the intellectual skills of human intelligence, posing serious competition to human labour and potentially even 'raising doubt over the end of human supremacy' (2017, p. 47). As such, algorithmic agency can no longer be sidelined in the discussion of digital entrepreneurship.

## ACCOUNTABILITY GAPS IN THE BODY ALGORITHMIC

Central to philosophical discussions of human volition, the notions of will and agency are relevant for algorithms as well. In its simplest form, an algorithm is a calculated programme for action. Algorithms can be usefully defined as socio-material computational processes comprised of three stages – input, calculation and output (Klinger & Svensson, 2018). Humans have relied on analogue algorithms for millennia, using them, for example, in cooking, mathematics, engineering, and navigation. However, contemporary understandings of algorithms as a means by which machines may be made 'intelligent' are a product of the 20th century (Čerka et al., 2017). While there is still significant debate around the definition of artificial intelligence (AI), the term describes a wide array of processes designed to generate a set of intellectual skills within machines, such as 'the ability to understand, learn and make autonomous decisions independent of the will of the developer or user' (Čerka et al., 2017, p. 687). Čerka et al. stress it is the *independence* of SAI that set them apart from other kinds of computer algorithms (2017). They suggest that because SAI engage in learning, analysis, and solution generation 'independently of the will of their developer (programmer)' that 'they are able to operate autonomously rather than automatically' (2017, p. 686).

The notion of agency, as it relates to humans, is composed of a variety of interrelated biological, psychological and sociological elements, such as experience, reflexivity, intention, will, capability and action. While ontologically inseparable in human agents, these dimensions can be analytically abstracted into cognition (processes related to calculation, such as reflexivity and capability) and conation (processes related to intention and will). Algorithmic cognition is a frequently explored topic, but algorithmic conation less so. Cognition, and thus autonomous functioning, within SAIs is often enabled through a method called machine learning. In this method, which includes deep learning and neural networks, statistical techniques are employed to train algorithms in data gathering, decision making, and learning processes (Rahwan, 2018). Yet, despite contemporary efforts to develop more transparent and explainable SAI, how the algorithms arrive at their conclusions is still poorly understood. The workings of such processes can be extremely opaque to programmers and data scientists, and are often referred to as a 'black box' (Andersen et al., 2016; The Lancet Respiratory Medicine, 2018). Thus, if SAI are acting independently of a developers' will, it is reasonable to ask whether there is a will attributable to the system itself, and if so, whether the SAI or the overarching algorithm powering it can constitute an agentic subject.

Critical realist philosopher and sociologist Dave Elder-Vass defines an agentic subject as 'a person who has the capacity to experience, to reflect on his or her actions and circumstances, to make decisions and thus, influenced by a social context, to act with some degree of autonomy' (Elder-Vass, 2012, p. 184). Similarly, critical realist philosopher and sociologist Margaret Archer (2007) conceives of human agency as characterised by reflexive deliberation about a constellation of concerns. SAI are composed of what would normally be conceived of as inert matter, such as plastic, metal, and minerals, through which electricity is conducted and resisted. Yet they possess the causal powers of processing information in such a way that produces the ability to deliberate, make decisions and act upon them – albeit not in a way identical to, or equatable with, that of humans. In other words, the capacities programmed into SAI that enable autonomy endow them with a type of machinic, or algorithmic agency, and a set of related causal powers. As SAIs increase in complexity and capability, the definition of agentic subjects as solely limited to human persons may need to be challenged. A broader definition could explicitly include those entities built of both machinic and algorithmic components, enabling a kind of cognition and conation analogous to our own. Adapting and applying notions of subjecthood across the human/non-human divide for the purposes of developing social and in particular legal understandings is a process not wholly unfamiliar; for example, corporations are considered legal persons (Lawson, 2019), a concept to which we later return. *Agents*, in this expanded definition, are causally powerful entities possessing *agency*, or the non-trivial capacity to cognitively evaluate circumstances and act according to volition. For these reasons, SAI are herein argued to be agentic subjects, motivated by algorithmic agents; they are thus held to exhibit *algorithmic agency*.

Not only is this algorithmic agency causally powerful, but it can be so in ways that are not necessarily beneficial or even harmful. Critical race and technoscience theorist Ruha Benjamin presents a tradition of co-production, in which it is assumed that technoscience and society are co-produced and thus shape one another (Benjamin, 2019a). She outlines the notion of discriminatory design, 'a conceptual lens to investigate how social biases get coded, not only in laws and policies, but in many different objects and tools that we use in everyday life' (Benjamin, 2019a, p. 5). Taking this view, we can see that like any technology (Wajcman, 1991, 2010), SAI and the algorithmic agents they empower are far from socially neutral. The outputs of contemporary SAI reflect the biases not only of tech founders and developers, who are typically men from dominant racial and class or caste backgrounds (Alfrey & Twine, 2017; Braguinsky, Klepper, & Ohyama, 2012), but also of the input data from which they learn. For example, algorithms employed in popular online translation systems are already exhibiting gender bias (Benjamin, 2019b; Caliskan, Bryson, & Narayanan, 2017). Widespread reliance upon such algorithmic decision-making has been found to reproduce and exacerbate the intersectional systems of oppression that structure society at large, such as anti-Blackness, sexism, and punitive over-policing of the poor and working classes (Benjamin, 2019b; Eubanks, 2018; Noble, 2018). Data scientists warn of further concerns arising as AI is given increased agency in society (Benjamin, 2019b; Caliskan et al., 2017). Clearly, then, the growing significance of SAIs for society, business and entrepreneurial activity raises new and important questions about their governance and accountability that have not yet meaningfully entered the academic conversation on digital entrepreneurship.

Realist philosopher and economist Tony Lawson (2019) offers a social ontology that supports a clearer conceptualisation of algorithmic agents centred upon his articulation of the relationships between social positioning, rights and obligations. He argues that all forms of social being rely on the establishment of social positions, attached to which are specific rights and obligations: notably, such positions exist not only for humans, but also for inanimate objects, or artefacts, that humans use to meet their needs and expand their capabilities, the causal powers of which 'tend, thereby, to be referred to as the positioned object's functions… as a component of the system' (2019, pp. 65–66). Currently, our conceptualisation of the *positions* of algorithmic agents in society lags behind the rapidly increasing ubiquity of their use. While our understanding of the potential causal powers of SAIs is increasing, the same attention has not been given to developing a common understanding of how they should be positioned, and thus the rights and obligations that should be bestowed upon them. As a result, these are still extremely vague. In general, debate around algorithmic ubiquity tends to be polarised into existential fears (Olhede & Wolfe, 2018) or uncritical promotionalism (HMG, 2016) – what Black feminist technology scholar Safiya Noble calls 'big-data optimism' (Noble, 2018, p. 169). Digital entrepreneurship theory and practice tends towards the latter, bolstered by underpinning techno-deterministic ideologies – in which technology, rather than society or even their interplay, is the primary driver of change (Benjamin, 2019b; Wajcman, 2010). In the context of late capitalism, this attitude encourages humans, and the organisations they design and drive, to participate competitively in the advancement of technological capacities, disregarding any potential negative consequences.

Building on Lawson's argument, when the rights assigned to agents exceed the scope of their obligations, I argue that what emerges is an accountability gap, in which it becomes difficult to meaningfully hold agents accountable for their actions. This may be because it is difficult to identify the responsible party, because responsibility is easily evaded, or because no effective mechanisms exist to incur responsibility. Furthermore, with the techno-optimistic orientation of contemporary entrepreneurial culture, the rights of algorithmic agents currently far outstrip their obligations. Therefore, as technical capabilities advance apace, it grows ever more urgent to ensure clarity on the positions and roles of SAI in society. In particular, the facility to hold them and their owners accountable for harm should be central to whatever frameworks of rights and obligations are adopted. Yet where the culpability should lie is itself a matter of debate (Reitinger, 2015). Although there are ways to utilise existing legal and policy frameworks to hold algorithms accountable, this is not yet common practice. Kroll et al. (2017) argue that progress in our collective communication and understanding of partial information regarding algorithmic decision-making is a precondition for utilising existing systems of governance to do so: 'Lawmakers and policymakers should remember that it is possible to make an algorithm accountable without the evaluator having full access to the algorithm' (2017, pp. 704–705). To advance theory on such positioning, it would be helpful to establish some common conceptual ground with which we can, as a species, begin to explore the various positions that algorithms occupy, and the associated rights and obligations generally associated with each.

Humans are increasingly agentifying algorithms through collective socio-cultural, technical, political and economic processes, to produce an emerging algorithmic leviathan – one that constitutes, rather than a body politic, a *body algorithmic*. Despite the novelty of this phenomenon, resulting from the greater affordances of digital technologies to more widely distribute entrepreneurial agency, a parallel can be drawn with a fundamental figure from Western political philosophy: Hobbes' Leviathan (König, 2020). Hobbes posited that society was created with the generation of an artificial person, in the form of the state – the Leviathan – the 'soul' of which, at the time of his writing, was the sovereign. The Leviathan was understood to produce and rule society through collective engagement in a social contract whereby individual members of society consolidate some aspects of their distributed agency, and thus their power, and renounce these to the sovereign. The state, then, can be understood as a human-generated, non-human entity with significant agentic powers. Yet today, in the era of digital entrepreneurship, what appears to be emerging is an ever-increasing distribution of entrepreneurial agency and causal power across not only other humans, but also algorithmic agents. König (2020) suggests what we may be witnessing is the gradual shaping of a new type of social contract in which humans renounce some aspects of our power not to the sovereign, but to algorithms.

It is important to note that both in this critique and at this stage of technological development, entrepreneurial algorithmic agents are still not on par with human founders – SAIs do not currently possess the ability, although it is arguably within the scope of a possible future, to envision and generate a business based on the identification of a potential entrepreneurial project. Instead, they are typically enlisted in service of an entrepreneurial founder or innovative team. Many contemporary digital start-ups or spin-offs are founded upon the development of a platform that employs an SAI with a specific remit. Thus algorithmic agents are argued to occupy a unique space as both entrepreneurial *resource* and *commodity*. SAIs working simultaneously produce emergent outcomes that are the result of the collective algorithmic agency of a vast number of agents. This body algorithmic manifests and operates in a number of modes, explored here through the notion of the Weberian ideal type, a heuristic research device that outlines general 'complexes of meanings and motives' (Eckstrom, 1992, p. 114) and illuminates causal relationships. Four types – algorithmic agent as oracle, trader, manager and enforcer – are here described, and the accountability gaps they open critiqued.

**Oracle**

The primary function of many algorithmic agents is that of prediction. Algorithmic agents serve an oracle-like function in a number of different use cases; for example, predicting the reliability of borrowers, as in the case of Wonga.com (Andersen et al., 2016), the likelihood of committing crimes (Benjamin, 2019b), or identifying eligibility for welfare benefits (Eubanks, 2018). However, treating algorithms like oracles presumes that the data used to inform such predictions is itself trustworthy. On the contrary, critical scholars of technology have exposed the encoded biases within such data, revealing the ways in which such predictive algorithmic agency is likely to compound and cement social disadvantage and inequality (Benjamin, 2019a, 2019b; Eubanks, 2018; Noble, 2018). As Benjamin puts it: 'Algorithmic neutrality reproduces algorithmically sustained discrimination' (2019b, p. 143). She describes an example in which Amazon realised an AI recruiting tool, built primarily on men's resumes and ranking applicants for their company fit, was discriminating against women (2019b). Women's profiles were downgraded unfairly and applicants excluded from the recruitment process prior to the bias being discovered; although Amazon eventually scrapped the tool, the damage was done (Dastin, 2018). Algorithmic oracles of this nature are certain to form the commodities upon which many new entrepreneurial projects and firms will be based. This opens a significant accountability gap regarding who is to be held responsible. In this example, when qualified candidates are struck from the list, who should be culpable: the technologists programming the SAI, the salespeople and managers responsible for the product's distribution and use, the selection panel that has used the SAI to make decisions while not critically assessing the outcomes it produced, or perhaps all of these? Accountability here becomes hard to imagine: recompense to those qualified women who were turned down is extremely unlikely, and yet predictive algorithmic agency played a significant role in denying them employment opportunities.

## Trader

Trading, or the ability to identify and act on opportunities to combine and/or mobilise resources to produce new means-ends relationships, is a classical entrepreneurial function (Jackson, Joshi, & Erhardt, 2003; Kirzner, 1979; Politis, 2005; Shane & Venkataraman, 2000). Algorithmic agents have been employed since the 1990s to automatically execute profitable trades in financial markets; they are widely used, and in 2011 were handling 50–60 per cent of all stocks traded in the US and EU (Chaboud, Chiquoine, Hjalmarsson, & Vega, 2014; Nuti, Mirghaemi, Treleaven, & Yingsaeree, 2011), a figure that will only have increased in the past decade. Much of this trading is based on the fine-grained analysis of market trends, the results of which are used to generate automated trading signals, entry and exit strategies (Nuti et al., 2011). As such, they work well in relatively stable trading conditions, but can perform poorly in response to sudden changes, as in the case of 2021's Gamestop stock price being driven up by users on Reddit's WallStreetBets forum (Kahn, 2021). Chaboud et al. (2014) highlight that algorithmic traders have been blamed for a number of trading disturbances in the equity market, noting that while they clearly offer potential advantages over human traders, they can also produce adverse effects. The accountability gap that arises here is wide – as adverse effects could impact an entire market, yet the activity that generated them was widely distributed across many algorithmic agents, working for many different firms. In such cases it is difficult to assess to whom, if any, responsibility for negative impacts can be assigned.

## Manager

The managerial function is another classical manifestation of entrepreneurial agency (Van Praag, 1999). Algorithmic agents have in many cases already replaced human managers, for example in the ride-hailing and delivery applications ubiquitous within the gig economy. In many of these cases, the algorithmic agent metes out incentives and consequences to produce specific behaviours in the human workers. In heavily service-based economies, the workers choose these modes of income generation simply because there are few, if any, better options, yet the companies claim that they are empowered entrepreneurial agents. Drucilla Cornell has said that the gig economy is characterised by the 'displacement of exploitation creating a confused ideology', and that what we are in fact witnessing are new forms of primitive accumulation (Aultman, Brown, Crandall, McMahon & Padilioni, 2021; Gordon & Cornell, 2021). The increasing levels and new techniques of exploitation enabled by algorithmic managers form an ongoing area of concern for scholars of work and labour (Davis & Sinha, 2021; Estévez, 2020; Fleming, 2017). Despite obvious relevance to the shifting of everyday working norms, companies using such algorithms have done little to acknowledge or address the technology's role in, and thus the organisation's responsibility for, the intensification and/or degeneration of working conditions. Negative effects are typically disguised in the managerial, neoliberal language of efficiency and choice, overlooking sectoral trends that leave gig employees who switch companies in search of better conditions frequently exchanging like-for-like.

## Enforcer

Algorithmic agents powering SAIs that drive autonomous machines, otherwise known as intelligent robots, are already being used to carry out the operations of the military and prison industrial complexes. These are algorithmic enforcers: patrolling streets and borders, and hunting down human targets, for example through drone strikes (Columbia Law School Human Rights Clinic, 2012). A newer recent example is Boston Dynamics' Spot, a robot 'dog' whose capabilities have recently been enhanced with AI (Caroll, 2020) and which has recently been seen patrolling New York City streets controlled by NYPD officers. Algorithmic enforcers are set to power a wave of innovations in border patrol, securitisation and other expansions of the carceral state (Benjamin, 2019a; Bhattacharyya, 2018). However, algorithmic enforcement is likely to follow the pattern of unaccountability that has characterised the use of such technology by the state for decades. As such, an accountability gap for the harm done to individuals yawns between the government agencies, including police and private police employed by the state, carrying out such activities, and the entrepreneurial firms that develop and sell such technologies to them.

## TOWARDS AN ACCOUNTABLE ALGORITHMIC FUTURE

I posit a potential inverse relationship between certain aspects of algorithmic and human agency: the more autonomy algorithmic agents are given, the less able humans will be – especially historically marginalised, under-resourced and vulnerable populations – to resist the impacts of their decisions. While I do not envision a Matrix-style 'rise of the machines', attention must nonetheless be paid to the wider impacts of accelerating the agentification of the algorithmic leviathan, with explicit focus upon the effect of SAIs on not only the futures of the entrepreneurial agents who leverage them to solve problems and create wealth, and the members of society who use them, but on those people and environments likely to experience intensified harm and suffering as a result. I propose a reconfigured critical perspective on the distributed agency of digital entrepreneurial activity, one that asks challenging questions, such as: Who will take responsibility for the so-called 'negative externalities' produced by biased algorithms working for unaccountable corporations? When algorithmic agency already operates beyond the realm of human comprehension, and algorithmic outputs are increasingly being used to train humans rather than vice versa (Eubanks, Noble, Boyce, Waterhouse-Cooper, & Martinez Dy, 2020), who is in control? And finally, how might scholars, policymakers, and the public mitigate against the extension of the historical trend of unaccountable corporate agents to other non-human entities such as SAIs, particularly in light of the fact that it is digital entrepreneurial companies driving both the growth and agentification of the algorithmic leviathan?

Regarding the latter question, some scholars and practitioners identify moves in this direction; for example, the code of conduct released by the UK National Health Service (NHS), encompassing ten principles and five commitments intended to 'ensure data-driven technologies are harnessed in a safe, evidence-based, and transparent way' (The Lancet Respiratory Medicine, 2018, p. 801). But more than transparency (Goodman, 2016), guidance or even regulation will be needed to resist and move away from the path dependency resulting from a set of tendencies and causal chains centuries old, supported by the durability of multiple social structures of domination and oppression. Critical scholars of technoscience are exploring what this path-breaking could entail. Rahwan (2018) proposes an algorithmic social contract, or pact between human stakeholders that is programmed, debugged and maintained. While algorithmic cognition may be much more capacious than its human counterpart, its synthetic nature means that there are at least three aspects it lacks in comparison – first, human instinct;

second, our ability to learn from the emotional and relational aspects of our experiences, and third, the intuition that ties these together, all of which contribute substantially to our ability to evaluate and make decisions. Therefore, ensuring that humans are empowered to question, challenge, interrupt, amend and end algorithmically agential processes and outcomes is crucial. Furthermore, *which* humans are involved in designing and training the algorithms is also relevant: currently, there is little, if any, meaningful co-creation with the marginalised groups most vulnerable to the specific SAIs' potentially harmful effects. Fairly compensated collaboration and co-design between not only technologists and users, but crucially, those affected by SAI decisions, might form the basis of an effective and ethical algorithmic social contract. Further aims and principles that may guide such a contract could include: increasing understanding of algorithmic decisions and keeping humans in the loop (London School of Economics Media Policy Project, 2016; Rahwan, 2018; Voosen, 2017), increasing regulation by developing, using or tailoring existing legal and policy frameworks to hold humans and organisations accountable for algorithmic actions (Kroll et al., 2017; Noble, 2018, pp. 132–133), including and improving failsafe mechanisms, and continuously critically evaluating and widening data sources to reduce bias and increase accuracy prior to deployment.

In this algorithmic social contract model, the body politic strives to maintain control over the body algorithmic. But as long as the capitalist imperative is a primary driver, the continued dominance of rent-seeking, carceral and extractivist ideologies over innovation are likely to impede this strategy. Instead, Benjamin suggests a revolutionary reconfiguration of our socio-technical imaginary, one that not only challenges discriminatory design, but also collectively imagines and enacts alternatives to what she calls the 'techno quo': 'business as usual when it comes to technoscience' (2019a, pp. 5, 12). Along with other abolitionist feminists, she argues that only by imagining alternative potential futures can we develop and harness the collective agency and resources required to power ourselves towards them. To prepare us for such futures, we must imagine and design the positions, rights and obligations of algorithmic agents, and complement this with the development of appropriate, effective and dynamic models of incentives and consequences for individuals and companies producing and employing potentially harmful SAIs, and for SAIs themselves that cause harm. In fact, this work is past due.

## CONCLUSIONS

In general, entrepreneurship literature is functionalist in orientation, following the disciplinary adherence to a capitalist imperative, whether implicit or explicit (Marlow, 2020). At the same time, digital entrepreneurship literature, like much other work in the technology field, is characterised by an implicit technological determinism (Benjamin, 2019a; Wajcman, 2010). The awareness of such limitations within the mainstream literature suggests an alternative approach is needed: one that not only highlights the socio-technical and economic benefits of digital entrepreneurship, but also challenges unquestioning positive beliefs in entrepreneurship as the driver of economic activity, and technological advancements as signals of social progress. In the vein of critical entrepreneurship studies, this work immanently critiques some of the standard assumptions made about entrepreneurial agency, and focuses in on the possibilities of digital entrepreneurship's negative effects, as well as widens the lens to increase the visibility of other manifestations and outcomes of the phenomenon. Drawing on feminist science and technology (STS) studies, in particular the cyber and technofeminist perspectives in which society and digital technologies are assumed to co-constitute each other, producing both positive and negative effects (Russell, 2020; Wajcman, 2004), the critique presented here seeks to slow us down and pull digital entrepreneurship scholarship away from deterministic views of technology and uncritical tech solutionism (Benjamin, 2019b). For, as feminist STS scholar Haraway (2016) admonishes, in order to remedy the current global crises and catastrophes in which we currently find ourselves, we must begin by thinking deeply and comprehensively about the nature of the problems we face.

This exploration of algorithmic agency as key to digital entrepreneurial activity highlights the need for both socio-technical critique and social scope to make new, less harmful action pathways for algorithmic agency possible. As this kind of digital entrepreneurial agency proliferates, new collective algorithmic agencies emerge, increasing accountability challenges and decreasing agential possibilities for many historically marginalised and disadvantaged humans, while increasing the wealth, power and control of a very few. Human entrepreneurial agency is typically associated with path creation rather than path dependence (Garud, Kumaraswamy, & Karnøe, 2010), and social transformation rather than reproduction (McMullen et al., 2020). Yet, as the distribution of digital entrepreneurial agency moves increasingly towards SAIs and algorithmic agents, we may end up mindlessly reproducing the most destructive aspects of society, and engineering socio-technical systems in which no one is answerable for their harmful effects.

## ACKNOWLEDGEMENTS

Many thanks to the editors, anonymous reviewers, and Dave Elder-Vass for constructive and insightful commentary on a previous draft of this chapter. Thank you to Thomas Higgins for valuable conversations illuminating important differences between human and algorithmic cognition. Any omissions or errors are my own.

## REFERENCES

Alfrey, L., & Twine, F. W. (2017). Gender-Fluid Geek Girls: Negotiating Inequality Regimes in the Tech Industry. *Gender and Society*, *31*(1), 28–50. https://doi.org/10.1177/0891243216680590
Alvarez, S. A., Barney, J. B., McBride, R., & Wuebker, R. (2017). On Opportunities: Philosophical and Empirical Implications. *Academy of Management Review*, *42*(4), 726–730. https://doi.org/10.5465/amr.2016.0035
Andersen, J. V., Lindberg, A., Lindgren, R., & Selander, L. (2016). Algorithmic Agency in Information Systems: Research Opportunities for Data Analytics of Digital Traces. *Proceedings of the Annual Hawaii International Conference on System Sciences*, *2016-March*, 4597–4605. https://doi.org/10.1109/HICSS.2016.571
Archer, M. (2007). *Making our Way Through the World*. Cambridge: Cambridge University Press.
Aultman, B., Brown, R., Crandall, E., McMahon, J., & Padilioni, J. (2021, April 15). Interview: Jane Anna Gordon and Drucilla Cornell on Always Already Podcast. Epistemic Unruliness 36. *Always Already Podcast*. Retrieved from https://alwaysalreadypodcast.wordpress.com/2021/04/15/creolizing-rosa/
Balocco, R., Cavallo, A., Ghezzi, A., & Berbegal-Mirabent, J. (2019). Lean Business Models Change Process in Digital Entrepreneurship. *Business Process Management Journal*, *25*(7). https://doi.org/10.1108/BPMJ-07-2018-0194

Baron, R. A. (1998). Cognitive Mechanisms in Entrepreneurship: Why and When Entrepreneurs Think Differently Than Other People. *Journal of Business Venturing*, *13*(4), 275–294. https://doi.org/10.1016/S0883-9026(97)00031-1

Benjamin, R. (2019a). *Captivating Technology: Race, Carceral Technoscience, and Liberatory Imagination in Everyday Life* (R. Benjamin, Ed.). Durham, NC: Duke University Press.

Benjamin, R. (2019b). *Race After Technology: Abolitionist Tools for the New Jim Code*. Hoboken: Wiley.

Bhattacharyya, G. (2018). *Rethinking Racial Capitalism*. London: Rowman & Littlefield Publishers.

Block, J., & Koellinger, P. (2009). I Can't Get No Satisfaction - Necessity Entrepreneurship and Procedural Utility. *Kyklos*, *62*(2), 191–209. https://doi.org/10.1111/j.1467-6435.2009.00431.x

Blundel, R. (2007). Critical Realism: A Suitable Vehicle? In H. Neergard & J. P. Ulhoi. (Eds.), *Handbook of Qualitative Research Methods in Entrepreneurship* (pp. 49–74). Cheltenham, UK and Northampton, MA, USA: Edward Elgar Publishing.

Braguinsky, S., Klepper, S., & Ohyama, A. (2012). High-Tech Entrepreneurship. *The Journal of Law and Economics*, *55*(4), 869–900. https://doi.org/10.1086/666488

Brown, K. C., & Wiles, K. W. (2015). In Search of Unicorns: Private IPOs and the Changing Markets for Private Equity Investments and Corporate Control. *Journal of Applied Corporate Finance*, *27*(3), 34–49.

Calás, M. B., Smircich, L., & Bourne, K. A. (2009). Extending the Boundaries 'Entrepreneurship as Social Change'. *Academy of Management Review*, *34*(3), 552–569. https://doi.org/10.5465/AMR.2009.40633597

Caliskan, A., Bryson, J. J., & Narayanan, A. (2017). Semantics Derived Automatically from Language Corpora Contain Human-Like Moral Choices. *Science*, *356*(April), 183–186. https://doi.org/10.1145/3306618.3314267

Cantino, V., Devalle, A., Cortese, D., Ricciardi, F., & Longo, M. (2017). Place-based Network Organizations and Embedded Entrepreneurial Learning: Emerging Paths to Sustainability. *International Journal of Entrepreneurial Behaviour and Research*, *23*(3), 504–523. https://doi.org/10.1108/IJEBR-12-2015-0303

Caroll, J. (2020). Artificial intelligence Software Expands Capabilities of Boston Dynamics' SpotRobot. *Vision Systems Design*, *September*(11), 1–15.

Carter, S., Kuhl, A., Marlow, S., & Mwaura, S. (2017). Households as a Site of Entrepreneurial Activity. *Foundations and Trends® in Entrepreneurship*, *13*(2), 81–190. https://doi.org/10.1561/0300000062

Čerka, P., Grigienė, J., & Sirbikytė, G. (2017). Is it Possible to Grant Legal Personality to Artificial Intelligence Software Systems? *Computer Law and Security Review*, *33*(5), 685–699. https://doi.org/10.1016/j.clsr.2017.03.022

Chaboud, A. P., Chiquoine, B., Hjalmarsson, E., & Vega, C. (2014). Rise of the Machines: Algorithmic Trading in the Foreign Exchange Market. *Journal of Finance*, *69*(5), 2045–2084. https://doi.org/10.1111/jofi.12186

Chrispal, S., Bapuji, H., & Zietsma, C. (2020). Caste and Organization Studies: Our Silence Makes Us Complicit. *Organization Studies*. https://doi.org/10.1177/0170840620964038

Christophers, B. (2019). The Rentierization of the United Kingdom Economy. *Environment and Planning A*, 1–33. https://doi.org/10.1177/0308518X19873007

Collins, P. H. (2019). *Intersectionality as Critical Social Theory*. Durham, NC and London: Duke University Press.

Columbia Law School Human Rights Clinic. (2012). *Counting Drone Strike Deaths*. *2011*(October), 1–65. Retrieved from http://web.law.columbia.edu/sites/default/files/microsites/human-rights-institute/files/COLUMBIACountingDronesFinal.pdf

Dastin, J. (2018, October 11). Amazon Scraps Secret AI recruiting Tool that Showed Bias Against Women – Reuters. *Reuters*, pp. 1–6. Retrieved from https://www.reuters.com/article/us-amazon-com-jobs-automation-insight/amazon-scraps-secret-ai-recruiting-tool-that-showed-bias-against-women-idUSKCN1MK08G

Davidson, E., & Vaast, E. (2010). Digital Entrepreneurship and its Sociomaterial Enactment. *Proceedings of the Annual Hawaii International Conference on System Sciences*, 1–10. https://doi.org/10.1109/HICSS.2010.150

Davis, G. F., & Sinha, A. (2021). Varieties of Uberization: How Technology and Institutions Change the Organization(s) of Late Capitalism. *Organization Theory*, 1–15. https://doi.org/10.1177/2631787721995198

Du Gay, P. (2004). Against 'Enterprise' (But Not Against 'Enterprise', For That Would Make No Sense). *Organization*, *11*(1), 37–57.

Duffy, B.E. (2017). *(Not) Getting Paid to Do What You Love: Gender, Social Media and Aspirational Work*. New Haven and London: Yale University Press.

Duffy, B. E. & Pruchniewska, U. (2017). Gender and Self-enterprise in the Social Media Age: A Digital Double Bind. *Information, Communication & Society*, *20*(6), 843–859. https://doi.org/10.1080/1369118X.2017.1291703

Eckstrom, M. (1992). Causal Explanation of Social Action: The Contribution of Max Weber and of Critical Realism to a Generative View of Causal Explanation in Social Science. *Acta Sociologica*, 35, 107–122. https://doi.org/10.1007/978-94-009-6317-7_12

Elder-Vass, D. (2012). *The Reality of Social Construction*. Cambridge: Cambridge University Press.

Elder-Vass, D. (2017). Material Parts in Social Structures. *Journal of Social Ontology*, 89–105. https://doi.org/10.1515/jso-2015-0058

Ellmer, M. (2015). The Digital Division of Labor: Socially Constructed Design Patterns of Amazon Mechanical Turk and the Governing of Human Computation Labor. *Momentum Quarterly*, *4*(3), 174–186.

Estévez, A. (2020, May 13). Zoomism and Discipline for Productive Immobility. *Critical Legal Thinking*. Retrieved from https://criticallegalthinking.com/2020/05/13/zoomism-and-discipline-for-productive-immobility/?fbclid=IwAR3By_LRMlpKywLYToxHfiQG9us-KIGtUlQqCcTtSfB4ZAkcxxLlg3Ba6L8

Eubanks, V. (2018). *Automating Inequality: How High-Tech Tools Profile, Police, and Punish the Poor*. New York: St Martin's Press.

Eubanks, V., Noble, S., Boyce, S., Waterhouse-Cooper, B., & Martinez Dy, A. (2020). 'Tech and Inequalities in the Public Sector' [webinar]. Ulster University. 17 September. https://www.ulster.ac.uk/faculties/arts-humanities-and-social-sciences/events/tech-and-inequalities-in-the-public-sector

Fairlie, R. W. (2006). The Personal Computer and Entrepreneurship. *Management Science*, *52*(2), 187–203. https://doi.org/10.1287/mnsc.1050.0479

Faraj, S., & Pachidi, S. (2021). *Beyond Uberization: The Co-constitution of Technology and Organizing*. https://doi.org/10.1177/2631787721995205

Feldman, M., Kenney, M., & Lissoni, F. (2015). The New Data Frontier: Special issue of Research Policy. *Research Policy*, *44*(9), 1629–1632. https://doi.org/10.1016/j.respol.2015.02.007

Fleming, P. (2017). The Human Capital Hoax: Work, Debt and Insecurity in the Era of Uberization. *Organization Studies*, *38*(5), 691–709. https://doi.org/10.1177/0170840616686129

Forson, C. (2013). Contextualising Migrant Black Business Women's Work–Life Balance Experiences. *International Journal of Entrepreneurial Behavior & Research*, *19*(5), 460–477. https://doi.org/10.1108/IJEBR-09-2011-0126

Frese, M., & Gielnik, M. (2014). The Psychology of Entrepreneurship. *Annual Review of Organizational Psychology and Organizational Behavior*, *1*, 413–438. https://doi.org/10.1146/annurev-orgpsych-031413-091326

Gartner, W. B. (1990). What are We Talking About when We Talk About Entrepreneurship?. *Journal of Business Venturing*, *5*(1), 15–28.

Gartner, William B. (1989). 'Who Is an Entrepreneur?' Is the Wrong Question. *Entrepreneurship Theory and Practice*, *13*(4), 47–68. https://doi.org/10.1177/104225878901300406

Garud, R., & Giuliani, A. P. (2013). A Narrative Perspective on Entrepreneurial Opportunities. *Academy of Management Review*, *38*(1), 157–160. https://doi.org/10.5465/amr.2012.0055

Garud, R., Kumaraswamy, A., & Karnøe, P. (2010). Path Dependence or Path Creation? *Journal of Management Studies*, *47*(4), 760–774. https://doi.org/10.1111/j.1467-6486.2009.00914.x

Goodman, B. (2016). A Step Towards Accountable Algorithms?: Algorithmic Discrimination and the European Union General Data Protection. *29th Conference on Neural Information Processing Systems (NIPS 2016), Barcelona, Spain*, 1–7.

Gordon, J. A., & Cornell, D. (2021). *Creolizing Rosa Luxembourg*. London: Rowman & Littlefield Publishers.

Haraway, D. (2016). *Staying with the Trouble: Making Kin in the Chthulucene*. Durham, NC: Duke University Press.

Hjorth, D., Holt, R., & Steyaert, C. (2015). Entrepreneurship and Process Studies. *International Small Business Journal: Researching Entrepreneurship, 33*(6). https://doi.org/10.1177/0266242615583566

HMG. (2016). Artificial Intelligence: Opportunities and Implications for the Future of Decision Making. Government Office for Science.

Holst, A. (2021, February 5). Amount of Information Globally 2010–2024. *Statista*. Retrieved from https://www.statista.com/statistics/871513/worldwide-data-created/

InnoCentive takes the Incentive: How Open Innovation Boosts R&D. (2005). *Strategic Direction, 21*(8), 6–8. https://doi.org/10.1108/02580540510606611

Jackson, S. E., Joshi, A., & Erhardt, N. (2003). Recent Research on Team and Organizational Diversity: SWOT Analysis and Implications. *Journal of Management, 29*(6), 801–830. https://doi.org/10.1016/S0149-2063

Jones, C., & Spicer, A. (2009). *Unmasking the Entrepreneur*. Cheltenham, UK and Northampton, MA, USA: Edward Elgar Publishing.

Kahn, J. (2021). The 'stonks' market caught the A.I. algorithms off guard, too. Retrieved from https://fortune.com/2021/02/11/stonks-stock-market-gamestop-reddit-wallstreetbets-ai-hedge-funds-losses-gme-amc/

Kalber, S. (2005). *Max Weber: Readings and Commentary on Modernity*. Oxford: Blackwell.

Kautonen, T., van Gelderen, M., & Fink, M. (2015). Robustness of the Theory of Planned Behavior in Predicting Entrepreneurial Intentions and Actions. *Entrepreneurship: Theory and Practice, 39*(3), 655–674. https://doi.org/10.1111/etap.12056

Kirzner, I. M. (1973). *Competition and Entrepreneurship*. Chicago: University of Chicago Press.

Kirzner, I. M. (1979). *Perception, Opportunity, and Profit: Studies in the Theory of Entrepreneurship*. Chicago: University of Chicago Press.

Kitching, J., & Marlow, S. (2013). HR Practice and Small Firm Growth: Balancing Informality and Formality. In G. Saridakis, & C. L. Cooper (Eds.), *How Can HR Drive Growth* (pp. 26–40). Cheltenham, UK and Northampton, MA, USA: Edward Elgar Publishing.

Kitching, J., & Rouse, J. (2017). Opportunity or Dead End? Rethinking the Study of Entrepreneurial Action Without a Concept of Opportunity. *International Small Business Journal: Researching Entrepreneurship, 35*(5), 558–577. https://doi.org/10.1177/0266242616652211

Klinger, U., & Svensson, J. (2018). The End of Media Logics? On Algorithms and Agency. *New Media and Society, 20*(12), 4653–4670. https://doi.org/10.1177/1461444818779750

König, P. D. (2020). Dissecting the Algorithmic Leviathan: On the Socio-Political Anatomy of Algorithmic Governance. *Philosophy and Technology, 33*(3), 467–485. https://doi.org/10.1007/s13347-019-00363-w

Korsgaard, S. (2011). Entrepreneurship as Translation: Understanding Entrepreneurial Opportunities through Actor-Network Theory. *Entrepreneurship & Regional Development, 23*(7–8), 661–680. https://doi.org/10.1080/08985626.2010.546432

Kroll, J. A., Barocas, S., Felten, E. W., Reidenberg, R., Robinson, D. G., Yu, H., ... Rev, U. P. L. (2017). Accountable Algorithms. *University of Pennsylvania Law Review, 165*, 633–705.

Latour, B. (1987). *Science in Action*. Boston: Harvard University Press.

Lawson, T. (2019). *The Nature of Social Reality*. Oxon: Routledge.

London School of Economics Media Policy Project (2016) Algorithmic Power and Accountability in Black Box Platforms. https://blogs.lse.ac.uk/medialse/2016/01/22/algorithmic-power-and-accountability-in-black-box-platforms/

Makridakis, S. (2017). The Forthcoming Artificial Intelligence (AI) revolution: Its Impact on Society and Firms. *Futures, 90*, 46–60. https://doi.org/10.1016/j.futures.2017.03.006

Marlow, S. (2020). Gender and Entrepreneurship: Past Achievements and Future Possibilities. *International Journal of Gender and Entrepreneurship, 12*(1), 39–52. https://doi.org/10.1108/IJGE-05-2019-0090

Martinez Dy, A. (2022). Levelling the Playing Field? Towards a Critical-Social Perspective on Digital Entrepreneurship. *Futures, 135*, 1–16. https://doi.org/10.1016/j.futures.2019.102438

Martinez Dy, A. (2020). Not all Entrepreneurship is Created Equal: Theorising Entrepreneurial Disadvantage through Social Positionality. *European Management Review*, *17*(3), 687–699. https://doi.org/10.1111/emre.12390

Martinez Dy, A., & Agwunobi, J. (2019). Intersectionality and Mixed Methods for Social Context in Entrepreneurship. *International Journal of Entrepreneurial Behaviour and Research*, *25*(8), 1727–1747. https://doi.org/10.1108/IJEBR-12-2017-0498

Martinez Dy, A., Marlow, S., & Martin, L. (2017). A Web of Opportunity or the Same Old Story? Women Digital Entrepreneurs and Intersectionality Theory. *Human Relations*, *70*(3), 286–311. https://doi.org/10.1177/0018726716650730

Martinez Dy, A., Martin, L., & Marlow, S. (2014). Developing a Critical Realist Positional Approach to Intersectionality. *Journal of Critical Realism*, *13*(5), 447–466. https://doi.org/10.1179/1476743014Z .00000000043

Martinez Dy, A, Martin, L., & Marlow, S. (2018). Emancipation through Digital Entrepreneurship? A Critical Realist Analysis. *Organization*, *25*(5), 585–608. https://doi.org/10.1177/1350508418777891

Matlay, H., & Westhead, P. (2005). Virtual Teams and the Rise of e-Entrepreneurship in Europe. *International Small Business Journal*, *23*(3), 279–302. https://doi.org/10.1177/0266242605052074

McAdam, M. (2020). Digital Girl: Cyberfeminism and the Emancipatory Potential of Digital Entrepreneurship in Emerging Economies. *Small Business Economics*. https://doi.org/10.1007/s11187 -019-00301-2

McClelland, D. C. (1961). *The Achieving Society*. Princeton: D. Van Nostrand Company.

McMullen, J. S., Ingram, K. M., & Adams, J. (2020). *What Makes an Entrepreneurship Study Entrepreneurial? Toward A Unified Theory of Entrepreneurial Agency*, 1–42. https://doi.org/10 .1177/1042258720922460

McNeill, D. (2016). Governing a City of Unicorns: Technology Capital and the Urban Politics of San Francisco. *Urban Geography*, *37*(4), 494–513. https://doi.org/10.1080/02723638.2016.1139868

Minniti, M. (2004). Entrepreneurial Alertness and Asymmetric Information in a Spin-Glass Model. *Journal of Business Venturing*, *19*(5), 637–658. https://doi.org/10.1016/j.jbusvent.2003.09.003

Mole, K. F., & Mole, M. (2010). Entrepreneurship as the Structuration of Individual and Opportunity: A Response Using a Critical Realist Perspective. Comment on Sarason, Dean and Dillard. *Journal of Business Venturing*, *25*(2), 230–237. https://doi.org/10.1016/j.jbusvent.2008.06.002

Nambisan, S. (2016). Digital Entrepreneurship: Toward a Digital Technology Perspective of Entrepreneurship. *Entrepreneurship: Theory and Practice*, (414), 1–27. https://doi.org/10.1111/etap .12254

Nambisan, S., Wright, M., & Feldman, M. (2019). The Digital Transformation of Innovation and Entrepreneurship: Progress, Challenges and Key Themes. *Research Policy*, *48*(8), 1–9. https://doi.org/ 10.1016/j.respol.2019.03.018

Newlands, G. (2020). Algorithmic Surveillance in the Gig Economy: The Organization of Work through Lefebvrian Conceived Space. *Organization Studies*. https://doi.org/10.1177/0170840620937900

Noble, S. U. (2018). *Algorithms of Oppression: How Search Engines Reinforce Racism*. New York: NYU Press.

Nuti, G., Mirghaemi, M., Treleaven, P., & Yingsaeree, C. (2011). Algorithmic Trading. *IIIE*, (November), 61–69.

Olhede, S. C., & Wolfe, P. J. (2018). The Growing Ubiquity of Algorithms in Society: Implications, Impacts and Innovations. *Philosophical Transactions of the Royal Society A: Mathematical, Physical and Engineering Sciences*, *376*(2128). https://doi.org/10.1098/rsta.2017.0364

Pittaway, L., & Thorpe, R. (2012). A Framework for Entrepreneurial Learning: A Tribute to Jason Cope. *Entrepreneurship and Regional Development*, *24*(9–10), 837–859. https://doi.org/10.1080/08985626 .2012.694268

Politis, D. (2005). The Process of Entrepreneurial Learning: A Conceptual Framework. *Entrepreneurship Theory and Practice*, *29*(4), 399–424.

Rahwan, I. (2018). Society-in-the-Loop: Programming the Algorithmic Social Contract. *Ethics and Information Technology*, *20*(1), 5–14. https://doi.org/10.1007/s10676-017-9430-8

Ramoglou, S., & Tsang, E. (2016). A Realist Perspective of Entrepreneurship: Opportunities As Propensities. *Academy of Management Review*, *41*(3), 410–434. https://doi.org/10.5465/amr.2014 .0281

Reitinger, N. (2015). Algorithmic Choice and Superior Responsibility: Closing the Gap between Liability and Lethal Autonomy by Defining the Line between Actors and Tools. *Gonzaga Law Review*, *51*, 79–119.

Ross, J., & Tomlinson, B. (2010). Who are the Crowdworkers? Shifting Demographics in Mechanical Turk. *CHI 2010: Imagine All the People*, 2863–2872. Retrieved from https://dl.acm.org/doi/abs/10.1145/1753846.1753873?casa_token=lx7-qNHLO2AAAAAA%3A8DPrabbu2MKpIME3Fu40y6csp_SQ0R9bl2nb-wwg-FJxZekRBUAs0FLIF2f6HPQvApOpfNbby8Tf

Russell, L. (2020). *Glitch Feminism: A Manifesto*. London and New York: Verso.

Russon, M.-A. (2021, February 19). Uber Drivers are Workers not Self-employed , Supreme Court Rules. *BBC News*, pp. 1–12. Retrieved from https://www.bbc.co.uk/news/business-56123668

Sahut, J. M., Iandoli, L., & Teulon, F. (2019). The Age of Digital Entrepreneurship. *Small Business Economics*, 1159–1169. https://doi.org/10.1007/s11187-019-00260-8

Sample, I. (2017, October 18). 'It's Able to Create Knowledge Itself': Google Unveils AI that Learns on its Own. *The Guardian*, pp. 1–6. Retrieved from https://www.theguardian.com/science/2017/oct/18/its-able-to-create-knowledge-itself-google-unveils-ai-learns-all-on-its-own

Sarasvathy, S. D. (2001). Causation and Effectuation: Toward a Theoretical Shift from Economic Inevitability. *Academy of Management Review*, *26*(2), 243–263. https://doi.org/10.5465/AMR.2001.4378020

Scrambler, G. (2021). An Ideal Type of 'Rentier Capitalism'. Personal Blog, 15 May. http://www.grahamscambler.com/an-ideal-type-of-rentier-capitalism/

Schumpeter, J. A. (2010). *Capitalism, Socialism, and Democracy*. Oxon: Routledge.

Shane, S., & Venkataraman, S. (2000). The Promise of Entrepreneurship as a Field of Research. *Academy of Management Review*, *25*(1), 217–226.

Standing, C., & Mattsson, J. (2018). 'Fake It Until You Make It': Business Model Conceptualization in Digital Entrepreneurship. *Journal of Strategic Marketing*, *26*(5), 385–399. https://doi.org/10.1080/0965254X.2016.1240218

Sussan, F., & Acs, Z. J. (2017). The Digital Entrepreneurial Ecosystem. *Small Business Economics*, *49*(1), 55–73. https://doi.org/10.1007/s11187-017-9867-5

The Lancet Respiratory Medicine. (2018). Opening the Black Box of Machine Learning. *The Lancet Respiratory Medicine*, *6*(11), 801. https://doi.org/10.1016/S2213-2600(18)30425-9

Thompson, N. A., Verduijn, K., & Gartner, W. B. (2020). Entrepreneurship-as-Practice: Grounding Contemporary Theories of Practice into Entrepreneurship Studies. *Entrepreneurship and Regional Development*, *32*(3–4), 247–256. https://doi.org/10.1080/08985626.2019.1641978

Thompson Jackson, J. (2009). Capitalizing on Digital Entrepreneurship for Low-Income Residents and Communities. *W. Va. L. Rev*, *112*, 187–198.

Ucbasaran, D., Westhead, P., & Wright, M. (2009). The Extent and Nature of Opportunity Identification by Experienced Entrepreneurs. *Journal of Business Venturing*, *24*(2), 99–115. https://doi.org/10.1016/j.jbusvent.2008.01.008

Van Praag, C. M. (1999). Some Classic Views on Entrepreneurship. *Economist*, *147*(3), 311–335. https://doi.org/10.1023/A:1003749128457

Voosen, P. (2017, July). How AI Detectives are Cracking Open the Black Box of Deep Learning. *Science*. Retrieved from http://www.sciencemag.org/news/2017/07/how-ai-detectives-are-cracking-open-black-box-deep-learning

Wajcman, J. (1991). *Feminism and Technology*. Cambridge, MA: Polity Press.

Wajcman, J. (2004). *Technofeminism*. Cambridge, MA: Polity Press.

Wajcman, J. (2010). Feminist Theories of Technology. *Cambridge Journal of Economics*, *34*(1), 143–152. https://doi.org/10.1093/cje/ben057

Watson, T. J. (2009). Entrepreneurial Action, Identity Work and the Use of Multiple Discursive Resources: The Case of a Rapidly Changing Family Business. *International Small Business Journal*, *27*(3), 251–274. https://doi.org/10.1177/0266242609102274

Watson, T. J. (2013a). Entrepreneurial Action and the Euro-American Social Science Tradition: Pragmatism, Realism and Looking Beyond 'The Entrepreneur'. *Entrepreneurship & Regional Development*, *5626*(December 2016), 16–33. https://doi.org/10.1080/08985626.2012.754267

Watson, T. J. (2013b). Entrepreneurship in action: Bringing Together the Individual, Organizational and Institutional Dimensions of Entrepreneurial Action. *Entrepreneurship & Regional Development, 5626*(December 2016), 1–19. https://doi.org/10.1080/08985626.2012.754645

Webster, A., Svalastog, A. L., & Allgaier, J. (2020). Mapping New Digital Landscapes. *Information Communication and Society, 23*(8), 1100–1105. https://doi.org/10.1080/1369118X.2020.1784507

Welter, F., Brush, C., & de Bruin, A. (2013). *The Gendering of Entrepreneurship Context* (No. 1). https://doi.org/10.2139/ssrn.701181

Zaheer, H., Breyer, Y., Dumay, J., & Enjeti, M. (2018). Straight from the Horse's Mouth: Founders' Perspectives on Achieving 'Traction' in Digital Start-ups. *Computers in Human Behavior*, (March). https://doi.org/10.1016/j.chb.2018.03.002

# 15. Digital entrepreneurship in a rural context: the implications of the rural–urban digital divide

*Paolo Gerli and Jason Whalley*

## 1. INTRODUCTION

Despite the emphasis placed by policymakers and scholars on the potential of digital entrepreneurship for economic growth and social inclusion, its implications for regional and rural development remain largely unexplored (Sahut et al., 2019). This chapter aims to address such as gap in the extant literature by focusing on the relationship between rural and digital entrepreneurship.

Rural entrepreneurship is traditionally constrained by a number of factors, such as the limited size of local markets, the lack of entrepreneurial ecosystems, or a shortage of human and financial resources (Clausen, 2020). Digital technologies are expected to help mitigate some of these constraints, in addition to making the entrepreneurial process less spatially bounded (Nambisan, 2017; Soluk et al., 2021). However, there is increasing evidence that digital entrepreneurship remains geographically concentrated in spatial clusters, usually located in major cities (Geissinger et al., 2019; Zaheer et al., 2019).

Some scholars have, therefore, concluded that the process underlying digital entrepreneurship remains influenced by the social context wherein it takes place (Martinez Dy et al., 2018; McAdam et al., 2019). The latter affects both the viability of digital start-ups and the type of digital entrepreneurship that individuals undertake (Martinez Dy, 2019).

Researchers usually distinguish between mild and more advanced forms of digital entrepreneurship (Hull et al., 2007; Martinez Dy, 2019; Fossen & Sorgner, 2021). Mild digital entrepreneurship refers to the use of digital technologies as an input into entrepreneurial processes (Hull et al., 2007): with examples being an Airbnb host or the owner of an eBay shop (Martinez Dy, 2019). Advanced digital entrepreneurship, in contrast, entails the use of digital technologies to create new products and services (Hull et al., 2007), such as in the case of self-employed ICT professionals or start-ups developing new online platforms (Martinez Dy, 2019; Fossen & Sorgner, 2021).

Extant literature has evidenced how different existing socio-economic backgrounds affect the ability of individuals to engage in either mild or advanced digital entrepreneurship (Martinez Dy et al., 2018; McAdam et al., 2019). This chapter further contributes to this debate, exploring the relationship between digital entrepreneurship and the digital divide, a concept commonly used by researchers to describe and analyse inequalities in the digital economy (Lutz, 2019). In particular, we focus on the rural–urban digital divide (OECD, 2018), to explore how the inequal distribution of digital infrastructures and skills affect the emergence of digital entrepreneurship outside of cities.

To date, the relationship between the digital divide and digital entrepreneurship remains largely unexplored from both a conceptual and empirical perspective (Sahut et al., 2019). We address such a gap by developing a framework that illustrates how the different levels of the digital divide affect the scope and intensity of digital entrepreneurship. This framework draws upon a review of the literature of the relationship between digital divides and entrepreneurship, as well as interviews with entrepreneurs, trade organisations, and multiple organisations with a stake in rural and digital entrepreneurship.

Focusing on two European countries, Italy and the UK, our qualitative analysis highlights how bridging the digital divide is essential to enabling any form of entrepreneurship in rural areas, as accessing and using broadband has become essential for entrepreneurs. However, for digital entrepreneurship to thrive in a rural context, more targeted measures are needed to sustain the development of those digital skills that are required to act upon digital entrepreneurial opportunities.

This chapter is structured as follows. A review of the extant literature on the digital divide and entrepreneurship is presented in Section 2. After a brief overview of our methodology (Section 3), Section 4 illustrates the findings of our case study analysis. These are discussed in Section 5, which is followed by concluding remarks and policy recommendations (Section 6).

## 2. A REVIEW OF THE LITERATURE ON THE DIGITAL DIVIDE AND ENTREPRENEURSHIP

This section explores the existing literature on the relationship between the digital divide and entrepreneurship. The different layers of the digital divide are presented and discussed in Section 2.1. The following sections, in contrast, explore how entrepreneurship is affected by the different types of digital divide.

### 2.1 The Three Layers of Digital Divide

The concept of the digital divide was defined by the OECD (2001, p.5) as "the gap between individuals, households, businesses and geographic areas at different socio-economic levels with regard both to their opportunities to access information and communication technologies (ICTs) and to their use of the Internet for a wide variety of activities". Such inequalities have been observed between different genders, geographic areas, and age groups (van Deursen et al., 2011; Bowen & Morris, 2019) and described as the combination of three different layers (Scheerder et al., 2017).

The first layer – access divide – refers to the lack of material access to broadband networks and digital devices (van Dijk, 2002). Gaps in the availability of Internet access reflect failures in broadband markets, which constrains the supply of connectivity in rural and deprived regions (Gerli & Whalley, 2021). The access divide is also influenced by the affordability of connectivity and ICT devices, which affects the extent to which low-income households and SMEs can access online services and digital technologies (Reddick et al., 2020).

However, some decide not to use Internet and ICT even when they have access to it. This is referred to as the usage and skills divide, as it reflects the extent individuals are able to use digital technologies (van Dijk, 2002). The latter require specific skills, labelled as digital skills or competences.

Multiple taxonomies have been proposed to conceptualise digital skills and competences. Initially the emphasis was placed on the technical know-how necessary to utilise ICT for both operational and strategic goals (van Deursen et al., 2011; Ng, 2012). Later conceptualisations also encompass those intellectual capabilities and behavioural attitudes that allow individuals to maximise the benefits of ICT and minimise the risks deriving from its use (Vuorikari et al., 2016; van Laar et al., 2017).

Previous research found that the skills divide is influenced by socio-economic variables such as age, the level of education and income (Scheerder et al., 2017). In a business context, the adoption of ICT is linked to both internal and external factors, such as the level of internationalisation and skilled workforce, the attitude of leaders and the existence of competitive and regulatory pressures (Giotopoulos et al., 2017; AlBar & Hoque, 2019).

More recently, scholars have conceptualised a third layer of the digital divide, namely the digital outcome divide. This reflects how individuals and organisations obtain different (and not necessarily positive) outcomes[1] from the use of digital technologies (Stern et al., 2009). The digital outcome divide is also influenced by social and personal factors (Scheerder et al., 2017), but research on this type of digital divide is still in its infancy. In particular, the digital outcome divide in a business context remains largely unexplored.

The concept of a digital divide provides an established and comprehensive framework to study inequalities in the digital economy and society, highlighting the influence of both individual and contextual factors on the attitude of users and organisations towards digital technologies (Lutz, 2019). Consistently, the three levels of digital divide have been used to explore how various aspects of digital technologies can affect entrepreneurship, as discussed in the following sections.

## 2.2   Access Divide and Entrepreneurship

Multiple quantitative studies have confirmed that a positive relationship exists between broadband availability and entrepreneurship, with such an effect being higher in innovative industries such as high-tech manufacturing and professional services (Audretsch et al., 2015; Prieger et al., 2017; Hasbi, 2020). Prieger (2020) also suggests that the impact of broadband on business start-ups is more significant in areas with a higher unemployment rate, while others have highlighted that the effect of digital technologies is influenced by the level of human capital (McCoy et al., 2018; Hasbi, 2020).

Although researchers agree that the availability of broadband contributes to determining the location of entrepreneurial activities (McCoy et al., 2018; Hasbi, 2020), conflicting views have been expressed on the impact that broadband has on economic agglomeration in rural areas. Focusing on rural Canada between 1999 and 2003, Cumming and Johan (2010) suggested that the expansion of broadband favoured the agglomeration of entrepreneurial activities in larger communities, as users in remote locations had become able to access products and services produced elsewhere. Conversely, the analysis by Mack (2014) concluded that broadband access facilitated both the retention and attraction of businesses in rural Ohio, thereby contributing to overcoming the agglomerative disadvantages of remote locations.

Overall, the literature suggests that the persistence of a rural–urban access divide constrains entrepreneurship in rural areas and the effects of broadband unavailability are more pronounced in innovative industries. The literature also demonstrates the mediating role of human capital in the relationship between broadband access and entrepreneurship. This aspect is further explored in the following section, with a specific focus on digital skills.

## 2.3    Skills Divide and Entrepreneurship

Digital skills are often mentioned among the competences required by entrepreneurs (Bacigalupo et al., 2016), yet the relationship between digital literacy and entrepreneurship remains largely under-researched. Oggero, Rossi and Ughetto (2020) found that individuals with digital skills are more likely to become entrepreneurs and this effect is greater for men. Their analysis, however, was based on a narrow definition of digital skills (the ability to use a computer for financial services). Conversely, Neumeyer, Santos and Morris (2020) emphasised the dynamic nature of digital skills and distinguished between four levels of digital literacy – basic usage, application, development and transformation – that entrepreneurs can take advantage of to start up a business.

These studies suggest that some level of digital literacy is required for any entrepreneurial activity to occur. On the other hand, researchers agreed that even individuals with basic digital skills can act upon entrepreneurial opportunities emanating from digital technologies. In fact, some digital entrepreneurial opportunities only require the ability to interact with an existing app or to add content onto an existing platform: this is the case, for example, of Uber drivers, eBay shops or professionals in social media marketing (Martinez Dy, 2019; Gustavsson & Ljunberg, 2018).

However, advanced digital skills are required to exploit those digital entrepreneurial opportunities that generate the highest value (Martinez Dy, 2019). For example, to create a new platform or device, nascent entrepreneurs need programming skills or the technical know-how to combine existing digital artefacts together (Gustavsson & Ljunberg, 2018).

Thus, the literature suggests that the digital skills divide affects entrepreneurship in multiple ways. The absence of digital skills limits the scope for any form of entrepreneurial activity, but a further distinction should be made between those with basic skills and those with advanced digital competences. The former can rely on existing platforms and devices, but cannot act on those opportunities that generate the highest value. As a consequence, the level of digital skills determines to what extent entrepreneurial individuals can act upon both traditional and digital entrepreneurial opportunities.

## 2.4    Outcome Divide and Entrepreneurship

Research has shown how individuals can obtain a wide range of economic, socio-cultural and personal benefits from the use of ICT (Wei et al., 2011; Ghobadi & Ghobadi, 2015), but the digital outcome divide remains under-researched in the context of entrepreneurship. Some scholars have explored how the performance of entrepreneurs varied with the use of digital technologies (Bowen & Morris, 2019; Millán et al., 2021), while others have focused on their impact on the ability of certain social groups to engage in entrepreneurial activities (Martinez Dy et al., 2018; Leong et al., 2020).

Focusing on rural Wales, Bowen and Morris (2019) observed that the lack of broadband access and digital skills had constrained the development of entrepreneurial activities among farmers and the internationalisation of SMEs in the food industry. Millán et al. (2021), in contrast, compared how the use of digital technologies affected the earnings of entrepreneurs in 35 countries. They found a non-linear relationship, suggesting that entrepreneurs need to continuously practice and develop their digital skills in order to maximise the outcomes of ICT use.

*Table 15.1*     *Distribution of interviewees across countries and typologies*

|  | Italy | UK |  |
|---|---|---|---|
| Public authorities | 3 | 2 | 5 |
| Organisations promoting rural development | 2 | 3 | 5 |
| Broadband providers | 3 | 3 | 6 |
| Business organisations | 3 | 3 | 6 |
| Entrepreneurs | 2 | 4 | 6 |
| Representatives of local communities | 2 | 4 | 6 |
| | **15** | **19** | **34** |

With regard to the impact of digital technologies on the inclusivity of entrepreneurship, Leong et al. (2020) emphasised the role of digital enablers, that is, organisations that help microbusinesses in emerging economies to overcome entrepreneurial constraints and maximise the outcomes deriving from digital technologies. Focusing on female entrepreneurship in Saudi Arabia, McAdam et al. (2019) confirmed the transformative effect of digital technologies, although the latter may be mediated by the economic status and social class of the entrepreneurs. Likewise, Martinez Dy et al. (2018) highlighted that the ability to act upon digital entrepreneurial opportunities in the UK remains constrained by socio-economic factors such as race and income.

These studies illustrated how the entrepreneurial outcomes of digital technologies may vary across different social and geographic contexts. With specific regard to rural areas, the extant literature suggests that the digital divide affects the performance of entrepreneurs and SMEs, but little has been said on its implications for rural digital entrepreneurship. This latter issue is further explored in the following sections

## 3.    METHODOLOGY

In order to understand the implications of the digital divide for digital entrepreneurship in rural areas, we conducted 34 interviews across two European countries (15 in Italy and 19 in the UK). As detailed in Table 15.1, the interviewees included entrepreneurs, spokespersons of business organisations, representatives of local communities and organisations promoting rural development, managers of broadband providers and public officials contrasting the rural digital divide. The business organisations included two chambers of commerce, two associations of SMEs and two farmers' unions. Among the interviewed entrepreneurs, three operated online businesses in different industries (event management, digital marketing, e-learning), two were freelance ICT consultants and one ran a rural business park.

Participant observation was also used on five occasions: two IT workshops run by local authorities in northern England, two IT workshops run by the volunteers of a community network in the UK, and a meeting between rural stakeholders and industry experts to discuss the benefits of digital technologies for the rural economy in Italy. The primary data were collected over a two-year period between June 2016 and June 2018.

Primary data were integrated with and triangulated by secondary sources, such as policy documents, consultancy reports and articles from the trade press (Yin, 2014). A thematic analysis of the data was conducted with NVivo (Wiltshier, 2011) to identify how the different levels of digital divide affected the development of entrepreneurial activities in rural areas, with a focus on the creation of digital start-ups.

## 4.    FINDINGS

A considerable access divide still exists between rural and urban areas in the case study countries. As of 2020, fixed broadband was available to 98% of the rural households in Italy, but 24% of them did not have access to next-generation access (NGA) networks.[2] Conversely, only 1% of urban premises were not provided with superfast broadband (EC, 2020). In the UK, Ofcom (2020) reported that, as of September 2020, only 81% of rural premises had access to superfast broadband, while the latter was available to 98% of urban premises.

Interviewees emphasised how the lack of broadband access impedes rural entrepreneurs to carry out the most basic activities, including the compliance with government regulations that "expects all farmers to complete their forms online and all businesses to do their VAT online" (Interview UK13). However, it is not just the lack of access to affect rural entrepreneurs: the quality of broadband also matters. Slow connections were described as "a deadweight that force many rural businesses to use obsolete techniques and processes" (Interview IT13), as well as a factor undermining their productivity, as explained by the founder of an events management company, based in rural England:

> every second you spend waiting for a file to upload or download is a waste of time and when you multiply that over a team of people, over the whole working day, for all us, the amount of time lost is quite significant. (Interview UK5)

Over the past decade, both national and local authorities have taken a number of measures to reduce the rural access divide. Since 2011, the UK public sector has spent £1.9bn to deliver superfast broadband to 5.3m premises (BDUK, 2020), while the latest plan launched by the Italian government earmarked €5bn to subsidise NGA rollout in rural areas (MISE, 2015). Such a considerable commitment of public resources was justified by the fact that superfast broadband is the "essential premise for the digital growth of the economy" (MISE, 2015, p.7) and "vital (…) especially to small businesses who are so often the engines of innovation" (BIS, 2010, p.2).

Entrepreneurs confirmed that getting access to superfast broadband has been "an enormous game changer" that allowed their operations "to be practically 80% online" (Interview UK16) and "more economically viable" (Interview UK15). However, some interviewees questioned the direct correlation between the availability of superfast broadband and the digitalisation of existing or nascent businesses. The representative of a chamber of commerce in Italy clarified that "the increased availability of superfast broadband did not automatically lead to the digital transformation of the economy" (Interview IT12). More specifically, enhancing the quality of Internet connections was not sufficient for rural businesses to fully exploit the benefits of digital technologies, as highlighted by the chief technology officer of a local authority in the northwest of England:

> for lots of people [it] isn't speed of broadband that makes a difference. It is how actually you change your business model, you exploit speed, that makes a difference (Interview UK6)

The broadband plans of national and local authorities in the UK also made explicit references to the role of connectivity as a driver of entrepreneurship – such references were, in contrast, missing from Italian policy documents. For example, the national government stated that "faster broadband also helps to support the creation of new businesses" (BDUK, 2014, p.3) and a county in the northeast of England assumed that superfast broadband will result in "increasing enterprise start-ups in remote rural locations" (Digital Durham, 2011, p.9).

Although Ipsos MORI (2018, p.64) estimated that in the UK "the number of firms (…) rose by 0.4 percent in response to the installation of new broadband infrastructure", a spokesperson for SMEs in the northeast of England doubted that "because they rolled out superfast broadband in some of the smaller villages, then all of a sudden there's been this rush of people that want to start up" (Interview UK4). Instead, interviewees suggested that bridging the access divide could favour the relocation of existing businesses to rural areas. The volunteers of a community network reported that entrepreneurs were moving to their village and "one of their reasons had been that the fibre network will reach the business units" (Interview UK3). According to the owner of a business park in rural Cumbria, the availability of superfast broadband could eventually help rural areas to attract more innovative companies than they have now:

> we're more likely to have some firms that want to use the fibre… because the firms that we have, they're really grateful it's here and it's much better for them, but it hasn't made a massive difference. (Interview UK15)

The analysis confirmed the existence of a usage divide in Italy and the UK, as many in rural areas still struggle "to understand the benefits of moving to superfast broadband" (Interview UK2) and "how and why superfast broadband works" (Interview IT8). According to the spokesperson of a rural charity in the UK, this reflected the fact that they "haven't basic digital skills" (Interview UK10), while the manager of a chamber of commerce in Italy noted that "the lack of digital culture is the main obstacle" (Interview IT12).

A need to provide rural businesses and entrepreneurs with ad hoc training emerged from the analysis. However, the comparison highlighted how the skills divide in rural areas was not addressed on a systematic basis, as had happened for the access divide. In the UK, less than half of the local authorities put in place specific digital literacy programmes to complement their interventions in support of NGA supply. In Italy the nationwide programme against the access divide was not integrated by any measure against the skills divide in rural areas. The latter were left to the initiative of trade organisations and chambers of commerce because neither public authorities nor ICT companies "took the onus to go to the actual or nascent entrepreneur and explain what they could do with broadband" (Interview IT8).

Digital literacy programmes in the UK included generic workshops for the rural communities reached by NGA networks as well as tutorials specifically targeting local businesses. Both were provided by local authorities in partnership with commercial ICT suppliers and trade organisations. The participation to two of these workshops clarified that these initiatives primarily aimed at raising awareness on the benefits of superfast broadband rather than addressing the digital skills divide:

> The first part of the presentation emphasised superfast broadband as something that could potentially solve or at least offset some of the negative trends affecting the local economy, such as the declining population, the lack of jobs and the low wages. (…)
> The presenter showed the applications that users can access with superfast broadband. The first one to be analysed was cloud computing. He did not provide technical details or showed how to use it: he just presented a list of alternative providers, such as Dropbox, Google, etc. (Observation UK1)

As to the tutorials for rural businesses, secondary data highlighted that most of them targeted existing SMEs in order to encourage the use of online services and digital technologies. These initiatives primarily focused on digital marketing: for example, out of 35 workshops organised by Leicestershire County Council between December 2014 and November 2015, 33 treated the potential of different digital platforms and applications (e-commerce, blogs, social media, email, Google tools) for marketing and advertising purposes (ERS, 2015).

Similarly, the digital literacy programmes run by the chambers of commerce in Italy were designed to "acquire basic digital skills to utilise the main digital platforms and manage the online presence of a company" (Crescere in digitale, 2021). Initially limited to digital marketing skills, the training provided by the chambers of commerce were later expanded to include more complex issues and advanced technologies such as cybersecurity and big data. However, these programmes remain focused on "exploiting the opportunities in the new digital labour market" (Unioncamere, 2019, p.55) without specific references to the potential of digital technologies for entrepreneurship.

Overall, the cross-country analysis showed that national and local initiatives aimed to reduce the digital divide largely overlooked the skills divide in rural areas. When training was provided, it was designed to support SMEs and to enhance the quality of the workforce by developing basic digital skills. Little consideration was given to the potential of emerging technologies, such as Internet-of-Things (IOT) and Artificial Intelligence (AI), for the development of new entrepreneurial activities. This may eventually undermine the potential for digital entrepreneurship in rural areas, as emerged during a meeting between technology experts and rural stakeholders in Italy:

> A researcher highlighted that Internet access is treated as a sort of right, and given for granted, but skills are also important and lacking. Superfast broadband supports the development and use of new technologies and services, such as precision farming and smart villages. Without skills, farmers and rural communities cannot take advantage of these opportunities. If human capital is not developed, this will compromise the competitiveness of the rural economy. (Observation IT1)

Interviewees emphasised the need to provide ad hoc training to rural entrepreneurs, with "local champions to teach people how to leverage the potential of broadband" (Interview IT8). Other sources stressed the importance to partner with educational institutions in order to offer "enhanced tailored support for high-growth businesses" (ERS, 2015, p.43). Indeed, the ethnographic analysis of two IT clubs run by a community network in northern England provided anecdotal evidence that the collaboration of multiple local actors can encourage local individuals to act upon digital entrepreneurial opportunities:

> During the club, an old man was showed how to set up a profile on eBay to sell some items. Participants also share tips and ideas among each other, i.e. on the different VoIP services available or the devices to use to boost the Wi-Fi signal. I was told by a volunteer that one of the users, after coming to the club, had the idea of installing a webcam in his barn to monitor the ewes during lambing season. (Observation UK3)

The network's users had a problem with their alarm systems (that only work with traditional telephone lines). The voice spread across the villages and then a local entrepreneur came up with a solution, developing a new alarm system that is entirely digital and does not require a traditional telephone line. (Observation UK4)

## 5.    DISCUSSION

The previous section has begun to shed light on the relationship between digital entrepreneurship and the digital divides that exist in Italy and the UK. In both countries, bridging the rural–urban access divide was not deemed as sufficient to spur digital entrepreneurship, even though the increased availability of fast and reliable connectivity may favour the digital transformation of rural businesses and encourage the relocation of innovative businesses from urban to rural areas.

In order to support rural digital entrepreneurship, tailored initiatives are needed to address the lack of digital skills in rural areas. To date, both public and private programmes in support of digital literacy have primarily focused on the development of basic digital skills that only enable existing and nascent entrepreneurs to use existing platforms or services. Little has been done to foster the know-how of emerging technologies and the development of advanced digital skills.

Figure 15.1 draws on the previous sections to outline the complex and dynamic relationship between broadband, digital skills, and digital entrepreneurship – these correspond, respectively, to the connectivity, skills and outcome layers of the digital divide that have been identified within the literature (see Section 2).

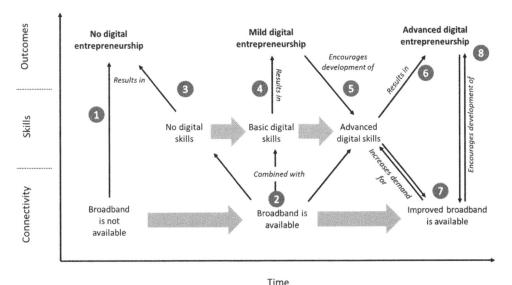

*Figure 15.1*    *Exploring the dynamic interplay between connectivity, skills and digital entrepreneurship*

The access divide inevitably stifles digital entrepreneurship, as the lack of broadband impedes the ability of individuals to act on those entrepreneurial opportunities derived from the use of digital technologies (point 1, Figure 15.1). However, the lack of connectivity potentially undermines any form of entrepreneurial activity, as Internet access has become essential for entrepreneurs to perform the most basic activities and to comply with government regulations. This applies to existing as well as nascent entrepreneurs, suggesting that the access divide may lead to the relocation of already established businesses to areas with (better) connectivity and deter the creation of new enterprises in rural areas.

Once broadband is made available to rural and remote areas, the extent to which individuals can act on digital entrepreneurial opportunities will depend on their level of digital skills (point 2, Figure 15.1). For some, having access to broadband will have a limited impact as they do not possess the basic digital skills to engage in digital entrepreneurship (point 3, Figure 15.1). Some will possess a limited set of digital skills, which, when combined with broadband connectivity, enables mild forms of digital entrepreneurship, that is, they will be able to use existing online platforms and digital devices to undertake new entrepreneurial ventures (point 4, Figure 15.1). For example, a connected farmer could diversify into hospitality services, becoming an Airbnb host. Likewise, an individual with craft skills could take advantage of e-commerce portals to set up an online shop.

The presence of broadband and mild digital entrepreneurship may encourage some individuals and businesses to gain advanced digital skills (point 5, Figure 15.1). This will allow for advanced digital entrepreneurship to occur in rural areas (point 6, Figure 15.1), resulting in the creation of new digital services and products. For example, an individual with programming skills could combine existing sensors to develop new smart farming technology or could develop a new e-commerce platform for the promotion of local produce and touristic attractions.

As individuals and businesses obtain advanced digital skills, they may also start to demand improved connectivity (point 7, Figure 15.1), since a broader and more intense use of online services and digital technologies requires faster download or upload speeds, and reduced latency. Having said this, the relationship between digital skills and broadband quality flows both ways. As improved broadband connectivity is made available within a community, some individuals and businesses may be encouraged to improve their digital skills. This, however, requires that potential users are made aware of the benefits associated with improved connectivity from the marketing that the infrastructure providers (and others) engage in, or through word of mouth, and so on.

Furthermore, an increase in digital entrepreneurial activities will place greater demands on the existing broadband infrastructure, which may result in slower speeds, reduced latency or (infrequent) outages. This will, in turn, encourage users to demand improved broadband connectivity so that their online activities, whatever they may be, are not negatively impacted by the quality of the broadband infrastructure that they rely on (point 8, Figure 15.1).

In summary, the combination of broadband availability and the possession of either basic or advanced digital skills creates the conditions for digital entrepreneurship, which may be varied in nature, to occur in a rural context. This does not mean it will necessarily occur. Other structural factors typically constrain rural entrepreneurship, such as the lack of financial resources or the limited access to transportation infrastructures (Clausen, 2020). Some have suggested that digital technologies may mitigate such constraints, thereby favouring entrepreneurship in a rural context (Nambisan, 2017). However, our analysis suggest that the rural–urban digital divide may significantly influence to what extent individuals located outside transport corridors can act on entrepreneurial opportunities emanating from digital technologies.

What emerges from the above discussion of Figure 15.1 is how digital entrepreneurship is based on the twin foundations of broadband and digital skills, which resonates the importance of both infrastructures and human capital for entrepreneurs (Zaheer et al., 2019; Hasbi, 2020). One without the other will prevent digital entrepreneurship in rural areas from developing, and it is only with both developing in parallel that the entrepreneurial opportunities emanating from digital technologies will be maximised.

While developments in the two areas are, in practice, unlikely to be exactly aligned with one another, the gap between them needs to be minimised to ensure that the rural digital entrepreneurship is not held back by either the lack of digital skills or broadband availability. If the gap in their development widens to the point that one negatively impacts on the other, then the scope for digital entrepreneurship is impinged upon and the associated benefits constrained.

This may lead to the emergence of an entrepreneurial outcome divide, which reflects how the unequal distribution of connectivity and digital skills determines the extent to which individuals can act on entrepreneurial opportunities emanating from digital technologies. If both the access and skills divides remain unsolved, some regions will struggle to retain their existing entrepreneurial activities let alone create new enterprises. As a result, digital entrepreneurial activities will converge on those areas characterised by advanced digital skills and improved connectivity. This will, in turn, further compromise the economic vitality of rural regions unless specific measures are undertaken to bridge the rural–urban digital divide.

Likewise, the persistence of digital divides is undermining the empowering potential of digital entrepreneurship, alongside other socio-economic factors that constrain the ability of individuals to act on digital entrepreneurial activities (Martinez Dy, 2019; McAdam et al., 2019). This is particularly worrisome if we consider that both access and skills divides tend to primarily affect those social groups that also encounter the highest barriers to entrepreneurship (Prieger, 2020).

With this in mind, it is arguably disappointing that our two cases demonstrate a preference for initiatives that tackle the access divide over those that would support the development of digital skills. In some respects, this is unsurprising. Broadband has been often described as the panacea for economic growth and policymakers have been led to believe that the provision of connectivity would be sufficient to trigger the creation of start-ups. Furthermore, improvements in broadband availability are easier to manage, with a clear pathway of improving DSL- and fibre-based broadband existing, and a target of connecting ever more premises being relatively simple to operationalise and measure. These allow those intervening against the rural digital divide to claim that the various initiatives being implemented are on target to or have met their objectives.

In contrast, the development of digital skills is more difficult to clearly articulate, in part because of their scope but also because of their dynamism. Quite simply, as software and hardware technologies develop, the technical skills needed to use digital technologies also evolve (Neumeyer et al., 2020). Furthermore, with more and increasingly complex challenges emerging in the digital economy (such as, for example, cybersecurity and the governance of big data), the nature of the skills required by digital entrepreneurs is also evolving, encompassing a broader set of competences like ethical awareness, critical thinking and problem solving (van Laar et al., 2017).

This complicates the development and support of digital skills, nationally as well as in rural areas. One aspect of this is whether the support should be forward looking, providing cutting edge skills to individuals and businesses in rural areas, or focus on existing and already well understood skills instead? Moreover, the constantly changing nature of digital skills questions the appropriateness of one-off interventions, but the provision of support over time is costly in terms of how the training is delivered as well as ensuring its relevance.

While there are challenges associated with ensuring the relevance of digital skills regardless of geography, in rural areas this will be compounded by the diversity of online tasks undertaken by some living and working in rural areas. A farmer, for example, with multiple sources of income is likely to require a broad array of digital skills so that (s)he is able to engage in e-commerce, interact with their suppliers and the government, employ emerging technologies for digital agriculture, and so forth. Providing in-depth digital skills in all of these areas is challenging, not least because the farmer may undertake some online activities infrequently or use bespoke applications.

While there are undoubted benefits of providing everyone with the same set of digital skills, not least of which is the efficiencies that can be achieved in the delivery of such support, a failure to tailor them to the specific rural context will impinge on entrepreneurial activity. In other words, if the development of digital skills in rural areas is supported by programmes and initiatives that reflect an urban context, then the emergence and growth of rural digital entrepreneurship (outcomes divide) will be negatively affected.

## 6.    CONCLUSION

This chapter has focused on rural digital entrepreneurship. More specifically, the chapter has highlighted the multi-faceted nature of the digital divide that many rural areas face. Connectivity in rural areas is typically poor and, in some cases, lacking altogether, creating a series of challenges for individuals and businesses wishing to be entrepreneurial. These challenges are, however, compounded by the lack of digital skills that limit the ability of would-be rural entrepreneurs to identify and then exploit the online opportunities that emerge. What emerges in the worst-case scenario – that is, when connectivity and skills are absent – is no digital entrepreneurship.

We have, however, argued that improvements in connectivity and skills can bring about changes resulting in digital entrepreneurship. The dynamic relationship between connectivity, skills and digital entrepreneurship, which correspond to the three levels of the digital divide identified in the literature, is shown in Figure 15.1. Improvements in connectivity give rise to a wider array of online entrepreneurial opportunities, but for these to be turned into revenue-generating activities those individuals and businesses located in rural areas require digital skills. At any one point in time, digital skills are varied in character reflecting the plethora of activities that can be done online, but they also change over time as technologies emerge and evolve.

This gives rise to our first conclusion, namely, that although connectivity is necessary for digital entrepreneurship in rural areas, it is not sufficient. For the opportunities of digital entrepreneurship to be maximised, rural entrepreneurs need access to both appropriate levels of connectivity and the relevant digital skills to identify and then exploit the opportunities that emerge. Our analysis demonstrated that initiatives in Italy and the UK to tackle the digital divide focus on connectivity, perhaps because of the challenges and costs associated with providing digital skills. Thus, a second conclusion that can be drawn is that the lack of digital skills provision needs to be addressed. Significantly, the support that is provided needs to be varied in terms of its content but also provided over the longer term. This provision of support over time is necessary, as time-limited initiatives are likely to fossilise the available skills and thus negatively impact on rural digital entrepreneurship.

Related to this is a third conclusion, that if the digital divide between urban and rural areas is not to widen, then investment needs to occur that is substantial and skewed in favour of rural areas. Through increased and sustained investment in connectivity and digital skills, the digital divide will narrow while the opportunities for digital entrepreneurship grow. The investment needs to be sufficiently large to kickstart the positive relationship between connectivity, digital skills and entrepreneurial activity that is outlined in Figure 15.1.

This chapter focused on the rural digital divide in order to untangle the effects of both digital and spatial inequalities on digital entrepreneurship in rural areas. This shed light on the influence of the socio-economic context on digital entrepreneurship and its emancipatory potential, taking into account those structural inequalities existing in both the digital economy and the rural society (Martinez Dy, 2019; McAdam et al., 2019).

The framework in Figure 15.1 outlines the relationship between digital entrepreneurship and the rural–urban digital divide. Other forms of digital divides exist (for example, between genders and different ethnic groups) but were not considered in this chapter and deserve to be further explored. This would contribute to the development of a comprehensive theorisation of how structural inequalities affect entrepreneurial agency in the digital economy, while also providing useful insights for policymakers committed to promoting digital entrepreneurship in socially disadvantaged context.

## NOTES

1. The literature review by Scheerder et al. (2017) distinguishes between economic, social, cultural and personal outcomes to reflect the wide variety of (positive or negative) effects that can be derived from ICT use.
2. NGA networks refer to broadband networks, partially or entirely composed of optic fibre, which are capable of delivering faster speed than legacy telephony networks. In this work we use the denomination of Ofcom (2020), which distinguishes between decent broadband (at least 10 Mbit/s in download) and superfast broadband (at least 30 Mbit/s). Download is among the parameters that determine the quality of a broadband connection (Stocker & Whalley, 2018): a faster speed is required to access bandwidth-intensive services, such as eHealth and cloud computing.

## REFERENCES

AlBar, A. M., & Hoque, M. R. (2019). Factors affecting the adoption of information and communication technology in small and medium enterprises: a perspective from rural Saudi Arabia. *Information Technology for Development, 25*(4), 715–738.
Audretsch, D.B., Heger, D. & Veith, T. (2015) Infrastructure and entrepreneurship. *Small Business Economics, 44*, 219–230. https://doi.org/10.1007/s11187-014-9600-6
Bacigalupo, M., Kampylis, P., Punie, Y., & Van den Brande, G. (2016). EntreComp: the entrepreneurship competence framework. Luxembourg: Publication Office of the European Union, *10*, 593884.
BDUK (2014). *Superfast Extension Programme Funding Guidance.* London, UK.

BDUK. (2020). BDUK Local Body Information Spreadsheet. www.gov.uk

BIS (2010). *Britain's Superfast Broadband Future*. London, UK.

Bowen, R., & Morris, W. (2019). The digital divide: Implications for agribusiness and entrepreneurship. Lessons from Wales. *Journal of Rural Studies, 72*, 75–84.

Clausen, T.H. (2020). The liability of rurality and new venture viability. *Journal of Rural Studies, 73*, 114–121.

Crescere in digitale (2021). *Obiettivi del corso*. crescereindigitale.it

Cumming, D., & Johan, S. (2010). The differential impact of the internet on spurring regional entrepreneurship. *Entrepreneurship Theory and Practice, 34*(5), 857–884.

Digital Durham (2011). *BDUK Broadband Delivery Project. Local Broadband Plan for Durham and Gateshead*. Durham, UK.

EC (2020). *Broadband Coverage in Europe 2019*. Brussels, Belgium.

ERS (2015). *1-2-1 Business Support Service Programme. Final Evaluation Report*. Bristol, UK.

Fossen, F.M., & Sorgner, A. (2021). Digitalization of work and entry into entrepreneurship. *Journal of Business Research, 125*, 548–563

Geissinger, A., Laurell, C., Sandström, C., Eriksson, K., & Nykvist, R. (2019). Digital entrepreneurship and field conditions for institutional change: Investigating the enabling role of cities. *Technological Forecasting and Social Change, 146*, 877–886.

Gerli, P., & Whalley, J. (2021). Fiber to the countryside: A comparison of public and community initiatives in the UK, *Telecommunications Policy*, 102222.

Ghobadi, S., & Ghobadi, Z. (2015). How access gaps interact and shape digital divide: a cognitive investigation. *Behaviour & Information Technology, 34*(4), 330–340.

Giotopoulos, I., Kontolaimou, A., Korra, E., & Tsakanikas, A. (2017). What drives ICT adoption by SMEs? Evidence from a large-scale survey in Greece. *Journal of Business Research, 81*, 60–69.

Gustavsson, M., & Ljunberg, J. (2018). Entrepreneurship in the digital society. *ICIS 2018 Proceedings*.

Hasbi, M. (2020). Impact of very high-speed broadband on company creation and entrepreneurship: Empirical Evidence. *Telecommunications Policy, 44*(3), 101873.

Hull, C.E., Hung, Y.T.C., Hair, N., Perotti, V., & Demartino, R. (2007). Taking advantage of digital opportunities: A typology of digital entrepreneurship. *International Journal of Networking and Virtual Organisations, 4*(3), 290–303.

Ipsos MORI. (2018). *Superfast Broadband Programme Evaluation. Annex A: Reducing the Digital Divide*. London, UK.

Leong, C., Tan, F. T. C., Tan, B., & Faisal, F. (2020). The emancipatory potential of digital entrepreneurship: A study of financial technology-driven inclusive growth. *Information & Management*, 103384.

Lutz, C. (2019). Digital inequalities in the age of artificial intelligence and big data. *Human Behavior and Emerging Technologies, 1*(2), 141–148.

Mack, E. A. (2014). Businesses and the need for speed: The impact of broadband speed on business presence. *Telematics and Informatics, 31*(4), 617–627.

Martinez Dy, A. (2019). Levelling the playing field? Towards a critical-social perspective on digital entrepreneurship. *Futures*, 102438.

Martinez Dy, A., Martin, L., & Marlow, S. (2018). Emancipation through digital entrepreneurship? A critical realist analysis. *Organisation, 25*(5), 585–608.

McAdam, M., Crowley, C., & Harrison, R. T. (2019). "To boldly go where no [man] has gone before" – institutional voids and the development of women's digital entrepreneurship. *Technological Forecasting and Social Change, 146*, 912–922.

McCoy, D., Lyons, S., Morgenroth, E., Palcic, D., & Allen, L. (2018). The impact of broadband and other infrastructure on the location of new business establishments. *Journal of Regional Science*, 509–534. https://doi.org/10.1111/jors.12376

Millán, J. M., Lyalkov, S., Burke, A., Millán, A., & van Stel, A. (2021). 'Digital divide' among European entrepreneurs: Which types benefit most from ICT implementation? *Journal of Business Research, 125*, 533–547.

MISE (2015). *Strategia Italiana Banda Ultralarga*. Rome, Italy.

Nambisan, S. (2017). Digital entrepreneurship: Toward a digital technology perspective of entrepreneurship. *Entrepreneurship Theory and Practice, 41*(6), 1029–1055.

Neumeyer, X., Santos, S.C., & Morris, M.H. (2020). Overcoming barriers to technology adoption when fostering entrepreneurship among the poor: The role of technology and digital literacy. *IEEE Transactions on Engineering Management*.

Ng, W. (2012). Can we teach digital natives digital literacy? *Computers & Education*, *59*(3), 1065–1078.

OECD. (2001). *Understanding the Digital Divide*. Paris, France.

OECD. (2018). *Bridging the Rural Digital Divide*. Paris, France.

Ofcom. (2020). *Connected Nations 2020*. London, UK.

Oggero, N., Rossi, M. C., & Ughetto, E. (2020). Entrepreneurial spirits in women and men. The role of financial literacy and digital skills. *Small Business Economics*, *55*(2), 313–327.

Prieger, J.E. (2020). Entrepreneurship in minority areas: The roles of broadband availability and financial constraints, paper presented at *TPRC48*, 17–19 February 2021.

Prieger, J.E., Lu, H., & Zhang, H. (2017). *The Importance of Transportation, Broadband, and Intellectual Infrastructure for Entrepreneurship*. Pepperdine University, Working Papers n. 68.

Reddick, C. G., Enriquez, R., Harris, R. J., & Sharma, B. (2020). Determinants of broadband access and affordability: An analysis of a community survey on the digital divide. *Cities (London, England)*, *106*, 102904. https://pubmed.ncbi.nlm.nih.gov/32921864

Sahut, J.-M., Iandoli, L., & Teulon, F. (2019). The age of digital entrepreneurship. *Small Business Economics*. http://link.springer.com/10.1007/s11187-019-00260-8

Scheerder, A., van Deursen, A., & van Dijk, J. (2017). Determinants of internet skills, uses and outcomes. A systematic review of the second- and third-level digital divide. *Telematics and Informatics*, *34*(8), 1607–1624.

Soluk, J., Kammerlander, N., & Darwin, S. (2021). Digital entrepreneurship in developing countries: The role of institutional voids. *Technological Forecasting and Social Change*, *170*, 120876.

Stern, M. J., Adams, A. E., & Elsasser, S. (2009). Digital inequality and place: The effects of technological diffusion on internet proficiency and usage across rural, suburban, and urban counties. *Sociological Inquiry*, *79*(4), 391–417.

Stocker, V., & Whalley, J. (2018). Speed isn't everything: A multi-criteria analysis of the broadband consumer experience in the UK. *Telecommunications Policy*, *42*(1), 1–14.

Unioncamere (2019). *Analisi della domanda di competenze digitali nelle imprese*. Rome, Italy.

van Deursen, A.J.A.M., van Dijk, J.A.G.M., & Peters, O. (2011). Rethinking internet skills: The contribution of gender, age, education, Internet experience, and hours online to medium- and content-related Internet skills. *Poetics*, *39*(2), 125–144.

van Dijk, J.A.G.M. (2002). A framework for digital divide research. *The Electronic Journal of Communications*, *12*(1–2).

van Laar, E., van Deursen, A.J.A.M., van Dijk, J.A.G.M., & de Haan, J. (2017). The relation between 21st-century skills and digital skills: A systematic literature review. *Computers in Human Behavior*, *72*, 577–588.

Vuorikari R., Punie Y., Carretero Gomez, S., & Van Den Brande, G. (2016). DigComp 2.0: The digital competence framework for citizens. Luxembourg: Publications Office of the European Union.

Wei, K.-K., Teo, H.-H., Chan, H. C., & Tan, B. C. Y. (2011). Conceptualizing and testing a social cognitive model of the digital divide. *Information Systems Research*, *22*(1), 170–187.

Wiltshier, F. (2011). Researching with NVivo 8. *Qualitative Sozialforschung / Forum: Qualitative Social Research, 12*(1), article 23. doi: https://doi.org/10.17169/fqs-12.1.1628

Yin, R. K. (2014). *Case Study Research. Design and Methods*. Thousand Oaks, US: Sage Publications.

Zaheer, H., Breyer, Y., & Dumay, J. (2019). Digital entrepreneurship: An interdisciplinary structured literature review and research agenda. *Technological Forecasting and Social Change*, *148*, 119735.

# 16. Data are the fuel for digital entrepreneurship— but what about data privacy?

*Wolfgang Koehler, Christian Schultz and Christoph Rasche*

## 1.   INTRODUCTION

The main advancement from digitization lies in collecting, analyzing, and translating formerly unknown amounts of data into relevant information and finally into action as monetization processes (Mikalef et al., 2017). With the rapid introduction of new technologies, digital innovation refers to the continuous adaptation of digital technologies to original market offerings (Nambisan et al., 2017). In a business world that is increasingly digital, new and established companies need to continually evolve their data analytics capabilities and competencies to achieve sustainable business success and perform under platform economics conditions. Due to Porter and van der Linde (1995), regulation can provide additional incentives for innovation by encouraging the creation of new technologies, products, and markets and the discovery of overlooked efficiencies. Changing requirements for handling data require a rethinking of various processes, which opens many business opportunities for digital entrepreneurs, even if "innovation cannot always completely offset the cost of compliance, especially in the short term before learning can reduce the cost of innovation-based solutions" (Porter & van der Linde, 1995, p. 100).

Data are considered an essential raw material for all key digital technologies of the 21st century. The collection and processing of large amounts of data are crucial for training artificial intelligence (AI) algorithms and advancing the Internet of Things (IoT), where data are seamlessly exchanged between devices, platforms, and sensors (Neely, 2019; Schmidt, 2020) to enable new products and services.

From a digital entrepreneurship point of view, the processing of personally identifiable information (PII) is especially attractive. It enables a variety of digital services and does not cause high additional costs, as there are very few significant technological limitations on processing vast amounts of data. However, not everything that makes business sense and is technologically feasible is also permissible and compliant. From a legal perspective, processing PII is—depending on the jurisdiction—rather highly regulated. Generally, companies that violate data privacy laws face harsh consequences in the form of monetary penalties, a collapsing reputation and a loss of customer trust, which will inevitably negatively affect their sales and business prospects. The widespread ignorance of data protection rules and the resulting fear of being guilty of data misuse poses severe obstacles for organizations in the process of becoming truly data-driven. Management must implement data protection measures that reflect the different legal data privacy spheres (e.g., the EU, the USA, and China) as prerequisites to utilizing value-adding data processes. With different data governance systems, there is a risk of data opportunism regarding IT-law dumping. Ultimately, effective data privacy management leads to the availability of legal data input for the improvement of digital product quality.

This chapter draws from the relevant literature streams and, especially in the third section, the authors' practical insights from the management of a leading global accounting firm's data risk projects over the last ten years. It provides answers to fundamental questions in data privacy areas for digital entrepreneurs and presents different digital entrepreneurship opportunities. First, we define the term data and differentiate it from related areas, for example, information or processing, and show what contributes to the value of information and the underlying data. Second, we highlight the significance of data for digital entrepreneurs. Then, we demonstrate how entrepreneurs can cope with data protection laws and use the laws to their advantage.

## 2.    DATA AND INFORMATION VALUATION

The availability and processing of personal data play a critical role in the success of digital platforms and digital service companies and in providing public services ranging from the storage of medical histories (digital patient files) to the creation of digital identity cards. Digital platforms represent new business models that use technology to connect people, organizations, and resources in an interactive ecosystem where exceptional value can be created and exchanged (Parker et al., 2017). Almost every conceivable industry for which information is a crucial component is a prime contender for the platform revolution (Gawer, 2014). Advanced analytics and artificial intelligence can provide consumers with entirely individualized solutions that are delivered in milliseconds (Gawer, 2014). Transaction costs are decreasing due to the increased speed of online dealmaking through digital agents.

What distinguishes data from other resources is its unique characteristics. The production of data through existing sensors or cookies is almost free. Once data are collected, they are not consumed in processing activities as other resources are. Moreover, the value of data is enhanced when insights gained from the data are sustained as a part of an overarching competence-building process, for example, through the regular exchange of experiences and findings from applied data analytics projects. There is an only minimal variable cost in creating value through processing (Tonetti & Jones, 2020). Unlike physical resources, invisible assets mostly incur no depreciation when employed in value chain activities. The value of data may increase when used in advanced artificial intelligence and data transformation technologies. Through data combination, machine learning, trained algorithms, pattern recognition, data cleaning and semantic contextualization, data evolve into information, knowledge and competence. Challenging the status of the most valuable companies in the world inevitably leads to a paradigm shift. In the digital era, value creation accrues to brick-and-mortar business models; companies such as Google, Amazon, Alibaba and Facebook take advantage of digital platform economies and scalable invisible asset business models.

On the surface, data are not in short supply in the digital age, where processes are mainly digitized, online behavior leaves traces, and everyday objects are connected to the internet (Internet of Things) (Reinsel et al., 2017). The International Data Corporation (IDC) forecasts that by 2025, the global data sphere will have grown to 163 zettabytes (that is, a trillion gigabytes)—that is, ten times the 16.1 ZB of data generated in 2016. However, a mass of data does not automatically translate into a huge benefit for a company, for example, in anticipating consumer behavior (Knape et al., 2020).

## 2.1   What are Data, Information, and Processing?

The terms "data" and "information" are frequently used synonymously in a wide variety of contexts. The professional and scientific literature supports many different definitions of data and information, depending on the discipline. A fundamental definition of data is that data are unorganized and unprocessed facts, for example, raw numbers, figures, images, words, or sounds, derived from observations or measurements. Data by themselves do not possess inherent meaning (El-Amir & Hamdy, 2020). The transformation of data to information occurs by adding value in terms of meaning, relevance, and purpose (Davenport & Prusakv, 2000). Data by themselves are abstract and can be meaningless, while information always has a meaning. Value is added, according to Davenport and Prusakv (2000), to data when data are:

- Contextualized      *e.g., the purpose for which the data were gathered is known*
- Categorized         *e.g., the units of analysis and critical components are known*
- Calculated          *e.g., the data have been analyzed*
- Corrected           *e.g., errors have been removed*
- Condensed           *e.g., the data have been summarized.*

Policymakers and legislators worldwide increasingly regulate the processing of data. In this context, it is essential to understand what "data processing" is. According to the European Commission and based on Articles 4(2) and (6) of the General Data Protection Regulation (GDPR), processing covers a wide range of operations performed on personal data, including through manual and automated means. It includes collecting, recording, organizing, structuring, storing, adapting or altering, retrieving, consulting, using, disclosing by transmission, disseminating or otherwise making available, aligning or combining, restricting, erasing, and destroying personal data. The GDPR applies to personal data processing wholly or partly by automated means and by nonautomated means if part of a structured filing system.

Information and underlying data are some of the most important assets of many companies. Lee et al. (2017) show that it is increasingly important for investors to know how well companies handle data. Data are considered as a non-asset under accounting standards and are therefore not recognized as an asset on balance sheets. Data are intangible assets with unique characteristics that preclude the assignment of a universally accepted value. This realization is an important starting point for an overview of all information valuation approaches. Publicly available data are public goods for which no market price is determined. According to the SECI knowledge model (Nonaka et al., 2000), public and explicit knowledge can be transformed into private, implicit, and tacit knowledge through sophisticated learning trajectories. Likewise, Kollmann (2016) observes that the difference between physical and electronic value creation activities lies in the special handling of information.

Just collecting enormous amounts of high-quality data is insufficient to generate a monetary or even competitive advantage. Data are valuable in organizations if they are high-quality, functional, and able to be evaluated by decision-makers ("data intelligence"). Data intelligence is, therefore, crucial to organizations' success. Visconti et al. (2017) describe a useful approach to determine the dynamic data value-adding with five stages: (1) creation and collection, (2) storage, (3) processing, (4) consumption, and (5) monetization. In the early phases, namely, data creation, collection, and storage, the data value remains low, while in the data processing and data consumption phases, the data value increases considerably. Data-driven business models can create the maximum value from available data in the final stage of monetization.

The model shows significant value generation for companies that have suitable business models and monetization-driven organizational planning (Li et al., 2018).

Further, it is not trivial to track or measure the value of data to different users and for different purposes over time because data consumption is non-rivalrous. The use of data by one person or organization does not deprive other users of the ability to use the data or diminish its value. These characteristics make it particularly difficult to determine the value of and exclusively monetize specific data products' benefits (Slotin, 2018). As a consequence, different data valuation approaches surface.

Another approach focusing on the quality of data provides that the value of unstructured or erroneous data remains low regardless of the quantity of such data. The criteria of the 3-V model and their extension are useful to evaluate data quality (Chen et al., 2014; Freiknecht, 2018):

- **Variety**: In what way are the data available?
  Data can be structured or unstructured and are either stored centrally or distributed. In the latter case, linking and further processing becomes considerably more difficult. Typical examples of data that are difficult to process are user-generated content on social media platforms, decentralized collected sensor data, and data collected through cookies.
- **Velocity**: How quickly are the data updated?
  Data that are updated at very short intervals will only generate substantial benefits if they are evaluated quickly, preferably in real-time.
- **Volume**: How large is the available mass of data?
  There is no objective measure for this criterion. Moreover, in an environment with a continually increasing volume of data, it is difficult to set a meaningful limit, as it can be assumed that data become obsolete relatively quickly.

Although the 3-V model is considered the standard, various authors (Lokhande & Khare, 2015; Shim et al., 2015) extend it by including the characteristics of veracity, variability, and value:

- **Veracity**: Are the data unbiased?
  It stands to reason that only correct and unbiased data can provide valid results. However, data can also be incorrect or biased under certain circumstances and still be relevant for data processing. Examples of such circumstances include tweets with misspelled names or incorrectly assigned hashtags.
- **Variability**: To what extent do the data change?
  The changeability of data depending on the situation is another criterion.
- **Value**: What is the value of the data?
  This category primarily refers to the utility value of the data in terms of the results to be derived, which can often be improved by adequate processing procedures.

Many companies fail to understand the value of their existing data assets and the mechanisms that can increase data value. Based on this section's precise delineation of the terms data, information, and processing and its description of the current methods for capturing the value of information and the data on which they are based, the following section discusses possible means of concretely measuring the value.

## 2.2    How can we Measure Information Value?

To capture and consistently harvest information value over time, organizations must first clarify how to evaluate information as an asset and then develop a comprehensive data strategy to drive value enrichment (Deloitte Touche Tohmatsu Services, 2020). It is paramount that organizations understand their own data's potential value in the respective context and measure it concretely from a management perspective. Different approaches to information valuation exist. While PwC (2019) limits its valuation methods to the income (net cash flow benefits), market (the traded price in an active market), and cost (the cost of reproduction or replacement) methods, the Global Partnership for Sustainable Development additionally accepts the benefit monetization (an estimate of the monetization of the benefits associated with the data product) and impact-based (an assessment of the economic and sociocausal impact of the data's availability on outcomes) approaches. While these methods have their merits, Duncan and Jones' (2020) measures provide an overview of information valuation and help adequately capture information value in organizations. In their sophisticated categorization they differentiate between external (direct), internal (indirect), and liability measures.

- External or direct economic measures distinguished into "Market Value" and "Economic Value" of information are used when it is possible to clearly measure the creation of financial goodwill. This approach is beneficial if the data at issue are sold or traded as products or services or contribute directly to the business through profit or loss. These measures are useful for organizations that need to know how information assets should be valued relative to other assets and how to invest in their processing, management, and security. Additionally, the value of information in an enterprise plays an increasingly important role in measuring enterprise value for investors in mergers and acquisitions (Duncan & Jones, 2020).
- Indirect or internal measures subdivided into "Intrinsic Value", "Business Value" and "Performance Value" of information are particularly applicable when the focus is on identifying opportunities to improve business operations. The effectiveness or efficiency of existing business processes should be positively influenced without affecting the core business. The quality and potential of an information asset versus its actual benefits can be better evaluated to ultimately improve business strategies. Furthermore, indications of the potential for external or direct economic benefits can be provided (Duncan & Jones, 2020).
- Liability measures "Cost Value", "Waste Value" and "Risk Value" of information describe a variety of possible negative financial impacts on an organization. Factors such as system failures resulting in data loss, low data quality, data security breaches, noncompliance with data protection laws and other regulations, or faulty processing are just a few examples of possible causes (Duncan & Jones, 2020). Several challenges inhibit the transformation from concept to reality, making a calculation of the value and risk associated with data a complicated task. The evaluation of various liabilities and risks and the assessment of their short-, medium-, and long-term impacts can be supported by comprehensive analyses. However, the responsibility for determining potential information monetization and business risk based on a comprehensive liability analysis for all data processing steps is distributed across different business roles (Chief Digital Officer, Data Privacy Officer and others) (Duncan & Jones, 2020).

Management may apply a collection of these information valuation measures to identify and illustrate the value of information assets. The application of information value measures works best if logical data groupings of related information assets are formed beforehand. Each grouping or class (e.g., customer data or employee data) is treated as a portfolio. It may be necessary to combine several different valuation methods. Which measures an organization can adequately use and under which circumstances depends on its business objectives (Slotin, 2018). Recently, Gregory et al. (2020) raise a new point about the role and value of data and use Tesla as an example to demonstrate their concept of a data network effect. The authors' main point is that the more of the users' driving data the company agglomerates, the better their AI for autonomous driving becomes, and consequently, the more valuable the Tesla platform becomes to each user. Gregory et al. (2020) formulate different implications for managers to reap the benefits of this data network effect. First, managers need to make sure that adequate quantities and quality of data are continuously available through effective data governance. Second, companies need to focus on user-centric design so network effects can result in a perceived superior user experience. Third, managers need to consider responsible privacy principles. If the data network effect is real and what long-term implications it might have is an ongoing discussion (Clough & Wu, 2020).

## 3. DATA AND DIGITAL ENTREPRENEURS

Digital entrepreneurship is a critical pillar for economic growth and innovation and is recognized by many countries as a very important element of economic development and job creation (Block et al., 2018; Zhao & Collier, 2016). Digital start-ups are organizations that fully rely on digital technologies to create and transfer value and to market, deliver and support digital products or online services (Ahrens et al., 2019; Berger et al., 2019; Zhao & Collier, 2016). Digital entrepreneurs develop innovative digital technologies to create new ventures, business models, digital products, or services or to transform the existing businesses (Ahrens et al., 2019; Audretsch et al., 2017).

Currently, digital entrepreneurs possess a wide range of opportunities to introduce efficient business models that use digital technologies. In addition to using digital technologies to improve coordination, communication, planning, and control, digital entrepreneurs use them internally to enhance (in-)tangible forms of decision-making. This approach affects products and services produced by the organization (software and hardware) directly and helps to scale their venture more quickly (Recker & von Briel, 2019). For this purpose, technologies such as AI (machine learning and deep learning), natural language processing, big data analytics, virtual reality, the IoT, 3D printing, or cloud computing are appropriate (Beck et al., 2017; Rippa & Secundo, 2019; Schulte-Althoff et al., 2021). While business models and their underlying technologies undoubtedly develop rapidly, regulations and legislation governing data handling are catching up with this pace worldwide. Data privacy regimes target the usage of PII, likely to be valuable assets, as the subject of legislative action. Firms should make frequent use of nonmarket strategies to achieve competitive advantages regarding regulations, legislation and legal regimes (Rasche, 2020).

In this section, we outline the relevance of data for digital entrepreneurs from different perspectives. Then, we describe regulatory spheres, risks, and how privacy regulation supports digital entrepreneurs' innovations.

## 3.1    What is the Role of Data for Digital Entrepreneurs?

As outlined before, the sheer volume of collected data and data triangulation capabilities has increased dramatically. These rapid technological developments create new challenges for businesses of any size, but especially for new companies, digitization creates opportunities as Porter and Heppelmann (2015, p. 19) "believe that the exponential opportunities for innovation presented by smart, connected products, together with the huge expansion of data they create about almost everything, will be a net generator of economic growth" and that "there will be more innovation and many new businesses." The environment for digital entrepreneurs is rather positive as the latest technologies allow companies to use data for unprecedented purposes in their operations. For example, in the automotive industry, the car turns more and more into a cyber-physical-system with a multitude of sensors and processing power (Karnouskos & Kerschbaum, 2018), where existing and new companies can compete with their service offerings. One of these relatively new and quickly growing segments with high economic potential are connected car services (CCS) which include various services around an improved user experience, for example, personalized settings (seating position, radio), remote services, automated logbook, concierge services, dynamic overview of fuel prices, predictive maintenance, driving style adjustments, online appointment booking, maintenance service, in-car-payment services or different functions-as-a service offerings (additional torque or improved electronic suspension) (Seiberth & Gruendinger, 2018). The key to profit from CCS is continuous access to the user's data and a proper business model. Just as the automotive industry, other industry sectors are undergoing an inevitable transformation process where products' added value continuously shifts from hardware product specifications and quality measures to software quality and solutions.

Digital entrepreneurs must identify potential economic sectors in which their ideas are competitive. In areas where digital transformation is far advanced, digital entrepreneurs may face fierce competition with established players. A well-known example is the social media platform market, where new competitors have to deal with market dominance by Facebook, which is so difficult to cope with that even Google, as a resourceful competitor, was unable to establish their service Google+.

For digital entrepreneurs focused on leveraging their potential or monetization, it is helpful to build in-depth knowledge and broad skills related to information valuation methods. Expert knowledge in recognizing the data's value makes it possible to demonstrate the value of digital products and services to (potential) customers and clients. This contributes to competitive differentiation and, in the best case, supports the development of additional sources of revenue or new lines of business.

## 3.2    What is the Role of Data Privacy for Digital Entrepreneurs?

Among other factors, the repeated and extensive misuse of personal data led to a discussion of and sensitivity to data privacy issues in society. A prominent example is an allegation that misuse of PII assisted in Donald Trump's election. In early 2018, the scandal surrounding Facebook and Cambridge Analytica came to light. The defendants exploited data from more than 50 million users without their consent or even knowledge and used it to target political information and fake news with the aim to manipulate public opinion and, as a consequence, the national election of 2016.

The incentives to collect as much data as possible and to transform it into information as quickly as possible to target customers accurately or offer new services, raise serious questions of legitimacy for public authorities, particularly legislators and ethics committees. Especially the privileged access to data by large digital platforms, for example Facebook, Amazon, or Tencent strengthens their market position. So monopolistic market structures and consequently unfair competitive practices are serious possibilities that would hurt the consumer. Thus, digital governance regimes on the macro-, meso- and micro-levels are needed to set codes of conduct regarding compliance issues.

The growing importance of data ensures the dynamic development and continuous improvement of laws across industries and countries. Regulations and laws on data protection and privacy are rather vast. Currently, there are more than 130 national privacy laws, and this number is increasing (Greenleaf, 2019). In many respects, these privacy laws are comparable. However, there are still country- and jurisdiction-specific requirements for the collection, processing, transfer, and storage of data, as well as transparency and documentation obligations.

Matching regulatory requirements, on the one hand, and technical developments in business, on the other hand, is a key challenge. Data governance and compliance require the analysis and implementation of a wide range of business areas and processes. Complexity arises in many respects from the diversity and continuous amendment of data regulations. The focus of digital entrepreneurs is rarely limited to one market and, therefore, they are rarely subject to only a single but multiple national data privacy laws. Additionally, customers are not limited to specific areas, services, or products. People cross borders and legal jurisdictions with possibly contradictory regulations while using smart devices or connected services with ongoing data processing and transmission. Such use cases may have consequences for data controllers and processors; thus, transparency regarding international laws, the application of those laws and their differences are required. Different regulations focusing on protecting subjects such as individuals, businesses, and market or national security often exist in parallel in each jurisdiction.

The superficial view is that the European Union passed particularly tough data protection laws that were adopted in the member states in 2018. The US more or less follows a laissez faire approach which gives their US-based but worldwide active technology companies a competitive edge. And in China, data privacy doesn't exist.

With a closer look, it becomes clear that the limits of these assertions are not clear cut. It is true that in China, data privacy is not recognized as an individual right, but data privacy laws have expanded since the 1980s. Yao-Huai (2020) opines that data privacy protection will continue to have a character that will adhere to Chinese values that favor the state's collective objectives over individual interests. Nothing makes this point more vivid than the rollout of the social credit system, where through close surveillance and big data applications, citizens are rewarded for good and punished for bad behavior. Authors who nurture a discussion if China has taken the direction of a third way in privacy protection (Pernot-Leplay, 2020) underestimate the fact that China is ruled by the communist party and separation of the powers of legislative, executive and judiciary doesn't exist in practice (He, 2012). Chinese data laws favor defined domestic national champions in using data to develop and exploit new technologies.

The EU GDPR, the California Consumer Privacy Act (CCPA), and the Brazilian General Data Protection Law (LGPD) are prominent examples of privacy laws and bills worldwide that mainly focus on protecting natural persons' rights and freedoms. Their focus is on individuals and the protection of personal rights, mostly informational self-determination and the right to privacy, and the implementation of security and transparency obligations for the processors of personal data. When raising national or regional requirements to the international level, the issue of cross-border data transfer is of fundamental importance. Single laws can affect different entities, even if the primary focus is on one.

Similar to privacy regulations, some data regulations focus on protecting businesses and markets. For example, the EU Directive on the protection of trade secrets, the EU directive on copyright in the digital single market, and the EU regulation on the free flow of nonpersonal data are laws that focus on protecting and supporting businesses or markets. Furthermore, data localization obligations, which require the local storage and processing of data and the operation of servers and data centers in the respective countries should be mentioned. One well-known example is the Russian Data Localization Law. When collecting personal data, including through the information and telecommunication network, an operator must document the recording, systematization, accumulation, storage, adjustment (update or alteration), and retrieval of the personal data of citizens of the Russian Federation using databases located in the territory of the Russian Federation (see Article 2, paragraph 1 of Russian Federal Law No. 242-FZ). Additionally, parts of the previously mentioned laws serve economic protectionism and national companies' interests. International data regulations with business as the subject of protection are also diverse and continuously changing.

As shown in Figure 16.1 and in addition to individual privacy and business emphases, some data regulations shall ensure national security or the protection of the state and the public interests. On the one hand, data protection concerns the area of national security, such as the pro-

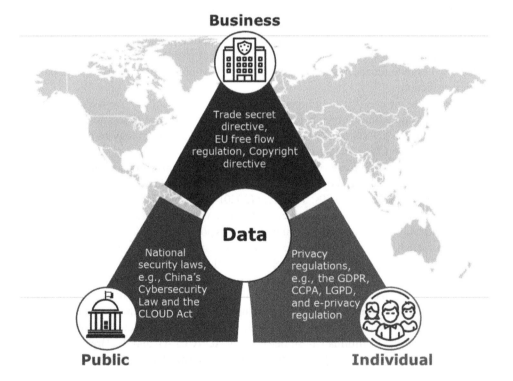

*Figure 16.1     Subjects of data regulation*

tection of important organizations whose undisturbed operations can directly affect national security, for example, organizations in the energy and telecommunications sectors, and in the international context in terms of restricting and controlling access by foreign states to specific information. On the other hand, data must be continuously monitored to ensure compliance with national legislation and to assist law enforcement. In particular, the Clarifying Lawful Overseas Use of Data Act (CLOUD Act), as well as parts of the Cybersecurity Law of the People's Republic of China (CSL), should be emphasized here. The CLOUD Act allows US federal law enforcement agencies to compel US-based technology companies, by warrant or subpoena, to provide data stored on servers upon request, whether the data are stored in the US or on foreign soil. The CSL requires critical information infrastructure operators ("CIIOs") to store personal information and important data generated from China's critical information infrastructures. Regulations from this realm may be particularly contradictory to national privacy laws that seek to protect natural persons' rights and freedoms. The aforementioned contradictions exist, for example, concerning third parties' access to data or the transfer of data to third parties (e.g., various authorities).

As outlined above, data can become valuable in different dimensions. It is essential to note that the monetary value of data can only be legally manifested through compliance with data privacy laws, which means a solid legal basis for data processing needs to exist. Furthermore, data can only be shared between different legal entities and further processed at another location (e.g., a head office) under certain conditions.

The narrow interpretation of the principle of informational self-determination (e.g., via consent) and the right of any citizen to control his or her personal information (the right to privacy) place the possibility of realizing the monetary value solely in customers' hands. Transparency and the right to privacy continue to be the focus of legislators' attention in the digital economy. Data protection laws thus also implement ethical restrictions in ongoing macroeconomic processes, the necessity of which is beyond question based on various incidents from the recent past.

Reputation, trust, and, above all, the actual realization of customer control over personal data are decisive factors today and will be in the future. Processing operations that exceed a contract's fulfillment and legitimate interest are, depending on the applicable law, wholly or partly in the customer's hands. Transparency, both internally and externally, regarding data processing practices is indispensable both as proof of compliance and as the operational realization of necessary amendments or actions, for example, the fulfillment of data subjects' rights. Noncompliance with data regulations is a significant risk for enterprises in the digitalization era and poses severe obstacles to their transformation into data-driven organizations. The organizational dilemma is that missing out on the potential of data monetization can lead to competitive disadvantages and organizational inefficiencies. In contrast, noncompliance with data regulations can lead to high penalties, market bans, lawsuits, and reputation loss. Corporate political strategies, nonmarket strategies and hybrid strategies can be seen as solutions to this dilemma (Rasche, 2020). The unlawful processing of personal data entails enormous financial risks in the form of claims for damages and fines (Art. 83 GDPR) or even an official ban on the processing of data, threatening the existence of digital products and services. In addition, inadequate protections can increase the risk of a data breach or a deliberate violation, which can have disastrous consequences for a company's reputation. For example, British Airways had to cope with reputational damage after a massive passenger data breach caused by a malicious cyber-attack on the BA website between August 21 and September 5,

2018 (ICO, 2020). All of this increases the pressure on those individuals who are responsible for acknowledging data protection requirements, many of which have been in place for a very long time and implementing them in a focused manner. Firms are increasingly challenged to achieve fair, competitive advantages and to engage in corporate social responsibility activities because influential stakeholders and investors are often no longer willing to accept breaches of rules and moral standards.

Martin et al. (2019) describe how privacy regulation simultaneously stimulates and constrains innovation. The researchers identified innovation constraints such as product exclusion in cases of fundamental incompatibility with compliance regulations, entrepreneurial deterrence where concerns related to privacy regulation discourage potential entrepreneurs from starting firms, and as mentioned above, barriers to access to data, especially PII.

Implementing and maintaining regulatory requirements in organizations requires effort and generates costs. Implementing the requirements ties up capital and capacities without directly contributing to value creation, but start-ups may undertake significant innovations in response to regulations—designated compliance innovations. The authors described compliance innovation as changes that make ideas or products compliant (e.g., more privacy-friendly default settings or the use of anonymized PII). The fundamental architecture and value proposition of a product are unaffected, meaning that compliance innovation is primarily about product design. Changes in supply chains (e.g., new partners or suppliers) to ensure that final products consist of compliant components and services are also included (Martin et al., 2019).

Furthermore, the regulation of privacy creates a market for technologies that support data protection and compliance. While regulations impose restrictions on some companies, they also create a potential market opportunity for developing innovative solutions. These solutions can help companies achieve compliance without impacting their regular production and value-added activities. These solutions are sold to others affected by regulations or are developed by companies to cope with their internal compliance activities. Martin et al. (2019) refer to advances in this sector as regulation-exploiting innovations.

## 4.    OPPORTUNITIES IN DATA PRIVACY FOR DIGITAL ENTREPRENEURSHIP

In addition to innovative approaches that can contribute to evaluating, structuring, processing, or analyzing data, a broad business opportunity arises from data processing regulations. Rapidly changing markets, the development of new technologies, and the swift parallel development of regulatory frameworks and legislation are challenges for all market players. With every new requirement, the question arises of who can provide the best and most efficient solution. Current research shows that regulation, in this case, privacy legislation, is not just an obstacle or barrier to start-up innovation.

In this section, we outline opportunities for digital entrepreneurs to benefit from data privacy regulation. We show the importance and advantages of technical compliance innovations before highlighting digital entrepreneurs' opportunities concerning technology, software, and IT innovations.

The GDPR increases the importance of IT security and refers to having 'appropriate technical and organizational measures' (TOMs) in place. Article 32(1) of the regulation states as follows:

*Table 16.1*     *Security measures supporting data privacy*

| Security Measure | Examples |
| --- | --- |
| Pseudonymization | Replacement of PII by one or more artificial identifiers or pseudonyms |
| Encryption | Encoding a file so that it can only be read by certain people |
| Confidentiality | Protecting data against unauthorized or unlawful processing |
| Integrity | Protecting data from unauthorized changes to ensure that it is reliable and correct |
| Recoverability | Generation of regular backups and use of data recovery centers |
| Evaluation | Regular review of TOMs on effectiveness and plausibility |

*Source:*     Compiled from Art. 32 GDPR.

Taking into account the state of the art, the costs of implementation and the nature, scope, context, and purposes of processing as well as the risk of varying likelihood and severity for the rights and freedoms of natural persons, the controller and the processor shall implement appropriate technical and organizational measures to ensure a level of security appropriate to the risk.

Different security measures are mentioned (see Table 16.1).

The implementation of these measures is essentially about matching the risks that arise from processing. It is necessary to regularly check whether the used measures are appropriate.

With the trend towards processing increasing amounts of data and more categories of data, and with more processing purposes and techniques, maintaining adequate protections requires the ongoing development of security measures. Simultaneously, new standards and norms for processing data, the development and usage of algorithms, and the protection of processed data continually evolve. State-of-the-art measures are moving targets that require the continuous development of standards within organizations. For entrepreneurs, developers, and existing service providers, these underlying conditions create a permanent need for new products and services.

The GDPR does not prescribe any standards for how to implement the respective protections in an organization. Digital entrepreneurs can develop and implement genuine technical solutions that fulfill these requirements. The areas with increasing demands on data processing and simultaneously increasing processing volumes that can be aided by technical solutions or support tools are incredibly diverse. Table 16.2 illustrates selected topics.

In addition to the implementation of measures to comply with legal requirements, another perspective is the design and implementation of appropriate processes and systems that support necessary follow-up measures in the event of a data breach. The focus is on immediate measures regarding the identification, assessment, documentation, and reporting of incidents on time and in an appropriate form and scope.

Artificial intelligence can be used to quickly and accurately identify compliance risks and derive early warning information in the event of a data leak or unlawful data processing. Furthermore, Romeike (2019) elaborates on the benefits of machine learning and multilayer learning for maintaining data compliance. The former enables the identification of potentially criminal acts (e.g., money laundering), whereas the latter supports the identification of and defense against previously unknown malware or cyber-attacks (Romeike, 2019).

The IBM Security and Ponemon Institute (2019) describe the benefits of investing in data breach detection technologies in their annual Data Breach Report. The faster data breaches are detected and contained, the lower the resulting costs. Organizations can improve their ability to contain security breach damages through security automation and intelligent orchestration capabilities that provide visibility to security operations centers.

*Table 16.2        Advantages of using technical compliance innovations*

| Specific advantages of a technological deployment and implementation | Closer view |
|---|---|
| **Category: Transparency** | |
| Optimized identification and structuring of (personal) data as well as complete, effective, and efficient implementation of documentation requirements | By visualizing data streams and processing activities and the associated increased transparency, it is possible to understand data processing within the organization, whether their collection and |
| Visualization of data streams and processing activities | documentation correspond to current requirements, and whether, |
| Improved integration with upstream systems and collaboration and exchange between available IT systems | in addition, processing activities exist that are not considered and therefore unknown to the organization. |
| **Category: Efficiency and Productivity** | |
| Increased efficiency and productivity | Efficiency and productivity can be increased by reducing |
| Centralized and standardized process management and data acquisition from various IT systems | manual workloads and process complexity and by reporting and preventing data compliance incidents. This is achieved due to, |
| Increase of product quality and process flexibility | e.g., the fact that errors caused by humans, such as accidental |
| Optimization of decision-making processes | deletion or overwriting of data, are prevented to the extent |
| Cost reduction through simplification/automation | possible and are largely eliminated. |
| **Category: Compliance and Liability** | |
| Minimization of compliance risks and follow-up costs | The transparency of the entirety of the existing data processing |
| Faster verification and monitoring of compliance conformity | activities and the associated completeness ensure the ability |
| Strengthening relationships with customers and business partners as well as the company's reputation | to check compliance and to make flexible adjustments to the processing activities in the event of any infringements of the |
| Real-time adaptations to changing conditions (legal or internal) | applicable requirements. This is achieved by central control in the sense of the uniform collection of all processing operations through complete identification and standardized structuring of all data collected and processed within the whole organization. |

Currently, however, technology, software, and IT innovations focus on the methodology of data processing, which is increasingly being used to support various compliance measures within organizations. In an article of Deloitte Touche Tohmatsu Limited (2019) the authors address the potential of using "regulatory technology innovations" as artificial intelligence to ensure regulatory compliance with the help of intelligent compliance technologies. They refer to the intersection of requirements and technologies as regulatory technology. This includes compliance solutions that provide efficient added value based on smart technologies and remediation. Technologies of this type are based on data mining systems, robotic process automation, and predictive analytics and help to efficiently implement the flood of new compliance regulations, monitor regulatory changes, ensure high compliance quality, optimize compliance, and automate compliance testing processes (Deloitte Touche Tohmatsu Limited, 2019).

Wicke and Püster (2019) investigate the opportunities for and risks of using big data, data analytics, and artificial intelligence to meet data protection requirements. The study shows that efficient data use and processing using self-learned algorithms can also be effective with unstructured data. In this way, the balance between regulatory compliance requirements and the technologies' strategic usability can be maintained. Furthermore, the authors noted that data processing regulatory requirements are subject to continuous change and that flexible designs of operational compliance processes using AI algorithms are therefore necessary (Wicke & Püster, 2019). While restrictive data governance regimes and provisions may contribute to lowering cybercrime, they may suffocate entrepreneurial creativity.

*Table 16.3*    *Development of privacy management software providers between 2018 and 2019*

| Company | Year established | Revenue [million USD] | Turnover development [2018–2019] |
|---|---|---|---|
| OneTrust | 2016 | 283.2 | + 141.6 % |
| TrustArc | 1997 | 83.7 | + 20.7 % |
| BigID | 2015 | 42.0 | + 92.6 % |
| Securiti.ai | 2018 | 39.7 | + 3,506.4 % |
| Crownpeak | 2001 | 24.3 | - 23.2 % |
| WireWheel | 2016 | 12.5 | + 108.2 % |
| Exterro | 2004 | 12.4 | + 44.5 % |

*Source:*    Turnover development from O'Leary (2020).

In addition to applications that support single areas such as data structuring, data detection, or risk analysis, the market for so-called privacy management tool software to achieve and maintain compliance with privacy laws and regulations is growing strongly. These tools are often modular in design and offered as platform solutions, enabling providers to continually expand their service offerings or adapt them to changing conditions and allowing organizations to purchase technical support tailored to their needs. The modules focus on specific processes, specifications, or requirements of individual laws, such as supporting or conducting privacy impact assessments (PIAs) under the GDPR or focusing comprehensively on the requirements of countries or regions such as the GDPR in the EU or the CCPA in California. In addition, provisions from other laws and guidelines, such as website tracking regulations under the EU Cookie Directive, are integrated into the platforms. The variation of software functionalities is broad and continually evolving.

In addition, legal requirements such as documentation and transparency obligations result in an enormous amount of manual effort both during implementation and in maintaining compliance with privacy laws and regulations. Businesses use data privacy management software to automate manual processes, support transparency requirements, and leverage applications to manage their internal privacy programs, centralize control and visualize various organizational compliance processes via dashboard functions.

A few years ago, most of the current privacy management tools did not exist. The increased regulation of data processing and data transmission (especially personal data) creates new unsolved problems.

A need for new solutions can arise directly from changes in legal or regulatory frameworks, so start-ups with data-driven business models or data processing and management capabilities should closely follow legislative developments. A current example of a regulatory change resulting in a need for action is the so-called "Schrems II" ruling in which the European Court of Justice declared the "Privacy Shield," a formerly suitable guarantee for sending EU citizens' data to the USA and further processing it there, invalid. Those who implemented the regulation were able to follow how the legislators work on new standards because of the ruling, with a considerable impact on many businesses.

In general, there are many opportunities for digital entrepreneurs to develop technical solutions for businesses to meet the growing challenges of data processing, structuring, valuation, and monetization. New big data technologies, such as AI, process mining, data mining, and predictive analytics are increasingly used in new applications to ensure data compliance and to develop new approaches and solutions. Digital entrepreneurs can satisfy new requirements through known and possibly adapted methods or through the development of new techniques and technologies. It is safe to say that the market for data privacy will continue to grow since individuals and institutions want to preserve their digital gestalt and identities.

# REFERENCES

Ahrens, J.-P., Isaak A. J., Istipliler B. & Steininger, D.M. (2019). The star citizen phenomenon & the 'ultimate dream management' technique in crowdfunding. In: *Proceedings of the 40th International Conference On Information Systems (ICIS)*, Munich, pp. 1–9.

Audretsch, David & Belitski, Maksim. (2017). Entrepreneurial ecosystems in cities: establishing the framework conditions. *The Journal of Technology Transfer*, 42. 10.1007/s10961-016-9473-8.

Beck, R., Avital, M., Rossi, M. & Thatcher, J. B. (2017). Blockchain technology in business and information systems research. *Business & Information Systems Engineering*, 59(6), pp. 381–384. DOI: 10.1007/s12599-017-0505-1.

Berger, Elisabeth, Von Briel, Frederik, Davidsson, Per & Kuckertz, Andreas. (2019). Digital or not – the future of entrepreneurship and innovation. *Journal of Business Research*, 125. 10.1016/j.jbusres.2019.12.020.

Block, J. H., Fisch, C. O. & Van Praag, M. (2018). Quantity and quality of jobs by entrepreneurial firms. *Oxford Review of Economic Policy*, 34(4), 565–583. https://doi.org/10.1093/oxrep/gry016.

Chen, Min, Mao, Shiwen & Liu, Yunhao (2014). Big data: a survey. *Mobile Networks and Applications*, 19(2), pp. 171–209.

Clough, D. R. & Wu, A. (2020). Artificial intelligence, data-driven learning, and the decentralized structure of platform ecosystems. *Academy of Management Review* (forthcoming). (Pre-published online, October 30, 2020.)

Davenport, T. H. & Prusakv, L. (2000). *Working Knowledge: How Organizations Manage What They Know*. Boston, MA: Harvard Business School Press.

Deloitte Touche Tohmatsu Limited (2019). *Künstliche Intelligenz im Compliance-Umfeld von Banken & Co.* https://www2.deloitte.com/content/dam/Deloitte/de/Documents/risk/Whitepaper-K%C3%BCnstliche-Intelligenz-im-Compliance-Umfeld-von-Banken-und-Co.pdf

Deloitte Touche Tohmatsu Services (2020). *Data valuation: Understanding the value of your data assets*. https://www2.deloitte.com/content/dam/Deloitte/global/Documents/Finance/Valuation-Data-Digital.pdf [accessed Oct 02, 2020].

Duncan, A. D. & Jones, L. C. (2020). *Applied Infonomics: How to Measure the Net Value of Your Information Assets*. Gartner 2020, ID G00463621.

El-Amir, H. & Hamdy, M. (2020). *Deep Learning Pipeline. Building a Deep Learning Model with TensorFlow* (p. 114). New York: Apress.

Freiknecht, J. (2018). *Big Data in der Praxis: Lösungen mit Hadoop, Spark, HBase und Hive. Daten speichern, aufbereiten, visualisieren*. 2. Auflage, München: Carl Hanser Verlag.

Gawer, A. (2014). Bridging differing perspectives on technological platforms: Toward an integrative framework. *Research Policy*, 1239–1249.

Greenleaf, G. (2019). Global data privacy laws. 132 national laws & many bills (February 8, 2019). *Privacy Laws & Business International Report*, 14–18. SSRN: https://ssrn.com/abstract=3381593.

Gregory, R. W., Henfridsson, O., Kaganer, E. & Kyriakou, H. (2020). The role of artificial intelligence and data network effects for creating user value. *Academy of Management Review*, 46. 10.5465/amr.2019.0178.

He, W. (2012). *In the Name of Justice: Striving for the Rule of Law in China*. Washington, DC: Brookings Institution Press.

IBM Security & Ponemon Institute (2019). Annual study: The cost of a data breach report. https://www.ibm.com/security/data-breach.

ICO (2020). The UK Information Commissioner's Office (ICO), Enforcement Information: British Airways. https://ico.org.uk/action-weve-taken/enforcement/british-airways/.

Karnouskos, S. & Kerschbaum, F. (2018). Privacy and integrity considerations in hyperconnected autonomous vehicles. *Proceedings of the IEEE*, 106, 160–170. 10.1109/JPROC.2017.2725339.

Knape, T., Hufnagl, P. & Rasche, C. (2020). Dashboardconsulting im Gesundheitswesen – Digitalisierungsoptionen und Anwendungsfelder. In Pfannstiel, M., Rasche, C., Braun von Reinersdorff, A., Knoblach, B. & Fink, D. (eds.), *Consulting im Gesundheitswesen – Professional Services als Gestaltungsimperative in der Gesundheitswirtschaft* (1–27). Wiesbaden.

Kollmann, T. (2016). *E-Entrepreneurship: Grundlagen der Unternehmensgründung in der Digitalen Wirtschaft*. Wiesbaden: Springer Gabler-Verlag.

Lee, H., Kweon, E., Kim, M. & Chai, S. (2017). Does implementation of big data analytics improve firms' market value? Investors' reaction in stock market. *Sustainability 2017*, 9, 978. https://doi.org/10.3390/su9060978.

Li, W.C.Y., Nirei, M. & Yamana, K. (2018). Value of data: There's no such thing as a free lunch in the digital economy, Presentation at the *Sixth IMF Statistical Forum*, Washington DC, November 2018 https://unstats.un.org/unsd/nationalaccount/aeg/2018/M12_3c2_Data_SNA_asset_boundary.pdf.

Lokhande, S. A. & Khare, N. (2015). An outlook on big data and big data analytics. *International Journal of Computer Applications*, 124(11), 37–41.

Martin, N., Matt, C., Niebel, C. & Blind, K. (2019). How data protection regulation affects startup innovation. *Information Systems Frontiers*. 10.1007/s10796-019-09974-2.

Mikalef, P., Pappas, Ilias O., Krogstie, John & Giannakos, M. (2017). Big data analytics capabilities: A systematic literature review and research agenda. *Information Systems and e-Business Management*, pp. 1–32. Springer.

Nambisan, S., Lyytinen, K., Majchrzak, A. & Song, M. (2017). Digital innovation management: Reinventing innovation management research in a digital world. *MIS Quarterly*, 41. 10.25300/MISQ/2017/41:1.03.

Neely, A. (2019). OpenDataScience. Data valuation – what is your data worth and how do you value it? https://opendatascience.com/data-valuation-what-is-your-data-worth-and-how-do-you-value-it/.

Nonaka, I., Toyama, R. & Konno, N. (2000). SECI, BA and leadership: A unified model of dynamic knowledge-creation. *Long Range Planning*, 33(1), 5–34.

O'Leary, R. (2020). Worldwide data privacy management software market shares, 2019: OneTrust dominates the competition. Framingham: International Data Corporation (IDC).

Parker, G., Van Alstyne, M. & Choudary, S. (2017). *Die Plattform-Revolution: Von Airbnb, Uber, PayPal und co. lernen: Wie neue Plattform-Geschäftsmodelle die Wirtschaft verändern*. Frechen: mitp Verlags GmbH & Co. KG.

Pernot-Leplay, E. (2020). China's approach on data privacy law: A third way between the U.S. and the EU?. *Penn State Journal of Law & International Affairs*, 8(1), SSRN: https://ssrn.com/abstract=3542820.

Porter, M. & Heppelmann, James E. (2015). How smart, connected products are transforming companies. *Harvard Business Review*, 93(10), 97–114.

Porter, M. & van der Linde, C. (1995). Toward a new conception of the environment-competitiveness relationship. *The Journal of Economic Perspectives*, 9(4), 97–118.

PricewaterhouseCoopers (PwC) (2019). *Putting a value on data*. https://www.pwc.co.uk/data-analytics/documents/putting-value-on-data.pdf.

Rasche, C. (2020). Nicht-Markt-Strategien im Gesundheitswesen – Wettbewerbsvorteile durch indirektes Management. In: FOR-MED, *Zeitschrift für das Management im Gesundheitswesen*, Ausgabe 04/2020, 9–19.

Recker, J. & von Briel, F. (2019). The future of digital entrepreneurship research: Existing and emerging opportunities. *40th International Conference on Information Systems*.

Reinsel, D., Gantz, J. & Rydning, J. (2017). Data age 2025: The evolution of data to life-critical: Don't focus on big data; focus on the data that's big. Framingham: International Data Corporation (IDC).

Rippa, P. & Secundo, G. (2019). Digital academic entrepreneurship: The potential of digital technologies on academic entrepreneurship. *Technological Forecasting and Social Change*, 2019, 146(C), 900–911.

Romeike, F. (2019). RiskNET. Von Im Risikomanagement die Stärken von KI nutzen. https://www.risknet.de/themen/risknews/im-risikomanagement-die-staerken-von-ki-nutzen/.

Schmidt, K. J. (2020). *Datenschutz als Vermögensrecht – Datenschutzrecht als Instrument des Datenhandels*. (M. Cornils & L. Specht-Riemenschneider, eds.) Wiesbaden: Springer Fachmedien Wiesbaden GmbH.

Schulte-Althoff, M., Fuerstenau, D. & Lee, G. M. (2021). A scaling perspective on AI startups. Proceedings of the 54th Hawaii International Conference on System Sciences (pp. 6515–6524). Honolulu: Hawaii International Conference on System Sciences (HICSS).

Seiberth, G. & Gruendinger, W. (2018). Data-driven business models in connected cars, mobility services and beyond. Berlin: BVDW Research, No. 01/18, April 2018.

Shim, J., French, A., Guo, C. & Jablonski, J. (2015). Big data and analytics: Issues, solutions, and ROI. *Communications of the Association for Information Systems*, 37, 797–810.

Slotin, J. (2018). What do we know about the value of data?. *Global Partnership for Sustainable Development Data*. http://www.data4sdgs.org/news/what-do-we-know-about-value-data.

Tonetti, C. & Jones, C. I. (2020). Nonrivalry and the economics of data. *American Economic Review*, 110(9), 2819–2858. DOI: 10.1257/aer.20191330.

Visconti, R.M., Larocca, A. & Marconi, M. (2017). Big data-driven value chains and digital platforms: From value co-creation to monetization. *Social Science Research Network*. SSRN: https://ssrn.com/abstract=2903799 or http://dx.doi.org/10.2139/ssrn.2903799.

Wicke, J. & Püster, K. (2019). *Strategische Datennutzung und Datenschutz*. In M. Reich & C. Zerres (eds.), *Handbuch Versicherungsmarketing* (pp. 307–324). Berlin: Springer Verlag GmbH Deutschland.

Yao-Huai, L. (2020). Privacy and data privacy issues in contemporary China. In Miller, K. & Taddeo, M. (eds.), *The Ethics of Information Technologies* (pp. 189–197). London: Routledge. https://doi.org/10.4324/9781003075011.

Zhao, F. & Collier, A. (2016). Digital entrepreneurship: Research and practice. The 9th Annual *Conference of the EuroMed Academy of Business*, 2016.

# Index

Printed and bound by CPI Group (UK) Ltd, Croydon, CR0 4YY

16/04/2025